RENAISSANCE MAN

RENAISSANCE MAN

Agnes Heller

translated from the Hungarian by
RICHARD E. ALLEN

ROUTLEDGE & KEGAN PAUL
LONDON, HENLEY AND BOSTON

Originally published as
A Reneszánsz Ember
© *Akadémiai Kiadó, Budapest 1967*
This translation first published
in Great Britain in 1978
by Routledge & Kegan Paul Ltd
39 Store Street,
London WC1E 7DD
Broadway House,
Newtown Road,
Henley-on-Thames,
Oxon RG9 1EN and
9 Park Street,
Boston, Mass. 02108, USA
Set in 10 on 11 pt Times
by Kelly and Wright, Bradford-on-Avon, Wiltshire
and printed in Great Britain by
Lowe & Brydone Printers Ltd, Thetford, Norfolk
© *Agnes Heller 1978*

British Library Cataloguing in Publication Data

Heller, Agnes

Renaissance man.
1. Man   2. Philosophy, Renaissance
3. Philosophy, Medieval
I. Title
128'.09'023   BD450   78-40552

ISBN 0 7100 8881 7

CONTENTS

CONTENTS

vi

Acknowledgments

For their help in the writing of this book, I am indebted to the late Georg Lukács, and also to Ferenc Fehér, György Márkus, Mihály Vajda, and Dénes Zoltai.

A.H.

INTRODUCTION
Is there a 'Renaissance ideal of man'?

The consciousness that man is a historical being is a product of bourgeois development; the condition of his fulfilment is the negation of bourgeois existence. During antiquity a static concept of man prevailed: his potentialities were circumscribed both in his social and individual life; the ideal was one of objective limits, not of the subjective projection of aims and desires. Medieval Christian ideology dissolved these limits. Either perfectibility or depravity can be a limitless process, at least in the earthly sense of limits; the beginning and end of the process are, however, fixed by the transcendence of beginning and end, original sin and Last Judgment.

With the Renaissance a dynamic concept of man appears. The individual has his own history of personal development, just as society has a history of development too. The contradictory identity of individual and society makes its appearance in every fundamental category. The relationship between the individual and the situation becomes fluid; past, present, and future are human creations. This 'humanity', however, is a generalized, homogeneous concept. It is at this time that 'liberty' and 'fraternity' are born as immanent ontological categories. Time and space become humanized and infinity becomes a social reality. But however dynamic man may be in his interaction with history, anthropologically he is still eternal, generalized, and homogeneous. Man creates the world, but he does not re-create mankind; history, the 'situation' remain external to him. The concept of man does not go beyond the notion of *corsi e ricorsi*, the cyclical movement does not turn into a spiral. In one respect, with their concrete analysis of the human psyche and human behaviour, the seventeenth and eighteenth centuries widen the

1

search for man, despite a seeming regression from a historical conception of humanity, making possible a real historical anthropology and the notion of the self-creation of man. From Hobbes to Rousseau the *past of mankind* becomes – on a higher plane – history. After the French Revolution the present, too – in such central figures as Hegel and Balzac – becomes history. Finally, with Marx and the negation of bourgeois society, the future as well makes its appearance as history.

The concept 'Renaissance' signifies a total social process, extending from the social and economic sphere where society's basic structure was affected to the realm of culture, embracing everyday life and everyday ways of thinking, moral practices and ethical ideals, forms of religious consciousness, art, and science. We can really speak of the Renaissance only where all these appeared together and in the same period, on the basis of certain changes in social and economic structure: in Italy, England, France, and – partly – in the Netherlands. The Renaissance current of thought which is customarily called 'humanism' is actually no more than one (or several) of the ideological reflexes of the Renaissance, in ethical and scholarly form, detachable from the social structure and the realities of everyday life, and hence capable of taking on a relative life of its own and gaining ground in countries where the Renaissance, as a total social phenomenon, never existed. But in those countries it necessarily remained without roots, gaining adherents only in the upper reaches of social life (albeit among the political and intellectual aristocracy) and quickly becoming isolated. Thus it was that in Germany the Reformation swept humanism away. Thus it was that in Hungary the precocious absolute monarchy of Matthias Corvinus – whose foundations had been laid by his father, János Hunyadi, the greatest of the *condottieri* – vanished almost without a trace.

The Renaissance was the first wave of the protracted process of transition from feudalism to capitalism. Engels rightly spoke of it as a 'revolution'. In that process of transformation a whole social and economic structure, an entire system of values and way of life were shaken. Everything became fluid; social upheavals succeeded one another with unbelievable speed, individuals situated 'higher' and 'lower' in the social hierarchy changed places rapidly. In these eruptions and rapid turns of fortune the process of social development can be seen unfolding in all its plurality; I will discuss some of its concrete problems later in a separate chapter. In any event, the Renaissance takes its place between two more stable social and economic systems: between feudalism on the one hand, and a state of equilibrium of feudal and bourgeois forces on the other. And from this point of view it is immaterial how long that equilibrium was maintained in different countries (and that varied greatly). The societies which preceded it and followed it were equally closed societies (though closed in different ways) compared with Renaissance society, of which Shakespeare's Henry VII so tellingly said that

> True hope is swift, and flies with swallow's wings
> Kings it makes gods, and meaner creatures kings.

But the Renaissance was the sort of social and economic revolution in whose final phase individual revolutions proved abortive, finding themselves eventually in a cul-de-sac. Certainly Italian, Spanish, and, in part, Netherlands developments led up a blind alley: daybreak was not succeeded by day. But even where it was – as in England, the home of the classical course of historical development – this 'day' turned out to be much more problematic and contradictory than it had appeared in the rosy light of dawn. I might say that the thinkers of the Renaissance already recognized this themselves. Let us take Thomas More as an example: in the first part of his *Utopia*, as is generally known, the inhuman world of primitive capital accumulation stands clearly revealed. But the sharp light cast there on social contradictions still illuminates no more than 'anomalies'. The same Thomas More willingly became Lord Chancellor at the court of Henry VIII, for no other reason than his sincere belief that the ruler would take steps to put an end to those contradictions; as a true 'Christian Prince' he would create as just a society as was possible given the existing state of 'human nature'. And More's friend Erasmus (writing in 1517, when Luther was already preparing his theses at Wittenberg) set forth his predictions of perpetual peace and of the noble future existence of the great family of a humanistic and tolerant Christian humanity. If we compare More the critic with Swift the critic the difference between their two epochs becomes palpably clear to us, even in that same England whose development (with that of France) proved the only viable path of development among the various courses offered by the Renaissance.

The Renaissance was the dawn of capitalism. The lives of the men of the Renaissance, and hence the development of the Renaissance concept of man, were rooted in the process by which the beginnings of capitalism destroyed the *natural* relationship between individual and community, dissolved the *natural* bonds linking man to his family, his social estate, and his 'ready-made' place in society, and shook all hierarchy and stability, turning social relations fluid, the arrangement of classes and social strata as well as the placement of individuals within them. Marx in the *Grundrisse* compared as follows the 'natural community' and the individuals who belonged to it with the kind of individuals characteristic of capitalist development:

> Property in the conditions of production was posited as identical with a limited, definite form of the community; hence of the individual with the characteristics – limited characteristics and limited development of his productive forces – required to form such a community. This presupposition was itself in turn the result of a limited historic stage of the development of the productive forces; of wealth as well as of the mode of creating it. The purpose of the community, of the individual – as well as the conditions of production – is *the reproduction of these specific conditions of production* and of the individuals, both singly and in their social groupings and relations – as living carriers of these conditions. Capital posits the *production of wealth* itself and hence the universal development of the productive forces, the constant overthrow of its prevailing presuppositions. . . . The result is: the tendentially and potentially general development of the forces of production – of wealth as such – as a basis. . . . The basis as the possibility of the universal development of the individual, and the real development of the individuals from this basis as a constant suspension [*Aufhebung*] of its *barrier*, which is recognized as a barrier, not taken for a *sacred limit*. . . . Hence also the grasping of his own history as a *process*, and the recognition of nature (equally present as practical power over nature) as his real body.[1]

In societies where the community still exists the object of a man's work does not appear to him as a product of labour, but seems 'naturally given' (findet sich vor als Natur); it is a condition of his existence, something belonging to him as much as his sense organs or his skin. The fact that 'man is a member of the community' is for him 'a reality given by nature'. His relationship to the community is identical with his relationship to 'defined existence'. To step outside the bounds of the given community is equivalent to destruction, and any kind of development is possible only within this circumscribed, untranscendable framework. With the development of capitalism, as the generation of wealth becomes the goal, all pre-existing social characteristics can and do become restricting, and man 'does not wish to remain what he has become, but lives in a constant process of becoming'. Life in the community gives 'satisfaction from a limited standpoint: while modern [life] gives no satisfaction; or, where it appears satisfied with itself, it is *vulgar*'.[2] In the endless process of production 'natural necessity in its direct form has disappeared; because a historically created need has taken the place of the natural one'.[3]

Marx's analysis shows succinctly how, parallel with the development of the bourgeois forces of production, the social structure and the individual within it have become *dynamic*. According to a naïve commonplace still found today even among scholars, the inhabitants of Italy in the course of their voyages became acquainted with the luxury of the East and a little later with the culture of antiquity, and comparing them with their own circumstances, became dissatisfied with the latter; thus under the influence of antiquity new ideas emerged, which in the course of their development came into conflict with the feudal system, the ideology of the church, and so forth. But in fact nothing of the sort happened. The first forms of capitalist productive forces and bourgeois social relations emerged from the *immanent* development of feudalism; as they gradually corroded and dissolved the latter, men simply found themselves in a new situation, where they *had* to act, feel, and think differently about the world and about themselves, than in the naturally given communities of the system of estates. A new way of behaving and a new manner of life, as it developed, sought out its own ideology, finding it partly in the ideas of antiquity but, as will be discussed later in more detail, *to at least as great an extent* in certain tendencies of Christianity. There was no question of a 'renewal' of antiquity because, so far as the relationship between individual and society was concerned, there was more in common (as is clear from Marx's analysis) between the Greek polis and the medieval system of estates than between the Greek polis and the social structure of the Renaissance era. In some of its forms the ideology of antiquity did indeed prove important in many ways for the ideology of the Renaissance, but, as we shall see, it served rather as a storehouse of thought to be transformed at will than as a model for imitation. I can cite, as random examples, two such basic categories as 'liberty' and 'equality'. In Italy – and in Florence even as early as the thirteenth century – 'liberty' and 'equality' were political slogans; at first they were the slogans of the upper bourgeoisie against the landed nobility, then of the middle and petty bourgeoisie against the *haute bourgeoisie*, and finally of the people against the whole bourgeoisie. The representatives of 'liberty' soon discovered the costume of antiquity (we need think only of Cola di Rienzo), and

Brutus soon became the ideal of liberty. But in content this liberty had little in common with liberty as Brutus understood it, as is shown by its far from accidental pairing with 'equality'. The concept of 'equality' was quite unknown to antiquity. Engels was right in observing that this notion first appeared in Christianity, as the concept of equality before God. Liberty as equality is a combination of two concepts, appearing at a time when commodity production is becoming general; in its very structure it indicates that here, too, antiquity was no more than an inherited and freely interpreted tradition.

A comparison of Athens and Florence provides the most telling proof for the differences between ancient and Renaissance conditions, as Marx indicated them. I have chosen these two city-states precisely because there were many similarities between them, not all of them merely apparent. In their time and compared with other city-states, both were industrially well-developed: handicrafts and small-scale manufacture were the basis of their commerce, with carrying trade (so important in ancient Ionia and Renaissance Venice) playing a smaller part. They were alike also in the storminess of their history: their great ages were marked by constant and violent class conflicts. Both tended towards democracy, inclining even towards the direct democracy of the polis. Both began to fall apart at their very peak, amid conditions of economic and social expansion. Last but not least, their cultures during their great eras were model, classical cultures. Clearly these similarities do not spring from the fortuitous act of setting the two side by side. The direct democracy of the polis, appearing at a relatively high level of technical culture, was the precondition and foundation of a universal and model general culture.

If we cast a backward glance at these two city-states from the vantage point of the future, the total picture is modified. Both cities fell; that is, they ceased to be independent city-states. But the fall of Athens was more than just the destruction of her existence as an independent city-state; it was almost the symbolic expression of a more general trend. With Athens the entire Greek world collapsed (though the complete process took centuries), and with it the entire *mode of production* on which the greatness of Athens had rested. The Athenian city-state had exhausted the last possibilities of *its own mode of production*. For here – to refer to Marx's discussion – the urban community had turned out to be a *limit* whose dissolution was synonymous with the dissolution of its mode of production. With Florence, on the other hand, the situation was radically different. The mode of production on which it was based did not vanish

6

with the fall of the Renaissance city, but vice versa: the city fell because a new mode of production was not capable of breaking out of the framework of the city-state, but remained within its limits, even though for modern, bourgeois production these limits were not just boundaries (*Grenzen*), but limits or barriers (*Schranke*). Even at the beginning of the sixteenth century such thinkers as Machiavelli and Michelangelo recognized this fact, to take two individuals of quite different character. They knew even then that the only way to preserve and extend Florentine culture was to make an end of the city-state and create a *unified Italy*. Both hoped for it from the two ill-fated later Medici, Lorenzo II, to whom Machiavelli dedicated his *Prince*, and Giuliano II, for whom Michelangelo designed the tomb in which Florence's future would be interred. But – in contrast with Athens – the mode of production on which the Florentine city-state rested did not perish with Florence; it went on to develop further in those countries where absolute monarchy assisted in breaking down the barriers to bourgeois production.

Let us cast a brief glance, however, at Athens and Florence during their most flourishing epochs. I have said that both were democracies of the polis. But, as is generally known, in Athens a real democracy existed, based on a real institution of slavery. It was a peculiarity of Florentine democracy, however, that on the one hand it was still *direct* democracy, while on the other it was already a *formal* democracy. Bruni, in his *Oratio in funere Johannis Strozzae* (1426), declared the existence of equality before the law and of an equal right to office. Formally, this equality extended to the *popolo minuto* and *sottoposti* as well as the *popolo grasso*, to the petty bourgeoisie and workers as well as to the great bourgeoisie. But *in fact* only the great and middle bourgeoisie held office. Hence springs the paradox that in its golden age the culture of Florence, which proclaimed the principle of equality, was *more aristocratic* than Athenian culture at its height. I have mentioned that both Athens and Florence were distinguished by the sharpness of their class struggles. But in the Athens of the classical period class conflict was seen ultimately as *a negative phenomenon*; the goal of its statesmen was to put a real end to class struggles (which of course was not possible there either), while its philosophers sought a 'good' or ideal form of society, in which class conflict could be brought to an end or at least reduced to a minimum. But in Florence the attitude of thinkers and political figures towards the class struggle was far from being so unequivocal as that. Here, too, there were of course those who saw it as a purely negative phenomenon, but they were surpassed in number and importance by those who thought to find in class struggle a useful leaven in society and who in theory and practice *encouraged* it. In this respect there is no difference in principle between Petrarch's enthusiasm for Cola di Rienzo and the enthusiasm of Pico della Mirandola, Michelangelo or Machiavelli for Savonarola. Again, the reasons are plain. Above all, a considerable proportion of the class struggles in Athens went on *within* a single class, while the Italian city-states of the Renaissance were characterized by a *plurality of ruling classes*. The centuries-old conflict of the Guelphs and Ghibellines in Florence was not carried on for the same simple reason as that of the Athenian aristocrats and democrats, merely for a share in political power; it was conducted primarily for the victory of different economic forms. (That, of course, should not lead one to underestimate the role of struggles for political power or of struggles between various strata of a class.) The class struggle, which in antiquity had indeed dissolved the community, was for the capitalism of the early Renaissance a source of ferment in economy and society. The philosophers and ideologues who in the first case attacked it but in the latter instance defended it were merely giving expression to the real state of affairs – among other things the difference which existed (to return again to Marx's starting-point) between the life of the community as a 'limit' or 'boundary line' and as a 'limitation' or 'barrier'.

My comparison of Athens and Florence was merely an example designed to show the novel character of the economic and social relations of the Renaissance. Wealth as a goal, production for the sake of production, production as an *endless process* constantly dissolving and transforming things, and hence the dissolution of all given, natural communities: *all the imperatives with which the new situation confronted men* led to the development of new types of men and consequently of a new concept of man, different from both the ancient and the medieval concept: *that of man as dynamic.*

The concept of dynamic man is an *undefinable* concept. It may be summed up by saying that *every* conception of human relations became dynamic. Conceptions of value shift; infinity (the infinity of space, time, and knowledge) becomes not merely an object of speculation but an immediate experience, a component of action and behaviour; perfection is no longer an absolute norm, for where everything is in process there can only be a constant striving after perfection, but no absolute perfection in the sense of ancient *kalokagathia* or Christian sainthood. As Max Dvořák wrote perceptively of the art of the period, 'the canon of perfection was not an abiding norm, as in antiquity, but was joined to a subjective will, as a more or less transient stage in the general process of development, already surpassed almost as soon as it was attained'.[4] The same dynamism characterized man's relationship to society. The choice of one's destiny is synonymous, in a social sense, with *an infinitude of possibilities* (at the given level of social development, of course). To be sure, the consciousness of the members of various classes conforms more or less closely to their class consciousness. But the life and consciousness of each class was itself rapidly changing, and moreover the individual could, as an individual, rise out of his class, for now he belonged to a class as a result of his place in the productive process, not in consequence of his birth. Destiny thus came to depend more and more on 'what I have done and what I have made of myself'; it became a question of rightly apprehending the dynamism of society. Since man's destiny took shape amid the *general movement* of society, it was there that the individual's relationship to that society emerged – as the relationship of an individual. Answering the question, 'How can I live and succeed amid the given movement of society?' gradually became an *individual* matter; convention could not serve as a basis for feeling out the trend of social movement, for this feeling-out was itself opposed to convention, and on the other hand the later bourgeois routine had not yet developed either. And it was precisely the emergence of an individual relationship to society, the choice of one's own destiny, which made necessary an ever more individualistic outlook, sense of values, and way of behaving – in a word, what we call with some oversimplification 'Renaissance individualism', though it had little in common with the individualism of mature bourgeois society. We might better speak of the cult of the 'self-made man', with the qualification that what a man made of himself was not entirely synonymous with the possession of power or money (though very often it was in fact one or the other), for the chief consideration was *how far he had placed his own stamp on the world.* The first symbol of this kind of self-made man is the equestrian statue of Gattamelata before the basilica in Padua. Thus the individual began to shape his own destiny, and not just in an ethical sense. The dialectic of man and destiny became the central category of a dynamic concept of man.

The development of a form of production carried on in order to acquire wealth, and the dissolution of the system of feudal estates, gave rise to another central category of this dynamic concept of man: that of versatility or many-sidedness. It was this that Marx called the emergence from 'the state of limitedness' (*Borniertheit*). Often he interpreted it as a case of man's not yet being bound to the division of labour, as did Engels in his writings on the Renaissance. But that is true only in so far as we compare the Renaissance with the later development of bourgeois society; it is not at all so by comparison with antiquity. Pericles was much less subject to the division of labour than Lorenzo de' Medici; the Florentine burgher, who spent the greater part of his days looking after his financial speculations and his manufactures, was far more the captive of the division of labour than the citizen of the Athenian polis, and the Florentine craftsman, toiling from dawn to dusk in his workshop, was less able to concern himself with philosophy than the unpropertied Athenian. It is true that during the Renaissance there was a larger number of broadly cultivated men than during the later stages of bourgeois development; the arts and sciences were themselves less differentiated. The estrangement of public and private life from each other was only beginning, though it is true that during the last century of the Renaissance it proceeded at a rapid pace. When Marx spoke of 'manysidedness', however, it was not primarily this kind of versatility he had in mind. The versatility of the Renaissance man sprang from two factors: the emergence of bourgeois production, and its still relatively low level. It was the former on which Marx laid emphasis. For him, many-sidedness meant primarily the end of *feudal one-sidedness*. In this sense the life of the landed gentleman was one-sided, even if some gentlemen at one and the same time sang and fenced, wrote verses and rode on horseback, and even philosophized. The beginnings of versatility lay, according to Marx, in the expansion of production, its becoming universal, the general development of productive forces, 'the possibility of the universal development of man', and with all these things the endless growth and expansion of needs as *social needs*. With the progress of bourgeois production man became universal, though this universalization occurred more and more in alienated forms. During the Renaissance this process of alienation was only just beginning, but the emergence of universality was only just beginning, too. The Renaissance was the starting-point for the development of versatility, just as it was the *starting-point* for bourgeois production and bourgeois society, but its society and mode of production were *still not* bourgeois society and the bourgeois mode of production themselves. Ancient Athenian versatility attained its most comprehensive form at the most developed level of the given mode of production; social and individual versatility by and large coincided. The *individual* versatility of the Renaissance was much more ambiguous. It was the appearance of the first forms of bourgeois production which made it possible, forms which in the future would create, over the centuries, an unimaginable wealth of *social versatility*. It is true that because of the extension of the division of labour and of alienation certain forms of individual versatility could not come into existence; thus Renaissance developments may indeed be regarded as a model of individual versatility, but with many qualifications. For even though individual and social many-sidedness closely paralleled each other here, just as in the ancient polis, they rested on social foundations which, in contrast to those of antiquity, were leading to a cleavage between the two; and finally, but not least important, the development of bourgeois production would eventually create much greater possibilities of *individual versatility* than was imaginable during the Renaissance. Hence we must draw the conclusion that the versatility of the Renaissance and its concept of versatility, were themselves, by contrast with their ancient counterparts, *dynamic*, and laden with objective contradictions. Precisely because of the undeveloped state of bourgeois production and the close connection between social and individual many-sidedness, the path of Renaissance versatility could lead backward as well as forward, towards refeudalization, into the cul-de-sac of a partial restoration of the one-sidedness of the system of social estates. In the concrete analysis of the concept of versatility we will often be confronted with these perspectives of 'forward' and 'backward'.

It is a favourite commonplace in discussions of the Renaissance that at that time 'man became the focus of interest'. But it would be just as true to say that nature became the focus of thought. Yet, the problem does not really lie here, but in the question: how did the Renaissance interpret the relationship between nature and man (or society)? First of all, the notion that man can 'conquer' something from nature, creating from primary nature a 'second' nature, dates from the Renaissance. The recognition of the 'conquest of nature' parallels the discovery of the concept of 'humanity', which in turn is inseparable from the idea of the *development* of humanity. The category of humanity, as we shall see, appears in a general anthropological and socio-philosophical light. The concept of the development of humanity first arises, however, in a concrete context, in connection with the 'conquest of nature'. Edgar Zilsel, in his study of the Renaissance's conception of technical co-operation and technical development, quite rightly sees in Bacon the most significant formulator of this tendency.[5] All these influences worked to transform radically the ontology of nature, and the relationship between ontology and the theory of knowledge as well. Nature came to appear as an object having its own laws (no matter, from our standpoint, if most of these laws were interpreted in an anthropomorphic way), and it became the continual duty of the human mind to gain knowledge of nature. Equal weight was placed on

11

the human mind and on the *continuous, ongoing character* of the process. The emphasis on the mind implied that the results of cognition are *in no way dependent on ethical behaviour*, while the stress on continuity separated the process of knowledge from logic; in this connection there arose attempts like that of Ramus to transform the structure of logic in such a way as to make it fit the categorical requirements of that process. Ramus's effort, despite all its interest, turned out to be a blind alley; the true course of development demanded a complete divorce of the two. The subject – man, or humanity – now stood face to face with a nature having its own laws; to learn to know this nature, intensively and extensively, became an infinite task. It was Nicholas of Cusa who first formulated both these tendencies – the divorce of the process of knowledge from ethics and logic, on the basis of a conception of an infinite nature acting out of its own necessity – in his conception of a '*docta ignorantia*'.

Everything I have said about a dynamic concept of man entails the notion of *immanence*. A focusing on earthly life did not emerge separately in the life and thought of the Renaissance; secularization in this sense cannot be regarded as a special chapter in the development of the Renaissance. With the dissolution of the corporate system of estates, the social structure on which Thomas Aquinas's world-view rested also vanished objectively (though I must add that in his own country Aquinas never became popular, precisely because of its very early bourgeois development); new ways of life, among them the cult of the self-made man, produced a kind of individual initiative and independence of judgment and desire that rendered nugatory any kind of dogma. But here I must also add (I will discuss it in more detail later) that the appearance of an interest in the things of this world did not at all imply irreligiosity. Outright atheism was very rare during the Renaissance. The decline of an age-old ideological tradition is an extremely lengthy process in any case, and during the Renaissance a practical interest in the things of this world did not conflict with the survival of religious ideas. But Renaissance religion was characterized by the disintegration of dogma: religion became multifarious and many-coloured, as if to express the fact that belief was now less strict, was 'free' and could be freely chosen.

In some philosophical conceptions, the Renaissance has been too much likened to the Enlightenment, on the grounds that the ideology of both eras was *polemical* in character. This emphasis on the polemical does indeed make them kindred periods, for in both cases a revolutionary ideology expressive of new social relations came

12

forward to attack the old; but the relationship of the Enlightenment to the Renaissance was the relationship of the last battle to the first one, and so the two were conducted with entirely different weapons. Socially, the course of the Renaissance might just as well have led backward towards refeudalization; developments might have become frozen in their tracks, for the process of the constant reproduction of bourgeois society had not yet begun. But there was no longer any going back from the social foundations on which the Enlightenment rested (and the problem of political reaction did not really change this in any way). The ideology of the Renaissance was already a bourgeois ideology, for it grew out of the beginnings of bourgeois production, *but it was far from becoming the conscious ideology of the entire bourgeoisie*; moreover, it left the plebeian strata almost untouched, while at the same time striking root and developing further among the nobility. The Enlightenment, by contrast, was a *universal* bourgeois ideology; differences among the various strata of the bourgeoisie were expressed by the differences *within* the ideology of the Enlightenment (we need think only of the kind of polarization that existed between the Rousseauian and Holbachian wings). A real and sincere social relationship linked early Renaissance absolutism to the ideology of the Renaissance, while the relationship of later, enlightened absolutism to the Enlightenment was ambiguous. A further reason for the great diversity in the substance of the polemics (in practice almost indistinguishable from the foregoing one) was the development which science had undergone between the two periods – the progress which extended from Galileo to Newton, the appearance of problems of method, the advance of analysis *clare et distincte* in philosophy, and so forth. The standpoint of immanence could no longer be reconciled with a religious ideology. The polemic was now conducted against feudalism and religion at the same time, either in openly atheistic form as in Helvétius or Diderot, or by converting religion into a religious need and thus stripping it of its ideological pretensions, as in the case of Rousseau. Of course, no strict historical borderline divides the two different ideologies: there is already a great deal of the Enlightenment in Hobbes, for example, while Goethe in many respects was still carrying on the rearguard battles of Renaissance ideology, as in his polemic against Newton on the theory of colour.[6] or his reworking of the Faust legend. To illustrate the difference, let me cite another example: the attitude towards reason. For the Enlightenment reason was synonymous with light or illumination; this was already an inheritance from Spinoza and Descartes. But during the Renaissance reason was still regarded as a power fraught with contradictions, especially ethical contradictions, often indeed in outright league with the devil. We need only compare Leonardo's allegory of the cave with Diderot's allegory of the candle in order to feel this difference. For Leonardo, reason is symbolized by the restless curiosity with which man leaves the bright daylight to grope about in the unknown, mysterious darkness of the cave; for Diderot it is a candle which illuminates the darkness of the forest (if only, at this early stage, with a flickering light).

With regard to religion, then, the dynamism of the Renaissance finds expression in the variegated character of religion and in the fact that one may choose his religion for himself. And here I must add that, as might be expected, idealism and materialism had not yet become differentiated during the Renaissance, or rather that the first steps in that direction were taken only at the end of the period.

Now I must ask: is there a unitary Renaissance ideal of man? Does the existence of a common concept of man as dynamic imply the existence of a common ideal of man?

During antiquity the ideal of man essentially *coincided* with the concept of man; at the same time, all of antiquity – excepting Rome in the period of its decadence – had a unitary ideal and concept of man. When Socrates said that man, knowing the good, can do good, he was also saying that the ideal man is the one who, knowing the good, does do good. When Plato declared that man's capacity to contemplate the idea was his most essential and most sublime quality, he was simultaneously taking as his ideal that man who attained to the contemplation of ideas. In Aristotle's eyes man was a social animal, and so his ideal was social man. When Epicurus taught that nothing exists for man in lesser degree than his own death, his ideal was the man who could live in such a way as to take no heed of his own death. Of course Socrates did not believe that every man was capable of recognizing the good and of doing good. But the individual who did not, had not yet attained to the concept of man, that is, the ideal of man. Nor did Plato believe that *every* craftsman and cultivator was sober and moderate, every warrior brave and every ruler wise – but in that case they 'still' did not conform to the concept and ideal of the craftsman, cultivator, warrior, or king. Aristotle's conception of a 'social animal' was not a mere conceptual interpretation of man, either, as it is now often considered to have been; it also postulates the sort of man who withdraws from public life, thus failing to fulfil the concept and ideal of man.

So much for the coincidence of the concept of man and the ideal of man. My other assertion, that concept and ideal of man were

identical, is more difficult to grasp. In any event we must treat
Sparta as a separate case, and rightly so, for in Sparta a special ideal
of man developed, but no concept of man ever evolved. Thus we
must restrict ourselves to the Attic, Ionian, and early Hellenistic
world and to the Roman Republic and the early Empire. But this
'restriction' is not at all arbitrary; we seek to understand the line of
development in its *classic* or typical form. Even within the mainstream, of course, the differences are seemingly great; in their conception of man it is customary to regard Plato and Aristotle, and
stoicism and epicureanism, as pairs of opposites. This opposition,
however, exists only in the *interpretation* of the concept of the ideal[7]
– in the answer given to the question 'Why?' on the one hand, and
in the emphasis placed on one or another aspect of the matter, on
the other. But who could deny, for example, that the notion of
kalokagathia was the *common* essence of all these concepts and
ideals? Or that the essence of all of them was the 'man of inner and
outer beauty' exercising his capacities in the given community,
living at peace among tempered pleasures, well-balanced physically,
spiritually, and morally, absorbed in the contemplation of truth?
If stoicism and epicureanism taught withdrawal from the world
(though in different forms), they did so in order to condemn a world
in which those ideals could no longer be realized. The prosaic basis
and starting-point of this ideal, moreover, was none other than
the idealized citizen of the Attic-Ionian polis. Stoicism and epicureanism sought to preserve that ideal, once real enough in the everyday
life of the remote past, for the sake of exceptional men living in a
hostile environment. And the social basis of this unity of concept
and ideal, and of their common character, was (as I have already
indicated) the communal nature of the ancient polis, its static
quality and lack of transcendability. In the later Empire this unity
dissolved: the concept of man and the ideal of man continued to
coincide, but concept and ideal themselves became pluralistic. This
was true, in germ, of Neoplatonism with its religious colouration,
by contrast with the stoic and epicurean ideal, but the process
reached its culmination with the development of the Christian ideal
and concept of man. This cleavage survived until the disintegration
of the Empire in the West.

I have no space here to analyse the social and economic bases of
that event, least of all in connection with the concept of man held
by medieval Christianity. Of the latter it is enough to say that its
concept of man and its ideal of man were in sharp contradiction to
each other. Its concept of man was founded on the idea of depravity,
its ideal of man on the idea of grace. By contrast with that of

antiquity, this dualistic conception was pre-eminently ideological. It never expressed a real status quo (for then belief and morality would really have coincided), but it proved to be a genuinely valuable ideological device in the age of the settlement of the barbarian tribes, the consolidation of feudal society, and the re-establishment of the fundamental norms of social life. Apart from its dualism, the Christian concept of man contained many elements that were new by comparison with antiquity. Among them were the idea of equality (equality before God), the notion of personal salvation (in which man's relationship to a personal God was separated from his relationship to the community), and the idea of free will which, while bound up with the idea of human depravity, still raised the question of a particularly individual kind of freedom.

Man's communal existence was thus split in two: on the one hand the individual man was a member of one feudal order or estate against other estates, while on the other he was a member of the Christian community as against others (infidels, heretics). This duality was not the expression of a looser relationship to the community, as it had been during antiquity. It was a double *subordination*, and as such reflected the extremely narrow range of movement allowed to the individual, even by comparison with antiquity. But at the same time it allowed much more flexibility to the particular movements of individual estates, strata, and communities within the general system. It was always possible to play off one form of subordination against the other: it was on this simple structure that the ideology of even the earliest heretical movements was based (and heretical movements are as old as Christianity itself). No social stratum of antiquity was ever able to confront another stratum with a different interpretation of its ideology. Brutus was 'Roman' and Caesar, too, was 'Roman' – the question never arose which was the 'true Roman'. We might say that the fact of 'ideological struggle' is a development of the Middle Ages. For antiquity, the symbol of voluntary death was Socrates, dying because he respected his country's laws (though he found its social order unjust); the Christian martyr rebelled in the name of religion against earthly power, even though that earthly power might also come forward in the name of Christianity.

The Christian concept of man and the Christian ideal of man were sharply dualistic; their content was, as a result, far from being unified *in the same sense* as during antiquity. For the latter, as we have seen, the basis of unity was an idealized image of an actual community. The ideological character of the Christian concept and ideal of man, on the other hand, offered much greater possibilities for a multiplicity of *substantive interpretations*. The abstract-ideological level of the contradiction between concept and ideal, and the multiplicity of substantive interpretations, were not, of course, the result of any kind of conscious decision. They were based precisely on the system of dual subordination, within which both the 'social' and the 'Christian' had each to have its own separate sphere of action. It is within the former, of course, that the concrete human ideals and auto-stereotypes and heterostereotypes of the various social orders must be interpreted. The abstract-ideological ideal and abstract-ideological concept of man, and the conflict between them, were still in *the last analysis* unitary: therein lay the *dogmatic* unity of the whole Christian world.

During the Renaissance the social basis of the Christian conception of man ceased to exist. Alongside the dual subordination to estate and to religion and, more and more, *above it*, appeared a third: the *national* (at first a local loyalty to the city-state, later national in the modern sense). The new interpretation of Christendom was no longer one of estates and certain social strata as opposed to a total hierarchy, as it had been in the heretic movements, but of individual nations as contrasted with other nations. Shaw correctly saw in *Saint Joan* that it was here the seeds of Protestantism were to be found. One's relationship to the nation, however, rests not on a system of estates but on class relations; and in a system of class relations the fact and the concept of personal subordination are both meaningless. At the same time ecclesiastical subordination was shaken too. Men more and more sought *individual* paths to God, because now they *could* seek them; here again we meet with the seeds of Protestantism. It is undeniable that the ideological preconditions of these changes were rooted in the medieval Christian concept of man, in medieval conceptions of personal salvation and abstract equality and in the dual subordination of medieval Christianity. But in a new and revolutionary context these concepts were radically restructured. The traditional medieval Christian concept of man was, as we have seen, gradually displaced by the Renaissance's dynamic concept of man, and for a long time the Christian ideal of man was forced into the background too (by which we do not mean to assert that most of the proponents of the new human ideal were hostile to religion – on the contrary, they were themselves religious).

The Renaissance's dynamic conception of man was just as unitary as the ancient conception. No thinker of the Renaissance ever harked back to a static (harmonious or dualistic) conception of man, so that this advance had to be conceded even by the Counter-Reformation and the baroque age. Within this dynamism the *two* extreme poles were the greatness of man, and his littleness. Which of the two is emphasized is often only a matter of the *point of view*. Giordano Bruno now speaks of man's littleness (compared to the infinity of the universe), now of his greatness (in the conquest of the world). Under the influence of historic events first one extreme and then the other may be stressed. Thus Michelangelo's tomb of Julius II and the Sistine frescoes are designed to express man's greatness, while the *Last Judgment* symbolizes his smallness before the judgment of fate. Differences of time and place play their part: it was natural for Pico della Mirandola, during Florence's golden age, to exalt the greatness of man, while in a France torn by the wars of religion Montaigne mocked at human pettiness. But to repeat: whether 'great' or 'small', man is always a relatively autonomous being, creating his own destiny, struggling with fate, making himself.

At the same time, if we look at the Renaissance's *ideal of man*, we are struck by the fact that *it is no longer possible to speak of a unitary human ideal. An unusual wealth of concrete human ideals* is revealed to us. And the concrete human ideal is no more than an idealized image of *actual* men – whether we recognize them as real men, or interpret them as ideals, or project them into the future as utopian figures.

If I mention only a few examples here, it is because I will return to these problems in more detail later. I must point first of all to the Renaissance interpretation of the figure of Christ. While the ideal content of the medieval Christian depiction of Christ is always the same (that of a suffering and redeeming Deity), Renaissance representations of Christ are characterized by a multifariousness of ideal content (the King, the Lord, the thinker, the plebeian with a heart of love, and so forth). We must add that at the same time the ideal of the suffering, tormented Christ fades away completely – at least in the period from Giotto to the late Michelangelo and Tintoretto, the classical period of the Italian Renaissance – and when it is rediscovered, it comes to appear as only *one* ideal and *one* interpretation among many. Similarly, the figure of Mary also turns into a pluralistic ideal. In the use of subjects from antiquity, it is more common for contrasting ideals to be represented in contrasting historical figures. Thus some thinkers of the Renaissance saw in Caesar the ideal 'hero', while others preferred Brutus, or Cicero, or the Gracchi.

The way in which ideals became pluralistic is most strikingly manifested in the appearance of a *pluralistic system of moral values*. Once again we are dealing with a phenomenon which sharply distinguishes the Renaissance from both antiquity and the Middle

Ages. However much controversy went on during antiquity over the interpretation of moral values – as in Aristotle's defence of the principle of the 'mean value' against the Socratic interpretation of ethical rationalism, or Plato's identification of scientific knowledge and virtue, or the dispute of stoics and epicureans over the interpretation of the concept of pleasure – *the major values remained unshakeably the same in them all*: wisdom, courage, moderation, and justice. These values could be supplemented with others, they could be dissected from the standpoint of differences in nuance, they could be ranked differently according to sequence or order of importance, but still their primary and fundamental character could never be denied. The same is true of the seven cardinal sins and seven cardinal virtues of medieval Christianity. Here, too, their order was fixed only in dogma – heretics often reversed it – but still the virtues and sins always remained the same for everyone. Who would have asserted that charity was not a virtue or that vanity was not a sin?

With the Renaissance the reversal is complete. Here the first step was a secular interpretation of the traditional virtues and sins: in my judgment Antal is correct in regarding the allegory of justice in Giotto's fresco in the Arena Chapel as an interpretation of justice in a secular republican spirit.[8] What was decisive, however, was the next stage: *the dissolution of the unitary medieval system of values*. Since this question is taken up in more detail below, I will merely mention a few selected examples here in order to indicate the process. In Castiglione's or Machiavelli's system of values 'thirst for glory' is one of the prime virtues; Cardano rejects it. For Vasari, 'haughtiness' is an object of respect; for Thomas More it is the source of the worst evil. Petrarch and Shakespeare deemed the passion for revenge wicked and senseless; Bacon places it among the positive values. 'Faith' is sometimes wreathed in respect, at other times it is the object of ridicule. The value of 'moderation' is central for Pico, but Giordano Bruno puts the immoderation of passion ahead of it. One after another new values are born to replace the traditional ones: patriotism, tolerance, tact, integrity, to mention only a few.

Machiavelli, Montaigne, Bacon, and Shakespeare – the four crowning glories of the Renaissance, leaving aside for the moment the fine arts – carried through theoretically and artistically a *separation of value, ideal, and table of virtues*, opening the way for the development of a realistic ethics in an age when a given, relatively small community was no longer the set limit of human action and hence the measure of the validity or invalidity of action, but where, on the contrary, the individual had to find grounds for moral action in a situation where values and interests had become relative and contradictory. As I have shown elsewhere, the Aristotelian sense of the 'mean value' still retained its significance and validity, but discovering the measure no longer meant the realization of 'virtue' in concrete circumstances and individual situations but only the discernment of the best possible relative good in the midst of a constantly shifting social reality.

A unitary – but dynamic – concept of man, and a plurality of human values, were two sides, necessarily linked, of one and the same development. The dynamism of the concept of man reflected the same revolutionary transformation of social life and human life as did the disintegration of the unity of the ideal of man. But here I would like to emphasize another aspect: a plurality of human ideals emerged *within* one and the same concept of man. Thus it is not simply a question of two lines of development which presuppose each other. I cannot stress enough: *the most contradictory human ideals cannot themselves be interpreted except by means of a dynamic concept of man.*

I have been obliged to return to this relationship in order to refer again to everything that was 'new' in the Renaissance and everything that was 'old'. With the beginnings of bourgeois economy and the advance of bourgeois social relations (even if, for the time being, it still went on within the framework of a feudal society) the concept of man and the ideal of man were split in two again. The elaboration of a dynamic concept of man is seventeenth-century philosophy (speaking now only of its mainstream) breaks with the problems of the human ideal; it takes a polemical stand against the existence of an ideal of man, or the need for one. (I will be examining the beginnings of this attitude soon in Machiavelli and Bacon.) The theory of egoism from Hobbes to Helvétius posits as 'man' the bourgeois individual, the kind of man developed by bourgeois society, and relates the sphere of action and the potentialities of everyday life, as well as of morals and politics, to this kind of individual. The *ultimate* unification of the concept of man and the ideal of man, by Spinoza with the aid of a renewed ethical rationalism, was a *rearguard action* of the Renaissance, a process traceable, as I have shown, all the way down to Goethe. I have stressed the 'ultimate' unification and the 'rearguard action' in order to emphasize that all these efforts aimed only at reuniting the concept of man and the ideal of man, but no longer came forward with the demand that the human ideal be bound to a table of values and virtues. But Spinoza was still the last for whom the ideal of man was objective and present; for those who later clung to the ideal of man as a formative principle or criterion belonging necessarily to the ethical man or to the moral substance of man, the ideal of man was projected into the future (postulated) and became subjective or, as with Kant, subjective and formal. The first major attempt to develop a historical concept of man, a concept of man in history, and to overcome the identification of 'man' with 'bourgeois man', is linked with the name of Rousseau; it took place under the sign of a new unification of the concept of man and the ideal of man. This effort of reunification was not, of course, a product of immanent philosophy; it was rooted in the special plebeian attitude and point of view with which Rousseau regarded the progress of his century. Rejecting both the present and the seeds of the future (a bourgeois future) lurking in the present, reacting in despair against both the feudal and the bourgeois systems of values, and their practical morality, Rousseau was able to save the ideal of man which he as a revolutionary spirit needed and still see men with some bitterness as they were, only by asking: were they always like this, and how and *why did they come to be like this?* In this manner – by raising the question in *historical* terms – he found the key to the reunification of the concept of man and the ideal of man, in so far as it became possible for a 'worthier' ideal human community to evolve from those human communities which were not yet or not completely depraved. The key, however, still would not open the lock. As we have said, for Rousseau it was still only the past that appeared as history. Present and future, too, had to become recognizable as history for the concept of man and the ideal of man to be reunited again.

The anthropology of Marx resolved the age-old dilemma of concept of man and ideal of man. These two were rejoined, and to that degree the heritage of antiquity and the Renaissance was renewed. But it was no longer either the static harmony of Greece or the plurality of ideals of the Renaissance. In the harmonious but static Greek world man was identified, in a bounded, finite way, with the ideal possibilities of a given, unchanging system of values. The plurality of ideals of the Renaissance was a reflection of the disintegration of society ('free' society) into social classes. In the various stages of bourgeois development, whether arrested or ongoing, each class, stratum, social group, and city had its own ideals and its own concrete system of values. Both humanity (as a being-for-itself) and man's individuality were in the process of genesis. With the progress of bourgeois development this plurality of concrete ideals necessarily turned into a set of abstract ideals, in what way and with what further possibilities we have seen – at least for those who still retained a need for ideals. Marx, however, always rejected these abstract ideals, and it was in this sense that he declared that the proletariat had no ideals to realize. Marx did not subordinate ideals to an abstract concept of man, nor did he build his concept of man on a set of human ideals. On the contrary: in Marx a concrete historical concept of man itself becomes the ideal of man.

György Márkus has analysed the content of the Marxian concept of man in terms of societality, labour, consciousness, freedom, and universality.[9] All these generally characterize man (humanity) – it is these traits which *distinguish* man, raising him above the animal world. But in the course of humanity's prehistory every step in the emergence of the human essence has been at the same time a moment of alienation; the development of the whole species took place at the expense of individual men, classes, and peoples, and the enrichment of humanity demanded the impoverishment of some men. Man was always a social being, but his societality-in-itself became a societality-for-itself only with the creation of a universal humanity by the world market, while humanity (man, hence every single human being) will become the master of its social relationships only in the future, becoming humanity-for-ourselves. Again, labour as a goal-setting activity, labour as the means of creating human society and human nature, will only become labour-for-ourselves when the possibility is created for every single human being to appropriate the use of the means of production left him by earlier generations, in such a way as to place thereby the stamp of his own individuality upon his creations, when goal-setting activity comes to entail the realization of his own goals. Man by definition is free, for he has alternatives and adjusts his actions to his conscious intentions; that is why this process bears the name of action. But freedom will only become freedom-for-ourselves when we become capable of being masters of nature, society, and ourselves. Man is universal-in-himself, but we will only become universal-for-ourselves when every man has the possibility of many-sided development, so that it is no longer only humanity as a *whole* which is the bearer of universality. Consciousness will only become consciousness-for-ourselves when human knowledge, as the aspect of praxis and the motor of freedom, becomes the consciousness of us all. Thus humanity, or 'man-for-all-of-us', is not derived from some subjectively set goal or from wishful thinking, but from the essence of man and its development: it is the ultimate tendency of human development. *The ideal of humanity and the ideal of man are none other than the concept of this possible end result.*

Until now I have spoken of the differences between the ways the concept of man and the ideal of man coincided during three historical periods – the conceptions of antiquity, of the Renaissance, and of Marx. Now, however, I must emphasize the common roots of the fact that this coincidence did indeed exist. The ages of the ancient republics (above all the Greek city-states) and the Renaissance (chiefly the Italian Renaissance) were those moments in history – always brief and transient, hitherto – *during which the individual's and the species' potential for development approached closest to each other*; during these periods the discrepancy between the two was smallest, so that it was possible, by 'extension' of the qualities of the given age and of man as given in each age, to attain to a concept of man and an ideal of man. True, both were decidedly ages of *transition*; nor does it matter from our point of view that the first was headed for destruction while the other gave rise to a new set of social and productive relations on a higher plane of development. This transitoriness finds perhaps its best expression in the sequence of the plays of Shakespeare. The atmosphere of the first comedies itself practically suggests what I have said about the parallelism of the development of individual and species. Rudeness, brutality, conventionality, stupidity, miserliness, and cupidity always lose out in the end in their contest with human nature or the 'natural man'; the terrible cataclysms of the historical past are swallowed up, too, in this world of affirmation. But the contours soon darken. If in the history plays the laws of an old order were still capable of destroying human values step by step in everyone, progressively and inexorably, *Richard III*, which closes the cycle, and the contemporaneous comedies posit the emergence of a 'human situation' productive of the values of a more humane world. Yet in the late tragedies 'man' himself becomes a doubtful entity. Brutus and Horatio are Shakespeare's last human ideals; thereafter no ideal of man in the Renaissance sense is to be found in Shakespeare's world.

As we have seen, the identity of the Marxian ideal of man and concept of man springs from the fact that Marx recognized the abolition of the discrepancy between the individuals' and the species' development – and its abolition by men themselves – as the immanent goal of historical development. Thus far his attitude was sharply *critical* (towards capitalist progress) and at the same time profoundly *affirmative* (with respect to the tendencies of future development). With its historical conception Marxism was able to create an ideal *from that which exists, even when in a certain sense that which exists still does not exist as yet.*

So we have seen what it is that connects the most 'normal' form of the 'natural' communities (the Greek world) and the 'most normal' of the forms born on the borderline of the 'natural' communities and 'purely societal' society open towards the future (Renaissance development) with the inner tendency of the 'normal development' of mankind. In this sense and for this reason we can regard Renaissance man and the Renaissance ideal of man as *a measure and a paragon*, just as much as the man and the ideal of man of ancient Greece.

Every ideal of man has *always* been accompanied by an *ideal of society*. The interpretation of man has always necessarily been bound up with the ideas that thinkers have formed about the various forms of social intercourse which have been familiar to them. Thus the Greek ideal of man was accompanied by a static ideal of the state, one free from class conflict; the final conjunction of the two ideals is presented effectively in Plato's *Republic*. By the same token, the principle of egoism was accompanied by a picture of society in which *homo homini lupus* was the watchword – we need only think of one of the most clear-cut expressions of that principle, Mandeville's *Fable of the Bees*.

Disputes about the ideal of man are expressions and reflections of struggles whose motive force (usually openly avowed, but sometimes tacit) is a definite ideal of society; nor was this any different during the Renaissance. In his *Discourses* Machiavelli still had an ideal of society, the polis-republic, and so he had an ideal of man as well. When, in *The Prince*, he rejected out of hand any ideal state, he was at the same time rejecting any ideal of man. When Aretino spoke scornfully of Tintoretto's figures while praising the portraits of Titian, he was opting for an aristocratic alternative of political development in the Venetian state and against a plebeian one, and for the rearguard defence (now a little apologetic) of a relatively harmonious age in a world of crisis, heavy with real antagonisms. In Thomas More's social Utopia the people are everyday men of the age, but in the learned utopia of Campanella wide knowledge is also an integral part of the ideal of man.

I have mentioned these commonplace-sounding connections only in order to point up more strikingly the *uneven* development of the concept of man and the concept of society. As we have seen, a concept of man existed both during antiquity and during the Renaissance; in both cases the question, 'What is man like?', was indistinguishable from the problem of 'What is man?' The problem of man was thus eminently an ontological problem, both psychologically (as the concept of the soul became secularized) and socially. The same was not true of the concept of society. Most important, an explicit concept of society was very belated – it is a product of capitalist development. *During antiquity, the concept of society never*

24

became distinguished from the concept of the state. That does not, of course, mean that some specifically social phenomena existing independently of the state were not examined at all. Aristotle had done that much in his *Politics*, whether in discussing the exchange of goods or in sketching the difference between slave-holding and slave-acquiring societies. But *the social structure as a whole* remained synonymous with the structure of the state. The Renaissance harked back strongly to the tradition of antiquity in this regard; it interpreted events in society as first and foremost *political events.* True, even here there was a recognition and examination of some social phenomena. Class conflict, for example, was not grasped exclusively as a struggle for political power between nobles and commoners, but as an eternal controversy between rich and poor; efforts were made to penetrate to the economic basis of individual historical events (see, for example, Machiavelli's analysis of the revolt of the Ciompi). But when it is a question *not of mere description*, nor of the interpretation or evaluation of individual historical events, but of formulating a comprehensive concept to grasp the subject *in its totality*, then recourse is always made to the concept of the state. The ideas formed about the movement of society do not order themselves into a concept of society; they remain descriptions. *Society does not become an ontological category.* This is true even of a thinker like More, who (as we will discuss later) went furthest in the analysis of a particular social structure. The condition for the birth of society as an ontological category was the existence of a science of political economy; and the condition for the birth of political economy was a society which brutally demonstrated the priority of economic facts, brutally splitting man into the bourgeois on one side and the citizen on the other, and thus overturning an age-old tradition which had identified state and society.

PART ONE

Uneven development

PART ONE

Uneven development

The basis for the uneven development of the Renaissance era was of course the uneven development of the forces of production in the social structure of the Middle Ages – but the 'unevenness' of the Renaissance displays important differences, quantitative and qualitative, by comparison with the earlier age. I will single out only a few essential factors. As it became possible to develop the forces of production at an *accelerated tempo*, existing and ever-growing *differences in tempo*, ranging from stagnation all the way to maximum exploitation of the possibilities of development (the beginnings of capitalist reproduction on a large scale) were accentuated. As a result, there appeared a number of decisively different possible paths and forms for the emergence of capitalist relations of production. After the nation became the economic unit, these various paths and forms came to appear as *national* paths and national forms, going to shape the varieties of national character; henceforward national character was to have its effect on the further development of the economic structure, on one hand, and gradually to set its stamp on the tone of each culture, on the other. The differentiated and uneven development of the various nations was made even more explicit by the transformation of history first into *European history* and then, later, into world history. Those nations whose development was more rapid and took classical forms left a more pronounced mark on the total historical process – but without being able to stop the stagnation of other nations; within a unitary Europe advanced and backward nations appeared, and with them *an awareness of advanced development and underdevelopment* was also born. Petrarch, travelling in France and Italy, observed only

29

differences in customs and manners; any idea of 'development' and 'underdevelopment' was entirely foreign to the world of his thinking. But Vives thought he had found in England a country that was 'not Spanish' and a society that afforded a path towards greater possibilities; Machiavelli in his polemic against mercenary armies cited the superiority of the popular levies of the Swiss war of independence; Giordano Bruno all but fled from Italy to the countries where real or imaginary freedom of thought existed; Galileo regarded his colleagues in Holland with justified envy; Campanella asked and received asylum in France. Common to the last three examples was a fear of the Inquisition. But the revival of the Inquisition in sixteenth-century Italy was itself one factor in the process of refeudalization.

The fact of the unity of European development – and at the same time its unevenness – appears in all its explicit brutality only in the sixteenth century. It is linked with three dates (the dates, of course, are only *conjunctures* at which previous differences in development came to a head, creating the basis for a further parting of the ways). These dates are 1517, 1527, and 1579 (or 1588). The first marks the Reformation, embodying and setting off the first great *popular movement* of the age (culminating in the Peasant War), and at the same time making possible the expression in religious and ideological terms of the parting of ways among the nations; Calvinism would create the religious form *most appropriate for the development of capitalism* (as Max Weber recognized, while reversing the terms). In 1527, with the Sack of Rome, the fate of the Italian Renaissance was sealed; hopes for a united Italy, and hence for the further development of Italian capitalism, were shattered once and for all; the influence of Spanish power worked on the Church to give an unequivocal answer to the Reformation: the wing led by Sadoleto, which strove to humanize the Church in the spirit of the Renaissance, had to give way to a hard-fisted Jesuit leadership supported by the Inquisition; *and thus the process by which the Church had begun to accommodate itself to the new situation created by capitalism came to a reactionary end.* Again, the growth of Spanish influence was itself a consequence of an earlier economic conflict, the exhaustion of the financial resources of a Florence (the party of the Black Guelphs) which had supported the Renaissance papacy, when in the new European situation the Church needed a far broader material basis to survive – but that is a problem which we cannot touch upon here.

In the general course of social development 1579 and 1588 may be regarded as forming, in the last analysis, one date. They mark *the failure of the Spanish path* of bourgeois development as well.

The year 1579 saw the triumph of the Netherlands war of independence, the first modern war of national liberation, led and supported
by the national bourgeoisie, and 1588 brought the destruction of the
'Invincible' Armada. Here already we meet with the *results* of the
first English wave of primitive capital accumulation; at the same
time the last obstacles to the *classical* course of capitalist development fall away.

The greatness of the thinkers and artists of the sixteenth century
is to a great extent determined by *how deeply they experienced or
thought through* these critical passages. From this point of view it is
all the same whether they were natural philosophers or social
reformers, painters or poets. (Of course, the question of whether
they experienced them or thought them through arose only to the
degree that the conflicts came to the surface in a given place. Thus
Tintoretto's vision of reality became a tragic one only after Lepanto,
for in Venice it was only then that the critical turning-point came.)
Nor does it matter *whether they affirmed or rejected* the new course
of development – though it does matter *what* they affirmed in it and
what they rejected. Here I should only like to characterize in a few
words the main types. Here one finds Aretino, unwilling to understand anything, immersing himself in the world of the Venetian
aristocracy and going on playing the fool as if he were still at the
court of Leo X. Here is Castiglione, recalling with no small amount
of resignation the harmonious life of the High Renaissance, at a time
when its foundations had already become eroded. Here is Erasmus,
who foresaw nothing of the cataclysms of the century, dreaming,
together with Vives and More at the court of the young Henry
VIII, of a world in which the *pax romana* would return, a rationalized
and universal Christianity would reign, the feudal world would go
down to defeat, and knightly ideals would die away and be replaced
by gradual social reforms and the trained humanists who would
bring them about, the 'knights of Christianity'. But the critical
junctures arrived just the same. Erasmus *saw* the situation but was
unable to deal with it; he could neither formulate the new problems
nor understand them. Hence the bitter but undirected trenchancy
of the *Praise of Folly*; but the wit and veracity of the details cannot
conceal the confusion of the *total* conception. Erasmus clung to a
literate humanism whose time had already gone by, but at the same
time he was too much the plebeian to be satisfied with a bookish,
intensive kind of humanism, such as the Counter-Reformation was.
He clung even more to a unitary *devotio christiana* and to the
compromising over of conflicts, and, as a consequence, he was
unable to join the movement which attracted others with a plebeian

31

attitude like his: the Reformation. At the same time he was sceptical about capitalist development: he viewed both the unfolding of productive forces and the advance of scientific thinking with a sceptical eye. Before 1517, an abstract synthesis of all the forces of the Renaissance still seemed possible; at that time Erasmus's viewpoint was not a profound one, but it was certainly not compromising either. Between 1517 and 1527 the same attitude became objectively both compromising and superficial. We are far from accepting Stefan Zweig's interpretation of Erasmus, which makes of the philosopher of Rotterdam a cringing petty bourgeois opposed to any kind of *engagement*. Nothing was further from Erasmus than fear of making a commitment. It was simply that, as a result of his own standpoint, there was no longer anything to commit himself to; his compromise, be it repeated, was not a subjective but an objective one, which did not exclude personal honour and courage.

Thomas More's stance may be understood as a counterpoint to that of his friend Erasmus. More, in contrast to Erasmus, recognized the new situation for what it was, and knew that things had happened which were irrevocable. It was in this vein that he dealt with the demand that he act as some sort of 'philosophical tutor' to Henry VIII: he realized that Henry VIII would never be a 'Christian prince' and that the age of 'Christian princes' generally was over. He saw, too, that the reception and official approval of Calvinism would open the gates to the process which we call 'primitive accumulation', and that thereby the social reforms which he and Erasmus had dreamed of would become impossible once and for all. He did not doubt for an instant that it was necessary to shoulder the consequences which sprang from his recognition of these facts; his martyrdom only sealed his readiness to do so. The same profound understanding of the age provides the pathos of Giordano Bruno's life, though with the terms reversed. It must be emphasized that Bruno was not the only man summoned before the Inquisition during the first wave of the Counter-Reformation. But the majority of thinkers kept to the age-old custom of making a *formal recantation*. Later, when Galileo did the same thing, he was not acting in any unusual way; he was merely following the ancient custom amid changed circumstances. Thus it was that in his day Valla retracted his discoveries of fabrications of the Bible, Nicholas of Cusa his denial of original sin, and Cardano the many medical discoveries of his which had appeared in magical trappings. Of course, we must emphasize the changed circumstances of the Counter-Reformation, for these found expression in the consequences as well. Not only did

32

Valla and Cusa go on living as free and respected men after they had made their recantations. Nicholas of Cusa even retained his ecclesiastical office; the Renaissance popes themselves regarded the retractions as a formality. During the age of the Counter-Reformation, however, severe punishments were imposed on the victims of the Inquisition; though they might save their lives, they were often condemned to life imprisonment. The Church's demand for recantation was no longer a formality: it implied an *ideological victory* over the opponent. Bruno recognized the fact *when he broke the tradition of recantation* and accepted the ideological struggle, regarding the Church as the enemy of his efforts. Bruno treated the Copernican picture of the cosmos not as a scientific discovery, but as a new world-view which entailed the affirmation of the changes that had taken place. For he regarded the great changes which the century had brought as irrevocable; he took the side of Calvinism as a movement, while viewing its concrete Genevan form and its religious content with growing reservations and eventually rejecting it, and taking his stand for an English type of solution he went to do battle, on the basis of this conscious world-view, with the Counter-Reformation. If, among those who deeply understood the age, we wish to refer to an artist, we must mention the name of Michelangelo. He became the *universal* artist of the epoch because in *every* period of his long life he lived through and generalized the conflicts of his time. One and the same man represented in the *David* the symbol of the Florentine polis and in the Medici tombs the ruin of its hopes, and made magnificent compositions of the idea of man deified in the tomb of Julius II and of the historical vision of man as dynamic in the Sistine frescoes; and the same man gave expression to the latest cataclysms in the *Last Judgment* and to a despairing sorrow in the last *pietás*.

In discussing the uneven pace of development and the conjunctures of world-historical importance which marked the sixteenth century, we cannot escape the problem of mannerism. This designation for the art (chiefly the Italian art) of the period following the Sack of Rome is rather unfortunate, for it employs a secondary formal characteristic to define a whole historical and artistic period. But however inadequate the concept of mannerism may be, it contains a most important problem: the fact that after the Sack of Rome (the date, of course, is only an approximation) Italian art can *no longer* be regarded as Renaissance art, but can *not yet* be considered baroque. Max Dvořak applies this term (correctly, we believe) to Cervantes as well, a creative artist in a nation where, as in Italy, the course of development had become 'petrified'. (At the same time he applies it – mistakenly – to all of Shakespeare, for in England artistic problems and categories evolved differently as a result of decisive differences in social development.) The marks of mannerism are the dissolution of harmony, a shift in the proportions of subjectivity and objectivity in the direction of subjectivity, the depiction of conflicts which remain artistically unresolved, and a greater prominence of the tragic and the comic; in their unity and complexity these are indeed characteristics which sharply distinguish the artistic *experiments* of the period from the *manifold but still unitary course* of Renaissance art. The category of 'mannerism' also obscures the essential distinction which can be drawn between the purely formal innovators and conformists of the period, like Veronese or Bassano, and those whose search for new forms sprang from an experience of new problems, like Parmigianino or Tintoretto. For our purposes, the important thing in this connection is to establish that the depiction of man by the most profound artists who are usually considered mannerists is no longer essentially a part of the problematics of the Renaissance concept and ideal of man, and can be dealt with only in terms of the dissolution of that concept and ideal.

In Italian philosophy the Renaissance character prevails for about half a century longer than in art. This was so first of all because the subject matter of philosophy was *much more international* and hence could take up the problems of social development beyond the frontiers of Italy as well. At the same time, the technical and scientific discoveries of the century, culminating in the Copernican picture of the universe, made it possible to deal with questions which gave such a powerful impetus to the immanent development of the earlier natural philosophy (and the attempts at an anthropology which were inseparably bound up with it) that philosophy was able to spill over the usual historical boundaries. And finally, the necessity of launching a counter-attack against the onslaught of the Counter-Reformation sprang primarily from the development of natural philosophy, which demanded a further elaboration of its categories. Italy's crisis found expression here in the fact that Italian natural philosophy *was unable to go beyond the limits of the Renaissance in posing the relevant questions.* When the creativity of Renaissance natural philosophy (and anthropology) came objectively to an end with Galileo, and a new methodology became necessary, there was no one in Italy capable of taking that step. While in France Montaigne and Charron were followed by Descartes, and in England Bacon was succeeded by Hobbes, in Italy the development of philosophy comes to a close with Campanella – the same Campanella

34

who, visiting France in 1634(!), sought the friendship not of Descartes but of Gassendi.

I have dwelt at length on the great international turning-points of the sixteenth century, those conjunctures at which the uneven pace of development suddenly burst out into the open, closing the golden age of the Renaissance in some places and opening the way to it in others. I should like to stress, however, that in between these great international turning-points local victories and disasters did not, of course, cease. I might cite the fact (important for our purposes) that Venice, the Italian republic most independent of the papacy, did not immediately feel the impact of the Sack of Rome. For Venice, the battle of Lepanto was the turning-point. On the other hand, the French occupation of 1500 had already put an end to the more superficial Renaissance development of Milan. French developments received a strong setback between François I and Henri IV from the wars of religion and the extirpation of a part of the Huguenots. These facts, however, do not alter the central importance of the dates cited above.

From the standpoint of the *emergence* of a dynamic concept of man the Italian course of development is the most important. But even this was uneven, from the very beginning of the Renaissance. We must often bear in mind the great differences in the concrete character of the economic base, of political forms, of the breadth of the Renaissance life style, and of the degree of its impact on the common people.

In grouping the Italian states first of all from the standpoint of their political forms, I will be considering one of the explicit criteria of *overall bourgeois development*. From the fourteenth to the sixteenth centuries *the kingdom of Naples* was, with respect to bourgeois development, the most retarded; here Renaissance cultures spread in a noble and aristocratic form and the people remained untouched by it. The principalities where 'tyrants' ruled – Ferrara, Milan, Urbino, and Rimini, to mention only the most important – were founded on an *equilibrium* between nobility and bourgeoisie; feudal distinctions still existed, but no single estate had an *economic* preponderance. From the fifteenth century – when the tyrants began to come more and more from the ranks of the *condottieri* – the stability of their social systems was based on a complicated and regular system of taxation, which was left unchanged; the assassination of the tyrant was a recurrent event but went on 'over the heads' of the people, and in no way overturned the whole system as similar political murders did in Florence, for example. The Renaissance manner of life and way of thinking were more or less general among the bourgeoisie of these towns, but the 'high culture' of the Renaissance was still peculiar to the courts of the tyrants. The golden age of their culture is bound up with the name and power of one or another of their culture-loving princes, and to this degree the Renaissance was a superficial phenomenon there too. The culture of Urbino is connected with the family of Montefeltro, the epicureanism which found favour in Rimini with the personal tastes of Sigismondo Malatesta; the name of Ludovico il Moro has left its mark on the golden age of Milan, and the Renaissance culture of the Este was also relatively short-lived (it is enough to compare the fate of Ariosto with that of Tasso).

Rome occupied an entirely different position during the whole three centuries of the Renaissance – though not because of any special character of its own as a polis, for the power of the papacy and the rivalry of the two great families of Orsini and Colonna prevented it from ever developing into a true polis. Rome had only one great 'historic moment', from the standpoint of its own potential evolution into a polis: the revolt and brief rule of Cola di Rienzo, an effort to create a plebeian republic ('plebs' is to be understood here, of course, as the *whole* bourgeoisie, for in Rome the concepts of 'patrician' and 'noble' had become fused, whereas in Florence the wealthy bourgeois was a patrician, leaving the petty bourgeois and workers as plebeians). One cannot read without emotion those letters of Petrarch in which he hails the deeds of that 'great spirit' (Rienzo), while fearing for the cause of 'liberty and the reborn republic' – only to accuse the leader himself of weakness in the end for giving up power.[1] But there were no economic foundations on which the success of this brilliant interlude might have been based. The foundations of Rome's bourgeois economy were *external*; they did not grow out of the internal development of the city, and so a polis-republic could only be an illusion in Rome. Two other factors were to determine the peculiar role of the Eternal City in the culture of the Renaissance. The first was the papacy itself: the court of the Renaissance popes was the richest single source of patronage and a centre of Renaissance culture in its aristocratic forms, especially during the pontificates of Julius II, Leo X, and Clement VII. The other was the survival in Rome, in their most vital form, of the traditions of ancient Rome. There it was not necessary to 'rediscover' antiquity. The Roman nobility pursued a genuinely patrician mode of life, not a feudal-chivalric one. Cola di Rienzo himself had large-scale excavations carried out. And, to speak for a moment of philosophy, Lorenzo Valla, too, was a typical example of those Roman patricians, with their attachment to antique traditions

36

of life. The natural continuity of the ties with antiquity on one hand, and the aristocratic character of Renaissance culture on the other, were the two factors which made the concept of *bellezza* the central category for the development of the Renaissance in Rome.

Still, the most solid foundations of the Renaissance were to be found in the poleis: Siena, Florence, and Venice. Sienese culture was founded on a markedly bourgeois basis and at the same time was more popular than that of Florence or Venice, but it faltered and went under during the first stage of the Renaissance. (Thus the principle of uneven development appeared early on even among the Italian polis-republics themselves). We do not know what brought about its collapse (at least I have not been able to find any material which satisfactorily explains the phenomenon). From our standpoint, however, Siena is not of the first importance; the culture of the Renaissance remained within the sphere of the fine arts there and never took on conceptual form. And so there remain Florence and Venice.

To begin with an informal analogy: *the development of Florence stands in relationship to that of Venice in the same way as, during antiquity, the development of Attica compared to that of Ionia.* I would like to indicate here two apparently superficial similarities. One is the phenomenon of stability as opposed to volatility. The social and economic system of the Ionian cities was comparatively stable; such cities as Miletus and Rhodes retained their economic and political power for several centuries. From the time of the fall of the tyrants a form of republican order took root which was not exposed to constant political struggles or oscillations of power, first in one direction, then in another. By ancient standards, the Ionian polis was relatively loosely organized; there was more scope for private life. The history of Athens, by comparison, was brief and turbulent; inside of a century the city climbed to its peak, only to disappear during the next century from the arena of history. A series of class struggles marked that century; political power was unstable; parties and leaders followed one another in quick succession; the public life of the polis was much closer and more demanding, private life only becoming possible later during the age of decline.

The difference between stability and volatility is also most striking if we examine the development of Florence and Venice. The whole history of Venice was hardly ever marked by class conflicts. State power was in the hands of the Council of Ten, which was elected by the entire aristocracy (i.e. the wealthy bourgeoisie). According to Burckhardt, moreover, participation in the Council was short-term and little sought after. The same was true of the office of doge. The poor citizenry were entirely excluded from the administration of the state, nor did they try to put an end to this state of affairs. Parallel with this there developed, as in the Ionian cities, a corresponding relationship of public and private life. From a very early date there was wide scope for private endeavour: increasing wealth could become a goal in itself, and did not necessarily involve the participation of a *social stratum* in power, for anyone who grew rich personally entered the aristocracy after a time and took part in the elections to the Council of Ten. Public life was narrowly defined and narrow in scope.

Precisely the opposite is true of the three centuries of Florence's golden age: sharp class struggles succeeded one another, upward and downward fluctuations of fortune were constant, individual strata gained power but were presently driven from their places. Here the individual could succeed only through the success of his *social stratum*. Public life predominated over private life; public affairs set the whole populace in motion, even the workers.

The other similarity – again only seemingly superficial – is observable in the development of philosophical thinking. Ionian philosophy was characterized from the very beginning (Thales) by the dominance of ontological problems, to be replaced increasingly from the fourth century B.C. onwards by speculation about nature, and medical and physical questions; ethics and social thought were either completely absent or were relegated to the second rank. Athenian thought, on the other hand, was dominated by ethical and social problems from the time of Solon, and when Plato first constructed an ontologically founded world-view, he did so (as Georg Lukács tellingly observed) in answer to the ethical and social question 'How should we act?': thus this ontology became consciously ideological. (In this respect Aristotle was not typical: he it was who carried through the synthesis of the Attic and Ionian philosophical heritages.)[2]

If we examine carefully the philosophical development of Florence and Venice, we find parallels once again. Questions of ethical and social philosophy also dominated Florentine thought for a long time; here it is enough to recall such names as Salutati, Bruni, Alberti, Palmieri, and Manetti. In pointing out its resemblance to Athens I am not, of course, thinking of any identity of *content* in their social and ethical thought. On the contrary, I believe that everything which has already been said about the divergent development of the two cities is sufficient so that we should not expect any such identity of content. Differences in substance do not, however,

38

alter the fact that both turned towards ethical and social questions. In Florence, moreover, ontology only appeared at a time when the crisis of the city had begun, during the rule of Lorenzo de' Medici. Nor was it an accident that it was precisely here, in Florence, that thinkers turned back to *Platonic* philosophy and *Platonic* ontology; for Ficino and Pico the Platonic system was the kind of ideological tradition in which they could seek an answer to the ethical and social question, "How should we act?'

I will return in another connection to the analysis of why Ficino called his system – and more than just formally – '*Theologia* Platonica'; for the moment it is only important for us to establish that *one* of his reasons was so as consciously to deal with the question in an ideological way. Here I might just mention, in order not to gain a one-sided idea of the evolution of Florentine philosophy through stressing the main line of development, that the level of technical development attained during the quattrocento made possible another course: the application of the ancient notion of activity to *technical* activity and an effort to explore the problems of natural philosophy on that basis. It was this course that Leonardo da Vinci took in his fragments. But in stressing that this second possibility existed I must still repeat that this was not to be the main line of Florentine development. From beginning to end Leonardo was an outsider in his own homeland, as his life history demonstrates.

If, on the other hand, we consider Venice – or rather its university and ideological centre, Padua – we may observe there the unequivocal dominance of *Aristotelianism*. Its main concerns were ontological and epistemological; the problems of ethics and social existence arose only *within* those, in a rather technical manner, with scholarly objectivity and devoid of pathos or passion. Its forms were much more conservative than at Florence. The scholastic method of disputation prevailed, Thomists and Averroists polemicizing with each other. But behind the scholastic method of disputation *the content was entirely secular*, directed not towards dogmatic issues but towards elucidating real ontological and epistemological problems. This secularism could be entirely free of compromise – it is well known that Venice was the only Italian city-state that was independent of the papacy; the Inquisition had no power there; the doge disposed of a certain amount of ecclesiastical authority. Thus Venice became the first home of the non-ideological quest for truth. The circumstance that it was precisely the *Neapolitans*, like Telesio and Bruno, living in the stronghold of *scholastic content* and with no Venetian course open to them, who eventually had to burst out of scholastic *forms* in natural philosophy does not detract from the scientific significance of Venetian Aristo-telianism, nor from the fact that the new natural philosophy (no longer scholastic even in style) owed a great deal to it. Natural *science* as well owed a great debt to it: Nicholas of Cusa, Purbach, Regiomontanus, and Copernicus all studied at Padua, and even Galileo did not remain untouched by that tradition, although by the nature of the case he was more conspicuous for his efforts to transcend it in his polemics. When Giorgione painted his *Three Philosophers* he depicted the three types of philosopher who epito-mized Venetian development: the Thomist, the Averroist, and the natural philosopher. A practical thinker in ethical or social philo-sophy, of Salutati's or Alberti's kind, never existed in Venice or Padua. And to point out yet another contrast: while in Florence the problem of *freedom* was the basic one, in Paduan philosophy it was the notion of *determinism* which was dominant.

I will close this comparison of the evolution of Venice and Florence with a distinction which has no counterpart in the history of Ionia and Attica: the special character of their fine arts. Here I would single out two factors. The first is the universality of the Florentine artists. It is common knowledge that in Florence almost every painter was at one and the same time an architect and a sculptor, too; every sculptor was also an architect at least, and so on. I need only point to Giotto, Donatello, Ghiberti, Brunelleschi, Leonardo and Michelangelo, not to mention the minor figures. In Venice, on the other hand, *there was not a single painter* who was at the same time a sculptor or an architect as well. The other factor can be seen in the circumstance that Florentine painting and sculpture are full of internal *conflicts*; to some degree the subject matter depicted is conflict-ridden, too, and collisions between individual trends in painting and sculpture are constant. In every period we may witness the clash of opposing artistic programmes; every two or three decades we meet with drastic innovations. In Venice the subject matter is devoid of conflicts: it is not drama that prevails in art, but rather *painterliness*. So harmonious and lucid an idyll as Gior-gione's *Reclining Venus*, for example, would have been unthinkable in Florence, just as Masaccio's *Adam and Eve* or Donatello's *Judith and Holofernes* would have stood out glaringly in Venice. The development of Venetian painting was *continuous*, too; one style of painting grew harmoniously out of the preceding one – until (as we saw with Tintoretto) the great break suddenly occurred.

I have briefly sketched the contradictory evolution of culture and political history. We will find the reasons for it in *the level and content* of the bourgeois development of Venice and Florence.

If we ask which of these two cities was a *more purely bourgeois* state from the very beginning, or where the bourgeoisie was *wealthier*, then undoubtedly Venice must receive the palm. From the time the city was moved to the lagoon Venice was a genuinely bourgeois polis, where no internal struggle ever had to be waged against feudalism. The citizen of Venice soon learned to 'reckon', book-keeping and statistics first developed there, the government kept a regular financial budget; economic life was 'rationalized'. Independence from the Church was only one reason why even at that time the religiosity of the Venetian gentleman was fairly *conventional*. Such passionate outbursts of religious needs as characterized Florence – consider the impact of Savonarola – are not to be found in Venice at this time.

Until the very end the kind of capital which determined the special physiognomy of Venice was *mercantile capital*. Trade was the main source of her power and wealth. Industry – as, for example, her very highly developed shipbuilding industry – was subordinated to the objectives of trade. Marx in several places emphasized the *conservative* effect of commercial capital. This conservative tendency appears in the case of Venice too. The dominance of commercial capital preserved the *stability* of the social structure; it crumbled only after the battle of Lepanto dealt the commercial power of Venice a serious blow.

Here we may return for a moment to the similarity with Ionia. The power and stability of the Ionian cities sprang, too, from their character as commercial centres; this was the basis of their economic strength. It must be added that, like every state founded on trade, Venice built up its *military* power *from without*: she made war with mercenary soldiers exclusively. The merchant does not know how to fight, nor does he wish to; a popular soldiery recruited from within, however, might destroy the system of government – thus a popular levy is out of the question. So I am not stretching the analogy too far in pointing out how helpless the Ionian cities were against the Persian army, which the far poorer cities of Athens and Sparta were able to defeat from their *internal* resources alone.

Let us consider Florence. Max Weber derived Florence's greatness from the fact that hers was an indigenous culture (*Binnenkultur*).[3] The autochthonous character of this development from one's own resources was, however, a consequence of the type of capital which emerged in Florence: from the very beginning it was *industrial capital*. From industrial capital money capital also developed. All this does not, of course, indicate an absence of commercial capital, but only that the commercial network which encompassed Europe

41

and reached even beyond it was in the service of industrial capital: Florence imported semi-finished goods and raw materials and exported finished wares. The two biggest guilds, the Calimata and the Arte di Lana, controlled the textile industry, as did, later, the Arte di Seta the silk industry and the Cambio money-changing. Here we may return to the parallel with Attica: the power of Athens also rested primarily on the *internal* development of her industry and technology; only the steady export of handicraft products made possible the steady import of grain. Again, we must not, of course, overlook the decisive difference: in Florence *capitalist entrepreneurs* stood at the head of the guild industries, looking after total production and, with the help of their constantly growing money capital, gradually tightening their control over it.

Here lies the reason for the special character of Florentine development, different from that of Venice. For industrial capital, in contrast to mercantile capital, is not conservative but *revolutionary*. The constant revolutionizing of production leads to a continuous transformation of productive relations. It constantly 'bursts' the limits which stand in the way of its development. (As we have seen, the basic reason for the check which Florentine development suffered was its *inability* to break out of the bounds of the city-state structure.) The starting-point for the development of the Florentine polis was the *violent* overthrow of feudal rule; this was followed by a many-sided economic struggle of various interest groups, breaking out each time in some kind of *violent* political crisis. *Internal* political authority was a mirror image of the economic and power struggle of social strata and branches of industry: *the changing of the guard among these strata necessarily reflected changed relations of economic power*. And not unworthy of mention among the consequences of her specifically industrial development was the fact that in Florence there developed for the first time a genuine proletariat, and that here appeared for the first time in history the class struggle of the proletariat, which broke out most sharply in the revolt of the Ciompi. (And to refer once again to what distinguishes Florence from Athens: *the Florentine process of development was much more protracted than at Athens*, where commodity production was never put on a capitalist basis yet still disrupted the existing community, at a stage which in Florence was only the starting-point for further development.)

This special 'indigenous' course of development necessitated for Florence a public life of the polis variety, for, objectively, private affairs had fused with public. And it made it necessary and possible for the political life of the state to be more than the particular affair of those in positions of economic and political power. Even if democracy was only formal (at those times when it existed at all) and if the middle and lower strata were still for the most part excluded from positions of power, *the stirrings of those strata none the less contributed objectively to the evolution of power relationships*, and so their interest in public life was far from being a mere illusion. By taking the side of certain movements even the lowest strata could win advantages for themselves – in Florence the tax system, for example, was far from stable. It was for this reason that problems of ethical and social philosophy occupied the centre of interest for the thinkers of Florence, that Florentine painting and sculpture are so dramatic, both in their subject matter and in the rapid succession of styles, and that the problem (and subjective experience) of 'freedom' forms the centre of attention during the golden age of Florence rather than that of determinism. Problems of praxis predominate over questions of the ontology of nature, which from a certain standpoint constitute an end in themselves; they have no immediate relevance to the question 'How should we act?' in the life and struggles of the polis. The scholastic method of examination, moreover, as a conservative way of thinking, cannot take root in a state where every step breaks conventions – however many real 'abstract' questions it enables one to take up.

And here I return to one more question already raised in the foregoing. I asked how it was possible that in Florence the painters were sculptors and architects, too, while in Venice we do not find one such case. Now the answer is simple: the reason is to be sought *in the universality of the industrial culture of Florence*. With the sole exception of Michelangelo, the artists of Florence came from the ranks of her craftsmen, where they had acquired a versatile craft skill almost as a paternal heritage. Artistic imagination could develop on the basis of that skill. (For a long time the Florentine artist was regarded as a craftsman just as much as the Athenian artist had been – his art counted as *techne*.) But the Venetian painter was, from the time of the Bellinis, an 'artist' in the modern bourgeois sense of the word. His culture did not develop on the basis of a many-sided bourgeois *techne* – hence the exclusiveness of his homogeneous medium. And, incidentally, the *content* of his painting also dealt less with public life than in Florence.

We must ask whether any kind of *hierarchical order* has emerged in the course of this comparison. The answer, in my opinion, considering the course of development *in its totality*, is 'yes'. I must emphasize that I do not regard Paduan-Venetian philosophy as less valuable than Florentine, and if in the fine arts I give Florence my preference (except for Giorgione), it is possible that that is merely a matter of taste. But since industrial capital was the basis of Florence's development, since that was the type of indigenous development in which individual phenomena can really be observed in their 'pure' and 'classical' form, since it was there that the first forms of bourgeois versatility emerged (in the Marxian sense of the word), and since there the development of the individual and the species (again in the Marxian sense) approximated each other most closely – I am not acting arbitrarily in regarding Florence as the classical home of the first period of Renaissance development.

Partly for this reason, and partly because Florentine development was broken up by a rapid succession of class struggles, with each period defining and evoking a new stage in the evolution of the Renaissance ideal of man, I should like to say a few more words in particular about the course of Florentine history and its main conjunctures.

The roots of the Florentine textile industry and textile trade go back to the twelfth century. First to develop was the guild of the Calimata, which performed the finishing work, and later the Arte di Lana, which took control of the entire textile industry in all its processes. It reached its peak at the beginning of the fifteenth century; the Medici family rose from the Arte di Lana. The triumph of the Lana over the Calimata demonstrated the changing structure of Florentine technology and society. The ascendancy of the Lana presupposed *the division of labour within a single branch of production*; the concentration of capital in the hands of a few great moneyed families disrupted the system of simple commodity production based on small craft industry, changing the small workshops belonging to the guild from independent commodity producers to outworkers, while also creating larger workshops employing early forms of manufacture. Here I should like to take issue with the view expressed in Jaroslav Kudrna's interesting *State and Society at the Dawn of the Italian Renaissance*[4] that the culture of the Italian Renaissance developed essentially on a basis of simple commodity production. Kudrna is right in saying that during the Renaissance there was still no capitalist reproduction – *but simple commodity production and capitalist reproduction are not separated by a no-man's-land, but rather by the period of primitive accumulation.* 'In Italy', wrote Marx,[5]

> where capitalistic production developed earliest, the dissolution of serfdom also took place earlier than elsewhere. The serf was emancipated in that country before he had acquired any

44

prescriptive right to the soil. His emancipation at once transformed him into a free proletarian, who, moreover, found his master ready waiting for him in the towns, for the most part handed down as legacies from the Roman time. When the revolution of the world-market, about the end of the 15th century, annihilated Northern Italy's commercial supremacy, a movement in the reverse direction set in. The labourers of the towns were driven *en masse* into the country, and gave an impulse, never before seen, to the *petite culture* carried on in the form of gardening.

In Florence, as we have seen, the situation differed only in so far as it was not commercial capital which dominated, as in the north Italian cities, and the breakdown of primitive accumulation was brought about by other circumstances. The most important of these was the fact that *although capital was continually being accumulated on one side, on the other the influx of free labourers came to an end.* Florence's limits as a polis made it impossible to go on expropriating the peasantry and generating free labour power.

In the twelfth and early thirteenth centuries, however, the outlines of the textile industry's development were still quite traditionally medieval. The city's political life, too, bore the marks of feudal anarchy; the half-historical, half-legendary rivalry of the Buondelmonte and Uberti families determined the course of society. While the two patrician families were exterminating each other the guilds, slowly gaining in strength, won self-government for the city; in 1247 a republican constitution came into existence, and the introduction in 1252 of a unitary currency, the florin, symbolized the victory of the upper middle class over the nobility. The subsequent struggle between Guelphs and Ghibellines was at first a movement of the victorious bourgeoisie against the remnants of the nobility; in 1282 the latter were completely excluded from the leadership of the city. Later the sides became more confused, partly because the Guelphs, the party of the great bourgeoisie, took the side of the Papal State and opposed a unitary monarchy, partly because the same upper bourgeoisie, having won its battle, placed its politics more and more at the service of the capitalist, *competitive struggle*, unwilling to allow the smaller guilds (the *popolo minuto*) to share in power and thus acquire a more advantageous position in the economic contest. As a result, the *par excellence* bourgeois sons of many an old Guelph family took the part of the Ghibellines, among them, for example, Dante. The victory of the *popolo grasso* over the nobility (which still ruled in the countryside around Florence) facilitated the beginnings of primitive accumulation; 'free' labourers moved into the city from the countryside, and a proportion of the old handi-craftsmen became outworkers. Machiavelli testifies thus to the morality of the bourgeoisie of this era in his *History of Florence*:[6]

> Oaths and promises have lost their validity, and are kept as long as it is expedient; they are adopted only as a means of deception, and he is most applauded and respected whose cunning is most efficient and secure. On this account bad men are received with the approbation due to virtue, and good ones are regarded only in the light of fools. . . . The leaders and movers of parties sanctify their base designs with words that are all piety and virtue, they have the name of liberty constantly in their mouths, though their actions prove them her greatest enemies.

Ideology, at this time, still had not gone beyond medieval tradi-tions. Giovanni Villani in his chronicle of Florence attributes every victory to divine providence. The first great example of architecture also reveal a traditional taste – the palace of the Signoria, on the model of a feudal fortress, and the two great churches begun in 1234 and 1246 respectively, Santa Maria Novella and Santa Croce, the one for the Dominicans, the other for the Franciscans. (We cannot enter here into an analysis of the problem of how much there is in the Florentine Gothic which is already Renaissance in character.)

From the end of the thirteenth century to the middle of the six-teenth the struggle of the middle and petty bourgeoisie for a share in power went on. In the course of this contest both parties developed their own particular cultural physiognomy. It must be stressed that the workers, too, took part in the movements of the middle and petty bourgeoisie. The ideology of the middle bourgeoisie was more religious than that of the *haute bourgeoisie*, and at the same time more *popular*. It was they who first cultivated the vernacular tongue and who created, with Dante, Boccaccio, and Petrarch, the first genuinely Italian literary culture. The characteristic difference between Dante's monarchical thinking and the militant republican outlook of Boccaccio was not a theoretical one, but sprang from the changing times. There was no contradiction whatever in the fact that Boccaccio simultaneously reproached Petrarch for casting Dante in the shade and for accepting the support of the princely courts (whereas at one time they had *both* been enthusiastic about Cola di Rienzo). Boccaccio's later, passionate devoutness, his expounding of the *Divine Comedy* to the people in church (in Italian), only underline how closely all of them were bound to the life of their society.

As Antal has shown quite convincingly, the process of secularization began primarily among the *popolo grasso*. Nor was that any wonder: it was they who first felt and saw that *they themselves* were guiding their own destinies, and it was among them that the need for religion first died out. At the same time they sought an ideology in conformity with their practical goals. That sort of semi-heresy which, like Averroism, was fashionable in Ghibelline circles (as in the groups around Dante and Guido Cavalcanti) did not correspond to their needs. Secularization appeared in its first forms in the fine arts. In 1294 they began to build the Duomo, which they called 'Santa Maria del Fiore'; *thus it bore the name of the city*, as the Parthenon had once borne the name of Athens, and it was called upon thereby to symbolize the unity and greatness of the city. The combination of a large nave with the small chapels of the wealthy objectively expressed the new social structure. Frescoes replaced mosaics; the subject matter became richer, though for the time being it still remained within the thematic limits of the New Testament. With Giotto begins the individual interpretation of events – we need only think of the legend of St Anne in the Arena Chapel. 'For the first time since antiquity the figures stand firmly on the earth in their natural positions at the time of their depiction', wrote Dvořák of this sequence of frescoes.[7] Antal is undoubtedly correct when he sees reflected in Giotto's art the outlook and world-view of a *popolo grasso* slowly becoming secularized – though in my opinion he is guilty of some oversimplification in linking the content of Giotto's art *in its entirety* to the aspirations of this stratum. He is also right in attributing the relative relapse into the Gothic between Giotto and Masaccio to the fact that at that time the *popolo minuto*, still conservatively religious, came to the fore and placed the stamp of their taste on the dominant art forms. But I must protest against his way of seeking *overly direct* connections between the interests of certain strata and the composition of some of the more Gothic pictures, for such an influence could make itself felt only through the mediation of a relatively uniform taste, especially within the narrow limits of the polis. There is no doubt, of course, that when Masaccio at the close of this period took over the tradition left by Giotto, a uniform bourgeois taste transcending the interests and strivings of particular social strata found therein expression. When Dvořák asserts that Masaccio's heroes express human dignity and the 'freedom of the will', and that in his works 'the group is made up of individuals, completely independent figures',[8] he sees in him the embodiment and portrayer of facts and ideals of life which by that time had become widely prevalent, and had through their ever wider dissemination placed their stamp upon general culture. Henceforward – as we know from Vasari's *Lives* – *every* important artist made his pilgrimage to the Brancacci Chapel to learn to paint, from whatever different social strata they may have come, like Michelangelo and Leonardo.

The development of Florence, especially in this early period, almost invites oversimplifying sociological generalizations. I can return once again to Kudrna's viewpoint, already criticized above. While Antal – whose merits I cannot emphasize enough – links the entire evolution of the fine arts during the Renaissance to the interests and tastes of the *popolo grasso* alone, Kudrna assures us that ideologically the *popolo grasso* always made their peace with feudalism, and for that reason it would be mistaken to regard Renaissance culture as a bourgeois culture, for truly progressive aspirations arose from the ranks of the petty bourgeoisie. But neither viewpoint yields a satisfactory explanation. I would in no way deny, of course, that amid the clash of social strata the special interests of those strata were mirrored both in ideology and in art. I would contend, however, that the beginnings of primitive accumulation in Florence as early as the end of the duecento, and more especially during the trecento, was an *integral* process which wrenched the *whole* city out of the framework of feudal traditions in every area, from manner of life to ideology, from religion to art. *Different problems of this ongoing transformation found expression in representatives of individual strata – but everywhere one finds people struggling to cope with the new problematic offered by the Renaissance.* Thus Renaissance culture cannot be tied to individual bourgeois strata. Of course it must be stressed (as I shall discuss later) that the Italian Renaissance, especially the Florentine, created a specifically aristocratic culture; the *sottoposti*, the numerous workers and petty bourgeois, did not have and were not going to have an *independent* culture, *and the peasantry*, negligible from this standpoint, *did not contribute to the creation of culture and are not even depicted in the products of that culture.* But in the last analysis this culture was still a public one, in so far as *every* stratum of society, more or less, found expressed in it their feelings and tastes. Those who did not produce culture could still enjoy it. In order to understand this special situation, we must cite two contrasting examples: Netherlands art, which by reason of the bourgeoisie's proximity to the peasantry was always more plebeian and more popular in its themes and outlook, and Venetian art, which not only was not a popular art (until Tintoretto), but which was not even a public one.

Let us return to the end of the duecento, to the victory of the *popolo grasso* and the beginnings of secularization. The first element of the religious ideology which had to be cast down was the ideal of poverty. Giotto wrote a hymn against poverty, asserting that it was the source of every evil: unwanted poverty leads to crime, while consciously desired poverty leads to hypocrisy. The case of the middle-class Boccaccio shows that here again we are not just dealing with the ideology of a single stratum; the protagonists' pursuit of money is depicted in the *Decameron*, in most instances, in positive tones. In 1323 the Guelph party succeeded in obtaining a papal bull according to which those who declared that Christ and the Apostles had never owned property were accounted heretics. (In the preceding century Thomas Aquinas had made a wide-ranging defence of lack of property as an ideal.)

The struggle of the middle and petty bourgeoisie with the *haute bourgeoisie* for a share in power, a reflection of their economic contest, set the *sottoposti* in motion too. The 'black Guelphs' frequently took refuge in the alliance of the expelled Ghibelline nobility. (Meanwhile this nobility had itself become partly bourgeoisified, with great noble families taking on bourgeois names, for example.) The advance of the middle bourgeoisie was irresistible, however, all the more so as those new economic powers, the guilds of the Lana and the Seta, played a leading role in their ranks. The base of the democracy grew broader, just as it had at one time in Athens. These developments reached their high point – and at the same time their turning-point – in 1378 in the revolt of the Ciompi in which 9,000 textile workers took part. Now they, too, formed an independent guild and had a share in power. For a characterization of the ideology of the rebellion, and in order to determine how far special workers' demands were intertwined with inherently bourgeois ideology, let me quote Machiavelli, who gives the following speech, certainly relatively true to its time, to one of the leaders of the revolt:[9]

Be not deceived about that antiquity of blood by which they exalt themselves above us; for all men having had one common origin, are all equally ancient, and nature has made us all after one fashion. Strip us naked, and we shall all be found alike. . . . We have no business to think about conscience; for when, like us, men have to fear hunger, and imprisonment, or death, the fear of hell neither can nor ought to have any influence

49

upon them. . . . All who attain great power and riches, make use of either force or fraud; and what they have acquired either by deceit or violence . . . they endeavour to sanctify with the false title of honest gains. . . . Faithful servants are always servants, and honest men are always poor.

Attention to the problems of the poor lasted only a short while, from 1378 to 1381. From 1381 on the government was again in the hands of the well-to-do citizens, with the demands of the middle bourgeoisie relatively satisfied. Then it was that the golden age of formal democracy began, and with it an irresistible new upsurge of Renaissance culture. In the fine arts, the creations of Brunelleschi, Ghiberti, Donatello, and Masaccio mark the new era. If the Duomo was the symbol of earlier progress, the symbol of the new age was its cupola, which the Arte di Lana commissioned Brunelleschi to build. When in 1425 the architect was elected to the Signoria, art *received its rights of citizenship*, becoming a form of merit and value in its own right. A change took place in the relationship between the citizen who commissioned the work and the artist who received the commission. The bourgeoisie realized, consciously or unconsciously, that if they felt the need to objectify their outlook and experience they *must* give a certain freedom of movement to the artist, and recognize him as an individual *of equal rank* with themselves. (This same awareness, and its recognition by the other party, the artist, find expression again a century later when the craftsman's son, Benvenuto Cellini, 'talks back' freely to Leo X and Clement VII.) One may note in passing that this period has often been called the golden age of 'works produced to order'; and yet it was not at all the practice of ordering works of art which dominated the relations of bourgeoisie and artist at this time, but rather the 'commissioning' of such works in a broader social sense. Those who gave the commissions only outlined in very general terms what had to be done; the concrete content depended entirely on the individual artist's own imagination. When during this period things happened otherwise, then conflicts were inevitable, as for example during the construction of the cupola of the Duomo.

The subject matter of art expanded greatly during this period, well beyond the bounds of the New Testament. Subjects from the Old Testament made their appearance, along with themes from anti-quity, new forms like the portrait, and depictions of nature. The return to antiquity and the 'discovery' of the nude are also a product of this age. A turning-point appeared as well in the kind of questions asked by ethical and social philosophy. Petrarch and Salutati still formally professed their belief in Providence, but Bruni no longer did so, not even formally. It was Bruni who revived the ancient ideal of the 'sage', coupling it with the demand of practical utility and 'patriotism'. The theory of this age is crystallized in the works of Alberti. In his versatility one finds summed up everything that the Florence of the golden age achieved in economic thought, art theory, technical knowledge, and social and ethical philosophy. His distinction is enhanced by the fact that he is free of all the apologetic tendencies characteristic of Bruni. Alberti was not a patriotic celebrator of Florence's present, but a sharp-eyed observer of the contradictions of the age, in particular of those social and economic conflicts which were to explode not long after. Here, then, universality was nourished by a talent sensitive to *both* ethics and the study of the world.

We have said that the golden age of formal democracy began in Florence in 1381, but it was also then that it began to be destroyed, albeit slowly. During the years of formal democracy the relations of power shifted; the Medici overcame the old bourgeois families, and the economic preponderance of the Medici family grew rapidly. Here again the source of economic power was still industry – the textile industry – but money capital was increasingly becoming the central factor and, what is more, money capital was used to finance the industry of *other* cities and countries. The Medici fortune came less and less to be – in Weber's expression – the fruit of a *Binnenkultur*, and increasingly became the product of an *Aussenkultur*. Beyond a doubt, it was the *external* orientation of the Medici which made possible their rapid rise.

But why should this 'external orientation' become a source of greater wealth?

I have spoken of the revolt of the Ciompi, and of the fact that the bourgeoisie had to yield (if only for a few years), and they made certain economic concessions to the workers later, too. At the same time the bourgeoisie, in their fear of the workers, *put an end to the Florentine army as a popular military force, which it had hitherto been*; from that time on the bourgeoisie of Florence made war with *condottieri* and mercenary soldiers, just as Venice and the north Italian despots did. One consequence of this change was a check to the expansion of Florence, and finally its restriction to the 'mother city'. War now ceased to be a national and popular cause. How true this was is shown not only by Machiavelli's cool, scholarly analysis, but can be read from the works of art left to us as well. The two statues of David by Donatello and Verrocchio, however different from each other, are still heroic, idealized symbols of the popular soldiery of the city. Their statues of *condottieri* still depict real, strong-willed heroes, true leaders (regardless of whether these *condottieri* really were such heroes). But now let us turn to the designs which Leonardo and Michelangelo prepared at the behest of the Signoria for a painting of the battle of Anghiari (a battle in 1440 in which, incidentally, not a single soldier was killed). Leonardo's sketches show faces distorted with hatred – not a trace here any longer of heroes. Michelangelo even more sharply turns his whole representation of the battle into a piece of grotesquerie, showing soldiers bathing who climb helter-skelter from the water and grab for their clothing on hearing the signal for battle.

But let us return again to the Ciompi. Why was it necessary to make concessions to the workers? Why were there fears of putting weapons in their hands? The prime reason was that at that time there was a *shortage of labour* in Florence. We have seen that the driving force behind the economic development and the culture of Florence was the first wave of primitive accumulation. Wealth continued to accumulate on the one side – but on the other side the supply of 'free' labour did not go on accumulating. Florence's efforts to win agricultural territory by warfare came to naught. There were no reserves of labour power; Florence was unable to deprive more peasants of their lands and means of production. Primitive accumulation could not go on; it came to a halt. And for this reason – because of the limits of the polis – the process of capitalist reproduction could not begin, and so there began, instead of the reproduction of capital, a process of refeudalization. Lorenzo the Magnificent was no longer able to invest the Medici resources in industry. In part he still carried on the financial operations of his grandfather Cosimo, but in addition he began *to buy landed estates*. An ever-growing share of the family property became a 'surplus'. The ascetic way of life of the founding fathers, and the modest setting of bourgeois existence, gave way to ostentatious wealth, luxury, pomp, and a princely style of living. For a short while this still provided a *material* basis for culture (the Medici were *individual* patrons), and for the purchase of international positions (right up to the papacy), but in the nature of things it soon faltered. Hence the rapid economic, political, and cultural decline which followed the golden age of the Medici.

This apparent age of ascent – deemed so because of its surrounding political 'brilliance', but in reality an age of decay bearing within itself the seeds of refeudalization – dates formally from 1343; it was that year that Cosimo de' Medici was called home from exile. Cosimo won the poorest sections of the populace to his side in the struggle against the middle bourgeoisie. Gramsci has shown how the popularity of the Medici *rested on their progressive system of taxes* (which they also paid – to themselves). When Lorenzo the Magnificent succeeded in excluding the entire *popolo grasso* from leadership and, in 1478, after the defeat of the Pazzi conspiracy, exiled their leaders from Florence, *formal democracy came to an end with the consent of the people,* and what remained was actually princely rule under the guise of maintaining the republic.

The breakdown in development became apparent only slowly; the age of Cosimo de' Medici was still an age of cultural flowering. It was then that the language and spirit of ancient Greece took root in Florence; Cosimo de' Medici, unschooled and uncultivated but highly intelligent, took delight in philosophy and supported Marsilio Ficino in his work. But the gathering clouds can already be seen in the immanent evolution of Ficino's work. He was the first philosophical system-builder in Florence, but also the one who (as I have already mentioned) developed his ontology from the question, 'How should we act?' But with the passage of time the ideological features of his work became more and more prominent; setting out from a renewal of the pagan ideal of beauty, he wound up trying to satisfy the needs of a reviving religious feeling. But in the last analysis Ficino still sought within the limits of the polis the answer to the question, 'How should we act?' In his pupil Pico, however, the ideal of the polis has already been lost. Pico was a man of morality, contrasting his own subjective conscience with the demands of public life. If until 1381 (the dates, of course, are only approximate) wealth and glory came in for praise, while between 1381 and 1434 the proper relationship between the common good and the individual's range of action was explored, then we may say that during the age of the Medici it was the demands of *asceticism,* of withdrawal from wealth and public life, which increasingly find voice, even in cultivated circles. The figure of Jesus of Nazareth was revived as an ideal. 'For if the Gospel is right' – the 'if' is characteristic –

> if it is difficult for a rich man to enter into the Kingdom of God, then why do we strive greedily to heap up riches? And if it is true that we ought not to seek the kind of praise which men bestow, but rather the kind that comes from God, why do we concern ourselves with the judgment of men?

wrote Pico in one of his letters to his nephew.[10] This admonition already bears witness to a *revival of religious needs* (needs which had never died out, but which in the earlier period had receded into the background; during that time religion became rather a matter of public observance and a common store of myth). The revived religious needs burst into view in the regime of Savonarola. That event, it must be stressed, was not a matter of the fanaticism of the 'ignorant populace', nor a movement of the devotees of the cult of the Virgin or of superstitious mass hysteria; *virtually the whole cultural elite of Florence sympathized with Savonarola*, the atheist Machiavelli as much as Michelangelo, Botticelli, and Leonardo.

Thereafter little remains to be said about the history of Florence; her fate was sealed. The last of her great sons to draw their ideas, their basic principles, and the problems with which they dealt, from Florentine soil – like Michelangelo, Leonardo, and Machiavelli – died in exile, sometimes self-chosen, sometimes enforced.

Thus it was not Florence (or Spain) which became the classical homeland of primitive accumulation and the starting-point for a new kind of development, but rather England (and France).

The evolution of England and France during the Renaissance – by contrast with that of Italy – is bound up with the emergence of a unified national state. In England, where development was essentially continuous during the rule of the Tudor dynasty, culture for the first time became centred in the capital city, and moreover – and this was decisive – both a relatively aristocratic culture and a decidedly bourgeois culture were found in one and the same capital (we need only think of the 'London Circle'). Similar tendencies prevailed in France during the reign of François I, too; only there the wars of religion seriously impeded those tendencies right up until the accession of Henri IV. The *national* character of Renaissance culture, however, was – to repeat – analogous in both countries.

The process of primitive accumulation in England is well known from the analysis given in *Capital*; it would be superfluous for me to repeat that presentation. From our standpoint the important thing is that the process of primitive accumulation in England, though it took place in several phases which shook and transformed the whole society, was still a rapid, sudden, and, moreover, continuous process. This profoundly *bourgeois* transformation (even if its bearers were primarily the new nobility) made England exceptionally receptive to the assimilation of the ideas which had developed in Florence and the other small Italian states. The emphatic experience that men could create their own destiny and their own society, and the idea of the mutability of fortune in particular, made the thinking and outlook on life of the Florentine quattrocento attractive. The choice of one's own religion, a demand enjoying increasing popularity in England, provided another link with the quattrocento. These ideas coming from Italy did not by any means remain the privilege of a 'humanist' circle, however, as in Germany; they became intermixed with *popular* needs, popular strivings, and popular life (taking the middle and petty bourgeoisie as the bearers of popular culture). It is enough to think of Shakespeare's *Merry Wives of Windsor* or Dekker's *Shoemaker's Holiday* to understand this popular character of the Renaissance bourgeoisie.

In this unitary national and, at the same time, bourgeois-popular transformation one can already see the expression of something which only the future would confirm: that English development would not falter. The abandonment of *all* traditional ties (something that was not characteristic either of the Italian city-states or of the Spanish empire) acquired form and shape in what was specific to English Renaissance culture: its *dramatic* character. Of the various Italian forms of development, the Florentine was the most dramatic; but it was a continuation of traditional forms to so great an extent that the sense of drama could find adequate expression in painting. In England, however, drama became the dominant genre of the Renaissance. In it we may witness, in condensed form, the disintegration of the old world and the birth of the new.

Its dramatic character and its 'openness' towards the future account for the fact that of all the Renaissance cultures it was the English which perceived most clearly *in advance*, almost at the moment of its birth, the contradictions of capitalism. If we wish to speak of the destructive role of money, then we must cite Shakespeare and Ben Jonson; if we wish to speak of pauperization we must refer to Thomas More. Do we not hear in *Pericles* the remark, cited so often later, that the big fish devour the little ones?

What makes the sense of drama so universal is the way in which these contradictions were thought through to the very end, by those who only thought out one side of them, by those who did not speak directly about them, and even by those whose proper genre was not the drama. The *New Organon* of Bacon is as dramatic as the speeches of More.

It can be said of the French Renaissance as well that to some extent it foreshadowed the fact that there, too, development would be 'open' – but in an entirely different manner from the English. The course of events in France was no less stormy than in England. The turbulence of French history did not, however, spring directly from the all-consuming force of the process of primitive accumulation (though, of course, it went on there too), but from the vicissitudes of *political events*, not least important among them the wars of religion. Here the old world did not die spectacularly, so that a new one might be born in all its beauty and squalor; rather, slow structural changes sought out – in bloody ways – their appropriate political forms. This peculiarity made *reflection* the dominant genre of the French Renaissance. Rabelais' novel, for all its ribald variety, is still a *roman à thèse*, in a way that the works of Boccaccio and Cervantes are not, while Montaigne on reflection reigns un-challenged on French soil. Rationalism and scepticism provide the content. Only reason and sceptical attitude were able to appreciate the dubious character of the absolute demands of the various contending political groups; against the background of chaos and fanaticism of the wars of religion only reason and scepticism were capable of assimilating the heritage of the Renaissance.

There is no line that leads from Ficino to Vico, or even from Machiavelli to Vico; but there is a line leading from More and Bacon to Hobbes and Mandeville, and a direct line leads from Montaigne and Charron to Descartes and Pascal.

PART TWO

Antiquity and the
Judaeo-Christian tradition

PART TWO

Antiquity and the
Judaeo-Christian tradition

The Renaissance – as we have already remarked – was in no sense a 'return to antiquity'. The thinking and the sensibility of the representative men of the Renaissance were rooted at least as firmly in the Judaeo-Christian tradition as in the newly rediscovered outlook of the Greek and Latin world. Here it is enough simply to indicate the thematic content of Renaissance culture. Pictorial art drew its subjects first of all from the world of Christian myth, secondarily from Jewish mythology; the myths of antiquity retained only a tertiary importance throughout. Philosophy, it is true, went back to the 'real' Plato and the 'true' Aristotle, but often it focused on problems which never arose during antiquity, like the question of freedom of the will. It was political writing which was most consistently concerned with antiquity; here the prestige of Plutarch and Cicero was unshakeable. Since the political structure of the city-states was similar to that of the ancient polis, since they had long ago accepted Roman law (at the time when simple commodity production became universal), and since the secular personalities of the time could find their peers only in the heroes of antiquity, the dominance of the ancient world in this regard is quite understandable. The burghers who in their lives experienced the alternatives of 'republic or tyranny' and 'republic or empire' thought in terms of Brutus or Caesar; this is true even of a work which rests as much on theological conceptions as does the *Divine Comedy*. If, moreover, the Roman tradition was in this respect the more powerful element of the legacy of antiquity, that was due not just to the reception of Roman law, to the fact that Rome in its long history had produced more great political figures, or to the circumstance that only there had the alternative of 'empire or republic' appeared, but to some extent to the 'national' character of the Roman tradition as well. The city-states of the Renaissance sought in the history of Rome the beginnings of their own 'national' history, dwelling endlessly upon the foundation of their cities in Roman times.

Almost the first spontaneous manifestation of Renaissance thought was the effort *to separate myth from history* (and from science). The 'critical spirit' was not directed against myth, but *against the historical verification of myth.* This attitude was characteristic of Petrarch and many of the artists, who saw in myth moral parables, 'stories' but not history, and who even turned religious events from the real historical past into 'stories' or myths, as Giotto did, for example, with the life of St Francis of Assisi. Political thought could not turn to the Christian tradition for its subject matter if only because it did not recognize it as *history*; while it did not necessarily deny the truth of the Christian tradition, it did not recognize it as historical truth. This, of course, was no longer the 'double truth' of the nominalists. The theory of 'double truth' did not deny that both kinds of truth were of equal value as far as *their relation to objective reality* was concerned. But now it is no longer a question of that: the truth of the myth can no longer be measured against objective reality, because it is no longer conceived as an expression of objective reality. Now it is conceived as a fable, as an aesthetic complex, as a spontaneous work of art. Its *'truth' or 'falsity'* is now measured *by its moral content and not by its historical content.* That is why the 'critical spirits' of the Renaissance do not battle against myth as their antique counterparts did.

Another, and frequently parallel, tendency is the inclination to analyse the historical truth-content of myth. Those who approach myth in this manner do not interpret it *as symbol* but as *allegory*,[1] and search for real-life content lurking *behind* the allegory. Even Valla makes this kind of attempt when he calls Moses and the Evangelists historians, thus calling their sacred character into question. The foremost example of this tendency is Pico della Mirandola's *Oration on the Dignity of Man*, in which he treats the creation of the world and of Adam allegorically. Thus Bacon in his *Wisdom of the Ancients* transforms Greek myths, allegorically interpreted, into scientific truths: in the Daedalus legend he sees the problem of the ambiguity of technical development, in Cupid the embodiment of the blindness of natural laws, and so on.

There is a third – and less trodden – way of exploring the relationship between history and the interpretation of myth: the transformation of the figures of myth into *historical personalities* and of the conflicts of myth into historical conflicts. Here it is enough to point to the two great masters of Umbrian painting, Piero della Francesca and Signorelli – though it is not at all clear why it was Umbrian painters who explored this set of problems. We need only think of Piero's *Flagellation*, a painting that calls up quite modern associations; it makes one think, almost involuntarily, of Anatole France's *Procurator of Judea*. The painting is divided into two parts, showing two interiors, side by side. In one, Christ is being scourged; in the other, Roman gentlemen are conversing serenely, quite possibly weighing the great questions of stoic philosophy. Christ is in the background, the Roman gentlemen in the foreground. It is not the *storied past* that this picture conveys, but the *actual historical* atmosphere in which Jesus appeared, as a historical personality rather than the Son of God. It is not Christ, the hero of the myth, who is the dominant figure of the picture, but rather those who dominated the actual history of the age. But His sufferings – by contrast with the complacence of the stoic gentlemen – enable us to discern in Him the hero of the future. In England, again, Shakespeare approaches myth in a similar way in *Troilus and Cressida;* but here the interpretation goes from the sublime to the grotesque. Only modern analogies come to mind once more: the historical dramas of Shaw and Dürrenmatt.

In taking up the separation of myth from history we were seeking to discover why it was ancient (chiefly Roman) examples which predominated in the political analysis of the day. But if we are to return to our starting-point, the analysis of how the Renaissance drew equally upon the ancient and the Judaeo-Christian traditions, I must speak briefly about the myths themselves.

In the course of the Renaissance there developed a *unitary body of myth* – and not just in the sense that poets, painters, and sculptors drew now on one, now on another of the available stores of myth (Greco-Roman, Jewish, or Christian) for their themes; more important, the stories and personae of the myths themselves *begin to fuse*. Cardinal Bessarion drew a parallel between Homer and Moses, emphasizing the respects in which they were *alike*; the people of Florence regarded Brutus and David as being equally symbols of their city; the figures of Christ and Socrates (likewise mythically interpreted) more and more merged into one. Charles de Tolnay nicely analysed the culmination of this tendency in the works of Michelangelo.[2] Michelangelo depicts the Christ Child as a *putto*; the Medici Madonna is actually a sibyl, looking down like a symbol of antique Fate on the tombs of the two Medici. The Christ of the *Last Judgment* is identical with Apollo; he stands like a powerful and vengeful sun-god in the centre of the painting.

True, it was only the cultural elite which carried out, and passed on, this fusion of myths. In popular imagination Christian mythology remained the only living and deeply felt tradition. It is true as well that in Florence the world of the Old Testament also left profound traces; various of its stories, especially the 'tales of liberation' with their marked dramatic character (Judith and Holofernes, Samson, Hamann and Esther, David and Goliath) held a powerful attraction for the participants in the city's dramatic history, alongside the traditional theme of the expulsion from Paradise; as yet there was no trace, however, of the popularizing universality which appeared only with Calvinism. As for the mythology of antiquity, it became a genuinely experienced, genuinely *lived* mythos only for the cultivated elite. We need only recall that the epic poetry of Virgil, so much read at the time, was never given representation in any significant measure by the artists of the day. Of Homer there is not even any need to speak, for mere *acquaintance* with his poetry in the original was only just getting under way at this time. The constant reference to the gods of antiquity, so characteristic of the lyric poetry of the age, was interpreted and experienced in a metaphorical and allegorical way. As for the pictorial representation of the ancient gods, it is never their histories (the myth itself) but rather their *figures* which occupy the foreground. It is typical of their allegorical character that, for example, in this respect nothing distinguishes Botticelli's *Birth of Venus* from his *Primavera;* while the focusing of attention on the figure can be seen from the fact that Giorgione's *Reclining Venus* – which might, for the rest, be any mortal sleeping nude – could be fully enjoyed for its own sake, without trying to turn the actual content of the antique myth into living flesh and blood. The conversion of the stories of ancient myth into a prime subject of the arts began only with the baroque, and represents a further break with the popular basis of art.

In this respect the Renaissance still had a closer and truer relationship to the mythology of antiquity than did the baroque. Even if the myths of antiquity were the property of the cultivated elite, the tendency, as I have observed before, was always in the direction of syncretism, of the fusing together of all available myths.

This assimilation did not take place in any formal way; rather, the values implicit in the various bodies of myth, their moral and dramatic content, and the kinds of human behaviour which emerged from them, were 'translated', i.e., one set of myths was seen in terms of another. In this way the ancient tradition was transmitted to the people as a whole, too. The figures of Jesus and Apollo, the Virgin Mary and the Sibyl, the Christ Child and the *putto*, in merging together in the work of Michelangelo, express *common values, common attitudes, and common conflicts.* The tradition of antiquity even if it does not become 'flesh and blood', at least becomes 'understandable'. *Here one is dealing with a process of historical and ethical homogenization whose impact extended ultimately to the whole society.*

Similar syncretic tendencies characterized philosophy as well. Today it is fashionable to contest the 'vulgar notion' that the Renaissance rediscovered ancient philosophy. It is quite correct to observe that early Christian thought was already full of Stoic and Neoplatonic elements, or to point to the cult of Aristotle in the classical period of scholastic philosophy. The 'vulgar notion', however, is not a mere product of ignorance. For in fact the Renaissance did discover ancient philosophy as an *autonomous* body of thought. To the men of the Renaissance, ancient philosophy was not just a *preparation* for Christian philosophy, any more than, in their view, ancient art was a preparation for Christian art. They treated the problems raised by the systems of Plato and Aristotle as independent problems internal to those systems, and accepted or rejected their solutions quite *independently* of the attitude the centuries of Christian philosophical tradition had taken towards those problems.

Yet this still does not mean that the new concern with the problems of ancient philosophy was, *objectively*, independent of the legacy of Christianity and Christian philosophy. The men of the Renaissance treated the thinkers and the thought of antiquity as autonomous, but they were themselves the heirs of Christian culture, and knew that culture well; the point of view from which they regarded the problems of philosophy and the new questions with which they confronted the classical solutions sprang from the development of Christian culture, *too.* (Here I need only mention again the problem of freedom of the will or the question whether the 'soul' which survived physical death was individual or collective; the problem of the immortality of the soul was, of course, known in antiquity, but the notion of collective immortality is specifically Averroist.) I have italicized the word 'too' above in order to stress – although this subject does not belong to our present theme – that, with the passage of time, the confrontation of ancient and Christian thought increasingly takes place with an eye to solving the peculiarly new, secular problems raised by the contemporary Renaissance.

Summarizing what has gone before, I should like to determine what *common* ground there was between the attitude of the Renaissance towards antiquity and its attitude towards Christianity. The answer is dictated in part by the very search for common ground; and what one finds here is the conflict between dogma and a critical spirit, between faith and knowledge. The relationship of medieval Christian philosophy with antiquity (and with the Christian tradition) was a dogmatic one; its basic attitude was one of faith, a faith which knowledge had to justify. The attitude of Renaissance philosophy towards both antiquity and the Christian tradition, on the other hand, was *critical*; *reason and knowledge* were the foundations on which it rested. In the course of this critical re-examination some ancient thinkers were weighed and found wanting, while others turned out to be paradigmatical; some categories were accepted, others rejected. The same is true of the Christian tradition; one Renaissance thinker will call one article of faith into question, another a different one, while at the same time they accept others. Thus the Averroism of Padua, for example, accepted the collective immortality of the soul, but as the solution of an immanent philosophical problem, not as an article of faith. In the last analysis, then, the thought of the Renaissance sought and found, both in antiquity and in the Christian tradition, *a cultural legacy and the raw materials of thought.*

The entire European intellectual tradition, right down to the present day, has two primary sources: it stems on one hand from Greek (and Roman) antiquity, and on the other from the Judaeo-Christian tradition. As C. Wright Mills writes:[3]

> If you ask to what the intellectual belongs, you must answer
> that he belongs first of all to that minority which has carried
> on the big discourse of the rational mind, the big discourse
> that has been going on – or off and on – since western society
> began some two thousand years ago in the small communities
> of Athens and Jerusalem.

Renaissance culture was the first to bring those two sources together consciously.

CHAPTER 1

Secularization

The premise for, and the consequence of, this union of the two heritages was the secularization of the everyday and ethical problems and strivings which had earlier appeared in religious guise. Before sketching these tendencies in outline, however, a few preliminary words must be said about the relationship between the religious spirit of the age and the Church.

Even during the early Renaissance, belief in the mission of the Church, recognition of the ecclesiastical hierarchy, and religious devotion had become sharply differentiated from one another. This was a phenomenon which had no parallel in the old heretical movements. The heretical movements came into existence *in spite* of the Church; their attitude towards the Church was a hostile one, and at the same time a *collective* and *organized one.* Their collective and organized nature, their character of a counter-movement, accounts for their fanaticism and made it necessary for them not only to retain, but even to enhance the *ideological* aspect of religion. They expressed the aspirations of *social* strata which strove against the secular power of the Church, too. The Church took a dual attitude towards these movements. Either it would win them over and thus 'tame' them, in that way returning rebellious social groups to the path of obedience, as happened with the Franciscan movement; or else it would strike down and annihilate them. (Today even St Francis of Assisi is sometimes accounted a Renaissance figure; but even though many themes appear in his hymns which later become common during the Renaissance, his ideological, or 'reforming', attitude towards religion makes him, essentially, not a Renaissance man but a 'heretic', just as much as Savonarola was at the end of the Renaissance, and for the same reasons.) During the Renaissance, on the other hand, it is increasingly common to find that the individual's attitude towards the Church is one of *indifference* or contempt, and that this indifference has no connection whatever with his religious sentiments or behaviour. Boccaccio's tale about the conversion of the Jew is well known, and its conclusion reflects the author's own attitude: Rome is a nest of sin, Wickedness, greed, and injustice, and if Christianity has survived *in spite* of the Church, that is the proof of its worth and grandeur. When he writes,[4]

> I tell thee, so far as I was able to carry my investigations,
> holiness, devotion, good works or exemplary living in any
> kind was nowhere to be found in any clerk; but only lewdness,
> avarice, gluttony, and the like, and worse,

that is his devasting judgment not only on Rome but on the whole ecclesiastical hierarchy. One finds similar reasoning, of course, in the heretical movements. But Boccaccio was no heretic; he did not wish to replace the religion prescribed by the Church with another, 'true' religion, he did not wish to codify a new, better, and purer faith or to organize a movement, he did not seek Church reform – he did not have in mind any kind of 'codification' at all. And here it must be emphatically added that such scornful private opinions did not interest the contemporary Church anyway, even when they were enunciated by holders of high ecclesiastical office. Petrarch was a bishop, but he could still write that Avignon (then the residence of the popes) was 'the modern Babylon', the city of hypocrisy, where 'to do any kind of service was empty and false'.[5] It occurred to no one to anathematize him or deprive him of his ecclesiastical office. I have already mentioned how in Florence it was the *popolo grasso* which first became secularized, and yet it was precisely this faction which financed the papacy and supported it against heresy.

It is possible to study the problem purely from the standpoint of the aspirations of the Papal State at that time. That, of course, is one aspect of the situation and ought not to be neglected. Burckhardt has analysed in detail how, in the fourteenth and fifteenth centuries, the Papal State itself set out on the road of secularization, and how its economic and power pretensions appeared more and more 'nakedly' as it threw off the cloak of ideology. Beyond any doubt, the papal throne itself wavered under Innocent VIII and Alexander VI (Machiavelli in particular sympathized with the Borgias because of their secularizing intentions). Those popes in fact did not pay any heed to attacks launched on a religious or personal basis; they only

66

strove to strengthen their power position and to acquire the material means necessary to extend it. Of course the situation was altered during the reign of Julius II and Leo X. After the fiasco of Alexander VI's policy, those popes began to realize that the Church could not employ the same methods as other, secular powers, *for its function in the power system of other countries* – as the case of Spain first made sufficiently clear – was *ideological*; it could not simply give up its spiritual hegemony over the French or Spanish peasant in exchange for the physical hegemony of Italy. But if Julius II and Leo X abandoned the earlier secularizing tendencies, as symbolized by the recommencement of work on St Peter's under Julius II, they continued to rely on the wealth of the Italian *bourgeoisie*, in particular the Florentine bourgeoisie, and tried to accommodate themselves to the general tendencies of the time, until two movements – opposed to each other – put an end to the process: the Reformation on one hand, and the rise of Spain to a position of world dominance on the other.

But the 'sinful epicureanism' of the Papal State and its relative indifference to ideological considerations are not an adequate explanation for the rift between religious piety and recognition of the ecclesiastical hierarchy. That was an outgrowth of the slow evolution of bourgeois circumstances of life. And those new circumstances produced two new attitudes towards religion (two attitudes which are frequently found together): a *conventional* posture, and an *individual, subjective* one.

Conventional piety does not mean simply that the manifestations of collective religious behaviour are bound to certain conventions or governed by them. That much is true of every religion and indeed of every collective expression of social life. But it does mean that external practices diverge from internal content; they become an end in itself, a mere ritual formalization of collective social life. The feudal era did not know a conventional piety in this sense. Religious ceremonies and feasts, whether they were understood or not, were personal experiences, and experiences in which contact was made with the transcendental. That did not mean an exaltation of the whole life, which was not required of ordinary mortals; but it did mean moments of deep religious devotion. During the Renaissance the conventionalization of religious observance came about in two ways. On one hand the church, the Mass, the feast day became a mere social custom, an occasion to meet and talk (we need think only of the tales of Boccaccio); for society's enlightened members, on the other hand, the growing artistic aspirations expressed in architecture, fresco painting, and the like transformed religious experience into artistic experience, replacing the former with the latter. When the artistic value of a *pietà* comes to matter, then it is no longer religious rapture which brings the bourgeois to contemplate the *pietà*, but aesthetic appreciation. At the same time the religious impulse did not die, especially among the lower and middle classes; but it was transferred from the 'official' scene to within the human being. Religion became a private affair. *In this regard Renaissance piety brought about in Italy the same change that the Reformation was soon to bring about elsewhere in Europe.* But – and the difference is essential for our purposes – this kind of 'private' or 'privately interpretable' religion, replacing the old one during the Renaissance, was profoundly different in its *content* from the religion of the Reformation. *It was a tolerant 'religion of reason', the first form in which deism appeared in Europe.*

Before turning to the analysis of this new, rationalized Christianity, which appeared in a great variety of philosophical forms, ranging from the raising of the issue of *docta ignorantia* all the way to the *devotio moderna*, I should like to emphasize, and to illustrate with a number of examples, the fact that what we are dealing with is the philosophical fall-out of a *general social and ideological process* extending over nearly two centuries. First of all, the sacred objects of the cult began to lose their sacred character in the eyes of the whole society. Alongside the registers of relics and holy places there began to appear lists of the notable sights of the city, equal in prestige to the former. Churches were no longer respected; almost every assassination of note took place in a church – like, for example, the attack on the two Medici brothers in the Duomo at Florence. The official, dogmatic cult of the Church became just *one among many superstitions*. This again was something quite different from the remnants of magic which survived during the feudal era. However strong beliefs of magical origin may have been, they either became intertwined with Christianity or remained subordinate to it. During the Renaissance superstition and religion 'lived side by side' – hence the view that the age was more superstitious than the preceding one, whereas in fact various deviant beliefs only appeared more openly, and frequently in a 'scientific' guise. *This demand for scientific verification is again of the greatest importance.* It, too, had been almost totally absent from the life of the Middle Ages. It now became expressive of the fact that even in the high culture of the day superstition, religion, and science coexisted peacefully on a plane of equality. Cardano, for example, was convinced that on one occasion he had been cured through the power of prayer, but also that a red sword-like apparition had appeared at the time his son was taken into custody and had remained there until he was executed, and that he was constantly watched over by a guardian spirit which had saved him from many mortal dangers. He regarded storms and nocturnal clamours as miraculous signs. Among scholarly superstitions, astrology played a prominent role; the position of the stars surely was considered to exercise the same influence as Providence. Describing the birth of Michelangelo, Vasari in one breath noted that it had taken place 'near . . . where St. Francis received the stigmata' and under an excellent horoscope, 'Mercury and Venus exhibiting a friendly aspect, and being in the second house of Jupiter'.[6]

One reason for the new link between religion and superstition was the fact that for many individuals religion – like superstition, whether in 'scientific' guise or not – came more and more to have value only as a view and an explanation of the world, *losing its ethical content*; the direct connection between the social and ethical behaviour of the individual, and his religious or non-religious outlook, became tenuous. This was the consequence of the *withering away* of the need for religion which gave birth to a certain kind of 'practical atheism', whose like we have already observed in the Athens of the age of Pericles.[7] It did not, of course, deny the existence of God or the gods, it frequently operated with transcendental theological concepts in explaining the world, and in everyday life often made use of religious formulas, but *in practice it behaved as if God did not exist*.

We need only recall to mind Cardano, superstitious in his everyday activities, convinced of the power of prayer. All of that did not influence him in the least either in his branch of science or in the important moral decisions of his life. He spoke scornfully of those who believed in the 'fortune' of the physician, for 'wherein should *Fortuna* attend the barber in order that he may shave, or a musician so that he may sing and strike the cords? Similarly in medicine *chance* is not to be counted on. . . .' And he added:[8]

I would not have anyone think that these things are far-fetched
or of a demon, or of astrology, but they are based on Aristotle's
idea of prophecy. True divination, says he, is an endowment
of the prudent and the wise only.

He was not willing to entrust a single patient to God or to a favourable horoscope. Religion no longer *dictated* the ethical content of human decisions either; at most it might utter a conventional 'Amen' over what one had already decided upon in a quite this-worldly way. In Benvenuto Cellini's *Autobiography* we read of two men who had sued him:[9]

One evening I wounded [one of them] in the legs and arms so
severely, taking care, however, not to kill him, that I deprived
him of the use of both his legs. Then I sought out the other
fellow who had brought the suit, and I used him also such
wise that he dropped it. – Returning thanks to God for this
and every other dispensation . . . I [turned to my household]. . . .

The ontological basis of the practical atheism of the Italian
Renaissance was essentially the same as during antiquity, especially
in Athens: a narrowing of the discrepancy between the development
of man as individual and as species being. In these exceptional
historical situations the individual was able to perceive his destiny
relatively clearly, and could experience with a relatively high degree
of certainty *the connection between his intentions, actions, and
choices on one hand, and their consequences on the other*. That connection was grasped most easily and most plainly in those cities, and
at those moments, where technical culture and democracy flourished
the most, above all at Florence. The sharpness of class conflicts
and the 'mutability of fate' made no difference for this practical
atheism, for – as we shall consider again later – the realization had
entered men's blood that it was possible to 'seize the time'. The
frequent rise and fall of factions under conditions of formal democracy reinforced the awareness of the individual's potentialities and
of opportunities seized or missed, whereas stagnant eras create
rather a feeling of helplessness and fatality.

During the great age of the city-state, it *became intuitively evident*
that man created his own life and his own world. Since I will be
returning to this problem later, here let me consider it only in
connection with the process of secularization. The first and most
important consequence of the new attitude, in this regard, was the
disappearance of the belief in Providence. Even in Dante an individual
Providence is already absent. With this step, however, the belief in
the relevance of Providence to the particular individual – the product
of genuine religious needs – ceases to exist. The problem of *universal*
Providence is a philosophical one, but it does not spring from the
individual's question, 'For what reason was I created?', nor can it
provide an answer to that question. The disappearance of the notion
of an individual Providence reflects the fact that 'For what reason was
I created?' ceases to be a living question. In its place the question
'What is to be done?' becomes dominant; the answer to that question,
however, simply by-passes the problem of individual Providence.

The felt experience that man is the maker of his own world and
his own fate always took hold of men within the context of the

possibilities of a given 'world', that of the city-state. To shape one's fate meant to live and act *together with others*, and not in a way determined by feudal rules of conduct, but *'freely'*: one's own activity proceeds in search of one's individual destiny and individual potentialities, but it goes on within the context of human society, amid the relationships of the larger community. This intimate relationship between the individual's sphere of action and the possibilities inherent in society – the point cannot be stressed enough – was borne in upon men *day by day* in their own personal experience. The measure of success or failure was a kind of 'consonance' with society's demands and with the possibilities that it offered. Thus society's norms – *the system of social norms as a concrete totality* – became the sole measure of individual morality and of the individual's system of values.

Darwin in one passage makes a nice distinction between feelings of shame and pangs of conscience. Shame, he declares, is characteristic of those communities, like the tribe, where the individual's actions are absolutely circumscribed by communal norms of customary behaviour. In such circumstances the individual feels ethically 'ill at ease' only if one or another of his actions *deviates* from what is customary, from the norms dictated by custom. If any such action is sanctioned by the community, even after the fact, he ceases to feel any ethical malaise; the individual's sense of proper ethical conduct is restored. In a bad conscience, on the other hand, there is always something *individual*. Even if others approve the deed, even if one has acted 'just as others do', feelings of guilt may remain; one must make one's peace with oneself if they are to disappear. Darwin quite properly places the emergence of conscience in the age of the dissolution of tribal society, and perceptively discerns the special part played by Christianity in shaping and fixing the sense of conscience. To this I should like to add that the ethical precondition and basis for the appearance of conscience is *morality*. Morality – i.e. an *individual* relationship and attitude to given customary and abstract norms – in fact develops simultaneously with the emergence of class society; from the time when the human being emerges, historically, into individuality, morality in this sense characterizes the ethical attitude of every man in every age. The spectrum within which this takes place is, of course, very broad; in some places a moral attitude can hardly be discerned, while at the opposite pole one finds the moralist seeking to validate his individual morality in the face of given customary norms.

Pure shame and pure remorse of conscience are the two extreme ethical reactions of the individual which may mark his psychic and

71

ethical state before, during, and after the commission of an improper act or thought. Since the dissolution of primitive communal society and the appearance of the individual there has never been an age or a social stratum where feelings of shame prevailed exclusively, nor has there been an age or stratum where individuals reacted to their actions exclusively with guilt. But still, there have been times and strata where the former, or the latter, was markedly dominant.

Early Christianity was typically characterized by the predominance of qualms of conscience in regard to ethical problems. I need not expatiate here on how far this reaction sprang from the general loss of validity of ethical norms in the declining Roman Empire or from the general spread of new ideas of individuality and morality, or on the degree to which it deviated from the system of values and ethical behaviour given expression in the New Testament. It is enough to consider that representative product of the age, the *Confessions* of St Augustine, to become vividly aware of the change. In it there is a turning away not only from the ethical universe of the New Testament, but also from the whole tradition of ethical thought of antiquity as well. It is true that morality had already made its appearance during antiquity; Socrates' daemon is a figurative and allegorical expression of the voice of conscience. But in Socrates – as in stoicism and epicureanism – a social standard still exists against which conscience can be measured. That standard was not identical with the accepted customary norms of the age; it was rather a social and human ideal. But at all events it was an immanent criterion and an earthly one. And here I should like to lay emphasis on a consideration which is important for my line of reasoning: remorse of conscience is not necessarily linked to the concept of sin; the precondition of its existence is merely that the *individual* should make the distinction between good and evil.

Let us now consider what is new in the type of conscience which began to appear in the Christianity of the Roman era, and which makes this such an important turning-point. The concept of evil and evildoing first arose not in connection with man's relationship to man, but in connection with *his relationship to God*. The community plays a *mediating* role; thus good deeds, so often emphasized and demanded, seem to have to do with men, but ultimately they relate to God. If we do a good deed, we please God – that is why they are absolute; their realization in this life, in society, is always relative and conditional and so man is necessarily 'imperfect', however righteous he may be. Thus the notion of *'evil'* – an earthly and relative concept, about which one may always ask *to what extent something is evil, for whom, and how irreparably* – gives way to the concept of *sin*. Every falling away from God is sin; thus sin is absolute, not relative. To that extent the *individual* cannot make reparation for it; contrition can prepare the way for *grace*, but in the last analysis grace is in the hands of God rather than of man. In the same way, 'saintliness' replaces the concepts of virtue and of good, which were also relative concepts. Saintliness, too, is absolute, a category based on one's immediate relationship to God; its premise is precisely a withdrawal from the normal human community and from the conditions of sin. Thus it can be seen that original sin and the notion of human depravity necessarily follow from the concept of sin itself. If evil is absolute and is synonymous with falling away from the absolute demands of the Deity, then *every man must necessarily be sinful*. The myth of original sin is merely a dogmatic, figurative formulation of this reasoning.

And here I must return in more concrete detail to my starting-point. I have said that, typically, Christianity was characterized by an attitude of remorse of conscience with respect to ethical problems. It was, moreover, a remorse of conscience at sin rather than at evil actions.

It is true, of course, that as Christianity began to be accepted as the state religion it became necessary to reconcile the fulfilment of one's duty to God with the fulfilment of one's duty towards men. That reconciliation is already evident in Augustine, and it is for that reason that I have called him a typical representative of early Christianity. The solution was achieved through the concept of *mediation*. Divine injunctions were mediated through earthly injunctions. But Augustine – and with him virtually the whole of medieval Christianity – stipulated that in case of eventual conflict one's direct relationship to God held priority over one's relationship to men as mediated through one's behaviour.

> What has been laid down as a general rule, either by custom
> or by law, in any city or nation must not be violated simply for
> the lawless pleasure of anyone, whether citizen or foreigner.
> For there is faultiness and deficiency in every part that does
> not fit in with the whole, of which it is a part. But when God
> commands that something should be done which is against
> the customs or institutions of any people, it must be done, even
> if it has never been done there before

writes Augustine in summarizing the argument of the *City of God*.[10]

Let us, after this brief aside, return to the world of Renaissance. The more men awakened to an awareness that they were the makers of their own fate – and the plainer it became that the social context of their actions was the given polis, in which the individual must seek scope for his activity – the more distinctly the notions of right and wrong, good and evil were placed in that context, and the more the old notion of 'sin' began to fade away. The men of the age began increasingly to measure their actions only by the prevailing norms of behaviour, and by their success (or lack of success: a problem to which I shall be returning more than once). Cardano sums up this attitude very well:[11]

> I determined upon a course of life for myself, not such as I would have, but *such as I could.* Nor did I choose perhaps exactly what I should, but *what I deemed would be better.* And in this my purpose was not single or constant . . . ; I acted *as seemed advantageous* when each occasion arose. . . .

Returning to Darwin's categories, one finds that in the Italian city-states of the fourteenth and fifteenth centuries *the sense of shame was far more prominent than remorse of conscience.* In so far as any action was sanctioned by society as a whole, accepted in some circles, or at least looked upon indulgently, very few individual doubts of conscience arose in connection with it. Thus Burckhardt was quite right in saying of the men of the Renaissance that[12]

> distinguishing keenly between good and evil, they yet are conscious of no sin. Every disturbance of their inward harmony they feel themselves able to make good out of the plastic resources of their own nature, and therefore they feel no repentance. The need of salvation thus becomes felt more and more dimly.

We have observed that the consciousness of sin is bound up with the notion of original sin; *as the consciousness of sin begins to die out, the idea of original sin necessarily disappears too.* If a man makes himself great (or small), he thereby makes himself good (or evil). The Renaissance man's way of thinking and way of life go to the roots of original sin and radically destroy them. If good or evil does not depend on one's relationship with God, then 'being forsaken by God' also ceases to have any meaning. If man is great and 'godlike' (a problem to which I shall return), then depravity is alien to the idea of man. Finally, if man is a social being, then outside society (at the moment of his birth) he cannot possibly possess ideas whose content is social like 'good' and 'evil'; he cannot inherit sin, nor can he, as an individual, be born in sin. As Castiglione put it:[13]

> Vertues may be learned . . . because we are borne apt to receive them, and in like manner vices.

74

And therefore there groweth a custome in us both the one and the other through long use, so that *first we practise vertue or vice, after that, we are vertuous or vitious.*

The contrarie is known in the thinges that bee given us of nature, for first wee have the power to practise them, after that wee doe practise: as it is in the senses, for first we can see, heare, feele, after that, we do see, heare, and feele: although notwithstanding many of these doinges bee also set out more sightly with teaching.

The relegation of religion to the status of a convention, and the emergence of a practical atheism, was only one aspect of the Renaissance – though one which was dominant during certain centuries. Simultaneously – and side by side with the development of human individuality – the idea of religion as a *personal* relationship to the Deity becomes individualized, and becomes ever more subjective. This tendency, as we shall see, becomes the dominant one during the sixteenth and seventeenth centuries.

This then was the basis of the 'rational Christianity' or 'tolerant religion of reason' of the Renaissance. In part it sought to bring together and summarize all those elements of *Weltanschauung* that conserved their common religious character in a world where men acted as practical atheists; while in part – and inseparably from the former – it took a critical stand against any kind of dogma which stood in the way of the individuality, variety, liberty, subjectivity, and free choice of any religious or semi-religious outlook. It broke a path for healthy scepticism, for the speculations of fancy, for scientific research and rational discussion, but also for personal ecstasy. It proclaimed for the first time that *specifically bourgeois programme* which during the Enlightenment would come to be called 'freedom of religion'.

Cassirer was right in asserting that Cusa's *docta ignorantia* was already a declaration in favour of scepticism and tolerance. But tolerance itself is older than its scholarly formulation. It is already present in Boccaccio's tale of the three rings. And just as the rejection of original sin attacked the social ontology of the Catholic dogmatics in its analysis of 'the Beginning', so too the fable of the three rings, and the idea of tolerance which is bound up with it, undermines that other pillar of a dogmatic ontology of society: 'the End', the myth of the Last Judgment.

When Christianity became the state religion, the Last Judgment was of course removed to a distant future, putting an end to its threatening imminence (which only chiliastic movements of heretics were to rediscover); but it always remained the end point of social existence, though projected into the mists of the future. In principle, the separation of the just and the unjust on the day of the Last Judgment would take place according to *religious* affiliation and religious sincerity; heretics of all kinds were condemned to horrible punishments. The whole schema of the other world was similarly religious in character; even in Dante it was still unshaken. What is new and bears a Renaissance character in Dante is the appearance of a hierarchy of morality and greatness within the framework of the traditional Christian hierarchy. The great personalities of the pagan world are still condemned to Hell; but in its hierarchy they occupy a distinguished position, already a sign of respect. But when the notion of the *equality of religions* becomes a conscious belief, philosophically formulated, then popularized, and finally a commonplace, the Last Judgment becomes not a religious but a *moral* tribunal, losing its concrete dogmatic content. Amid the social and moral cataclysms of the sixteenth century it appears again as the end of the world, but now it is a well-deserved punishment on humanity for everything it has committed *against itself*, or as a judgment of fate or history (Dürer, Michelangelo). The relationship between religion and morality is reversed. In the parable of the three rings true morality is no longer that which belongs to the true religion; on the contrary, true morality determines which is the true religion, if indeed there is such a thing at all. Faust and Don Juan are not condemned because they have fallen away from their faith, but because they have violated all norms of human morality; their loss of faith is merely one aspect of the latter. Thus no 'redemption' is possible for them, as it still was for the medieval knight Tannhäuser.

The religion of reason was developed into a philosophical system by Ficino in his *Theologia Platonica*. In evaluating this figure, we must take issue with an interpretation that is fashionable today. Just as the Hegelian or positivist histories of philosophy of the later nineteenth century laid one-sided stress on the Platonic elements in Renaissance philosophy, so today the most outstanding Renaissance scholars (like Kristeller and Randall) over-emphasize the importance of Aristotelian tendencies as against Platonic ones. Kristeller and Randall are right in preferring the scientific promise and precision of the problems which arose from the Aristotelian tendencies, over the Platonism of Ficino's sort; but they completely ignore Ficino's *historic accomplishment*, the creation of a philosophical system that is extra-religious and is meant *to replace religion*.

The unification of religion and philosophy *on a philosophical basis* was – let it be repeated – a historic accomplishment. Contemporary

76

Aristotelianism worked out its scientific problems *independently* of religion; it took account of religious problems only where it encountered them in immediate connection with epistemological or ontological inquiries, and for that reason it had no unified world outlook or system. Ficino, however, did have a unitary outlook and system; it was one of objective idealism, like Plato's or even Hegel's. And it must be said that the philosophies of nature of the following century, especially Bruno's could not have come into existence without this first great effort on Ficino's part.

Ficino's system was the product of reviving religious needs, and so it was an ideological system. To that degree it was more primitive and more elementary than similar attempts which were to be made in the sixteenth century. But what is decisive for us here is the fact that in creating an appropriate vehicle for religious needs, Ficino did *not* build on *traditional* religion. Alongside the *Theologia Platonica* no other religion can exist (including traditional Christianity).

If it be objected that Ficino's was not the first attempt to combine Plato (i.e. Neoplatonism) and Christianity, I must agree. But Ficino – in the spirit of the Renaissance – drew equally upon Christianity and the cultural heritage of antiquity. In his work, moreover, Christian elements are subordinated to Platonic ones (and to his own peculiar ethic, a stoic one in many respects), rather than the other way around. Here it was no longer simply a case of the secularization of one problem or another, as had occasionally happened before in Christian philosophy. Now Christianity itself was secularized. *Christianity itself became a secular philosophical problem as soon as theology was transformed into philosophy.*

It is true that Ficino's attempt was *unique*, just as the efforts of the 'London Circle', which flourished a little later, were unique. The London Circle (Colet, Vives, More, Erasmus) was, as I have remarked before, more plebeian than the cultivated elite of Florence, particularly that of the Medici era. They did not wish to create some 'higher' system of 'philosophy of reason'; what they wanted was a *uniform, rational faith* valid for all mankind, a *devotio moderna*, as they called it. Reason and tolerance were their watchwords. It was one of the basic principles of More's Utopia that 'No one should suffer for his religion'.[14] The inhabitants of the island, 'in desiring one thing and avoiding another, obey the dictates of reason'.[15] Among the great variety of religions there is only one common trait, belief in the immortality of the soul. But the Reformation shattered the illusion of a peaceful coexistence of faiths; hopes for religious toleration and freedom of religion were disappointed.

77

If we were to seek for a single word to describe the religiosity of this era and its efforts to create a common faith, we should have to settle on the word *deism* – though not, of course, in the meaning which the age of the Enlightenment gave to it. Later deism was a product on the one hand of the development of natural science; its God was the watchmaker who wound up the mechanism of the world of the demiurge who had set inanimate matter in motion. On the other hand, it was the product of religious needs, experienced in a moralistic or pragmatic way. But the deism of the Renaissance and the deism of the Enlightenment had at least one thing in common: for both, God did not intervene actively in the affairs of this world. The basis of this deism was – as we have seen – either *conventionality in religion*, or else an *individual, subjective 'choice of God'*.

One further word must be said about atheism in the Renaissance. It was, as has already been observed, a rare phenomenon, far from being of central importance. Those writers stood closest to atheism who realized (as Laplace did later, on the basis of scientific reasoning) that there was no need for God in the universe – neither in the moral universe nor in the natural universe. Bovillus, for example, when he writes that 'nature is the efficient cause of sensible species; the mind is the efficient cause of intellectual species',[16] leaves no place for God in the universe. Leonardo, too, openly contrasted knowledge with faith: he not only constructed his ethics and view of nature without God (if only aphoristically), but according to Vasari he claimed that the philosopher was superior to the Christian. This type – not yet militantly atheist in the modern sense, i.e. in the sense of the totality of his outlook – first comes to the fore in the sixteenth century, at a time when relations between the Church and science have reached breaking point.

During the process of secularization all those concepts and categories which had operated in the Christian philosophy of the Middle Ages in a theological context broke away from their theological matrix; thinkers began to examine the real problems of life that were implicit in them. The repertoire of categories had become much enriched even before the sixteenth century, of course, but the old familiar categories also reappeared again and again. And yet, since it is their real life-content and their immanent meaning and significance which cognitive efforts are now focused on, the function of these old familiar concepts in the philosophical systems of the day was *changing*. Since I will deal with these changes more concretely later on, I will restrict myself here to a few words about the *secularization of myth*.

We have already seen how the myths – those of the New Testament in particular – began to change, more and more, into moral parables; but not just moral parables of any kind, rather of a sort which reflected and exalted an ethic that focused on men's relations with one another, i.e. on relative and not absolute relations. That is why these ethical parables have no allegorical character; *they invariably reflect the ethical content of concrete social conflicts.* The story of the sufferings of Golgotha recedes into the background; it is replaced by subjects which touch on the theme of *calling* or *vocation* (one of the most important themes of the age), like the homage of the three kings or the Archangel's announcement to Mary; by subjects which express one's direct relationship to society, like that of 'the things that are Caesar's'; and by subjects which reflect conflicts inside a group, like the theme of treachery as depicted in the Last Supper. But that was only one aspect of the process which we may call the *humanization of myth.* Parallel to it, gods and saints alike become men. Mary is no longer the Queen of Heaven, but ever more often a mother fearful for her child, a more or less distinguished *bourgeoise*, or quite simply the ideal of feminine beauty. Saints, 'unveiled' in the literal sense of the word, display the real proportions of earthly life. Mantegna's dead Jesus is palpably dead – a death from which no resurrection will follow. No distinction is made in the depiction of 'divine' and 'human', as was the case in Gothic art, where the divine and sacred world was traced in ethereal spiritual beauty, while the world of ordinary mortals was often shown in a manner distorted and grotesque: the former depicted in abstract, idealized fashion, the latter in a naturalistic way. With the Renaissance, the depicted world becomes *homogeneous.* Beautiful and more beautiful still exist, along with virtuous and more virtuous, evil and more evil; but the 'earthly' figures grow to equal the divine ones in beauty, demonstrating that there are not two worlds but only one, and the *ethical hierarchy* is realized and made valid *within this one unitary world.* Even wickedness is not denied a certain beauty and grandeur – we need think only of contemporary representations of Judas.

In this creation of a homogenous store of myth two separate motifs can be detected: the humanization of the myth is at one and the same time the *deification of man* as well. As God becomes man, so, too, men are deified.

An awareness of *the creative and self-creative power of man* was one of the major experiences of the Renaissance world. During the early Renaissance these powers seemed boundless. One writer after another discovered that the attributes of God were in fact the attributes of man. The Biblical myth according to which man is made in the image and likeness of God divests itself of its theological content; there remains the awareness of man as a 'divine creature'. Cusa can already write that 'man is a god, though not absolutely, for he is still man. And therefore it follows that mankind's God . . . is a God in human form'.[17] Manetti is of the opinion that although man gratefully received the world from God 'it appears that he afterward greatly refined and beautified it';[18] the world as it exists today is at least as much man's creation as God's. Ficino goes even further, writing:[19]

> Who could deny that man possesses as it were almost the same genius as the Author of the heavens? And who could deny that man could somehow also make the heavens, could he only obtain the instruments and the heavenly material, since even now he makes them, though of a different material, but still with a very similar order?

We can observe in these statements the creative aspect of the process of deification of man. It is clear, especially in Ficino's formulation, that it is the process of productive development, the recognition of man as an actual demiurge, the progress in the creation of a 'second nature' that leads to the concept of 'divine humanity'. The naive immediacy of the references to the heavenly 'materials' and to the 'instruments' of divine creation bear sufficient witness to that. *The history of humanity – and of its ideology – had never before seen anything comparable to this.* Some may object here, citing the famous chorus from Sophocle's *Antigone*:[20]

> Many are the wonders of the world,
> And none so wonderful as man.

It is true that this chorus from *Antigone* is the first wide-ranging formulation of the idea of the greatness of man. I do not wish to minimize its sublimity and grandeur if I insist that the Renaissance notion of the 'divinity of man' goes far beyond it. First of all it implies *process* of deification: man is not born a god but *becomes* one, so that in this respect, too, the concept of man becomes a *dynamic* one. In the world of ancient thought, moreover, man's greatness was never 'in competition' with the divine order; if man did compete with the gods, then the ethics of the age regarded it as hubris, as an overstepping of man's limitations, as transgression, and so as evil. The early Renaissance did not recognize the notion of hubris, for it did not recognize any limits to human development. The fable of Polycrates' ring could never have been born in this atmosphere; in

Renaissance eyes man could never be *too* powerful, *too* rich, *too* famous, or *too* happy. (As we have seen, it is a *human* moral order which Don Juan and Faust violate.) Although – to speak for a moment of the pinnacle of ancient secular thought – the gods of Epicurus are mirrors of human behaviour, although they do not intervene in the affairs of the world, they still exist *as gods, as ideals of human behaviour*; even if men *can* live like gods on earth, it falls to very few of them to achieve that state. To that degree, Epicurus was still a captive of the ancient conception of 'deification', according to which only certain individuals – *heroes, exceptional men* – could become gods after their death. Among the Greeks this was the reward of earthly greatness (and fortune), in late imperial Rome it was a question of social standing – the emperors were *ipso facto* gods (as they had always been in the Orient). 'To become a god' was, nevertheless, at all times an exceptional thing, an aristocratic possibility. For Epicurus 'becoming a god' was this-worldly and immanent; it happened not after death, but in spite of death; and yet it was only an exceptional, aristocratic possibility. The problem of 'man' becoming a god, of the deification of humanity as a whole, was entirely foreign to the thought of antiquity. Until the notion of equality among men had come into existence, how should the idea of the equality of man and god have arisen?

And so this transcending of all restraints, the unlimited development of technique and production, and the idea of equality were all required in order to give birth to the concept of 'deification' in the sense that I have employed, that of the *creation* of reality. But we have seen that the Renaissance concept of deification has another meaning as well, that of *self-creation*; this I may term 'ethical deification'. It sets out from a belief in the *infinite perfectibility of man* and from the presupposition that this infinite process of perfection is the work of men themselves. (I should like to mention that this notion of deification could appear during antiquity to an even lesser degree than the first one. The ancient gods were anything but exemplars of pure mortals; their world was rather devoid of any morality.)

This ethical concept of deification stems from Ficino, too. In some of its forms it was closely bound up with the Platonic tradition, as we shall see when we come to analyse the Renaissance's ideal of beauty. I cannot expatiate here on the enormous contemporary impact of this set of problems; here I may simply mention the hymns of Lorenzo de' Medici. But I must say something more about the man who at once formulated and depicted the idea of deification most monumentally: Michelangelo.

Even his contemporaries recognized this fundamental theme and this basic pathos in Michelangelo's works. Varchi, for example, summarized the essence of the sonnets thus: 'Even in the midst of earthly life we are able to rise to heaven and to change from men into gods.'[21] The sculptor's human heroes, in their power, strength, uprightness, grandeur, and sometimes beauty, are divine figures. His David, by comparison with the scrawny little warriors of Donatello and Verrocchio, is like a Greek god; he reminds us of Hercules. Of his Moses, again, Max Dvořák writes with justice: 'Here is the apotheosis of the divinity that dwells in man, the deification of that force of will which knows no bounds, which governs men and scatters its enemies.'[22] That great admirer of antiquity saw perhaps most clearly of all the *difference* between antiquity and his own time. Perhaps that is why he undertook to create a work which in its totality is so alien to the spirit of antiquity, however reminiscent in its details of ancient models; for it depicts a dynamic concept of man, the dynamism of becoming divine: I am speaking here, naturally, of the monumental composition of the tomb of Julius II. The threefold division – recalling Ficino's system – represents man's path from a 'slavish existence' all the way to the union of the *vita activa* and *vita contemplativa:* to moral deification. The same process of ascent and deification is reflected in the basic motif of the Sistine frescoes. God creates man, but created man creates himself over again, rising once more to the height of divine existence. It is not the figure of God the Prime Mover, but the gigantic forms of great men, the heroes and makers of history, which dominate the composition.

For the sake of historical fidelity we should note that the idea of deification in Michelangelo, and its execution, takes on a different tone in different periods. In his youthful years (the time of the *David*) *joy* at the greatness and splendour of man predominates. In his middle years the revolt against Christianity provides the main motif; Dvořák is right when he says of the tomb of Julius II that it is 'a supreme challenge to the spirit of Christianity' and 'a rebellion against the Christian view of the world'.[23] During the period of crisis the idea of becoming divine recedes; the pagan Michelangelo becomes an adept of the religion of reason, that late product of the Italian Reformation, and seeks to carry on the contest with the divine oeuvre in the very cupola of St Peter's. For the old Michelangelo, deification has lost its meaning; man's wretchedness, his tragic fall and suffering take the place of the one-time 'God-man'.

And thus we find ourselves already in the sixteenth century, where the earlier course of development of religion and philosophy, science and philosophy, and science and secularization is interrupted and in part even reversed. (Again England forms an exception; for the time being More's tragedy proves to be only an interlude.) In the trecento and quattrocento city-states – above all in Florence – we find virtual freedom of religion emerging (based on a practical atheism), and religion subsisting peacefully side by side with science and philosophy; indeed science and philosophy, hand in hand with art, progressively appropriate the problems of religion and theology, discovering their hidden secular meaning. Every man could choose among the colourful multiplicity of individual interpretations, choosing 'for himself' his own religion and philosophy (or none at all). 'Sin' and 'penance' practically ceased to exist, and original sin and the Last Judgment disappeared from the lexicon of thought. Disputation went on among tendencies which displayed mutual respect for one another, and – reflecting as they did a single underlying historic process – strove for essentially the same goals.

But the precise reverse of all this is true of the sixteenth century. That age was characterized by *a sharpening of contradictions, and a declaration of war between science and philosophy on the one hand, and religion on the other*. To appreciate the change of attitude which marks the philosophy and the thinkers of that period, we need only single out the representative figure of Giordano Bruno. As a young novice in Naples he removed from his cell every other sacred image, but *left hanging there the crucifix*; and yet in 1600, when (having lived through literally every major conflict of his time) he saw the cross thrust towards his heretic's pyre, *he turned his face away from it*. The crucifix hanging in his cell was the symbol of a unitary Christendom and of a religion of reason; but half a century later the same crucifix became the insignia of fanaticism and reaction, of learning's most deadly enemy.

I have already described in Part 1 the new situation brought about by the Reformation and the Sack of Rome. When the wing of the Church standing under Spanish influence and led by Ignatius Loyola triumphed over the humanist wing led by Sadoleto (as early as the pontificate of Paul III), Catholicism launched its general attack not only on reforming 'heresy' but against any kind of individual learned interpretation of religion. Thenceforward every independent philosophical interpretation of the faith counted as heresy. (In principle that had been true before; but the rule had not been enforced.) At first, restoring the *moral* authority of the Church was the prime task; later, as a result of the spread of Copernican doctrines, the emphasis was shifted to apologetics on behalf of the ideological authority of the Church.

The central problem of moral authority was, as we have seen, the problem of sin and repentance; its ideological basis, again, was the concept of original sin and the related concept of human depravity. The Council of Trent (1545–63) explicitly declared the dogmas of man's depravity and of original sin to be fundamental tenets of Catholic belief.

> If anyone asserts that the sin of Adam – which in origin is one and which has been transmitted to all mankind by propagation, not through imitation, and is in every man and belongs to him – can be removed either by man's natural powers or by other remedy than the merit of the one mediation our Lord Jesus Christ – let him be anathema. . . . That man can be justified before God by his own works which are done either in the strength of Human nature or through the teaching of the law, apart from the divine grace through Jesus Christ – shall be anathema.[24]

The ideas expressed here do not deviate in the slightest from those of the conquering Protestantism of the same age. Luther emphasized the same thing in his earthier and more robust manner. In his *Table Talk*, for instance, he draws the following analogy:[25]

> Hair and beard do not cease to grow, so long as a man lives . . . even so, original sin survives and stirs within us so long as we live; but we have always to resist it, for such hairs must constantly be trimmed.

Man can no longer attain virtue – and only a constant, relentless struggle against his nature can make him eligible for grace. (Max Weber has aptly observed that Protestantism turned *all* of bourgeois everyday life into a monastic existence.) Once again the concepts of virtue and sin become meaningful only by reference to God; their relativity disappears. At most Protestantism is more democratic, in so far as it denies even the possibility of sainthood.

The relativization of sin and virtue in the life and thinking of the Renaissance necessarily linked right choice with a correct assessment of the situation, with human judgment – that is one of the reasons why I have called Renaissance deism a religion of reason. Now the very possibility of an ethically relevant and useful knowledge is denied; man's path in the world becomes a path of error. Calvin writes:[26]

> For the dulness of human mind renders it incapable of pursuing the right way of investigating the truth; it wanders through a

variety of errors, and groping, as it were in the shades of
darkness, often stumbles, till at length it is lost in its wanderings
thus, in its search after truth it betrays its incapacity to seek
and find it.

The moral result is in keeping with this: 'The mind of man is so
entirely alienated from the righteousness of God that he cannot
conceive, desire or design anything but what is wicked, distorted,
impure and iniquitous. . . .'[27] The identity of the ideas of sixteenth-
century Catholicism and Protestantism about original sin and
human depravity does, of course, span different practical positions.
For Protestantism – to mention only on – religion becomes a subjective relationship between the individual and God, and so the
threat of anathematization loses all meaning (which does not of
course imply a greater degree of tolerance by any means). But since
the Reformation and Counter-Reformation concepts of man do
not fall within the scope of this study, I can only indicate here the
direction taken in the further evolution of this problem.

We have seen that in sixteenth-century Italy (in some cities, like
Florence, even at the end of the fifteenth century) the progressive
course of development 'foundered'. The immediate signs of social
decline became ever more perceptible. Even more apparent were the
secondary signs, above all precisely in the ethical sphere. Even those
who hymn the greatness of man, like Pico della Mirandola, find
themselves increasingly confronted with the phenomenon which
they describe as '*the decay of morals*'. They are now no longer
confronted with concrete strata or classes of '*immoral character*', as
Petrarch had been at Avignon, but rather *with a universal process* of
moral degeneration, as widespread as that which took place in late
imperial Rome. And what they thus describe really existed. The
development of the forces of capitalist production was destroying
feudal ties, traditions, and norms of behaviour; faced with new
opportunities, men more and more rejected the abstract, absolute
norms of Christianity. The dissolution of the old systems of values
(of which I will have more to say later) brought about a disorientation
in values which opened the way for the triumph of the kinds of
ethical motives actuating bourgeois production: desire for gain,
self-interest, and so forth (only recall the passage in which Machiavelli characterized the morality of the victorious *popolo grasso*).
But so long as the possibility of further development existed – so
long as men could still more or less expand their potential for self-
realization – that disorientation and insecurity in values still bore a
positive sign: moral contradictions still did not assume the form of

'decay'. We need only recall that to be rich was still virtuous for Boccaccio, or in the early Shakespeare's world of values (cf. *The Taming of the Shrew*). When, however, this progressive trend came to an end, there stood the world of men motivated by gain, ready and waiting – but the quest for gain could no longer yield new values, either objectively or subjectively, nor did it offer any opportunity for self-realization. At the same time, refeudalization mingled bourgeois motives with new feudal characteristics; I have spoken of luxury, but might have referred to sexual licence just as well.

How did people of finer feelings react to the new situation? Above all with a revival of the attitude of morality, with the creation of a private morality *in opposition* to the prevailing ethical norms of society. Increasingly, they again opposed asceticism to luxury and sexual excess. And among them – as happened side by side with refeudalization among broad strata of the bourgeoisie and populace as well – *religious needs revived*. Once more an answer was needed to the questions: to what end am I here on earth? What purpose does my life have? In Germany, the home of the Reformation, where a typical Renaissance development was lacking, this felt religious need never died out. The revival of the same religious need goes far to explain the rapid *spread of the Counter-Reformation* in Italy and Spain, the scene of an abortive bourgeois development.

Of course the Counter-Reformation was only a last-resort answer to newly felt religious needs, and a retrograde one at that. During and before it we meet with many unsuccessful attempts to provide an answer: I need point only to the heresy of Savonarola or the reformation of Juan de Valdes. A special shading on this palette was provided by the religious ideas of the circle of Roman literati around Vittoria Colonna. The members of this group (like the late Michelangelo) strove to work out a subjective, personal concept of God. In this circle the Renaissance tradition still held good in so far as the image of God was a strongly individual one, and everyone could 'project' into it his own vital ideals, as Michelangelo did in identifying God with Beauty. But the dominant role of *belief and subjective devotion* were Reformation phenomena, as were the rejection of 'externals' and the effort to achieve an intimate, mystical union with one's God. (Of course the Counter-Reformation appropriated this last feature, too, but through dogmatization robbed it of precisely what linked it to the Renaissance tradition – its individual character.)

Until now we have dealt only with the social and moral roots of the religious developments of the sixteenth century, and with the social and moral problems they raised. But almost immediately religion had to contend with a new and more difficult set of questions, those posed by the first appearance of an independent scientific view of the world.

Here, too, of course, we are dealing only with an earlier process which has suddenly become explicit. For even before, the relatively rapid development of the forces of production had led to the appearance of a *Promethean* view of man. In his *works* man is the equal of God; all that separates him from God (as Ficino points out) is that he does not have the divine instruments and materials at his command. It was Luther once again who first perceived what a tough nut this problem was for religion. With radical consistency he struck man's works from the list of criteria of piety. Faith alone, not works, was the guarantee of a man's devoutness and morality. 'Good works do not make a good man, but a good man does good works',[28] he wrote; and more clearly formulated: 'It is clear then that a Christian man has in his faith all he needs, and needs no works to justify him.'[29] With this, Protestantism opened the way to detheologized works, and voluntarily withdrew to the regions of 'pure' faith and morals. With a like genius, Luther removed from the sphere of religious behaviour the category of 'right reason', so much favoured by Thomism and especially by Aquinas himself because it made some room for a rational conduct of everyday life which was not at all in conflict with the principles of religion. Right reason was indeed a useful guide to rational living so long as everyday life had not become impregnated with the findings of another world-view *in conflict with the religious picture of the universe*. As soon as the ideas of natural science and social science began to make their way into everyday life, however, and thus everyday 'common sense' found itself in constant conflict with religious dogmas that were held to be absolute, right reason became a useless category from the standpoint of religion. In sweeping right reason aside, Protestantism on one hand opened the way for scientific ideas to penetrate into everyday life, while at the same time it derationalized the daily demands of religion.

The Catholicism of the sixteenth century was characterized by great confusion on these matters. Playing upon religious needs and revived mysticism (of a sort that later culminated in the Jesuit baroque) could not give an answer to the problems described above. That fact emerged most clearly when the turning-point in the whole crisis of the religious world-view arrived, in the form of the question of how to reckon with the *Copernican system*.

When Catholicism openly turned against the Copernican universe, the polarization of religion and science began. Religion demanded the right to force a dogmatic ontology on science; science declared its right to an independent ontology which would not have to compromise with dogma. Ficino could still create a unitary ontology without exacerbating the conflict, or indeed without even thinking it through. Giordano Bruno, however, was compelled by the times *to think the conflict through*. And Bruno's greatness lies in the fact that he clearly understood the demands of the times. The Church had launched its offensive for the reconquest first of morals, then of *Weltanschauung*. Now Bruno *made a moral issue of loyalty to one's world-view*, snatching even martyrdom itself from religion.

At the beginning of the seventeenth century Catholicism found a way out of the confusion, developing the forms of its accommodation to capitalism. One of its most important ideological aspects was the principle worked out by Cardinal Bellarmine: science must be accepted because – and in so far as – it leads to practical results, but it is still the Church that will provide the *Weltanschauung*.[30] When Galileo withdrew his teachings, he consented in practice to Bellarmine's programme, abandoning science's aspirations for an independent world-view and with them the moral obligation to remain faithful to the scientific world-view as well. (Brecht's conception of Galileo, it seems to me, corresponds in considerable measure to historical fact.) Philosophy, however, in its greatest representatives, never gave up those aspirations; and to that extent the figure of Bruno rightly stands symbolically beside that of Socrates.

The new social situation (refeudalization in Spain and Italy and religious war in France, and hence a mounting sense of religious needs) and the new situation in science (the first open clash between religion and science) together created growing scope for *scepticism*. *Scepticism became the practical atheism of the age* – an ethical atheism that did not draw the last theoretical consequences, did not create a new world-picture. Charron formulated this new cosmological 'self-restraint' thus: 'The causes and prime mover of things are unknown, their seeds and roots are hidden. Human nature cannot, and should not, try to find them.'[31] But in the midst of the Church's offensive, in the shadow of burning pyres, the consequence of this scepticism was easily detected. Buffalo, the Papal Nuncio, declared *De la sagesse* 'a scandalous book, indistinguishable from the impious doctrine of Machiavelli and greatly harmful to the Christian religion'.[32]

We have reached the turn of the sixteenth and seventeenth centuries. The ideas of Bacon are about to appear, the pinnacle of Renaissance philosophy. Kepler's *Astronomia Nova* has not yet appeared, and years still separate us from Galileo's works and the new world they will open. One must wait a little while longer for the appearance of an exact and methodical exploration of nature. *But with Bruno and Bacon on one hand and French scepticism on the other the process of secularization has reached its conclusion.* The scientific-secular and religious *ways of posing the question* part company once and for all – despite all the efforts at a 'final reconciliation', of which we find so many in succeeding centuries. (Pascal, for whom the two ways of posing the question did not part company, stands outside this process.) By the turn of the century, then, the positions are clarified, and the adversaries, each armed now with their *own* weapons, survey each other with narrowed eyes.

CHAPTER 2

A glance at the past

The Renaissance was the first era which *chose for itself a past*. Sartre rightly saw in that one criterion of freedom, for it was indeed a *sign of liberation from the bonds of feudal or communal life*; those peoples who still live within the bounds of these communities receive their past ready-made and given, in the form of myth. They may transform those myths or reinterpret them, but they cannot select for themselves another past. For the Greeks, the Trojan War was not something chosen, nor did the stories of Abraham and Moses constitute a chosen heritage for the Jews. They were part of an inescapably present past. No less was true of the myth of Romulus and Remus for the Romans, or the story of the rape of the Sabine women. Virgil's attempts to select a new past for his people was likewise based on mythical material (though it was another people's myth); on the other hand, it was artificial and never sank roots. (Moreover, that undertaking grew from a social soil characterized by the slackening and, in part, dissolution of communal ties.) Choosing a past means that the peoples or classes of a given age *select* from the history of the past and from its myths, historically interpreted, those in which they find *affinities*, be they positive or negative. Thereby the whole process of seeking for *precedents* undergoes structural alteration. 'Precedent' plays a key role in the whole history of human practice – for whenever decisions are taken collectively or individually, the conviction that 'it's been done this way before', that 'there's an earlier example for this', provides moral and practical reassurance. Even if there is truth in Hegel's remark that nothing has ever been learned from history, we must still add that people would never have been able to make history

90

if they had not believed they had learned from it, so that they might justify their actions and decisions by reference to similar instances from the past. What precedent means for traditional societies, even in the world of their mythology, has been profoundly (if ironically) depicted by Thomas Mann in his *Joseph* tetralogy. This reference will suffice here. That this phenomenon has not lost its importance even at the present day is easily demonstrated. We need only consider how every new artistic movement, with whatever revolutionary claims and *avant-garde* assurance it may emerge, invariably reshapes the artistic past in order to discover there its 'forerunners'. Or – to stay with history – it is common knowledge how much the leaders of the French Revolution felt the need for the Roman cloak, and how much the revolutionary tribunals in their work needed to call on Brutus.

But, of course, the limitations on what precedents could be chosen were very precisely fixed in those ages before free choice of a past was possible. The fact that Alexander the Great wished to be like Achilles rather than like Hector reflects not just an individual taste; it also demonstrates that the choice of precedents made by men born into a particular situation was very largely determined, *even within the limits of given popular myths.* Now, however – beginning with the Renaissance – the choice of a precedent frequently becomes conditional in several ways. Within the framework of the commonly chosen past social strata, classes and individuals won some elbow room to make their *own* selection of precedents. Belonging to one class or another did not confer any 'right' to interpret the decisions of the past as precedents in one's own favour. It was the concrete situation that came to be decisive in the selection of precedents, rather than the position into which one was born. (These developments, of course, later made it possible for some to abstract even from the given situation in their decisions. Thus for Raskolnikov Napoleon's actions could serve as a precedent.)

The choice of a past is free to the degree that it *makes* it possible to forge links with any period or movement from the past *consciously,* rather than in a way 'determined by nature'. The content of this choice is never arbitrary. It is dependent upon a certain *objective similarity* of situation, or at least on the fact that, in its modern *interpretation,* the former age becomes similar to the present; it must point the way to action or – no less important – furnish historical lessons. If the choice of the past were a *completely* arbitrary one, it could no longer serve the very purpose *for which* we select a past: it could no longer serve us in any regard, either positively or negatively, as a precedent.

I have said that the choice of historical precedents on the basis of substantive or supposed similarity has gone on right down to the present day. But it must be added that, with the development of historical consciousness and the awakening of a genuinely historical attitude towards the past, this kind of choice of a past became *objectively obsolete* and anachronistic. It was already rejected in Hegel's system, whence the polemical remark mentioned above. And in the Marxian system its rejection is substantiated by a whole theory of history. Marxism regards every historical epoch as a particular and total complex in itself, even though each one grows organically and dialectically out of the previous era; for that reason *it rejects as barren, both in theory and in practice, every search for similarities which turns into a search for norms, and it particularly rejects precedent as a motive for the concrete social decisions and actions of men in history*. Those who have attained to the level of a genuine historical consciousness no longer have *any need* to look to precedent for a motive; on the contrary, doing so would impede them in correctly assessing the situation and in making their decisions accordingly. But while it is true that with Marxism the search for a similar past, one that will furnish precedents, comes in principle to an end, nevertheless even since that time every social movement has been characterized to a greater or lesser degree by that search. (The history of socialist movements is woven through and through with appeals to precedent.) The French Revolution may have been the last to play out its scenes in Roman costume, but 'disguises' of that sort have not at all vanished from history. The disappearance from social practice of these 'guises' – appeals to precedent – can only be the result of historical consciousness becoming general. Thus the choice of the past is only a means towards the recognition that *all* of history is ours, and forms our prehistory. Nor is any of this in conflict with the peculiar attraction or repulsion we distinctly feel for certain eras. And what I have said here about history in general applies equally well, *mutatis mutandis*, to the development of our own personalities. Here it certainly shows a relatively high degree of freedom if we can select from our past the things we want to regard as precedents and wish to pursue, 'forgetting' the rest; but here, too, the higher type of behaviour is to accept our whole past with its regressions and errors, regarding it as an individual 'historical background' for choices that are, in principle, new.

I have discussed how the Renaissance synthesized the heritage of ancient and Christian culture. But if I analyse the question of the choice of a past, I can unequivocally establish thus *that the past it singled out as similar – as a precedent – was always drawn from*

92

antiquity, more specifically from Roman history. The superficial signs of this are readily perceptible. The outstanding part played by Cicero, Lucretius, Polybius, Strabo, and others, the cult of the Latin language, which despite its aristocratic character determined the cultural features of the *literati* for almost two centuries, the dominance of the oration as a genre, the frequency with which ancient authors – especially Latin ones – were cited: all these are well known. This Latinized culture had a marked *imitative* character; in originality it lagged far behind the Italian vernacular culture which preceded it and followed it. This imitative character was not, however, a mark of lack of ability in the poets of the time writing in Latin – for there were first-rate artists among them – but rather the result, precisely, of an unhistorical relation to the past. Reliance upon precedent does not necessarily lead to disorientation in action – it may produce a kind of false consciousness leading to successful action – but *in art it invariably creates a derivative culture.*

There were, of course, two different ways in which the implications of the choice of the Roman past could be worked out artistically. The imitative Latin literature of the Italian *popolo grasso* was only one of these. The other was to experience and depict real *contemporary* events and conflicts, but *projected back* into Roman history. Shakespeare's Roman dramas are typical examples of the latter. In Shakespeare – as we shall see later on – a new way of depicting history has begun to ripen. In the construction of the characters, their behaviour and their relations to one another, he can make us understand completely whether he is writing about the actual historical antecedents of his time, or rather about the conflicts of his own age. Not only the history plays proper but even such later dramas as *Hamlet* and *Macbeth* belong among the works dealing with 'prehistory'. By the same token, not a single one of the plays reflecting contemporary conflict, whether tragedy or comedy, is set in England (or anywhere in Britain). We need not be concerned here with the particular aesthetic reasons for that; no doubt the kind of symbolic representation that was artistically demanded could not have been brought off with the raw materials offered by the England of that day. What is essential for us is the fact that most of the plays which depict the present are placed in a Roman or Italian setting – *Romeo and Juliet, Julius Caesar, Antony and Cleopatra, Othello, Coriolanus* – and one in Greece (*Timon of Athens*). Objectively we are dealing here, too, with 'costume dramas' (in the Marxian sense) rather than with historical dramas, and clearly these 'costumes' solve perfectly the same artistic problems with which Italian literature struggled quite vainly. These works were *true in the present*, and their present

truth found its form, through the kinds of similarities I have discussed, in tales from the past. (It is characteristic that for Shakespeare ancient Rome and the Italian cities of the Renaissance filled
precisely the same function in this respect). Here precedent was not
the starting-point for art, but its final outcome.

In the old communal societies there was only one source of
precedents: the earlier (mostly mythical) history of the society
itself. Now, simultaneous with the choice of a historical past, actual
prehistory and chosen history part company with each other. Blodus
di Forlì wrote the history of the Middle Ages as the prehistory of
his own time, but he by no means treated it as a chosen history. Or,
to return to Shakespeare: in his history plays Shakespeare writes
about actual prehistory, in his Roman plays about chosen history,
and these are two different worlds, which can be distinguished from
each other with precision.

The effect of Roman history (and, through Plutarch, of Greek) and
of Latin literature was felt long before the rediscovery of ancient
visual art, which became general only with the growth of interest
in Greek culture. True, Cola di Rienzo studied the architectural
beauties of Rome – though he was the first to do so; his purpose in
his *Descriptio Urbis Romae* was to raise the dead again from their
tombs.[33] The influence of classical fine art reached Florence, on the
other hand, only during the quattrocento. Ghiberti was the first to
collect Roman statues, while Brunelleschi and Donatello made their
pilgrimage together to Rome to discover its antiquities. The great
excavations, however, still fall into a considerably later age, the
cinquecento. It was only in the course of Julius II's diggings that
such works as the Vatican *Venus*, the *Laocoon* group, and the
Belvedere torso were brought to light. This 'difference in tempo'
is not to be explained by the difficulty of excavating – for we know
that taste in art was still quite different from the ancient taste, while
literary taste had long been founded on Roman poetry. The age took
'Je prends mon bien où je le trouve' for its principle, and never strove
to penetrate into the inner workings of its 'chosen' historical era,
much less to grasp its material and spiritual culture as a whole.
The discovery of ancient sculpture was 'belated' because the need
for it only awakened belatedly, in the age of the renewed spread of
Greek culture and especially of Platonic philosophy. And it happened then because at that time the ideal of *bellezza*, of beauty and
measure, became a central category of thought.

The attitude towards the *philosophical heritage* of antiquity was,
again, relatively independent of the choice of a historical past, with

94

one exception: those philosophies in which it was no longer the world-view that dominated but rather ethical behaviour. In these – stoicism and epicureanism – a common or at least analogous attitude towards ethics and the community was seen between the ancient models and men living and acting in the present. (I will speak further of stoicism and epicureanism in a separate chapter.) Interest in the great *systems* of ancient philosophy, on the other hand, those of Plato and Aristotle, was only aroused a good deal later, and for different reasons in different places and at different times. It cannot be denied that the capture of Constantinople, the personal efforts of Gemisthus Pletho in propagating Greek culture, and a familiarity with the original Greek texts all played their part. But it was just at this time that a need for such ideas began to stir in society. (It is worthy of note that even though some of the texts of Aristotle had been known before, there was no considerable Aristotelian tradition in Italy before the *High* Renaissance; he was much less read there than at Paris or Oxford.) The popularity of Plato and Plotinus in the Florence of the Medici's was, as we have seen, definitely rooted in the revival of the problem, 'What is to be done?', and the need for an ontology that would respond to it. That requirement was reinforced by the rise at this time of the ideal of beauty, whose economic basis lay in the faltering of the process of primitive accumulation, the reflux of money from industry into conspicuous expenditure, and the fading of republican practice in favour of a 'life of beauty'. In this process Platonic philosophy found a common ground with the aesthetic traditions of Florence. Aristotle, on the other hand, won popularity chiefly at those times and places where the need for an objective, demythologized ontology developed, or where scope was sought for a concrete ethic to govern the relationship of individual and community. Thus in the *Rhetoric*, for example, it was not just the rhetorical rules which attracted, but even more so the ethical examples themselves.

Of course, the principle of 'Je prends mon bien où je le trouve' applied to Plato and Aristotle too; the works of these much-read ancient thinkers were not treated as dogma. Just as everyone more or less had his own religion, so everyone had his 'own' Plato or his 'own' Aristotle. Philological 'accuracy' did not matter much in this sphere either. The polemics between the Platonic and Aristotelian tendencies bore no resemblance to the heated battles of the schools both earlier and later; they remind us more of a conversation in which the opposed parties mutually stimulate one another. The figures of the two thinkers in Raphael's *School of Athens*, amicably disputing with each other, reflect not only the views which had

95

developed by the early sixteenth century on the relationship between the Greek philosophers, but also the real relations of the 'schools' of the day among themselves.

In the course of this later evolution the choice of the past, the search for precedent, proved more fruitful than in the case of literature. The 'themes' were not concrete, but rather comparatively abstract philosophical questions, in regard of which repetitions and new inventions could organically be linked with each other. Taking over the ancient forms, concrete problems and all – as in the borrowing of the dialogue form in Ficino's *Symposium* – did not necessarily lead to mere imitation, as in the case of the adoption of ancient poetic forms; for in philosophy the connection between content and form is far from absolute. On the contrary; it is looser and more contingent; the same 'symposium', with the same participants and the same problems, can lead to new insights, even if the discussion of only one or two questions sets the participants to go groping almost spontaneously after new solutions, with the author's scarcely being aware of it.

Since the Platonic and Aristotelian systems of categories were constantly applied to the needs of the age and to its new problems, they were constantly altered, yet also retained their identity. (I deliberately omit conscious attempts to merge them with categories derived from other world outlooks or cultural traditions, such as Christian ideas, magical-mystical Persian elements, or – as in Pico – efforts to combine all the given cultural heritage into one great synthesis.) To illustrate this process, we may select almost any category at will. Let us consider, for example, two different interpretations of the Aristotelian principle of the mean. Castiglione makes the Aristotelian principle of the mean entirely his own. But when he comes to discuss the problem of what is meant by 'the measure' he speaks as follows:[34]

> Let [the Courtier] consider well *what* the thing is he doth or speaketh, the *place* where it is done, in presence of *whom*, in *what time*, the *cause* why he doth it, his *age*, his *profession*, the *end* whereto it tendeth, and the *meanes* that may bring him to it: and so let him apply him selfe discreetly with these advertisements to what soever hee mindeth to doe or speake.

Now let us look at Aristotle himself:[35]

> Thus it is possible to go too far, or not to go far enough, in respect of fear, courage, desire, anger, pity, and pleasure and pain generally, and the excess and the deficiency are alike

96

wrong; but to experience these emotions at the right times
and on the right occasions and towards the right persons and
for the right causes and in the right manner is the mean or the
supreme good, which is characteristic of virtue.

In examining the differences between these two formulations we are
not so much concerned that Castiglione's conception is a diluted
version of Aristotle's, for the Aristotelian 'in the right manner'
includes not only the behaviour demanded by the moment and the
social situation but also that component of behaviour which is
determined individually (not by the situation). The essential,
decisive difference for our purposes lies in the fact that Castiglione
calls Aristotle's reference points 'contingencies.' For Aristotle these
were not 'chance' circumstances, to which an existing virtue had
to be adjusted; the mean was *different* according to how these
reference points varied, and thus *virtue was also located differently
in each case*. Castiglione's categories of 'contingency' and of 'accommodation' to it already reveal the differentiation that is taking place
between *morality and legality* – to employ terms introduced much
later by Kant, but which describe very well the tendency of all
bourgeois development in the sphere of ethics. To take circumstances
into consideration is none other than to accommodate morality to
legality, to adjust virtue to concrete social requirements, up to and
including the rules of social decorum.

But let us glance at Bacon's reflections on this same problem:[36]
The path of virtue goes directly midway between excess on the
one hand and defect on the other. . . . And yet if it was to
perish one way, it must be admitted that of the two paths . . .
he [Icarus] chose the better. For sins of defect are justly
accounted worse than sins of excess . . . ; in every knowledge
and science, and in the rules and axioms appertaining to them,
a mean must be kept between too many distinctions and too
much generality – between the rocks of the one and the
whirlpools of the other.

Here Bacon analyses the theory of the mean in connection with
problems of a kind that play no part in Aristotle's reasoning. The
example of Icarus raises the question, 'For the sake of what is it
better to perish?' For Aristotle – as for antiquity in general – it was
only worthwhile to die for virtue; thus we do not choose why it is
better to die, but always why it is more virtuous. And even if for
him 'virtue' and 'the mean' was somewhat nearer to 'doing more',
it would still be quite foreign to the thought of Aristotle and of

antiquity to give currency to the exaggeration that perishing for the sake of 'more' was somehow 'worthier'. But in that age, when the concept of man was becoming dynamic, the mean necessarily shifted in the direction of 'more'; the extreme one-sided passion for more stirred visions of greatness and splendour, and aroused sympathy (I need only refer again to the legends of Don Juan and Faust). At the same time Bacon's usage was radically new, also in the respect that he applied the principle of the mean to knowledge and to the methodology of knowledge. Since, for antiquity, knowledge was pure speculation, aiming at the apprehension of the general, it was senseless to apply the principle of the mean to it. For Bacon, however, knowledge and practice were intertwined; and thus a 'principle of the mean' derived from practice became applicable to scientific knowledge too. Even more: if Aristotle had separated pure theoretical knowledge (knowledge and *epistémé*) from ethical knowledge and practical reason (prudence), the Renaissance strove to comprehend the ethical implications of scientific choices, choices of a *Weltanschauung* as we have already seen in the case of Giordano Bruno. Thus the concept of the measure could also be interpreted from this second point of view in an epistemological and methodological sense.

The concept of the 'golden mean' furnishes only one example of how the Renaissance, spontaneously or deliberately, reformulated the newly rediscovered categories of ancient philosophy. Resuscitation led to reinterpretation, naïve interpretation to a *programmatic* effort at reinterpretation. Here the change in Pico della Mirandola's standpoint is characteristic. Early in his philosophical career Pico regarded the thought of antiquity as something that *ought to be revived*; but as a mature thinker he had come around to the belief that, even if antiquity was the bearer of certain general values, it was still necessary to seize hold of these independent values *independently*, in the present, and to realize them anew. Here too, however, it was the sixteenth century that took a great stride forward.

For the thought of the sixteenth century was marked by a *critical attitude* towards antiquity, and by the constant growth of this attitude of criticism. It is least apparent in the sphere of ethics; we have seen how in ethical questions even Bacon frequently refers directly to the ancient Greeks. But so far as the philosophy of nature and the study of man are concerned, a realization of how *naive and primitive* the ancients had been was becoming ever more prevalent. In the light of new scientific discoveries – be it the compass, gunpowder, or the Copernican system – the scientific thinking of the ancients seemed immature. This criticism, of course, was quite as unjust as the earlier adulation. Not only was it incapable of evaluating ancient thought historically; staring into the sun of the 'new science' had, moreover, made it blind to the real accomplishments of the classical philosophy of nature. Let it be said in its defence that this criticism was heaviest in those countries – France and England – where Plato and Aristotle were still the idols of conservative scholasticism, rather than of the new philosophy. (The admiration of Telesio or Bruno for the two great thinkers was no less than that of the preceding century.)

The sharpest critic was Bacon himself. For him Plato and Aristotle were really 'dead dogs', and their teachings were to be relegated to the world of 'idols', of false notions. True, it was Bacon who 'discovered' pre-Socratic philosophy for posterity. But his respect for the pre-Socratics was circumscribed by an awareness that the thought of his own age far surpassed the simple questionings of theirs. His criticism is often shrewd and telling, as when he remarks that 'the philosophy of the Greeks, which in investigating the material principles of things is careful and acute, in inquiring the principles of notion, wherein lies all vigour of operation, is negligent and languid. . .'.[37]

But the consciousness of *the intellectual superiority of their own age* kept growing even among those who did not neglect the classics or some portion of them. Often this consciousness rose almost to the point of enthusiasm, as with Bruno. In comparisons with antiquity the present age always emerged victorious, and its victory was proclaimed loudly and passionately. Here is Cardano speaking of the circumstances of his own life:[38]

Among the extraordinary, though quite natural circumstances of my life, the first and most unusual is that I was born in this century in which the whole world became known; whereas the ancients were familiar with but little more than a third part of it.

Even more telling is the statement of Regius:[39]

Nothing prevents this age from producing in philosophy men as eminent as Plato and Aristotle, or in medicine as Hippocrates and Galen, or in mathematics as Euclid, Archimedes and Ptolemy, after the help which we get from their books, after so many observations and inventions made since then, after such a long experience in all things; so that, when we consider well, *there was never a century more happily placed for the advancement of letters than the present one.*

99

Edgar Zilsel is right to say that even at this time – and in these statements – there appear, in the discussion of technical progress, *the seeds of historical thought.* A direct connection is discerned between the forces of production, or technology, and discoveries, on the one hand, and the possibilities of scientific, and especially philosophical, speculation on the other. The thought begins to dawn that technical discoveries, and hence scientific discoveries, *build on one another;* their relationship is one of continuation and evolution. But despite all this I still maintain what has been said about the unhistorical evaluation of the ancient philosophers. For if the connection between technique and science (or philosophy) became discernible, and if the notion that 'one thing builds upon another' appeared in these areas, there is still *not a trace of all this in the analysis of the development of society.* The same thinkers who proclaim the development of technology and science do not even recognize the very problem of social development (I will discuss this in more detail in my analysis of Machiavelli). It had dawned on some that there was a connection between the technical backwardness of antiquity and the peculiarities of its science and learning. But there was still no awareness that it was society which mediated this connection, or that science and society lived in the same mutually conditioning relationship as did science and technology.

The evolution of the Renaissance attitude towards antiquity was thus the precise opposite of what the accepted commonplace would have it. According to that view, the men of the Renaissance found in the culture of antiquity something that was 'different', and went on from there to identify themselves with it. The truth, however, is that the discovery of antiquity started out from a sense of *identity;* the men of that age of unfolding bourgeois development thought to find more and more similarities between their time and the distant past. The recognition of *distinctiveness* was the product of a relatively high degree of development; it is bound up with the first great technical and scientific discoveries. The *sense of social distinctiveness,* however, only became a conscious one when *bourgeois social relations* had become recognizable. Then it was that social philosophy, with the theory of social contract, and ethics, with the *theory of egotism,* threw off the leading strings of antiquity. But that belongs to the history of the seventeenth century's concept of man.

CHAPTER 3

Stoicism and epicureanism

Every philosophy expresses at the same time a vision of the world and an active attitude towards it. To be a philosopher means two things above all: to create a vision of the world which illuminates its objective contents more comprehensively and more profoundly than before, and at the same time to incorporate in social and ethical attitudes the practical consequences of that new vision. For the philosopher personally the link between these two is *absolute*. But it depends to a great extent on the content of any philosophy – on *what* it says about reality – how far the *ordinary men* who accept it are obliged to apply the implications of its teachings in their daily practice (or at least should feel obliged to). It is a common experience, for example, for obsolete world-views to be accepted even when they no longer satisfy the needs of the age, while in practice their demands on conduct are neglected wittingly or unwittingly. We need only think of a simple pastor of the sixteenth-century, let us say, who naturally accepts without ado the Thomist view of the world, but who does not solve the moral conflicts that confront him in a Thomist manner at all. My assertion still holds true even if we take into account more up-to-date world-views and concentrate only on their contents. For an ordinary eighteenth-century Spinozan the injunction to live his ideas in practice was more absolute than for those who at that time accepted Locke's outlook; today one expects from a Marxist (even if he is not a philosopher) a close harmony of world-view and practice, of the sort one would never expect from even the most enthusiastic follower of, for example, Nicholas Hartmann.

In the history of philosophy there have been only two schools for whom this harmony was absolutely binding *on all those* who accepted their outlook: stoicism and epicureanism. For these two schools *no distinction existed even in principle between philosopher and layman.*[40] If we seek to grasp – as a first approximation – what is common to both and what distinguishes them from all other philosophies, we find that within the unity of world-view and conduct it is *conduct* that predominates in both. Since it is the sort of conduct adopted which makes one a stoic or an epicurean, one's adherence to one or the other of these schools can be measured, both objectively and subjectively, by one's conduct; so in principle there is no possibility of that discrepancy between outlook and practice which I pointed to in connection with the everyday functions of other philosophies. Instinctively, of course, everybody has always known this. If someone wished to cite an example of a great Aristotelian or a great Hegelian, his store of examples would consist exclusively of philosophers; but if he searched for a great stoic, then perhaps Brutus or Shakespeare's Horatio would come to mind first, rather than Seneca or Epictetus, and among epicureans he would as soon think of Danton or the mature Goethe as of Lucretius. Or – more likely – he would hit upon some great 'creative' personality of his own age; we find such men mirrored in art time and again. Giorgione's epicurean attitude towards reality is displayed in his paintings, while we know nothing of his philosophical conceptions, if indeed he had any. The inhabitants of Shakespeare's Forest of Arden are typical epicureans, and yet, though they 'philosophize', none of them is a philosopher. During the Renaissance this truth was formulated theoretically, too, at least in part. Thus Charron, completing his analysis of stoic conduct, summarized his conclusions as follows: 'To live happily and contentedly one need not be a sage, or a courtier, or any other sort of notable. Everything beyond what is common and natural is vanity.'[41] That is to say: not everyone can be exceptionally gifted, but everyone can be a stoic.[42]

The primacy of conduct in stoicism and epicureanism does not, of course, imply the absence of a vision of the world. But here we are first of all interested in the characteristic nature of these world-views.

In part, their character was determined, and can be explained, by the *genesis* of the two philosophical schools. Both arose at the time of the decay of the Greek polis; both were popularized and spread in the Rome of the Caesars. Both were forced to reckon with the loss of the morale and cohesion of the community, and both sought an individual answer to the question, 'How should we live?' – though only for the 'sage', of course: ancient stoicism and epicureanism always remained aristocratic, visions of the world accessible only to the elite.

True enough, Plato had already constructed his ontology around the question, 'How should we live?' – only Plato did not seek an individual answer. He was the last philosopher of the polis, whose ideal state, with its corresponding ontology, was designed to save the polis; the collapse of these hopes was the tragedy of his life, as his famous sixth letter tells us. Compared with Plato, Aristotle once again introduced a relative division of ontology from ethics. In his metaphysics he rejected the theory of ideas and returned (on a higher plane) to the Ionian philosophy of nature; his ethics – with social practice (*energeia*) as its central category – presupposes a looser kind of communal society, but ethical problems are still solved within the community, in the social arena, as with Democritus a century earlier.

After the decay of the polis both these solutions were untenable; only two possible courses remained open. One was to proceed further along Plato's path, answering the question 'How should we live?' with an ontological system that gave an *ideological answer about the meaning of life*; but this ideological answer no longer referred to the community, but to the individual. This was the course followed by Plotinus and Neo-platonism, creating thereby a rich spiritual soil for the reception of Christianity (we need think only of Augustine's ideological development). The other possible course was to retain the question 'How should we live?' – and likewise as a question addressed to the individual – but to base the answer not on man's heteronomy but on his *autonomy*, on that relative degree of autonomy, freedom, self-consciousness, conscious choice among alternatives, and mastery over the world and over oneself which emerged from the ancient (and especially the Athenian) polis and which, once formulated, remained valid even after the destruction of the polis as a postulate and an injunction: *to make oneself free in a world from which freedom was absent.*

The Platonic and Plotinist ontology of 'What is to be done?' – and in this regard I can certainly mention the two together – seeks the *goal* of human life in the world of transcendence, in one's relationship to the transcendent; the teleological structure of the transcendental world enables man, by contemplating it, to attain to its beauty and harmony. *The world beyond is a part of the human world*; an existence before and after death lends a meaning to human life. Once again the heteronomy of man in Plato and Plotinus must be stressed (not, of course, in the early Plato, not yet in the creator of a system): for them, as we have seen, man's end is determined by transcendent ends external to him.

103

In the world of stoicism and epicureanism (and in this regard there is no difference between them, in their classical forms) the relationship between man and the external world is radically different. Both took over from the Platonic heritage (as contrasted with the Aristotelian or Democritan) the interdependence of ethics and ontology, but 'merely' reversed their relationship. For both, the laws of the universe are given for every human being. Man is born into a world *given by nature*, a world without purpose which offers one neither an individual end nor any overall meaning in life. Here man's task (not, be it noted, his *end*) is to make *a sober accounting with objectivity*. He must win his freedom within and 'in accordance with' the world of the objectively *given*.

Ancient stoicism and epicureanism differed as to the *nature* of the objective laws, independent of men, with which they had to reckon in order to become free. Stoicism, at least in its classical forms, proclaimed the absolute necessity of the laws of the universe. On this view, it is the recognition of the laws of nature (and hence of 'human nature'), and a way of life 'according to nature', that makes man free. No less familiar is the theory of 'declinations' of epicurean atomism. Epicurus (and Lucretius) thought to demonstrate that the *objective existence of chance* made possible the attainment of human freedom, in defiance of concrete forms of necessity. These ontological differences gave rise to differences on the plane of ethical conduct as well. For the stoics – especially the late Roman stoics – the premise of absolute necessity justified a kind of 'double-entry bookkeeping': on the one hand *acting in accordance* with necessity, on the other the transformation of human autonomy into a purely *subjective autonomy*. The theory of declinations, again, confirmed the epicurean posture of complete and absolute withdrawal from public life. And these differences entailed, once again, new and contradictory consequences. For the stoic living 'in the world', the disciplining of his nature – asceticism – became obligatory. The epicurean, on the other hand, living far from the world, could objectively assert his autonomy (within narrow limits) by giving free rein to his affections; in the absence of a corrupting environment affections could be directed only towards noble and sound pleasures.

In certain concrete cases these differences could become decisive: a stoic emperor was possible, but an epicurean emperor was not. Or, to mention a more important consideration: the combination of asceticism and 'living in the world' made certain elements of stoicism attractive and assimilable for Christians at the time when their religion was becoming the dominant one in Rome. But the essential thing, even in antiquity, was the relativity of their differences. Once assimilated by Christianity, stoicism was no longer authentic. Why this was so appears clearly from the fact that stoicism and epicureanism always believed in common in the same free relationship towards *our future:* towards death.

For ancient stoicism and epicureanism the question was, 'How is the individual to live like a free, autonomous human being in a natural world and social world both independent of him and both having their own laws, among which necessarily belongs the inevitability of death, man's final annihilation?' This fundamental question, common to both schools, did not imply an unequivocal answer to the query, 'How?' Ancient epicureanism already existed in active and passive variants. The various types of conduct exhibited in the behaviour of various stoics, again, are well known; it is enough to mention Seneca and Marcus Aurelius, one put to death by an emperor, the other himself an emperor.

But as soon as we come to speak of modern – or even Renaissance – stoicism or epicureanism, we must reckon with the fact that not only do the answers to the question 'How?' vary now; to some extent the ontological foundations have changed as well. No longer did everyone regard the natural and social worlds as realities independent of men, with laws of their own. Of course, there were many who did; among them I need only mention Montaigne. But the number of those who saw the *human* world as the work of man, and man himself as his own creation, was growing constantly; they set out – if only partially and incompletely, like Machiavelli – from the fact that it was possible to actively transform the world. And yet it is no accident that we speak of a basically stoic-epicurean attitude in them as well – not just because, like the ancient stoics, they saw nature and human mortality as an unalterable fate which had to be staunchly confronted, but also because they preserved the stoic-epicurean attitude of accepting the consequences of their actions. Marx, in analysing Sue's *Fleure de Marie*, held the principle of 'what I have done, I have done' to be the unshakeable basis of stoic-epicurean morality (a principle which, incidentally, he accepted for his own).

Little by little stoicism and epicureanism abandoned those differences of detail, often significant in their day, which had characterized them during antiquity. Detached from speculations relating to the philosophy of nature (atomism, the theory of universal conflagration), from fatalism and the aristocratic attitude that necessarily went with it, stoicism and epicureanism finally merged. The process of fusion was already discernible during the Renaissance, although it was completed only at the end of the period.

105

Thus modern stoicism (or epicureanism) was far from being a concrete philosophy any longer, much less a philosophical system; it had become a basic attitude towards reality or an ethically tinged form of conduct, which might go together with quite different philosophical systems – though not, of course, with any and all philosophical systems. Still, it always retained a certain ontological foundation, in the absence of which that basic attitude could never have arisen. That was the existence of a reality we must deal with independent of our desires, dreams, and individualities, from which our actions must set out, in the knowledge that they will have further repercussions in this world, and that only we – through our conduct, our actions, and our whole life – can and *must* give a meaning to that world.

The stoic-epicurean attitude was one of the basic types of conduct of the Renaissance – but only one of them. Here I have omitted not only those whose works were dominated by religion and who thus left their ends in the Creator's hands, but also those who were unwilling to take account of nature's laws or of objective social possibilities, and who, regarding man's autonomy as practically (and sometimes theoretically) absolute, sought to overpower reality with their boundless passion. Once more it is only necessary to point to two typical heroes synthesized by the imagination of the age out of countless individual examples: Don Juan and Faust.

It is interesting that the age itself related this unbridled passion (or thirst for knowledge), exceeding all possibilities, to the transcendent: hence the oft-mentioned legend about a 'pact with the devil'. The story of Faust also demonstrates how such great and passionate personalities (often tragic personalities) become capable of 'repentance' in the very moment of confrontation with death. But whether they defy the world beyond with their 'No!', or whether in the final moment of their lives they place their hopes in divine mercy, they are all still foreign to anything that we call stoicism or epicureanism. It is particularly important to emphasize this in the case of Don Juan, for the common cliché regards epicureanism as synonymous with the pursuit of pleasure. Thus it must follow that anyone obsessed with pleasure-seeking, who seeks to gratify his desires as widely as possible, has to be considered an epicurean. Space is lacking here to analyse the relationship of epicureanism to the theory of pleasure; here I should only like to note that there is a theory of pleasure that goes with epicureanism, but that the connection is far from a necessary one. As for the Faust theme, be it remarked that here I am speaking, of course, of the Renaissance

Faust, in particular the Faust of Spies and Marlowe, and not of the subject of Goethe's drama.

Don Juan and Faust are extreme cases. The Renaissance was rich in personalities whose passionate recklessness sprang from a misunderstanding of reality, and who for that reason could not achieve a stoic-epicurean sort of autonomy. Such tragic heroes appear frequently in Shakespeare; we need only think of Lear. But the Renaissance also produced personalities who did not even desire to come to terms with their own 'natures' and who, once free of religious morality, threw off every restraint and thus lost above all their objective relationship to themselves; here it is enough to refer to such typical figures as the three Borgias. Often the individual's situation – or rather the reciprocal effect of situation and individual character – made it impossible for someone to achieve the stoic-epicurean ideal of conduct. We need only think of another Shakespearean hero, Hamlet, and of the respect with which – for that very reason – he looks *up* to his friend, the stoic Horatio.

But if the stoic-epicurean mode of conduct was only one of many which characterized the Renaissance era, still its special significance cannot be too strongly emphasized. The adoption and spread of this form of conduct in life was one of the ways in which the *secularization of ethics* was carried through. Often it appeared even in the thinking of believers, as a kind of ethical expression of a practical atheism. Frequently it found its way into the views of other schools of thought, like the Platonists. Among contemporary Aristotelians, too, it became almost a general moral attitude. Nor was that at all surprising: Aristotle's own original outlook was in many ways the point of departure for ancient stoicism and epicureanism, and those who were now returning to the 'original' Aristotle perceived this affinity and carried it further. It was not at all accidental that Luther called Aristotle an epicurean through and through. Burckhardt bears witness to the fact that in the course of this whole process we are not dealing with 'pure' schools when he notes that during this period everyone was called an epicurean who denied, or at least disregarded, the immortality of the soul.

From all of the foregoing it is clear that the stoic or epicurean of the Renaissance cannot be characterized as a *single* type. We must be aware of this plurality of types in dealing not only with philosophical and methodological premises, but also with the answers to the question 'How should we live?', which were implied by the common ontological foundation. Already during the Renaissance men who swore by different philosophers and even men who conducted themselves differently in life could with equal justice be called stoics or epicureans. We can only take note of this multiplicity, of course, while we first survey those *common premises* on which every stoic and epicurean of the age built, and around which he oriented his conduct. I shall then conclude my present train of reasoning with the analysis of several important and particularly revealing types.

PHILOSOPHICAL FOUNDATIONS OF STOIC AND EPICUREAN CONDUCT

'While We Live, There is No Death'

To take account of objectivity means, among other things, taking account of the inevitability of one's own death. For ancient stoicism and epicureanism this problem became a crucial one, for it was at that moment in human history that death first became a central and painful life-experience. So long as the community remained intact, the individual's life was a part of the community's life; so long as the community went on living – as it necessarily must – the individual did too. It was not only in the primitive community that life after death, the life of shades, was seen as punishment and pain rather than as a state to be desired; the Greeks' 'realm of Hades' was not an attractive place either, nor did it determine people's actions on earth in the slightest. Consider the legend of Orpheus: for Orpheus, Eurydice lives only so long as she lives with him and *on earth*. In his eyes the fact that she 'exists' in the realm of Hades is tantamount to her total extinction. Socrates simply treats the next world ironically; in the *Apology* he speaks of the possibility of 'questioning' the heroes in the next world, but remarks that if after his death he does question these heroes and sages in Hades, surely many of them will prove ignorant; then, however, it will no longer be possible to condemn him to death for it. At the same time Socrates (and with him, of course, the young Plato) takes up the other and real alternative, the idea of complete extinction. Complete extinction is comforting, for it is exactly like a sleep. (Leaping ahead for a moment to the figure of Hamlet: Hamlet, too, is comforted by the thought of complete extinction; he, too, does not fear death, but only the life after death.) We must, of course, note that this ancient indifference in the face of death was by no means equivalent to an indifference towards the death of *others*; for that was something that bore upon the *living*. Nor did it signify an indifference towards *when* or *why* we die; an early death made impossible the living of life in its entirety, a senseless death meant the conclusion of a senseless life. Thus the problem of death never appears as an immanent problem of death or as the misfortune of extinction, but rather as a problem or conflict belonging to life; and it is of interest only so long and in so far as it is *a part of life*. Thus when Epicurus wrote that 'while we live, there is no death', he was formulating as a theoretical principle something that Greek practice – especially in the Athenian polis – had actually realized in an earlier period. (This feature plays no small role in the stoic and epicurean image of Socrates.)

But at the time when Epicurus coined his saying, the ancient Greek city-state community no longer existed; the life of the community had ceased to be the 'natural' continuation of the individual life. The death of the individual had become synonymous with the death of 'the world'; fear of death became a basic sentiment of individuals living an increasingly senseless life. Epicurus' idea was thus anything but the simple recording of a given fact of life; on the contrary, it was a polemic and a challenge. The polemic was not, of course, directed exclusively against the fear of death. It had a positive content: the choice of a *meaningful life*, a life that has meaning only in and for itself and cannot be lived or judged from the standpoint of death. For death is outside of human life; man must reckon with death as *something that exists, but none of his actions can be motivated by it*.

During the Renaissance these ideas were revived, with an even more passionate polemical edge. Here we are at the end of a long historical epoch during which men had become accustomed to living their lives from a perspective of death and life after death. The stoic thinkers, and the ideas of Epicurus, disseminated by way of Lucretius, struck this world with the force of a revelation, for they put life back on its feet again, and sought the meaning of life in life itself, not above it or outside it. These ideas began to hold sway over people's lives even before they could be transformed into a conscious ideology. Consider the heroes and heroines of Boccaccio's *Decameron*: in the midst of a deadly plague they meet in a church – but instead of resigning themselves to divine grace, fasting in atonement for their sins or hysterically appealing for the help of saints or objects of devotion, they set out for the attractive garden of a castle to 'live a life of beauty'. And here the 'life of beauty' is synonymous with meaningful life: for these figures are seeking pleasure, but pleasure in 'harmony' and 'measure' – not in debauchery, the complement to religious hysteria, but in singing and dancing, telling witty stories, contemplating the landscape, in friendship and refined love; it is in these that they find their pleasure. The raciness of the stories only underscores the noble and sober

109

detachment of those who tell them; for those who themselves tread the path of beauty and goodness can safely listen to all that is ugly and evil as well as to all that is good and beautiful. During the whole time that the plague is raging, they do not think once of the possibility of their own death; they seem to embody in advance the demand of Spinoza that the wise man should think of life, not of death. It is not said of them vainly that 'death shall not vanquish these'.[43] Petrarch expresses a similar conception of life when he writes: 'Life makes us happy or wretched; and those who have conducted their lives virtuously down to their last breath have no need of anything more. . . .'[44] When Boscoli was condemned to death for having taken part in a conspiracy against the Medici, he *wished* to be converted, but he was *unable to*. His earlier stoic conception and conduct of life prevented him from becoming a Christian. ' "Ah," sighs Boscoli, "get Brutus out of my head for me, that I may go my way as a Christian." '[45] And when the monk who had come to convert him admonished him to bear death bravely, he replied: 'Father, waste no time on this; the philosophers have taught it to me already; help me to bear death out of love to Christ.'[46]

By the time Pomponazzi came to generalize this problem in a theoretical way, he was summarizing the experience of two centuries. His starting-point was the long-disputed question of the immortality of the soul, to whose analysis we shall return in another context. What is important for our present purpose is the following conclusion of Pomponazzi: 'The question of the immortality of the soul is a neutral problem.'[47] (His work 'On the immortality of the soul' stirred up a great storm. In his reply to these attacks he went even further than this statement; he no longer spoke of a 'neutral problem', but bluntly denied the immortality of the soul. But from the point of view of the ideas expressed in his earlier work, this neutrality was quite enough.)

Pomponazzi interprets 'neutrality' as follows: the immortality of the soul may be necessary for us in order to explain knowledge, since it would be extremely difficult to explain how the soul can have knowledge of conceptual essences if it is a purely material phenomenon – for only like can apprehend like. But it is unnecessary – indeed, it is to be rejected – *from the standpoint of ethical conduct*. True moral nobility appears in the extent to which a man is able to regard his life as a rounded whole:[48]

For the ancients also called life a purgatory, since man
receives it with the provision that he knows *he must give it back
to nature*. He will give thanks to God and nature and will always

be ready to die, nor will he fear death, since fear of the
inevitable is vain; and he will see nothing evil in death.

And as examples he cites Homer and Seneca.

Pomponazzi began here a polemic with Christianity whose
ripples have spread outward across the centuries, right down to
our own day. He attacked the value of other-worldly rewards or
punishments as guarantees of the practice of virtue in this world.
This-wordly virtue means a *social morality*; the motives of good and
evil are not other-worldly, but profoundly social.[49]

> Since then in choosing death for the sake of country, of friends,
> and of avoiding sin the greatest virtue is acquired, and it is
> greatly to the advantage of others, since men naturally praise
> an act of this sort, and nothing is more precious and more
> happy than virtue itself, it is above all things to be chosen.
> But in committing crime, *a man very greatly harms the
> community, and hence also himself, since he is part of the community.*

Abstracting from a number of other problems raised by this
quotation, which are important in other contexts, let us concentrate on what concerns us at the moment: the fact that
Pomponazzi radically restores the character of virtue as *an
end in itself*, one which carries with it its own reward. But in the
context in which the words appear it is not only the fact that Pomponazzi sets aside other-worldly rewards and punishments that is
important; it is also that *the stoic and epicurean idea of virtue as an
end in itself springs not from the individualistic morality of ancient
stoicism and epicureanism, but from the soil of the concrete morality
of Renaissance society.* Here we see clearly formulated the same
novel features which were already present in our earlier examples
from literature and real life. The stoic and epicurean behaviour of
Boccaccio's heroes, too, can only be understood within the context
of the given community, while Boscoli was 'unable to get free of
Brutus' because his stoicism expressed the real moral world of the
anti-Medici, republican community of Florence.

Pomponazzi groups men according to their degree of nobility,
perfection, and virtue. The most illustrious are those who choose
good (and avoid evil) autonomously, for its own sake (or for the
sake of the community, which is the same thing); these are the men
whose behaviour we have characterized as stoic or epicurean. They
have no need of violence or falsehood; their virtue springs precisely
from truthfulness and freedom. Less illustrious are those who
require rewards and punishments; for them the morality of the

111

community is not completely free, but is rather an imposed morality. Even less illustrious are those who have need of a legal order; while the most wretched are those who must weigh other-wordly reward and punishment in the balance. We have gone from *a free virtue to an imposed virtue, from autonomy to heteronomy, from voluntary confrontation with truth to the need for falsehood.* For Pomponazzi, the need for an afterworld (and, I might add, for religion generally) is a property of those who are morally weak.

Of this last, most wretched type of person Pomponazzi says:[50]

> But some from the fierceness and perversity of their nature are moved by none of these, as daily experience teaches. Therefore they have set up for the virtuous eternal rewards in another life, and for the vicious eternal punishments, which *frighten greatly.*

The more eminent and virtuous a man, the less he will be moved by *hope* and *fear*, the weaker and more vicious he is, the more he will be moved by them. The just man, 'fearing nothing, hoping for nothing, [remains] in prosperity and adversity ever the same'.[51]

In those periods when the communal life of the Renaissance was vanishing (and in those places where it scarcely existed) stoic and epicurean thinking and conduct came closer to the ancient point of departure. If, from Boccaccio to Pomponazzi, the individuals who shared the 'life of beauty' were individuals within a given community, who *collectively* ignored the prospect of *natural* death but were very much concerned (like Boscoli or Pomponazzi) with the problem of a chosen death (for friendship, for one's country, etc.), then we can say that those sixteenth-century humanists who during the first wave of the wars of religion were unable to make a firm decision (between two evils) once again stood face to face with the problem of life and death on an *individual* basis; for them virtue had once again become a question of the individual conduct of life, a matter of self-preservation in an evil, disjointed world. For them a death coming *from without* was still a *chance* affair even when it was social. That was not a matter of choice for them. But they had to choose a kind of life such that even the incendiary whims of contemporary 'Caesars' could cause them no harm. The most notable representatives of this kind of stoicism, which because of its outsider's attitude towards fanaticism necessarily goes along with scepticism, were Frenchmen, above all Montaigne and Charron.

From the point of view of the problem under discussion at present two questions ought to be singled out. First of all Montaigne, because he does not feel the support of a living community, feels (like Epicurus) that the ontological continuity of reality resides not primarily in society but rather in nature. He writes, for example: 'Your death is a part of the order of the universe; it is a part of the life of the world.'[52] Again, the attitude towards death acquires a dimension which was quite common in antiquity, but which had been almost completely missing during the two preceding centuries of stoic and epicurean thinking: the notion of the possibility of *suicide*. Let us recall Pomponazzi: among the variety of deaths which he lists there is death for one's country and death undertaken for the sake of a friend, but death undertaken for its own sake, a *wilful exit from the world*, does not figure there. Montaigne, however, writes: 'Now among the principal benefits of virtue is disdain for death, a means that furnishes our life with soft tranquillity. . . . Whenever we please, death can put an end, and deny access, to all our other woes.'[53] But so long as there is still some sense to life the alternative of a 'freedom' to commit suicide makes no sense; suicide can only be regarded as a reasonable conclusion to a life which can no longer be continued in an honourable and reasonable manner. In Shakespeare this theme appears again and again, not only with such consistent stoics as Brutus, for whom the failure of his cause makes life objectively unbearable, but also in a character like Othello, who is not a stoic to begin with but who, by committing suicide, also gives new meaning and splendour to a life that has become meaningless.

Bacon is, all in all, not a stoic figure. Still, I would like to close this discussion with his words, for with his ability to draw telling analogies he summarized what is common to the human condition, the position which stoics and epicureans took towards this common condition, and what was acceptable from their philosophy and ethics for a sober natural philosopher like himself, whose ontology could have served as an adequate basis for a stoic or epicurean outlook: 'Death is a friend of ours, and he that is not ready to entertain him, is not at home.'[54] Stoics and epicureans, however, *were at home* in the world.

Living According to Nature

To live according to nature means to take cognizance of nature as it is. Only thus can a man's life be *honourable and 'virtuous'*; and *he will feel at ease* in his honour and virtue only if he takes stock of what is necessary and unchangeable in nature, of where and to what extent there is free scope in it for the free activity of man, and of *how man can make use of an unchanging nature to make himself a free and honourable life*.

Three kinds of nature are intertwined in the stoic and epicurean view of life: nature proper, the *macrocosm*, independent of all

113

human will and striving; social nature, an outgrowth of the actions of men; and finally individual nature, which every human being at all times has had to contend with – nature as *general*, as *particular*, and as *individual*. I have deliberately stressed that they are intertwined. The stoic-epicurean relationship to these three natures is always *unitary*; it is determined by the way they are bound up with one another and by the specific way in which they interrelate. I have spoken, for example, of matters relating to life and death: death belongs properly to the 'first nature' – all human beings alike, in all societies, must die. But the development of a 'normal' attitude towards death is a necessary precondition if one is to remain virtuous with respect to the 'second nature', that of society and of own life. Montaigne writes that if you do not fear death you gain thereby 'the true and sovereign liberty, which enables us to *thumb our nose at force and injustice and to laugh* at prisons and chains'.[55] Those who do not measure life by death will have a different relationship towards the ensemble of their affections. They will never be 'pressed for time', they will never commit an unworthy deed lest, because of the shortness of life, they fail to attain what they seek. Not only will they be steeled against the blows of fate (as several stoics interpret it), they will also gain scope and courage to actively pursue right actions. But the interrelationship also works, as we have seen, in the opposite direction. The sense of Pomponazzi's example is that love of country or of a friend can impel a man to have no regard for death; here the pathos of the 'second nature' generates the normal relationship to the 'first nature'.

I have already discussed some of the problems connected with 'first nature'; now I would like to say a few words about attitudes towards 'social nature'. I will deliberately omit those who in this matter did not deviate from the traditional path of ancient stoicism or epicureanism. Nor will I mention the devotees of the *procul negotiis*, particularly numerous in the sixteenth century, nor those who took up once again the ambiguity of ancient stoicism, seeking to reconcile inner autonomy with a superficial and formal accommodation to external circumstances. Here I should like only to point to one or two new aspects and one or two new pioneering efforts.

First of all I should like to discuss the somewhat similar conceptions of Valla and Alberti, found in more comprehensive form, it is true, in the latter writer.[56]

Valla directs his polemics against monastic life, but his principles are valid for secular life as well. Only an integrity gained in social life can, according to him, educate us to be human beings; it is there

114

that we come into contact daily with contradictory demands and desires, and in this conflict we must decide; the possibility of deciding for the worse arises again and again. Those who withdraw from the world only believe that they are virtuous – it is possible that they commit no wickedness, but they do not acquire a faculty for virtue. In order to 'live according to nature', self-knowledge is necessary above all else. But there is an interrelationship between self-knowledge and praxis: only those can act adequately who possess self-knowledge, and self-knowledge can be won only through praxis by proving one's own integrity.

Thus Valla is far from regarding the given social order of the polis as good, and this sharply distinguishes him from the thinkers of the ancient polis, Plato and Aristotle. *In a relatively evil world man must find his own freedom and virtue, in the conflicts of the given world he must shape and develop himself* (and the world). And with this Valla gives a new meaning to the stoic and epicurean answer to the question. 'How should we live?' Here we can speak of a new tone of voice, for Valla describes the interaction of social demands, social education, and individual morality in a way that will become typical during *the great progressive age of bourgeois society.* The idea adumbrated by Valla is at the heart of every great *Bildungsroman*, from *Tom Jones* to *Wilhelm Meister's Apprenticeship.*

Alberti does not describe the 'great theatre of the world', as one of the favourite allegories of the age called it, as any earthly paradise either. The world is mad; there is no justice, loyalty, courage, or honour; religion, man's consolation, is itself the product of men, the fruit of fear. But that does not imply a withdrawal from the world either, but rather a dual 'obedience': obedience to righteousness and obedience to facticity. Man must participate in public life, shape it and be shaped by it; but he must not be absorbed by it totally. His behaviour combines *participation* and *distance.* The *heroism* lies in realizing that union. His means of doing so is *masserizia*, a method born of a combination of the Aristotelian and stoic-epicurean concepts of measure. *Masserizia* means the wise conduct of one's affairs. Nor does it refer only to 'virtue' as ethical behaviour, narrowly conceived. *Masserizia* may just as well mean the healthy governing of our bodies, or the harmonious and balanced direction of our family life, business affairs, time, interests, and fate. Alberti's fundamental principle, then, is one of living *without illusions.* But this freedom from illusion is not of a kind to breed despair; on the contrary, it protects us from despair. It is precisely this freedom from illusion which enables us to recognize the real possibilities which exist for good and beauty; 'living according to nature', man can become master of the facticity of nature and make it into a basis for 'truth'. *Man's true satisfaction lies not in resignation, but in the enjoyment of a full life, replete with contradictions, struggle, and difficulties* (this last expression cannot be found, to my knowledge, in Alberti, but that is still the content of his reasoning).

Again we can only indicate very sketchily what an immense problem and what *paradigmatic forms of conduct* Alberti discovered here. First of all, consider Shakespeare's world again, the world of *As You Like It*, where Shakespeare, too, pursues the dialectic of social and individual life. On one side are Oliver and the usurping Duke, both – to use Alberti's expression – completely 'facticity's' men. They want power – like the Duke – or else they simply want to give free rein to their worst instincts, like Oliver with his jealousy of his brother. They know neither virtue nor dignity, for those things are 'against nature'. At the other pole is Jacques, who loathes this ruined world. But because of his loathing and rejection he is unable to live and be happy. 'The sundry contemplation of my travels . . . wraps me in a most humorous sadness,'[57] he tells us. Jacques loves melancholy, and for that reason every ordinary thing of beauty in life, even love itself, evokes his scorn – even if it is an indulgent scorn. His way is that of the *procul negotiis*, of the 'cave left behind'. In that there is a certain consistency which is worthy of respect, and that is the reason the poet follows him so lovingly. But Shakespeare's true heroes, and his real favourites, are those who – to cite Alberti again – live according to *masserizia*: the banished Duke and his entourage. They see the world without illusions, but they do not withdraw from it for reasons of principle. They accept public life, be it in the form of friendly company or of a dukedom, whenever it affords them an opportunity to 'live according to nature'; it can be the scene (or battle-ground) of a just and honourable life, if not of perfection. Their outlook – and the poet's – is summed up in the famous song from Act II:[58]

> Freeze, freeze, thou bitter sky,
> That dost not bite so nigh
> As benefits forgot:
> Though thou the waters warp,
> Thy sting is not so sharp
> As friend remember'd not.
> Heigh-ho! sing, heigh-ho! unto the green holly:
> *Most friendship is feigning, most loving mere folly.*
> > The heigh-ho! the holly!
> > *This life is most jolly.*

116

The Forest of Arden is symbolic: nature is the symbol of the natural life.

I should like to illustrate the exemplary character of Alberti's analysis by discussing a situation, and an analysis, that arose some five hundred years later. Here is part of a letter written from prison by Rosa Luxemburg to Luise Kautsky, in 1917. The passage that concerns us reads as follows:[59]

> You have certainly lost your taste for music temporarily, as for so many other things. Your head is full of cares about a world whose history has gone awry. . . . Everyone who writes to me sighs and complains. That is too stupid. Don't you realize that the general smash-up is much too great to moan about? . . . I can get upset if Mimi falls ill or if something happens to you. But if the whole world gets out of joint, then *I try to understand what has happened and why it has happened, and if I have done my duty then I feel relieved again. Ultra posse nemo obligatur.* And then once again I have *everything* that I enjoy: music and art and the clouds and botanizing in the spring and good books and Mimi and you and so many other things. . . . I'm rich and I think I will remain so forever. To abandon oneself completely to the calamities of the day is intolerable and incomprehensible. Think with what calm composure Goethe looked at things. And remember what he experienced: the Great French Revolution – and seen up close it must have looked like nothing more than a bloody and utterly useless farce. And then from 1793 to 1815 an uninterrupted chain of wars until the world once again looked like a mad-house. And with what calmness and intellectual serenity he continued his studies on the metamorphosis of plants, on chromatology, and on a thousand and one other things! I don't expect you to write poetry like Goethe's, but *you can adopt his attitude toward life, his universality of interests, and his inner harmony* – at least you can strive to attain it. And if you say: But Goethe was not politically active, then I say that *a political fighter needs to be able to place himself above things even more urgently, or he will sink into the trivialities of everyday life up to his ears.*

If we read Rosa Luxemburg's passionate avowal carefully, we will see that her attitude towards reality is a straightforward continuation of Alberti's. It is an attitude mediated through the personality of Goethe, whom I have already described as one of the last proponents of Renaissance thinking. A direct line leads from the stoicism and epicureanism of the Renaissance, via Goethe and, no less, Diderot (and in Russia, Chernyshevsky), to the great philosophical and political figures of the Marxist tradition.

After this seeming excursion, let us return to the era of the Renaissance. We have seen how stoicism and epicureanism became the vehicle of a dynamic, dialectical relationship between individual and society. But Renaissance thought raised yet another new problem: could stoicism or epicureanism actually furnish a set of principles on which society could be organized? Could they provide a *universal norm* for men in society?

First let us consider stoicism. A positive answer to those questions was given only once, in More's *Utopia*. But that positive answer was tantamount to a negative one: for if the whole basic economic and political structure of society must change for stoic conduct to become the norm of a universal ethic operating with the force of custom and permeating the whole society, then it follows that every such aspiration is vain and unrealizable in the given social and economic circumstances. Machiavelli formulates his negative answer forcefully. The stoic who expects his own kind of virtue from everyone violates the principle of 'living according to nature', because he takes no account of facticity or the nature of *others*, which includes not only their own objective natural endowments but also their inclinations and their morality, which are a part of their own 'second nature' as it has already developed. It is in this sense that Machiavelli, in his *Discourses*, interprets the story of Manlius. Manlius is brave, honourable, irreproachable, and ascetic. But when he tries to make all these things into norm for others, he *necessarily* turns into a tyrant. Machiavelli generalizes the problem as follows:[60]

> When, therefore, a man of this kind obtains the rank of
> commander he expects to find everybody else like himself,
> and the boldness which characterizes him makes him order
> bold actions. . . . [But] when harsh commands are given, one
> should be harsh in seeing them carried out. . . .

Epicureanism as an organizing principle for society makes its appearance in only one place, Rabelais's Abbey of Thélême – though only with reservations, of course. The word 'abbey' is not only an ironic counterpoint to the Christian conception of life; it also indicates a *small community*, small enough to break away from the system of customs of the total society and to isolate itself from those whose sentiments are not honourable. To that extent it resembles Epicurus' garden more closely than More's Utopia.

118

All their life was spent not in laws, statutes, or rules, but according to their own free will and pleasure. They rose out of their beds when they thought good: they did eat, drink, labour, sleep, when they had a mind to it, and were disposed for it.[61]

Social control, then, is non-existent, there is only the freely chosen *mutual* existence of free men; here we are still in the garden of Epicurus. But – it seems to me – we are still justified in speaking here of epicureanism as a formative power in society. In Epicurus' garden 'labour' could not figure in the list of activities; in that regard, the garden is, in principle, decidedly a circle of aristo-cratic friends. The condition of its survival is the existence of all those, slaves and freemen, who create and reproduce day after day the material basis for the happy and harmonious community of the garden. In the Abbey of Thélême, however, labour plays no small part, in the form of voluntary, free work, carried out at will. The community is in principle 'self-sustaining'; thus the *creation* of *its own means of subsistence* is a part of its free, harmonious life. The notion of *free labour*, however, thoroughly reproduces the content and outlook of the epicurean garden. Yet however much Rabelais may limit himself to the small community of the abbey, in principle *there is no reason* why the abbey cannot be extended to include the whole people, or all of humanity.

What sort of an anthropology did Rabelais build the playfully serious theory of the Abbey of Thélême upon?

In all their rule . . . there was but this one clause to be observed: DO WHAT THOU WILT. Because men that are free, well-born, well-bred, and conversant in honest companies, have naturally an instinct and spur that prompteth them into virtuous actions, and withdraws them from vice, which is called honour. Those same men, when by base subjection and constraint they are brought under and kept down, turn . . . that noble disposition, by which they formerly were inclined to virtue, to shake off and break that bond of servitude, wherein they are so tyrannously enslaved; for it is agreeable with the nature of man to long after things forbidden, and to desire what is denied us.[62]

Here is the idea of 'do what you will', which was to play so large a part in future Utopias of epicurean hue, from Fourier's phalan-steries to Chernyshevsky's vision of the future in *What Is To Be Done*. It sets out from the premise that man by nature strives for the

119

good. Rabelais himself still formulates this principle a good deal more cautiously, for he speaks only of men moving in well-educated, free, honest society, thus giving a certain aristocratic tone to his utopia. At the same time he evades the philosophical core of the problem: how can a 'noble nature' emerge in men if it can only develop when given free rein, and if it is only allowed free rein in the Abbey of Thélême itself, where only men who are already free are to be found? Here is the 'vicious circle' of Enlightenment thought, all of whose efforts to get around it led to new contradictions. To escape this contradiction Rousseau's Emile must be educated outside of society, for only thus is it possible to bring out his 'true' nature. Fourier, on the other hand, simply ignores the problem of the transition from present society to future society. Rabelais was not obliged to think through all these consequences, because his literary and playfully polemical form did not demand it. But it was an act of historical significance to *formulate the new standpoint*: giving free rein to human aspirations and affections does not lead necessarily to anarchy, but may just lead to virtue and a harmonious coexistence. Here there appeared with graphic and powerful simplicity the ideas of freedom as *self-development* and of activity as *self-realization*, two aspects which are truly an integral part of human emancipation (even though only one part of it).

But with this we have already reached the third, or individual, level of 'living according to nature'. Man must – as we have seen – live according to his *own* nature. That again has two aspects: a man must reckon with everything in his nature which is *universally human* (another concept which, as we shall see, evolved during the Renaissance); on the other hand, he must also take account of the 'natural' *peculiarities* of his own personality. His view of life, choice of occupation, actions, and decisions must be adjusted to these 'natures'. But that is far from a slavish accommodation to 'nature' – knowledge and virtue shape, put to use, limit, perhaps even put a curb on nature. But in order to do all these things one must know their *object*, his own psyche and its degree of plasticity, the *limits of its potential*. The ancient injunction to 'know thyself' was broadened and became enriched with new content. It no longer meant simply becoming aware of one's assigned station, as in the original Apollonian sense, nor the confrontation with one's *own* conscience and morality, as in Socrates; it referred rather to the total sum of the individual's possibilities, both external and internal. Renaissance characterology, for example, accepted the Hippocratic types. Men were now obliged to take their own characters into consideration. Cardano, for example, writes, 'I am cold of heart, but ardent of brain.'[63] He knew that he was vengeful, and he saw that he was incapable of changing this basic characteristic. Thus he took care *deliberately to overlook occasions of taking revenge.* The truly virtuous man was the one who made the most of his own nature. As Montaigne wrote: 'It is an absolute perfection and virtually divine to know how to enjoy our being rightfully.[64] But this 'divine perfection' does not mean that every man can be of *equal* importance, equally wise or equally heroic. 'But this I ought not to call repentance, it seems to me, any more than my displeasure at being neither an angel nor Cato.'[65] The same theme appears here which Goethe later varied with the remark that every man can be equally complete. One may doubt whether anything truer can be said even today.

Common to every stoic and epicurean thinker of the Renaissance is the belief that we must know what is good and what in human nature and our own natures leads us towards virtue, and that we must guide our actions accordingly. But opinions diverge on what is good and what is bad and what should be fostered and what suppressed there. On that question epicureanism diverges most from stoicism. The stoics, for example, believe it possible to disregard suffering (like Pico), or to set limits to human needs (like More). Indeed Charron, already an expressly bourgeois thinker, puts pleasure on a plane with interest, referring to it, for the rest, as destructive of 'human nature'. Men are naturally good and follow evil only for its pleasure or profit.'[66] And, to cite a contrary example: Bacon often regarded the stoics as promoters of illusion. 'Herein I do not profess myself a stoic, to hold grief no evil, but opinion, and a thing indifferent.'[67] And he justly reproached them for treating self-knowledge and the practice of virtue as an achievement attained once and for all, over and done with. 'To speak truth, no man knows the lists of his own patience; or can divine how able he shall be in his sufferings, till the storm come, the perfectest virtue being tried in action. . . .'[68] Here 'living according to nature' becomes a *dynamic concept, conduct in motion,* evolving through praxis and constantly transformed anew.

There are still two questions which I should like to take up, both of them new: Valla's theory of pleasure and Vives's theory of the affections. Valla's *De voluptate ac vero* does more than rehearse again the questions taken up by the ancient epicureans; it is at the same time a forerunner of the French theory of pleasure of the seventeenth and eighteenth centuries. Its premises, combined with the theory of utility, lead on to the interpretations of the French Enlightenment, in particular the analyses of Holbach and Helvétius.

Valla denies the existence of self-sacrifice – in fact no one ever sacrifices himself, for that goes against 'human nature'. Every human being seeks pleasure; pleasure is the motive force, the goal and fulfilment of life. Differences exist among men only in that *different people find pleasure in different things*. Thus far Valla's reasoning scarcely varies from that of traditional epicureanism. From this starting-point, however, he soon arrives at a *classification* of pleasures. These are 'fine' and 'rude' pleasures, 'physical' and 'spiritual' ones; love of art, for example, is a spiritual pleasure, while a rude pleasure is a purely bodily one. Valla nevertheless does not classify pleasures as 'good' and 'bad'. Instead he examines them from an anthropological and psychological rather than an ethical standpoint. He starts from the *heterogeneity* of the human species. Since men are different, everyone will find enjoyment in something different. The hero takes pleasure in heroism, the saint in sanctity; and so forth. Of course, the question of wherein someone finds his pleasure is an ethical question *too*. But it is still not identical with the concept of 'virtue', nor does that exhaust its ethical content. By universalizing the motive of pleasure Valla rendered it *abstract*. But through this abstraction the question of *pleasure versus self-restraint ceased* to be the *central category*, and the main topic of discussion, of ethics. And the fact that many later thinkers kept returning to it and to efforts to 'classify' pleasures does not detract from Valla's historic accomplishment.

Dilthey believed that Vives's theory of the affections, as set forth in his *De anima*, had exercised a decisive influence on Spinoza's ethics. Leaving aside the question of any philological connection, the substantive resemblances are still obvious. According to Vives, human affections run towards what is *useful* (here for the first time the category of utility appears alongside that of pleasure); nature has implanted them in us so that we may avoid evil and grow rich in good things. Its manifestations are love and 'offence' (*offensio*). We love whatever does good to us or to someone we love. If our 'being offended' becomes fixed on an object, then hatred is the result. Our affections vary in strength; the nearer they touch our self-preservation, the stronger they are. A stronger affection will always overcome a weak one. Vives's model here is bourgeois existence, where no one pays any heed to what is more honourable, but only to what is more powerful, since their self-preservation (hence their stronger affection) demands it. Affections are uniform in all men. Stoic and epicurean conduct, however, is rooted in the attitude taken towards the affections. Judgment plays a part, deciding what is right and what is wrong; the wise and just man is one who is *able to make a correct assessment of the facts themselves.* Here, moreover, a proper estimation of things does not amount to a judgment of *vanitatum vanitas* in regard to wordly life, but a cognitive analysis of concrete situations *and* values. Clarifying what values are 'right for me' is just as important as the non-moral 'analysis' of the objective world. It is that sort of analysis for which Vives seeks to provide a methodology, as, for example, in the study of character, which is to say the study of man.

Here I must make one further observation. In many ways the theory of the affections of Telesio resembles that of Vives (I will return to this again later from another direction, in connection with natural philosophy). Telesio anticipated such ideas of Spinoza as the thought that whatever strengthens soul and body evokes joy, while anything that weakens them calls forth sadness. But – and for this reason I cannot accept him as a classic of contemporary stoic-epicurean thinking, comparable to Vives – Telesio shrinks before the inner contradictions of the principle of self-preservation, and returns to the concept of the immortal soul. He was right to recognize that a number of phenomena cannot be deduced from the principle of self-preservation, among them the fact that a man can choose his own death, or that he may adhere to what is right even when wrongdoing is more useful. But it would have been more consistent, in the face of such contradictions, simply to accept the contradictions rather than to seek a solution in the 'immortal soul'. For stoicism and epicureanism, as we have seen, are first of all codes of conduct furnished with a number of basic ontological premises, foremost among them the acceptance of immanence; those whose anthropology contains weak links and unexplained principles can still be consistent in their stoicism or epicureanism (like Vives with his affection of self-preservation), but those who, recognizing the weak spots or systematic inconsistencies in their anthropology, demolish their ontological premises in order to reconcile those inconsistencies, cannot be consistent stoics or epicureans.

The philosophical contradictions which sprang from efforts to synthesize the principles of self-preservation and utility, the theory of pleasure, and stoic-epicurean conduct emerged, however, in their classical form only in the seventeenth century's concept of man.

The Gods do not Intervene in the Affairs of the World
When Alberti wrote that the gods do not intervene in the affairs of the world, and so men are increasingly responsible for their actions, he did nothing less than link the ancient world-picture of Epicurus

123

with the moral consequences of the practical atheism of the Renaissance. Making that rather unique connection he transformed epicureanism from a *passive outlook on the world into an active ethic*. The aloof gods of ancient epicureanism were models for the conduct of human life; men, if they wished to remain virtuous, had to live in a kind of limbo, just like their gods. In the new epicureanism, however, the 'non-intervention' of the gods received an opposite interpretation. It no longer justified men's not intervening in the affairs of the world; on the contrary, it made it necessary that, *instead* of gods, men should direct the affairs of the world. Indeed, *it increased their responsibility*, for now the interpretation, evaluation, exploitation, and transformation of everything which a given 'nature' offered depended *exclusively* on them. The problem was no longer just one of creating a beautiful, harmonious, and honourable *individual* life, as it had been during antiquity; for beauty, harmony and honour, in the sense of *masserizia*, meant *intervention* as well. Intervention could vary in extent; it ranged from active political participation to an honourable private life which touched on politics only at important conjunctures. But one way or the other the ideal of an ethic of withdrawal ceased to exist.

Its disappearance is to be sought primarily in the social praxis of the age. Of course, we are dealing with a world in which – by contrast with the declining ancient world – it was still more or less possible and meaningful to intervene effectively, and so non-intervention lost all connotation of moral value, becoming a mere egotism, or cowardice. At the same time there began to appear that sort of praxis which came to be termed a 'calling'. Max Weber was right in linking the concept with Protestantism; the phenomenon itself, however, is earlier. It was the bourgeoisie which took the lead in propagating Renaissance culture, in the more important city-states of Italy and to some extent in France and England as well. The manner of life of that class is bound up with the *practice of an occupation* which, directly or indirectly, is social. Lorenzo de' Medici remained a banker, Leonardo was a painter and sculptor, Ficino a teacher, Cardano a physician, More and Bacon were Lord Chancellor – and not by reason of birth, but rather more in the modern sense of 'occupying a status'. Since their living was bound up with the practice of an occupation (which they regarded as a calling) they could not 'withdraw from life' after the pattern of their ancient predecessors. Such a thing was partly possible only if they could assemble the material means, as Bacon did towards the end of his life, but to a degree it was impossible even then, for without their calling their lives became empty. Living away from the world could turn into a banishment; then literary activity might become an extension of the 'calling', as in the case of Machiavelli's history of Florence or Cardano's autobiography. For that reason alone their wisdom could not consist solely of leading an – individual – life of beauty; it had to be manifested above all in the exercise of their calling. Thus in two different senses and in two different ways they came in touch, day after day, with the real conflicts of life and with ethical situations that were far from unequivocal. In those situations they had to declare themselves and make decisions, to act in consonance with *masserizia*, to display 'wisdom'. And thus the non-intervention of the gods receives new emphasis in the form of increased responsibilities and a heightened sense of responsibility.

If the gods do not intervene in the affairs of the world, that means not only that the gods neither further nor frustrate men's actions, neither punish nor reward; it also means that *they do not redeem anything*. What has happened has happened, and it is no longer possible to undo whatever has happened. Lazarus does not rise, Iphigeneia does not live on after her fiery death, nor does the sun stand still in the sky at Joshua's command. Time is nothing but the *irreversibility* of every happening. Only if we postulate a deity existing outside of time can events become reversible. Stoicism and epicureanism, which deal with nature as 'given', treat this irreversibility, too, as given.

We have already analysed this fundamental attitude in connection with death. But the same frame of mind characterizes stoicism and epicureanism with respect to *every* happening. It is not possible to undo a single situation once it has actually come into existence. The task is rather to deal with that which exists, and to deal with it *exactly as it is*: hence the steadfastness which we can observe in good fortune and misfortune alike, and the patience under the 'blows of fate'. Some have identified this behaviour with so-called 'stoic calm'. But the Renaissance recognized that '*calm*' *was in no way the real essence of the matter*. Whether someone reacted to a given situation, fortunate or unfortunate, with calmness or passion, coolly or angrily, was fundamentally a *matter of temperament, and not a question of attitude at all*. A man's basic attitude appeared in his ability to accept the given as final, to deal with it without damage to his personal substance, to regard it as an inescapable, 'natural' basis for possible action. Thus once again we see a readiness to take account of irreversibility.

That fact has a particular significance in the domain of ethics. The attitude of the stoic or epicurean towards his own actions is one of 'what I have done, I have done'. If everything that has happened

125

is irreversible, then my actions are irreversible too. A wrong is irredeemable once it has been done. Men's forgiveness is different from God's, for God – if he exists – could change the past, 'turn back the clock', but human beings cannot. This attitude implies first of all an intensification of responsibility. If every step of mine is irretractable, if no penance or contrition can 'do away' with it, then I had better watch my step very carefully indeed. But at the same time this attitude takes a burden off human shoulders. For if the deed is irredeemable and irreversible, *then it is senseless to be bound to the deeds – and sins – of the past.* I can act differently today from yesterday, I can be a *different man* from the one I was yesterday; the past can be written off because it *is*, once and for all, *past.* In ethics, accepting irreversibility is, in Aristotelian terms, a mean between two extremes: an irresponsible cynicism and a self-destructive remorse of conscience.[69]

It follows from the foregoing that an open recognition of the irreversibility of events makes possible reversibility in ethics. Reversibility here no longer relates to the individual deed, but to the *whole man,* to one's moral personality. Whoever can come to grips with his every action and with the unavoidable consequences can, in case of need, 'turn back the clock'; he cannot reverse events, but he can alter the ethical development of his own personality, expunging everything which earlier moved him to wrongdoing. Thus Othello, for example, regains the clear brightness of his character as soon as he can look the finality of his deed in the face, with all the causes that led him to commit it.

The stoic-epicurean of the Renaissance is thus a man *who stands on his own feet,* yet fully *within the currents of this world.* But all of these things – coming to terms with reality, sense of increased personal responsibility, acceptance of irreversibility, steadfastness, and attainment of the life of beauty – have a psychic precondition: *man must live without fear and without hope.* He remains, to quote Pomponazzi again, 'fearing nothing, hoping for nothing, in prosperity and adversity ever the same'.[70] And that was far from a merely aristocratic philosophy. At carnival time in Florence there appeared several times a figure of 'Prudence enthroned above Hope and Fear, which lay bound before her'.[71] (Once again it is no accident that Goethe later used this motif in *Faust.*) Of course this does not at all mean that stoics never felt fear and never hoped for anything. In this connection it is enough to point to the figure of Horatio (which I will analyse more thoroughly later). Horatio does experience fear when he finds himself face to face with the ghost of Hamlet's father. As for hope: in the sense that we may hope reality's mysterious ways will bring some unexpected turn of good fortune, it is not at all in contradiction with the stoic-epicurean attitude. The polemic over fear and hope is directed against those who allow their actions to be *motivated* by hope and fear, and against those for whom fear and hope become a *state of mind*. The two, in fact, go together; for those who constantly live in a state of fear and hope must necessarily be motivated by them, at least in part. Machiavelli neatly expresses the unshakeable objectivity of reality, the opportunities inherent in it for human action, and the proper role of hope, when it is not an overmastering motive or a permanent state of mind:[72]

> I assert once again as a truth to which history as a whole
> bears witness that men may second their fortune, but cannot
> oppose it; that they may act in accordance with, but cannot
> infringe, its ordinances. Yet they should never give up, because
> there is always hope, though they know not the end and
> move towards it along roads which cross one another and as
> yet are unexplored; and since there is hope, *they should not
> despair, no matter what fortune brings or in what travail
> they find themselves.*

SOME STOIC-EPICUREAN TYPES

The age of dynamic man and of a diversity of ideals of man naturally brought into being a remarkable variety of types of stoic-epicurean conduct. Here we can only mention a few examples of them.

The 'Courtier', or the Educator

Castiglione's courtier is not really a courtier. He is a stoic-epicurean sage, one who is not a ruler but an *educator* – and, we should add, *the ideal type* of the educator. And he is deliberately so, for his figure is synthesized by the members of the company in the course of their playful conversation, out of all those characteristics which they find good, true and beautiful. He is the sort of teacher who teaches primarily by *example*. He is an autonomous personality living his life in the social and political world, his abilities are many-sided, and his behaviour is imbued with grace and charm. At the same time he is an enlightener, in the same sense that Socrates was. He *teaches* his entourage about good and evil. To some extent, Castiglione shares the illusions of ethical rationalism: knowledge of the good entails good actions.

Therefore even as in the other artes, so also in the vertues it is
behofefull to have a teacher, that with lessons and good
exhortations may stirre up and quicken in us those moral
vertues, whereof wee have the seede inclosed and buried in the
soule . . . taking away the dim veil of ignorance, whereof arise
[in a manner] all the errours of men. For in case good and ill
were well knowne and perceived, every man would alwaies
choose the good, and shunne the ill.[73]

But here the stoicism of the educator intervenes. Knowledge of
good and evil *by itself* is generally not a guarantee of proper conduct.
A thorough knowledge of a person's nature is a contributing factor,
too. Distinguishing between good and evil involves *goals* and
tendencies. Knowledge of human nature is required to assess those
given characteristics and potentialities which can and ought to be
developed in the light of certain goals and tendencies.'Maisters
should consider *the nature of their scholars*, and taking it for their
guide, direct and prompt them in the way that *their wit and naturall
inclination moveth them unto*.'[74] And what is more: Castiglione
contends that there is no innate desire or capacity which is intrinsic-
ally incapable of becoming the ground of virtue; *every* ability,
properly recognized and properly directed, can be made virtuous.
'The affections therefore that be cleansed and tried by temperance
are assistant to virtue, *as anger, that helpeth manlinesse: hatred
against the wicked helpeth justice*, and likewise the other vertues are
aided by affections. . . .'[75] If virtue and knowledge of the good build
on the nature of man, then to be virtuous no longer means self-
mutilation, constant struggles with oneself, dubious victories and
defeats laden with guilt, but *inner ease and harmony*, and a constant
process of '*being in agreement with oneself*':

> So in like case this vertue not enforcing the mind, but pouring
> thereinto through *most quiet waies* a vehement perswasion that
> may incline him to honestie, maketh him quiet and full of rest,
> in every part equal and of good proportion: and on every
> side framed of a certaine agreement with himself. . . .[76]

How far the virtue, and the education, of Castiglione's courtier
represents a polemic with Christian ideals is a question that need
not detain us here. I should rather like to underscore *those features
which distinguish his ideal of education from the* paideia *of the ancient
Greeks and which make it a peculiarly modern (bourgeois) phenomenon.*
I am not thinking of Socrates, whose unequivocal ethical rationalism
simply bracketed men's 'nature', nor of Plato, for whom reason had a
restraining rather than a *stimulating* function, as in the image in the

Phaedrus of the coachman guiding two steeds with a single set of reins. But let us consider Aristotle, who recognized the dialectic of nature and ethics, who argued that good does not come from nature but is not against nature either, and who with his conception of the mean sought the possibility of turning many affections to good ends. It is thence that Castiglione derives his sympathy for the idea of the mean. In Aristotle, however, nature is always 'nature in general'. When he speaks of a 'mean' among affections, he takes into consideration, of course, that an affection may be stronger in some people and weaker in others, and so the task of finding the mean is not the same for everyone, nor is the mean to be found in the same place for everyone. But he speaks only of affections which are to be found *in everyone*, and he only admits the possibility of stronger or weaker affections, never the possibility of their presence or absence; nor does he ever speak of the *single individual as a concrete totality*, or of the various affections as they relate to this concrete totality. Castiglione, however, *focuses on the nature of the individual*; and that is quite proper, for Aristotle is writing of the education of *citizens*, while Castiglione deals with the education of *individuals who are also citizens only in certain respects*. For Aristotle, 'being at peace with oneself' is not a goal but a consequence; whoever attains virtue, i.e. serves the good of the state with success, must be at peace with himself. For Castiglione, however, this kind of harmony becomes a *goal* – almost, one might say, a *goal in itself*; now it is much more complicated to be an honourable, virtuous man than to be a 'good citizen'. The fact that harmony becomes an end in itself is a revealing phenomenon; it reveals that this harmony is not 'natural', and that there no longer existed social norms firm enough to make possible at one and the same time an unequivocal socially approved ethic *and* the individual's comfortable acquiescence in that ethic. For harmony to be a goal is tantamount to its being an ideal: *a social ideal which can only be realized by certain individuals*. Hence springs the need, in modern education, to discover the concrete totality of the individual, his 'individual character'. Castiglione's courtier educates the sort of men of whom Alberti spoke, the sort of people who live in Shakespeare's Forest of Arden. He shapes a man who will live in the world, but at a distance and according to his own nature. The educational ideal of Rousseau's *Emile* is a plebeian version of Castiglione's courtier.[77]

The Moralist and the Politician

These two types frequently make their appearance, not least of all in Machiavelli. I should like to examine their peculiarities in two figures from Shakespeare: Brutus and Cassius. Since I am dealing here with artistic types, the individual psyche and individual morality will receive greater emphasis than with comparable types in scholarly writings; but that should only make it easier, rather than more difficult, for us to gain some insight into the human ideals of the age.

In Shakespeare's gallery of types, to begin with, there was from a very early date no longer any clear line of demarcation between stoic and epicurean conduct. We know that Brutus is a stoic, while Cassius says of himself that he holds with Epicurus' teachings; but *that* does not create any significant difference between them – the differences which create conflict between them are differences between the conduct of the moralist and the conduct of the politician. Thus, for example, Cassius is a long way from manifesting the joy in life characteristic of epicureanism. Caesar rightly says of him:[78]

> He loves no plays,
> As thou dost, Antony; he hears no music;
> Seldom he smiles, and smiles in such a sort
> As if he mock'd himself, and scorn'd his spirit
> That could be moved to smile at any thing.

Not only is there no sharp boundary between stoicism and epicureanism, however; there is no sharp boundary line either between stoic-epicurean conduct on one side and non-stoic-epicurean conduct on the other. In the face of death Caesar displays exactly the *same* stoicism as Brutus:[79]

> Cowards die many times before their deaths;
> The valiant never taste of death but once.
> Of all the wonders that I yet have heard,
> It seems to me most strange that men should fear;
> Seeing that death, a necessary end,
> Will come when it will come.

At the same time stoicism and epicureanism do not imply the acceptance of a *static behaviour*. Self-control, self-discipline, and mastery of one's affections do not create the picture of tranquillity; and there is no human being, not even the most 'stoic', who is not overpowered at certain points in his life by his passions. Shakespeare depicts this brilliantly in Act IV, Scene 3 of *Julius Caesar*, in the heated altercation between Brutus and Cassius. Each of them breaks out in a passion, and they recklessly hurl the most serious accusations at each other; but they do not cease to be stoics for all that. The close of the scene is gripping, too, with its attitude of 'what I have done, I have done' towards the past; there is no self-reproach or asking of pardon, only a 'discharging' of the conflict.

But here, too, Shakespeare indicates the *varying depth* of the two men's philosophical conduct. Brutus' passion is evoked by extreme sorrow at the suicide of his wife Portia. Cassius' anger has no such justifiable reason; he sees that Brutus does not understand his policy, and that is what provokes his charges. His natural characteristics ('that rash humour which my mother gave me') make him quick to anger. But the fundamental difference in depth between the stoicism of Brutus and the epicureanism of Cassius is not to be found therein, but rather *in their attitude towards fear*.

The deaths of Brutus and Cassius are *different*; their suicides have a *different value content*. Shakespeare brilliantly foreshadows this on every occasion where the possibility of failure, destruction, and death comes up. The first occasion is during the Ides of March: the conspirators are approaching the Capitol when Popilius, who is not a party to the conspiracy, openly refers to their coming attempt ('I wish your enterprise to-day may thrive'),[80] and then goes to talk with Caesar. At that moment Cassius is seized with fear; his imagination already foresees the spectre of betrayal:[81]

> Brutus, what shall be done? If this be known,
> Cassius or Caesar never shall turn back,
> For I will slay myself.

But Brutus is not moved by fearful fantasies. He replies:[82]

> Cassius, be constant:
> Popilius Lena speaks not of our purposes;
> For, look, he smiles, and Caesar doth not change.

The same thing is repeated, on a higher plane, before the battle of Philippi. Cassius must once again face up to death. And now – if only for a moment – he begins to have doubts about his philosophy:[83]

> You know that I held Epicurus strong,
> And his opinion; now I change my mind,
> And partly credit things that do presage.

And projecting his own end before him again, he asks Brutus what he will do in the event of defeat. But Brutus again replies:[84]

> I know not how,
> But I do find it cowardly and vile,
> For fear of what might fall, so to prevent
> The time of life: arming myself with patience,
> To stay the providence of some high powers
> That governs us below.

131

And he goes into battle with the words:[85]

> Why, then, lead on. O! that a man might know
> The end of this day's business, ere it come;
> *But it sufficeth that the day will end,*
> *And then the end is known.* Come, ho! away!

And now motives have been provided for the two different deaths. Cassius becomes a victim of *error*; he sends his friend Titinius to find out whether Brutus' forces have won or been beaten, and then when he is surrounded by some of Brutus' men he thinks he has been captured by the enemy. As Messala says:[86]

> Mistrust of good success hath done this deed.
> O hateful error, melancholy's child!
> Why dost thou show to the apt thoughts of men
> The things that are not?

Brutus, however, fights his battle to the end and waits until the right moment for his death. And so for him death is not defeat but victory the culmination of a life well spent:[87]

> My heart doth joy that yet, in all my life,
> I found no man but he was true to me.
> I shall have glory by this losing day,
> More than Octavius and Mark Antony
> By this vile conquest shall attain unto.

So Brutus lives and dies unambiguously a stoic, while Cassius can only strive to be an epicurean; his nature prevents him from developing his personality into a unified, harmonious whole.

Shakespeare several times indicates the theoretical foundations of Brutus' stoicism. When Cassius is organizing the conspiracy, he succeeds in moving Brutus to action by saying:[88]

> The fault, dear Brutus, is not in our stars,
> But in ourselves, that we are underlings.

With consummate political feeling Cassius pulls the strings to break down Brutus' resistance. To win over Casca, on the other hand, Cassius pulls out all the stops:[89]

> You shall find
> That heaven hath infused them with these spirits
> To make them instruments of fear and warning
> Unto some monstrous state.

Prophecies incline the superstitious Casca's spirit to accept Cassius' plan, but the stoic Brutus can only be won by an appeal to the autonomy of man.

Brutus' tirade against swearing an oath springs from the same ontological basis. Twice he emphasizes the immanent character of their action. It is social conditions, just as they are, which inspire them, not the prompting or command of heaven; their pact, more-over, does not require any divine or supernatural guarantee, for that is a need felt by cowards. (Recall Pomponazzi's discussion of how only the weakest and least noble require supernatural sanction in order to practice virtue.)

> No, not an oath: if not the face of men,
> The sufferance of our souls, the time's abuse,
> If these be motives weak, break off betimes,
> And every man hence to his idle bed; ...
> *What need we any spur but our own cause*
> To prick us to redress? what other bond
> Than secret Romans, that have spoke the word
> And will not palter? and what other oath
> *Than honesty to honesty engag'd,*
> That this shall be, or we will fall for it?
> *Swear priests and cowards and men cautelous,*
> *Old feeble carrions, and such suffering souls*
> *That welcome wrongs;* ...[90]

What has been said hitherto indicates only, up to now, that the stoicism and epicureanism of Brutus and Cassius are rooted with varying degrees of intensity in their personalities. Brutus' tempera-ment and character display harmony and a sense of being at peace with himself, while Cassius' personality is torn by contradictions: his principles are constantly at war with his nature. Nor is his nature marked only by a propensity to sudden anger. Cassius in fact is eaten up by such affections as envy and jealousy; Mark Antony is right in saying, in his last speech at the end of the play, that Brutus alone was motivated exclusively by love of the common weal. But it would be a rude oversimplification to characterize Cassius as merely envious; love for the common weal and fear for Rome's liberty are not just rationalizations of his affections but sincere, heartfelt motives as well. The affair which permits Cassius to give free rein to his envy is *not* an accidental one. And of Brutus he is never envious, even though he knows that Brutus is more popular than he, and is in fact a more remarkable man than he is. On the contrary, Cassius sincerely admires, loves, and respects him.

133

The diversity of types appears in the fact that Brutus is a stoic moralist, while Cassius is a stoic-epicurean politician. Brutus is brought into the conspiracy from purely ethical motives and will not tolerate a single action which would stain his moral integrity. Cassius is a politician and an organizer: he is not primarily concerned with what is the virtuous thing to do, but rather with what will be effective in achieving success and making it secure. Every clash between Brutus and Cassius springs from this conflict. On the very night of the conspiracy they debate the fate of Mark Antony. For the sake of keeping their actions honourable Brutus wishes Mark Antony to be left unharmed, but Cassius wants him out of the way, since he foresees that Mark Antony will endanger the success of the affair. They are faced with the question whether to permit Mark Antony to deliver a funeral oration over the the body of Caesar. Brutus once more makes his decision as a moralist: no one is entitled to prevent a man from paying his final respects to his friend. Cassius, again, knows that this ought not to be allowed: Antony will stir up the people against them. Finally, the same conflict comes to the surface again twice in their camp. Brutus accuses Cassius of buying followers – yet Cassius knows perfectly well that to achieve victory he needs hired followers, too. Finally, Cassius wishes to await the enemy's attack in their secure positions, but Brutus is determined to anticipate him by marching to Philippi, to accept battle openly and courageously.

There is no doubt that in all matters of dispute Cassius, politically, is right. At every step the noble spirit of Brutus thwarts their success. *But from Brutus' point of view that is the consistent thing and the right thing to do.* It is no coincidence that Caesar's ghost appears in Brutus' tent shortly after his angry exchange of words with Cassius. That discussion has awakened Brutus to the fact that whoever sits in Caesar's place must be a Caesar; from virtuous motives he has killed someone *whose successors, occupying the same position, will not be any better.* Brutus sees that he has fallen into a vicious circle:[91]

> Remember March, the ides of March remember:
> Did not great Julius bleed for justice' sake?
> *What villain touch'd his body, that did not stab,*
> *And not for justice?* What! shall one of us,
> That struck the foremost man of all this world
> But for supporting robbers, shall we now
> Contaminate our fingers with base bribes,
> And sell the mighty space of our large honour
> For so much trash as may be grasped thus?

I had rather be a dog, and bay the moon,
Than such a Roman.

But Brutus is consistent indeed, and true to his 'nature'; he will not take a single step that runs contrary to his ethics. And in doing so he brings about the ruin of his cause, for he believes that if he cannot *succeed by ethical means then it is better his cause should not succeed at all, for in the latter event it would no longer be the same cause for which he was willing to strike.* Cassius, on the other hand, the brilliant politician who, so long as he is acting alone, shows tremendous firmness of purpose in bringing together within a short time a well-organized conspiracy, and who in the interests of success does not fear shady measures (like the letters deliberately thrown into Brutus' rooms)–Cassius does not remain true to his principles and to his nature. Cassius, who knows that (to use Chernyshevsky's expression) politics is not the smooth pavement of the Nevsky Prospekt and that in politics a man's hands get dirty sometimes, *still submits on all occasions to Brutus' decisions.* And the motive which brings him to submit, and to abandon his own ends and his own initiative, is the noblest of stoic-epicurean attitudes: *friendship.* He does not wish to lose Brutus' friendship, and for that reason he concurs every time in decisions which he is convinced are mistaken. It is that friendship – involving his respect for the superiority of Brutus' moral principles and of his whole personality, a kind of recognition of Brutus' human pre-eminence – which brings about Cassius' destruction. And never is there a word of reproach, never an 'I told you so', even when the fatefulness of Brutus' actions becomes clear. Cassius accepts the mistakes of his friend again and again, *and that is what makes Cassius a stoic-epicurean politician and not merely a 'politician-type' in general, and least of all a Machiavel.*

The Honourable Man
The honourable man, as a stoic ideal, may be found in the arts in Shakespeare's Horatio, and in theory in Charron's *'preud' homme'.*

Preud' homie is non other than honour, *or active goodness.* It is the central category in Charron's system of values, preceding even the great public virtues of patriotism, wisdom, courage, and the rest. It is decidedly a 'civic' virtue; it ought to appear in every man's conduct in life, regardless of his social station. It does not require special learning or unusual capacities; the honourable man is not someone singled out by fate, but a person who is free of all prejudice and who, knowing nature and his own nature, *rationally cultivates the natural goodness in himself:* 'a strong, active, masculine and

135

efficacious goodness, which is a prompt, easy and constant affection for what is good, upright, and just according to reason and nature'.[92]

We should not think, however, that *preud' homie* as a civic virtue stands for the choice of some 'more comfortable' way *vis-à-vis* the public virtues. On the contrary, it was precisely at the time of the dissolution of the traditional community and the loosening of systems of fixed, customary morality, when emerging bourgeois relations and money were putting an end to the solidarity of the family and the loyalty of friends, making treachery, flattery, denunciation, hypocrisy and two-facedness daily occurrences – it was precisely at that time that a special, even a *heroic* function was performed by virtues like straightforwardness, loyalty, simple honesty – all the things Charron calls *preud' homie*. Charron knew that this civic virtue of his was not at all lacking in pathos. He wrote: 'We must be moral because nature and reason command it, because the general order of the world to which man belongs demands it. We must be moral, no matter *what* consequences may go with it.'[93]

Stress must be laid on the *new* features in Charron's stoic ideal. The ontological foundations have, of course, come down to him from the past. The 'private' character of conduct would seem to bring him closer to certain ancient thinkers than to the stoics of the early Renaissance. But that is only the appearance, for his private virtue is still thoroughly *active*. Being true to ourselves is a prerequisite if we are to be good towards others; spiritual calm is not a goal in itself, but a starting-point for activity. The *preud' homme* turns not inward but *outward*, like the stoics in public life of the quattrocento; and 'outward' does not mean towards a circle of select friends or towards some 'garden of sages', *but rather towards all of daily life, just as it is*. It is incumbent upon everyone to practise active goodness. Thus the moral content of an immanent philosophy's practice evolved from the equality taught in principle by Christianity.

The field for active goodness and *preud' homie* is, to repeat, everyday life, where it is at least as difficult to remain honourable as in the glare of public life. That *civil courage* which Charron calls 'civic virtue' and which goes hand in hand with stoic behaviour was indeed *a new ethical attitude, appearing at a time when public and private were increasingly becoming separated;* and it became more and more attractive as that separation became more marked and as every aspect of private life became more and more permeated by capitalist money relations.

Shakespeare's Horatio is the epitome of *preud' homie*. He takes no active part in public life; he has neither function, nor calling, nor office. And yet he cannot be called a passive participant; he is always there to help if needed. Nor is he a mere plaything of fate; he comes to Elsinore of his own free will to support his friend, and with quiet loyalty goes about setting right whatever can be set right. His basic affection is also friendship, just as it was with Cassius. But how different is Horatio's friendship! In Cassius' case, friendship was a pact to free his country – a bond sealed in blood, and anything but the private affair of two patriots; it was a friendship on which the fate of an empire hung. Horatio, however, is no 'dignitary' in Denmark. When he says that 'something is rotten in the state of Denmark', and weighs the chances of war, he speaks as an *outsider*; his partners in the discussion are the guards or, as we should say today, 'the people'. He views the machinery of state with misgivings, but he does not think of intervening; he is dependent upon Denmark, not Denmark upon him. His friendship is purely a *private bond*; so are the circumstances of its origin, for he first met Hamlet during their student years at Wittenberg. He is nothing more than Hamlet's friend. But this 'nothing more' is a great deal, for Hamlet has no other friends. Apart from him, there are no upright men in Denmark – everyone dissembles, even the beloved Ophelia. There are no more honourable men – everyone is a spy or an informer; Polonius even sends someone to spy on his own son. There are no more friends – the Rosencrantzes and Guildensterns are betrayers and assassins. There is no one who lives rationally and according to nature – everyone is irrational and rotten to the core; even Hamlet receives from destiny a task which is not in keeping with his nature. Thus a *'mere' friend, a 'mere' upright man, 'mere' honour become unique, exceptional, almost a wonder.*

Cassius tells Brutus that the essence of man is best reflected in the eyes of his friends. This is how Horatio's personality is reflected in Hamlet's eyes:[94]

> Nay, do not think I flatter;
> For what advancement may I hope from thee,
> That no revenue hast but thy good spirits
> To feed and clothe thee?...
> Since my dear soul was mistress of her choice
> And could of men distinguish, her election
> Hath seal'd thee for herself; for thou hast been
> As one, in suffering all, that suffers nothing,
> A man that fortune's buffets and rewards
> Has ta'en with equal thanks; and bless'd are those
> Whose blood and judgment are so well commingled
> That they are not a pipe for fortune's finger

STOICISM AND EPICUREANISM

To sound what stop she please. Give me that man
That is not passion's slave and I will wear him
In my heart's core, ay, in my heart of heart,
As I do thee. . . .

The opening lines cite Horatio's good spirits and poverty; both are
of the essence. The first underscores *how foreign Horatio's personal
aura is to the atmosphere of Elsinore*. This exponent of the stoic-
epicurean attitude of 'good humour' is as remote from the wild
revelry of the court as he is from the exaltation of tragic passion;
hence we may speak of a stoic *who cannot be a tragic hero*. His
poverty is likewise an integral part of his being an outsider. It might
be added that Horatio is one of the few Shakespearean heroes *of
whose past we know virtually nothing*. Even his being a Dane is
fortuitous; he could just as well be English or French. The emergence
of great passions has to be motivated – as in the case of Hamlet,
Lear, Othello, Macbeth, Romeo and Juliet – but honour simply
is. Hamlet's later words exalt Horatio's *human autonomy* as against
both his own passion and the world (the one presupposes the other);
fate cannot toy with those who can harmonize blood and judgment.
Hamlet thus bows before Horatio's inner perfection, integrity, and
greatness, just as Cassius bowed before Brutus.

In *Hamlet*, however, the *objective hierarchy of values* is quite
different. Hitherto we have not examined Hamlet himself, but only
looked at Horatio through the prince's eyes. Now let us consider
Hamlet with our *own* eyes. If there were no Hamlet, only a Horatio,
nothing would ever change in Denmark, or anywhere else. Horatio
is always honourable, upright, and helpful – but he would never go
into battle against the existing order of the world or on behalf of a
new world order. That is why I have said that, unlike Brutus and
Cassius, he has no tragic aura. If Denmark is a prison and honest
men are few, then *preud' homie* is true heroism, a living example that
human dignity is *possible*, that the complete man *can* exist, that
beauty, harmony, and reason are not merely abstract ideals. To that
extent the 'honourable man' is a representative type. He is a representative type for those who are *different* – less harmonious perhaps,
but certainly bigger in terms of grandeur and power – and capable of
going into battle against the world, throwing their passions into
the scale; to them he is a proof that it was 'not in vain', that it was
'possible' and 'worthy'. Horatio's dignity only unfolds at Hamlet's
side; *preud' homie*, civic virtue, civil courage acquire their full
splendour in the glory of great public men and their deeds.

CHAPTER 4

Ecce Homo:
Socrates and Jesus

Socrates and Jesus together form the moral paradigm of the Renaissance.

It is important to stress the 'and'. The thinkers of the Renaissance did not see in the actions of Socrates and of Jesus alternative forms of conduct, nor even attitudes that were distinguishable in principle; Socrates and Jesus represented such abstract ideals that precisely *by dint of their abstract, ideal character they resembled each other.* Frequently formal parallels were drawn between them; Gemisthus Pletho, for example, discovered allegorical similarities in the circumstances of their lives and deaths, noting that the cock and the chalice played a part in the destinies of both men. Their cognate character appears in the phrase *ecce homo*, too; for the great majority of the thinkers of the Renaissance Jesus was just as much man as Socrates. His role as the Christ, his mission as the Redeemer, so central to the Christian myth, fade completely into the background; his life, his sufferings and teachings, become a human life and human sufferings and teachings. It is the exception when this identification of the two men works in the opposite direction, by deifying Socrates, as for instance when Erasmus writes: 'Very little prevents me from saying, Holy Socrates, pray for us!'[95]

The assimilation to each other of these two men as a moral exemplar was based, as we have said, on the *abstract* character of their ethos. Ethical features certainly played no small part in the other ideal figures of the time, but with all the others the function of ethics was specific and concrete; it is a question of integrity in pursuit of a circumscribed goal with a definite, limited content. Prometheus, too, is a martyr, but he is a martyr of technical

139

progress; Brutus, too, is a moral hero, but he is the moral hero of republican pathos. Thus all those who saw the dignity of man in his domination of nature and glorified *technè* as the vehicle of man's triumph over the gods saw humanity's great hero in Prometheus, or in his Old Testament counterpart, Adam. Those, on the other hand, who were the ideologues of democracy and the city-state – above all the Florentines – preferred the figure of Brutus. But Jesus and Socrates were taken as ideals by all of them in common. In the case of both Jesus and Socrates the content of their moral integrity was not specifically or concretely defined – or, more properly speaking, their stories made it possible for everyone to seek and find his *own* ideas and his *own* ethical content in the conduct of Socrates or Jesus. What is common to these two figures, and also abstract – i.e. what can be interpreted from any concrete ethical and social standpoint – *is the purposeful, consistent living out of one's own life, the acceptance of all moral consequences and of whatever fate may bring, up to and including a martyr's death, the idea of teaching (or rather the complete harmony of conduct and teaching), and finally the homely, everyday character of their lives.* The first is, of course, the most general of all stoic-epicurean ideals. It is no paradox to say that during the Renaissance the figure of Jesus enduring his sufferings receives a pronounced stoic impress; a finer and plainer example of faithfulness to one's nature and one's mission would have been hard to find. In the theme of martyrdom, likewise common to both, the note of a subjective morality can often be heard. There is no question here, either, of the fulfilment of some divine destiny, but of a stand taken against the majority of men and their prejudices, and against the decadence of prevailing morality. Their teaching lends the lives of both men a public character, without disturbing the basic conception of them as moralists. It is not just a matter of ideas, but of the readiness to make ideas effective – and whether one teaches in the forum at Athens or amid a circle of chosen disciples is immaterial. Finally, as to the plain, everyday character of their lives: both Socrates and Jesus, as ideal figures, are *democratic*. Socrates ceases to be the 'sage' just as Jesus has ceased to be the 'Son of God'; each of them is only *one among the sons of men*. Their teachings do not represent wisdom in any learned sense, but rather in the moral sense of the word, and thus their wisdom speaks to everyone; their way is open to every human being.

Of course, the democratic character of these two ideals does not at all mean, for example, that the contemporary image of Jesus became identical with that of the 'carpenter's son of Nazareth'.

'Democratic' does not imply any highlighting of the fact of poverty; it refers only to the universality of his teachings, and the interpretation of his conflicts as general human conflicts. No more than two instances come to mind where Jesus the 'poor man' receives as much emphasis as he had earlier in some of the heretical movements, for whom he was the 'redeemer of the poor'. One is Duccio's *Entry into Jerusalem*, a product of the rather more plebeian turn taken by Sienese painting; the other is Thomas More's interpretation of Jesus. In More's eyes the existence and exploitation of private property were already deviations from Jesus's teachings. The history of Christianity had been nothing more than the accommodation of Jesus's teachings to the dubious and contradictory demands of the world:[96]

> Preachers, slie and wilie men, followynge youre counsel (as I suppose) bicause they saw men evel willing to frame theyr manners to Christes rule, they have wrested and wriede his doctryne, and like a rule of leade have applyed it to mennes manners: that by some meanes at the leaste waye, they myghte agree together.

Here, however – and elsewhere as well – More does not dwell *solely* on the compromise nature of the reconciliation of property with Jesus's poverty, but rather on the overall contradiction between Jesus's alleged subjective morality and the customary morality of society. And in stressing this element More was not alone. But the heroic Christ rebelling on behalf of the oppressed, so prominent in the German and Flemish art of the period (we need only think of Cranach, Dürer, and Breughel), is rather a forerunner of the Reformation than a Renaissance ideal of man. Nor is it possible to relate this ideal to Socrates, for in his figure the appeal to the poor and oppressed is completely lacking. Even less can this Christ be interpreted as a stoic, for here is no teacher of humanity dismissing suffering lightly, with a smile, but rather suffering itself, passionately accepted and endured.

Universality, democratic appeal, active acceptance of fate, susceptibility to a stoic interpretation, abstract moral content lacking any definite, concrete end: these were the properties which made possible the transformation of the common or similar traits of Socrates and Jesus into the most general and the ultimate symbols of the Renaissance's ideal of man. Within these limits, nevertheless, interpretations were completely diverse, an expression of the plurality of the Renaissance ideal of man.

Here a few examples may be mentioned.

Pico della Mirandola was, as we shall see, the first subjective moralist to appear in the course of the development of Florentine thought, and one of the first to draw the contrast, in a sharply polemical way, between the ever more problematic ethical world of the Medici and an individual *absolute virtue*, only realizable on an individual basis. He interpreted the imitation of Christ as follows: [97]

If men praise you for living virtuously, then that virtue,
inasmuch as it is virtue, makes you like unto Christ. But
inasmuch as you receive praise for it it makes you unlike
Him who received from men, as a reward for His virtue, death
upon the cross.

It goes without saying that this notion of Jesus is far from conforming to the 'real' Jesus of the New Testament, who never rejected the praise of the disciples who flocked around him. Still, Jesus's *fate* can undoubtedly be interpreted in this way *too* – in so far as his fate is abstracted from the legends concerning his life. In this connection the words Pico borrows from the Apostle Paul take on a new meaning: 'The wisdom of this world is foolishness before God, and it is the foolishness of Christ which has overcome the wisdom of this world. . . .' [98]

Here we have no longer the opposition of a human community – specifically the *Christian community* – to the old and still-dominant pagan order, but rather the opposition of the *individual* to a whole system that calls itself Christian – not the contrast of new ethical norms with the old ones, but the contrast of an individual, self-sufficient virtue with *every* kind of social and communal ethic. We have no evidence to indicate whether Pico, who knew Socrates well and loved him, interpreted the Greek thinker in this same fashion. But it is certain that he would have interpreted him in much the same way that others did at the same time and later, right up to and including Kierkegaard in his youthful dissertation.

Coluccio Salutati, a public man, saw in Socrates, too, a representative of the public man. He it was who 'brought wisdom down to earth' and who, instead of speculating about the stars, concerned himself with 'human affairs'. That, too, was a one-sided interpretation, for it ignored Socrates' conflicts with the democracy of the Athenian polis. Castiglione, who as we have seen worked out the ideal of the stoic educator, looked for the stoic educator in Socrates.

And I reckon him onely a true morall Philosopher that
will be good, and to that he needeth few other precepts than
that will of his. And therefore saide Socrates well, that he

thought his instructions had brought forth good fruite, when
by them hee had provoked any one to apply his will to the
knowledge and learning of vertue. For they that are come to
the point that they covet nothing more than to be good, doe
easily attaine the understanding of all that belongeth
thereto. . . .[99]

Here Socratic *askesis* and ethical rationalism are transformed in
conformity with Castiglione's portrait of the educator. The *intention*
or will to do good is of no great importance in Socrates or in the
young Plato; *askesis* meant not the inclination of the will towards
good but the constant practice of righteousness. Thus Castiglione
simply ascribes to Socrates his own precept that rationality is the
expression of a passionate impulse towards what is good and right.
Again, however, this is not an arbitrary procedure, for in fact one
possible interpretation of the essence and influence of Socrates is
that of the 'educator' (an educator, moreover, whose principles
cannot be set down in writing).

If we examine Montaigne's portrait of Socrates, we will see that he
explicitly treats him in the context of the *separation of bourgeois and
citizen*. It might be added that that perspective is not so very far
away from the usual interpretations of Jesus either. It is striking what
a prominent place is occupied in the thematic repertory of the
Renaissance by the parable of the tribute due unto Caesar (especially
when we consider that, unlike the story of the Last Supper, it had
no particular decorative quality to attract the artist). The treatment
of the parable of the tribute due unto Caesar, from Masaccio to
Titian, displays precisely *this* duality. Jesus is the teacher of new
ideals and the representative of new forms of conduct and new ideas,
but at the same time he is a loyal subject too: he gives unto Caesar
the things that are Caesar's. Caesar has every right to claim the
subject for himself, for that is not the essence of Jesus's being; only
let Caesar have nothing to do with Jesus's ideas or teachings or with
anything that concerns his disciples. But to return to Montaigne –
this is what he has to say:[100]

Society in general can do without our thoughts; but the rest –
our actions, our work, our fortunes, and our very life – we
must lend and abandon to its service and to the common
opinions, just as the great and good Socrates refused to save
his life by disobedience to the magistrate, even to a very
unjust and very iniquitous magistrate. For it is the rule of
rules, and the universal law of laws, that each man should
observe those of the place he is in.

What Montaigne is discussing here is unquestionably something quite different from what existed in Socrates' case, for Socrates did not at all believe that his ideas had nothing to do with the larger society; it was precisely his ideas that he propagated. It was foreign to the spirit of antiquity to draw this kind of distinction between thought and deed, so common in bourgeois society, which invented the watchword 'freedom of thought'. For Socrates, moreover, there was no question of compliance or non-compliance with some kind of 'superior authority' – Socrates bowed to the will of a polis-democracy whose legitimacy *he himself* recognized, even though he considered its judgment unjust.

We have seen how closely Montaigne's portrait of Socrates resembles the Jesus who 'gives unto Caesar the things that are Caesar's'. But, of course, that portrait of Jesus is a one-sided one too. For the Jesus of the New Testament, 'giving unto Caesar' did not imply the loyalty of the subject, but rather a total indifference towards worldly affairs. Here, then, we are dealing with a Jesus and a Socrates who incorporate Alberti's principle, but in a much sharper form than Alberti ever would have imagined. This Jesus and this Socrates live a double life: a pure, consistent, internal 'private life' on one hand, and on the other the life of the citizen, freely chosen but full of contradictions. This is not the Jesus of the New Testament or the historical Socrates; but this, too, *can* be Jesus and *can* be Socrates.

It follows that these diverse and often mutually contradictory interpretations are far from being mere 'falsifications.' The place where latter-day interpretation leaves off and outright falsification begins differs with the kind of truth that is involved. Thus there is more scope for interpretation without falsification, in the re-creation of figures in the arts, than there is in the re-evaluation of historical personages. In the case of a historical figure, certain factors are decisive once and for all: their position in the social structure, their major and subsidiary purposes in life, an estimate of their progressive or regressive role, and our perception of the place they occupy in the scale of values. Anyone who goes wrong on any of these things falsifies, in that the figure he presents is not identical with the historical personage who serves as his original. Of course, this falsification is not necessarily deliberate – as, for example, when Machiavelli asserts that the Gracchi contributed mightily to the decline of Rome – but objectively it is still an error, and needs to be corrected. (Or, to cite a contrary example: Shakespeare countless times depicts the historically necessary downfall of human values which he himself greatly admires – like blind loyalty, for example.)

144

In the case of figures re-created in art, the important thing is that the interpreter should not do violence to the objective scale of values inherent in the work of art. Thus, for example, treating the comic in a tragic fashion – as happens with some frequency in the case of Don Quixote – is always a falsification. Within these limits, however, a shift in the relative weight of various motifs does not constitute a transgression of the bounds of authentic interpretation. It is with the figures of myth that interpretation can go furthest – not only because in them the ultimate types of popular imagination and experience always appear, but also because myth has no fixed historical or structural truth. There is only the *figure* and the *tale*, the *hero* and the *episodes* – an abstract and not a concrete theme, which only *variation can make into a concrete theme.* Thus the variation does not falsify the theme, for *it is* itself the theme. *Myth lives only so long as variations are woven on it, and the heroes of myth survive only so long as they change with the times* and so long as everyone can find in them his own heroes.

We know that such was the fate of other personages besides a mythically interpreted Jesus and Socrates. In the sense I have described, Adam, Moses, David, Mary, and Prometheus were all living figures during the Renaissance too. I have already discussed the reasons why Jesus and Socrates were pre-eminent among these heroic figures. The fusion of these two universal, democratic, and human teacher figures, or their hegemony, side by side, as the reigning mythic heroes, *was the most abstract and at the same time most tangible form in which the synthesis of the classical and Christian traditions was carried through.* It was a measure of the progress of secularization, of the emergence of a degree of human autonomy, and of the modern revival of stoic and epicurean ideals. To the extent that these two gigantic figures became 'ours', men recognized themselves as their own creation. As Montaigne wrote of Socrates:[101]

He shows [the soul] as neither elevated nor rich; he shows it only as healthy, but assuredly with a very blithe and clear health. By these vulgar and natural motives, by these ordinary and common ideas, without excitement or fuss, he constructed not only the best regulated but the loftiest and most vigorous beliefs, actions, and morals that ever were. . . . He did a great favour to human nature by showing how much it can do by itself.

PART THREE

Ethics and life:
man's practical possibilities

Part 2 has dealt with such questions as *the conquest of the past* and indeed the choice of a new past, and the synthesis of the two great cultural heritages of Western man; it has sought to illumine the relationship of the Renaissance's concept and ideal of man to the ancient and Christian concept and ideal of man. Part 4 will examine the *specific anthropology of the Renaissance*, its final theoretical formulation of radically new problems. But if the theoretical generalizations drawn from the new facts of life are to be understood we must examine *those new facts themselves*. Our sources here, of course, will rarely be accounts of the facts, customs, and mores proper; for the most part we will be forced to draw conclusions about life itself from works of art, aphorisms, and fragments of philosophical speculations and discussions, and to that degree Part 3, too, will not be free of philosophical generalizations. Withal, however, I still believe that the analysis which follows belongs rather to the genre of historical sociology.

CHAPTER 5

Everyday life

During the Renaissance science and scholarship, technology, and art were differentiated to a relatively small extent from everyday life. This fact must be stressed even in comparison with the Middle Ages, and most of all, of course, in the case of science. In feudal society scholarship was the scholarship of a caste-like social group.[1] It was either a prerogative of the Church, as with philosophy itself, or a complex of knowledge and skills preserved and practised by certain members of certain social estates, though *not in a professional way* (as with the more scientific branches of the 'seven liberal arts'), or else it consisted of *guild 'mysteries'* handed down from generation to generation, but only among the initiated. Thus the everyday lives of men – not only the lives of the exploited masses, but also those of most members of the ruling strata – were lived completely 'outside of science'; science, and the *magic which was not yet distinguished from it*, were covered with a veil of mystery and were often still associated with notions of the diabolical and sinful. Daily life did not fructify this science, and science in turn had no effect on daily life.

With the Renaissance all this radically changed. Above all else, the dissolution of the system of social orders put an end to the association of science with privilege. From that point of view the organization of the Platonic Academy in Florence was an epoch-making event: here was the first school of philosophy independent of the old framework of Church and university, and one that was entirely secular and 'open', to the extent that it was open in principle to every thinking man, at least to all who thought in a Platonic spirit. Its patron, Cosimo de' Medici, was quite unschooled in the traditional learning of the day. The universities, above all that of Padua, opened their doors more and more to young men whose

148

birth did not predestine them to study. Plebeian youths, who formerly had been able to acquire knowledge only by becoming priests, now managed to do so while avoiding a clerical career (along with many defrocked priests); the practice of scholarship and the liberal arts began to be a profession, and slowly there developed that new stratum which today we call the intelligentsia. From that point of view, the development of the social division of labour of a rising bourgeois society acted as a stimulus.

The disintegration of the feudal orders was, of course, only an expression of the immanent development of the means of production. Their dissolution was a stimulus not only in the way I have described; it also swept away the web of guild 'mysteries' or secrets. Zilsel has correctly pointed to the way in which the idea of the universality of science and of scholarly co-operation began to emerge. Such co-operation no longer tolerated the bequeathal of trade secrets from generation to generation, but demanded – in the interests of the development of the city, or of the nation as a whole – co-operation, publication, and the transmission of results. Now the scientist was no longer a mysterious magician; it was essential for him to 'make public' his secrets. He became a sorcerer who would be recognized as such only if he demonstrated the secrets of his sorcery and thus made them *reproducible* by others, *reproducible*, in principle, by *everyone*. That was important even with sciences where learning and individual intuition played an appreciable part, as in medicine. A Paracelsus or Cardano did not reject their own intuitions; yet they always set down the basic principles of their science, which everyone could acquire, and those basic skills which every physician, if he were diligent, could come by. The cult of the 'mystery' was quite foreign to both Cardano and Paracelsus.

It was a novelty of Renaissance science that it grew out of needs which arose in the course of everyday life, and in a way that was *immediate* and visible to everyone. Renaissance philosophy, too, sprang from ethical and other problems that were raised by people's everyday lives, again in a way that was *immediate* and visible to all. For that reason it is possible to *relate them back*, directly and continuously, to everyday life and everyday thinking. We have already seen one example of this in the way stoic-epicurean conduct was realized in the daily practice of 'average' men. But people's everyday outlook was changed in a similar way by geographical discoveries, the invention of gunpowder, printing, and the Copernican universe, to mention only the most important factors.

I must emphasize the lively mutual impact of science and everyday life on each other not only by comparison with the past, but also by comparison with the future – for by the seventeenth century the course of development had in some respects already 'transcended' that harmony. With the onset of the bourgeois cycles of accumulation, a constant interaction emerged between the needs created by the development of the means of production on one hand and the evolution of science on the other; and the collaboration between philosophical thought and the problems of life became more intense as well. But that immediacy which was so tangible during the Renaissance ceased to exist. The technical fruits (or curses) of the progress of the sciences became perceptible to everyone. But scientific problems themselves reached such a degree of abstractness and technicality as to be beyond the understanding and capacity of everyday human thought; science took leave of everyday thinking. *Renaissance science still remained within the bounds of everyday thinking*; its methodology had still not become divorced from everyday technique to such an extent that the layman could not grasp it relatively quickly, and its view of the world was sufficiently anthropomorphic to be responded to as a simple 'extension' of the everyday imagination. The first scientific discovery which scandalized the everyday imagination was the Copernican universe; to grasp it one had to abandon the sure footing of the testimony of the senses. Still, it could make its way into everyday consciousness relatively easily, partly because it served the strongly felt needs of practical atheism, partly because it could be made 'imaginable' with the help of a simple allegory (imagine two spheres, a large one and a small one; why should the large one revolve around the small one, was it not more natural that the small one should circle around the large?). It was this concreteness, tangibility, and anthropomorphic quality – or, to be blunt about it, the relative underdevelopment of science – which made it possible for not only the results of science, but also scientific problems in their entirety, to sink back into everyday consciousness. It must be added that in the Italian city-states this interaction was helped along by the fact that there scarcely existed a peasant stratum, bound to nature; in Florence, Venice, and Rome almost the entire population was directly involved in everything that affected shipping or industry. Scientific 'news' spread quickly in the little city-states; there hardly remained any strata untouched by it.

For art, unlike science, there was no sharp break between feudal and Renaissance society. Moreover, art and daily life were less differentiated during the Middle Ages than during the Renaissance. Religion was a part of everyday life, as was – for certain strata – the service of chivalry, and art was the servant either of religion or of chivalry. Music, poetry, and the graphic arts made their appearance on feast days, the high points of everyday life. And it is well known that artists, too, did not consciously set themselves apart from craftmanship on the one hand and entertainment on the other.

It follows from all of this that here, too, the Renaissance was a turning-point. It was at this time that art *detached itself* from *techné* and entertainment, and the artist consciously began to regard *art as such as his goal*, rather than as a by-product of religious or craft activity. The individuality and self-consciousness of the artist made their appearance, as did a hierarchy of artists. This last is very important, for there has never been a period in history, perhaps, which was able *to rank contemporaries so precisely and unequivocally from the standpoint of artistic greatness.* Thus Cellini and Vasari, for example, those two great rivals, placed the very *same* artists (Giotto, Masaccio, Leonardo, Giorgione, Michelangelo) at the pinnacle of their hierarchy of greatness. The separation of art from everyday life did, indeed, make possible their continual and fruitful influence upon each other. For now everyday life no longer simply generated art as an integral part of daily life itself, but created, honoured, and exalted it *as art*; while art, obedient to its own laws, reacted back upon everyday life as art, and permeated it. We need only recall what happened when statues commissioned by the municipality were unveiled before the palace of the Signoria in Florence. The day after a bad statue was unveiled, hundreds of satirical poems were attached to it (and tossed into the artist's quarters), while a good sculpture received just as many poems of praise – something that demonstrates the public character of art and artistic standards and also the good taste of the people (plus, incidentally, their readiness to write verses). It is no wonder that men who constantly lived in an environment of beautiful objects should be able to distinguish the beautiful from the crude and the successful from the unsuccessful; they regarded the creation of new beauty as an enrichment of their *own* lives. Of course, Florence in this respect was an exception even during the Renaissance. When Shakespeare writes that 'the censure of . . . one must in your allowance o'erweigh a whole theatre of others', he is referring to a situation which differed greatly from the Florentine. There is no doubt that the taste of the English Renaissance, less rooted in tradition and not cultivated by the city-state, was not such a reliable yardstick as that of Florence. But that does not alter the fact that the plebs of London also felt the drama and the theatre to be their own; there, too, the demands and interests of everyday life brought a theatre culture into being, and mutual interaction between the two was present. As a consequence of all these things, there *was not a*

151

single branch of Renaissance art which broke apart into a 'higher' and a 'lower' culture. Dante appealed to the taste of the aristocracy of culture, and yet it was the same Dante whom Boccaccio expounded to the people in church. There was nothing more popular than Boccaccio's tales, while Shakespeare and Ben Jonson appealed to the public of the Globe and to Queen Elizabeth alike. The narrower high culture, like that of Latin poetry, was more restricted not only in its effect but also in quality – and, incidentally, its store of ideas, metaphors, and expressions also 'filtered down' into everyday life, not only into the lives of the cultivated strata but also into the lives of ordinary people (as Boccaccio's tales faithfully attest).

Thus artistic activity became differentiated, subjectively as well as objectively, from everyday praxis; and precisely because of it there arose a brisk interaction between technical craftmanship (as, for example, in goldsmith's work and the skilled trades generally) and art on the one hand, and between the themes of art and the problematics of everyday life on the other; and these were the factors which assured a high general level of taste. In this respect, too, the Renaissance was a transition, and a fruitful 'mean', between the practice of the Middle Ages and that of bourgeois society.

All the more astonishing is the *tension* which existed during this same period between the *intrinsic ethic of the work of art and the ethics of daily conduct.* Daily life was dominated by the *brutality* of primitive accumulation; I shall return often to the analysis of how the old value systems were overthrown and how rudimentary and insecure, from the standpoint of the whole society, the new values still were. Only here I must circumscribe the meaning of the term 'work of art', for it is primarily with the graphic arts that we will be concerned. They inherited the myths which served them for subject matter, and with them their stories and hierarchy of values. And since modernization and reinterpretation could affect all things but one – the hierarchy of values – the beauty and autonomy of the Renaissance endowed these stories with a new beauty and splendour without 'accommodating' their hierarchy of values to the new age. It did not matter that it was the opinion – not just the practice – of the artist that it was no great crime to betray a friend, particularly if you could gain by it (and according to the testimony of contemporaries that was the opinion and practice of more than a few artists); all of that did not alter the scale of values expressed in the story of Jesus and Judas (nor did it occur to anyone to change it) – Judas's betrayal still remained a crime.

In the literature of the early Renaissance the situation was already not quite the same. I refer once again to Boccaccio, for he gives the most complete picture of the everyday life of his time, and in him we can read most clearly what attitude one of the most honest men of the day – almost a moralist – took towards everyday life. Let us then consider the facts which he depicts: brutality, a brutality which today is astonishing and almost unbelievable, was a fact of everyday life. 'Roussillon dismounted, opened Cabestaing's breast with a knife, and took out the heart with his own hands, wrapped it up',[2] took it home and served it to his wife for supper. Here envy makes its appearance. Presently we witness the exercise of his paternal authority, when he forces his daughter, who has given birth to an illegitimate child, to choose between poison and a dagger, then orders her to smash his infant grandson's head against the wall and afterwards to throw the remains to the dogs. Here a barbaric fantasy is at work, of the sort we know from the story of the House of Atreus – though, one must add, not a single Greek dramatist ever *depicted* the notorious supper of the Atreids. Boccaccio, of course, represents this kind of brutality as evil, but in no way surprising; he condemns it, but he is not astonished at it, and so in his writings there always remains a certain 'factuality'. There are more than a few tales, none the less, in which the hierarchy of values becomes problematical; in one place, for example, a body-snatching pirate turns into a 'positive hero'. Or consider the celebrated story of Ricciardo. Ricciardo is very much in love with Catella, the wife of his friend. When they have been brought together through a strata-gem and the woman still does not wish to have him, he tells her that if she will go to bed with him now, she can keep her reputation of a virtuous woman, but if she will not he will spread the report that she has initiated the whole affair and so ruin her. 'You are not the first, nor will you be the last to be beguiled,' he tells her; 'nor have I beguiled you to rob you of aught, but for excess of love that I bear, and shall ever bear, you. . . .'[3] It is beside the point that today no one would call this love, for at that time the notion of individual love was only just beginning to emerge. But I would underscore that the man's threats cannot be justified, on any moral basis, as charac-teristic of a righteous and intelligent man – yet that is the construc-tion Boccaccio puts on the matter.

To avert misunderstanding, let it be said that Boccaccio's tales *as a whole* display a clear, reasonable, and just hierarchy of values. Opt for what is pleasant, it *may* always be good – that is the message of the tales, from which it does not at all follow that everything pleasant must necessarily be good. I would only maintain that even in Boccaccio there are 'lapses', originating not in his character – for he was, to repeat, one of the outstanding moralists of the age – but rather in the facts of the everyday life of his time. It was a part of Shakespeare's greatness that by contrast with his contemporaries, with whom these 'lapses' were often much more pronounced and more numerous than in Boccaccio (think of *The Duchess of Malfi* or *The Revenger's Tragedy*), he displayed an unheard-of sureness in ordering his values into a hierarchy; for him brutality is never just 'a fact' but always something which brings men and the times to ruin (as with Macbeth, who has 'murdered sleep') and which provokes indignation (as with the servant who kills Cornwall after he has blinded Gloster).

When, in reading Machiavelli, we shrink from how 'natural' poison, murder, hanging, or treason appear, at least in politics; when in reading Cellini we marvel at the cool indifference with which he mentions his own murders:[4]

> I only gave two blows, for he fell stone dead at the second. I had not meant to kill him; but as the saying goes, knocks are not dealt by measure. . . . I went back alone through Strada Giulia, considering how best to put myself in safety.

At such times we should not forget that what we see here are not exceptions, but rather common practices – and not just the practices of 'high' society either. Burckhardt describes what an important part was played in the everyday life of the common people by the *bella vendetta*. He cites two peasant families who, in the space of a month, exterminated thirty-six of their members in the course of taking mutual vengeance. And he tells us that public opinion, almost without exception, took the side of the murderer.

This brutality and fluidity of values cannot at all be written off to the account of irreligiosity; it was a direct heritage of feudal anarchy. At most, the difference lies in the fact that since the Renaissance had in certain ways promoted the development of individuality, vengeance and the many other forms in which brutality was manifested became more individual, and appeared in areas of life where they could not have appeared before (as, for example, in striving to rise from below to the highest positions; compare the attitude of Shakespeare's Edmund or Iago).

In and of itself, the emergence of bourgeois relations of production could not put an end to the brutality of feudal anarchy. On the contrary, capitalist competition opened up new ground for the use of the same means; those who had struck at their family's enemies could now strike at their own personal enemies, at all those who stood in the way of their individual success. The adage *homo homini lupus* was put into practice in the most direct and most wolf-like way. What finally set bounds to individual brutality and put an end to people's taking the law into their own hands was none other than the development of the *bourgeois legal order*. In those Italian cities where a bourgeois legal system was most developed – where, that is, the law became independent of the persons of even the leading civil functionaries – the state became in some measure alienated even from the ruling class, and enforced its laws even against some individuals and groups from among the ruling classes; in those places the practice of violently taking the law into one's own hands never went so far as it did elsewhere. Such a place was Florence from the end of the fourteenth to the middle of the fifteenth century. *To that extent the emergence of a unified, centralized state and the creation of a more or less universal system of law contributed greatly to accustoming men to civilized forms of behaviour.* To some extent that was the work of the constitutional city-state; generally, however, it was the *absolute monarchy* that started and carried on this process, spreading the rule of law with fire and sword. We would scarcely assert that the number of those who fell victim to 'legal' murder under the absolute monarchies was smaller than the number of victims of the preceding age of arbitrary individual action. In some respects, moreover, judgment pronounced in the name of an alienated law is *less humane* than one pronounced and carried out personally – even where no 'judicial murder' is involved – for such judgment proceeds on formal criteria, and abstracts from the individual case and from the totality of circumstances; and yet at the same time it is *more humane*, for it removes vengeance and the decision about the degree and kind of vengeance from the hands of the subject and thwarts the unbridled rule of passions, by making the perpetrator responsible for deeds committed as a consequence of passion, too. It represses, in every sense of the word, the more primitive strata of the human psyche. Hegel in one place says resignedly that it is no longer possible to write Shakespearean drama because reward and punishment have been taken out of the hands of individual men; the greatness of Shakespeare's figures, for good or evil, rested on their ability to mete out reward and punishment. That, of course, is true. But Hegel omits to mention that in this respect Shakespeare's own viewpoint was undoubtedly that of the absolute monarchy. Othello is much more sympathetic than the justice of the Venetian Republic, with its disregard for the individual; and yet the arrest of Othello and Iago is not only legally justified, but a just one as well. Romeo has our sympathy when he takes revenge for Mercutio, but in the light of higher considerations the Duke's decree of exile is just. It may be true that the vacillating citizens of Rome are pygmies compared to Coriolanus; but they are pygmies whom personal emotion would never lead to commit treason. And here I will refrain from even mentioning those tragedies in which an unequivocal condemnation of feudal anarchy is expressed.

I have discussed the foregoing only to throw light on the unbridled violence of the Renaissance. We cannot ignore that a whole long epoch of bourgeois development, through ages of refeudalization to that of the bourgeois republics, has gone to create an ever more impersonal legal system, and in so doing has, in spite of every inhumanity, increasingly 'civilized' the individual. Hence it is no accident that even today one can decipher from the psyche of a people how long a period of bourgeois development it has had, and how long its experience of a bourgeois legal system has been. During the full flowering of the Renaissance there were a good many men who came to grips with this problem. In part, the stoicism and epicureanism of the age represented a struggle against giving free rein to the individual. But beyond that, the problem of one's *style of life* came into question, stirring even greater controversy.

During antiquity and the Middle Ages there was, essentially, no difference between way of life and style of life. One was born into a certain place in the community and the given division of labour, and that determined one's mode of life; at most the individual could 'vary' that way of life, but no more. The severance of the umbilical cord binding him to the community now created a new dynamics in this respect as well. A man's income and position in the division of labour still determined his mode of life; the breakdown of his working time and leisure time still depended on that, as did his means of employing his free time, his opportunities in public life, and the like. But now the way of life became, in a certain sense, only a framework; within its confines a man could work out *quite different ethical attitudes*, in accordance with his personality and moral choices – and, moreover, not just concerning the decisions made at life's great turning-points, but precisely in the affairs of *everyday life*. The conscious guidance of daily living within the given mode of life, through an ethical attitude that is relatively freely chosen – that is what we have called style of life or 'life-conduct'.

It was in this age, whose brutality I have depicted hitherto, that the demand first emerged for the *humanization of everyday life*, for the development of a humane type of conduct. The two things, of course, are connected. So long as feudal vengeance and the vendetta were blind custom, they remained a *necessary* part of the way of life. As soon as they ceased to be custom and became more individualistic, and thus could no longer be regarded as necessary in principle, then there could emerge, *by contrast*, a variety of modes of conduct, also autonomous, which were consciously directed against brutality. When we hear of the 'life of beauty' of the 'aesthetic life' during the Renaissance, that does not mean a life which had to be lived according to the laws of art; rather – as I have said in connection with the unique potential of the graphic arts – that the beauty and harmony depicted in art, the system of values incorporated in it, had to be re-applied to reality *as a system of values*. The hierarchy of values which had emerged in the world of beauty (and which, of course, had found its way there from the social world of ethics) had to be put into practice in daily life. Thus *the striving for a 'life of beauty' and for 'living a life of beauty'* – which I shall discuss at greater length in connection with Ficino – *represented a confrontation of the values of the Athenian and Christian myth-worlds, in secularized form, with the reality of the age of the Renaissance, and a desire to realize those ideals* vis-à-vis *the average morality of the time.*

Of course one finds many purely external aspects of 'living a life of beauty'. Thus grace and charm, for example, became basic values of conduct. But much more important than these was *tact*, which acquired a particularly prominent place in Castiglione's system of values. Tact, a sensitivity towards the human individual and the concrete here and now, is far from identical with the prudence of the 'mean'. *Prudentia* makes one capable of correctly judging the given situation and of being able to do the *right* thing accordingly. Its necessity appears, then, in ethical decisions. Tact is both less and more than *prudentia*. It is less, for of itself it cannot judge what is 'right' or 'good' – for that prudence is needed. It is more because it appears not only in connection with ethical choices, but permeates *all of life*; thus its practice is an everyday obligation, and it must operate even where there is no question of decisions of a moral content. Since it is oriented towards the individuality of 'another' being or of 'the others', its demands presuppose the individuality and autonomy of these other beings, and make 'accommodation' to them a norm (I have put the word in quotation marks because there is no question here of absolute accommodation). Tact, therefore, as a part of right conduct, is truly a decisive category; it requires taking into consideration other developed individualities in the course of daily life and mutual social existence.

Everyday life was at least as important a *theme* of Renaissance thought as the problems of ontology, epistemology, art, or ethics; more accurately, there was a constant and fruitful interaction between those 'technical' matters and the study and analysis of daily life. The former were, for the most part, an outgrowth of the examination of the latter. In *Die Eigenart des Aesthetischen* Georg Lukács has shown that in daily life various types of reflection – principally artistic and scientific – were still present in undifferentiated form. This lack of differentiation made it possible to appeal to everyday thinking when speaking of *any* form of reflection, and to draw far-reaching conclusions from its study. (We have already observed that this is true even with regard to natural science and philosophy, which were still anthropomorphic at that time.) Petrarch and Montaigne – especially the latter – made discoveries in ethics which were valid for centuries; yet they never started out from ethical categories themselves, but rather from day-by-day experience, and generalized from that. The *aphoristic* style was an expression of this movement of thought. It is especially characteristic that a return to the observation of daily life should always have led to a revival of the aphoristic style, as in La Rochefoucauld, Diderot, and Feuerbach. 'Imitation' was bound to be the fundamental category of art. But again, it was not restricted to art; rather it was held to be a phenomenon of *all* of life, whose special properties, as they appeared in art, had to be studied (compare Machiavelli and Leonardo). At the same time, Leonardo built his analysis of science and technics on the observation of everyday practice and everyday work – again in the form of aphorisms. New *sciences* emerged from daily experience: economics with Alberti, the science of politics and warfare with Machiavelli, legal and political science with Grotius, and so on.

It was Pomponazzi who first examined theoretically the ways in which everyday life on one hand, and scientific knowledge and specialized technical skills on the other, were drawing apart and interacting on each other in a new fashion. It is uncertain whether his genius is more to be praised, or whether a certain narrowness of later ages in raising this problem is to be blamed; but without a doubt he addressed the issue in a much more profound way than anyone had for a long time, and more profoundly than most have right up to the present day.

To all appearances he sets out directly from Aristotle, distinguishing the various faculties of the mind and the various forms of thinking. Aristotle distinguished *phronésis*, or ethical prudence; *epistémé*, or scientific intelligence; and *sophia*, or contemplative wisdom. Aristotle had already touched upon the problem that while everyone had need of prudence in order to make right and proper choices, and *epistémé* could be acquired by anyone, yet very few ever reached the stage of wisdom. But for him this was purely a question of people's *capacities*, and had no *connection with the concrete structure of the given society*. The two forms of knowledge, *sophia* and *epistémé*, were alike theoretical; only their objects differed. *Phronésis* alone was 'practical reason'. It was basic to both *techné* and *energeia*, the two forms in which it appeared; Aristotle made no distinction here between technical and ethical practice.

Pomponazzi takes this as his starting-point, but in such a way as to modify the contents, sources, and meaning of the whole classification. His three 'intellects', to begin with, are the *theoretical*, the *practical or operative*, and the *productive*. All scientific knowledge belongs to the theoretical intellect; thus it is the *type of thinking that is decisive, not the object of thought*. 'Wisdom' goes into the same category with scientific activity. At the same time *phronésis* is divided into two. 'Practical' or 'operative' intelligence remains the 'practical faculty' of ethics. But *techné*, a special facility for labouring activity, forms a separate type of intelligence, the 'productive intellect'.

Why this new distinction? The reason for it is that Pomponazzi does not regard distinctions between the faculties of the intellect as something *once and for all given. The differentiation between the faculties of the intellect is, for him, a consequence of the division of labour*. With this insight he created, at a decisive point, a dynamic concept of man; he analysed man in terms of his interaction with his concrete social and *productive* relations. I have not laid stress accidentally on the word 'productive'. For Aristotle it was simply a given fact that man was a 'social animal'. But now an answer is sought to the question: *why* is a man a social animal?

For the whole human race is like a single body composed of
different members, also with different functions, yet ordered
to the common advantage of the human race. And each gives
to the others, and receives from him to whom he gives, and
they have reciprocal functions. Nor can all be of a equal
perfection, but to some are given functions more perfect, to
some less perfect. And were this inequality destroyed, either the
human race would perish or it would persist with great
difficulty. . . .[5]

It would be difficult to establish from this quotation alone, of course, whether this is a simple rehashing of Menenius Agrippa, an application of the hierarchical, 'everyone-in-his-place' reasoning of Aquinas, or a premonition of the Leviathan of Hobbes and Mandeville. From what follows, however, it becomes clear that it is none of these. What sets it apart from both Menenius Agrippa's reasoning

159

and the traditional Thomist argument is the fact that for Pomponazzi the principle of 'everyone in his place' never relates to the function performed *in the social hierarchy*, but rather (as we shall see) to one's connection with a certain kind of work, independent – at least relatively independent – of the place one occupies in the social hierarchy. With this the feudal character of social co-operation really is at an end, and the way is open for commodity production and the bourgeois social system. At the same time, however – and it is important to take note of it here – we are still a long way from the conception of Hobbes and Mandeville. With those writers it becomes explicit how the bourgeois division of labour cripples the masses of men, how it creates poverty, ignorance, and misery for the multitude of individuals so that the whole, the state and society, may flourish in spite of all this, and because of it. Pomponazzi, however, is still filled with the illusion – a legitimate illusion in the Renaissance city-state, in this case Venice – that the division of labour, which assures the welfare and increase of the whole, at the same time makes possible the happiness of *every single person*. Pomponazzi is the enemy of every aristocratic conception of happiness – like the notion of the 'sage' – which denies the possibility or necessity of happiness for those in *any* branch of the division of labour:[6]

> Such knowledge demands a man of very superior ability, and
> moreover wholly withdrawn from worldly affairs, of a good
> constitution, that is, of a healthy one, and not lacking the
> necessities. But such men may be most rare; even in long
> centuries hardly one is found. This our daily experience
> teaches and history declares. But this is contrary to the nature
> of happiness, because that is a good appropriate to any man
> who is not disabled, since every man desires it.

As we shall see, Pomponazzi gives up the hope that every single human being can develop a many-sided personality, but he does not yet renounce the possibility that every human being can achieve *self-realization*. And in this, too, he expresses the character of the Renaissance as an age of *transition*.

Pomponazzi seeks the *objective possibility* of happiness and self-realization in the dialectic between the totality of everyday life and the specialized skills inherent in the division of labour:[7]

> All men in pursuing this sort of common end must share in
> three intellects: the theoretical, the practical or operative, and
> the productive. *For no man who is sound and of due age fails*

160

to possess something of these three intellects. . . . For each man has something of speculation and perhaps of each theoretical science. Because he knows the principles at least, as is said in Metaphysica, which are as the doors of the house which no one does not know. For who is there who does not know first principles like 'of anything it is said to be or not to be,' 'it does not happen that the same thing at the same time both is and is not'? Who is altogether ignorant of God? Of being, of one, of true, of good? . . . It is also clear of natural philosophy since those things are subject to the senses which first meet the intellect. In mathematics also it is clear to see, since human life could not be carried on without numbers and figures; and all men know hours, days, months, and years and many other things which are the business of astronomy. And no less, unless he be blind, does he know something of sight, which is the task of optics; and unless he be deaf, of harmonies, which belong to music. What shall I say, moreover, of rhetoric and dialectic . . . ?

Thus without exception all the sciences percolate down into daily life and, what is more, into *everyone's* daily life, which implies two things: on the one hand there is no sharp line of demarcation between science and everyday life, and on the other there is no sharp line of demarcation between the thoughts or the ability to think of various sorts of men.

And the same is true of the practical and productive intellect: 'Now in regard to the operative intellect, which is concerned with morals, public and private affairs, it is very clear, since to each is given to know good and evil, to be part of the state and family.'[8] And again: 'And as regards the productive intellect, it is plain, *since no man can maintain life without it. For without things mechanical and necessary to life man could not endure.*'[9] I consider this last element to be very important indeed. I do not agree with the view that during antiquity every kind of labour was despised; still, it is beyond doubt that the assertion of *the universal character of technical manipulation* became possible only in the epoch of the continuous development of the means of production. It is not simply a matter of discovering human labour as the element which maintains society. That had already been stated in the form of the observation that either everyone will perform his own work, or else society will collapse. The difference is that Pomponazzi seeks to characterize *man in general as the being that performs labour*, not limiting it to those classes and strata which in fact do carry out labour. And he

161

ascribes to this universal faculty, found in everyone, not only the power to create and produce but also that of technological manipulation, i.e. the *use of objects* created by man. Thus man is, necessarily, just as much a productive being as he is an ethical and cognitive being.

And here we return to the division of labour. What part does it have in the exercise of the productive, the cognitive or theoretical, and the operative faculties?

The theoretical intellect is not found in everyone in equal measure. It characterizes everyone's daily life, to be sure, but it appears in a developed and complete form only in the lives of those who have taken science for their *occupation*: 'Hence even if all men possess something of it, yet very few have it and can have it exactly and perfectly.'[10] In the case of the productive intellect the situation is similar, but the proportions are different – for a great many people are occupied with toil. 'But the productive intellect, which is lowest and most mechanical, is common to all men. . . . And this is most necessary, inasmuch as the greater part of men have been occupied with it.'[11] But it does not belong to everyone in equal proportion either. Those who are not occupied with the production of goods possess it in lesser measure. What is more, Pomponazzi differentiates *between different kinds of work* as well; he who is master of one trade cannot at the same time be master of another. 'One artisan ought not to spend his time at different crafts,' he writes.[12]

The situation is different, however, with the ethical intellect:[13]
Yet the practical or operative intellect is truly fitting for man. And *every man* not incapacitated *can pursue it perfectly*. And according to it man is called unqualifiedly and absolutely good and evil, but according to the theoretical and the productive intellects only relatively and within limits.

Thus morality is a universal social phenomenon, without reference to any division of labour. Goethe's notion that everyone can be equally 'complete' appears here for the first time, expressed and supported in theoretical terms.

There can no longer be any doubt, it would seem, that Pomponazzi's theory of the division of labour does not amount to a revival either of Menenius Agrippa, or of Thomist hierarchy-theories. For in his conception neither social strata nor medieval 'estates' have their own special and separate 'virtue'; the same moral criteria and values apply to every human being, and they apply to them as individuals, not as members of a social estate. Thus Pomponazzi's whole train of thought is based on the *equality* of men – on men's bourgeois equality, their equality as individuals subordinated to the division of labour and engaged in the exchange of commodities.

Here I must revert to Pomponazzi's views on universality and individual *happiness*, for they play no small part in his thinking.

From the social conditions of his time Pomponazzi drew the conclusion that *universality, as such, is characteristic only of the entire human species*; it is only ethically that individuals can be universal. For Pomponazzi universality is always a *teleological* category; he speaks of the *individual's* end in relation to the end *of the human species*. The individual participates in humanity's end, but only if, in his relative one-sidedness, he acts successfully: 'Not every man has the final end which suits the part, except as part of the human race. It is enough that he has the common end.'[14]

But the happiness of the individual can, as we have seen, be complete. For happiness – and here Pomponazzi follows the traditional reasoning – is the result of a life of virtuous conduct. But what is essential to a life of happiness and virtuous conduct? The essential thing is that a man should understand that he is only a *part* of the development of humanity as a whole; he should recognize *his own place* and the functions proper to his nature, and should fulfil them to the best of his ability, in the knowledge that thus he is participating in the end of humanity. In this way we return to the *stoic idea of live-conduct*. Stoicism appears here from a new angle – that of the division of labour. The honest performance of one's own work, the seeing of the 'whole' in the 'part': that is the special stoicism of the society of commodity production.

But it must be stressed once again: this is no apology, not even by comparison with the later Hobbesian conception. For Pomponazzi began from a social and human status quo where the division of labour did, of course, exist, but where the many-sidedness of individual men was yet assured within the given division of labour. According to Pomponazzi, 'participation' in the theoretical and productive intellects characterizes – to repeat – *everyone's daily life*; and what he wrote was *not simply a structural analysis of the interaction between everyday thinking and science, but a description of the status quo of his age*. That, in turn, was an age where (as we have seen) the unity of science, praxis, production, and ethics was much more effective than in succeeding centuries. And now I can give an answer to the question raised at the beginning of this exposition: was Pomponazzi's genius exceptional, or was it the narrowness of later thinkers in posing their questions that caused the disappearance or obscuring of his insights in the centuries that followed him? It is not out of any desire to minimize the greatness of Pomponazzi that

I reply: it was neither the one nor the other, but rather the fact that those two kinds of many-sidedness, that of the old world and that of the new, met temporarily during the Renaissance, but afterwards separated. Later it was much more difficult to find scientific thinking, broad practical abilities, and moral completeness in the everyday bourgeois existence of the ordinary person, the later 'common man'; it was more difficult to discover the creative link which connected undifferentiated everyday thinking with the differentiated forms of reflection (though that link always existed), and it was more difficult to describe or put into programmatic form the universality of man and of humanity. With few exceptions – and these were all rear-guard fighters of the Renaissance or forerunners of socialism – such a thing did not occur before Marx.

The democratic tendency of Renaissance science and philosophy, and its interaction with everyday life, did not prevent it from criticizing everyday life. Here above all it is Montaigne, one of the most thoroughgoing analysts of everyday life, who must be cited: 'He will sound the capacity of each man: a cowherd, a mason, a passer-by; he must put everything to use, and borrow from *each* man according to his wares, for everything is useful in a household. . . .'[15] And yet in many places he sensed what stumbling blocks lay in the path of everyday thinking – especially where it was evident how people's everyday practice and principles conflicted with erudite stoic ideals. Here we may mention one example: Montaigne discovered how everyday thinking is *bound to the particular*.

> We are all huddled and concentrated in ourselves, and our
> vision is reduced to the length of our nose. . . . When the
> vines freeze in my village, my priest infers that the wrath of
> God is upon the human race, and judges that the cannibals
> already have the pip.[16]

The reference to the pastor indicates that Montaigne saw how it was precisely religion which built on this short-sightedness, making a world-view out of man's bondage to the particular, out of his demand that *his own interests and the troubles* (or blessings) that affect *him* immediately be generalized in an abstract way.

It was, nevertheless, Bacon who went furthest in the critique of everyday life; in that respect (and chiefly in that respect) he is a true forerunner of the philosophers of the seventeenth century. I should like to lay stress on the fact that he, too, *consciously* built on everyday experience, polemically contrasting the results which sprang from it with the lifeless dogmatism and speculation of scholasticism. But for Bacon scientific thinking was not simply a systematized and abstracted extension of everyday thinking, as it was for the typical thinkers of the Renaissance; at the same time it was something that in certain aspects contradicted and denied everyday thought. To that extent, Bacon did not simply discover 'errors' in the structure of everyday experience, which science, as abstract and generalized experience, simply 'corrects'; rather, these were *typical* and *necessary* 'errors', which because of that fact can no longer be termed errors, but instead are forms of thought which *necessarily* belong to the *normal structure* of everyday thinking. Bacon arrived at the realization that (1) science and everyday thinking necessarily interact with each other and can be related to each other, but that (2) at the same time everyday thought has its own structure distinct from that of science, and thus everyday 'truths' have no scientific demonstration-value or truth-value; and (3) for normal human praxis, both kinds of thinking are equally necessary.

'For expert men can execute, and perhaps judge of particulars, one by one; but the general counsels, and the plots and marshalling of affairs, come best from those that are learned. . . . They perfect nature, and are perfected by experience,' Bacon writes.[17] I have deliberately singled out this passage, for here Bacon speaks not of natural science but of the direction of affairs, of government and business. This passage demonstrates that the three aspects of Bacon's outlook which we have just analysed do not refer solely to the relationship of experience, theory, and practice in dealing with the natural world, but relate to *every* kind of experience, theory, and practice.

The most concise summary of Bacon's reasoning is found in his *Novum Organum*. Under the heading of 'idols of the tribe' he analyses the typical features of the structure of everyday thought:

(1) 'The human understanding is like a false mirror, which, receiving rays irregularly, distorts and discolours the nature of things by mingling its own nature with it.'[18] Everyday thinking, then, is generally and necessarily *anthropomorphic*. And that becomes a special problem in the study of objects the existence and operation of which are completely independent of the human understanding.

(2) 'The human understanding is of its own nature prone to suppose the existence of more order and regularity in the world than it finds.'[19] Everyday thinking is marked by the hypostatization of regularities, like harmony or causal relationships, with the aid of which praxis can be more simply and easily organized. That is the

pragmatism of everyday thinking. So long as such an 'order' or 'universality' lends *certainty* in the great majority of actual cases of everyday practice it does not matter for everyday thinking that in certain – exceptional – cases this false universality can frustrate practice. (Science, in such situations, calls into question the whole theory, the system itself; even if it is only exceptional cases that do not conform with the theory, that theory as a whole still becomes problematical.)

(3) 'It is the peculiar and perpetual error of the human intellect to be more moved and excited by affirmatives than by negatives.'[20] In everyday thinking this gives rise to a system of *prejudices*. Once again, as in the preceding case, the root of this phenomenon lies in the orientation of everyday thought *towards practice*. Preconceptions and prejudices make it easier to orient oneself, decide, and act, just as do a hypostatized 'order' and 'universality'. But while the latter always refer to the whole and thus have the character of a *Weltanschauung*, preconceptions, springing as they do from hasty overgeneralization, refer to *single phenomena or groups of phenomena*, and thus their effect is limited. Of course there is always a more or less close connection between the system of preconceptions and the hypostatized world-picture. Naturally, not every preconception is a prejudice.[21] But the need for preconceptions in everyday practice is one reason for the existence and operation of prejudices.

The second part of Bacon's thesis deals with the other side of the same phenomenon. In daily life scepticism plays, objectively, a much smaller part than it does in scientific and critical thinking. (The sort of negation which is not sceptical in character is always, at one and the same time, an assertion as well.) *A sceptical world-outlook* always clashes with everyday practice; it is common knowledge that even those who are sceptics in their scientific world-view are obliged to abandon it relatively in the activity of daily life. In principle, *scepticism with respect to single concrete phenomena or groups of phenomena* can act as a stimulus in everyday practice too. In reality, however, this kind of behaviour is, as the result of a combination of other factors, exceptional. It may be remarked that during the classic centuries of the Renaissance this sort of attitude was much more common than usual, precisely because of the popularity and spread ot stoic conduct.

(4) 'The human understanding is moved by those things most which strike and enter the mind simultaneously and suddenly. . . .'[22] What Bacon has discovered here is the *economy* of everyday thinking. In every concrete instance ordinary reasoning stops at the first explanation or principle which seems *evident*, provided that with its

aid one can operate relatively free of error. Even mere *probability* – much less scientific certainty – has the force of patent truth. (If one waited for absolute certainty, in many cases one would be incapable of acting at all.)

(5) The human understanding always seeks the most general laws:[23]

> And then it is that in struggling towards that which is further off it falls back upon that which is more nigh at hand; namely, on final causes: which have relations clearly to the nature of man rather than to the nature of the universe; and from this source have strangely defiled philosophy.

Bacon here recognizes that objective link which connects *overgeneralization with anthropocentrism*. In the process of generalization, everyday thinking abstracts from mediating factors; with the help of unscientific induction, analogies, and inherent likenesses it overgeneralizes from the observation of a small number of phenomena (whether that observation be immediate or mediated). Bacon has already analysed the other aspects of this kind of overgeneralization. These – to recall – were anthropomorphism, the assumption of order and universality, the primacy of assertion over negation (anti-scepticism), and economy of thinking. Consequently, overgeneralization, too, is anthropomorphic, presupposes order and universality, has an affirmative character (combined with faith), and is economical and thus more comfortable. That, however, adds up to none other than a *teleological* picture of the world. We may just point to the fact that in everyday life the category of teleology appears in two connections. In the first, man seeks *his own ends* in a world which is given to him relatively ready-made. In the second, he looks for an answer to the question: *what purposes does the world have with him?* Those who follow the first course wish to give a meaning to their own lives and the lives of others; those who pursue the second course are seeking the 'meaning' of 'life'. The first sort of behaviour is stoic-epicurean, the second dominated by religious needs. The first – as I have said – does not hypostatize any kind of teleology at work as part of a general world-outlook but, on the contrary, consciously takes account of objective natural and social forces operating outside oneself. The latter attitude teleologizes the whole cosmos, in order to establish a direct relation between the world-process and one's own self. I have said all this only in order to emphasize that the kind of teleology which hindered the development of science was *one* aspect of the teleology that appears in daily life, but it was not the teleology of daily life in general. Bacon

167

does not distinguish between the two (just as he does not distinguish between preconceptions and prejudices) because here he is looking for those characteristics of everyday life which science must confront with criticism. And in so doing he makes no distinction between those forms of behaviour and structures of thought which are *consistently and necessarily unavoidable* in daily life if one is to act at all, and those which are not *necessarily characteristic of the structure* of everyday life (such as the absence of scepticism towards individual phenomena), even though they may generally be found in actual everyday life and *in everyday thinking as empirically given.*

(6) 'The human understanding is no dry light, but receives affections; whence proceed sciences which may be called "sciences as one would". For what a man had rather were true he more readily believes.'[24] Having examined the structure of everyday knowledge, Bacon now turns to search for its *psychological* basis, and theoretically approaches the phenomenon that Montaigne has already described metaphorically as the phenomenon of *particularity*.

Affections are not merely enrolled in the service of particularity, of course. They may just as well be a means for rising above mere particularity, like the understanding itself. But it is in that aspect that Bacon now examines them; for the present he does not consider the ways in which the affections (or passions) can sharpen the mind's eye, but the ways in which they can dull it.

We know from other passages that Bacon was aware of how the passions could work to sharpen the intellect. But we do not know how (if at all) he clarified in his own mind which are the concrete contents and functions of affections that make them the partisans of particularity, for there is no indication of that in the terse and aphoristic formulations of the *Novum Organum*. 'What a man had rather were true he more readily believes' may refer just as much to false consequences as to particularity. At the most we can opt for particularity through a process of elimination: Bacon nowhere touched upon the problem of false consciousness, and the notion itself is foreign to his whole system of thought. The analysis of classes, masses, and movements is nowhere to be found in Bacon, much less the problem of the consciousness of classes and social strata. If what we 'had rather were true' is the way social needs appear in an individual consciousness, then it *may* be connected with the phenomenon of false consciousness, but if it is only an individual's goals and 'desires' which colour his interpretation of reality, then we are dealing with the forms in which particularity appears. Here Bacon, as we have seen, makes no scientific distinction;

but what he is *thinking of* is, beyond a doubt, the phenomenon of particularity. And in the atmosphere of the time, permeated with stoic and epicurean thought, that is readily understandable; for in other connections (unrelated to knowledge or scientific thinking) it was common to theorize about the distorting effect of the affections and will on the understanding, and in these trends of thought it was customary to analyse the way in which the mind could be darkened by a will expressing purely individual interests and aspirations and by the unrestrained passions which accompany it.

Following the analysis of this 'idol of the tribe', it is important to emphasize once again the character of Bacon's critique of everyday consciousness as a transition from the Renaissance conception proper to the standpoint of the seventeenth century. What Bacon *demanded* – the realization of the function of science as a way of 'extending' experience and praxis, while critically rejecting everything which was a structural peculiarity of everyday thinking as such and which hindered the development of an *independent and systematic scientific representation of the world* – was already the common practice of Galileo and Descartes. What he for his own part *achieved* of this project was the culmination of the science and experience of the Renaissance.

CHAPTER 6

Time and space: past-orientedness and future-orientedness

The change in the concepts of space and time, the particular interpretation which the Renaissance gave to them, demonstrate once again how little scientific and everyday thinking were differentiated during that age. Neither category was ever interpreted in such a way as to go beyond the bounds of the *imaginable*. We can still say, however, that the Renaissance concept of space had already become *de-anthropologized*, while its conception of time remained to the very end related to man.

Hegel in his *Logic* makes a neat distinction between space (*Raum*) and position (*Ort*).[25] During the Renaissance *both* conceptions of space were to be found. But the first – *Raum* – never appears in connection with time; the Renaissance recognized a time-space correlation only between time and place or position (*Ort*). Space was a basic category of the philosophy of nature. It made its appearance in two connections: either as extension or the possibility of extension, or else as motion in space. In the philosophy of nature of the Renaissance opinions were divided as to whether the universe (which some thought finite, others infinite) was 'full', i.e. consisted of a compact and continuous substance, or whether it was, as in Democritus, composed of material substances and the void. Both schools nevertheless spoke of the motion in space of concrete things, objects, substances, 'forms', and assumed it to be independent both of human society and human consciousness. This unitary and homogeneous concept of space was in itself nothing new; it had already existed in principle for Democritus. Now, however, a *pantheistic* conception arose in polemics with the theological view of the world (as in Telesio and Giordano Bruno). Pantheism was

170

indeed the premise for the unity and homogeneity of the universe. With the declaration that *natura est deus in rebus* the Deity ceased to be something *outside* of space, just as the spirit or soul ceased to be independent of space. From that point of view it proved necessary to spiritualize substance; the world 'soul' and its function became something quite different from what they had been for the Florentine Platonists. For them, the world spirit was a derivative of ideas existing outside the world; for the former, the world spirit was coextensive with matter, which exists everywhere. *This 'soul' was subordinated to the universal laws of spatial extension.* With that step Renaissance philosophy of nature, despite its often theological character and frequent flood of scholastic speculation, created a theoretical basis for the development of modern science; in this respect, anthropomorphic speculation about nature removed an obstacle to the de-anthropologized study of nature. It was this theoretical point of departure which enabled Bruno to go on from the Copernican universe to a conception far in advance of contemporary science: that of the infinity of the universe and of the existence of an infinite number of worlds. In his reasoning place became – at least from the standpoint of the philosophy of nature – a form of appearance of space or spatiality.

As we have seen and shall see again, the philosophy of nature's concept of the homogeneity space was born within the framework of a philosophy that was, overall, anthropomorphic. To that extent, it did not free itself from the umbilical cord of everyday thought here either. At the same time, however, it is beyond doubt that this new conception of space, which, of course, goes hand in hand with an immanent interpretation of infinity, scarcely penetrated into the daily life of the Renaissance, not only as a result of its scientific abstractness, but also because this new conception was really developed only in the twilight of the Renaissance proper. And by that time, as we have seen, new religious needs were awakening which this new brand of truth could not satisfy. It is clear that in his *Galileo* Brecht was not without his reasons in depicting the truly *popular* character (in the strict sense) of the Copernican system, or the appearance of echoes of the controversy over it at the carnival of Florence. But it is also clear that this was an ephemeral phenomenon and one which did not have any genuinely far-reaching impact.

Everyday life was affected much more fundamentally by the change in *notions about terrestrial space*. That was a direct consequence of the great *discoveries*. Before science had changed the earth's position (and, by derivation, man's position) in the universe,

171

a new conception had already evolved of man's place in his own, terrestrial world. The change in ideas of 'large' and 'small' became a matter of everyday experience: it became a commonplace that the hitherto known 'world' was only a tiny part of the earth. That experience – at least during the classical period of the Renaissance – had an activating effect; it gave a spur to the discovery of new worlds. The vast and unknown attracted rather than repelled; its conquest was a challenge for the newly developed individuality, an adventure.

The change in notions about space permeated the world of imagination as well. Long before the great discoveries and the transformation of ideas about terrestrial distances, men had sought the real proportions between the world and man, the external and internal world. The search for the real proportions between the world and man also found expression in painting in the way *perspective* and the representation of perspective became a central problem. As the background 'opened out' towards the world, painting, too, began to demonstrate that man was no longer in contact with a transcendent world, but with a very human one, cut to the measure of man. And at the same time it also demonstrated (especially in the theories of perspective) that the appropriation of that world was the appropriation, on behalf of man, of an autonomous, *natural* world.

And what of the concept of time?

The *philosophy of nature of the Renaissance did not know any concept of time proper*. True, it recognized many phenomena which presupposed 'temporality', in the sense later given to that word. Among these were movement, development, cognition, finite and infinite process, transcience and eternity, and the like. But from all these natural and social phenomena it did not abstract the concept of 'time'. Nor is that to be much wondered at, for 'time' had been unknown to antiquity too. Similarity – turning to the future – it is common knowledge that an abstract concept of time is absent even from Spinoza's *Ethics*.

It may be objected that 'time' already had a place in Aristotle's system of categories, and thus those thinkers of the Renaissance who had studied Aristotle must have been familiar with it. The trouble is that *to interpret the Aristotelian 'when' as 'time' is erroneous, one of the most egregious errors of the Kantian interpretation*. It has been pointed out many times that the Aristotelian system of categories is *heterogeneous*, for it contains both genuine categories and others which are not genuine categories. But it has never been generally recognized – not to my knowledge at least – that the Aristotelian categories of time and space are not really categories of time and space at all. The Aristotelian 'where' is none other than Hegel's *Ort* (rather than *Raum*), that is to say concrete position or place, while Aristotle's 'time', or 'when', refers to the concrete *point in time*. In connection with space this misconception is not really confusing, for Aristotle does have a concept of 'space', even if it does not figure in his system of categories. But the difficulty is all the more serious in connection with 'time'. A false interpretation of the category of 'when' obscures the fact that Aristotle operated with a concept of time just as little as did Plato or Democritus.

If Renaissance philosophy of nature dispensed with the category of time, the same cannot be said in the slightest degree of the social philosophy of the Renaissance. *Time was one of the central problems for social philosophy.* But let us be clear: here there is no question, either, of 'time' as such, but of quite different concepts of time. Some of these notions also had meaning for nature in itself, but here again they appeared only in relation to society and human affairs; others can *only* be interpreted, objectively, in terms of society and of man's social praxis.

We have already spoken of the notion of *irreversibility*, in discussing stoicism. It implied the irretractibility of human choices and actions, the ontological basis of stoic-epicurean conduct. Above and beyond this, various other commonly accepted – and heterogeneous – concepts of time existed: time as a *point in time*, time as the *continuity of social events* and the *consciousness* of that continuity, and finally time as *rhythm*.

The heterogeneity of these concepts of time does not mean that there were no objective links between them, as will become clear when we come to their concrete analysis. Frequently there are links between them; indeed, at times they are inseparable. And the reason for that lies in the fact that behind all three concepts of time *lies the same social process and social experience*. The thinkers of the age sought to approach and describe this same social phenomenon from the standpoint of three different aspects of time.

What is common to these three aspects and to their *concrete* analysis is *the extraordinary, and hitherto unknown, dynamism of the history of the age*. On one hand there was the acceleration of development, the drama of the age of primitive accumulation and the awareness of its dramatic character, *the change in the rhythm* of the social process. On the other hand there appeared, with the dissolution of the framework of feudal orders, the chance for the individual to move 'up' or 'down', to 'plug into' the objective dynamism of society; *the 'right moment' had to be 'seized'*, so that one could move with the historical current. 'Rhythm' and 'the moment' become essential and altogether comprehensible within the 'process'.

173

These concepts of time, then, did not go beyond the generalizations of everyday experience. And so it is that they often appear as everyday concepts, and not at all *clare et distincte*. If, then, in our analysis we separate out these three aspects, we should remain aware that the distinction is merely a relative one.

TIME AS THE POINT IN TIME

The 'point in time', as I have said, appeared already in Aristotle's system of categories. The same is true of its application to social praxis. We may recall the importance of the 'right moment' in determining the ethical mean. Choosing the right time, determining the proper measure of virtue with respect to the given moment – these are all considerations which can be found in abundance in the *Nichomachean Ethics*. Here, too, Aristotle brilliantly worked out a generally valid schema of the ethical behaviour for every epoch. The brilliance is not reduced by the fact that in the course of history the content of the problem of the point in time has often been modified. Aristotle's world was a static one; the framework of the given community and its ethics set bounds to social dynamism. Thus it was that the question of the proper moment could appear only in an individual and ethical connection. From the standpoint of the course of social development the problem of the correct or incorrect moment could not arise. Every moment turned out to be the same; there was no hierarchy. Even at the peak of awareness of the crisis of the Athenian polis, in the time of Socrates and Plato, the notion of possibilities missed did not appear for an instant. That sort of problematic presupposes a certain dynamism, a social situation, a possibility of choice which will never return. Antiquity was aware, of course, that choices were not uniform in value, that there were basic choices in life whose consequences had later to be borne – otherwise tragedy could never have come into existence. But there was never a hint that it might have been possible to act otherwise or that it might have been possible to seize the 'time' in some other way. That is why we speak of them as tragedies of 'fate'. Even with Oedipus, Sophocles' most 'modern' hero, it never occurs for a moment that in the past he might have lived differently or acted differently, whereas in Shakespeare's heroes this is a constantly recurring motif, particularly at the moment of catharsis (we need only think of the tempest scene in *King Lear*). For that reason, of course, the ethical value-content of the 'point in time' is different for the Renaissance from what it was in antiquity. For antiquity – and for Aristotle, who in this regard sums up ancient practice – the moment was *one* of the modes of right ethical action; but during the Renaissance it receives a much more signal role. For the Renaissance, recognition of the moment becomes one of the main components of knowledge. Bacon writes:[26]

> And with regard to authority, it shows a feeble mind to grant so much to authors and yet deny time his rights, who is the author of authors, nay rather of all authority. *For rightly is truth called the daughter of time, not of authority.*

It is plain that here time does not in any way figure in the sense of *chronos*. To say that truth is the daughter not of authority but of time is as much as to say that striving to know the 'time', rather than understanding the old authorities or traditions, is the way to truth and to a correct praxis. In antiquity knowledge was a knowledge of one's situation, and knowledge of good and evil (Oedipus, for example, did not know *who* his father and mother were); the cognitive function could not be explained by reference to time. It was not a matter of discovering *what* the times *were like*, only of knowing that action had to be *adapted* to the here and now of the concrete moment. During the Renaissance, however, the *whole value-content of action became a function of knowing the times.* The reason and purpose of action came to nothing if someone acted blindly in opposition to the concrete demands of the historical moment. These demands, however, were constantly changing, just as the age itself was constantly changing. Knowledge – and hence ethical action, too – depended upon the sureness of one's instinct for the new, a specific sense of time. Thus Shakespeare's Richard II says:[27]

> How sour sweet music is
> When time is broke and no proportion kept!
> So is it in the music of men's lives.
> And here have I the daintiness of ear
> To check time broke in a disorder's string;
> *But for the concord of my state and time*
> *Had not an ear to hear my true time broke.*
> I wasted time, and now doth time waste me;...

Here we can observe the sense of missed possibilities ('I wasted time'), brought about by 'time broke', that is, by a changing society and the rise of disharmonies which did not exist before, and which the hero *did not recognize* ('had not an ear' for). And so there are the consequences: 'now doth time waste me'. Shakespeare depicts in their totality the causes, political and moral, of Richard's fall, but that totality is organized around the problem of time.

175

The dynamism of society, the central importance of choosing the right 'time', did not, of course, weigh equally on men in every sphere of life. The more responsible one's position, the more lives and empires hung upon one's decisions, the larger a part 'time' played in one's judgment and actions. Antiquity had not known this distinction either, nor for that matter had Christianity or the Middle Ages. Of course, they made far-reaching distinctions from the standpoint of moral grandeur and responsibility, among the decisions of men of varying social significance, but the *structure* of these moral decisions and of their ethical content was essentially the same. Now that structure necessarily became more heterogeneous. Objectively, the structure of choice had to be different for 'superiors' and 'inferiors'; objectively, the choice of the right moment had to play a greater part for the former. This constituted the socio-ontological basis of the differentiation of politics and morals or, more correctly, of the separation of political morality from ethics in general. When Machiavelli advances the theses of his *Prince*, when Shakespeare depicts the structural differences between the choices of 'superiors' and 'inferiors', they give expression to one of the most important and real problems in the development of dynamic man. The dynamism of society, and hence the need for a special political morality, figured among the causes giving rise to that division of labour the consequence of which is the appearance of the type of the 'politician'. Plato's illusions about the identity of the persons of sage and king were still, in his time, sensible illusions. But with the Renaissance they lost all sense, or else they preserved their significance only in those cases – as in the utopias of the age – where the model or ideal of society was itself *static* (More, Campanella, and – with respect to society – Bacon as well). Here, of course, I speak of the 'sage' in the ancient sense of the word. Inghirami, for example, identifies the ancient sage with the philosopher, while calling the politician 'the wise man'. For him, to be wise means to serve men and ourselves; the culmination of wisdom is 'glory and success'. Wisdom is a 'kind of civil and popular philosophy inciting men to actions splendid and glorious in the sight of the multitude and making them great, powerful, noble and, in short, the first of all men'.[28] The greatest sages have been Lycurgus, Pericles, Romulus, and especially Caesar. That being the case, wisdom lies in *time*; the wise man knows his time and changes with it; wisdom must be able to draw profit from every change. The stoic philosopher may stand by one opinion or one mode of conduct – the wise man never. This kind of interpretation of the concept of wisdom cannot obscure the fact that Inghirami carries out *exactly* the same sort of separation as Machiavelli

176

or Shakespeare. The fact that he does so by reinterpreting an old system of categories rather than introducing a new one does not indicate so much cloudiness of thought as *polemical* intent: Inghirami assumes a hierarchy between the 'wise man' (or politician) and the 'philosopher', and in that hierarchy the wise man has the higher place. Neither in Machiavelli nor in Shakespeare is there any sign of such a hierarchy, and with good reason.

For Inghirami the figure of the 'wise man' or politician is free of moral contradictions. The same is true of the philosopher, though on a lower level of the hierarchy. Machiavelli and Shakespeare, however, reveal the ethical – and more than ethical – contradictions, the dialectics of this new division of labour. Consider *Hamlet*: here, too, the situation is one of 'time out of joint'. The young Hamlet stands at the summit of Denmark's hierarchy, after the vicious king and queen; truly he is 'born' to set things right. Horatio rejects the prison of Denmark just as much as Hamlet does, but it is *not* his task to set the times right – hence it is much easier for him to remain an unblemished, unequivocal figure; Denmark expects nothing of him, nor does 'truth', the 'daughter of time', and so he can live and act calmly *sub specie aeternitatis*. The responsibility for setting things right is placed in Hamlet's hands. From this, however, springs the endless and insoluble series of conflicts. For Hamlet's character – as Goethe rightly emphasized, analysing it in *one* respect in *Wilhelm Meister* – fails to conform, in many points, to the task he has received.

First of all, vengeance, too, must wait for its *time*. Those who think to find in Hamlet's indecisiveness the key to the tragedy forget that vengeance requires an occasion, and Hamlet's first objective opportunity really comes only when he interrupts the king at his prayers. Kyd had already touched upon this problem in his *Spanish Tragedy*. There Hieronimoe, feigning madness, reasons as follows:[29]

> Wise men will take their opportunity,
> Closely and safely fitting things to time.
> But in extremes advantage hath no time;
> And therefore all times fit not for revenge.

This motive, too, counts for Hamlet. But what is more important, Hamlet recognizes how contradictory is the task before him from the standpoint of *his own morality*. He is not afraid to kill; in that respect he is characterized by the same 'lightheartedness' as his contemporaries. Without a second thought he stabs Polonius to death and sends his former friends to eternity. But Hamlet's morality is a Renaissance, *humanist* morality; it is the emerging morality of a *lawful order*, whose principle is *audiatur et altera pars*. That is why the play-within-the-play scene is *necessary* for him. Hamlet wishes not to take vengeance, but to *do justice*, to really be 'the child of the time'; for that, however, he must know whether he is really doing justice. Justice – but not in a *political* sense! – for 'Denmark is a prison' and in a political sense the assassination of the usurper is justified in any case; but rather justice in a *legal* sense, which in this case also provides the *moral justification* for punishment: to punish the crime. Hamlet behaves like a *judge*, not like a *politician*. If he had already been placed at the top, with the law in his own hands, he would not have been faced with these conflicts. But as it is, his conflict is truly unresolvable. The beauty of Hamlet's personality lies not least in the fact that he *knows* this in advance; his cry of 'O the shame of it!' is an indication that he does not consider himself fitted to carry out his task, and not from indecision, but because of his own morality.

The interaction of task, character, and 'the time': here again is a new problem springing from the dynamism of man and history. But, it may be objected, why is it new? Were there not historical figures before – like those Inghirami cites – whose greatness lay in the fact that they were 'in tune' with their times and responded satisfactorily to the demands of the times?

I would not assert either that the dynamism of the Renaissance came out of nowhere, but only that it bore new qualitative characteristics. First of all, before the Renaissance being 'in tune' with one's times was characteristic, or not characteristic, of one's entire life. Whoever was able to grasp the demands of a new age was able to grasp them once and for all. To take the historical rather than the legendary figures whom Inghirami cites: Pericles represented the culmination of an evolution of long standing, Caesar was one of the first to grasp a new situation – but they had to realize only one kind of 'time'.

Here we must revert to the socio-ontological meaning of the 'point in time'. In terms of the ontology of nature the point in time is the 'now' of an instant. In terms of *the ontology of society, however, the point in time has meaning only in reference to man, and only in various concrete relations. Here the point in time, the 'moment', is never just a 'moment' in the sense of a measured unit of time* (a second, or some fraction of it). I do not wish to assert that in the life of man the moment, the measured instant of the clock, never has any importance. In connection with *psychological reflexes* it may often have a major part to play. If a soldier in wartime turns aside at precisely the moment when otherwise a bayonet thrust would have struck him, and thus the thrust misses its mark, then of course that moment was decisive in that soldier's life. But here either there is no inter-action between character and 'time' (purely reflex actions can be entirely independent of moral character), or else, if there is, such an instant plays only a subordinate role in the overall interaction of character and time. The fact that someone has good reflexes does not make him a Napoleon in war, though of course it was relevant to Napoleon to have good reflexes in war. But if we go beyond the sphere of purely psychological reflexes, we find that the point in time is actually an *interval of time*; the question is, how great is this interval in different connections? In the life of the individual, the *span of life* sets a limit to the 'point in time'; on the whole, 'now' means the 'now' of a lifetime, during which the appropriate tasks and opportunities for choice are presented by the ethics and possi-bilities of the age. In adulthood, childhood with all its possibilities is 'past', just as in old age most of adulthood is 'past'; 'now' is the 'point in time', the seizing and use of the opportunities of the given age in life. Through all these 'nows', character develops.

Let us consider, however, the 'nows' of history. The historical 'point in time' is an integral *historical period which demands unitary and identical attitudes and modes of action from those who live in the flux of that period.* In the interaction of history and character, a decisive role is played by the way in which *the rhythm of history is related to the rhythm of the individual life.* During antiquity and the Middle Ages the individual historical moments or 'points in time' were sufficiently intervals of time so that they far exceeded one man's lifetime (and frequently even exceeded the span of life of generations). But during the Renaissance the relation was reversed, and ever since then this reversal has (exceptional points apart) affected all of European history: historical 'moments' have become shorter than the span of human life (taking the normal human lifetime as a basis). Character, ways of thinking are scarcely formed, when they are obliged to accommodate themselves to changed demands and to take account of new human characteristics. The elderly cease to be unquestioned authorities; what is more, age, and experience acquired long ago, can become obstacles to the acquisi-tion of new knowledge. In Athens the aged still counted as the chief authorities, the old, blind seers who had 'seen a great deal'. But now it is the Cesar Borgias, the young, the *homines novi* who understand the message of the age and the 'time'. From this time forward Goethe's saying 'Stirb und Werde' becomes valid for every human life, if not always in the same way. Only the man who is constantly developing, dying and being reborn, can keep abreast of the times;

only the man who remains receptive to the very end, amid the flux of change, and at each new moment is capable of acting differently, can be a politician and statesman. Where did Pericles or Caesar have need of that?

Once again it was Machiavelli who formulated the problem most neatly. I might cite one passage among many:[30]

> I also believe that he is happy whose mode of procedure accords with the needs of the times, and similarly he is unfortunate whose mode of procedure is opposed to the times. . . . From this it results . . . that two men acting differently, attain the same effect, and of two others acting in the same way, one attains his goal and not the other. On this depend also the changes in prosperity, for if it happens that time and circumstances are favourable to one who acts with caution and prudence he will be successful, but if time and circumstances change he will be ruined because he does not change his mode of procedure. *No man is found so prudent as to be able to adapt himself to this, either because he cannot deviate from that to which his nature disposed him,* or else because having always prospered by walking in one path, he cannot persuade himself that it is well to leave it.

Here Machiavelli touches upon a particular but decisive aspect of the dialectic of character and the point in time. To anyone familiar with the comparable train of thought in Plutarch's *Lives*, it could not have been a strange notion that a certain kind of 'nature' or character could be an advantage or disadvantage in coming to grips with certain 'times', that is, with perceiving and carrying through special historical tasks. But the idea that time and history could 'outrun' the flexibility of a man's perceptions and character is a newly hatched thought. Machiavelli recognizes and tries to explain the often contradictory ebb and flow of history, in which one wave brings the individual to the surface while the next casts him down into the depths again. He gives three reasons, each equally important. One is the basic nature of a man (for example, of an indulgent prince in quiet times); then there is force of habit; and finally there is our personal stake in our past, a clinging to our own past. It is true that Machiavelli does not recognize or analyse the degree to which flexibility wears a Janus-face. If a man (and above all a politician) has firm social goals and a fundamental moral attitude, and these remain more or less the same, then flexibility is a mere *tactic* in the pursuit of a unitary strategy. To that degree flexibility and a feeling for the ever new aspects of time's onrush constitute a remarkable virtue, an eminently political virtue. We need only think of politicians as great as Napoleon and Lenin. If, however, flexibility is merely the power of accommodation, and if the ability to recognize the time is no more than an instinct for personal success at a given time, then those abilities turn into their ethical opposite, and we have to deal with the most unprincipled historical figures, the Talleyrands and Fouchés. It is quite true, of course, that both those types are rare enough. The more common, and constantly recurring, kind of political personality is able to take one or two waves, but the third or fourth necessarily buries him under. At such times, there appears the phenomenon – all the more clearly the more history 'hurries' – that a whole *series* of individuals is required to fulfil *one* historic task; in the onrush of history they constantly succeed one another. We need only think of the sequence of great personalities in the French Revolution, from Mirabeau to Condorcet and from Danton to Robespierre. The oft-cited saying that the revolution devours its own children is simply a description of that fact, of the inter-action of character and task, of the changing of the political guard in circumstances where 'time is rushing onward'.

At the beginning of this discussion I observed that, in the hierarchy of motives for human activity, the ability to select the 'moment' did not occupy one and the same position; the closer someone came to political activity, the more important it became. The more one's activity was centred on a social sphere which, in its reproduction and its way of life, remained comparatively stable amid the rush of events, the less important it was. The distinction is, of course, only relative. Great historical cataclysms shake the *whole* of society, and at those times the moment acquires an importance for the lower reaches of society just as much as for the upper. Walter Scott again and again depicts a mediocre bourgeois hero who is suddenly thrust into the stream of history; abruptly and without previous 'practice', he is forced to display a certain feel for the 'here and now'. During the Renaissance, however, when the masses, even in the most cruel stages of primitive accumulation, were still passive rather than active participants in history, such a thing still happened only rarely (Shakespeare, for example, still depicts only the 'upper reaches' of society). Still, we must stress once again that all this is relative. For in bourgeois society, seizing the 'moment' has a significance above and beyond the realm of political history. It has no small role *in the economy itself*, for the 'rush' of history is only a reflection of the 'rush' of production. The right moment plays no less a part in the struggle of competition than it does in political activity. That was clear to Bacon, who called attention to the importance of the 'moment' in connection with economic praxis just as much as with political praxis. It is interesting that he compares fortune to the market: 'Fortune is like market; where many times, if you can stay a little, the price will fall.'[31] And in speaking of the market, he says: 'There is surely no greater wisdom than well to time the beginnings and onsets of things.'[32]

Despite all this, however, I still believe it is correct to speak, in connection with the significance of the 'moment', of a specific political rather than a specific economic morality. In the case of the politician, and of all those who as a result of the historical movement come into positions which are decisive for society, the individual's decisions have an effect on masses of people; the *consequences* of his decisions reach far beyond the individual and his immediate environment. And since weighing the consequences is one of the decisive components of morality and moral responsibility, we face here a specifically ethical structure. As for business or activity on the 'market', however: there is no doubt that for the *individual* and his immediate environment finding the 'time' is no less important here either, for one's enrichment or impoverishment depends upon it; but since the consequences affect only the individual and his immediate environment, commercial life has objectively no ethical structure peculiar to itself. Here again, as in so many other areas of life, what we find is only a special *form* of expression of the *unitary* essence of man. (If it be objected that selling good merchandise, for example, or not cheating others, makes up a specific 'business morality', we can retort that it is considered the honest thing in general not to cheat others, and so on.) But all this would take us far afield from the problem of the 'moment', the 'point in time'.

TIME AS CONTINUITY

Time as moment is itself a category in which history, historical change, and a sense of history are latent. There, however, time is always 'present time', and a sense for the present moment amid changing times. Time as continuity is likewise a socio-ontological category; it is, however, a more historical one in so far as it is directed towards comprehending *humanity's road to the present* (that is, its past) as a *temporal process*. Yet it is true that, while the concept of the 'moment' was applicable to every aspect of human praxis (though most pregnantly expressed in terms of political action), the category of time as continuity appeared during the Renaissance *exclusively in connection with science or technical development*.

Time, like every category, is a universal concept. Its various aspects can be grasped only where in one or another respect an idea of its universality has emerged. We have seen that the abstract universality of the 'when' (the point in time) is already found in Aristotle; since this 'when' pertains to everything that exists in the present, it was enough to recognize this simple fact for a universal concept of the point in time to develop. In antiquity, however, it was impossible to grasp the past as a temporal process; *chronos* was nothing but the beginning. In the Judaeo-Christian religious *Weltanschauung*, *chronos* was replaced by the Creation. The world was created 'ready-made'. What happened afterwards was the history of a people or of a small group within it, or the ensemble of these histories. There was no trace of 'one building upon the other'. The genealogies (think of David's or Jesus's) do not describe a building *up*, but rather a *descent*. The concept of redemption is in contradiction to every notion of time as continuity. A concrete image of a world governed by an Eternal Being (no sparrow can fall unless He wills it) turns human life and the life of peoples into an endless succession of discrete, unconnected 'moments'.[33] With the advent of the practical atheism of the Renaissance, these obstacles to comprehending the temporality of the past fell away. Causality became a this-wordly causality, process a process in this world. All this, however, was still not enough for an idea of universality to develop. Irreversibility as the impossibility of the individual's recapturing lost possibilities, as the uniqueness of the opportunity to grasp the historical occasion, could have emerged clearly long before the notion of the irreversibility of the *whole* historic development could make its appearance. We have discussed before and will discuss again how often antiquity was viewed simply as a *repeatable* example, leaving out of consideration what a difference separated the present from the remote past; it was the recognition of *parallels* that prevailed, rather than the recognition that one epoch built upon another. Now the causes of the historical phenomena and types of a given era came to be sought in that era itself; moments determined by God no longer stood independent of one another in their infinity, but various periods and social structures still appeared separate and apart, independent of one another. It was seen that social structures are born and die – but in this birth and death, coexistence or sequence, no common substance was perceived, existing *in spite of* the birth and death of societies. I have observed in my introduction that the concept of 'society' had not even evolved; how then could the notion of 'social development' come into existence?

The thread which an integral social evolution follows, through every contradiction and retrogression, is the development of the means of production. A unitary socio-ontological category of time as continuity can only emerge after this relationship has been clarified. The Renaissance was still a long way from that; but here, too, as in so many other instances, the first steps were taken towards working out the new category. It is true that this took place only on the 'last wave' of the period, but still it took place.

I am referring to Bacon and Giordano Bruno, who recognized the unitary and successive character of the development of science and the means of production – though, to be sure, they did not see their interaction with the development of society. For them, the organic development of science and the means of production was not one 'thread', one index of human development; rather, it *was* general human evolution, *the* evolution of society. In scholarship, there emerged a 'sense of time'; in judging the scientific development of the ancients the yardstick was no longer an absolute one, for now the question came up: at *what time* did they live? But this 'time' always referred only to the 'time' of technical proficiency, of the state of development of science and the means of production; it is never social 'time'. Giordano Bruno, for example, writes as follows: 'Judgment could not be so ripe in Eudoxus, who lived shortly after the rebirth of astronomy, if indeed it was not reborn with him.' We are older, there is a longer period of time behind us than was the case for our predecessors, so far as experience is concerned.

> Copernicus saw more. . . . But if many of those who came after him were not more astute than their predecessors, and if the bulk of those who are alive today are no sharper, that is because they did not relive, and do not relive, their predecessors' times, and, what is worse, are dead even to the world of their own times.[34]

It is by living through others' years, by appropriating the technical and scientific expertise of earlier generations, that man becomes the child of time. If he does not appropriate it, if he does not participate in this continuity, he 'drops out' of time; time 'goes forward' with the objective development of science and technology (and humanity goes forward with it). The individual, however, and individual groups of men, may live out their years as if 'dead' (though Bruno does not say that there may be objective reasons for this 'living as if dead').

Here Bacon goes a step further. He attempts to formulate dialectically the successive character of the evolution of science and the

184

means of production. For him, too, the substratum of continuity, the bearer of progress and its absolute measure, is science and technology *exclusively*. But he does not put the responsibility for periodic retrogressions in the development of science and technology on men who live 'as if they were dead'. 'In times no less than in regions there are wastes and deserts. . . . And therefore the first cause of so meagre a progress in the sciences is duly and orderly referred to the narrow limits of the time that has been favourable to them.'[35] As the comparison indicates, Bacon here, too, sets out from the parallelism of space and time (both, of course, conceived in an anthropocentric way). For Bacon the course of development of science and technology is not determined simply by the accumulation of experience or by an insensitivity towards experience, but follows rather from the needs and possibilities of given epochs; the evolution of the whole involves progress and regress, in the form of leaps ahead followed by periods of stagnation, with the periods of stagnation lasting longer than the leaps forward. Thus Bacon sensed, so far as science and technology were concerned, the category of uneven development. Of course, Bacon gives no answer either to the question of what the concrete cause or causes are that make one age a 'desert' and another a fertile oasis. But the fact that he raised the question is significant. The answer to the question why there were 'deserts' and 'oases' would have to wait for a long time. Bacon's age did, however, react immediately to another aspect of the problem. It did so by discovering the rhythm of time.

TIME AS RHYTHM

'Time as rhythm' is actually an imprecise expression, for it is not time that has a rhythm, but rather events that have theirs. And yet we do not mention the 'rhythm of time' – in the consciousness of its imprecision – in a purely allegorical way. In using the expression, we are simply taking heterogeneous components and making them homogeneous. In some historical periods the *whole* tempo of social and human development speeds up, while in others it slows down; and the acceleration or deceleration of the individual factors – the various heterogeneous components – is far from being parallel and proportional at all times: indeed, contradictions can even appear between certain factors at times. In that event we have to do once again with one of the forms in which uneven development makes its appearance. (The rhythm of change may vary not only in different areas of life but also, at various points of the social structure, in the same sphere of existence. We need only think of Marx's analysis of old India, which saw in the village communities rapid changes of fortune among the upper strata and complete immobility among the lower.) The 'rhythm of time', then – as we have said – is a concept that tends to homogenize: it serves to express the tempo of development of the *whole* society.

So far as the whole society was concerned, the Renaissance marked, by comparison with the Middle Ages, a quickening of the pace. That is the reason why the concept of 'time' appears so often in the sense of 'rhythm'. But the fact that the concept of time was so often interpreted in this way does not at all mean that people became conscious of everything that I have just described. For the most part they did not speak of the 'acceleration' of time *in general*, but of some of its concrete manifestations. Thus Bruno, Bacon, Bodin, and Regius understood by the 'speeding-up' of time the sudden surge in the development of science and technology; we have already cited the saying of Regius in which the French philosopher calls his own century the 'happiest' for precisely this reason. When Machiavelli, again, mentions 'onrushing time', he is referring rather to the acceleration of social changes.

Shakespeare in his history plays was the first to depict the rhythm of time as a uniform, homogeneous social phenomenon. Here, too, Shakespeare was a child of his age, though in the artistic formulation of its problems he pointed far beyond it. Shakespeare's history plays are *authentically* historical in that *the acceleration of the sequence of historical events is indicated by a constant acceleration of the dramatic rhythm*. This acceleration is *total*, for it relates not merely to the course of events, but to the development of character, the conflict of character, and the restructuring of worlds of feeling and systems of moral values as well. I will go into this in more detail later; for the time being I should like merely to illustrate what has just been said. The first in the series of history plays, *Richard II*, proceeds at a leisurely pace, up to the moment of Bolingbroke's return. With his return, rebellion, and seizure of the throne, with which a 'new era', that of the final agony of feudal anarchy, begins, the tempo of the whole drama is suddenly stepped up. Systems of values are 'suddenly' overturned, men 'suddenly' begin to learn things which they never suspected before in their lives, history swoops down suddenly on the heads of some (York), while it 'throws up' others. Richard II's soliloquy on time, already quoted, is the first conscious recognition of this change in rhythm as such (compare his analogy of 'broken time'). The tempo of the two parts of *Henry IV* is more even (quicker than that of the beginning of

186

Richard II, but slower than the section beginning with the usurpation of the throne). At the same time, Shakespeare brilliantly makes things homogeneous here: the 'mediating' role of the young Prince Hal makes it possible to introduce the 'lower' alongside the 'higher', and we see that the rapid transformation of men and morality which has taken place in the sphere of 'majesty' has also been going on just as rapidly, though in a comic, grotesque form, among the 'lower' orders as well. In spite of that, the tempo slows down in the two parts of *Henry IV* itself; thus the poet signals that a 'condition of equilibrium' is approaching, as we near the reign of Henry V. Here history 'holds its breath', both 'above' and 'below' – only to plunge into a rapid acceleration in *Henry VI*: there the same change of tempo sets in as in *Richard II*, on a higher plane (albeit morally on a lower level). The acceleration now goes on irreversibly; with the second part of *Henry VI* (the beginning of the Wars of the Roses) it becomes almost demonic, as murders and betrayals follow, surpassing one another in number and horror, and so through Henry VI's first fall and on up to his assassination. And since we know that Shakespeare wrote these plays at various times and not successively, we must marvel all the more that everything is in its place. The new demonic 'acceleration' is marked again by a soliloquy on time, in this instance Henry VI's:[36]

> O God! methinks it were a happy life,
> To be no better than a homely swain;
> To sit upon a hill, as I do now,
> To carve out dials quaintly, point to point,
> Thereby to see the minutes how they run,
> How many make the hour full complete;
> How many hours bring about the day; . . .
> How many years a mortal man may live.
> When this is known, then to divide the times:
> So many hours must I tend my flock;
> So many hours must I take my rest;
> So many hours must I contemplate; . . .

Henry here contrasts the old time, even, measured time, 'certain' time with 'historical' time, accelerating time, uncertain time, the rhythm of time. Henry sees clearly that that time in which one can 'measure out' one's whole life in advance, whose tempo does not change, which is never crossed by other forces and which is not subject to change, is not the time of kings and not the time of townsmen or peasants either, but the time of shepherds, that is, of those *who stand outside society. An even time-rhythm is the time-rhythm of nature, not of society.* Thus whoever wishes to escape from this time must escape from history.

The high point of the dramatic rhythm is finally reached in *Richard III.* Until now, one king at most has fallen in one history play (*Richard II*); for the most part it has taken two or three plays to cover the reign and destiny of one king. *Richard III* begins in the reign of Edward, with Richard's actions only in the planning stage. But from its very beginning, from Richard's first soliloquy, everything races without any side action towards its 'end'. And the 'end' is now an end in two senses: it is the end of Richard and the end of an era.

This changing rhythm, moreover, marks nearly every tragedy of Shakespeare's; I have referred to the history plays because there the process can be traced most clearly and continuously. This is not the place to discuss aesthetic considerations, but I must simply note that the problem analysed above is not identical with the distinction between objective and experienced time, one of the most important principles of composition in the novel. The 'drawing out' of experienced time as presented in the novel springs from the richness of the experiences of its hero. An amorous hand-clasp can be described for a hundred pages if it has a decisive, culminating significance in the life of the protagonist. But the novelist – as Fielding put it so well – is the chronicler of private life. The dramatist, however, is the chronicler of public life, and for that reason – and because of the totality of the action – in drama the rhythm of the individual life always approximately expresses, and must express, the rhythm of history.

But if we remain with the problem of *experienced* time and with the question of the substantiality and experiential content of a span of time in the minds of various subjects, we will see that Shakespeare has put that into words, too, if only in jocular form. (I have never come upon this sort of interpretation of the concept of time anywhere else.) I am thinking of Rosalind's whimsical characterization in *As You Like It*:[37]

> Time travels in divers paces with divers persons. I'll tell you
> who Time ambles withal, who Time trots withal, who Time
> gallops withal, and who he stands still withal.

Time as the point in time, time as rhythm, time as process, and time as experience, too; time as present and time as past, as experienced present and experienced past. And the future. Did the *futurum* occupy no place at all in the Renaissance's conception of time? To answer that question, I must say a few words about attitudes towards past and future.

Until capitalism first began to emerge every society was oriented towards the past. That is to say that in the minds of the members of society the future did not appear as something 'different'; it did not appear as a *prospect*. Their idea of the future was of a simple continuation and repetition of the past, with some – quantitative – displacement of the proportions of the present, but without becoming different, without a substantial transformation of the present. It may be objected that the prospect of freedom or liberation is as old as class society itself; oppressed men and peoples have always dreamed of 'freedom' as a different kind of future. That, of course, is true; but 'liberation' in this sense does not necessarily imply a future which is totally different. It is well known that the dream of slaves was never more than to return to their old homeland – hence it was bound up with an orientation towards the past; the ideology of various people's struggles for freedom was one of regaining some old freedom; even the migration of the Jews to Canaan, the Promised Land, was a 'return' and they wished no more than to become an equal nation in the ranks of the other peoples. Or the example of the later chiliastic movements may be raised against us. But the objection is not valid here either. *Parousia* in its original form implied the destruction of the world; but orienting oneself towards the destruction of the world is only necessary if there is not and cannot be any immanent historical perspective, any orientation towards the future. An orientation towards the future first glimmers in the chiliasm of Joachim da Fiore, but that was an idea which already had roots in the culture of the Italian city-state which was emerging at that time; and there, too, it only glimmered, for it never lost its transcendental character.

Of course, a social consciousness and praxis growing out of a type of development which proves to be objectively a cul-de-sac is oriented towards the past in one way, while a kind of development which is not objectively a blind alley is related to it in a different way – though it is useful to analyse the differences only in terms of the concrete forms in which they manifest themselves. During the Renaissance, as we have seen, the development of society was dynamic and went forward, for a time, at a constantly accelerating tempo; from the standpoint of the overall development of society it was an 'open' period, for the mode of production which was emerging at that time did indeed have a future. At the same time, *some* of the possible roads leading to capitalism did turn out to be blind alleys, like the Italian and Spanish ones (as I have already mentioned). Other paths, again, were all the more 'open', like the English and in part the French. The evolution of technique and of the means of production, however, displayed an accelerating tempo *everywhere* during the Renaissance; there, for the time being, the stepping-up of the rhythm was not broken. Thus certain contradictions, and a certain tension, arose between the development of society and the development of the forces of production. Of course this was not simply a matter of tempo. It was becoming obvious already, even in the period of the emergence of capitalist society, what profound internal contradictions, social and moral, this form of society brought with it, and more and more people saw clearly these two things – the development of technology and science, and the growth of social and moral contradictions – necessarily went along with each other. Thus those who opted for the prospect of technical development did not envisage any 'different' kind of society in the future – different from that of the most developed and most nearly bourgeois country of the age (usually England). *An orientation towards the technological future was not coupled with an orientation towards the social future.* Those, on the other hand, who were sceptical about the fruits of technical development possessed no sort of orientation towards the future whatever.

Thus orientation towards the future, as a general attitude, only characterized those who measured historical progress by the development of technique and of the means of production – all those, in other words, who (to refer back to my earlier argument) grasped time as process and succession. And – to reverse what I have said – it was precisely their orientation towards the future which enabled them to comprehend time as process. If the generations build on one another and each starts out from the 'experience' of its predecessor, then the present, too, is only a 'starting-out', a point of departure for new, never-before-seen, unimaginably rich and wondrous 'experiences'. Giordano Bruno called his own time a 'dawn' following a long 'night' – but dawn, of course, is followed by day, the true light of human knowledge: that is the resplendent future. Cardano exults as follows:[38]

> What is more amazing than pyrotechnics? Or than the fiery
> bolts man has invented, so much more destructive than the
> lightning of the gods? Nor of thee, O Great Compass, will I be
> silent. . . . The fourth marvel is the invention of the typographic
> art. . . . What lack we yet unless it be the taking of Heaven
> by storm?

The past is null, the present is everything, and the future holds the overthrow of the power of God. These thinkers saw in everything they did not a consummation, but a *beginning*. The very titles of

Bacon's works indicate this enthusiasm for the future, titles like '*Instauratio*' *Magna* and '*Novum*' *Organum*. Bacon speaks scornfully of those sceptics who go about 'making it believed that whatever has not yet been discovered and comprehended can never be discovered or comprehended hereafter'.[39] These future-oriented 'technicians' always interpreted *their own* work, too, as a starting-point. A. C. Keller cites many examples of this attitude: Cennini, Roriczer, the young Dürer, Peter Apian, Regius, and others. Bodin, for example, writes: 'Nature has countless treasurers of knowledge which cannot be exhausted in any age.'[40]

I have asserted, then, that with respect to past-directedness and future-directedness, the social-historical consciousness and the technical-scientific consciousness parted company. But what, it may be objected, of the utopians? *It would be an error to ascribe to Renaissance utopianism any kind of orientation towards the future.* Neither in More nor in Campanella is there any sign of such a thing. It is not at all accidental that for both More and Campanella the framework for their utopias is some kind of journey, in the midst of which they 'happen' upon the island of Utopia or the City of the Sun. In that there is more to be seen than simply a reflection of the age's taste for travel and the proliferation of descriptions of voyages. It is significant indeed that both the island of Utopia and the City of the Sun exist in the *present*, although *somewhere else*; thus they are remote *in space* rather than *in time*. Neither More nor Campanella believed that the ideal society they were describing could ever be the 'future' of humanity or of their own societies. They were creating an *ideal* by which the reality of their age could be measured, an ideal of a 'normal' human society in comparison with which the contradictoriness, pettiness, and inhumanity of their own time would emerge more clearly. Campanella had no other purpose. Of More, on the other hand, we can say that he did not consider it impossible for one or two elements of his Utopia to be attained in real life, but only as a part of the life that *already existed*. In that respect, Renaissance utopianism truly stood halfway between that of antiquity and the modern utopianism of the eighteenth and nineteenth centuries, from Morelly to Fourier and Cabet. Ancient utopianism was decidedly oriented towards the past. I am thinking not only of the variations on the legend of the Golden Age but also of Plato's state, which was a consciously retrograde utopia; it sought to sweep away all those social and productive (and artistic and scientific) accomplishments in which Plato thought to see the forces that were destroying the polis. The sort of utopianism which first appeared in the eighteenth century was truly future-oriented (just as the

Enlightenment in its entirety was oriented towards the future). Renaissance utopianism, however, lived in the present. The reason Bacon broke off writing his *New Atlantis*, in my opinion, was that his technical future-directedness simply could not be fitted into the typical framework of contemporary utopianism. Consider Solamona, the first legendary king of New Atlantis, who 'did ordain the interdicts and prohibitions which we have touching entrance of strangers; which at that time . . . was frequent; doubting novelties, and commixture of manners'.[41]

In the domain of science and technology, then, some thinkers of the Renaissance learned to regard the present from the standpoint of the future. The future was something that was evolving infinitely, constantly changing into something else and becoming perfected; the present, by comparison, was a beginning, an imperfect starting-point. Their attitude towards the present was thus determined by a sense of *perspective*. In the study of the structure of society, however, it was not the future that dominated. The present was either simply *described* or at most analysed from the standpoint of what *action was immediately called for* (as with Machiavelli), or else measured against some ideal. The attitude of writers on society towards the present was thus determined either by *Realpolitik* or by an ideal. A 'social perspective' still did not exist.

The fact, however, had in its turn a far-reaching effect on the perspectives of technical development. A technical perspective without a total social perspective is not only abstract but decidedly unhistorical (and may even become anti-historical). The past as process (compare my discussion of time) was an *unhistorical* process; moreover, it was abstracted from history. It became an accumulation of experience on one hand, and a series of errors, blunders, and inexplicable retrogressions on the other. It will be recalled that when Bacon spoke of the 'deserts' of time he gave no reason as to what made one age a 'desert', useless from the standpoint of the development of science. The social basis, consequences, and interactions of scientific and technical development – these were problems that held no interest for him. In the *Novum Organum* he even went so far as to set up a hierarchy between politics and 'discoveries', claiming that the benefits of politics are restricted to one group while 'the benefits of discoveries may extend to the whole race of man'.[42] I have said that an orientation towards the technical future alone is unhistorical and may even be directly anti-historical. Such are the 'technological utopias' of the twentieth century. They employ the same basic structural formula analysed above, either in grotesque and fantastic form, as in Wells, or with a pessimistic thrust, as in Huxley and Orwell, or naïvely and apologetically, as in science fiction. It turns out that a purely technical future-orientation is compatible with *any* kind of world-picture, up to and including an updated Last Judgment.

The technical future-directedness of the Renaissance, however, cannot be condemned from that point of view. Something may be unhistorical but it can hardly be anti-historical in an age when the notion (and even the possibility of the notion) of historicity has not even evolved as yet. Historical thinking developed step by step, and even the emergence of technical future-directedness was a step in the right direction. Similarly, the future-orientation of the Enlightenment was another such step with respect to social development, despite all the mystifications of romanticism (we can say this of Helvétius just as much as of Diderot). *If we wish to avoid seeing the Renaissance through modern spectacles, we must avoid two extremes. One is to assume that historical thinking existed during that age, and the other is to suppose that anti-historical thinking existed at that time.*

But if no *futurum* existed in the social science and social philosophy of the era, does that mean that none existed in the everyday life of the individual? Do we not meet with any future-orientation in the daily life and thinking of Renaissance man?

In speaking of the ancient and Judaeo-Christian traditions I made mention of many examples of their orientation towards the past, and in particular of the fact that precedent was so important in the social practice of the men of the Renaissance; how often did they not believe they were simply repeating the past, how often did they not seek (and find) parallels between past and present! But at that same time I also mentioned that in all this search for precedent, in this often quite conscious 'repetition' and allegorization, there were frequent instances of *false consciousness*. One aspect of this false consciousness was the fact that *objectively they did not act in a way that was oriented towards the past, even though they often thought they did.* In men's daily life the dynamism of society constantly thwarted and closed off the possibility of *really* acting in a past-oriented way. *The ideal often lay in the past, but it was still the present which guided the individual's steps.*

As a result of rapid changes in technique and social conditions an orientation towards the real past turned out to be an unprofitable line of conduct. Let us, for the moment, consider production. In the Florentine textile industry tradition long preserved for itself a very great role indeed; the young learned their trade from their more experienced elders, and it was many years before they became 'mature' workers themselves. During the quattrocento, however, the situation gradually changed, partly because with the spread of manufacture there was more and more use of unskilled labour, which did not require a lengthy period of training, and partly because – most significantly – innovation came to play an unbelievably large role. If we look at the most striking example, the technique of the fine arts, we can see what a remarkable number of technical innovations were born within the span of half or even a quarter of a generation. Artists were no longer content to go on for even ten years with the technical equipment which they had acquired from their masters, but went further and further in the search for new methods. Technical innovations gave rise to entirely new artistic genres, as, for instance, the majolica reliefs of the Della Robbias. If we read Cellini's autobiography carefully we cannot help noticing what an extraordinary role technical innovations played in his life; without them he would have lost his patrons every ten or fifteen years. The skilled worker, handicraftsman, or artist who remained oriented towards the past was simply 'left behind'.

The area of human relations present much the same picture. Once traditional forms of life have disintegrated, the tradition of the fathers and grandfathers can no longer offer a guide to the individual in his daily life (we are not speaking, of course, of the countryside, where a traditional outlook survives much longer). In morals, way of life, behaviour, dress, and the like the individual had constantly to change and accommodate himself to the demands of the present, demands which in themselves were constantly changing. Hence *fashion* came into being. The rule of fashion is, of course, only an extreme instance of the way in which the loss of the validity of tradition is manifested. Changes in custom in the broader sense point to the same phenomenon in a more decisive sphere of life. When Castiglione writes that it is impossible to strive for absolute and eternal perfection because customs are constantly changing and perfection can only be related to custom, he is only drawing the consequences of that same phenomenon. (It is, incidentally, precisely because of the rapid *change* in customs that the category of custom becomes a *problem* – but that is a subject to be dealt with in a separate chapter.)

It is clear from all of this that however past-directed the thinking of Renaissance man may have been in some respects, in practice he lived entirely *in and for the present*. The past was the ideal, but keeping pace with the present was the true – and dynamic – motive of action. There have been few periods in history in which men gave themselves over so unconditionally to the present as they did during the Renaissance. In saying this, I do not wish to imply a moral

194

judgment either for or against. Living for the present, in a dynamic, changing world, may possess two different value-contents – to take into account only the two extreme cases: either merging completely in the moment, with the dissolution of individuality and a moral relativism, or else a constant attention to the real demands of the present while preserving one's individual substance. Here I might refer back to the views of Alberti, analysed above, in which he seeks to discover a 'mean' between the demands of society and the autonomy of the individual, or to those stoic and epicurean thinkers of the Renaissance who assessed and ordered these ever-renewed demands without fear or hope, according to their 'naturalness', i.e. their 'justice'.

Living in the present none the less presupposes a certain kind of orientation towards the future. In eras of dynamic social development, when (as we have seen) the rhythm of social change is more rapid than that of the individual life, the man who wishes only to live in the present as it is today must objectively 'fall behind' a present which is constantly changing into something new. Thus there develops in men, and above all in the leading strata of society – and here I mean not necessarily the political leaders, much less any aristocracy of birth or intellect, but those people or groups which form the vanguard of change in their own field – an attitude of 'facing towards the future', an alertness to the stirrings of the future, its evolution, and its possibilities. They relate their actions not only to their own individual goals – for that has existed ever since the individual has existed – *they also measure the individual goals to which they relate their actions by the possibilities and perspectives of the age* (one might add that it is only in this case that the conflict of ends and means becomes typical). Men do not attend to what *is* but rather to what *will be* or *might be*. That, too, is a prerequisite for 'seizing the moment'.

I should like to illustrate with an example how this kind of future-directedness in the conduct of everyday life need not imply a historiosophical or scientific orientation towards the future. The fact that everything is changing and in concrete situations one must ever be on the alert for change does not contradict the wisdom of Solomon's saying that 'there is nothing new under the sun'. (Bacon, incidentally, greatly valued this saying of Solomon's, deeming that it expressed the same wisdom as Plato's notion that all knowledge is recollection.) My example is drawn from Shakespeare's *Henry IV*. Following Northumberland's treason there is an interesting discussion between the King and Warwick about whether and how it may be possible to see into the future:[43]

K. Henry: O God! that one might read the book of fate,
            And see the revolution of the times. . . .
Warwick: There is a history in all men's lives,
            Figuring the nature of the times deceas'd;
            The which observ'd, a man may prophesy,
            With a near aim, of the main chance of things
            As yet not come to life, which in their seeds
            And weak beginnings lie intreasured.
            Such things become the hatch and brood of time; . . .

For Warwick, then it was no great 'wonder' that Richard had foreseen Northumberland's defection. That betrayal was already present 'in its seeds'. King Henry, however, had ignored those seeds, from which the future, the 'hatch and brood of time', sprang. Thus Warwick appeals to a kind of thinking and conduct that is future-oriented. But on what sort of historical and philosophical conception does he base this appeal? He bases it on the notion that history only presents the lessons of *past* times ('Figuring the nature of the times deceas'd'), and in an approximate way ('With a near aim'). What is new, sudden, and surprising from the standpoint of concrete action may, from the standpoint of history, be old and repetitive.

The men of the Renaissance did not, then, set for their goal the creation of a 'new' and 'better' society; their actions were not determined by that kind of outlook, as the actions of the men of the Enlightenment later on were. Thus they could not have a future-oriented praxis. By way of illustration it is sufficient to cite Shakespeare again. Not one of his heroes made it his purpose to create something new, and yet Goethe was right to say that in every one of his tragedies an old world is crumbling and a new one is struggling to be born. And that new world, again, is not an absolute, timeless one, but once more a *concrete beginning*. To cite Jan Kott's telling observation:[44]

> When a hero of Racine's kills himself, the tragedy is over, and, simultaneously, the world and history cease to exist. In fact they have never existed. When Antony and Cleopatra kill themselves, the tragedy is over, but history and the world go on existing.

CHAPTER 7

Individuality, knowledge of men, self-knowledge, autobiography

It is common knowledge that the Renaissance was an age of great and many-sided personalities. Science, politics, philosophy, and art could all boast their great representatives during the Renaissance. Similarly, we find examples of versatility and of the most fanatical and passionate one-sidedness, of stoic-epicurean moderation and of uninhibited unscrupulousness. Burckhardt rightly asserts that no one was afraid of being conspicuous, of appearing to be different from the others; men stubbornly followed their own course in life and the laws of their own personalities.

Amid the cavalcade of diverse personalities there is, nevertheless, one common feature that appears repeatedly. That is a *turning towards the world*, what we today call, with a common expression from psychology, extroversion. This turning towards the world was typical right up to the sixteenth century, when amid the deepening crisis of that age it gave way to a turning away from the world, men's withdrawal into inner concerns and 'introversion'. This sharp historical break is the best proof of the extent to which 'extroversion' and 'introversion' are not innate forms of human behaviour, but are shaped by the needs and possibilities of the age – though always, of course, on a given psychological foundation. The typical Renaissance individual's lack of inwardness cannot be emphasized enough, and it is on this decisive point that we must take issue with the overly rigid and overgeneralized concept of 'individualism'. Individuality, as it now exists both in reality and as an ideal, is the product of a long historical evolution. Different historical epochs have contributed differently to its development – and the Renaissance contributed a great deal – but even here one can still observe a certain continuity, a successive building of one age upon another. The ages that have gone by since the Renaissance – even those periods of much greater conformism – have brought out new features of individuality; they have enriched and refined the structure of individuality and given it greater self-awareness. To give but one example (albeit a decisive one): interpersonal emotions were much less individual during the Renaissance than, for example, at the beginning of the seventeenth century. Again, the need for freedom was, in its content, much narrower. If we should ask someone today whether he would like to live in More's Utopia or Campanella's City of the Sun, he would certainly reply with an alarmed 'no'. And if we should insist on knowing why, he would undoubtedly answer that these societies leave no scope for the unfolding of the individual personality, and for that reason it would be like a stifling captivity for him to live in such conditions. But during the Renaissance no one, not even its most striking individuals, felt that way about it. In the dialogue in More's *Utopia* a great many things are brought up against Raphael and many counter-arguments are raised against his principles, but individuality has no place among the counter-arguments. (Similarly, not a single contemporary – not even Aristotle – ever said of Plato's *Republic* that in it the individual was not free.)

Engels rightly remarked that during the Renaissance giants were needed, and so the age gave birth to giants. But a special kind of giant was required – and it was for that reason that the kind of individuality which emerged at that time was a *special kind* of individuality, corresponding to the needs of the day.

We have already seen that the demands of the day were: to keep abreast of new, constantly changing situations, to sense the 'time', to seek out and find opportunities for individual action in the ebb and flow of reality, to come out on the crest of the wave – and not only to move with events, but to move them as well – to move ahead with onrushing time or even anticipate it. All of these are tasks which spring from a public situation, demand it and react back upon it. *The glare of publicity illuminated the path of these heroes; rather, they could only become heroes if they were willing to stand in the glare of publicity.* Everyone necessarily lived 'outwardly'. Here I should like to refer back to two phenomena already discussed. The first is the fact that few epochs were ever able to establish the hierarchy of merit of their own contemporaries in art so precisely as did the Renaissance. Later ages were unable to 'discover' a single Renaissance artist who – if he was truly great – had not been popular and recognized in his own time. We cannot even say (as we can with antiquity) that misunderstood geniuses had perhaps perished. On the contrary: some of them were forgotten by posterity, for it is common knowledge that even in Goethe's time Renaissance art began essentially with Raphael. But if we read Castiglione, Leonardo, or Vasari we will see that contemporary estimates recognized as 'famous' and 'great' all those whom posterity later forgot and whom the nineteenth century rediscovered. The other phenomenon I wish to call attention to is the fact that the stoics and epicureans of the period also lived outwardly, for the *procul negotiis* was only rediscovered in the sixteenth century.

Meeting the challenges described above not only required great energies and abilities (antiquity and even the Middle Ages had often demanded as much), but often required peculiarly individual energies and abilities as well. A non-communal social structure made possible a kind of *competition* between one individual and the other which was unknown in communal society with its set and rigid bounds. The individual could realize himself only *against* others. Thus Renaissance individuality was always a form of individualism, and its motive force was *egotism*. Hatred, envy, jealousy of all those who had done better or might do better was no small part of the Renaissance personality. And that was true not only of public figures in the narrow sense. If we read Vasari's lives of the great artists we will find even there none but envious and ambitious men, with the sole exception of Donatello and to some extent Michelangelo. And the interesting thing is that Vasari describes all this envy and ambition as quite natural, and does not find it reprehensible in the least. Cellini, likewise, saw in Vasari and every other contemporary of his a 'back-stabbing' striver (and, incidentally, also describes *himself* as such). I should like to remark by the way that Renaissance egotism was not at all synonymous with egocentrism – outward-directed men are never egocentric.

Egoism alone does not, of course, make anyone an individual. Renaissance egoism was nevertheless an egoism of individuals. They staked their future on action, threw themselves into the currents of the age, acted and created; hence their egotism cannot be interpreted as so negative an ethical attitude as the common, egocentric egoism of developed bourgeois society. Renaissance egoism was an egoism of *creation*. It was not oriented purely towards the particularity of the individual human being, but first and foremost towards his work. The work was none the less the work of an individual and its success was inseparable from the individual's success.

Bringing to fruition one's own work became so important as a *motive* as a result of the peculiarly transitional character of the

Renaissance (and we have seen that individual and work were closely bound up with each other). *For tradition was no longer a motivating force, and conformism had not yet become one.* The structure of motives in stoic-epicurean conduct was the same, except that there the 'work' was a life of beauty and righteousness. The individual's work was not only a motive, but at the same time an end as well. That, of course, is something which should not be misunderstood. The citizens of the Renaissance city-state (for example, Florence) consciously served their city-state; some wished to create for humanity, others for the sake of learning or art – that is why we have said that their individual motives cannot be reduced to sheer particularity. But it was *they* who wished and *they* who sought to serve humanity. If someone had told them to live their lives in obscurity, for their work would still survive, they would have laughed; for the success of their work was inseparable from their own – personal – success.

The Renaissance individual, then, was an individual because he externalized himself, and in that process of externalization came to know himself and to take delight in himself. But externalization does not simply mean objectification; it implies *success* as well. Of course, perfect objectification is a success in itself. But typical Renaissance men had need of other forms of success as well: money and fame.

With the Renaissance, then, the *self-realization and self-enjoyment of the personality became a goal.* To that degree Renaissance individualism realized a great deal of what we today consider the essence of individuality. But that identity remains an abstract one. *Wherein* did this self-realization lie, *what* did this self-enjoyment consist of, *what* did these men interpret as success? That was determined by how much of this 'human essence' the individualism of various Renaissance personalities managed to realize. The hierarchy is clear: from the inessential to the essential, it leads from money through fame to 'pure' creation.

The hierarchy was clear; yet during the Renaissance very few people were aware of it. Since, on the whole, the individual had become fused with his work, men had not yet learned to differentiate between self-love and self-interest, self-preservation and egoism. The motives of money and fame were combined in self-realization and self-enjoyment. Of course we do not wish to assert that every Renaissance personality was money-hungry; but almost without exception they thirsted after fame, and there are very few of whom we know or suspect that in their attitude towards life they deprecated such particular motives. Vasari, for example, gives dozens of examples of the mingling of general and particular motives. Giotto 'repaired to Padua, where he painted several pictures, and adorned many chapels . . . from which he derived both honour and profit'.[45] Thanks to the discoveries of the della Robbia brothers, 'the arts of design, and the world generally, were enriched by the possession of a new, useful, and beautiful decoration – from which, too, the master himself derived perpetual fame and undying glory'.[46] Cardano wrote of himself that from the very beginning his greatest passion was to make his name live for ever. The culmination of Petrarch's life was his crowning with the laurel. Or we may cite once more Inghirami's 'principle of success', according to which wisdom is 'a kind of civil and popular philosophy inciting men to actions splendid and glorious in the sight of the multitude and making them great, powerful, noble and, in short, the first of all men'.[47]

With the sixteenth century this lack of differentiation comes to an end. The pronounced emergence of human inwardness or subjectivity, a consequence of the crisis-ridden character of the period, taught men to make distinctions between the various areas of self-realization. It is not that men became 'better' – only that, during the early Renaissance and to some extent the high Renaissance, there was *no objective contradiction* between the 'self' as it represented humanity's consciousness and self-consciousness, and the needs and strivings of individuals. In plain language: *generally* (and not only in exceptional cases) it was possible to 'succeed' through genuine creation and to acquire money and fame through greatness and force of will. In the sixteenth century, after the Church (or rather, churches) put their ranks in order again and began to exert strong pressure on every kind of creation, opposition to official 'expectations' became increasingly a precondition of creation; thus an objective contradiction appeared between that 'self' and particular interests, and the former lack of differentiation had to come to an end. In Montaigne this contradiction is apparent in a particularly pronounced form.

This 'separating out' of particular aspirations from the general concept of self-realization went forward in different countries at different times and in different forms, in tune with the course of history itself. I may refer once again to Shakespeare, for the process is clearly observable in his work and system of values. In the comedies of the young Shakespeare, the desire of his heroes to acquire property is not at all a reprehensible motive. Even more: those who strive after goods are often more sympathetic and more normal than the 'old-fashioned' characters. In *The Taming of the Shrew* Petruchio says:[48]

> If thou know
> One rich enough to be Petruchio's wife,
> As wealth is burden of my wooing dance. . . .
> I come to wive it wealthily in Padua;
> If wealthily, then happily in Padua.

And this is how he asks Kate's father for her hand:[49]

> Then tell me, if I get your daughter's love,
> What dowry shall I have with her to wife?

Petruchio is indeed superior to Kate's bourgeois suitors, with their mimicry of aristocratic courting – and he wins the only woman worth having. In *Two Gentlemen of Verona* the perfidious Proteus takes this for his principle:[50]

> I cannot now prove constant to myself
> Without some treachery us'd to Valentine. . . .

Here self-realization is identified with one's special interests. It is true that Proteus is an unsympathetic figure in the play, but in the end Valentine, and the poet, forgive him. But the scale of values goes on changing; in *As You Like It* money (success) and humanity come into direct conflict – though only for a moment. Yet how far that is from *King Lear*, *Timon of Athens*, or even from the desperately happy ending of *All's Well That Ends Well*! For in those plays success, money, and power are blind and self-mutilating in principle.

Leonardo da Vinci was the first Renaissance personality to react against a hierarchy of money, fame and *oeuvre*, and for him *only the work* was a criterion of self-realization. We do not know whether his unhappy lot in life brought him to that conclusion, or whether, conversely, it was that principle which made his lot an unhappy one. For Leonardo, the sole measure of a man's worth was his work, but his work had to have a *moral content*; and these two were now inseparable from the moral bearing of the creator.

> Lo some who can call themselves nothing more than a
> passage for food, producers of dung, fillers up of privies, for of
> them nothing else appears in the world, nor is there any virtue
> in their work, for nothing of them remains but full privies.[51]

For Leonardo, men solely concerned with their own particular interests, and content to pursue them, are fillers up of privies (compare Marx's analysis of the vulgarity, narrowness, and baseness of complacency).

The decline of the 'principle of success' reflected the new social status of art. Never before in history had art – real, new, original, profound art – been an official art to the same degree as during the Renaissance. It is enough to compare Rembrandt's lot, not with that of such successful artists as Raphael or Titian, but with a 'difficult personality' like Michelangelo, to see how striking was the difference. I have purposely spoken of the graphic arts, for until the very end of the sixteenth century Renaissance literature (including lyric poetry and work of Ariosto) was not a literature of inwardness, in that respect resembling the productions of the graphic arts, despite its non-spatial character. A subjective art emerges in the sixteenth century, rather towards the end of the century. Dénes Zoltai has shown the growing importance of music in Florence at the end of the century (Vincenzo Galilei, the Camerata group, and so forth).[52] This inwardness, on the other hand, is thoroughly characteristic of Shakespeare's dramatic art, more precisely the depiction of the conflicts between the outer and inner life.

The dominant Renaissance striving for self-realization, whether in the form of the success-principle or as mastery over one's particular interests, was *a concomitant and a result of secularization*. The justification of a man's existence was a thoroughly this-wordly one; it was a secular justification which he demanded and sought. Paradoxical though it may sound, it is still true that in this not at all minor respect the figure of Luther was the *culmination of the process of secularization*. Luther – though unconsciously, of course – beat religion on its own ground. It was Dilthey who perceived that Luther was not a 'saint' and not one of the elect, but 'simply' a personality made to act and dominate, and that it was thence his extraordinary personal influence sprang. 'He dominated the men of his time, for they thought to see in him what their own selves might be,' he wrote.[53] Luther essentially differed from all previous renewers of religion, not because he was oriented towards the world (many others had been as well), but because the notion of election had no part in his ideology and practice. God had not singled him out for higher purpose (no more than any other man); it was not a mysterious appeal that called him to work, but rather the sight of the decay of the Church and religion. He was a *man*, in no respect a superhuman figure; he was a man who recognized his possibilities, sensed the 'right moment', saw his 'task', fulfilled his 'calling', and realized the ideas that sprang from these perceptions. He was a man unshamed of his particularlity, unlike St Augustine; on the contrary, he accepted it (for, as he tells us, he could never think of a woman without desire). Whatever Lutheranism may have become in the future, with Luther the preaching of religion became a human affair, and was itself secularized.

Let us turn now to the philosophical thought of the Renaissance: how was the new individuality reflected in it?

It appeared above all in the way the immortality of the soul was interpreted. The Thomist concept of the soul followed the principle of dual subordination: the human spirit was 'personal' and individual, and after death it would be immediately united, as such, with the divine spirit. The soul as a separate entity was, however, far from an individual soul. Since man's whole earthly existence was fitted into an objective hierarchy, his activity within that hierarchy determined the forms and content of virtue and vice; the salvation or damnation of the individual soul depended on the overall conduct of the man who found (or did not find) his place in this objective hierarchy (and, of course, upon grace as well). The opinion of the Averroists that men are not personally immortal, but are immortal through the mediation of the universal part of their souls, their intellect, was a step in the direction of secularization, in so far as it reincorporated the myth of the soul's immortality into philosophy. During the Renaissance, however, even that idea became obsolete, for Renaissance individualism did not tolerate depersonalization even in immortality. The solution could not, however, be a return to the Thomist conception, for now men wished to become immortal in their *earthly personalities*. Since I will return later to the analysis of the problem of the soul, I shall simply indicate here the main directions which the answers to this question took. According to Ficino, for example, the body, too, is immortal; thus man lives on in the entirety of his *individuality*. Pomponazzi theoretically treated immortality as individual and total, yet at the same time (as I have said) he did not regard that as being normative or orientative in everyday life and moral practice. On the other hand – as J. H. Randall writes – 'the later Averroists, like Zimara, came more and more to identify this unity of the Intellect with the unity of the rational principles in all men'.[54]

The world was coming to appear, more and more, a world made up of individuals, a kaleidoscope of individual personalities. From now on, the individual becomes the theoretical point of departure for all psychological-ethical systems. For Vives and Telesio, *self-preservation* is the starting-point of human conduct. Every sensation, every virtue and vice is reduced, in the last analysis, to self-preservation. *Society, the* status civilis, *also comes to appear as a set of ties binding together individual units which resemble one another.* *Commiseratio* is the motive which prompts us to social activity;

'putting ourselves in the other man's place' becomes the psychic point of departure for social compassion. Here we can see the beginnings of the modern bourgeois principle of egoism, the anthropological source of all theories of social contract. Here was the first attempt – if only from one single aspect – to construct society from the 'atoms' of individual men. In the beginning, then, was – not the society, but the individual.

Individuality came to appear, finally, in nature itself. I would not assert that that is the *sole* foundation of Bruno's monadology; but *in Bruno's monads individualism certainly becomes a concept constituting a whole new picture of the world*. Giordano Bruno's 'entities' are not the abstract, mathematical units of Cusa, but individual beings, unities of body and soul, concrete, self-sufficient, closed totalities. And the one infinite universe is made up of an infinite number of monads, just as society consists of concrete totalities made up of units of body and soul – of individuals.

The appearance of a specifically Renaissance individual changed *the structure of character as well*. Character no longer grew organically from the tasks and expectations fixed in advance by the system of feudal orders; it was self-chosen, winding its way along relatively autonomous paths in the direction set by social expectations, especially the hope of success – and thus it drifted away from the general and approached ever closer to the individual. Thence springs the constantly repeated effort of Renaissance thinkers to create new character typologies above and beyond the Hippocratic typology of temperaments, so that they might make it easier for men to 'recognize themselves' amid the new plurality of characters. In painting, especially from the fifteenth century on, the portrait became more and more important, and even in the choice of subjects for historical or mythological canvases the individual won himself a larger place (as in Donatello's second period). Several of Leonardo's paintings can be regarded as deliberate character studies. Max Dvořak is quite right, in my opinion, when he interprets the *Last Supper*, too, in this way. Leonardo set out to show how the Apostles, with their different personalities, would react *in different ways* to the same news (of Judas's betrayal); he sought to grasp artistically the connection between individual personality and mode of reaction. Giambattista della Porta, again, examined in his *De humana physiognomia* how human character was expressed in facial features. But he added that he was only presenting conjectures since, given men's free will, they were capable of deceiving us with their facial characteristics.

The dissolution of the system of feudal orders and the emergence of a multiplicity of characters in itself placed new demands, more substantial than ever before, in the way of gaining knowledge of men. In feudal society one could more or less tell from someone's social position, previous life, connections, and temperament how he would act. *And that was all the more true because unexpected situations arose only within well-defined limits.* One could foresee whether in a given case a person would or would not take vengeance, to what degree, in a passion or in cold blood. Now, however, knowledge of men became ever more difficult. The situations which might confront men became 'unstructured', unexpected, incapable of being defined in advance; what more or less defined them *now was not just circumstances or objective relationships, but, to a considerable degree, character itself*, so that all the possible situations which might arise for men could be defined, even approximately, only with the help of a knowledge of human character.

But that was only the beginning of the problem. What made it even more difficult to acquire knowledge of men was the appearance of 'roles' and role-behaviour. In feudal society, a man did not 'play a role'; he *was* what he had been born to be. Capitalist division of labour and the loosening of the social hierarchy made it possible, however, for one and the same person to occupy quite different rungs of the social ladder; he could be active in quite different branches of the division of labour, becoming a barber one day, a writer the next, and a *condottiere* the third, adopting quite different forms of behaviour one after the other and yet remaining, all the while, the same man. Since each particular place in the social structure and each particular occupation entailed different manners and a different complex of rights and obligations, *one man could identify himself with different manners, different sets of rights and obligations, and different concrete norms, and yet 'he' would not become 'them'.* Of course, it was more than the extension of the social division of labour which brought role-behaviour into existence. For that, emerging capitalism had to dissolve every community, so that a man could assert himself only through the mediation of the position he occupied in the social division of labour, so that economic status (and not humanity as a community) could become the universal norm. Only in this way could that duality arise according to which man, as man, is independent of the position he occupies in the division of labour (everyone is equally a human being), while at the same time men can only realize themselves through the place they occupy in the division of labour (economic status is the sole universal norm). *Thus man became divided, relatively speaking, into 'individual' and 'role'.*[55]

The attenuation of the link between men's personalities and the functions they performed in society not only made it possible for some people to display various kinds of behaviour *one after the other*; it also allowed them to show different kinds of behaviour *side by side*. To mention only one key example: the separation of bourgeois and citizen foreshadowed the division of public life from private life. The representatives of the classic Renaissance, like Alberti, devoted great theoretical and practical efforts to bridging this gap and to creating a dynamic, substantial interaction between public and private life. But we have seen that by the sixteenth century these efforts more and more ended in failure. As Montaigne wrote: 'Society in general can do without our thoughts; but the rest – our actions, our work, our fortunes, and our very life – we must lend and abandon to its service.'[56] 'Freedom of religion', the 'free' practice of one's faith, freedom of 'conscience' or subjective belief – all these were demands which codified the growing separation, if not actual conflict, of the norms of private and public life. As the norms and ethics of the 'world' increasingly showed their inability to realize the ideals of the Renaissance and even began to depart from them more and more, 'privacy' and subjectivity came increasingly to preserve these trampled ideals, while the simple citizen or 'subject' living in bourgeois society, possibly amid conditions of refeudalization, was obliged in his 'outward' behaviour to accommodate himself to the demands of the new age. Confidently, but with no small bitterness, Charron wrote:[57]

> In the end each of us must seek to distinguish, in his public
> role, his own self, *for each of us plays two roles and consists
> of two persons, of which one is external and the other essential.*
> We must be able to distinguish the skin from the shirt . . . and
> we must learn to deal with the world as it is, while at the same
> time regarding it as something alien to us.

As we have seen, Charron regarded an awareness of the existence of this 'dual role' as the condition *sine qua non* of a knowledge of men. To distinguish the skin from the shirt – that is where knowledge of men begins.

True, the contradiction between 'external' and 'internal' was not characteristic, in this extreme form, of the classical Renaissance. But even at that time the beginnings of role-behaviour, and of *hypocrisy as an attitude*, characterized to an increasing degree the whole range of human activity, from daily life to politics. That was almost a natural consequence of the competition for status among egoistic individuals and of the principle of 'success'. For when individuals struggle to win themselves a place in the world – and frequently do so *against* others – then in order to attain their goals they must often disguise their intentions; they must show themselves to others as something different from what they really are, they must 'play a role'. Of course, it was nothing new for men to feign or to conceal their identity. To cite Biblical examples alone: Jacob dissembled and concealed his identity when he received Isaac's blessing, and Joseph in Egypt concealed his origin and dissembled before his brothers. But in these ancient examples hiding one's identity, and dissimulation, *did not involve any ethical contradiction.* Jacob was acting according to his own morality (and that of his community) when he accepted the blessing; Joseph was professing his own morality (and that of his people), and he succeeded in validating it even in Egypt. With the Renaissance, however, this kind of dissimulation came to conceal an ethical contradiction. Men gave themselves out as different from what they really were, pretending to be good if they were wicked and wicked if they were good; they lied about their real purposes, professing different ones, even where these were, morally, directly contrary to their real goals. Dissimulation turned into a *regular form of behaviour*, and so it became more than just dissimulation or hypocrisy. Thus arose the split between people's 'real' nature and their other, 'not real' nature, and with it a permanent contradiction between essence and appearance.

Knowledge of men always remains one beat behind the actual evolution of character types. During the Renaissance that 'beat' proved to be a long one. Those who did not become aware of this double game (because it remained foreign to their moral natures) suffered extraordinary shocks and disappointments. Those great catastrophes caused by a lack of knowledge of men, which we meet time and again in Shakespeare, are reflections of a problem which affected the lives of all. The attentive reader of Ariosto, too, can see what a fateful and key question this was. Only on rare occasions does Ariosto stray from his tale in order to point a moral for contemporary experience from the story. But when he comes to speak of enchantresses, he cannot keep himself from sighing:[58]

> Oh strange enchantments used now adayes,
>   Oh charmers strange among us dayly found
>   That find so many charms and subtle waies,
>   Wherewith they hold fond lovers hearts fast bound,
>   Not with conjured spirits that they raise,
>   Nor knowledge of the stars and skills profound,
>   But blinding mens conceits, and them fast tying
>   with simulation, fraud, deceit and lying.

And that sigh refers not just to dishonest ways of winning people's affections, but to all those forms of deceit by which one man can get another into his power.

For the active hypocrisy of the Renaissance did indeed have for its object to destroy the other man or get him into your power. Efforts to gain knowledge of men either collapsed before this hypocrisy, or else sought to accommodate themselves to it. Accommodation, however – assuming an honourable man – could be of two kinds. It meant, on one hand, *'training' oneself to know men*, developing the ability to see behind the mask. On the other hand, it meant working out forms of defence, of *covering one's own exposed spirit* and limiting one's unlimited confidence. Only the two of these together could guard one against catastrophes, failures, and disillusionments. And so when Charron writes that men must distinguish the shirt from the skin, the words have a double sense. One must learn to discriminate in dealing with others (sharpening one's knowledge of men), and at the same time draw a shirt over one's own skin (defending one's own exposed spirit).

Thus even during the Renaissance (especially during the sixteenth century) *there appeared what we may call the 'incognito', with two different sorts of content and purpose*. The offensive incognito was an active dissembler, toying with others in order to achieve its goals; the defensive incognito was not a dissembler or a hypocrite but sought, by barricading the self, to prevent others from toying with it.

It is no accident that these two forms of incognito, and the moral, psychological, and socio-philosophical problems surrounding them, were analysed and described in all their complexity in England. It was in Elizabethan England that there emerged, together and simultaneously, those phenomena which gave rise to this new, double incognito, and not slowly and gradually as in Italy, but quite abruptly. Primitive accumulation, the dissolution of old traditions, the decay of feudal restrictions, and the restructuring of values all took place during the sixteenth century, at a time when inwardness and subjectivity had already developed. Thus it became possible to survey the whole problem in all its complexity. Such attempts can be seen above all in the works of Bacon and Shakespeare.

Bacon set out very often indeed to analyse the problem of our knowledge of men. He started out from the conviction that character had to be 'sought after' – it was not possible to perceive it immediately, and moreover *not every* situation was suitable for becoming acquainted with it. 'A man's nature is best perceived in *privateness*, for there is no affection; in *passion*, for that putteth a man out of his precepts; and in a *new case of experiment*, for there custom leaveth him.'[59]

209

It would seem unnecessary to analyse the cases listed; anyone can easily see that Bacon shrewdly put his finger on those situations which really bring out a man's essential nature. I should like to make two observations here, however. The first is that Bacon did not have in mind, by any means, conscious dissemblers alone. He was aware of the more modern forms of role-playing as well, which do not necessarily spring from deliberate deceit but from *conformist* principles and practices, and which are likewise products of the capitalist division of labour. If we constantly adjust our principles and practices to 'other people', without ever asking whether they are right or not and without ever seeking to realize ourselves in our principles and practice, then the separation of essence and appearance must follow – and what is more, a loss of essence – even without any conscious intention to harm or deceive. But it is also true of this type of person that passion, or a new, unexpected situation, can knock him out of his rut, for it is precisely in such situations that stereotypes frequently fail to stand up.

The other point worth exploring is the expression 'experiment', together with that of a 'new case'. These terms indicate that Bacon was no stranger to the idea of enriching our knowledge of men by consciously 'putting it to the test', that is by placing a character to be studied into an artificial situation planned out in advance. Here is a problem which we will meet again in connection with Shakespeare.

In another place Bacon deals at length with the various forms of defensive dissimulation. He discerns two basic principles. The first: without a certain amount of dissimulation one cannot defend one's life and individuality. The second: if dissembling turns into a person's regular behaviour, if it becomes hypocrisy, then that person is lost once again, for he loses what is most important, his moral individuality. *Absolute sincerity and hypocrisy are the extreme forms of conduct. A 'mean' between them has to be sought.*

Let us see what Bacon thinks of the two extremes. 'Nakedness is uncomely, as well in mind as body,'[60] he writes in one place. And again: 'The discovery of a man's self by the traits of his countenance is a great weakness and betraying.'[61] But on the other hand: 'A general custom of simulation ... is a vice',[62] because it 'depriveth a man of one of the most principal instruments for action; which is trust and belief'.[63] These maxims themselves are highly characteristic. The disapproving passage about 'nakedness of mind' is a direct appeal to decorum. Unconventional aspects of decorum, such as may combine the formalities of human behaviour with a sense of the concrete situation, may appear in the form of keeping back one's own thoughts in word and behaviour, or outright concealment (I have already discussed, in another connection, the matter of tact). And this reticence is one way of checking that brutality which, as we have seen, was an everyday occurrence during the Renaissance. Facial expression, as a direct mirror of feelings, comes under criticism from Bacon from two points of view. It is imprudence in so far as through it a man 'gives himself away'; and it is 'weakness' in so far as he cannot keep himself under control, but frequently violates tact, decorum, and humanity (and as such it is a manifestation of lack of cultivation, recklessness, and brutality).

Let us now turn to the principles raised against hypocrisy. The first is purely ethical, while the second refers to the success of one's practice; but the two are closely connected. Bacon clearly felt that hypocrisy as a regular form of conduct, as a 'vice', was in the end doomed to failure in practice as well. Thus we ought not to underestimate men's moral reserves. Those moral reserves can be the source of practical success, too. And first among them are *fidelity and trust*. Let us take note of them, for we will meet with them again in Shakespeare.

Between his extremes Bacon distinguishes three main types of self-concealment or incognito:[64]

> The first, *Closeness*, Reservation, and Secrecy; when a man
> leaveth himself without observation, or without hold to be
> taken, what he is. The second, *Dissimulation*, in the negative;
> when a man lets fall signs and arguments, that he is not that
> he is. And the third, *Simulation*, in the affirmative; when a man
> industriously and expressly feigns and pretends to be that he is not.

There are several stages, then, leading from a defensive, passive incognito to an offensive, active one. But Bacon is quite clear about the fact that no Chinese wall separates these stages from one another. A man who chooses 'Closeness' may occasionally slip over into 'Dissimulation', while someone who does not wish to go beyond dissimulation may sometimes, willy-nilly, slip into active hypocrisy or 'Simulation' (and may also, in certain circumstances, revert to 'Closeness'). There is always a certain amount of 'elbow room' for the incognito; whoever wishes to remain true to his own incognito must leave himself a little space, so he can move freely in one direction or the other. 'No man can be secret, except he give himself a little *scope* of dissimulation; which is, as it were, but the skirts or train of secrecy.'[65]

Thus Bacon is far from regarding the various sorts of feigning as being entirely unproblematical. In all feigning, even the most elementary, there is a risk, and that risk, moreover, is both moral and practical: the greater the risk, the more easily and imperceptibly one can slip from ordinary self-concealment to the level of hypocritical conduct. It is true that complete sincerity has its own hazards as well, and these, too (as we have seen), are not only moral but also practical (disregard of decorum, of the right moment and the situation, tactlessness). What then is the right choice?

Here Bacon has recourse, unwittingly, to the Aristotelian principle of the mean. First of all, he writes, *the individual's choice of conduct must be in keeping with his own character*. From that point of view, however, the most important character trait is wisdom or sagacity (*phronésis*). With Bacon the Aristotelian concept of *phronésis* is expanded to include a new dimension, that of knowledge of men. The man who knows other men well, who possesses *phronésis*, can allow himself to be sincere so far as his general conduct or dominant attitude is concerned, for with the help of a sound knowledge of men he will be able to sense at what point in his contact with people he must abruptly withdraw into himself again. A bad judge of men, however, lacking sagacity, must necessarily turn to hypocrisy in order to maintain himself, for he is unable to sense which men and which junctures are dangerous. Insincerity is the greater danger for the former, sincerity for the latter.

> For if a man have that penetration of judgment as he can
> discern what things are to be laid open, and what to be
> secreted, and what to be shewed at half lights, and to whom
> and when . . . to him a habit of dissimulation is a hinderance
> and a poorness. But if a man cannot obtain to that judgment,
> then it is left to him to be close, and a dissembler.[66]

Truly astute men could be open and sincere, 'for they could tell passing well when to stop or turn; and at such times when they thought the case indeed required dissimulation . . . they used it. . . .'[67]

It turns out, then, that *knowledge of men is that aspect of* phronesis *around which the other values range themselves*, and on which the morality and success of men's actions turn. Only a good judge of men can be, at one and the same time, both honourable and successful; the others *either* come to grief *or* lower themselves, or else they both abase themselves *and* come to grief.

Shakespeare presents us with a whole gallery of villains who manipulate the contradiction between essence and appearance, and who, recognizing the trust, good faith, and helplessness of honourable men, withdraw into their incognitos in order to toy with them.

212

Something of the sort is present in germ even in the first usurp̣
Henry IV. He, too, presents a good front until he becomes king,
and then he turns against his former supporters. But in Henry IV
this trait is present, indeed, only in germ, for he lacks what is
common to Shakespeare's other villains: an awareness of the game
they are playing, a conscious use of their own intellect and will – the
cat-and-mouse spirit. The first who approximates to this type is
Richard, Duke of York, and even in him both old and new features
are mixed. He would never, for example, be Machiavellian in
dealing with his own family. To a greater or lesser degree Suffolk,
Somerset, and most of the other members of Henry VI's court
follow the same course, each according to his own character. It is
from this *common* soil that Shakespeare's classical villain springs,
Richard III, who violates every old restraint and works his wickedness on everyone and everything without distinction.

In the figure of Richard III the transformation of essence and
appearance into a conscious opposition turns into role-playing, and
dissimulation into a principle of life:[68]

> Why, I can smile, and murder while I smile,
> And cry, 'Content,' to that which grieves my heart,
> And wet my cheeks with artificial tears,
> And frame my face to all occasions. . . .
> I can add colours to the chameleon,
> Change shapes with Proteus for advantages,
> And set the murd'rous Machiavel to school.

Thus Richard speaks already in *Henry VI*.

Later, in *Richard III*, he gives Buckingham a lesson in his art:[69]

> Come, cousin, canst thou quake, and change thy colour,
> Murder thy breath in middle of a word,
> And then again begin, and stop again,
> As if thou wert distraught and mad with terror?

And this lesson finds a practical confirmation in the scene of the
election of the king.

Richard's deceitfulness sometimes comes close to comedy, for he
not only hides his real self and wraps his villainy in an incognito; in
addition, he constantly lays emphasis upon his own honesty and
innocence. 'I am too childish-foolish for this world,' he tells Margaret.[70] And the result is that only Margaret really sees through him,
while his own men do not, for she, too, is a conscious deceiver.
Even after Richard has given the order for his execution, Hastings
can still say of him:[71]

> I think there's never a man in Christendom
> Can lesser hide his hate or love than he;
> For by his face straight shall you know his heart.

In his conscious manipulation of the contradiction between essence and appearance, the internal and the external, Iago displays a very similar psychology. (At present I am analysing these figures of Shakespeare's only in this one regard. It hardly need be said, of course, that there are qualitative differences among them, not only as regards the totality of their personalities but also in their order of greatness. Even in his villainy Richard is a great man, while Iago is petty. It is no accident that the first is the hero of a tragedy, while the other is only an intriguer.)

Iago reveals the duplicity of his character thus:[72]

> In following him, I follow but myself;
> Heaven is my judge, not I for love and duty,
> *But seeming so, for my peculiar end:*
> For when my outward action doth demonstrate
> The native act and figure of my heart
> In compliment extern, 'tis not long after
> But I will wear my heart upon my sleeve
> For daws to peck at: *I am not what I am.*

These Shakespearean villains know what moral autonomy is; they are aware that man chooses relatively freely between good and evil, and that in that choice *reason* plays a guiding role. "Tis in ourselves that we are thus, or thus,' says Iago. 'Our bodies are our gardens, to the which our wills are gardeners. . . .'[73] Edmund, again, philosophizes as follows:[74]

This is the excellent foppery of the world, that, when we are sick in fortune, – often the surfeit of our own behaviour, – we make guilty of our disasters the sun, the moon, and the stars; as if we were villains by necessity, fools by heavenly compulsion, knaves, thieves, and treachers by spherical predominance, drunkards, liars, and adulterers by an enforced obedience of planetary influence; and all that we are evil in, by a divine thrusting on. . . . My father compounded with my mother under the dragon's tail and my nativity was under Ursa major; so that it follows I am rough and lecherous. 'Sfoot! I should have been that I am, had the maidenliest star in the firmament twinkled on my bastardizing.

Richard, Iago, and Edmund are all convinced that reason enlarges a man's freedom of choice and action, and gives him a kind of *security* in his actions, for reason can discern certain necessary tendencies – whether those tendencies lie in objective social laws, or in the laws of individual men's characters, or perhaps in the interaction of the two. When they toy with men who trust in them, there is a secondary purpose to their sport alongside their main goal, which is always power and gain. That is to test their strength and their wits, and to enjoy the feeling that they know men and the world and know how to play with them at will. 'If thou canst cuckold him, thou dost thyself a pleasure, me a sport,' says Iago to Roderigo.[75] Here the power of reason is realized, and yet at the same time it is perverted by its negative moral content. For toying with people always has a negative content, even when it is done for its own sake, without any intention to harm. For at such times, too, one man becomes a mere *instrument* in the hands of another. That is always inhuman, whether it is done for a negative purpose or only to test the ingenuity of the agent, for whenever it is done one man's moral autonomy is realized only by depriving others of theirs. Thus Iago takes away Othello's freedom of action and Edmund takes away Gloster's, bringing them to actions which do not follow from their essences and thus turning men into things. (I will return later to analyse the fact that, in Shakespeare, these villains are never ultimately successful.)

The possibility of a conflict between the external and the internal, appearance and essence, does not necessarily manifest itself only in conscious evildoers. It may also appear – and in Shakespeare's world it does appear – with the signs reversed, when certain still unrecognized new virtues lie hidden beneath the outer shell, unfamiliar, unaccustomed, suspicious virtues.

> Opinion's but a fool, that makes us scan
> The outward habit by the inward man,

says Simonides,[76] referring to just this phenomenon. Social rank, an impressive manner, decorous behaviour, and the like are not at all expressive of inner content.

The problem of knowing men thus becomes very complex for Shakespeare; and, as a result, we can discern even in his great, rational, morally upright heroes a behaviour or procedure which at first glance resembles his villains' propensity for toying with people. That is the practice of *putting people to a test*. The greatest Shakespearean heroes often put men to the test in order to learn more about them, to find out what lies behind the front they put up. They devise artificial circumstances which will produce one reaction or another, good or bad, in the men whom they wish to study, so as to acquire certain knowledge of their real selves. Thus Hamlet tests Claudius, and Prospero tests not only the scoundrels but Ferdinand as well. These trials have nothing in common with the medieval trial by ordeal, for there chance (allegedly, God) made the decision; here, however, men's own behaviour is decisive, as positively or negatively evaluated by the person who puts them to the test, with his knowledge of men. *In principle*, the boundaries between test and sport are quite firm and clear. The purpose of a test is always a moral purpose with a positive value-content (Hamlet tries to find out whether Claudius really deserves to be condemned to death); toying with people, on the other hand, is partly a goal in itself, and partly serves the advantage of the manipulator. Later on, these two types of conduct became even more polarized, with that polarization reaching its culmination during the Enlightenment. Toying with people is exposed as the most extreme form of aristocratically inhuman conduct in Laclos' *Les Liaisons dangereuses*, while being put to the test becomes one means of humanist education (compare the *Nouvelle Héloïse* or *Wilhelm Meister*). But if in principle the differences are clear and unequivocal, Shakespeare saw clearly – more clearly than the writers of the Enlightenment did later on – that in practice the two forms of conduct can approximate to each other and that the dividing line can become blurred. Who can judge whether Posthumus is testing Imogen, or whether he is toying with her? At the same time, anyone who puts others to the test must manipulate himself, too, just as the villain-figures do (though this self-manipulation has a different content). He must not give away his real self. Thus Hamlet plays the madman, Prospero the tyrant. The truly great and upright testers are those who (unlike Posthumus) preserve in the midst of every game the integrity of their essential selves, never identify themselves with their roles and at the same time never play an unworthy role, and remain at heart something that cannot be 'performed' or acted out. As Hamlet says:[77]

> I know not 'seems.
> 'Tis not alone my inky cloak, good mother,
> Nor customary suits of solemn black,
> Nor windy suspiration of forced breath,
> No, nor the fruitful river in the eye,
> Nor the dejected 'haviour of the visage,
> Together with all forms, moods, shapes of grief,
> That can denote me truly: these indeed seem,

For they are actions that a man might play:
But I have that within which passeth show;
These but the trappings and the suits of woe.

If we examine the plays of Shakespeare we can see that there is
always some identity of substance among those figures who know
men well, and among those who know them badly. Let us consider
first those tragic figures who are *trusting to the point of naïvety*, and
who come to grief because of their naïve trust. The most prominent,
in the order of their creation, are Gloster, Othello, Lear, and Timon.
The sources of their blind trust are various, and so the content of
their catharses varies. But common to them all is the fact that their
naïvety and their absolute trust is the source of their greatness as
well. Beyond a doubt, Shakespeare depicted this type of hero with
affection. The unsuspecting, honest psyche, untouched by the calculating intellect, incapable either of toying with people or of putting
them to the test, was in and of itself the most attractive type of
character in the eyes of the English dramatist. But he clearly saw –
and to an ever-increasing degree – that that type of character was
no longer for this world – not so much because it inevitably came to
grief, but rather because, in its naïve trustfulness, it lent itself to the
triumph of evil. Prospero, looking back on his youthful trustfulness,
put it thus:[78]

I, thus neglecting wordly end, all dedicated
To closeness and the bettering of my mind
What that . . .
. . . in my false brother
Awak'd an evil nature; and *my trust*,
Like a good parent, *did beget of him*
A falsehood in its contrary as great
As my trust was. . . .

The awareness that naïve confidence in others fosters evil, its
opposite, developed slowly in Shakespeare's work and successively
modified the author's attitude towards these great naïve figures.
Gloster is still an unequivocally noble figure, free of contradictions.
True, his naïve humanity is one of the causes of England's becoming
a prey to the noble houses who are contending in the Wars of the
Roses, but he himself works no evil, his hands and his heart remain
clean to the very end. Othello goes on to commit his tragic crime;
his naïvety gives rise to his murder of Desdemona. But his terrible
error, the outcome of his trust in Iago, is motivated by the plotting

of an intriguer, which Othello cannot see through; and for that reason the sublime integrity of Othello's moral being is not dissipated. With Lear, again, the situation is already different. At the beginning of the tragedy Lear appears as a stubborn, obstinate old man. He is promptly warned – as Othello was not – that his confidence in his two daughters is unfounded and mistaken. Lear loves flattery – already a flaw of character – and for that reason he takes Cordelia's openness and sincerity for disdain. Thus Lear's kind of naïvety is morally suspect from the very outset. Lear rises to the plane of moral and human candour only when he faces up to the evil his wrong-headedness has produced, after he has come to know suffering. The same is true of Timon in even greater measure. While he places an absolute trust in his friends, almost his whole entourage sees that that confidence is unfounded. Apemantus and the Poet warn him several times – but all to no avail. In Timon elements of self-conceit are already mingled with his lack of knowledge of men. For he sees relatively clearly that men in general may leave one another in the lurch, but he is convinced that this cannot happen *to him*. He blindly attributes to his own personal attractiveness the goodwill which he has bought with his generosity. For Timon – by contrast with the other great naïve figures – there is not even a catharsis at the end.

From the succession of these great naïve protagonists, and the changes in their characters, we can draw certain conclusions about the alteration of Shakespeare's outlook on the world. As the possibility of a divergence between essence and appearance, the internal and the external, grows ever more likely, and as the demand for a new, more complex knowledge of men grows ever more exacting, naïvety comes to lose not only its effectiveness but also its moral worth as well. Magnanimous human conduct in a world which is becoming more and more a breeding ground for evil – we may recall in this connection Prospero's words, Shakespeare's own swan-song – gradually becomes problematical and ceases to be magnanimous human conduct any longer. Not only is the *world* of great naïve figures waning, but with it also the very possibility of *great* naïve personalities existing at all.

It is a common trait of character in Shakespeare's naïve figures that when they are deceived in their trust the whole world always collapses for them. Othello, thinking to have acquired proof of Desdemona's unfaithfulness, bids farewell to his *whole life*, not only to love but to the wars and the service of Venice as well. Lear in the tempest scene sees his whole past as useless and vain. Trapped by one or two men, they conclude from these single acts of wrongdoing that the real

218

world is evil in its entirety. As Claudius says in *Much Ado About Nothing*, in the scene where the play takes a tragic turn:[79]

> But fare thee well, most foul, most fair! farewell,
> Thou pure impiety, and impious purity!
> *For thee I'll lock up all the gates of love,*
> And on my eyelids shall conjecture hang,
> To turn *all* beauty into thoughts of harm,
> And never shall it more be gracious.

The psychological switch-over from general trustfulness to general mistrust is proper to every one of Shakespeare's naïve characters. But just as their natures grow problematical ethically, so too does disillusionment sharpen into *misanthropy*. They do not withdraw their confidence in those places where they ought to, they do not trust people they should trust – in a word, they always lose the right measure. The loss of all measure characterizes the last of the naïve figures, that of Timon, when he says:[80]

> Burn, house! sink, Athens! henceforth hated be of Timon
> man and all humanity!

And a little later he curses all of mankind:[81]

> The gods confound – hear me, you good gods all –
> The Athenians both within and out that wall!
> And grant, as Timon grows, his hate may grow
> To the whole race of mankind, high and low!
> Amen!

While Gloster, Othello, Lear, Timon, and their like perish in their naïvety, Shakespeare's clever villains are all excellent judges of men. (The qualification 'clever villains' is very important, for a Macbeth or Caliban is not distinguished by great knowledge of men.) In Richard, Iago, and Edmund knowledge of men becomes a principle of evil, and an instrument by which men can be manipulated. These scoundrels know perfectly those whom they wish to deceive. Consider, for example, Iago's analysis:[82]

> The Moor is of a free and open nature,
> That thinks men honest that but seem to be so,
> And will as tenderly be led by the nose
> As asses are.

There is, however, a psychological rub to this kind of knowledge of men, and that is the fact that it springs from a contempt for human beings. Shakespeare's clever villains see all men as knaves or fools,

219

or at least as such whose good qualities themselves can be turned to bad ends. In the Shakespearean reality they are the bearers of a pessimistic world-view. The source of their scorn for mankind is some sort of injury, just as in the case of the naïve heroes who turn into misanthropes. And it is the size and legitimacy of this grievance which determines, among other things, the weight of these evil figures. Of the three villains we have mentioned, Iago has the smallest grievance – Othello has not made him his lieutenant, though by reason of his seniority the position should have been his, and allegedly the Moor has slept with Iago's wife Emilia. Edmund's injury is greater: he cannot put his abilities to use because he was born a bastard, and thus ranks as someone beyond the bounds of society. The disappointment which has made Richard scornful of men is not only quantitatively greater but also qualitatively different. As his father's most able, most intelligent, and bravest son he has risked his life fighting for his crown, only to see it go to his brother Edward, who, for the sake of his pleasures, bargains away England's interests and who would have been succeeded by Clarence, the previous traitor to the common cause of the House of York. And he must accept the fact that his weak brothers have come to peaceful terms with those who had a part in the murder of his father and younger brother. These are the offences which have made him contemptuous of men. But whatever the root of these men's scorn, their common feature is a denial of the existence and power of virtue on this earth.

That, however, is the only trait in common between the trusting spirits who, deceived, turn into misanthropes, and the scoundrels who become contemptuous of men: a deprecation of human values. The villains feel at home in a world they think devoid of any values, while the naïve, disillusioned heroes are unhappy – for contempt for people is a coolly dispassionate feeling, while hatred is only love reversed. The fact that the world is evil gives the scorners of men their psychological balance, while the misanthropes have lost their human equilibrium because of that same fact. This contradiction emerges time and again in the resolution of the tragedies. For both types are again mistaken. Those who are contemptuous of men are forced to recognize that there still remain in the world human values which stand up against their wickedness. Iago does not reckon with Emilia's testifying against him, nor Richard with the fact that his despairing nobles (like Stanley) will risk everything for Henry's victory, nor Edmund with his brother Edgar's loyalty to his father. Similarly the great naïve heroes, too, are 'deceived' again in their despair. Othello must learn that Desdemona was true to him, Lear

220

that Cordelia is a loving daughter, Timon that his servant Flavius will not leave him even in his misery, and Posthumus that Imogen has not deceived him. For the despisers of men, the survival of values calls into doubt their whole behaviour and their pessimistic world-picture. They have been deceived twice in the world and they die as its enemies. They have lost the game. The great naïve figures, however, find themselves again in this second 'disillusionment'; their existence acquires a new meaning and justification. And for that reason they are exalted even in their destruction. Was it, then, really the great naïve characters who were poor judges of men, and the scoundrels who were good judges? Shakespeare's moral world does not suggest that conclusion. Those who trusted blindly did not recognize the power of evil, and so they were unable to orient themselves in a world growing evil. The clever villains, on the other hand, did not recognize the power of goodness. For that reason they make their way not just better, but for the most part with great precision as well, and yet in the end they always come to grief. During the period of the great tragedies Shakespeare still thought that in the last analyses those who constantly renew their trust in human beings are right. Jan Kott, the outstanding Polish Shakespeare scholar, is wrong in speaking of the pessimism of Shakespeare's entire life-work. It is in Shakespeare's tragedies, if anywhere, that pessimism is rejected in the end.

It is true that the content and tendency of the representation changes during the dramatist's last period. The way in which the figure of Timon is depicted is characteristic of that change. Timon is the only naïve Shakespearean hero who experiences no catharsis, remaining a misanthrope to the very end; even his servant's faithfulness cannot convince him of the one-sidedness of his feelings. But even here the world has not become completely hopeless – for Flavius belongs to that same world, too; it is not that the world has darkened completely (at most, *nearly* completely) – rather naïve, blind trust, always liable to swing over into misanthropy, has lost its former worth.

Is there any kind of human conduct which points beyond the alternatives of naïve (good) blindness and shrewd (evil) knowledge of men? Shakespeare again and again presents this *tertium datur*, in the form of heroes who have learned to know the world through their own experience and who are able to live rationally, without becoming either misanthropes or scorners of men, because they can recognize good as well as evil. The most prominent among them (again in the order of their creation) are Henry V, Hamlet, and Prospero.

Falstaff and Hotspur are the two figures counterposed to Henry V. Hotspur is the embodiment of the noblest passions of knightly chivalry, but he knows men – and the new world – so little that his ardour sometimes comes near to obtuseness. Falstaff, on the other hand, is well aware that the old norms are becoming relative – only recall his monologue on honour – and from that he draws the conclusion that a man must be cynical and cowardly. Henry V, while he is still Prince Hal, learns to know the world, but not in order to adapt to it. Warwick rightly says of him:[83]

> The prince but studies his companions
> Like a strange tongue, wherein, to gain the language,
> 'Tis needful that the most immodest word
> Be look'd upon, and learned. . . .
> . . . And their memory
> Shall as a pattern or a measure live,
> By which his Grace must mete the lives of others.

Undoubtedly Henry V does not belong, all in all, among Shakespeare's best-drawn characters. True, all those properties which the playwright sketches in his figure, even in *Henry IV*, make him capable of becoming, in principle, a great king. But for such a character to get through the perils of the age, a certain utopianism is necessary on one hand, and, on the other, an increased flexibility and adaptability, qualities which destroy the unity of his personality. But however that may be, Shakespeare here tried to create a positive hero who would observe a proper 'measure' between cynicism and blind faith, not only in the moment of his triumph but throughout his entire life. Thus in creating his other great and favourite figure in the person of Hamlet (who fails, for in *Hamlet* Shakespeare is indulging in no utopias), the dramatist expresses his own conviction when at the end of the play Fortinbras says that had he reached the throne, Hamlet would have been a great king.

Hamlet knows the world in which he lives. His studies at Wittenberg, the horrible experience of seeing evil lodging in his own house, and the injury of having been deprived by murder of his crown, have all taught him that 'the time is out of joint'. For that reason he is characterized, even at the beginning of the play, by a hostility and suspicion towards the dignitaries of the castle of Elsinore, a hostility and suspicion which never lays hold of the spirits of the naïve heroes who do not know that the time is out of joint. With them, suspicion never develops until later and never finds its real target. Hamlet's suspicions, however, are always well-founded. Even in the opening moments his remarkable knowledge of men and situations is demonstrated. Goodness does not escape his attention any more than evil. (In that he once more resembles Henry V, who after the discovery of the conspiracy does indeed lose his faith in men for an instant, but then, when his spiritual equilibrium has been restored, learns to trust again.) In the second scene Hamlet asks Horatio what has brought him to Elsinore, and when Horatio answers, 'A truant disposition, good my lord', Hamlet rejoins:[84]

> I would not hear your enemy say so,
> Nor shall you do mine ear that violence,
> To make it truster of your own report
> Against yourself; *I know* you are no truant.

Questioning people, drawing prompt conclusions from their answers and from what he reads in their eyes, the emphasis on 'I know' – all these are typical of Hamlet's methods of getting to know about them. They are evident in his first scene with Rosencrantz and Guildenstern. At first he greets his two old friends with complete trust. But then suspicion quickly grips him, and in order to be certain, he questions them, quickly drawing the conclusion from their vacuous answers that he must take care, these men are enemies. This is the place to suspend all confidence and to hide his real self behind a mask. 'Were you not sent for?' he asks Rosencrantz and Guildenstern, and when they temporize he tells them:[85]

> You were sent for; and there is a kind of confession in your
> looks which your modesties have not craft enough to colour:
> *I know* the good king and queen have sent for you.

His method of questioning is repeated in the great scene with Ophelia. At the beginning of their conversation, Hamlet has no idea that they are being eavesdropped upon. That is why, in coming to terms with his love, he first accuses himself. The first suspicions are planted in his heart by Ophelia's own behaviour. It is then that he asks her: 'Where's your father?' And it is only after her reply 'At home, my lord' that he displays malice, even hostility towards her. The stage direction introduced, in particular, in the Olivier film version, of having Hamlet at that moment accidentally catch sight of Polonius and the king lurking behind the arras, is quite superfluous. It detracts from the essence of Hamlet's character, his uncanny knowledge of men. The man who could read something from Rosencrantz and Guildenstern's eyes as they answered his quick question could certainly see the lie in the eyes of someone better known and beloved to him!

Hamlet's intellectual knowledge of men makes it possible for him to play with others, while raising an absolute barrier to their efforts to toy with him. He tells his alleged 'friends':[86]

Why, look you now, how unworthy a *thing* you make of me.
You would play upon me; you would seem to know my stops;
you would pluck out the heart of my mystery; you would
sound me from my lowest note to the top of my compass; and
there is much music, excellent voice, in this little organ, yet
cannot you make it speak. 'Sblood, do you think I am easier
to be played on than a pipe?

As I have said, it is characteristic of Hamlet's conduct to put people to the test, rather than to toy with them. The latter he reserves for small-bore scoundrels, flunkies, and favour-seekers, whom he really does despise but does not hate. In that sense, even toying with people gains a relatively positive ethical content; it is a way of doing justice, as with Polonius:[87]

Hamlet: Do you see yonder cloud that's almost in shape of a
             camel?
Polonius: By the mass, and 'tis like a camel, indeed.
Hamlet: Methinks it is like a weasel.
Polonius: It is backed like a weasel.
Hamlet: Or like a whale?
Polonius: Very like a whale.

In Hamlet's eyes, knowledge of men is not just a means of doing justice, but a means to honour and to life itself, and a moral value in itself. In the great scene with his mother it is primarily for her lack of knowledge of men that he finds fault with the queen. That, according to Hamlet, involved her in crime:[88]

Look here, upon this picture, and on this;
The counterfeit presentment of two brothers. . . .
              . . . Have you eyes?
Could you on this fair mountain leave to feed,
And batten on this moor? . . .
             . . . What devil was't
That thus hath cozen'd you at hoodman-blind?
Eyes without feeling, feeling without sight,
Ears without hands or eyes, smelling sans all,
Or but a sickly part of one true sense
Could not so mope.

224

Of all Shakespeare's heroes, then, Hamlet is the best judge of men, able to perceive good and evil and to elevate knowledge of men into a general means, even a means of *doing justice,* and to consider knowledge of men an ethical value in itself. But then we still must ask: how does this Hamlet come to grief precisely through faulty knowledge of men, when he fails to see through the part which Laertes has to play in the conspiracy that has been woven against him?

We can immediately dismiss the king's explanation:[89]

> He, being remiss,
> Most generous and free from all contriving,
> Will not peruse the foils. . . .

The king, a calculating villain, identifies honesty with naïvety. Moreover, he knows only the former Prince Hamlet, as he was before becoming disenchanted. The new Hamlet has always played a role in front of him. And yet the king is right. Hamlet does not examine the foils. But only because he is unsuspecting? Is a man unsuspecting who is capable of creeping into his former friends' cabin by night, stealing the king's letter from them, reading it, and then calmly sending his two 'friends' to the executioner? There are very special and concrete reasons for Hamlet's lack of suspicion, for the first and only lapse in his knowledge of men. First of all, he has known Laertes for a long time, but he has not had occasion to study him in the disturbed state of mind into which the death of his father, Polonius, has cast him. Nevertheless, Laertes' behaviour at Ophelia's grave becomes offensive to Hamlet, and so he insults him there. And now that insult proves Hamlet's own undoing. He is troubled by guilt *vis-à-vis* Laertes. Hamlet, who is so careful not to be unjust to anyone, feels that he has been unjust with someone whose lot is comparable to his own. He puts it all to Horatio thus:[90]

> But I am very sorry, good Horatio,
> That to Laertes I forgot myself;
> For, by the image of my cause, I see
> The portraiture of his: I'll court his favours:
> But, sure, the bravery of his grief put me
> Into a towering passion.

His concern about his own misdeed, and the desire to 'court the favours' of Laertes, blind Hamlet, and so he accepts the challenge to a duel.

The best judge of men can go wrong once, but it is only very rarely that that mistake is irreparable. In Hamlet's case the irreparability springs from factors that go well beyond the problem of knowledge of men. I cannot analyse here the content of, and the reasons for his tragedy. At this point it is enough to say that Hamlet sought with the help of his knowledge of men to put right a time that was out of joint; that was what he felt to be his mission and his duty. Time out of joint, however, *could not* to be set right any longer.

That is the lesson drawn by Prospero in *The Tempest*. He, too, has attained to knowledge of men at the cost of grave disillusion-ment, and has grasped the truth that, in a world of villains, trust only works to the advantage of the wicked. Practically every major type of Shakespearean villain appears on stage in *The Tempest*, from Caliban to Antonio. Through his wisdom Prospero curbs them all and forces them to serve him, or at least obliges them, under threat of compulsion, to act properly in spite of their own intentions. Here, as with Henry V or Hamlet, knowledge of men is an ethical value and a means of doing justice.

And yet that is true only with several qualifications. First of all, Prospero triumphs over evil not in the real world, but rather in a fable, in imagination – that is, in the world of art. He turns appear-ance into reality, but he is incapable of turning reality into appear-ance. After he breaks his magic staff, his power of *cognition* is no longer joined to an effectiveness in *action*. The unity of knowledge and deed, which in the real world has become problematic (Hamlet), is restored, but only in the world of art. Prospero returns to Milan, but not to govern, for he cannot govern without the power of magic.

At the same time, Prospero no longer wishes to set right a time that is out of joint. His figure is characterized by resignation. He can no longer defeat evil in the real world, since it has become general; and in a world where goodness appears in the shape of the vacuous Gonzalo, such an enterprise would be but a vain hope. Doing justice appears here in the form of *forgiveness*. Prospero says of the assembled scoundrels:[91]

> They being penitent,
> The sole drift of my purpose doth extend
> Not a frown further. . . .

Leontes in *The Winter's Tale* had to wait sixteen years for forgive-ness, but the villains of *The Tempest* do not need to wait at all. And why? If men in general are such, then we can do nothing else but forgive them – but in such a way that we keep them in our power. Here the leitmotif of Mozart's *Così Fan Tutte* first makes itself heard in world literature.

At the same time, Prospero's resignation is still only relative. He has seen through men, and yet there is still a place in the world for naïve trust. Miranda, newly awakened to love, is filled with it when she first comes upon earthly creatures:[92]

> How many goodly creatures are there here!
> How beauteous mankind is! O brave new world,
> That has such people in it!

And Prospero's ironic rejoinder, "'Tis new to thee', does not at all contest the justice of his daughter's rapture and wonder.

In Shakespeare's eyes, those who can recognize and follow the proper mean between cynicism and blind trust, naïvety and contempt for mankind, are the ones who in their true nature are capable of standing their ground in a world whose norms are in dissolution. From that point of view – and, to repeat, abstracting from other sides of the matter – they are the ones born for this world and born to rule. But they are made only for a world in which it is still possible and worthwhile to rule. Henry V is still a great king, who achieves in the real world the unity of knowledge and deed. Hamlet might have been a great king, living in the real world, but in him the unity of knowledge and action is broken. Prospero, finally, is the king of the world of art, in whom that unity is restored again – but only in imagination. In the eyes of the aging poet the kingdom of reality is no longer a region where great men can realize themselves and govern.

Shakespeare always reveals how complex is a good or bad knowledge of men. Some of his great naïve figures, for example, are poor judges of men only *vis-à-vis* the new phenomena thrown up by a 'time out of joint', but they are very good at evaluating the possibilities afforded by ability and character in other aspects of life. Lear recognizes instantly that the disguised Kent will make a loyal servant, because in dealing with servants he has a good eye. Othello certainly knew very well how to choose men for battle; he quickly recognized who would be a good or bad *soldier*, as his victories attest. There is a type of Shakespearean hero who in his knowledge of men misses the measure. Buckingham, for example, sees through Richard very well; but he measures him by his own villainy, and for that reason he can not foresee the consequences of his own momentary vacillation.

Shakespeare often demonstrated that there is no such thing as *all-round knowledge of men. Julius Caesar* documents that fact most comprehensively. Caesar and Cassius are first-rate judges of men where it is a matter of evaluating someone's *political* character. At the same time Brutus – as it turns out in every single instance – is incapable of assessing his rivals realistically from a political standpoint. All his political judgments are wrong. When Cassius and the other conspirators want to make an end of Mark Antony, Brutus repeatedly assures them that Caesar's young adherent is harmless:[93]

> For Mark Antony, think not of him;
> For he can do no more than Caesar's arm
> When Caesar's head is off. . . .
> . . . For he is given
> To sports, to wildness, and much company.

Cassius wishes at all costs to prevent Mark Antony from speaking at Caesar's bier. He knows Mark Antony will stir up the people. But Brutus only says, 'It shall advantage more than do us wrong.'[94] And Brutus's political blindness is a major reason why the supporters of the republic suffer defeat.

Does that mean that Brutus is a bad judge of men in general? Not at all. For his knowledge of men's moral character is greater than either Caesar's or Cassius's. Brutus perceives better than either of them who is an honest man and who a scoundrel, who can be regarded as a friend and who cannot. From that point of view, the contrast between the death of Brutus, and the deaths of Caesar and Cassius, is characteristic. (That is not altered by the fact that Brutus is incapable of assessing – as in the case of Mark Antony – just what an unscrupulous man is capable of.)

Let us consider Caesar. He gives a perfect diagnosis of Cassius, whom he deems to be a good judge of men politically and a rival:[95]

> Would he were fatter! but I fear him not:
> Yet if my name were liable to fear,
> I do not know the man I should avoid
> So soon as that spare Cassius. He reads much;
> He is a great observer, and *he looks*
> *Quite through the deeds of men*; he loves no plays,
> As thou dost, Antony; he hears no music;
> Seldom he smiles, and smiles in such a sort
> As if he mock'd himself, and scorn'd his spirit
> That could be mov'd to smile at any thing.
> Such men he be never at heart's ease
> Whiles they behold a greater than themselves,
> And therefore are they very dangerous.

How can it be that Caesar, who can peer into Cassius's soul with such clinical precision, still regards Brutus as a friend, almost a son, and thinks it unimaginable that Brutus should hatch any scheme against him? The answer is that Caesar has no knowledge of men's moral character. He is unable to comprehend what an adept of stoic morality can make up his mind to, even against the inclination of his heart. Hence his incredulous shock at the moment of his death, expressed in the despairing cry, 'Et tu, Brute!' Cassius suffers no such shock at the time of his death. Nor is it an accident that the man who has often bought his supporters with money – for which Brutus rebukes him in their quarrel scene – finds that the first servant he asks is willing to kill him, in the hope of gaining his own freedom. Brutus, on the other hand, cannot find a single servant who will, at his request, drive home the sword. And thus he draws the last lesson of his life, in the lines already cited:[96]

> My heart doth joy that yet, *in all may life,*
> *I found no man but he was true to me.*
> I shall have glory by this losing day,
> More than Octavius and Mark Antony
> By this vile conquest shall attain unto.

Shakespeare shows here in classical fashion that the unfolding or stunting of one or another aspect of knowledge of men is not an innate psychological datum, but develops very much under the influence of moral forces and of one's outlook on the world. Brutus' *Weltanschauung* and conduct are those of the *moralist*. Thence proceed directly the atrophy of his political knowledge of men, and the refinement of his private, moral knowledge of them.

In the world of action, the conflict between appearance and essence, the external and the internal, must always be resolved. For when a man acts, his real self must in fact come to the surface; he cannot remain cloaked in his incognito. That is the common ruin to which Shakespeare's clever villains come. Emilia loved the semblance of Iago, but as soon as his essence was revealed to her, her love was at an end. Richard III could pretend to be devout until he was made king, but afterwards he could not but show how he would rule. Then his real self appeared: he was capable only of murder. The semblance had been shattered. Behind the unctuous, unfortunate cripple the outlines of the odious tyrant took shape. When villainy ceases to give itself over to independent action, exposing its existence to fate, when it becomes common and general, then goodness cannot be an independent, autonomous agent any longer either – and drama is on the wane. When the essence can no longer be discovered behind the appearance, and when appearance loses its individual character, then that is the end of tragedy. *The soliloquy on money in Timon of Athens is the swan-song of tragedy.* That is the reason why this play is not in fact a tragedy, and one of the reasons why in *The Tempest* Shakespeare was obliged to take his leave of the stage.

In speaking of how, as gaining knowledge of men became more difficult, people began to seek refuge in an incognito, I have constantly stressed that this was a matter of *individuals'* incognitos. Outright accommodation, whether gradual or instantaneous, to systems of role and custom in which the individual is drained of his own essence and ceases to be an individual: that was a phenomenon which scarcely appeared at this time, for the age was one of striking individual personalities. Self-concealment, feigning, hypocrisy were still conscious; the individual still knew who he was but, in order to gain certain objectives, he wished to appear something different. Bacon, indeed, touched upon certain problems relating to other types of incognito, but these were never central for him. Man's absorption in his role, and the loss of his essential being, became commonplace only in the ever more conformist world of developed bourgeois society. The incognitos in Shakespeare's tragedies and comedies reveal only the physiognomy of conscious dissemblers; the exploration of the new type of incognito which developed with the rapid spread and generalization of role-behaviour was left to bourgeois drama. In that respect Peer Gynt, who goes through a whole series of adventures without becoming an individual, and whose soul resembles an onion without a central core, is the programmatic type of the hero of bourgeois drama.

Self-knowledge, then, is not problematical *in the same sense* as knowledge of other men. Knowledge of others became more difficult as dissembling, hypocritical attitudes became more widespread, but the same was *not* true of knowledge of oneself. The man who posed, played a role, and deceived others knew very well who he actually was himself. There was no question of 'Who am I?'

That is to say that during the Renaissance, men were generally aware that in realizing themselves, in practice, and in the pursuit of knowledge they successively became acquainted with their own selves as well. *Acquiring self-knowledge was not some sort of 'separate' activity – it came about simultaneously with the theoretical or practical appropriation of reality.* According to Charron, for example, all wisdom is self-knowledge. Animals lack self-knowledge (their knowledge is unaccompanied by self-knowledge), and therefore they are lacking in wisdom as well. The stoic-epicureans of the age believed, as we have seen, that knowledge of one's own nature was a precondition of correct action. But they did not separate that, in principle, from acquiring knowledge of nature in general. Nor did the question ever arise whether it is possible at all to gain knowledge of our own natures. A *positive* answer to that question was always *self-evident.*

230

Self-knowledge, as the study of human nature, means two things. It means, first, a general anthropology – acquiring knowledge of 'human nature', and the investigation of oneself as an individual belonging to the species 'man'. Since I will revert later to the problems of anthropology, I should merely like to note here that *anatomy*, too, became an organic part of self-knowledge. Man made his own organism and its biological functions an *object* of study. Second, there was the constant analysis of particularity. With an almost scientific objectivity individuals analysed their desires, passions, and secret thoughts. Hamlet says:[97]

I am myself indifferent honest; but yet I could accuse me of
such things that it were better my mother had not borne me.
I am very proud, revengeful, ambitious; with more offences at
my beck than I have thoughts to put them in, imagination to
give them shape, or time to act them in.

The birth of striking and colourful individual personalities, a greater degree of autonomy, the possibility of a rich and adventurous life, and the appearance of analytical forms of self-knowledge together made the Renaissance an *age of great autobiographies*.

In his study, *Design and Truth in Autobiography*, Roy Pascal has tellingly demonstrated that autobiography is a genre *peculiar to European civilization*. It is unknown in the oriental tradition; when it appears, as for example in the case of Gandhi, it already represents an instance of the adoption of the European tradition. But even in Western culture it appears relatively late.

There are numerous autobiographical statements in classical
Greek and Roman literature, accounts of things done or works
written, communings with the self. But never is the unique,
personal story, in its private as well as public aspect,
considered worthy of the single-minded devotion of the author,

writes Pascal.[98] St Augustine's *Confessions* are the first true autobiography. After that, however – in the Middle Ages – the form recedes into the background again. In medieval 'autobiographies', observation and description of the external world completely disappears behind the depiction of spiritual facts and experiences. Abélard's *Historia Calamitatum* is based on the *contradiction* between personal destiny and religious belief; it is limited to the revelation of erotic and religious experiences, obligations, and conflicts. Suso's *Dieners Leben* is no more than a parable of the fulfilment of God's will, while the hysterical visions of Margery

231

Kempe testify precisely to her insincerity and her lack of self-knowledge. Pascal reckons the revival of autobiography from Petrarch's *Letter to Posterity*; the three major works of its first efflorescence are those of Cellini, Cardano, and St Teresa.

Before we attempt to answer the question of why this was so, let us briefly review the characteristics of autobiography. Roy Pascal singles out the following: for the writer of autobiography, everything is *experience* – external and internal experience, and the unity of these experiences. Mere *facticity*, of the sort which has not been transformed into personal experience, may find a place in memoirs, but not in the autobiography. Pure subjectivity which has never taken on objective form may have a place in diaries or confessions, but not in autobiography. Thus the peculiarity of autobiography lies in the way it mirrors the unique *mutual interaction of the world and the individual's development*. And therefore the precondition for the validity, and even for the very rise, of autobiography is the existence of a *significant individual personality* and a *representative world*.[99]

Every autobiography is the history of the formation of a personality. To the extent that it describes how experiences educate a human being and how through those experiences he shapes himself, it is a *Bildungsroman*. One's lot in life abounds in mistakes, but these mistakes, and the fresh mistakes to which they give rise, nevertheless carry the whole man forward: experience means learning from the errors of the past. The individual is *enriched*; the successes, even if they are accidental, are the successes of his own personality, and the failures are relative, for they serve as lessons; *one's life is never a fiasco, even if many aspirations meet with defeat*.

This process of education has several aspects – *education for social life*, moral education, the development of one's capacities, education in one's *calling* or *craft*. Whichever autobiography we examine, all these aspects can be found together in it.

Let us consider now why in antiquity there was no autobiography, even though concern about education (*paideia*) occupied the very centre of attention for both thought and praxis. We can approach the answer by singling out a secondary phenomenon: in the ancient world only education for social life and morality presented a problem, so much so that in the last analysis the two were almost synonymous (the supreme good, according to Aristotle, was the good of the state), while the problem of education for a calling or trade simply did not exist. Think for a moment of Plato's noble letter written in old age, in which he looks back on his whole past life. Its great turning-points – those with which he had to come to terms and from which he had learned – were his meeting with Socrates, his master's condemnation to death, his disillusionment with the new Athenian city-state, the hopes he placed in the Sicilian tyrant Dionysius of Syracuse, his disillusionment with the latter, his disappointment with his pupils, and the like. These are all direct social experiences and theoretical moral lessons. It never occurred to Plato to speak of how or why he came to be a philosopher, why and how his theories developed as they did, in what way he became attracted to Socrates' ideas and how he later moved away from them, or how he moved towards 'the truth'. The impassioned pages whirl past with complete indifference to the person, or personality, of Plato. Does that mean that Plato had no personality, no individual physiognomy? I would scarcely assert as much. I have already said that during antiquity individuality was different in many respects from the individuality of modern times, but that is not the essential thing here either. The heart of the matter is that in the communities of the ancient world education for social life, and for the morality which was synonymous with it, always took place in a direct and immediate fashion. Man and citizen had not gone their separate ways; education for manhood meant the same thing as education for citizenship. Since division of labour was not to be found in the leading class of society, it was a matter of indifference from the standpoint of training for manhood or citizenship that someone should acquire a calling or 'trade'. By writing philosophy, Plato also fulfilled his duty as a citizen, but he was not a better citizen for being a thinker. Plato had to absorb the communal ethos before he could become Socrates' pupil; and so he did not see, and could not see, in his own philosophical development any 'growth' morally or in terms of 'citizenship'. The mistakes of which he speaks in his letter were errors in judgment of men or in his estimation of situations, not of moral principle or attitude. To understand that more clearly we need only look at his *Republic*. There the 'guardians' are those who are called to watch over the security of the state. If one of them distinguishes himself as a morally complete citizen, then he is designated king, so that he can concern himself with wisdom and philosophy; thus ability and ethos do not arise from the practice of an occupation. It was *a priori* impossible for someone to rise to the level of full humanity, socially and morally, *simply by reason of his calling*, and impossible for his *paideia* in good and evil and his mistakes in right and wrong to evolve solely in connection with his finding, practising, and perfecting his profession, in a world in which the demands of *sociality were primary and one's calling only secondary*, and where no separate, 'special' calling was necessary.

233

Only at the time of the dissolution of the ancient communities did a situation arise in which the idea of a calling could point towards a specific ethic, and hence education for a calling could become a means to the individual's moral and social development. And here we can see how far the problem we set out from was a secondary one. The primary question is: *is the sociality and morality into which the individual must 'grow up' essentially homogeneous or heterogeneous stable or dynamic?*

Of course the morality of the ancient communities was not absolutely homogeneous, but varied with different social strata. But we have already spoken of how ethical ideals were homogeneous. Nor was society, on any absolute measure, stable; it grew, flowered, and declined, but because it was not a future-oriented society all this took place within a relatively constant, fixed framework. In Rome of the late Empire, however, just this relative homogeneity ceased to exist. Within the boundaries of the Empire countless different social structures developed or declined; among others, the first seeds of feudal economy appeared. A plurality of ethical ideals came into existence, too; alongside the relatively unitary antique ethos Christianity made formidable advances, along with a great variety of other religio-mythical moralities. Thus one's calling,[100] its particular form, content, and tendencies, became here a means of *selection*, a signpost and guiding thread amid the plurality of social and moral values and outlooks. And, vice versa, the acceptance of certain values and a certain kind of outlook determined one's calling and developed one's consciousness of that calling. One's calling (and later one's craft or art) thus became a necessary factor in one's appropriation of reality, in one's education; *it mediated between the individual and the world, in so far as it contained, objectively, both a person's most characteristic individual aspirations and the kinds of values, ideology, and sociality which he chose.* From that point of view it is all the same whether that calling lay in preaching religious faith, as with Augustine, in craftmanship and sculpture, as with Cellini, in medicine, as with Cardano, in poetry, as with Goethe, or in philosophy, as with Rousseau. Where this factor is missing, there can be no question of true autobiography. Thus Casanova's autobiography is a mixture of adventure novel and exhibitionism, and its insincerity, to which Roy Pascal also refers, springs from that fact.

I have spoken of the late Roman Empire, where for a brief space there first developed the preconditions for autobiography, giving rise to Augustine's *Confessions*. Not only did a representative world and a significant personality meet here, but also a dynamic world with a pluralistic system of values and an individual prepared to

234

choose his own way in that world. However much Augustine's words may be addressed to God, however much prayer, supplication, and religious argumentation may interrupt the actual narrative of his life, the book is, as autobiography, typically *worldly*. That is why it could become truly great and could never be surpassed by the writers of confessions of the Middle Ages. For above all Augustine was not simply a man who, having previously ignored the accepted laws of God and Christ, or having deviated from them, 'returns' to his Lord and Saviour – rather he was a man *seeking the truth for himself* amid a welter of countless other equally accepted, 'official' truths and courses of conduct. Augustine – to repeat – sought *for himself* and found *for himself* a faith and a content for his life, and it was his merit, his strength, and his greatness that he did so. He himself attributed all this to the grace of God – that was a part of the truth he had found – but the reader still marvels constantly at the sharply outlined, striking personality of the writer of the auto-biography, his tireless search and his conscious shaping of his own life. At the same time Augustine did not 'grow away' from the world, as did the medieval writers of religious confessions; his was an education precisely for the world, like that of any other writer of autobiography, choosing from among various worlds *his own*. He would not become a teacher of rhetoric, a married man, and the like, but a Christian bishop; yet, in his day, being a Christian bishop was not a smaller but a more significant, more far-reaching social calling than being a teacher of rhetoric. Moreover, Augustine – like every later hero of autobiography – arrives at the truth only by passing through a succession of mistakes. And though Augustine himself judges his mistakes to have been deviations from truth and goodness, objectively he still depicts how he learned and grew through them, and how his errors were steps towards the truth. Here one more word about the calling is in order. It is common knowledge that Plato changed his mind in many respects on individual philosophical questions. Yet nothing was further from his mind (or from Aristotle's) than to condemn his earlier views as 'errors'. Nor was there any need to do so; since philosophy had not yet become a calling, the true and the erroneous did not carry such a heavy charge, in terms of *Weltanschauung*, as they later did. Standing firm for one's philosophy was, of course, a *sine qua non* of philosophical thought even then; but it meant standing one's ground for one's *present* views. Philosophical self-criticism was born when philosophy became charged with the burden of a *Weltanschauung*.

As we have seen, the Middle Ages were not a favourable period for autobiography. The world became more stable again, and its system of values – albeit a dual one now – also became stabilized. The possibility of choice among various worlds and various moralities was lacking; so was the opportunity for the unique individual personality to manifest itself in that choice, and the mediating role of a calling was absent, too. The appropriation of the world by the individual – what Roy Pascal calls 'experience' – faded into the background. Only with the Renaissance was it possible for auto-biography to flower again.

For Augustine, Christianity could still create the psychological preconditions for the writing of autobiography. At that time, even on relatively favourable historical soil, an entirely new self-image was required before autobiography could make its appearance. Insight into the inner depths of the soul, self-analysis, the illumina-tion of past mistakes, and psychological description became possible only after the new Christian ideology and the Judaic, Biblical tradi-tion had been experienced and absorbed. During the Renaissance, however, when self-consciousness and self-analysis became secul-arized, autobiography was secularized as well.

With Augustine, a tension still existed between the life described and the ideology (even though – to repeat – it was the ideology which made it possible to give that kind of description of the life at all). The life shows a relatively autonomous human agent struggling for his own world-view and his own calling in a changing, turbulent world, while the ideology speaks of divine election and omniscience, where the end is already implicit in the beginning. *But the world-view of the autobiographies of the Renaissance is based on a practical atheism and on the image of man creating the world.* The course of the lives described is in a harmony with this ideology. The individual creating himself and his own destiny exemplifies mankind creating itself and its destiny. But in spite of that there still remains some structural similarity, indicating that it is, nevertheless, Christianity which has become secularized. That is the idea of a *vocation*. Cellini and Cardano are both convinced that even in their cradles they had a vocation, that the world 'awaited' something from them, and that in their persons men were born to the world who must necessarily set the stamp of their personalities upon it. Their self-portraits, then, were *teleological*. With their lives, in which they would make choices, blunder, seek, and find, they would 'fulfil' that vocation, bearing out all those signs which declared their greatness in advance. This teleological self-conception was a spontaneous outgrowth of one of the biases of everyday thought, and that everyday bias was a survival of religious needs or – if the occasion offered – a fertile soil on which religious needs might blossom again. In Cardano and Cellini, as we

236

have seen, this teleological outlook was accompanied by a practical atheism, for in them the idea of a vocation gave rise merely to superstitious fancies, and did not lead back to theology. With St Teresa, however, all the constructive achievements of Renaissance autobiography were channelled back into the religious sphere, demonstrating that the notion of the vocation, too, had to be transcended in order for the classical and modern type of autobiography to develop. That step was finally taken with Rousseau and Goethe, even though the former was as closely involved with religion as Cardano or Cellini (perhaps even more closely), and yet the atmosphere which he creates is entirely of this world. There are no more signs and there is no longer any election; the stars do not portend a man's future greatness; the individual is, first and last, alone with the world which has given him birth and which he in turn creates anew.

A great, significant, dynamic age, with great, significant, dynamic personalities: that in itself made it a fruitful soil for autobiography. But the beauty of the classics of Renaissance autobiography lies in the richness with which they incorporate the age's plurality of values. Rarely can such *different* personalities be seen, such *different* systems of values, attitudes, and habits, as in the case of Cellini and Cardano. And yet the unity of the age still emerges clearly. No historical knowledge is needed to read these two accounts and know afterwards, with perfect certainty, that the tale is told of *one and the same world*. Here is an instance of the happy union of the objective and the subjective, the universal and the individual.

Before examining the differences between them, I ought to refer to the similarity in the social backgrounds of these two writers of autobiography. Both of them came from *plebeian* families. Cellini had farther to climb than Cardano, but that does not alter the fact that both alike had to fight their way up from below. They had to fight for everything, pay the price for everything, overcome every difficulty; nothing was handed them ready-made. Their calling was not a spiritual one, as Augustine's had been, but a practical one; the physician was then as much a master craftsman as the goldsmith. They had to raise not only themselves, but also their *craft* – the goldsmith's trade into an art, medicine into a science. And both – and this is the decisive fact – both wrote success stories. From that point of view it is no matter that Cardano's personal life was unhappy, that his favourite son was put to death while the other became a vagabond, that his daughter was sterile, that the end of his life was spent in the prisons of the Inquisition. For both succeeded in elevating the status of their craft. Later, with Rousseau, we can witness – seemingly – the same kind of triumph. For Rousseau, too, was a plebeian, and came from as far down the social ladder as Cellini. But despite every formal resemblance Rousseau's auto-biography is closer, in this respect, to that of Goethe, the *haut bourgeois*. For he did not *create* bourgeois culture but rather appro-priated it; he did not develop his ideas out of his craft but by break-ing with it and with his bourgeois environment, and his plebeian character is reflected much more indirectly, in the content of his morality and ideology.

Let us review briefly the differences in attitude between Cellini and Cardano. Cellini belonged to that type of the self-made man of the Renaissance whose extroverted character we have spoken of already. There are many aspects to 'living outwardly'. Morally, he was an egoist, avid of money and fame, envious, proud, aggressive, belligerent, a player of roles. As for his interests – the world in its entirety interested him, everything from history and great events down to the slightest happening. Gossip about servant girls intrigued him as much as gossip about kings. He looked outside himself, seeking hidden motives, studying character and depicting it master-fully. But above all else it was his own self that interested him – his self but not his 'soul', for it was his works, his successes, his interests, passions, and aspirations that riveted his intention. He measured the world partly by his own self – yet not by his inner subjectivity, rather by the ensemble of his interests. Psychologically, his passions and angers were always directed towards others; they were never turned on himself or against himself. He was a stranger to con-science and remorse, and after every transgression easily made peace with himself. He knew that he was inclined to anger and regretted it. but he made not the slightest effort to overcome it, even when he knew that he was doing a shameful thing. As for his social praxis, Cellini loved to move among the great, but without being in the least impressed by them. He was unjust to superiors and inferiors alike. He loved to take an active part in great historical events, like the defence of Florence or Rome; but for him that sort of thing was not an ethical problem, but an adventure. In art, he saw his work as the best token of both his self-realization and his success. He was as taken with his creations as he was with himself: a conscious crafts-man and no dilettante, in the full (and exaggerated) awareness of his own worth.

Cardano's, on the other hand, was a struggling nature. We can see in him already the encroachments of subjectivity. (The difference was one of situation, not of the age: Cellini flourished in the Rome of the Medici popes, while Cardano was active in Milan in the aftermath of the French invasions.) Cardano was a private person rather than a public man, and so it was the private events of his life which occupied the forefront of his attention; his experience was centred on his work and its conditions (lack of money, lack of employment), on his family, the fate of its members, and the like. His manner of life was already that of the *bourgeois* scholar. In his judgments on heroism, political greatness, and the common weal he was more than sceptical. 'How foolish, then, for Brutus to seek a place for noble virtue in the midst of his sedition,' he wrote in one place.[101] But this remark itself shows that resignation was the basis of his scepticism. Cardano no longer has any democratic illusions; he has seen that in public life actions are taken over the heads of the citizens and against their wishes. 'There is no reason why one should vaunt his country. What is one's country save a cabal of petty tyrants for the oppressing of the weak, the timid, and those who are generally innocent?'[102] He passed his life, essentially, without adventure. It was not the opportunity that was lacking; he did not want to seize that opportunity. He was invited to England, for example, to become Edward VI's personal physician, and he did indeed set out, but he never accepted the position. He was moved by medical considerations alone; the chance to associate with the great was never as attractive for him as it was for Cellini. And yet the whole world pulses through these other, unadventurous experiences just as much as it does through the broader swath of Cellini's life – not only because the 'great world' is always present as horizon and framework, but rather because it figures as more than horizon and framework: for Cardano is always able to select from private life and the events of private life those characteristic *junctures* where the destinies of the individual and the world *meet*.

A scholarly type of this sort, withdrawn into private life, can only be a representative figure if he possesses a richer, more profound subjectivity. (Without it, his autobiography would be of no interest.) That subjectivity did not entail an abandonment of his orientation towards the world. Cardano, too, strove to succeed and to win immortality for his name, and he, too, was convinced of his destiny and his genius; true, by success he meant primarily his works, money only secondarily (for Cellini money was another expression of his dignity). In Cardano, subjectivity appears in the form of a *gaze directed inward*. Constant self-examination, self-analysis, study of and insight into his own personality, psyche, and behaviour run through his autobiography. In describing every action he seeks his own essence. Here is a *conscious* sincerity. Cellini, too, is sincere, but his is a naïve sincerity. He acts spontaneously and makes spontaneous judgments on his actions; his judgments make no pretension to moral or psychological depth. That is why he can love himself so unthinkingly, with humour, irony, and indulgence. Such spontaneity, however, is completely absent from Cardano. He *wants* to be sincere (and he is), but he *does not love himself*, he does not take delight in himself. He never enjoys his worst impulses or his physical and spiritual deficiencies; his is a true self-analysis, the furthest thing in the world from exhibitionism (think only of his description of his temporary impotence). That is why, despite every superficial similarity, Cardano's autobiography cannot be considered 'modern', in the twentieth-century sense of the word. But it cannot be regarded as Christian either. Augustine, too, was not enamoured of his youthful self; he, too, analysed his earlier behaviour mercilessly. But he regarded as sinful everything in himself which sprang from his particularity. Cardano, on the other hand, if he is not enamoured of himself, at least does not reject his own self either. He never considered himself a 'sinner'. Whatever he was, he was as the given circumstances *permitted* him to be. 'I determined upon a course of life for myself, not such as I would have, but *such as I could*.'[103] Cellini spontaneously followed the ethics of the age, while Cardano struggled to work out consciously an ethic for himself; yet that ethic was always a *concrete* one, an ethic of the possible, not mere moralizing or cynical self-conceit. The parallel with Hamlet's soliloquy, cited earlier, comes spontaneously to mind: 'I am myself indifferent honest; but yet I could accuse me of such things that it were better my mother had not borne me.' Here, too, *equal* stress is laid on integrity and self-accusation.

If Cardano's 'inward-directed gaze' reveals a richer subjectivity than Cellini's, it is also marked by a greater degree of *objectivity*. Comment has often been made on the extent to which he views and analyzes himself from outside, almost like an object of scientific study. His is a physician's analysis of his own body and soul; but it is the sort of medical analysis which is not devoid of ethical content and ethical commitment.

If we can enjoy in Cellini the colourful description of one man's life and in Cardano the unity of life-conduct and reflection, then what appeals to us in Montaigne is the way in which reflection itself becomes individualized.

'I am the sole subject of this book' – thus programmatically does Montaigne write in analysing his own *Essays*. Such a plan – though, of course, he does not carry it through – is eloquent in itself. It bears witness to the evolution and deepening of subjectivity. Montaigne's searchlight is pointed in the opposite direction from Cardano's. The Milanese doctor deflects it from the milestones of his

240

life onto his own soul; Montaigne sets it up on the pedestal of his own personality and turns it outward, upon the world. Montaigne's programme is fulfilled to the extent that his thoughts are not simply theories and reflections, but *experiences of life transformed into reflection*, and not simply experience become thought, but *thought become experience*. Yet since his experiences (whether personally lived or stemming from his reading) originate at the points where a representative, eventful world meets a significant personality full of character, his reflections tell us something *about the world*; the external is filtered through the internal, but the content of the ideas is *the external internalized*. And that is true not only when he speaks immediately or generally of others, but also when he is speaking about himself. Here again, then, a greater degree of subjectivity goes along with a greater degree of objectivity; the scientific tradition does not give way to random snippets of reflection, but *to the experience of a self studied and analysed with the same scientific objectivity*.

The appearance of autobiography as a genre is a sure sign of the meeting of a dynamic age and a dynamic personality. But, of course, the union of self-knowledge and knowledge of the world, of intro-spection and experience of reality, appears in countless forms and variations. Here it is the *self-portrait* that first comes to mind. Dürer's series of self-portraits, for example, also reflects the evolution of character. We see the gradual development of personality; one portrait takes up where the last one left off, for features indicated only sketchily in one emerge more clearly in the next and – conversely – the innocence of adolescence survives only in a hidden way in the portrait of Dürer as bridegroom and in the so-called *Renaissance Portrait*. But this evolution is not in the least immanent; at every stage the demands of the age and calling are reflected, and the tasks and conflicts which made up the man's experience of the world find expression. We need only examine how the cataclysms of the sixteenth century are mirrored in the last two self-portraits in the series. To feel how the self-confidence of Renaissance man, and his orientation towards the outside world, were translated into hope and despair, spiritual struggle and suffering, we need only put side by side the *vir dolorum* and the 'Renaissance' self-portrait which preceded it.

But even where there are no self-portraits or other immediate representations of self, personal experience can be seen to progres-sively gain ground. Once again I must revert to Michelangelo. I have already remarked upon how consistently Michelangelo, in his long lifetime, reacted to the vicissitudes of his age. Now, however,

241

I should like to add to that something else: he always did so through the mediation of *personal experience*. There is something of the self-portrait in the statue of David, even if there is no exterior likeness, for its spirit resembles that of its creator. There are elements of self-representation, in the same sense, in the statue of Moses as well. The entire plan of the Medici tombs might have been designed to express Michelangelo's personal view of the world, while the late *pietàs* reflect the agony of the sculptor's broken spirit, like Dürer's *vir dolorum*. It is true, of course, that the personality of the artist finds realization in *every* work of art. But here it becomes more and more a matter of the direct reflection of the maker's world of experience and feeling; sculpture begins to aspire, within certain limits, to the specificity of lyric poetry. (It is not at all accidental that Michelangelo also expressed in his sonnets the things he expressed in his sculpture.) The qualification 'within certain limits' is important; for when the representation of subjective experience and feeling makes it impossible to produce works that are three-dimensional bodies in space, sculpture ceases to be a great art. It is probably there that we should seek the reason why during the baroque period sculpture was no longer the leading art (Bernini was still a child of mannerism), ceding its place to music. Michelangelo, however, is still characterized by the same aspiration which we have observed in Cardano and Montaigne: alongside a growing and deepening subjectivity appear strivings for a conscious objectivity. I refer not only to the tendency towards a more abstract generalization, or the famous anecdote to the effect that the statue 'is already in' the marble, but above all to the predilection for large, comprehensive compositions in which self-portraits (like depictions) of emotional states and 'self-expressions' are 'fitted into' the course of world history (the Sistine frescoes), into the conception of the deification of man (tomb of Julius II), or into the vision of the *Last Judgment*, receiving thereby an objective position and a place in the system of values which is appropriate to them.

But I do not need to refer only to Michelangelo in discussing the objectivity of autobiographically charged motifs; there is Shakespeare as well. In this respect, Shakespeare stands in the same relation to the great Greek dramatists as Michelangelo does to Phidias or Myron. Only the most insensitive can overlook how often intense personal experiences find expression in the actions, soliloquies, and destinies of Shakespeare's favourite heroes. It is enough to point to Hamlet or Prospero. Of course there is no more question here of self-depiction *per se* than there is of self-portraiture in Michelangelo. Shakespeare is neither Hamlet nor Prospero, any more than

242

Michelangelo is David or Moses. The fate of his heroes is different from his own, an immanent destiny developing in close conjunction with their situations. But they project emotions which are to be found in their creator as well, they experience disillusionments of the kind which he has experienced (even if not the very same disillusionments), and they reflect on problems which he has reflected upon. But here, too, as in Michelangelo, *objectivity has become conscious*: no particular motive or individual experience of the author is allowed to intrude uncritically into the moral or spiritual physiognomy or world of feeling of the characters. Here is one of the characteristic features of modern bourgeois literature, particularly of its greatest representatives, and here it appears for the first time. When Corneille attempted in many of his plays to return to objectivity of the ancient type, the result was vacuity. When Schiller accepted subjectivity but (at times) without conscious objectivity, he opened the way to that rhetorical and ideological manner of writing drama which Marx called *Schillerisieren*, and which reached its culmination (in non-ideological form) in the romantic and modern art of pure 'self-expression'.

In Shakespeare and Michelangelo, then, it is an individual experience – a dynamic individual's experience of a dynamic world – that finds objectification, just as it does in autobiography; that is another reason why they can make such free use of traditional material, Biblical, legendary, and historical. No figure of Christ departs as far from the traditional one as the Christ of the *Last Judgment*; nor did any ancient dramatist transform the motives of his heroes so freely as Shakespeare did with Othello, Lear, and Macbeth (not even Euripides, who went the furthest in this respect, and likewise because, out of all antiquity, his age saw individuality and the characteristics of the private individual emerge most strikingly). I must, of course, repeat that all this does not imply any strictly autobiographical content. There is a sharp distinction here between what is experienced and what is lived through. The artist depicts a whole gallery of figures whose behaviour and psychology he has experienced; but those are far from being types of behaviour and types of psychology which he has lived through. (Shakespeare, for example, did not 'think himself into' Iago's mind, did not 'become' Iago; he merely lived through the shock of apprehending that mind.) In autobiography, on the other hand, we learn of every experience solely through the mediation of that which has been lived through. Cellini, for example, did not think himself into Vasari's spiritual world either, and yet the figure and mind of Vasari appear to us only through Cellini's eyes; for us there is no other

Vasari but the one Cellini saw, while there is another Iago for us than the one Othello saw.

Another sign of the growing importance of individual experience, emerging alongside autobiography and parallel with it, was the rise of *lyric poetry*. The *Vita Nuova* of Dante already represents *both*. Tibor Kardos thus distinguishes the traditional sources of the work: 'Dante actually takes over the *razon* of the troubadours, their analysis of experience, and fuses it with another, closely related genre, that of the troubadour autobiography.'[104] The word 'fuses' says a great deal: we do not know how far it was done spontaneously and how far consciously, but in fact Dante attempted to root lyric poetry firmly in individual experience. Lyric poetry itself could never have fulfilled that function; in its themes, forms, and expressions it was still general, even when speaking of individual sorrow, personal loss, and trouble – as general as folksong; everyone could read his own feelings into it, and yet it had no 'here and now' of its own. In the *Vita Nuova* Dante is looking for that 'here and now' when he designates his own *individual* development as the locus of 'great experiences' and analyses the motifs of lyric poetry – a device brilliant in itself, yet one that could be discarded later on. Petrarch's lyrics are, already in their content, even more individual; again it is no accident that their author was the man who left us in his letter to posterity the first self-analysis in the modern sense of the word, opening with these proud words: 'Perchance you will want to know what manner of man I was, and how my writings fared.'[105] Shakespeare's sonnets again, despite the conventional form, breathe the individuality of the author; here, indeed, only personal experiences and sentiments find a place (as, for that matter, in Michelangelo).

Finally, a word must be said about philosophy and science. Montaigne's reflections constitute one of the philosophical pinnacles of the age. Bacon's and Leonardo's thinking is full of references to their own personal experience. In an age when obsolete scholasticism was being demolished or had already been overthrown, and a de-anthropomorphized natural science had not yet emerged, the practice of starting out from individual experience and constantly referring back to it, and of describing the *genesis* of ideas in the individual's personal life, flourished as never before or since. Nor did it matter, in this respect, whether inductive or deductive thinking was involved. For the tendency to root ideas firmly in the history of an *individual* process of thought is one which permeates Descartes' *Discours* as much as it does Bacon. The questions 'What is the essence of the matter?' and 'How did I arrive at the essence?' are intertwined.

In speaking of Cardano and Cellini I have said that their history is not simply one of two plebeian citizens finding their place in a ready-made world, but rather the story of how their world, their art, and their science arose and took root. And in general this age was not only the one in which bourgeois philosophies and sciences, bourgeois scholars and philosophers appeared, but at the same time the age in which 'modern science' and 'modern philosophy' were born. The life of science and philosophy is identical with the life of scientists and philosophers. They uncover the problems of the world – the problems which will dominate science and philosophy for centuries to come – in much the same way that Abraham, in the legendary world of the Bible, once discovered the God of Israel.

CHAPTER 8

Measure and beauty—
emotional ties

I must refer once more to what has been said about everyday life: different homogeneous spheres of being and consciousness had not yet become sharply distinguished from one another. And that was particularly true of aesthetics, ethics, and politics. Until the end of the quattrocento no awareness existed that there might be contradictions between the beautiful and the good, the beautiful and the useful, the good and the useful.

Throughout the Renaissance the concepts of measure and beauty presupposed each other. Recklessness and immoderation might indeed often appear fascinating and sympathetic, yet they were never regarded as 'beautiful', but rather as great or (to use a Kantian expression which I have never met with in the Renaissance) sublime. Immoderation attracted, but at the same time repelled. It aroused pleasure, but also fear, while beauty only attracted and only aroused pleasure: *for beauty was the object of love.* 'The measure of love corresponds to the measure of beauty,'[106] wrote Ficino.

Though measure and beauty always presupposed each other, the two concepts (and ideals) did not always develop side by side. The category of 'measure' was to be found even in the early Renaissance, as the maintenance of proper measure in conduct (Petrarch), as moderation (Bruni), and as the Aristotelian principle of the mean (Alberti). It received, moreover, an ontological foundation: for Nicholas of Cusa, man was 'the measure' because he was the union of the finite and the infinite. The aesthetic and the 'utilitarian' were united in this concept of measure. To be temperate, to live with moderation, to observe the measure – all these were not only good and beautiful for a man, but useful to him as well. This unity was most natural in Florence. No conflict could arise between utility and a dominant morality containing the notion of 'measure' so long as the city-state structure remained intact despite partial revolutions in economics and politics, and so long as the individual's possible range of conduct remained within social bounds which were also ethical bounds, so that the anti-social character of any purely individual recklessness was immediately recognizable and the general opinion could immediately react against it. To repeat, then: the concept of measure embraced ethics, aesthetics, and utility as well, but in such a way that the *ethical aspect was the fundamental one*. Thus 'measure' was a social habit, and yet one which was far from being 'natural', or just a usage grown habitual; it was always a *norm* as well. It was one of the concrete norms of conduct of the age.

But I have already singled out as the basis of Florentine development the process of primitive accumulation, which is characterized precisely by the fact that it is boundless and infinite, transcending all measure! And I have several times spoken of the emergence – even in the fourteenth century – of the corresponding attitude of mind, one which knows no bounds. I refer again to the words of Marx: 'capitalist development disrupts all communal limits, which presently become obstacles to it.' And yet – as I indicated in my earlier discussion – in Florence the process of primitive accumulation came to a halt *before* it could burst the limits of the city-state. That is why a tendency towards unbounded expansion set in, in the economy, even while fixed bounds and limitations still prevailed in the political structure. In the economic sphere gain was more and more the motive of men's actions, but in political life individual advantage was still something to be ashamed of; here the good of the republic was the real (and not just the pretended) norm of conduct. Where money-making was concerned, there were no limits to how far one might follow individual interest, but in political activity there was indeed a 'measure'. Measure, then, was a customary norm, though not a universal one (it did not include the economic sphere), nor was gain or utility, egotistically interpreted, a universal norm either (it did not include the political and social spheres). It is not at all accidental, then, that the theory of utility – whose essence lies precisely in its presenting a *universal* conception of individual advantage – makes its appearance, even in germ, only in the sixteenth century.

From this point of view, then, that part of the Renaissance which closes with the end of the quattrocento occupies a middle position between the ancient city-state republics and the Enlightenment.

247

In the ancient polis *mezotés* (measure) was a *universal* category; it applied to getting rich just as much as to art, to knowledge, or to one's attitude towards the emotions. It was, moreover, a custom of universal character which made homogeneous one (common) aspect of every relationship in one's *whole* life. To violate *mezotés* was always to commit *hubris*, even when the act had a positive value content, as in the case of Electra. In developed bourgeois society, on the other hand, *utility* becomes universal. It is likewise a concrete norm (i.e. a customary norm) but of a sort whose every form of manifestation is limitless and whose consistent pursuit means at the same time a constant breaking of the norm itself. The *Manifesto of the Communist Party* formulates it with clinical precision:

> The bourgeoisie, wherever it has got the upper hand, has put an end to all feudal, patriarchal, *idyllic* relations. It has pitilessly torn asunder the motley feudal ties that bound man to his 'natural superiors,' *and has left remaining no other nexus between man and man than naked self-interest, than callous* 'cash payment.'. . . It has resolved personal worth into exchange value, and in place of the numberless indefeasible chartered freedoms, has set up that *single*, unconscionable freedom – Free Trade.[107]

> The constant revolutionizing of production, uninterrupted disturbance of all social conditions, everlasting uncertainty and agitation distinguish the bourgeois epoch from all earlier ones. All fixed, fast-frozen relations, with their train of ancient and venerable prejudices and opinions, are swept away, all new-formed ones become antiquated before they can ossify.[108]

'Idyllic relations', in Marx's usage, is a reference to ages when 'measure' prevailed, wholly or in part. The italicizing of the word 'single' (italics are only rarely employed in the *Manifesto of the Communist Party*) is designed to place unusual emphasis on the *homogenizing* character of the utility relation.

The bourgeois thinkers of the seventeenth century had already observed that the quest for gain had a homogenizing effect on conduct in bourgeois society. That recognition brought into being the theory of utilitarianism in the broader sense (that of egoism), and also attempted to reduce all the phenomena of human existence – first and foremost, all *ethical facts* – to the principle of utility, and/or to derive them from the same principle. I have dealt with the various tendencies inherent in utilitarianism elsewhere,[109] and so I will not elaborate upon them here. For the present it is enough to note that attitudes and systems of thought of quite different content have been erected on the basis of this principle (Hobbes and Mandeville, Spinoza and Rousseau, Helvétius and Diderot, and others). The common weakness of all these thinkers, in varying degree, was that from the fact that the quest for utility has a homogenizing effect they drew the conclusion that utility – striving for gain, egoism, and the like – was the *cause* of every other sphere of existence and knowledge. They believed, for example – and here is the most important matter – that because utility governs the moral activity of men in their everyday lives, it must follow that ethics are derived from utility. And so, of course, every moral principle or practice which was not motivated by personal advantage (from abstract norms to self-sacrifice) became objectively inexplicable; the most varied devices were necessary to press them into the Procrustes' bed of utility. Thus they made distinctions between reasonable self-interest and unreasonable self-interest, between 'true' utility and 'false' utility, between justified self-love and unjustified self-love, often to the point where the original concept of utility – and the one which always remained dominant in bourgeois society – was completely obscured. For morality cannot be derived, of course, from utility, any more than it could be derived from the concept of measure.

Bourgeois utilitarianism did not bother to give any explanation at all of values which were hostile to the bourgeois world and which, moreover, denied the universality of utility relations. The first to come to grips with this problem seriously was Rousseau, who rejected the social relations of both feudal and bourgeois society. He sought to transcend the contradictions of utility theory in the one way that was possible, through a historical analysis of psychology and ethics. A captive of tradition in so far as he, too, derived ethics from an *amour de soi-même* sublimated into a psychological drive, Rousseau nevertheless broke tradition by treating bourgeois self-interest (*amour-propre*) as a type of motivation which had arisen historically, along with the world of private property; and thus he explained utility, as it existed in bourgeois society, not as the *creator* of the moral universe, but as a force which had transformed it. For him, then, there did exist an *autonomous* moral order and *autonomous* moral values which denied the validity of the utility principle and its world.

Here it is necessary to return once more to the problem of measure. With Rousseau the category of measure reappears, though now only as an *ideal*, an *abstract* norm. Rousseau postulates a world in which measure, not gain, is the homogenizing force, whether he projects it into the historical past or posits it in the idyllic world of Clarence. It is an ideal because Rousseau knows not only that this 'world shaped by measure' does not exist here and now, but also because he sees no concrete ways and means of bringing it into existence. But it is the sort of ideal which well expresses his own peculiar kind of 'double negation'. Later on, romanticism, too, would wage its polemic with bourgeois utility, but the ideal which it opposed to it was an ideal of universal excess, and moreover, of the excess of subjectivity. It is a revealing feature, and it reveals again what we already know from the late Georg Lukács's studies in romanticism: romanticism was a bourgeois movement through and through. Rousseau's ideal of measure, on the other hand – coupled as it was in his thought in particular with a special theory of beauty – was indeed a programme of radical double negation.

If the 'intermediate' character of the Renaissance, between ancient and bourgeois society, is to become perfectly clear, we ought not to overlook here, either, the problem of beauty and art. *Measure, as a homogenizing relation, of course embraces, and creates, beauty.* We may rightly call the world of the ancient polis, including its everyday life, a world of beauty. The art which reflects that world shows us a world of beauty. Every ancient art, *without exception*, took an attitude of *absolute affirmation* towards its time and the world of its time. And that was true even of those who (like Aristophanes) depicted the concrete politics or politicians of a specific period as wicked or petty. Aristophanes, basing himself on an affirmation of the given world, its beauty and even idyllic character (think of the idyllic figures of his cultivators of the soil), rejects from that perspective the demagogues and warmongers with their pettiness and their treachery. (I am deliberately leaving aside Rome in the period of its decadence, for here I am comparing social formations in their progressive phases.) The ideology of inconoclastic movements always contended that art did *not* sufficiently represent the beauty of reality; Plato's *Republic*, for example, was based on an ideal unity of measure and beauty in comparison with whose harmony even Homer's poetry was thought to be too rugged. Statues were never seen as more beautiful than the young men who were their models; in antiquity it would have been ridiculous to raise against art the charge that it 'beautified' reality. The world of measure was, to repeat, a world of beauty as well, and for that reason art had no need to take an adversary or polemical stance, whatever contradictions, tragic or otherwise, the artist may have seen and depicted.

Turning, now, to the opposite pole of my comparison: *utility, as a factor tending to render reality more homogeneous, and permeating all aspects of life, is not in harmony with beauty.* There may be points where they coincide (as in Chernyshevsky's famous example of the waving ear of wheat which is beautiful to the eye of the husbandman even while he estimates its value to him), but these are accidental and ephemeral. When Marx wrote that capitalism is the enemy of art it was this sort of thing he was thinking of, not so much the fact that artists are bought and sold, while their works become commodities. We may even reverse the Marxian thesis – since capitalism is the enemy of art, art is also the enemy of capitalism. The art of the capitalist era is one long – and continuous – protest against utility relations. Thus the relationship of the artist to the world changed, too. He ceased to affirm it and to be in harmony with it. The artist comes essentially to deny the world in which he lives. He denies its morality in its entirety. In speaking of Athens I said that even the artist who stood in opposition to the concrete developments of his own age (like Aristophanes) still affirmed his world as a whole. Now, however, I can say: in the capitalist era even the artist who is *in agreement* with the concrete developments of his age still denies, in the final analysis, his world as a whole, and above all its morality. It is enough to think of the figure of Blifil in *Tom Jones*, a typical – and not accidental – product of capitalism, or of Walter Scott, in many of whose novels the morality of the Scottish clans comes through as much more elevated than the ethics of that bourgeois progress which, in the last analysis, the author sees as justified. In saying all this I do not, of course, wish to identify the sphere of art or of aesthetics with beauty; I am only asserting that the affirmative or negative relationship of the artist and his art to the general tendencies of the age is to a great extent a function of how far and how generally that age makes it possible for beauty to emerge *in life itself.*

The world of the Renaissance takes its place halfway between the ancient era of 'measure' and the modern, bourgeois period of 'utility'. (I am, to repeat, taking into consideration for the present only developments up through the middle of the quattrocento, and those only in Italy.) Capital accumulation is already characteristic of economic life, along with boundless opportunities for profit; the ideals of infinitude and limitlessness come increasingly to the fore in all those areas which constitute the basis and motive force of economic development. That is true, above all, of everything that relates to the *development of the means of production and the effort to acquire knowledge of nature.* In ferreting out the secrets of the world there is no longer any *hubris.* Ficino, for example, writes of man:[110]

251

He *alone never rests* during his whole life, he alone is *never satisfied* to remain where he is . . . [God] created him for the infinite, to be dissatisfied with everything finite, no matter how great, so that he alone might seek out on earth the infinity of nature. . . .

Here a dynamic concept of man is based explicitly on a refusal to acknowledge any limits. In this connection Randall writes perceptively of Leonardo da Vinci: 'In his mathematical vision of the world, Leonardo seems to belong to the realm of "dynamic" and "Faustian" attitudes, rather than to the static geometrical perfection of Greek thought.'[111] But – as we have seen – it is not only in these spheres of high endeavour, but in the accumulation of wealth as well, that there are no longer any 'bounds'. It is impossible for Boccaccio's merchant heroes to have so much money that they do not yearn for more, and Marlowe's Faustus, too, is urged by the Evil Angel to 'think of honour and of wealth'.[112] In social attitudes, nevertheless, measure still prevailed for the time being. The same Ficino who speaks of the eternal restlessness and dissatisfaction of the human mind in exploring nature still clings, in the sphere of ethics, to the ancient virtues of fortitude, justice, wisdom, and moderation, and the last plays no small role in his thinking.

Measure then, even if it had no homogenizing effect, was still an existing, functioning ideal and norm for the beginning of the Renaissance. Its world was a world of beauty as well, above all in Florence. Yet while the thought of the fourteenth and fifteenth centuries is characterized to the very end by the categories of measure and moderation, beauty as a 'separate' ideal makes its appearance only in the middle of the fourteenth century. Max Dvořak is right in saying that 'it is striking . . . how this period of the Renaissance did not know the word "beauty", which admirers of the period have so often used in connection with it'.[113] *The ideal of beauty appeared at the moment when the Renaissance city-state was on the decline*, at the moment when beauty, as an integral component of everyday life, as one of the forms in which social morality, social life, and 'measure' were made manifest, was, together with all these, on the decline. So long as the structure of the city-state gave a certain 'form' to men's lives and moral custom gave a certain form to human conduct, the concept of beauty could not become an abstraction. Abstracting beauty, postulating it as an ideal, and placing it – teleologically – in the centre of things was a symptom of decay, an attempt at an ideal restoration in the small community (Ficino), in art (Raphael), and in philosophy (the Platonists) of something which in reality had ceased to be general.

252

Objectively, the decline of the city-state was an indication that utility had already begun its homogenizing work, slowly penetrating every area of life. It was possible to approve this process (Machiavelli, Bruno) or to reject it (as many did from Ficino to Savonarola) – but it was impossible to disregard it. Machiavelli firmly separated the good, the beautiful, and the useful, expressing his belief in the autonomy of the useful. Savonarola called measure to his assistance against utility, but thought to find that measure in a Christian type of *askesis*. (It should be added that this was an attempt at a relatively plebeian solution, for an appeal to Christian moderation could still seize hold of those who, having been destroyed economically, were now seeing their last support, their country and the formal democracy of the city-state, pulled out from under them.) We ought by no means to ignore the fact that the restoration of the splendour of the polis was a part of Savonarola's programme. Giving the ideal of beauty a central place in philosophy, art, and personal relations (for the latter, compare the friendly circle of the Florentine Academy or Raphael's painting of *The School of Athens*) was a relatively aristocratic protest against the tyranny of utility – aristocratic not as designating a social stratum, but in the sense of an express aristocracy of spirit. For the rest, no Chinese wall separated the idealization of beauty from the course followed by Savonarola. In this connection it is enough to point once more to the well-known sympathy which a Pico della Mirandola or a Michelangelo felt for Savonarola. Michelangelo, as is generally known, refused to follow the Dominican friar in only *one* respect, in his condemnation of beauty.

The graphic arts demonstrate splendidly the extent to which the *ideal of the unity of external and internal beauty* prevailed during the first Medici period not only in Florence but also, under Florentine influence, in Rome. Dvořak has already shown how the style of the later Donatello changed in keeping with the ideal of beauty. But I could just as well point to Botticelli (not just to the *Birth of Venus* or the *Primavera* but to the paintings of an inconographical character as well), to the young Michelangelo and Leonardo, or to Raphael. Dvořak has likewise analysed the extent to which Raphael's style, the *maniera grande*, expresses an ideal corporeality in which there is no conflict between body and spirit, in which *kalokagathia* prevails. It must be stressed that this is decidedly a *beauty of measure*, yet not of the sort that comes as a natural result of the representation of reality itself, such as we see in Giotto, Masaccio, or even Fra Angelico; it is definitely the result of a programme. I should add that Venetian painting, for example, never acknowledged the exclusive claims of measure as Florentine painting did. In the paintings of Crivelli or the Bellinis it was precisely disproportion which prevailed, albeit in different ways. In this respect the art of Giorgione forms the exception rather than the rule. When the ideal of beauty gained the upper hand in Venice, beauty itself came to appear in immoderate forms. We need only think of the nudes of Titian or the early mannerists (Veronese, the young Tintoretto), with their overblown, deliberately exaggerated corporeality. This kind of absence of measure already points towards the baroque. It would not be too daring, perhaps, to venture the hypothesis that the epigone character of Florentine painting in its age of crisis springs from the ideal of measure and beauty. *Kalokagathia* was no longer fitted at all to express the tragic atmosphere of the sixteenth century; and so it should not strike us as accidental that the painter who best summed up the conflicts of the age – Tintoretto – sprang from Venetian soil.

During the Renaissance, the beauty of measure and proportion held sway – to repeat – only for a historical moment; it was not a permanent condition, as in ancient Athens. Even those who extolled it most highly began to grow uncertain about their point of departure, the unity of physical and spiritual beauty, the necessary harmony of the external and the internal. In Michelangelo, for example, the ideal of beauty was gradually transferred from the external to the internal.[114]

> Lo, all the heavenly things we find on earth
>   Resemble for the soul that rightly sees
>   That a source of bliss divine which gave us birth:
> Nor have we first-fruits or remembrances
>   Of heaven elsewhere. Thus, loving loyally,
>   I rise to God and make death sweet by Thee.

Here (and in other places which could be cited) beauty is treated as a unitary whole. *Every* kind of beauty is a mark of our heavenly origin (and indeed the *only* one); the contemplation of *every* kind of beauty raises us to heaven. In this there is nothing which separates Michelangelo from Ficino or Castiglione. But let us consider another, later poem (again only one example from among many).[115]

> Just as we put, O Lady, by substraction,
> Into the rough, hard stone
> A living figure, grown
> Largest wherever rock has grown most small,
> Just so, sometimes, good actions
> For the still trembling soul

254

Are hidden by its own body's surplus,
And the husk that is raw and hard and coarse,
Which you alone can pull
From off my outer surface;
In me there is for me no will or force.

Here the comparison speaks plainly, in two senses. On one hand, the harmony of physical and spiritual beauty has been broken. What is truly beautiful is the soul; the body is only a husk. On the other hand, the artist who carves the work out of stone is the one who draws forth the soul from the body; the beauty of the work is to be sure objective and objectified, but it is the soul which is objectified in it. We have come a long way from Alberti and his theory of mimesis.

And so we have once more drawn close to the peculiar character of the religious needs which arose during the sixteenth century – though I must emphasize that here, with Michelangelo, there is no trace of any wish to revert to any codified religion. Religious needs involved, at one and the same time, a *need for beauty*; the soul which these two needs inhabited, and whose 'beauty' was a proof of man's heavenly origin, was identical with *subjectivity*. The prevalence of subjectivity in its relationship to objectivity, which distinguishes Michelangelo from the aesthetic creeds of the preceding age, is likewise an attempt to preserve beauty, and the old Florentine and Renaissance values generally, in a world where they were going under and where only great-hearted *beaux esprits* could bear them aloft any longer. *A heightened degree of subjectivity, and the domination of a subjective, more abstract beauty over the material objectivity of everyday life – in that age that was the only way in which the once high-spirited Florentine artist and patriot could remain true to the ideas of his youth* and still follow with sensitivity the new conflicts of the age. Through subjectification of beauty, through a more abstract conception of objectified beauty, Michalangelo completed a truly Herculean labour, the final synthesis of the ideals of the Renaissance.[116]

The ideal of beauty played an autonomous and central role – to repeat – only in Italy, from the end of the quattrocento to the middle of the cinquecento; elsewhere it did not fulfil the same function. The reason is to be sought in the success of the Italian polis in preserving the idea of measure: 'measure' governed *one* aspect of life (public life, public morality, politics) in some of the city-states, particularly in those whose culture left its stamp on the development of Italy *as a whole*. Where bourgeois utility relations did not dissolve the framework of the city-state but instead penetrated into a world of feudal anarchy, making it even more chaotic even while bringing it to an end, the problem of measure and beauty arose only marginally. That world was not entirely exempt from its influence or from the influence of the Platonic philosophy which mediated it; examples would not be hard to find in Ronsard's poetry or in Shakespeare's sonnets. But it was only one theme among many, and it appears almost exclusively in connection with love.

We can scarcely help noticing this if we set alongside each other two literary works, one from Italy, one from Spain. Both deal with the theme of chivalry, and each in its own fashion does so in a modern way. Both are masterpieces. The two works are, of course, *Don Quixote* and *Orlando Furioso*. The contrasts between the two are not at all fortuitous − Don Quixote himself refers several times to Orlando and his story. To avoid misunderstanding, let it be said that Cervantes does not at all ridicule Ariosto's poem itself, but he does question the validity of the value-system of Ariosto's heroes in a thoroughly different, and prosaic, world. The half-century which intervened between the two works does not satisfactorily account for their radically different attitudes. In Ariosto's time the Italian Renaissance had become at least as problematical (despite the relatively late flowering of the Este family and their world) as the Spanish Renaissance had in Cervantes' time. Here only differences in tradition can provide us with an explanation.

I have emphasized that both works regard the world of chivalry in a modern way. In the case of Cervantes' novel, it is not necessary for me to demonstrate that fact. But it is all the more essential to demonstrate it with Ariosto's poem, which − as one example of the 'art epic' − is customarily set alongside Tasso's *Gerusalemma Liberata*. Yet nothing could be more misleading. Tasso − whose poem I cannot analyse here − takes the world of Christian chivalry *seriously*. Fabulous elements are not absent from his poem, and yet the whole work is still *stylized history*. It is a quest for tradition in a historical subject matter in which his people (and this applies as well to all of Christendom at the time) had no real traditional roots. Imposing in its particulars, it is on the whole a misconceived attempt at the literary creation of the sort of prehistory which Tasso's contemporary, Shakespeare, succeeded in creating out of the material of his own national history. Ariosto's poem, on the other hand, is truly a *fable*. It was the first attempt − and a brilliant one − at creating a new variety of *parable*. The parable is a special kind of fable, one that points a moral. Its first examples took the form of animal fables. The modern parable, however, draws its events not from the animal world, but from *fabulous adventures* rich in happenings, comprehensible to all, poetic and, at the same time, more or less stylized. The reference to present-day conflicts, and the 'moral', are generally explicitly drawn, but these, too, can be omitted if they are sufficiently obvious. The wealth of events and the universally comprehensible character of the genre indicate its *plebeian* nature. The moral which is drawn speaks to the many, not the few. That is the reason the form is especially favoured by periods of enlightenment. The stylization and the poetic character, on the other hand, are an essential condition if the fable is not to be too obvious and the moral neither forced nor pedestrian, and if the aesthetic character of the representation is to be preserved. The line of descent of this sort of poetry extends through Diderot and Lessing all the way to Anatole France and Brecht. Nor is it difficult to find all these properties in *Orlando Furioso*. The adventures and the stylization consciously point up (by contrast with Tasso's work) the fantastic cut of the story. Each section of the tale, however, closes with a *moral* (and often individual sections are interrupted to draw a moral); and the lessons thus drawn refer to contemporary truths, which the story does not reflect, but rather poses in the form of a parable. But the allusion to contemporary reality, and the moral lesson, never put a stop to the internal dialectic of the story's thread; the adventures go on in response to a law of their own, with their own special atmosphere. For that reason, the fable never spills over into allegory. In discussing knowledge of men I have already cited one such 'moral', and I will introduce several more in analysing ties between men, and the content of those relationships. Here – partly in order to characterize the style, partly for the sake of my later analysis – I will examine but one such instance.

The story of *Orlando Furioso* tells of the havoc wrought by a fearful 'gigantic' technical discovery, whose superhuman power is meant to symbolize the effect of gunpowder. The poet adds:[117]

> O wicked and foul invention, how did you ever find place in
> a human heart? Through you the soldier's glory is destroyed,
> through you the business of arms is without honour, through
> you valor and courage are brought low, for often the bad
> man seems better than the good; through you valor no more,
> daring no more can come to a test in the field.

I must stress once again: the improbability of the story is deliberately brought out. The heroes are not characterized; they possess only a few, abstract, functional properties, like the heroes in folk-tales. Time and place are purposely vague and dream-like. The dismal wilderness shrinks to the dimensions of a garden, distances contract and then expand, time adjusts itself to the rhythm of each hero. Ariosto's world of time and space resembles that of modern surrealism, with the qualification that he is constantly, and ironically, underscoring its unreal character.

Fable does not always lend itself to being the stuff of parable. It can become suitable material only if the narrator will *distance* himself from the tale. That distance finds expression in the lack of verisimilitude, in the subdued irony that goes with it, and in the very realistic lessons that are drawn. It was because such a distance prevailed in the attitude of the poet that a chivalric tale could change, in Ariosto's hand, from myth to parable. *Ariosto thus stood as far from the world of chivalry as Cervantes, only in a different way.*

But to return to the lines just quoted: what is said about gunpowder expresses a certain nostalgia. The question is: is this a nostalgia for the world of chivalry?

Of that sort of nostalgia there is no trace. With his fable Ariosto lays a world to rest, just as much as Cervantes does with his satire. But on the other hand Ariosto and Cervantes are profoundly related again in their recognition that much of human significance was expressed in the value system and world of feeling of chivalry, including many things which were perishing in a society permeated by motives of gain. For Ariosto, his heroes' willingness to sacrifice themselves for friendship, their sense of honour, and their fidelity in love were as remarkable as Don Quixote's pure humanity was for Cervantes. But the fact that 'it is only a story' puts those honoured values in their place, just as does Don Quixote's tilting with windmills. Indeed, we might even say that for Ariosto it is even less an evocation of the beauty of purely chivalric virtues. *For in the eyes of the Italian poet the world in which men's greatness, heroism, and self-sacrifice were decisive in battle was not primarily the world of chivalry,* but the world of the city-state republics in their prime. For the inhabitants of the Italian peninsula, overrun by mercenary armies, the heroic world of legend became intertwined with their own heroic past. I need only refer back to the revealing expression 'business of arms' in the lines just cited, an expression which is anything but chivalric and is drawn in fact from the world of handicrafts.

We have said that parable is a plebeian genre. And in fact Ariosto's poem is a deeply plebeian work, every bit as much as Cervantes' novel. It is hardly accidental that when the hero of Gottfried Keller's *Der grüne Heinrich* looks around for reading matter for the peasant girl Judith, his choice should fall on *Orlando Furioso*. Judith is enthusiastic about Ariosto's poem, and does what the parable intended her to do – she relates the happenings to her own life, discovering what she has in common with the heroes and heroines of fable, above all Bradamentis.

In Italy, what made the parable the vehicle for a confrontation with the past, for a juxtaposition of values, and for expressing the conflict of poetry and prose was none other than the attachment to *beauty*. The world of *Orlando Furioso* is a world of beauty; terror, despair, and the monstrous are all resolved in it. It should be added that this was truly a pagan beauty. Charlemagne's struggle with the Moors forms the background of the story, but it remains literally a backdrop; in the last analysis the beautiful appears united with the good, immanent and this-wordly.

But if *Orlando Furioso* radiates an atmosphere of beauty, that does not at all mean that beauty is reflected as an unproblematic presence, even within the limits of the fable. The poem is a parable, but a parable of the *present*, the vision of beauty of Ariosto's age. Thence springs one of the central ideas of the work, *the notion of beauty as the unattainable* (in connection with Orlando and Angelica); thence, too, is the idea of *beauty as the demonic* (in the many figures of sorcerers). If there is any nostalgia after all in Ariosto's poem, it is a nostalgia for beauty.

I have lingered over Ariosto's work and over the contrasts and parallels it displays with Cervantes' novel in order to underscore the special role reserved for beauty during the Italian Renaissance. Now, in order to further illustrate what has been said above, I should like to say a few words about Shakespeare. For Shakespeare, there is no separate world of 'measure' and no separate world of 'gain'. Beauty is always present in the early comedies, as one aspect of reality, joined with freshness and gaiety. This beauty was of his *own* age, and it disappeared step by step from his plays just as did gaiety and the atmosphere of trust generally. It was a *natural thing*, as it had been for the early Italian masters; it was not an ideal, nor did it ever become an ideal. Shakespeare's system of values was a system of moral values, his ideals were moral ideals; beauty was secondary, the result of moral grandeur and righteousness, a derivative of one's whole attitude as a human being. *For him beauty in itself was not a value*. It might provide a cover for wickedness, as in Lady Macbeth, in whom wickedness is not demonic at all, but very calculating indeed. Or it may simply be a weakness, and thereby a source of dishonour. We need only think of Hamlet's words:[118]

The power of beauty will sooner transform honesty from
what it is to a bawd than the force of honesty can translate

259

beauty into his likeness: *this was sometime a paradox, but now the time gives it proof.*

Would such words have been thinkable on the lips of a Leonardo, Michelangelo, Ariosto, or Ficino?

Love and friendship so dominated the emotional relationships of the Renaissance that I will not deal in detail with other sentiments. *Both love and friendship were placed above those emotional ties which sprang from blood relationship.* Melantius in *The Maid's Tragedy* expresses the common conviction of the whole period when he declares that[119]

> The name of friend is more than family
> Or all the world besides. . . .

Hamlet gives voice to a prevailing sentiment when he cries:[120]

> I loved Ophelia: forty thousand brothers
> Could not, with all their quantity of love,
> Make up my sum.

The same thing happened much earlier in the Italian city-states where, with the destruction or bourgeoisification of the old noble families, feudal ties of blood ceased to have any social function, and family solidarity became an increasingly destructive force, constantly coming into conflict with the bourgeois legal order of the small Italian states. A Lucius Brutus who executed his own sons, a Marcus Brutus who assassinated his 'father' – these could be and indeed were ideal figures. In Shakespeare, even those who revolt against their own families are often heroes: Romeo and Juliet, Desdemona, and Cordelia as well.

The dissolution of the feudal family was the process which left its mark on the era and, side by side with it, *the development of bourgeois family relations.* English Renaissance drama (above all, the works of Shakespeare) depicts the tragedy of the dissolution of the feudal family in all its terribleness. Family solidarity and staunchness in defence of family honour have become, by the time power is won in the Wars of the Roses, the source of the greatest cruelties and inhumanities, until finally the lust for power turns against its own seed: in *Richard III* the House of York, victorious in the Wars of the Roses, exterminates *itself.* In the third part of *Henry VI* there is a heart-stopping scene in which appear, successively, the father who has killed his son and the son who has murdered his father – that is the final outcome of the world of feudal family solidarity. But the bourgeois family which is taking shape in its place does not offer a more encouraging prospect. Here gain is the binding force; human relations are mediated through interest. We may recall that in *The Taming of the Shrew* the motive of interest is still, to a degree, sympathetic, for here we are still in the shadow of the family struggles of *Henry VI*. But in the later works of Shakespeare an air of resignation, almost despair, surrounds marriages dictated by interest (*Measure for Measure, All's Well That Ends Well*). The plot of the latter, be it noted, is from Boccaccio, and Boccaccio's marriages are, for the most part, marriages of interest.

Family relationships came to be permeated by utility relations sooner than did friendship or love. Love – in keeping with medieval tradition – could flourish as adultery or in the form of an ideal spiritual bond, and that in turn did not necessarily have any effect on how an individual made his mark in an increasingly dog-eat-dog world. The atmosphere surrounding friendship was also 'freer'. The family, however, was an economic unit, under capitalism, too. There the interests at stake were immediate and vital. Thus the least scope existed there for love relationships divorced from considerations of gain.

In saying this, I do not at all wish to assert that the Renaissance completely emptied family relationships of their emotional content. The increasingly common transformation of the iconographic theme of Mary with the infant Jesus into a secular, family scene of the 'mother with child', and the stress on family intimacy in the depiction of the birth of Jesus, do not indicate that at all. Here, however, painting selected a sphere of emotional and family relationships which remained relatively untouched by the motive of gain, in which 'natural beauty' and harmony still prevailed, untorn by concrete social conflicts. The tie between the still naïve infant and the mother or parents was necessarily free of conflict; an air of joy and pride suffused it, whether the surroundings were magnificent or humble. The dominance of this theme illustrates, too, how Italian Renaissance art sought to select from the material of life everything that was simultaneously beautiful, natural, harmonious, and yet true as well. At the same time we cannot help noticing how alien the depiction of the grown family was to the art of the period, portrait painting only excepted. If we take a close look at Ghirlandaio's *Old Man and His Grandson* or Signorelli's *Mary and the Child Jesus* we can see that the emotional relationships portrayed there are not family relationships but rather the ties between teacher and pupil – a loving, understanding teacher and an assiduous, intelligent pupil.

But family sentiment, and the values inherent in it, were not limited to, or solely reflected in, the mother-infant or parent-infant

261

relationship. Where deep and intense emotional links developed between parent and child, however, or between one sibling and another, they were precisely ties which *had* developed, which had been *chosen* in exactly the same way as in cases of friendship or love. Here, too, new social relations put an end to 'naturalness'. According to the feudal value system it was equally natural, fitting and proper that Juliet should be obedient to her parents, Ophelia to her father, Cordelia to Lear, and Miranda to Prospero. But Juliet did not obey – and therein lay her greatness, Ophelia obeyed – and therein lay her weakness. Cordelia disobeyed, and *thereby* remained her father's only true daughter, while Miranda was obedient because she loved and respected – with reason – the man who was her father. Fidelity to blood relationships was no longer a value in itself, but only if one had chosen that relationship anew for oneself. Fidelity to friendship or love were, autonomous values *in any event*: they were ties which had *necessarily* to be chosen.

The fact that family solidarity was a species of natural solidarity already elevated the importance of love and friendship. For the family was no longer the unconditional support which it once had been; the new individualism could shake off those ties at any moment. Nor did that rejection always have a negative value-content – as with motives of gain in view, for example; it could have a positive content, as in the case of the rebel. Gradually, chosen ties became individuals' sole support. As we will see, they were not always reliable or secure. But their security and reliability depended to a great extent on the person who did the choosing, on his values and above all on his knowledge of men. Ties of blood were 'natural'; each person was delivered over to them as a manifestation, in himself, of nature. Love and friendship, however, were attempts, successful or not, to live a life of human autonomy, independent of natural bonds. The dominant position occupied by love and friendship among the emotional bonds of the men of the Renaissance represents, then, another step in the process of humanity's 'growing up'.

Renaissance love and friendship wore many faces. It is no longer customary to call attention to that many-sidedness, for posterity has preserved and enriched it (especially in the case of love), so that it has become a familiar thing for us. But the great variety of types of these two feelings developed during the Renaissance, is one, very important aspect of the birth of a plurality of values and of dynamic man.

What is most important, these sentiments ceased to be the privilege of a class or feudal order. For until the Renaissance both love and friendship appeared and flourished only *among certain social orders* and *in certain situations*. Thus in antiquity friendship applied only to the feelings of free citizens. Aristotle distinguished three types of friendship: friendship growing out of custom, friendship bound up with mutual advantage, and friendship springing from virtue. Only the last was genuine and sublime. The second could flourish only so long as lasting mutual advantages existed. Virtue as *energeia*, however, could only arise through the constant practice of civic activity, defence of country, and the enjoyment of the arts and sciences – could it then arise among those who had no access to all those things? (Thus it was not accessible even to the entire free population.) Aristotle likewise noted that differences in wealth and social status were an obstacle to friendship. Even among free citizens, then, true friendship could only develop if other virtues (primarily greater knowledge) could compensate for a certain, not overlarge difference in wealth.

So far as love is concerned, it is common knowledge that a freely chosen emotional relationship between man and woman was unknown to antiquity. The power of custom (Philemon and Baucis) or feelings of erotic attraction (the Roman lyricists): that was as far as the content of love went during antiquity. As for the feudal era, the network of feudal obligations restricted opportunities for friendship even more than could have been imagined in the ancient city-state. A friendship can only be formed horizontally; but vassal relationships were vertical, and as relationships of subordination and superordination they friendship an impossibility from the very outset. Deep human attachments could indeed be formed between members of different of orders (as between master and servant), but they never took on the character of friendship. Equality, which Aristotle astutely held to be the cornerstone of friendship, was quite excluded in such a situation. Friendship, moreover – where it existed – had very narrow boundaries of moral custom set to it, by the obligations of knights to one another, for example. Individuals could work some variations on these forms, but it was not possible to 'overstep' them. Of the friendships of the serfs of the time we know nothing. But it is quite improbable that they went beyond mutual assistance and solidarity; they certainly did not take on a distinct, individual form. On medieval love, we can only repeat what Engels so tellingly wrote: individual love did indeed emerge at that time, but primarily among the knightly strata and even there in the form of adultery (as in the story of Tristan and Isolde). Individual love was unknown to the non-knightly orders and the peasantry, and even the nascent bourgeoisie was scarcely aware of it. Class boundaries were not an obstacle to love which, unlike friendship, was not necessarily a relationship between equals; but – and this is the heart of the matter – it was always the *exceptional thing* wherever it appeared, arousing astonishment and alarm, as in the case of Abélard and Héloïse. Marriage, of course, had little to do with love. Like social relationships in general, it was regulated, down to the slightest details, by convention.

During the Renaissance the feudal limitations to friendship and love fell away; those feelings became universal, the property of all mankind. Friendship and love, as sentiment and ideal, came to occupy a dominant place in life, in city and country alike, among superiors and inferiors, rich and poor. For that reason alone, they were not bound by any hard-and-fast forms. How could *identical* conventions fix the forms which feelings would take in such different social milieus and such diverse situations? For fixed conventions are more than just forms, of course; they presuppose a definite content. So long as love and friendship appeared only in the same situations and among the same social orders – so that their forms could become fixed – there might indeed be differences in depth or intensity of feeling, even individual modifications, but no plurality of types of feeling could arise. Now, however, there did appear, in love and friendship, a *plurality of types*. For the old knightly orders love was one thing, for the merchant classes another, and for the peasantry still another. Love makes its appearance as part of a *totality* of values and sentiments, and that totality was always different. Love emerges, in all its richness, in many forms, from the sublime to the ridiculous, from the conventional to the passionate, from spiritual companionship to sensual beauty. And similarly, friendship can no longer be defined within the limits of the tripartite Aristotelian division, nor by the rules of chivalry or the laws of solidarity, but takes on an infinity of forms and contents.

The transformation of love and friendship into something universal, accessible to all men, went hand in hand with the process of *individualization*. The man seeking his own way as an individual, freed from feudal restraints, would also tread the paths of love and friendship as an individual. Until now, it had been possible, and justified, to classify the types of love and friendship. 'Chivalric love', for example, denoted a certain well-defined form and content, common to *every* enamoured knight. From now on, however, there were no longer to be any such static types of love and friendship. That, indeed, was one of the reasons why the typifying activity of art had to be shifted in the direction of the individual and particular. And where that did not happen – as, for example, in the *Cid* – love seems less convincing to us; we no longer experience emotion where that emotion is not thoroughly individual. (After this, song was the only form which could preserve its generalized character.)

It was Shakespeare, once again, who depicted the universal spread of love, and the multiplicity of its individual variations, in the greatest number of shades and nuances. We need think only of *As You Like It*, where side by side five different love stories run their course. They vary in content, in depth and moral level; among them there are long-tried passion and suddenly inflamed desire, good sense and bad, but each one is still love. Or we could cite the amorous world of *A Midsummer Night's Dream*, from the wedding of Theseus to the adventures of Titania and Bottom.

In distinguishing certain features which went to make up the content of Renaissance love and friendship, I would not go so far as to assert that those features were typical of every Renaissance love or friendship (or, rather, of those significant ones which are known to us from life or art) – only that those features are expressive of a *new* value-content, and for that reason they tend to acquire an ever larger place in the ideals of the Renaissance. They include voluntary choice, an attention to personal value-orientation, many-sidedness, reciprocity, and an absence of compulsion. I must emphasize that their progress was realized in the realm of *ideals*. For even though the evolution of the surrounding social reality made their emergence a possibility and even sometimes a reality, bourgeois utility relations still stood in the way of their general realization. *The same developments which made them possible took away the opportunity to put them into practice*; at a time when they might have become concrete norms of behaviour, they turned instead into abstract norms. *Here, too, the development of humanity and the development of individual men came into conflict*, as in every area of bourgeois existence.

The more *autonomous* was the choice of a friend or beloved, the higher it stood in the Renaissance's scale of values. The criterion of choice was *personal merit*. In different times and places, for different thinkers and writers, personal merit was interpreted in very diverse ways. It might mean – as we shall see – sensual attractiveness, wit, beauty, intelligence, or integrity. Desdemona loves Othello for his heroism and sufferings, Juliet simply loves Romeo – the motive is unimportant. Montaigne wrote of his friendship for La Boétie: 'If you press me to tell why I loved him, I feel that this cannot be expressed, except by answering: Because it was he, because it was I.'[121] In the ideal, one thing was essential: external factors, unrelated to a person's human substance, ought not to influence the unfolding of one's feelings. *Comprehensiveness*, again, appeared in the conviction that these feelings should not just govern one department of life, more or less independent of or detachable from the others, but should pervade one's whole outlook; the *whole* individual was manifest in his feelings. Each partner, whether in love or in friendship, wished to participate in the *entire* existence of the other; the ties between them had an absolute character. *Reciprocity* had always been a part of friendship, but it had never before been a necessary component of love. Chivalric love, moreover, had even elevated one-sidedness and unrequitedness to the level of the highest value. But it is easy to see how, in the emotional world of the Renaissance, unrequited love became extinct. The relationship of Dante and Beatrice is, in this respect, still medieval; the object of love is relegated to a pedestal, for it is only the sentiment that is important. For Boccaccio, however, unrequited love is nothing but the first step in the direction of requited love, and the same is true of Bandello and Shakespeare. Romeo thus explains to Friar Laurence why his love for Juliet has so suddenly taken the place of his feelings for Rosaline:[122]

> I pray thee, chide me not: she whom I love now
> Doth grace for grace and love for love allow;
> The other did not so.

In the whole body of Shakespeare's work there is not a single example of unrequited love!

The elimination of force and compulsion was likewise a fundamental prerequisite for the emergence of feeling. In the emotional world of the Renaissance, autonomy meant that the autonomy of the *other* person must be acknowledged too. Thus it was an unwritten rule that a friendship or love could truly be good only if the other person also found it good. In the whole range of Boccaccio's amorous tales there is not a single embrace where the enjoyment is not mutual. Craft and subterfuge are allowed, but only if 'all ends well' – and for both parties.

I have said that, even as ideals, these common features were but incipient tendencies, which the men and women of the Renaissance created or made their own only gradually, step by step. Now I should like to add the further qualification that, while autonomy and freedom from compulsion occupied an important place in the emotional world of the Renaissance from the very beginning (the latter in particular having been inherited from chivalric love, and given a new content), attention to personal merit, reciprocity, and emotional comprehensiveness did not become general ideals until the sixteenth century, the end of the period.

A few words must be said about the relationship of love and friendship to each other. Here, too, the Renaissance occupied a position halfway between antiquity and the modern world. During antiquity, friendship occupied the very pinnacle of the scale of emotional value. The reasons for that are well known: the predominance of public life over private life, the extreme moral, emotional, and intellectual inequality of women, and the like. Friendship then often displayed the same symptoms that love did later: it was absolute and exclusive, for example, or demanded to be exclusive. In the modern era the ascendency of love over friendship is undisputed. Only love is absolute and exclusive; in friendship, even of the closest kind, such a thing is considered excessive, a violation of normal proportions. During the Renaissance these two sentiments were of equal weight. Frequently they even became fused, and not only in the same way as during antiquity, when friendship often took on the character of love; often love, conversely, turned into a deep bond of friendship, as in the attachment which joined Michelangelo and Vittoria Colonna. The question of which emotion was the loftier was one of the favourite topics of debate of the age. Here opinions wavered. In *The Two Gentlemen of Verona*, for example, it is the shallower of the two youths who betrays his friend for love; the nobler of the pair sacrifices love for friendship. Romeo risks his life not only for Juliet, but also for Mercutio (and that against his better judgment). But Othello, on the other hand, has no friends; perhaps that is why his passion takes on such an unequivocally destructive form. *Individuals for the most part decide which to place first, love or friendship, but for society as a whole no firm hierarchical order emerges; the issue remains in flux.* So long as men are still wholeheartedly involved in public life (as in the ancient world), while at the same time a relatively independent sphere of intimate, individual private life is emerging (as in bourgeois society), so long will love and friendship hold equal sway, side by side.

But let us trace – even if only sketchily – the triumph of love, or, better said, *how love is conquered.* The story of love's becoming universal, and of the unfolding of its contents in all their richness, extends over two centuries and a half. Here we are dependent on literary examples, and not at all accidentally. Paradoxical as it may sound, *the graphic arts are not fitted for the depiction of love*, at least in so far as we mean love in its totality, a unified complex of emotions which developed during the Renaissance. The fine arts could express, and indeed did express again and again, sensuous love, attraction and desire, up to and including the outright erotic. It could depict the *object* of love, the sort of man or woman who was worthy of love and ought to be loved, the ideal beloved, whether drawn from a model or shaped by fancy (Giorgione's *Venus*, or the *Mona Lisa*).

Art could *allegorize* love, as in the figure of Cupid or Amor; the allegory, moreover, could be immediate, as in Titian's *Sacred and Profane Love*. But neither the expression of sensuality, nor the representation of the object of love, nor its allegorization, is identical with the depiction of love; what is left out of all these is love itself, the concrete human totality of emotion. That emotion is dynamic, it is *movement* itself; what is lacking is Lessing's 'creative moment' in which it can be grasped. It is only to be sought in the succession of moments, the flux and reflux of passion; and for that reason it can be depicted only in those artistic media which are temporal, not spatial, and are therefore more suited to presenting the contents of subjectivity: literature and music. Since Renaissance music has left no outstanding individual compositions which are still evocative today,[123] we must rely here upon literature. (Parenthetically, be it noted that everything said here of love is true of friendship as well. The fine arts of antiquity, an age which prized friendship very highly indeed, never depict actual friendships but only the objects of friendship, and of love: handsome men and women. At the same time literature, beginning with the story of Achilles and Patroclus, provided many fine examples of friendship.)

Dante, Petrarch, Boccaccio, Ficino, Michelangelo the poet, Ariosto, Ronsard, and Shakespeare are the most prominent names in the process we have to consider. The 'conquest of love' proceeds step by step. A new experience here, a new implication there – out of such building blocks is the edifice of modern love constructed. And here, too, the sixteenth century marked an important turning-point, creating a fertile synthesis of all these new elements.

Individual love – to repeat – developed during the Middle Ages; love poetry was not in itself any novelty. One reason for this, though the least decisive, was the fact that the poet, after all, belonged to those same classes of men to whom, by virtue of their social rank or occupation, love 'pertained'. He had to write love poems just as much as the painter had to paint sacred subjects. Dante and Petrarch were not new in writing amorous verses (nor was Cavalcanti); what was new about them was that *they were not troubadours*, not poets by reason of their noble status, and yet they became almost the 'official' authors of love sonnets. They were poetic *individualities*, but they were also – even *primarily* – Florentine citizens, living in voluntary or enforced exile. The epicurean gentleman, the Ghibelline bourgeois, and the humanist bishop of bourgeois origin represented in their own persons the process by which *love was becoming universal*, no longer a feudal privilege but something which could and did belong to everyone. By comparison with this great change it is an altogether secondary question how much is new in the *content* of Dante's and Petrarch's lyrics, and what the new elements are in comparison with the medieval love lyric. Certainly many stylized turns of phrase remain in their verse, and the experience of love often serves only as an occasion for the expression of generalized feelings of joy and sorrow (by which I do not mean to deny their beauty of expression). It is also true that the demand for reciprocity scarcely appears; we can in no way speak of a comprehensive, all-embracing love in Dante, for whom Beatrice is a symbol of pure maidenhood. In Petrarch, to be sure, the emotional content is more comprehensive; but the weight of the past is revealed again, in Petrarch as well as Dante, in the factt hat neither considered (nor could consider) love as something that could be connected with marriage or family. Posterity has greatly wondered at the fact that Dante, while still filled with loving memories of Beatrice, could none the less go ahead and, without any conflict, contract a marriage appropriate to his family's position; while Petrarch's actual love life was a far cry from the sentiments expressed in his sonnets. It would not be proper, however, to measure this duality by the standard of later bourgeois hypocrisy and split-consciousness. At a time when a unitary kind of love had not yet developed, this was not a sign of duality or divided consciousness (of the sort that appeared later, after an integrated love had arisen), but the only natural and honourable procedure possible; by reason of that, the poet's feelings were not insincere, but at most one-sided, and even then only if we regard them in retrospect.

To analyse the poetry of Dante and Petrarch in further detail, elucidating the new shades of feeling which appear in it, is not part of my purpose; I have singled out those features which permit me to say with assurance that here the Renaissance conquest of love had its beginnings.

If it was Petrarch who set out to explore the emotional many-sidedness of love, I can certainly say that *it was Boccaccio who discovered the erotic in its modern form.* And it is the modernity which must be emphasized. So far as the techniques of eroticism are concerned, Boccaccio's imagination does not come up to that of a refined age of decadence, like that of late Roman poetry. Boccaccio's is not an eroticism of stratagems and amorous dalliance, however, but rather one of *conquest.* Moreover, it is not concerned with conquest in general; it is the concrete conquest of a concrete individual that is involved. Boccaccio's eroticism is never 'generalized': it always adapted to the individual, his situation, and his experience or lack of it. In the eroticism of Boccaccio, *sensuality becomes individualized.* The sunny atmosphere of the tales (disregarding for the moment the few stories which end tragically) springs not from sensuality itself, but from the way it is combined with the 'ideologizing' of sensual pleasure, which is always concrete and always individual. What is erotic about the tale of Alibeh is not just the fact that the hermit introduces the heroine to the joys of love, but the whole turn of events where they decide to 'drive the devil back into hell'; similarly, the exploitation of the repentant husband's stupidity, and the 'cathing of the nightingale', take on an erotic vibrancy from the concrete circumstances of conquest and enjoyment, and from their 'ideologization'. It is easy to see, from the tales of Boccaccio, that they are products of an age that created the legend of Don Juan and not that of Tannhäuser.

Boccaccio's concept of sensual love is profoundly epicurean and profoundly un-Christian. It cannot be said that he was alone in that: it is enough to refer again to Cavalcanti, or to Walther von der Vogelweide. But he gave expression to his attitudes in a series of tales depicting every stratum of Italian society, rather than in scattered lyrics, and that makes his work programmatic and universal. *Boccaccio separated the notions of sensuality and sin, and he joined together once again the pleasant and the good* – not in such a way that everything pleasant was necessarily good, but so that anything that was pleasant *could* be good. The command of nature could not be a prompting to sin, and to follow nature was tantamount to pursuing good. 'I, and others who love you [ladies], follow the promptings of nature, whose laws whoso would withstand, has need of powers pre-eminent, and, even so, will oft-times labour not merely in vain but to his own most grievous disadvantage,' he writes in one place.[124]

It is noteworthy how Boccaccio here expresses his belief in the *universality or general character of human nature.* For Boccaccio, the sphere of the sensual and erotic is – one might say – *democratic.* In their desires, all human beings are equal; lord and servant, nobleman and bourgeois, man and woman: 'Thou seest that in regard of our flesh we are all moulded of the same substance, and that all souls are endowed by one and the same Creator with equal faculties, equal powers, equal virtues.'[125] I said before that, by contrast with antiquity, love became individualized during the Renaissance; I can add to that that *in the tales of Boccaccio love becomes something universally human.*

Much has been written about Boccaccio's 'immorality'. *Yet a very strict system of values is to be found* in the *Decameron. Reciprocity* is an absolute requirement; the other person's pleasure is at least as important as that of the initiator, the woman's enjoyment as important as that of the man's. While joy and pleasure are an absolute good in themselves, moreover, third parties must not be hurt except where they deserve it, by reason of their being grasping, foolish, dishonest or – most notably – tyrannical. To outwit a tyrant is always meritorious: that involves more than just sensual pleasure, it is an act of liberation as well. And finally, but not least important: all love is voluntary and freely chosen, *and so a love that is bought is sinful.* Everything is possible for love, but nothing is permissible for money. Here the 'immoral' Boccaccio is not sparing with his strictures:[126]

> I affirm that she that allows herself to infringe [her chastity]
> for money merits the fire; whereas she that so offends under the
> prepotent stress of Love will receive pardon from any judge
> that knows how to temper justice with mercy. . . .

At the outset of this study, I spoke of how wavering and uncertain the *Decameron* is in its ethical judgments. That uncertainty does not appear, however, in its judgments on sensual pleasure – rather in its poetic evaluation of other actions and other types of conduct, going beyond the sphere of the erotic. And here it is necessary to emphasize once more – though it does not in the least detract from the great liberating and artistic significance of the *Decameron – that while Boccaccio did indeed capture the essence of modern eroticism, he did not capture the essence of modern love.* What Boccaccio's heroes and heroines felt as love and held to be love – what, indeed, was love for them in their age – was not love in the sense which that word has acquired over the past two hundred years. If in Petrarch the emphasis is on abstract sentiments, in Boccaccio those elements recede completely into the background. But that does not really form a contrast between the two. Emotional elements, in the form of *generalized* sentiments, may often appear in conjunction with a concrete, individual eroticism. But to desire an individual in his or her totality, and to desire *only* that totality – neither Petrarch nor Boccaccio demands or requires that. That sort of emotion is a kind of 'love before love'; it stands in relation to modern love in the same way that Shakespeare's reworking of the story of Romeo and Juliet stands to Boccaccio's original story of Guisquardus and Gismunda.

A new approach to love was made by way of *beauty.* That was the work of the quattrocento, the age when Plato was discovered anew and when beauty became an ideal. The representatives of that era saw in love an expression of the yearning after beauty. 'If we speak of love, you must understand by that a longing for what is beautiful',

271

wrote Ficino.[127] And Castiglione: 'Love is nothing else but a certaine coveting to enjoy beautie.'[128] I have already described Michelangelo's views in this connection. For further illustration of how deeply the idea that the longing for beauty was the motive of love had sunk into the consciousness of that age and the succeeding one, I need only cite a sonnet of Ronsard:[129]

> I would burn away everything imperfect in my human shell in
> order to soar to the skies, immortalizing myself like
> Alcmene's son, who took his place all fiery among the gods.

> My spirit, already caring its boon, strides about rebellious
> within my flesh, setting a pyre *to immolate itself by the light
> of your eyes.*

> Oh holy fire, oh flame fed by a fire divine, may your heat
> burn away my earthly husk so well, that I may leap at a
> bound, pristine and free, beyond the sky, there to adore
> *that other beauty, from which yours is sprung.*

Ronsard was one of those who set out upon the conquest of love in its *entirety.* Among his poems there are some which are merely piquant and erotic, others which mirror abstract sentiments, and still others which express an adoration of beauty. He approached love – a unitary, integrated love – from several different directions, but without yet achieving a synthesis. Only with Shakespeare does love appear as a passion that can be attained and experienced by everyone, bound up with one person, carrying the whole individual along with it and oriented towards the whole individual; not just an exceptional thing but rather an exemplary one. *Shakespeare took possession of individual, total love on behalf of the consciousness* of mankind. Art – to cite one of Georg Lukács's basic theses – is humanity's self-consciousness of its own development. Only what finds reflection in art becomes an irrevocable part of that self-awareness. Thus it is fair to say that with Shakespeare modern love is born.

The conquest of love came about only in the sixteenth century. Before then – as I have said – no deeper sphere of subjectivity had been opened up, and without the subjective outlook created by an individual range of emotion a real modern individual is an impossibility, and so modern *amour passion* is impossible too. Nor could these emerge at all in the sixteenth century or afterwards, in those regions which were behindhand in their bourgeois development, despite the awareness that a crisis was at hand. We must bear these things in mind in order to understand the notions which the utopianism of the Renaissance had about love.

Thomas More's *Utopia* gives some space to love. There men and women choose their partners on the basis of *attraction*. Thus marriage is founded, to some extent, on sensual and emotional ties. That in itself is already very modern and bourgeois – it is evident that we are in England. This, however, is the *only* autonomous action permitted in connection with love, the *sole* opportunity for choice. Pre-marital relations are punished with a deprivation of freedom, for secret lovers are forbidden to marry. The same loss of freedom awaits the adulterer, while those taken twice in adultery are punished with death. The law according to which a couple wishing to marry must present themselves to each other naked is, in our eyes, a ludicrous interference with the life and morality of the individual. At that time, however, it was not. In those days it seemed a further guarantee of freedom, for in that way the individual 'got acquainted' with the object of his choice before that choice became final. Before these dispositions of More's could come to seem inhuman a centuries-long evolution of the individual, of subjectivity, and of the idea of intimacy had to be completed.

Campanella's ideas on this score are even more absurd. For him, love is synonymous with procreation, which is under proper and all-encompassing state control. Within his strict ordinances even the details of sexual intercourse are regulated by a high official bearing the name of Love. Consider his cool, objective style:[130]

And so, after they have washed carefully, they give themselves
over, every third evening, to intercourse; tall, handsome
women are paired only with tall, strong men, heavy women
with slender men and vice versa, in order to strike a mean. . . .
They proceed to intercourse only after they have fully
digested their evening meal, and have prayed. . . . The hour is
determined by the Astrologer and the Physician. . . .

The racialists of the twentieth century have often referred to Campanella as a forerunner – but quite without justification, for in his theories Campanella always regarded the perfection of the species as the outcome of *ethical* choices, within the meaning of traditional forms.[131] According to his theory, one's ethics were determined by one's character, and it is difficult for anyone born with a bad character to be virtuous, while someone possessing a good character finds that virtue comes much easier. (We will see later how common this idea – the distinction between virtue and goodness – was in the thinking of the Renaissance.) Procreation, however – so Campanella thought – decisively influences character, and so if we encourage 'good breeding' we will produce human beings whose character will incline them, of their own accord, to pursue goodness. But the reference to Campanella as a forerunner of racialism is not just theoretically unjustified. It is unwarranted also because Campanella expressed his ideas at a time and place (Naples, far behind in its bourgeois development) when the demand for a free choice of marital partners had scarcely even emerged. Thus his was not a case of individual free choice being supplanted by an enforced constraint, but of *one kind* of constraint being replaced by *another*. Neither the social status of their parents, nor their material situation, was to determine young people's choice of partners, but rather their physical suitability for each other. From the standpoint of human freedom, however, it is all the same whether one's parents choose one's partner, or the state, nor does it matter in that situation what considerations dictate the choice. Why is it more humane if it is the elder Capulet who demands that Juliet marry Paris, when for her that is a fate worse than death?

Fourier declared that the degree of liberation of women is a measure of how free society is; and Marx added the observation that the degree to which man's nature has been humanized is precisely expressed by the relationship of men and women, for in the relations between the sexes the social values inherent in the most elemental natural relationship find expression. The Renaissance was the dawn of feminine equality. It was of course only the dawn, the beginning of a process whose end we have not yet reached today. The expansion of opportunities for autonomous action, and the weakening of feudal ties, also provided women with a greater scope for action and with more opportunities to choose – though, of course, for the time being only in the higher reaches of society, where the cares of earning a daily living did not deliver them over to the mercy of men. One after another great feminine personalities appear, among them a striking number who take their place on the political stage; but the organizers and inspirers of cultural life, too, are, in increasing number, women. They are no longer saints, nor even muses, nor simply the passive objects of masculine passion, but active shapers of the age, of taste, and of the world of ideas: Vittoria Colonna, Elizabeth I of England, Margaret of Navarre, or – not to neglect less reputable personalities – Catherine de' Medici. But even disregarding women who made history, cultivated women frequently set the tone in the intimate circles of the Renaissance courts and philosophical schools, as Castiglione's *Courtier* so amply testifies.

Even the Middle Ages put women higher than antiquity, at least in its ideals: in the persons of the Virgin and the saints, they were accorded the greatest respect and homage – yet not in their womanly character, but rather in their incorporeal essence. The Renaissance was the first age to esteem women as *whole human beings*. It is true, of course, that that too was mostly an ideal, and became a reality only within very narrow circles; but we have already seen in many instances that the appearance of new ideals reveals the existence of new realities in life, even if later the new realities of life disappoint hopes of establishing those ideals in practice.

In formulating its theory, or rather theories, of 'human nature', without making any distinction between the sons of Adam and the daughters of Eve, Renaissance philosophy programmatically declared the unity of the human species. I have mentioned in connection with Boccaccio how that was immediately translated into practice, with the acceptance of women as equals. Or I might as well cite Ariosto, in whom an enlightened attitude appears perhaps most directly, and who here, too, consistently carries through on the identification of naturalness with goodness and worth. Here are the words with which the knight Rinaldo defends a lady who has slipped out of her castle at night to make her lover happy and who, according to the letter of the law, must pay with her life for it:[132]

> Rinaldo paused, and after thus he spake,
>   Why then (said he) must this faire damsell die,
> That for her true and secret lovers sake,
>   Did condescend within his armes to lie?
> *Accurst be they that such a law did make*,
>   Accurst be they that meane to live thereby,
> Nay rather point a punishment and paine
> For such as do their lovers true disdaine.

> Sith like desires the fancies doth possesse,
>   Both of the male and of the female gender,
> *To do that thing that fooles count great excesse*
>   And quench the flame that Cupid doth engender,
> To grant the men more scope, the women lesse,
>   Is law for which no reason we can render.
> Men using many never are ashamed,
> But women using one or two are blamed.

Sexuality, then, is good and beautiful; its cultivation is virtuous, and equally so for both sexes, if it leads to fulfilment in love. Ariosto's standard is the same as Boccaccio's: if that same sexuality becomes involved with considerations of interest, or money, or gain of any kind, then it immediately becomes sordid, for one sex just as much as for the other. Thus sexuality is to be regarded within the setting of the overall ethics of the whole person, in the context of one's whole essence and object in life – and that applies to both men and women alike. The attitude of Ariosto's heroes towards women reflects the socialization and humanization of nature to a high degree. It is, of course, the reflection of an ideal, a reflection of aspiration rather than reality. The form of the didactic fable was what made it possible for such a work to succeed without infringing upon artistic truth. In Shakespeare, on the other hand, the writer who depicted the most all-encompassing loves of the age and their conflicts, we can see how far away the greatest and most complete love was from Ariosto's ideal.

In the sixteenth century love – and friendship – took on a new face (or faces). I have discussed how different aspects of love were fused into a single synthesis and how, enriched with a new subjectivity, love was deepened while becoming, in its emotional content, more individual. Now, however, I should like to touch upon other aspects of the subject.

So long as beauty and measure reigned – at least in the superstructure of society – love was a part of the beauty of everyday life; it was *one* aspect of human activity in all its multifariousness and relative harmony. Men had many kinds of ties, and love was one of them. It was an accustomed thing without having become a fashion, a pleasure without having become a ruling passion: it was frustration that generated the formula of passionate devotion. Amid the cataclysms of the sixteenth century, however – when the ground once thought to be so firm was slipping rapidly from under men's feet, when refeudalization and Counter-Reformation here, war and the Reformation there, and the advance of utility relations elsewhere were shaking communal foundations and making ethical norms and the bases of life itself shaky and uncertain, when treachery was a daily occurrence and one could only grope about for knowledge of men – love and friendship became much more important in life generally. Love and friendship, especially the former, were something to cling to on the brink of the abyss, a piece of flotsam to hold on to on a stormy ocean, the only certainties, the only havens. Love was man's salvation; it was the redeemer of those who no longer believed in a traditional God but still needed a redeemer. Love was all that bound men to life in a terrible world. Shakespeare's strikingly powerful sixty-sixth sonnet again brings home in an eternally valid way the sustaining power of love:[133]

Tired with all these, for restful death I cry,
As, to behold desert a beggar born,
And needy nothing trimm'd in jollity,
And purest faith unhappily forsworn,
And gilded honour shamefully misplaced,
And maiden virtue rudely strumpeted,
And right perfection wrongfully disgraced,
And strength by limping sway disabled,
And art made tongue-tied by authority,
And folly doctor-like controlling skill,
And simple truth miscall'd simplicity,
And captive good attending captain ill:
    Tired with all these, from these would I be gone,
    Save that, to die, I leave my love alone.

Those Shakespearean heroes who are deceived in friendship or love (or think they are) always find themselves bereft of *the whole meaning of their lives*. We need only think of Othello, in whom this conflict appears most sharply, for he has *only* love (and thus he has everything), but if he loses it, then he no longer has anything. If Desdemona is untrue, then 'chaos returns'. That is why, when he first begins to believe Iago's calumnies, he says:[134]

              O, now, for ever
Farewell the tranquil mind! farewell content!
Farewell the plumed troop, and the big wars,
That make ambition virtue! O, farewell!
Farewell the neighing steed, and the shrill trump,
The spirit-stirring drum, the ear-piercing fife,
The royal banner, and all quality,
Pride, pomp and circumstance of glorious war!
And, O you mortal engines, whose rude throats
The immortal Jove's dread clamours counterfeit,
Farewell! Othello's occupation's gone!

But at the same time that love was becoming a source of support, partly against the world, but partly, too, so that one would not have to wage alone the struggle for one's own world, another process was beginning as well: *love was becoming the fashion*. Chivalric love had not been fashionable, but rather an obligation incumbent on social rank; the love of the troubadours was no fashion, but the necessary concomitant of a poetic attitude; the everyday love of the early polis was not a fashion, but one expression of an overall *joie de vivre*, one form of release. The fashion made its appearance only after an individual outlook had emerged; it appeared in individual instances (which in the aggregate could be quite numerous), but the number of significant individuals could never become legion, and thus attitudes towards love acquired forms which were not autonomous but conformist. That was the price of love's becoming universal and general in emerging bourgeois society. It became universal as a kind of quasi-love, occupying a place in everyone's life and expected of everyone (and therefore appearing in everyone), an emotion subordinate to considerations of interest, a veneer overlaid on those considerations. 'Authentic' and 'inauthentic' love are not of course sharply defined, exclusive alternatives, but rather the two extreme poles of a whole range of possibilities. But the two poles still exist, and they exist from this time forward. Every troubadour sang of love with equal 'sincerity'; but can we say the same of Tom Jones and Squire Blifil? In *Much Ado About Nothing* Beatrice takes up the cudgels against this love *à la mode*, the kind of 'love' which 'blooms' as follows:[135]

Don Pedro:	No child but Hero; she's his only heir.
	Dost thou affect her, Claudio?
Claudio:	. . . Now I am return'd and that war-thoughts
	Have left their places vacant, in their rooms
	Come thronging soft and delicate desires,
	All prompting me how fair young Hero is,
	Saying, I liked her ere I went to wars.

And Beatrice says: 'Manhood is melted into courtesies, valour into compliment, and men are only turned into tongue, and trim ones too: he is now as valiant as Hercules that only tells a lie and swears it.'[136] In Shakespeare this conflict becomes ever more pronounced.

In the medieval Christian *Weltanschauung* love was split into two parts: a sensual component which was sinful, and a pure spirituality which was sacred. From the early Renaissance on, the integrity of love was restored: there was no longer any such thing as a sinful love. Love was natural, good, and beautiful; it could only become destructive *if the world was out of joint* – the emotion itself was always right. In the sixteenth century, when love had come to be seen and experienced as a passion involving the whole person, his or her integral human essence and individuality, this unproblematic outlook once again ceased to exist. No longer was love 'always good', nor was it either 'sinful' or 'sacred' – love was, above all, of a piece with the person who loved. Lady Macbeth's love did not arouse horror because it was 'sensual', but rather because it was the love of an evil woman. Titania's amorous passion for an ass is, for all its

278

grotesqueness, no less horrible, and again not simply because it is an error of 'sensuality' but rather the result of a *blind* and *stupid* desire. Jealousy was 'not right' either; with the emergence of individual love and the recognition of the human equality of women, jealousy, far from being curbed, turned into a destructive fury. *The great achievement of the humanization of man*, in its character of a *new* achievement, could become a source of inhumanity. For there was no longer a 'heavenly' love and an 'earthly' love, and what was 'noble' could no longer be distinguished so easily from what was 'sinful'; only the concrete passions of concrete human beings in a concrete situation could be deemed good or bad. At different moments, in different situations and relations, one and the same passion could be beautiful or sordid, pure or ignoble; greatness and baseness alike could spring from it (as in the case of Othello). With the birth of an *integral* love, an infinite variety of forms of love came into existence. In its new diversity love could no longer be reduced to types, as Plato had done in the *Symposium*; in its new variety love became as fluid and contradictory as man himself and the concept of man in all its dynamism and infinitude. Its contradictoriness was, among other things, the contradictoriness and open-endedness of human values themselves. Its values were no longer rigid and fixed, but formed a moving scale, even changing over, in extreme cases, into their opposites.

CHAPTER 9

Values and ethics

To recapitulate what has been said before: the Renaissance no longer knew a single, unequivocal, universally valid scale of values. At any given moment the system of values was a pluralistic one, and at the same time it was constantly changing; considerable differences existed, too, in the interpretation of one and the same value.

New ideals of value, and new sets of values, came into existence only gradually, of course, in the wake of changes that had taken place in the morality of the age. Pluralism grew out of the needs of the time, giving expression to an ethical structure which was much more complex than any previous one, and hence more difficult to fix through norms and ethical precepts. Men's social relationships became so many-sided that the behaviour realized through and demanded by them could not be pinned down in any definite set of prescriptions or ethical system. That was true even where this versatility or many-sidedness existed only potentially. The less the concrete actions could be prescribed, the less was it possible to fix once and for all the value-content of any action (for then it would have been necessary to rank an infinite number of variations according to their ethical value); all the more, then, did ethics tend to split in two. On one hand, various social strata organized their various ethical practices into concrete systems of morals, where, however, the values themselves were not 'basic', but very much partial, local, and customary. On the other hand, there appeared a general human attitude, bound up indeed with certain abstract norms (and hence with certain abstract traditional values), but according to which men themselves 'picked out', on the basis of a positive ethical attitude, the right values to guide their concrete actions at any time.

But how did this positive ethical attitude arise, if not by adaptation to some fixed system of values? And how can this attitude be measured, if not against a fixed system of values? The philosophy of the seventeenth and eighteenth centuries would presently throw out the whole notion of values at one stroke, in order to seek a quite different criterion for settling the question; it thus came to derive all morally positive action from self-love (and altruism), from rational egoism, or from the categorical imperative. During the Renaissance, however, this process was only just beginning. Renaissance thinkers still sought – at least at first – to go on linking proper action with *definite* virtues, hence with a system of values. True, stoicism and epicureanism made an attempt to trace every action of positive value back to some basic attitude, and then give the latter an ontological foundation. But the stoics of the age were not consistent in doing so, for along with emphasizing basic attitudes many of them also clung to fixed hierarchies of value, above all, of course, that of antiquity. Thus the dissolution of communal relationships did not have as its immediate consequence the rejection of all fixed sets of virtues but – as we have seen – a plethora of mutually contradictory systems of value, and a variety of interpretations of individual virtues, again often mutually contradictory. By the end of this epoch in the sixteenth century, however – as we shall see – the situation was ripe for the complete separation of ethics from fixed values (virtues).

Those fixed sets of values themselves had not, of course, been put together at random. They incorporated, even if in a rigid form, all the traditional ethical attitudes which the men of the age had assimilated, whether as ideal or as practice. With the decline of feudalism the dominant values of the Middle Ages more or less lost their validity in real life, as did the Christian value-system which had, in part, codified them. Thus the ethical writings of the time are filled with polemics against the feudal and Christian hierarchy of values; often, in fact, they preserved even less of those values than did the lower strata of society. It is a commonplace to observe, for example, that during the quattrocento the *popolo minuto* of Florence clung more tenaciously to certain Christian virtues than did the *popolo grasso*. Of course the ethics of the elite also absorbed many values evolved by medieval Christianity, even though their content was constantly being altered; thus the Renaissance concept of 'love' was a good deal closer to medieval *caritas* than to ancient *philanthropia*. Similarly, certain virtues that were, strictly speaking, chivalric – like loyalty, or respect for women – were taken over, though once again in modified form. But it was still predominantly the ancient model which at first set the tone for attempts to establish some

281

fixed set of values. Ficino, for example, described the proper scheme of values as follows: 'Wisdom, fortitude, justice, moderation.'[137] Castiglione operated with a much richer and more refined Aristotelian variant; his roster of values consisted of fortitude, steadfastness, justice, modesty, magnanimity, wisdom, generosity, pride, desire for fame, etc.

There is no need, in the light of the new directions taken by ethics from the seventeenth century on, to qualify these efforts as primitive. It is true, of course, that from the time the 'natural communities' began to break up, and the modern individual to emerge, it was no longer possible to describe ethical conduct by listing a set of values, nor was it even possible to approach it through such a list. If we were to 'supplement' the foregoing, quite comprehensive list with twenty-five values more, we would still not exhaust the toll. But even that is not the important thing; what is essential is the fact that today we cannot say (as one could in Aristotle's time) that the ethical man is one who 'follows' these virtues, who acts in conformance with them. And what if a person is able to realize only some of them, but achieves those to a very high degree? And what if, among the great diversity of virtues – often interpreted in a contradictory way – he attains some at the expense of others? We could go on with such questions.

Bourgeois ethics have, however, in my opinion, taken a defeatist attitude in their judgment of systems of value. For there is no question that at certain periods, among certain peoples and classes, and in certain defined situations there are leading values around which the others range themselves, and that it was a great merit to have recognized these leading values. It might be added that, while philosophy was remiss, literature often did recognize them. For if we look at the great literary creations of an age we can determine with precision what were the leading values of that era; there we can read the *concrete* system of values. Balzac, for example, was right in considering the degree of one's steadfastness in the face of money and success the leading value of the France of his time. Of course the hierarchy of values is always concrete. And yet the values which, with their concrete implications, currently occupy the pinnacle of the hierarchy are still basically and in substance traditional; they have found a place before in those often ridiculed lists of values (which may be enriched in content, as we have said, and of course every age does tacitly or explicitly enrich their content). What is true of 'virtues' is equally true of 'vices'. Just as there are leading virtues, so, too, are there leading vices, relative to each age, social stratum, class, and situation.

In turning now to analyse briefly some of the leading values found among the enumerations left by the Renaissance I will not strive for completeness. I will examine the content of those virtues and vices which recur again and again and find mention most often. I shall try to demonstrate how pluralistically they were interpreted, though restricting myself to the more characteristic of those interpretations. Besides examining new interpretations of traditional values, I shall have to devote some space to the analysis of certain entirely new values, too.

But first of all I must mention a category which strikes our attention precisely because of the fact that it appears so much more rarely than in earlier systems of ethics. That is the concept of the highest good. The 'supreme good' was the crowning glory of the ancient ethical systems, and in two senses: as the highest good *for man*, and as the supreme good in the objective hierarchy of values. For man, the supreme good was always *happiness.* In the objective value-system it could be the good of the state – as in Aristotle, who in this regard simply formulated the common consciousness of antiquity – or it might be the idea of the Good, as in Plato. The 'supreme good' for man is distinguished from the objectively existing 'supreme good', *but* not as regards *their value-content* – for it was precisely the identity of their value-content that made both the 'highest' of goods. If, for example, the supreme (objective) good for Plato was the idea of the Good, then the supreme good for any human being – his happiness – lay in the contemplation of that idea. If for Aristotle the supreme good was the good of the state, then the supreme good for man, and hence his happiness, was to be founded in the unstinting service of the good of the state. Two things were necessary for that, 'virtue' and goods of fortune. Happiness thus equalled virtue plus goods of fortune. The happiness of the individual was realized in the maximum service and enjoyment (the two coincide) of the objective 'highest good'. The whole fixed value-system is clearly based on the communal character and homogeneous ethical structure of the polis, in which the individual could 'take part' as an integral part of the polis as a whole.

So it is no wonder that, no matter how sweepingly Renaissance philosophy went back to the virtues of antiquity, it was unable to galvanize the concept of the 'supreme good' back into life again. Occasional efforts were made to revive the formula of the supreme good by resuscitating Christian traditions and religious needs in the form of a philosophically sublimated deity (Pico); but there, too, the idea of 'the supreme good for man', of happiness as a state of perfection and the acme of life, faded into insignificance.

But we can also find instances where the same sort of separation was made from the opposite direction. Pomponazzi, for example, writes of happiness that 'it is *a* good appropriate to any man who is not disabled, since every man desires it'. That man is happy who can attain his *end*. That, however, is far cry from the 'supreme good'. 'There must be assigned to each thing as its end not what is good to a greater degree, but only according to what suits its nature, and has a due proportion to it [viz. good in the widest sense].'[138] It must be emphasized again that in Pomponazzi this is not a survival of feudal thinking, although no doubt the Thomist notion that certain men's ends do not necessarily coincide with the end of the whole made it easier to dismantle the ancient ideal of the 'highest good'.

The dethronement of the 'supreme good' meant not only that any firm hierarchy of values was shaken; it also meant that *happiness ceased to be the central category of ethics*. (And ever since then it has appeared as such only in the most obtuse, philistine discussions of the subject.) The relegation of the concept of happiness to the periphery of ethics was a necessary consequence of that process of development whose driving force was constant dissatisfaction, which is characterized by dynamism, and in which everything static is only a phase and never a fulfilment, for in so far as it is a fulfilment it is already something bounded. (We need only recall those propositions of Marx which provided us with our starting-point.) The ancient concept of happiness expressed a state, the state of fulfilment. The adjective 'supreme', the goal beyond which there was no other (nor did there need to be another goal 'beyond' it): these things signalized a condition of stasis and fulfilment. *In a static age it is possible to achieve and maintain the maximum and, moreover, the preservation of the maximum is really a value.* Thus it is not without reason that happiness becomes an ethical category. *In a dynamic age, however, the state of happiness is not* a value, since it is a state of fulfilment; but for a dynamic age there is nothing 'supreme' beyond which something 'even more supreme' does not exist. Goethe's interpretation of the Faust theme advances a powerful symbolic treatment of this new situation: anyone who relaxes in the happiness of the moment is damned.

But let us analyse the ancient concept of happiness a little more thoroughly. Two separate, and quite different, experiences are bound up together in it. One is that of the *rational conduct of life*, the other that of the *enjoyment of the moment*. They were truly bound up with each other, for in every ancient thinker *both* were present; what is more they were often present in undifferentiated form. For Plato the happy man was the one who practised virtue (that was rational

284

living). But the person who through the mediation of beauty and love identified himself with the idea was also happy (here is the enjoyment of the moment). For Aristotle virtue plus goods of fortune, and working for the good of the state, makes for happiness (again, the rational life). But for the same Aristotle the pinnacle of happiness is the contemplation of the sage (again, experience of enjoyment). It is unnecessary to waste many words demonstrating this absence of differentiation: for in both Plato and Aristotle the most rational life is the life of contemplation and, conversely, the contemplation of truth is a practical value (with Plato the philosopher-king, with Aristotle wisdom as the supreme virtue). In ancient stoicism and epicureanism rational living, and contemplative or sensual experience, were even less differentiated – for in them the demand for a social praxis, still so important in Plato and Aristotle, was lost as well. Rational living, for the stoics and epicureans, meant not least the preservation of an unchanged system of values in a changing, and disintegrating, world.

All ancient ethics were necessarily eudaemonic – but in the modern world all eudaemonic ethics are, just as necessarily, without meaning. It is most short-sighted to describe the utility theory or the theory of rational egotism as 'eudaemonic' simply because their starting-point is the real man in his totality, and his aspirations (even when this real man is the concrete man of bourgeois society). To take the striving for pleasure or enjoyment as the starting-point of human behaviour does not at all entail a eudaemonistic conception. A theory of eternal dissatisfaction can just as well be built on the basis of the pursuit of pleasure, and indeed that has often been done. These thinkers, especially since Vives, Telesio, Descartes, and Spinoza, simply sought to interpret *ethical* facts on a purely *psychological* basis, and for them the starting-point was never the culminating point. For the ethics of happiness, however, happiness was not a psychological but an ethical fact, not the basis but the culmination. *The growing intrusion of the categories of enjoyment, pleasure, interest, and self-love into the foreground of modern ethics does not at all contradict, then, what I have said about the dethronement of happiness.* Spinoza already did not contrast happiness with unhappiness, but freedom with slavery. Freedom was becoming just as central a category for modern ethics as happiness had been for ancient ethics. Had it still been possible to speak about a 'supreme good', modern ethical philosophers surely would have said: 'Freedom is the supreme good.'

I will discuss the concept of freedom at greater length below, in the fourth part of this book. Here, then, let us return to banished happiness. From the time of the Renaissance, happiness was no longer an ethical concept, but rather a *category of everyday life*. Its undifferentiated and heterogeneous character restricted it to that sphere. That restriction did not, of course, represent a degradation. The concept of happiness, like happiness itself, has a meaning and a place in everyday life. It is always significant if someone feels happy, knows himself to be happy, and says so. Nor is there any 'confusion' if by happiness different people mean quite different things, or if the same person at different times and in different connections uses the word in different senses. That is no more a source of confusion than if someone says that he finds beautiful a beloved woman, a dress, a piece of music, a dog, an action, and the like. The 'feeling of well-being' or 'feeling of lasting well-being' which the expression 'happiness' serves to denote cannot be defined scientifically – nor is it necessary to do so – while ethically it is neutral, for its meaning is entirely dependent on its content. The sociophilosophical interpretation of happiness is equally meaningless. One occasionally hears it said that 'we intend to create a happy society'; that phrase, however, means only that we wish to create the kind of conditions in which some of the more frequent causes of unhappiness will be eliminated, such as poverty, oppression, meaningless toil, and the like. It does not at all mean that 'everybody will be happy', which is meaningless and not even desirable.

Although the everyday concept of happiness is, by its very nature, heterogeneous, we can still distinguish in it two basic tendencies. They are identical with the two features which characterized the Greek concept of happiness: rational living, and the experience of happiness.

To live a rational life means to give some reason to life, to set goals of a kind which 'fit into' the overall trend of human development and at the same time satisfy one's own desires – goals of a sort which always breed new goals, but whose partial achievement or approximation creates that feeling of pleasure which is characteristic of happiness. That lasting feeling of pleasure which marks a rational life is, of course, life's final lesson, the result of a last balancing of accounts; it does not rule out moments or periods of bitterness or despair. In that sense every rational life is a 'happy' life, even if it meets with an untimely end. Thus Othello dies truly happy, for he has regained the sense of his life. Rational life is indeed a moral value. With that, can we introduce happiness back into ethics again? To a certain extent we can, but not as a goal, nor yet as an end result either, but rather as a subjective emotional projection of that goal and result. In this very ultimate sense I can indeed repeat the ancient saying: 'He who is virtuous is happy.' But here the 'mediating' link is again that category which antiquity scarcely understood in an ethical sense: freedom. And since there is no such thing as freedom attained – for the process of becoming free is all that exists – I can best formulate it by saying that *happiness is an experiential concomitant of the process of becoming free. But it is never a value in itself,* for the accompanying experience can never be separated from the process itself.

The other, extreme manifestation of happiness lies in the experience of happiness. It may appear at certain moments of a rational life – but only at moments, for its duration is very brief; euphoric completeness is never more than an interlude. But even if we analyse it outside the context of a rational life it still retains its momentary character. Plato's insight was brilliant when he linked this type of happiness with *love* and the *contemplation of beauty.* In love and in the enjoyment of beauty there are indeed moments of absolute ecstasy when one is fused completely with the present instant and would only ask that it last for ever, if one could speak at all. Here happiness recaptures its ancient meaning: it is not a process, nor is there in it any yesterday and tomorrow, any doubt or dissatisfaction. Here it reigns as a state of self-identity. But even if we were to call these the most beautiful moments of life (something which the present writer would not maintain anyway), we still could not assert that these moments are of a sort that can be apprehended in an ethical way, much less that they form the 'supreme good'. Here, too, we remain on the level of everyday life, even though it is the level of its red-letter days.

The dismissal of the 'supreme good', and the gradual elimination of the concept of happiness from ethics (at least from its central position there), demonstrated that Renaissance ethics already reflected altogether new moral processes and a new ethical reality. The uncertainty and spontaneity of that 'dismissal', however, indicated that the new processes were still only beginning; the old categories were still peeling off them, like flakes of old paint off a wall, but only slowly, piece by piece.

Let us take a look now at how the values inherited from antiquity were reinterpreted. We can only mention a few examples, of course, but they should indicate how, in content, values were becoming increasingly pluralistic.

Practically every Renaissance thinker listed *moderation* among the cardinal virtues. But it was not necessarily viewed in the same way as during antiquity. *Among the ancients, moderation was a category of consumption.* Since no regular accumulation of capital existed at that time, the general relationship to products or commodities was a relationship of consumption. The moderate man was one who consumed neither too much nor too little and who, in his pleasures generally, held to the rule of *mesotes*. The Renaissance preserved this meaning, but in its outlook there was a new polemical edge: 'moderation' was contrasted with Christian asceticism, seen as a form of 'excess'. Castiglione, for example, wrote that[139]

> continencie may be compared to a Captaine that fighteth manly, and though his enimies bee strong and will appointed, yet giveth he them the overthrow, but for all that not without much ado and danger. But temperance free from all disquieting, is like the Captaine that without resistance overcommeth and raigneth.

It is obvious that in this polemic moderation ('temperance'), in the sense of measure in consumption or enjoyment, also acquires a new content. It becomes synonymous with *autonomy and freedom* as they manifest themselves in pleasure and enjoyment. The old category is pervaded by a new conceptual content. That new content is evident in the notion (which we met in examining Rabelais' Abbey of Thélème) that if we choose the forms and content of our pleasures ourselves we will never go to extremes, but will keep to right proportions of our own accord. Moderation thus loses its function as a *norm* and becomes a *consequence* of one's all-round conduct. The notion that moderation is an outgrowth of autonomy thus makes it possible to apply the concept of moderation in the realm of *praxis*, too, detaching it from consumption. Parallel with the process by which stoicism and epicureanism went from being passive forms of conduct to active forms of behaviour, moderation became a universal category of praxis, until often it fused to the point of indistinguishability with the demand to 'keep the measure'. This was a great deal more than just the reinterpretation of an existing category. 'Moderation' was *one* concrete *virtue* (with the stress on 'one' just as much as on 'virtue'). It was *one* virtue in an array of *many* other concrete virtues, and it was a *virtue*, a distinct value unequivocally desirable in itself. But if it is transformed into the general concept of 'measure', if we say that to practice moderation means to observe a due proportion and measure in action, if it consistently becomes identified with a modern version of the Aristotelian concept of the mean, the moderation is no longer *one* virtue among many but the general standard of correct ethical behaviour; it is no longer a single circumscribed *virtue* but a universal *method* of exploring ethical conduct. Then – in this case at least – ethics becomes separated from a rigid set of virtues, and at the same time one of the ancient 'virtues' loses its individual and absolute character and its limited sphere of reference. Pomponazzi, for example, writes that 'we first suppose that to each thing a proportionate end is assigned. For if man will be moderate, he will not desire the impossible, nor does it suit him'.[140] And again: 'It is characteristic of the temperate appetite to desire as much as it can digest; so it is characteristic of the temperate man to be content with what suits him and what he can have.'[141] Here consumption serves only to provide an analogy. This concept of moderation, however, is completely bound up with the position each person occupies in the social division of labour. Its component elements are a recognition of one's position, a feeling for one's concrete possibilities, a willingness to adjust one's desires *and goals* to the given situation and given possibilities, and a relative degree of contentment. I have underlined the application of the concept of moderation to the setting of one's goals because it illustrates that here we are no longer dealing with just a problem of consumption. Here, too, then, the concept of moderation is deprived of its character of a concrete, normative virtue. To accommodate our actions to our possibilities – that is no longer a concrete virtue, but rather a general attitude towards life and a general mode of behaviour.

Something similar happened to the category of *justice* as well – similar, but not exactly the same. While moderation lost its character of a virtue, justice remained an absolute value. Moreover, it began to take over a very important, basic place in the system of values. What it lost was not its character of a value, but rather its *unequivocal* character. In the ancient world, the main thing was *to be* just. The question of *how* to be just was a subordinate one. Justice could be based upon distribution according to right proportion (everyone gets what is due to him), or upon equal distribution. There might be local and temporary conflicts between justice, the law, and the state, but no general tension among them could persist. It was the conviction of antiquity that the state was just, or else ought to be just; the legal system at most ought to be supplemented with some degree of 'equity'. The early Renaissance still shared this conception – rather, it held this conception anew, for the Renaissance vindicated it again in the face of the Middle Ages' transcendent concept of justice. As Max Dvořak's analysis has shown, Giotto's allegory of *Justice* is indeed an unambiguous representation of the justice of the polis. In the course of the later Renaissance, side by side with the emergence of bourgeois social relations, the concept of justice lost its unambiguous character, and the problem of *how* pressed ever more into the foreground. It turned out that it was not equally possible for everyone to do right, and not everyone had the means to do so; moreover, what was just in one connection might be unjust in another, and acting justly towards one person might mean doing an injustice to someone else. We must take care not to confuse this with another problem, the fact that the stronger, the exploiter, the person in power regards his own interests as just and interprets that as 'justice'. That problem also existed for antiquity (we need only think of Thrasimachus' argument in Plato that justice is the will of the stronger), and not just in connection with the institution of slavery; the story of the wolf and the lamb also stems from ancient times. The new problem for the Renaissance was rather that even a conscious desire to do right could become entangled in unresolvable contradictions. Let us compare two acts of judgment: the judgment of Creon on Antigone, and the prince's judgment on Romeo. Creon clearly did not act justly, though he acted according to the law; the prince, on the other hand, acted both justly and unjustly. Or we might take two instances of the execution of an individual judgment. Orestes could be a tragic hero because he acted justly, and in the end his justice became law. Brutus, too, is a tragic hero, but he acted justly and yet at the same time unjustly; and the 'judgment' of the play does not absolve him even at the end.

Wisdom as a value-category was likewise transformed. With the aid of Eugene Rice's fine study,[142] that transformation can be followed step by step. Wisdom as knowledge and wisdom as praxis begin to be sharply separated. The Florentines generally treated wisdom only as praxis, but that attitude took root elsewhere, too, reaching its culmination in the ideas of Charron. (As we have seen, Charron *completely* separated scientific knowledge from ethics.) Bovillus took the notion of wisdom as knowledge to its furthest, writing: 'The wise man, who knows the secrets of nature, is himself secret and spiritual. He lives alone, far from the common herd. . . . He keeps to himself, needs no one, abounds in every good. He is perfect, consummated and happy. . . .'[143]

Whether wisdom as an ethical category was practical or theoretical, and whether it was embodied more fully in active or passive behaviour, was of course a subject of discussion for antiquity too. But at that time it was not possible to identify wisdom, as a value, *completely* and *exclusively* with contemplation, much less *solitary* contemplation; nor was it possible to divorce it *completely* from knowledge as a cognitive activity directed at discovering truth. For the connection between knowledge and practice was, of course, much more *immediate* then than during the age of emerging capitalism, and knowledge itself had scarcely been differentiated as yet into individual sciences; in the last analysis all 'searching after truth' either set out from philosophical thought or flowed into it, and thus was necessarily a direct expression of a practical commitment. During the Renaissance, however, the division of labour began to affect knowledge, too. To be wise came less and less to mean possessing universal knowledge. People were wise *about something*; in plain English, they became specialists. This process was only at its very beginning, of course, during the Renaissance, but its outlines can already be perceived. 'Specialized knowledge', however, is no more an ethical value in science than it is in a handicraft. That is certainly not to say that it has no value-content at all. Not just in the social sciences (like politics, which became a separate science at this time), but in the Renaissance's study of nature as well (as in astronomy, chemistry, and the like), so many questions loaded with implications for the investigator's world-view arose that moral commitment and consistency were often required in selecting, addressing, and solving them. But the virtue of 'wisdom' was not required. Wisdom could be a 'separate' virtue (here I am still speaking only in respect of pure knowledge) only so long as the realm of truth to be apprehended was a relatively homogeneous one, not requiring the co-operation of the most diverse ethical virtues for a person to find his way to it; rather, he need only be the same as his fellows, but dispose of the additional benefit of wisdom. The ancient 'sage' was a citizen who had a deeper understanding of the same things that everyone else was thinking about. The Renaissance scientist, on the other hand, was a man able to raise new questions and uncover new 'secrets' in *one* area (an area not the object of everyone's thinking), and for that a special configuration of moral forces was necessary. It did require virtue – though not the virtue of 'wisdom' itself – for someone to be a scientist, and the kind of knowledge that he attained (though ethically valuable in itself) did not at all qualify him to be a universal counsellor of men, as the ancient *sophos* had been; for he was 'wise' in only one or a few matters. In connection with theoretical knowledge the demand for the value of 'wisdom', and the expression itself, progressively vanished. Later, with the further evolution of bourgeois society and the ongoing individuation of the sciences, theory also began to separate itself from the whole complex of moral commitment and content, culminating in Kant's sharp separation of practical and theoretical reason, and taking its most up-to-date form in the constant effort of modern positivism to separate judgments of fact from moral judgments. But that is a later story.

This negative insistence on separating value and knowledge was still completely foreign to the Renaissance; only the distinction itself is characteristic of that era. 'Wisdom', indeed, was finished when the separate sciences took their leave of philosophy, but moral steadfastness for the sake of truth and, what is more, a recognition of the value-content of truth were not yet, of course, at an end.

But if it is a problematic – and ephemeral – undertaking to dignify a purely theoretical (individual) science with the title of 'wisdom', it is just as problematical (and ephemeral) to characterize pure praxis as 'wisdom'. Would a good statesman, an honourable man, a moralist treading the path of virtue be 'wise'? Here, too, wisdom as a 'separate' virtue has no meaning, for no new feature would be added to a good and honourable man, or an unusually effective statesman, if we were to call them 'wise'. Ancient wisdom was truly a *distinct* value, for it denoted a kind of knowledge which as such had an ethical content and 'contributed' to the enhancement of actions springing from other virtues, and to making one's judgments and counsels more effective. If – as Charron, for example, maintained – wisdom were only the sum of all virtues, that would just mean that wisdom is not a virtue, but rather a name for the aggregate of virtues, a sort of collective term. As a result, then, of the rupture of the relative unity of theory and practice, wisdom no longer has any meaning in connection with practice either. True, here too the concept still maintained itself longer than in the world of pure theory. Even the writers of the French Enlightenment still regarded the legislator as 'wise'. Behind the ideal of the 'practical sage' there still lurked the thought of Plato's philosopher-king, a notion which humanity has not been prepared to dispense with until our very own time.

It may be objected that what I have said about the rejection of wisdom as a separate virtue contradicts what I expressed earlier in connection with the values of self-knowledge, knowledge of other men, and knowledge of one's situation – for (as we have seen) a good knowledge of men in some form does still 'contribute' to other abilities, and thus it has an independent value in itself. Here, however, we come up against a problem which is much more general than the question of 'wisdom' as a virtue. That is the whole problem of the function of knowledge generally in ethical action. (One could, for example, discuss it in connection with the ability to foresee consequences.) There can be no doubt, of course, that the strength and depth of our knowledge powerfully influences our ethical decisions. But the ethical content of our knowledge is a function of our entire moral personality, of our situation, and of other personal factors. As we have seen from the example of Iago, someone can have a brilliant knowledge of men without that being a genuine virtue in the case of this *concrete* man. The ancient sages knew men well, but knowledge of men can hardly be regarded generally as 'wisdom' in the ancient sense.

However we look at it, then, it is clear that the category of wisdom, as an ethical category, became devoid of meaning when, during the Renaissance, it was subjected to two sharply distinct interpretations, a theoretical one and a practical one. The thinkers of the Renaissance did not draw that conclusion. They still held to a category of 'wisdom' as an independent virtue, but without really regarding it as a *separate*, absolute virtue on a par with the others.

Of the traditional ancient virtues, the one least analysed was courage. That, however, is true only of its direct analysis. For it was *cowardice* that was the object of discussion (and depiction); the negative pole agitated minds more than the positive (for reasons which we shall presently see). But I will return to this whole subject later.

There were two virtues which figure even more prominently than the traditional ones, and which I should like to discuss briefly. I have already mentioned one of them, honesty (in some earlier epochs, *honour*). In Charron's *preud'homie*, or in the figure of Shakespeare's Horatio, it came to occupy the very pinnacle of the hierarchy of values. Antiquity did not know any such separate virtue. It had its place, of course, in the chivalric code – but not as a culminating virtue, rather as a necessary prerequisite. An 'honourable' knight was still a long way from being an outstanding knight, much less a heroic one. Honour was a minimum requirement; it was essential if one was to consider oneself a knight at all. He who lost his honour lost everything; he was not a knight any longer but a nobody. When, however, the secure ethical foundations of the communal life began to crumble and the value-system was shaken and grew uncertain, 'honesty' took on a special significance. It became something secure in the midst of uncertainty, something to hold to in a wavering world. As a 'fixed' value, a certainty to cling to, it moved to the top of the hierarchy of values. The honest man was the one who could be counted on, who was there to help when there was trouble, who would not commit treachery. These were the simplest and most elementary values, but at a time when all other values were uncertain these fixed, elementary values could become central. Pylades played a more active part at Orestes' side than Horatio did for Hamlet; Pylades was more than just an honest man. And yet he was also less than that: for he was Orestes' friend in a world where everyone was like him and like Electra, not in a world where friends were of the calibre of Rosencrantz and Guildenstern.

Loyalty, too, received the same maximum emphasis as a value. Like honesty, loyalty was only gradually transplanted from the medieval world. But the practice of this virtue was more difficult, for the matter was more complicated and, at the same time, loyalty as a value was more exceptional. In the feudal world it was *personal* loyalty that was absolutely required; only faithfulness to God and religion was placed higher. Since society rested directly on personal relations (and since these did not appear in a reified form as later under capitalism), reliance on personal ties, steadfastness, and the fulfilment of personal obligations formed one of the chief ethical bonds of society; and that was true both of horizontal and of vertical loyalty (friend to friend, servant to master, vassal to lord, and so on). Since loyalty acted as a direct bond of social relations, it was the social system and social custom which prescribed relationships of loyalty. One could not 'choose' to whom one would be loyal: one *had* to be loyal (ethically as well) to whomsoever had been designated as the object of one's loyalty. The serf did not 'look to see' if his lord was right when he served him body and soul in a fight with a neighbouring lord over a piece of ground; the vassal in serving his king did not 'look to see' if his royal master was good or bad, better or worse than the neighbouring king. Nor could a woman have any voice in deciding who should be the husband to whom she would owe unconditional loyalty. These were sharp, clear, unmistakable requirements. They could lead to conflict only where there was a clash between two equally binding demands for loyalty (as between loyalty to husband and loyalty to king).

By the time of the Renaissance all that was long a thing of the past. Loyalty 'from inferior to superior' had, for the first time, become problematical. The process had begun even under feudalism, as commodity production became general and the separate interests of the various feudal orders came increasingly to the fore; gradually the feudal estates developed a consciousness of themselves as separate estates, and the serfs an awareness of themselves as a class. To the degree that lord and serf, great lord and small landowner became adversaries, loyalty itself became laden with contradictions: loyalty to one's lord *could* mean disloyalty to one's social estate, and vice versa. All this, of course, did not destroy the value of personal loyalty at one blow. That survived for a long time still – through the Renaissance and beyond – in those relationships which still remained personal (the king and his knights or immediate vassals, for example, or the lord and lady and their servants). This process again wore a Janus-face. It was destructive in so far as interest came more and more into conflict with loyalty, and service became something that could be bought; no one knew any longer whom he could 'count upon', for betrayal had become an everyday occurrence. It was constructive in so far as loyalty did not die out but became transformed from spontaneous fidelity to a designated person into *autonomous* fidelity, to a bond that had been freely chosen.

In different places and at different times during the Renaissance, now the one aspect of loyalty came to the fore and now the other. If I had to describe the direction of development, I would say that the early Renaissance saw positive value rather in the decline of the old, feudal type of loyalty, while in the latter part of the era the problem became more one of the development of a new type of loyalty. Thus the concept of 'loyalty' changed in content, and as it changed it once more rose in rank in the value-system until – as we shall see – by the sixteenth century it had regained one of the highest positions.

Boccaccio is our best guide to the early Renaissance's interpretation of loyalty. I need waste few words to demonstrate that in Boccaccio's tales feminine infidelity is not only pardonable but, in some instances, almost commendable. I should, however, like to point out that the very same thing is true of the Florentine attitude towards fidelity in servants. In one of Boccaccio's romances a woman takes a liking to her husband's servant and sends for him. The servant is attracted to the woman, too, but wishes to remain faithful to his master. The servant 'is minded to evince his loyalty at my expense', complains the woman, then sends her maid to him to argue:[144]

> No such loyalty is demanded between servants and masters as
> between friends and kinsfolk; rather 'tis for servants, so far as
> they may, to behave towards their masters as their masters
> behave towards them. Thinkest thou, that, if thou hadst a fair
> wife or mother or daughter or sister that found favour in
> Nicostratus' eyes, he would be so scrupulous on the point of
> loyalty as thou art disposed to be in regard of his lady?

Her arguments, of course, are effective. And we must add that they are true. Boccaccio, like his heroine, started out from the *equality* of all human beings. Ethical relationship and ethical obligation can exist only between equal persons. It is valid only if it is *mutual*. And as soon as loyalty becomes a freely chosen loyalty, it is a mutual loyalty.

Thus Boccaccio also underscores the fact that even if an unchosen fidelity is meaningless, that still does not deprive a chosen, mutual loyalty of its meaning. Still, it is primarily the liberating effects for human self-development of the decay of the old concept of loyalty which he brings out. In Shakespeare, on the other hand – skipping ahead to the late Renaissance – we find depicted the destructive forces loosed by the dissipation of loyalty. Sometimes even the old type of fidelity seems desirable in a world of selfishness, money-relationships, and treachery. Orlando in *As You Like It* tells his servant Adam:[145]

> O good old man, how well in thee appears
> The constant service of the antique world,
> When service sweat for duty, not for meed!
> Thou art not for the fashion of these times,
> Where none will sweat but for promotion,
> And having that, do choke their service up. . . .

And yet in spite of that, every kind of loyalty which Shakespeare depicts is, in some respects, loyalty of the new type.

First of all, in Shakespeare fidelity rests upon a value-judgment. It is not 'naturally' given, but freely chosen. A naturally dictated loyalty is not, in itself, of ethical value. Catesby, for example, is true to Richard III. But that is no merit of his, first of all because in dealing with a villain the virtuous thing is to betray him, and, second, because what motivates Catesby's sticking it out to the end is only necessity anyway (he can do none other). But Adam's loyalty to Orlando – to take another example – is already not simply dictated by nature. True, he has been the father's servant and thus has an obligation to remain at the son's side (here are the traditional features); but at the same time he is the one who most clearly appraises Orlando's special merits and who condemns a world which does not appreciate those merits:[146]

> Why are you virtuous? why do people love you?
> And wherefore are you gentle, strong and valiant? . . .
>   . . . Your virtues, gentle master,
> Are sanctified and holy traitors to you.
> O, what a world is this, when what is comely
> Envenoms him that bears it!

Thus Adam is a rebel. He despises the world he lives in, and *because of that* he is faithful to the man he deems honest, a man whom that world treads underfoot.

At the same time, fidelity in Shakespeare is, for the most part, *mutual*. Shakespeare never makes any distinction, for example, between man's loyalty and woman's loyalty. Nor is fidelity a one-sided affair in the servant-master relationship, either. Antonio, in *Twelfth Night*, has saved Sebastian's life and has (of his own free will) served him. When he mistakes Sebastian's sister Viola for his master, and accuses his supposed master of ingratitude, Viola – with complete conviction – responds:[147]

> I hate ingratitude more in a man
> Than lying, vainness, babbling, drunkenness,
> Or any taint of vice whose strong corruption
> Inhabits our frail blood.

When Lear, following the tempest scene, says of Edgar (disguised as a madman), 'I will keep still with my philosopher', that is likewise an expression of loyalty; the king, suddenly fallen from his high station and taught a lesson in the misery and misfortune of the world, has learned the value of reciprocity and the meaning of obligation to 'inferiors' as well.

But even where loyalty is still traditional in form, and not reciprocal, it still manifests itself, *in its concrete content and style*, as a new, freely chosen value. We need only think of Kent's loyalty. Here is a vassal who remains true to his king; beyond a doubt, we have to do here with a traditional bond. Here, moreover, is a vassal who completely identifies himself with his lord: for Kent, life itself no longer has any meaning after his master's death. But loyalty, in his case, does not mean identifying himself with the other person's *every* action, either. Kent makes distinctions; he distinguishes good from evil; he is loyal, but only in what is *morally good*. His angry, open break with the unjust king, and his service, in disguise, of an increasingly rejected and unfortunate master, resolves for him this dual ethical challenge. Here, too, the value 'loyalty' has been drastically reinterpreted. Nor is it only in Shakespeare that we see how much blind fidelity has lost of its value. Castiglione, for example, held that the first prerequisite of loyalty towards the prince was to speak the truth unconditionally (just as Kent did).

Finally, the concept of loyalty was no longer restricted to *personal fidelity*. (In the Middle Ages, as we have seen, only loyalty to God stood higher than that.) Here the Renaissance went beyond Christian values, reaching back to the ancient universe of values. Symbolically, the relationship between Jesus and the Apostles was characteristic for the Christian value-system. The highest personal loyalty, and fidelity to God and religion, were combined in loyalty to Jesus. On the other hand, the idea 'I love Plato, but I love truth more' was compatible with the ancient value-system, as was the ideal of Brutus the assassin of Caesar (acting in the name of loyalty to his country and his beliefs). During the Renaissance it became self-evident once more that it was possible to be 'true' to an idea, belief, or *Weltanschauung*, that this kind of fidelity was more binding than any personal tie (including the personal bond with the transcendent, the *imitatio Christi*), and that in the name of this fidelity to a higher, more general truth it could be right, fitting, and just to disregard the most personal ties. Here, too, however, the return to antiquity was a complex one, for the ideals that were set above personal ties were often not general ones; they were still new and untried, often only an ideological cover for individual interests. It should be added that this subject only grew more complex as the Renaissance progressed, so that we can witness a succession of revivals of the idea of personal loyalty as the only 'sure' loyalty.

Until now I have spoken mainly of the cardinal virtues. But I should add that during the Renaissance many human reactions and character traits came to be valued which until then had been regarded with indifference, and many 'finer', more individual values were born which earlier ages had not known. I have already spoken of *tact*, for Castiglione a central category. But I could just as well speak of laughter, of the sense of humour. For both antiquity and the Middle Ages, the 'serious' man was the ideal. In the *Nicomachean Ethics* Aristotle went so far as to declare it unworthy of a noble spirit to laugh aloud – and with good reason, for what provoked laughter was most often a coarse jest. Even if we look at so refined a writer as Aristophanes we must admit that what moved the audiences of his time to laughter was not really humour, not even wit in the modern sense of the word (which was already evolving during the Renaissance); what set them laughing was either parody or plain ribaldry. In saying that comedy imitates low persons Aristotle was quite correct so far as the comedy of his time was concerned. In the Middle Ages laughter was still fitting the ideal, hearty laughter was the mark of some rude entertainment, and the person who made others laugh was a buffoon, a jester: a servant. We need only take a glance at the literature of the Renaissance to see how radically the situation has changed. Laughter and joking are no longer 'servile' – they are quite noble indeed. The humanist Galeozzo Marzio collected the stories and anecdotes about Matthias Corvinus, king of Hungary; in them Matthias is seen to laugh and joke and, what is more, we can laugh at him, too. Nor did that do any damage to his dignity and greatness; on the contrary, his sense of fun was one of the great king's virtues. In Shakespeare's comedies dukes and princes and, what is more, his most beloved figures of young women, all love to joke, laugh, and make others laugh. When Caesar says of Cassius that he seldom smiles, or when Falstaff says of the Machiavellian Lancaster that 'a man cannot make him laugh', these are derogatory remarks, and justly so. England's greatest king was a man who, while he was heir to the throne, did not scorn the grossest jests, laughing in the tavern and on the highways with Falstaff and his mates.

There is no room here for me to analyse *why* this turn of events came about. I should only like to remark that the reasons are to be sought in the multifarious richness of human relations, drawn together only in the unity of human character, and in the fact that men's lives began to move less 'on a single plane' and more through a sequence of decisions and situations of varying degrees of import- ance, with solemnity making its appearance at the decisive points of life, while at other times people could relax and 'let go'. That relaxation, however, no longer manifested itself as an absence of civilized behaviour; rather, as overall conduct became humanized, it too became more humane, if less 'disciplined'. Prince Hal, for example, adopts a more lofty bearing at moments when important decisions must be made, only to lapse into the world of gaiety and laughter again when those moments have passed (as in the wooing scene). If some people were unable to relax and let go, that meant (in the eyes of the thinkers and writers of the Renaissance) only that they had not been truly humanized, that in their heart of hearts they were still uncouth, 'fearing' to abandon their dignity because they thought thereby to lose their humanity as well. In the Epilogue to the *Decameron* Boccaccio takes issue with those who describe anything piquant, and the laughter which accompanies it, as crude, because they are 'afraid' of it. For – he writes – 'these stories, such as they are, may, like all things else be baneful or profitable according to the quality of the hearer'.[148] Laughter then, and humour, are virtues.

In opposition to the cardinal virtues stood the anti-values or *Unwerte* ('sins' is not an apt expression for it, nor is 'vices'); of these the most prominent, and indeed almost the only one of importance, was *cowardice*. I have already described how stoic-epicurean morality, and those portions of public morality influenced by it, held fear to be the worst human impulse. 'Courage' and 'cowardice' referred to ethical conduct related to feelings of fear. The noblest man was the one who did not know fear (because he took no heed of death). The man who mastered his fears was noble (he was the courageous man), while the most ignoble was the one who gave himself over to his fears and allowed himself to be led by them: he was the coward. The archetypes of courage and cowardice varied accordingly as the things which men were afraid of changed. In the ancient polis-republics at their peak (including the flourishing age of the Roman Republic) and during the Middle Ages courage was primarily a martial virtue, for fear, above all the fear of death, gripped men chiefly on the field of battle or in single combat. That sort of courage – staunchness as opposed to flight on the field of battle – played scarcely any part in the Renaissance. In Italy fighting was a mercenary's trade; the classical age of the English Renaissance was a peaceful one, while in France the Wars of Religion made military activity least attractive of all there. Machiavelli, to be sure, wished to arouse 'martial' courage, yet he regarded it as something foreign to the spirit of his time. For a full appreciation of how little martial courage counted as an important value, we must turn again to Shakespeare. Brave soldiers (like Iago) often appear among his basest and most vicious protagonists, while more than one sympathetic hero flees (like Mark Antony) from the field of battle. But what is true of martial courage is not true of courage in general.

Even during antiquity, stoicism and epicureanism had worked out a new concept of courage. Lonely fortitude in the face of tyranny, steadfastness in adversity, composure in the presence of illness, poverty, or abandonment: these received the name of 'courage'. Aristotle's concept of courage was already broader than was customary, for it referred to fortitude as a *whole*; yet here Aristotle was not consistent for he held this more broadly interpreted sort of courage to be likewise related to fear – and with reason, for in an age when communal ties were loosening and some individuals (though they were the exception) sought to withdraw to a position of *procul negotiis*, fear did not make its appearance on the battlefield; tyranny, misery, illness, early and senseless death really were the things men were afraid of. This kind of concept of courage was very well suited to the social situation of the Renaissance and to the challenges facing the men of that age. Stoic-epicurean philosophy was indebted not least to this concept of courage for the great popularity it enjoyed during the Renaissance. When, for example, Bacon wrote that 'the virtue of Prosperity is temperance, the virtue of Adversity is fortitude',[149] he was thinking not of any sort of martial virtue but rather of courage in this stoic-epicurean kind of interpretation.

Courage came more and more to mean the virtue of *constancy* in one's principles and values; such a thing was all the more necessary the greater the sacrifices that went with such constancy, from loss of one's goods to sacrifice of one's life. Thus it was that at this time courage became purely a *moral* value. So long as it remained primarily a martial virtue there were still many *psychological* elements in it. The psychological was not of course absent from the new interpretation; psychological factors have a share in courage as 'constancy', but no more so than in justice, moderation, or loyalty, just as fear is not necessarily a stronger emotion than self-love or love of pleasure, with which those other values were primarily (though not exclusively) bound up. In the old, martial concept of courage, however, the condition and nature of the psyche received much greater emphasis than was the case with the other virtues. The gradual transformation of courage into a moral virtue reflected, on the other hand, the fact that it was becoming a virtue not necessarily associated with common activity (battle) or with action regulated by communal ethical norms (the duel), but often, even preponderantly, a requisite attitude for the conduct of the individual who stands *alone*. Here I do not have primarily in mind the fact that courageous conduct may come to be called for amid circumstances of *physical* isolation. That much is common enough even where courage is only a martial virtue or means only the observance of communal norms. Fenimore Cooper's Indians, for example, act bravely while alone in captivity among white men, but for all that their bravery is still a typically 'martial' virtue. We must take 'standing alone' in a *moral* sense – in the sense that some men must stand their ground for their chosen principles and ethics even though they do not belong to a community that is firmly grounded ethically, even though their community may not demand such conduct from them in a given case, even though the community with its own set morality may not even pay any attention to their actions. Certainly a different kind of courage is demanded of the servant who kills the murderous Cornwall, unexpectedly, against all usage, and in the full knowledge that he must pay for it immediately with his own life, than is demanded, for example, of Brutus, who dies as a Roman on the field of battle, before the eyes of other Romans who expect from him a heroic and 'beautiful' death. These two kinds of courage can come into conflict with each other, and there also exists the possibility of choosing between them. When, for example, Romeo *contrary to* the customary ethics refuses to fight Tybalt, he can be regarded in the eyes of the traditional ethics as a coward; but in terms of the morality he has *chosen* for *himself* he is brave, braver for having borne the semblance of cowardice as well. This kind of courage is what we call 'civil courage'. Romeo's steadfastness in observing the imperatives dictated by his love, the servant's outraged and liberating act, Cordelia's truth-telling, Emilia's rebellion are all examples of it. Civil courage occupies a prominent place in ages when traditional systems of values have been overturned and no great movements have yet arisen to orient people towards new ones. So it is in Shakespeare's world, in Montaigne's, and in Bacon's.

Let us return for a moment to the opposite pole, that of the anti-value. Traditional martial valour had only one contrary, cowardice. Civil courage, however, has two, cowardice and *weakness*. Everyone knew that martial courage was the proper thing – so if anyone did not display it he must have acted out of fear, hence he was a coward. Civil courage, as we have seen, is the courage of the man who stands alone. Here one's staunchness and integrity may come to grief not merely on the emotion of fear, but because one's inner values have become unreliable: that is weakness. In such cases men are usually clear enough about their values, but they feel very strongly the pressure of such ideas as 'Nobody does this sort of thing', 'Everything recommends my doing the opposite', 'What can you do anyway at times like this?'. Civil courage breaks down in the face of a stronger will.

Thus in the value-system of the late Renaissance (especially the sixteenth century) weakness and cowardice, the opposites of civil courage, were the most dangerous of faults. They opened the way for tyrants and poisoned the innermost reaches of life as well. In Shakespeare's history plays a whole gallery of types of cowardice and weakness takes the stage. Henry VI is not simply an 'easily influenced' ruler; the problem is not that he lets the helm of state slip from his hands, but rather that he knows exactly what is right and what is wrong, knows what he ought to do, sees who is honest and who is treacherous, and yet simply cannot do anything for the good and against the wicked because he is alone and uncertain, and never takes on himself the courage to decide. He calmly endorses the death of his uncle, Gloster, and then sighs afterward:[150]

> Even so myself bewails good Gloster's case
> With sad unhelpful tears, and with dimm'd eyes
> Look after him and cannot do him good,
> So mighty are his vowed enemies.
> His fortunes I will weep and 'twixt each groan
> Say 'Who's a traitor? Gloster he is none.'

Richard III really can get away with *anything*, for *everyone* around him is cowardly or weak. There is not a single character who does not lose his presence of mind in Richard's proximity – not only Hastings and Buckingham, but even Anne as well. Richard's contempt for the world is profoundly justified. And every time that he 'breaks' someone else that contempt only grows. After his scene with Anne he cries out, almost in despair:[151]

> Hath she forgot already that brave prince,
> Edward, her lord, whom I, some three months since,
> Stabb'd in my angry mood at Tewksbury?...
> And will she yet debase her eyes on me,
> That cropp'd the golden prime of this sweet prince,
> And made her widow to a woful bed?
> On me, whose all not equals Edward's moiety?

The scrivener, having read Hastings's indictment, sums up like a Greek chorus the parade of weakness and cowardice:[152]

> Here's a good world the while! Why who's so gross,
> That seeth not this palpable device?
> Yet who's so blind, but says he sees it not?
> Bad is the world; and all will comme to nought,
> When such bad dealing must be seen in thought.

The age also saw very clearly the destructive effects of cowardice and weakness. Both showed up not only as passive failings, only indirectly harmful, but also as active, directly destructive faults. Machiavelli gives many examples to illustrate how princes have committed politically unnecessary and harmful murders and other crimes out of fear, and Shakespeare's Richard II prophesies:[153]

> The love of wicked men converts to fear;
> That fear to hate, and hate turns one or both
> To worthy danger and deserved death.

Montaigne, for his part, writes:[154]

> What makes tyrants so bloodthirsty? It is concern for their
> security, and the fact that their cowardly heart furnishes them
> with no other means of making themselves secure than by
> exterminating those who can injure them ... for fear of a
> scratch. ...

Alongside cowardice and weakness, sins related to the emotion of fear, the Renaissance regarded as most dangerous those which sprang from egotism and which could turn aggressive and destructive. These included envy, jealousy, and pride. *Pride* was still one of the Christian cardinal sins. It never entirely divested itself of its origins; the writers who most stressed its dire consequences were those who contrasted to the dog-eat-dog world of primitive accumulation an ideal system of equality, making appeal to the ideal equality of Christianity (Thomas More, and, for that matter, Luther and Calvin as well). More, for example wrote:[155]

> And I dowte not that either the respecte of every mans private commoditie, or else the authority of our savioure Christe . . . wold have brought all the worlde longe agoo into the laws of this weale publique, if it wer not that one only beast, the princesse and mother of all mischiefe, pride, doth withstande and let it.

The remark also reveals that even More no longer used the word 'pride' in a completely Christian sense. Healthy self-interest – 'every mans private commoditie' – was a reliable guide; pride was a form of self-interest that was not healthy, the individual's effort to place himself – his whole particularity – above every other interest and end. Thus it had no overtones of *superbia*, as in the Christian value-system, and its opposite certainly was not 'humility'; rather it meant 'individualism', and its opposite was 'having regard for the other person's interests', 'going along with the pursuit of common goals', and the like. What More calls 'private commoditie' Bacon terms 'self-love'. As soon as it goes over to aggressiveness it becomes 'the wisdom of rats', of foxes and crocodiles. *Envy* is the product of this sort of egotism. It springs from constantly comparing ourselves with others: 'Envy is ever joined with the comparing of a man's self. . . .'[156] Bacon regarded envy as the vilest affection, for it always has some object, some material to work with. Other failings require some occasion, but there is always occasion for envy, since there is no situation in which it is not possible to draw comparisons. It is hardly necessary to demonstrate that in Shakespeare, too, envy and jealousy stand at least as 'high' in the hierarchy of vices as weakness and cowardice.

I have already touched, in my discussion of knowledge of men, upon the place of *hypocrisy* in the age's catalogue of vices. Here I should only like to emphasize that the extraordinary seriousness with which hypocrisy was regarded was due to its novelty and unfamiliarity, to the relative difficulty of detecting it, and to its ever-increasing commonplaceness. 'As for this new-fangled virtue of hypocrisy and dissimulation, which is so highly honoured at present, I mortally hate it,' wrote Montaigne. 'It is a craven and servile idea to disguise ourselves and hide under a mask. . . .'[157] And mention must still be made of *cynicism*, which became widespread at this time, as in every age which has become uncertain of its values. I cannot analyse here the problem of cynicism, either in its hypocritical or its open form. But we may observe that the best minds of the age clearly felt the ethical difference between hypocritical cynicism and open cynicism. The value-content of hypocritical cynicism was always negative, for in appearance (externally) it acknowledged the traditional roster of values while internally, in the secrecy of the incognito, it regularly acted contrary to those values (as, for example, in the case of Richard III). Open cynicism, however, wore a Janus-face. It was a frank attack on certain values, and its own value-content depended on *what kind* of values it took issue with. If they were obsolete, ambiguous, or trivial, or if they were not even approximately realized in actual reality, then cynicism was relatively justified, being in effect a form of scepticism, evolving into a life-attitude. Some of Shakespeare's most sympathetic heroes and heroines are openly cynical in this way, like Jaques in *As You Like It*, who in his polemics against supposed values actually defends truer ones (as do Beatrice and Benedict). To the problem of political cynicism, again, I shall return later, in discussing Machiavelli.

With this I have obviously not exhausted the cardinal sins of the age, just as I did not exhaust the list of its cardinal virtues either. I wished merely to indicate that the hierarchy of values (both positive and negative) underwent rearrangement and redefinition, and that although the resulting value-system was far from unitary the 'important' virtues and vices were still those which in the new situation of the age were most necessary, or most likely to appear, whether they were humanistic values or anti-human ones.

Of the varieties of ethics which rested upon a system of virtues, the most flexible variant stemmed from Aristotle. For him, as for all ancient writers, moral goodness lay in the realization of virtues, but in each individual case it was for *phronésis* to decide which concrete actions were virtuous. True moral merit lay not simply in acknowledging the right values or in incorporating these value-claims and virtues into character, but rather in the 'astuteness' with which virtue and virtues were applied. It was of no use, for example, for someone who was unable to decide when, where, with whom, how and why he should be magnanimous to have a 'magnanimous' character; he possessed this 'virtue' to no purpose since he did not know how to act magnanimously, and if he did not practise magnanimity he would finish by losing value and 'virtue' alike. It was this flexibility which made Aristotle's ethics so popular during the Renaissance. I have already mentioned the direct influence of the theory of the mean on Castiglione and Bacon, and one could as well mention Cardano, who more than once complains that he is wanting in

305

phronésis. Here, however, the flexible Aristotelian theory of value begins to go over – almost imperceptibly, to be sure – into a new type of ethic, one that does not rest on virtue. When, for example, Cardano writes that not all kinds of perseverance make sense, for everyone must view Diogenes as a silly fool for exposing himself to the scorching sun in summer and clasping his frigid pillars in winter, while admiring Bragadino for enduring the severest torments at his enemy's hands, he is not simply repeating the theory of the mean. For he does not say that Diogenes was not really steadfast while Bragadino was (since steadfastness means persevering when, where, and in whatever context it is appropriate); what he is saying here is that perseverance itself, as a virtue, is not always sensible, good, and honourable. Practising certain virtues does not necessarily mean that a man is moral.

Cardano analyses the question from the other direction, too. A man can be moral even though he does not always pursue and realize the virtues. Here, again, is the way he characterizes his own ethic: 'I determined upon a course of life for myself, not such as I would have, but *such as I could*. . . . And in this my purpose was not single or constant . . .; I acted as seemed advantageous when each occasion arose. . . .'[158] One must know what is good, but one must act with a view to what is possible; that much flexibility is necessary if one is to remain honourable and yet not go to rack and ruin. So long as there existed an immediate communal ethic, where only a difference – but no contradiction – obtained between concrete and abstract norms, men could find a secure guide by holding fast to the existing system of norms. As such times there could emerge a viewpoint like that of Socrates, according to which it suffices for the realization of the good to recognize it, or that of Aristotle who amplified this requirement by presupposing in addition the necessity of a basic disposition of character towards the good on the part of the subject. If, however, there is no firm communal ethic, then neither Socratic ethical rationalism nor its Aristotelian modification is satisfactory. The problem is not only whether we will know the 'good' (i.e. the system of virtues, which is also a generalization and idealization of the customary ethic), or even whether character, training, and long-standing habits permit us to follow that known good; the problem is that the good itself becomes ambiguous. What does it mean to be just? What does it mean to be steadfast? In themselves – abstractly – these categories meant less and less. They would become internal moral imperatives (at least for some) – but moral in a sense different from that of Socrates. Socrates was the first representative of morality as differentiated from ethics, yet for him it was a once-living, concrete system of customary ethical norms that was transformed into a set of inner, subjective postulates, in an age when the former system had lost its validity. Now, however, the situation is completely different. Modern morality, reacting to man's situation in bourgeois society – and hence beginning with the Renaissance – opposes to the existing system of ethical custom not some concrete system of ethical norms, but rather a set of abstract norms; or, more correctly, it tries with the help of those abstract norms to orient itself within the existing system of ethical custom. Here is the origin of that contradiction between 'morality' and 'legality' which Kant so rightly recognized. And yet – and here we return to the Renaissance's problem, the separation of ethics from the roster of virtues – real action can never be based on that antinomy. Ethical judgment may accept the attitude of pure morality – and in that event it would conclude that the world belongs to scoundrels; every value in it has become valueless, nothing moral exists, society has been overwhelmed by baseness and squalor. And of course ethical judgments could accept also the viewpoint of pure legality: whatever people generally do is right, all the rest is mere preachment, since the world is as it is. But when people come to act they rarely can act on a basis of pure legality, and never on a basis of pure morality. The former implies an absolute conformism and the extinction of the 'private' conscience. On the other hand, it is impossible to act from a purely moral standpoint because at every step one strikes contingencies, relations, and situations in which absolute systems of value have foundered or provide us with no bearings whatsoever. Hamlet knows that he must be just. That in itself is nothing, however. The problem is, how is that possible? In what case will he be just? Ophelia wants to remain honest. But how? There is no general, customary system of ethics which offers firm ground from which to answer that question (Hamlet envies Fortinbras precisely because for him there *is* such a system of values). But if neither pure morality nor pure legality offer any opportunity for genuinely ethical action, can ethics itself be possible?

Assuredly it can. But it will be much more bound up than before with individual choice, with an ability to take account of the situation, with the mutual interaction of character and situation, and will judgment. The concept of *phronésis* took on a new meaning. Not only must general values be applied in a manner appropriate to the individual, concrete situation; in each concrete situation the hierarchy of values must constantly be re-created, with some values being rejected and others reinterpreted, in the search for the 'mean value' between the general and the subjective-individual, between

307

what is demanded and what is possible. That is the new ethic whose birth we can witness, an ethic of grouping for a 'mean' between morality and legality, an ethic of the possible; and the passages cited from Cardano display a profound awareness of the new problem.

From the time of the Renaissance, then, there was a need for an ethic divorced from any fixed value-system, in search of the possible, resolving in practice the contradiction between morality and legality. Of course, that does not at all mean that this challenge, which faced all humanity, was taken up and solved by every single human being. On the contrary: most common of all were those who clung to one or the other pole of this opposition. There were those who imposed on themselves and others the postulates of morality, and who – since they could never hope to live up to them in practice – had thus to wrestle constantly with a guilty conscience; they made abstract and rigorous demands on others, too, and if it was impossible for them to be thus virtuous they did succeed in making themselves and others unhappy. And there were those who followed the common opinion and common practice in pursuit of their immediate interests and who, having thus become pure conformists, lost their human essence – though that rarely happened permanently, and they too eventually wound up struggling with guilt or facing the contempt of the hypocritical public opinion which they had aroused. Only a few, having arrived at an awareness of the new ethical status quo, recognized and realized the dialectic of integrity and possibility, becoming neither conformists nor moralists but practical stoic-epicureans instead, and sparing themselves the pangs of guilt. There had been many more of these people during the Renaissance; in the Chapter dealing with autobiography I have analysed this morally triumphant type from Petrarch to Montaigne. In the later course of bourgeois development their number constantly shrinks, but of course they do not die out altogether. Citing literary figures as examples, we can point to Tom Jones and Wilhelm Meister.

If we wish to see clearly how radically the separation of ethics from the roster of values was carried through, it is enough to compare the plays of Shakespeare with the tragedies of antiquity. Who could be a dramatic hero, and what *concrete* virtues the hero had to have, were very clearly defined for antiquity. There is not a single ancient tragic hero who is not courageous; as for the other cardinal virtues, either they characterize the tragic hero or else it is precisely for lack of one or another of them that he commits his tragic offence and comes to ruin. It is not least of all for this reason that it is so important for the tragic hero to be *unwitting* in his tragic wrong-doing. They are not ignorant of the virtues – for in that case they

308

could not be tragic heroes in the ancient sense – but rather of the circumstances amid which they act (compare Oedipus). Yet even where it is not a matter of unwitting action, what we have to do with is a violation, not of virtue, but of the standard or measure. Agamemnon, Clytemnestra, Electra, Orestes – all are right-minded. But as a result of changes in the system of communal custom (and hence of changed standards as well) Clytemnestra's action proves worthy of condemnation, while her children's actions can be forgiven. Creon, too, violates the measure in not yielding to Antigone. In ancient drama, then, only *great personages* come into conflict with one another; everyone is right to some extent; and, finally, the conflict is never between good and evil, for evil, as a non-value and a deficiency, can never be characteristic of the tragic hero.

Consider, by contrast, Shakespeare's heroes. Some are weak (Richard II, Henry VI), others mediocre (Henry IV), unsure of themselves (Hamlet), unjust (Coriolanus, Lear), evil and clever (Richard III), evil and crude (Macbeth), voluptuous (Antony and Cleopatra). The cardinal virtues will no longer serve to describe these figures. Whether a hero is good or bad, and what role he fills in the moral hierarchy, is always decided *in the actual, concrete course of a concrete conflict*. Thus it is not the 'virtues' that are now concrete, i.e. fixed; the hierarchies of values must be crystallized out, again and again, around the conflict itself. And there are no two plays, no two conflicts in which the *same* hierarchy of values is precipitated out.

We may take as an example the 'virtue' of chivalric honour. Its most characteristic representative, in the history plays, is Harry Hotspur. Hotspur's knightly code of honour is, in itself, rather appealing. And so it remains, just as long as his obligations are the traditional chivalric ones: to fight in the service of his king. But as soon as his family, on behalf of a very modern kind of self-interest, take advantage of his old-fashioned chivalry to win him to their service, until finally he takes up arms against Henry IV, it immediately becomes apparent that knightly honour is, in the circumstances, foolish; it makes Hotspur seem almost ludicrous, and is no longer a form of grandeur but of pettiness. Thus in the course of the conflict Hotsput 'slips' ever further down the concrete value-scale, until finally we have no tears left for him when he falls. Value thus is labile: the moral 'locus' does not depend upon the concrete virtues. And so – by comparison with ancient tragedy – it is not just the value-content of chivalric virtue which changes, but its order of grandeur as well, while nothing has changed the place of, for example, Clytemnestra in the 'order of greatness', even though the time for her ethic has passed away.

But let us continue further: in Shakespeare's plays, by contrast with ancient tragedy, we no longer face the conflict of greatness with greatness. In general, there are at least as many distinct degrees of greatness as there are different moral orders. It has long been remarked of Shakespeare's tragedies that they are full of comic and grotesque figures. That fact is a reflection of the heterogeneity of social life. The same conflict could be 'approached' in quite different ways, depending upon one's membership in a social estate or class, one's individual ethics, general perspective, and so forth. Here we can witness a variety of individual ways of resolving the dialectical relationship between legality and morality. The judgment of society and history emerges as the *final outcome* of these various, individual 'approaches' and judgments. This process is the opposite of that which took place in ancient drama; there, since a communal ethic existed within which every individual could find reliable norms of value, the general social framework was already 'given' when the action took place. That is why the chorus, as the embodiment of the communal ethic, could play a part and render its judgment in the drama.

We must devote special consideration to the depiction of the grandeur of evil. A glance at antiquity's system of ideals will suffice for us to see that there evil is never great. There are no true 'villains' in tragedy, nor in comedy either, where wickedness always goes with meanness and ridiculousness. Wickedness as greatness appears only on the margin of a decaying antiquity. But then it is always an unequivocally *negative* force, and an unequivocally *destructive* one. Its embodiment is Satan, a transcendent being from whom all terrestrial evil springs. Thus, although evil can be a great, demonic force, it has a predetermined place in a fixed system of values. All sin springs from the transcendent principle of evil (and everyone knows what sin is). From that standpoint it does not matter whether one is dealing with a Catholic or Manichean conception of Satan. Satan, or sin, lays hold of his victims through the medium of the three human weaknesses: love of money, sexuality, lust for power. Christianity, both in antiquity and during the Middle Ages, judged these three impulses in an unequivocally negative way. The power of Satan, or evil, dissolved but did not build, destroyed but did not create. If we struggled with him and defeated him, then the world of 'goodness' would be restored, a world of pure positivity.

The practical atheism of the Renaissance sounded the knell of this kind of interpretation of evil. (If it was revived in Protestantism and in the Counter-Reformation – though only relatively – that is a subject to be taken up elsewhere.) First of all, the three sins by which

Satan could find his way into the human soul ceased to be sins. In the early Renaissance – as we have already pointed out – love of money was no longer a sin, nor was sexuality, nor was lust for power. Again, it is necessary only to refer to the stories of Boccaccio. The carpet has been pulled out from under Satan. In the same period, the problematics of evil also recede into the background. The ancient notion that evil can never be great is revived again, particularly in the city-state republics.

At the end of the fifteenth century, however, and in the sixteenth century, history and ideology again take a new turning. With the final dissolution of the polis, and the merging of the hitherto developed forces of capitalism with a resurging feudalism even in Italy, the sublimation of power-hunger and cupidity into something 'ethical' comes more and more to a stop. The quest for money and power comes to stand out in an even more glaring light in England, where the process of primitive accumulation was carried through to a successful conclusion. (I omit mention of sexuality because it appears as a 'demonic' force only in the legends of Faust and Don Juan, and never becomes universal.) Once more it becomes clear that lust for power and lust for money are *evil* forces. And gradually it also becomes clear that they are *great* forces, since they more and more carried all of society along with them, homogenizing society's relations and giving it its underlying tone. But it also becomes apparent that they are very concrete forces indeed. Evil as something great and powerful, as seen and depicted during this period, is no longer a Satanic principle, abstract and transcendent; it is very much a concrete spirit, the spirit of capitalism.

Money is no longer simply 'gold'; what sends men off in pursuit of it is not the *aurea sacra fames*. I will not cite Shakespeare's well-known lines from Pericles about the 'big fish' which devour the 'little fish', nor the famous soliloquy from *Timon of Athens* on money, analysed earlier by Marx. Instead, let us take a less-known passage in order to characterize the concrete ideologies of the day, Volpone's apostrophe to his gold in Ben Jonson's play:[159]

> Well did wise poets, by thy glorious name,
> Title that age which they would have the best;
> Thou being the best of things, and far transcending
> All style of joy, in children, parents, friends
> Or any other waking dream on earth: . . .
>   . . . Thou art virtue, fame,
> Honour, and all things else. Who can get thee,
> He shall be noble, valiant, honest, wise.

311

The value of gold, then, does not lie in the *pleasures* it can buy (as was characteristic of the allure of the Christian Satan), but in the general extension of commodity relations, the transformation of money into a general equivalent of value, the development of all human relationships into utility relations; when everything can be bought, the person who has money is *everything*, and the person who has none is *nobody*.

Similarly, power too means something different than formerly. The dramas of power are concerned not with the demonic use of inherited power, but rather with the *acquisition* of power. Old forms of power offered opportunities for its *abuse*; the new opens the way to the overthrow of every previous ethics, set of norms, and system of custom. Power is now a manifestation of *autonomy*, a product of choice – a choice by which one can opt not only for some position but also for the content of that position and how to make use of it.

Thus traditional 'evil' takes concrete shape here, in the spirit of capitalism. One must not, of course, oversimplify. There are few villains in Renaissance drama who merely 'symbolize' capitalism; perhaps Volpone himself is the sole clear-cut example. We could hardly say as much of Richard III or Edmund, or even of Marlowe's Faustus and his demon. In the words of the latter those *concrete* desires appear which had taken root in the soul of Renaissance man:[160]

> Settle thy studies, Faustus, and begin
> To sound the depth of that thou wilt profess;
> Having commenc'd, be a divine in show,
> Yet level and at the end of every art. . . .
>
> Be a physician, Faustus, heap up gold,
> And be eternis'd for some wondrous cure.

To sound the depths, to 'level at the end of every art', to be something 'in show' which one is not in reality, to acquire wealth and fame, to achieve power – these were, as we have seen, the most common aspirations which capitalism released in the men of the Renaissance. Of Richard and Edmund, whose historical function is quite different, we can at least still say that they owe their creation and existence to a recognition of the same problem.

And so the enormity of evil once more becomes the stuff of reality and the subject of artistic representation. The question, however, is: does evil appear in the same light as it did for Christianity?

It is enough to look at the Faust story to see that it did not. Evil is a great force, sinful, amoral. But at the same time it is definitely not an absolutely negative force. To put it better: its moral negativity, its sinfulness, still did not make it generally negative, unequivocally destructive. Evil no longer owed its grandeur to its power of destruction alone but also to its *ambiguous* character. Capitalism gave birth to that phenomenon which Hegel (writing after the gathering of dusk, when Minerva's owl had begun to take its flight) called the world-historical role of evil.

I must first of all speak of the thirst for knowledge. *Objectively*, sounding the depth of every mystery, the revelation of the secrets of nature proceeded side by side with the evolution of capitalism. The development of the means of production, and the general extension of the utility relation, were two facets of one and the same phase of historical development. Symbolically, all this could be summed up in the formula: vice can be the catalyst of good.

That, of course, was only the abstract point of departure; in actuality art and ideology went far beyond it. Vice and evil carry out the judgment of history; with relentless malice they can sweep an evil world away. That is what Richard III does, and that is why Margaret, acknowledging the historical role of evil, says:[161]

> Richard yet lives, hell's black intelligencer,
> Only reserv'd their *factor*, to buy souls
> And send them thither; but at hand, at hand,
> Ensues his piteous and unpitied end. . . .

But evil – as greatness – can fulfil its historical mission in other ways too – not least of all through political action. There, what is morally wrong in the abstract can have a good result, while what is morally good may have bad consequences. An example of the latter is Shakespeare's Brutus, who with his moralizing brings his and Cassius' common enterprise to grief. If we wish to speak of the former situation, however, we must turn to Machiavelli.

Up to now, I have been analysing the ways in which morality became detached from the roster of values. Now, however, it is time to examine how this process was mirrored in the ethics of the age. Machiavelli was the genius who grasped the process in all its implications; in his writings he presented a comprehensive analysis of the dialectic of morals in the Renaissance and, in so doing, formulated theoretically the historical function of evil. Here, then, we must to some extent recapitulate what has already been said in our discussion of the system of virtues, only this time from the point of view of ethics.

313

It was Florentine philosophy which traced most rapidly the course of development leading from communal ethics to the divorce of ethics from any fixed roster of values. Inside of fifty years it had covered this 'classical' path. Here we must refer back again to points of similarity with Athens, and points of difference. In both these city-states a relatively secure communal ethic had evaporated. The first ethical reaction to its dissolution, in both communities, was the appearance of a form of conduct based on *morality* (Socrates, Pico della Mirandola). In Athens, however, this was not followed by a split between value-system and ethics, while in Florence that was almost a direct response to the problems raised by morality. Here I can only mention the reasons for that. First of all, the communal ethic was already more heterogeneous in Florence, and while commodity production was a purely disintegrating force in Athens, in Florence it did further develop social relations in their basic tendencies, even while bursting the bounds of the city-state. That is why Florentine philosophy, above all Machiavelli, could pose for posterity *questions* to which answers are still being sought at the present day.

The communal ethic (*Sittlichkeit*) prevails unbroken right up through Ficino. This is what the Florentine Platonist has to say about it:[162]

For man everything that is bad is immoral, and what is moral must be regarded as good. Undoubtedly, every man strives to conduct his life in such a way as to avoid what is immoral and to practise morality. Even an immeasurable amount of time, precepts, and teachings can scarcely achieve that, but love makes it possible within a short time. For the feeling of shame restrains men from immorality, and the desire to distinguish themselves leads them to morality. Both can be attained most easily and quickly through love.

Ficino thus sets out from the following premises: (1) for the individual, the good is whatever is accounted ethical in the community; (2) every person strives to attain it; (3) ethics is laid down in a variety of precepts and teachings, and deviating from them causes feelings of shame; and, finally, (4) the ethical can most easily be approached and attained through *amore*, love (this is what specifically characterizes Ficino's philosophy).

With Pico della Mirandola *all* these premises have been transformed into their opposites. For him what counts as ethical in the community is, for the most part, not good; the good is what one is persecuted for, what one does in the teeth of the world. Men's customs are *bad* customs, their opinions *false* opinions. 'For they

314

do not know themselves what they do, but let themselves be swept away, as swimmers in a river are swept away by the force of the current', he writes,[163] and to his favourite nephew he gives the following advice: 'Let them whine, let them grumble, let them snarl – go thou thine own way, unshakeably, to the very end.'[164] Here a purely personal morality stands contrasted with the customary ethic of the world: a man's only support is himself, and he must go his own way in opposition to others. And what is the teaching which affords us, against the world, a way of laying hold of this pure morality? According to Pico it is the gospel.[165]

> For if the gospel is right in saying how difficult it is for a rich man to enter into the kingdom of heaven, why do we strive to heap up treasures? And if it is true that we should seek the glory that comes not from men but from God, why are we constantly concerned with men's judgment?

It is not as if Pico were more religious than Ficino, of course. As the dissolution of the Florentine polis became obvious, rather, it was the purely *negative* features of bourgeois development that became, as a result, more apparent; an ethic of money-grubbing had to be countered with the gospel, and not simply the gospel but its anti-capitalist interpretation.

This is the challenge that Machiavelli took up. His judgment on the Florence of his day, and on its ethics, was as negative as that of Pico or Savonarola. But with him protest developed into a *programme*, and indeed a programme of *alternatives*: either return to the old polis and its communal ethic, or else reject the polis-ideal altogether and move ahead towards the creation of a unified absolute monarchy for Italy, accepting the ethical situation which contemporary capitalism had brought about and, moreover, carrying it through to a consistent conclusion. The centuries-old controversy and the many misunderstandings which have surrounded the figure of Machiavelli stem from this way of posing the problem in terms of two alternative courses. It is the reason some have seen in him *exclusively* an advocate of absolute monarchy and, moreover, the apostle of a cynical bourgeois ethic, political 'Machiavellianism'; while others saw *only* the republican and plebeian who (as Rousseau, for example, thought) took up the subject of the *Prince* in a purely satirical vein. I will return later to the analysis of Machiavelli's political conceptions; here I should like to examine briefly its ethical consequences.

Like Rousseau – who was right to see here a connection – Machiavelli distinguishes between 'corrupt' and 'unspoiled' peoples.

315

The mores of unspoiled peoples are sound, their men are ever ready to defend their country, the laws are kept by all. Such an unspoiled people were the Romans, for example, until the advent of the Empire. Machiavelli speaks with great enthusiasm indeed of 'sound morals', but such sound morals – he writes – exist only in secure republican communities. 'Where the mass of the people is sound, disturbances and tumults do no serious harm; but where corruption has penetrated the people, the best laws are of no avail. . . .'[166] What is it that brings about the decline of morals? It is none other than the development of *inequalities of wealth*. Where society is divided into rich and poor the best laws may exist, but they will still not preserve good morals. Such a society can no longer be governed in the old way; since there *no longer exists* a communal ethic of the old type it would be absurdly idealistic, in politics, to rely for support on that sort of ethic. Politics and ethics must come to terms with the new situation; otherwise society will go to rack and ruin.

Machiavelli's overall conception is not only clear; it is true as well. The great polis-republics were based on a relative equality of wealth (both at Athens and in early Rome), and too sharp distinctions of wealth, inside the ruling strata, did indeed cut short the flowering of the polis. Alongside this great insight the frequent inaccuracy of Machiavelli's individual historical interpretations fades into insignificance. (Thus, for example, Machiavelli holds the Gracchi responsible – among others – for the decline of the Roman Republic, whereas with their agrarian legislation they actually acknowledged the same problem he did.)

Machiavelli has no doubt, however, that the people of his own age are 'corrupt' (in that he is once more in agreement with Rousseau), and so their ethic is different from that of unspoiled peoples and demands a different kind of action. In analysing it, he separates ethics from the roster of values.

In respect of the interpretation of 'human nature', however, the conceptions of Machiavelli and Rousseau are far apart. Nothing is more remote from Machiavelli's mind than the standpoint of a historical anthropology. As far as anthropology is concerned, he is rather a forerunner of Hobbes; he hypostasizes the 'nature' of the men of his time into 'human nature'. The expression 'unspoiled' does not just mean 'not yet spoiled'; rather, it refers to the ethical attitude of a long historical epoch during which people became accustomed to ethical conduct in the polis. 'Unspoiledness', then, is not to be understood in relation to the *history of humanity*, but only in reference to one people in one historical *cycle*. True, it does also refer to the 'beginnings' of human history. Men at first live scattered, like animals, they 'associate' around a chief, and presently the idea of justice develops. Only then does actual political life begin, and an order based on ethics proper. This starts with a prince, continues with the rule of the nobles and then popular government, which is then succeeded (whether on a higher level or not) by the authority of a prince again. 'Such is the circle which all republics are destined to run through', Machiavelli writes.[167] Amid all these historical vicissitudes, however, *human nature remains the same*; only its functions change, and the forms in which it manifests itself.

What, according to Machiavelli, is this 'human nature'? 'Whoever desires to found a state and give it laws', he writes, 'must start by assuming that all men are bad and ever ready to display their vicious nature, whenever they may find occasion for it.'[168] And again: 'Men act right only upon compulsion; but from the moment that they have the option and liberty to commit wrong with impunity, then they never fail to carry confusion and disorder everywhere.'[169]

In constructing his ethics, then, Machiavelli starts out not from any system of values, but from 'human nature'. True, that was in a certain sense the usual point of departure for stoic-epicurean thinking, too. But stoicism and epicureanism advanced the norm of 'living according to nature' only in connection with one's *own* nature. A conscious and high-minded individual (such as the stoics and epicureans were) can take his own 'nature' into consideration without thereby rejecting the traditional system of moral values. For trying to lead a good and honourable life was the main purpose of conduct in life, and so taking one's nature into consideration was tantamount to recognizing those courses and opportunities through which one could realize abstract and general ethical principles and attitudes in terms of one's own nature. Machiavelli, however, starts by taking into consideration the 'nature' of the *other* person. One must always reckon, in action, with another person, or more correctly, with an endless multitude of others who are not high-minded individuals, and who for the most part are not in the least striving for ethical objectives. If one reckons thus with the nature of the 'other', and guides one's actions and judgments accordingly, two solutions are possible: either condemn mankind as 'evil-natured' (that is the attitude of 'morality', Pico's solution and Savonarola's), or else try to find that margin of activity with the help of which 'bad natures' can be directed towards relatively good actions and results. The latter is Machiavelli's solution.

Let us examine more closely what this 'bad' nature consists of. It is not 'evil', a conscious striving after the vile; it is merely the absence of any striving for good, for ideal ethical goals. Concretely:

317

'Human desires are insatiable. . . . This gives rise to a constant discontent in the human mind and a weariness of the things they possess. . . .'[170] Above all, then, it is the absence of the old restraints of the polis, eternal dissatisfaction, the human situation created by bourgeois production and bourgeois social relations. Again: only 'a small part of [the people] wish to be free for the purpose of commanding, whilst all the others, who constitute an immense majority, desire liberty so as to be able to live in greater security'[171] – a necessary consequence of the split between bourgeois and citizen, as a result of which the people are alienated from politics and seek, amid the storms of primitive accumulation, a very dubious security. And again: 'Men are bad, and would not observe their faith with you.'[172] 'And men have less scruple in offending one who makes himself loved than one who makes himself feared; for love is held by a chain of obligation which, men being selfish, is broken whenever it serves their purpose. . . .'[173] The most powerful motive, the incentive of every human action, is self-interest. Self-interest, however, demands immediate satisfaction. Men are looking for gain, and quickly; they must be satisfied promptly, or else one must have the means to employ fear in order to appeal to their self-interest:[174]

> Thus it comes about that all armed prophets have conquered and unarmed ones failed; for . . . the character of peoples varies, and it is easy to persuade them of a thing, but difficult to keep them in that persuasion. And so it is necessary to order things so that when they no longer believe, they can be made to believe by force . . . as happened, in our own time with Fra Girolamo Savonarola, who failed entirely in his new rules when the multitude began to disbelieve in him, and he had no *means* of holding fast those who had believed nor of compelling the unbelievers to believe.

But the striving for immediate gain and the desire for the quick satisfaction of self-interest often make men stupid, blind, attached to appearances and pliable; men are so fatuous and so obedient to momentary necessity that anyone who wishes to mislead them will always find some whom he can deceive:

> For it may be said of men in general that they are . . . covetous of gain; as long as you benefit them, they are entirely yours. . . .[175]

> Men forget more easily the death of their father than the loss of their patrimony.[176]

318

If we go over all the statements in which Machiavelli analyses the 'badness' of human nature, we will not find any instances of *deliberate striving after evil*. What Machiavelli describes as 'bad nature' is no more than an ethics homogenized by the profit relation, not more than the general ethical practice of bourgeois society. Machiavelli here anticipated those ethical facts which I introduced at the beginning of Chapter 8, quoting from the *Communist Manifesto*.

Thus Machiavelli recognized that interest is the motive of human actions, not ethical principles and norms, values and virtues. But by that he did not mean to assert that norms, values, and the like *may* not act as motives or incentives. They may indeed do so, when they are in harmony with interest. The ethical realm has, then, a certain autonomy, power, and ability to shape motives, but it is only secondary and derivative, for the ethical realm itself is very often determined in many ways by interest. Machiavelli, nevertheless, still does not claim – as many later exponents of the bourgeois theory of egoism did – that pursuing one's self-interest *necessarily* leads to good, but only that it *may* lead to good, though in itself – as a value in itself – it is in no way good. If in our actions we count upon the other (or others) being motivated by interest, and assume that ethics is merely a cover for the latter, then our actions – even though, judged in terms of their own worth, they may be bad – can, in their *results*, still lead to good; if however we set out (mistakenly) from the premise that men are guided in their acts by values, then our actions (though in their own terms good) will have bad consequences, for they will go wide of the mark.

I must emphasize once again that Machiavelli does not deny, in principle, that ethics play a part in motivation. But – as we have seen – he derives their function not from 'human nature' but from *custom*, which in his view also rests, in the last analysis, on interest. 'Unspoiled' peoples are those which have grown used to virtuous action and to following ethical motivations. That is why there is not the slightest logical contradiction in the fact that Machiavelli in *The Prince* can thoroughly analyse how men may be manipulated through interest, and yet at the close of the work can suddenly write that 'the ancient heroic virtue is still not dead in the hearts of Italians'.

We might say that Machiavelli opposes to ethical speculation an *ethic of experience*: the unbiased observation of facts. He discloses reality in all its rawness, even sharpening its outlines. That sharpening leads to a certain one-sidedness, but it is the one-sidedness of all great discoveries. With a flick of the wrist Machiavelli swept away the ethics of virtue, replacing them with an empirical theory of interest. In this theoretical context, *consequences* became for him the basic criterion.

Not that ethics had hitherto left consequences out of account: according to an ethics of virtue (such as those of Plato and Aristotle) ethical judgment must take into consideration the consequences of action, too. For them, however, consequences were an *extra-ethical factor*. On one hand, they were regarded as accidents which might prevent the realization of a good intention, or turn a bad intention to a good end. On the other hand, the consequence was – for Aristotle, who perceived this brilliantly – a question of *knowledge*. According to Aristotle, *ignorance of circumstances* could frustrate the best intentions. But it followed from that that someone who was not well aware of the consequences and hence sought the good unsuccessfully still remained just as 'good' as if he had succeeded, even though his *action* was not good. A just man could commit an unjust deed and an unjust man a just one. Of course if a just man committed an injustice repeatedly he could grow accustomed to it, and then he could become unjust. But that was no longer merely a question of the consequences, but of a series of acts which influence the future motivation of the acting subject. Philosophy, then, was as little aware as was tragedy of the conflict aroused by the unexpected, unwanted result.

In Machiavelli, however, the problem of consequences does not arise in this connection – at least not exclusively in this connection. Machiavelli advances the seemingly paradoxical proposition that some good deeds sometimes *cannot be realized with good motives*; negative motives are necessary to the achievement of some positive consequences. Further, he maintains the seemingly even more paradoxical view that if someone with bad motives and bad actions achieves a good result, not only is the deed good though the doer is still bad (as for Aristotle) – on the contrary, the agent is better than if he had accomplished a band end with a good motive:[177]

> Cesare Borgia was considered cruel, but his cruelty had brought order to the Romagna, united it, and reduced it to peace and fealty. . . . He was really much more merciful than the Florentine people, who, to avoid the name of cruelty, allowed Pistoia to be destroyed.

Finally – and here we return to our old problem – the precondition of proper action is *knowledge of men*. It is, moreover, a knowledge of men *which always assumes the worst about people*. When, for example, Machiavelli seeks to prove that a prince should not keep his word, he argues: 'If men were all good, this precept would not be a good one; but as they are bad, and would not observe their faith with you, you are not bound to keep faith with them.'[178]

Machiavelli saw very clearly that the broader the repercussions of one's activity – the more people are affected by it – the greater must be the importance of the consequences in our judgment of it. In the ethics of the public man, politician, statesman, or prince, the result must be *solely* decisive. For them it is an *ethical* imperative not to shrink from *any* kind of evil in the interest of a good result. The more someone is a private person, the more he can 'afford' to avoid wrongdoing, for the effects of his actions do not reach far and so are of little consequence. I shall speak later of Machiavelli's political ethics *sensu stricto*. Here I should like only to remark that there is no Chinese wall separating political ethics from general ethical conduct. That is so first of all because statements about 'human nature' and human motives are, of course, true in general; these motives confronted the private person just as much as the politician. Second, if the private person can afford to avoid certain wrongs (murder, breaking faith, and the like), he cannot hold either to any fixed roster of virtues, since they are not realized in practice. Third – but not least important – Machiavelli, though he did see them as less fraught with ethical problems, still did not greatly esteem the way of life and the morality of the purely private man. The main passion of his life centred around the resurgence of Florence and of all Italy; public political *pathos* permeated his every thought and action too deeply, and he saw the fateful social abyss into which his country was about to plunge too clearly to think those truly great, praiseworthy and exemplary who withdrew into a quiet burgher's existence and 'kept their nose clean', in comparison with those who were prepared to take a moral risk in order to restore Italy:[179]

> This opportunity must not, therefore, be allowed to pass, so that Italy may at length find her liberator. I cannot express the love with which he would be received in all those provinces which have suffered under these foreign invasions, with what thirst for vengeance, with what steadfast faith, with what love, with what grateful tears.

It is important to understand this sentiment if we wish to appreciate the one-sidedness which – as we have seen – characterized Machiavelli in his judgment not only of political ethics but of ethics in general. In England, where the Elizabethan era finally opened a clear road to capitalist development, much more opportunity was afforded to expose the *internal contradictions* of the sort of ethical conduct brought out so sharply by Machiavelli. In his analysis of hypocrisy, for example, Machiavelli had emphasized only that it was necessary in political action (and more often than not in any kind of action) and that it led to good consequences, and so was not to be condemned from a moralistic standpoint. Bacon, as we have seen, raised the problem of *how far* hypocrisy is reconcilable with honesty, and in what circumstances it leads to the moral ruin of the hypocrite. It is with Shakespeare, however, that the whole moral dialectic of the problem comes to the surface. Like Machiavelli, from whom he learned a great deal, Shakespeare saw clearly that evil often comes of good, and good from evil – and not only in politics (where I have cited more than once the example of Brutus) but in the realm of private life as well (as in the conflicts in *Measure for Measure* or *All's Well That Ends Well*; even the title of the latter is programmatic). But in most of his plays the question is not whether bad can generally come from good, or good from bad, but rather: *what kind* of evil can come to good? *How far* can one go in evil and *in what ways*, and still achieve a good result? *When* does it ruin the agent morally, and when does it not? We might say that in the concrete conflicts of his tragedies Shakespeare applies the theory of the mean to the Machiavellian conception as well.

It is not easy to apply the name of moralist to Shakespeare, a playwright whose favourite hero runs his fiancée's father through without a qualm, and blithely consigns his two childhood friends to their death. And yet – as I have said – *in every concrete instance* the outlines of 'when', 'towards whom', and 'how far' are concretely delineated. To take a few examples: Shakespeare's villains – the ones whom wrongdoing has ruined morally – are never the figures who commit but one crime; they are guilty of a whole series of transgressions. In that 'series', moreover, there is *without exception* one crime, usually the culmination of all the wrongdoing: *the murder of a child*. The murder of a child can never be made good, not only because it strikes the innocent (and hence is not justifiable even in Machiavelli's terms), but rather because it is *senseless* and *needless*, for its motive is always *fear*. And yet – and this is quite new by comparison with Machiavelli – these rulers of Shakespeare's do not arrive by accident at those senseless, needless acts, outrageous both in themselves and in their consequences. They follow necessarily from their whole attitude. And here I touch upon an area where Shakespeare's insights served as a definite corrective to Machiavelli: the question of the ambiguity of *lust for power*. Only one kind of craving for power existed for Machiavelli. It was the motive which made the prince a prince and impelled him to act. He writes: 'The desire to acquire [territorial] possessions is a very natural and ordinary thing, and when those men do it who can do it successfully, they are always praised and not blamed.'[180] But Shakespeare knew and demonstrated that the significance of a thirst for power and conquest depends in a far-reaching way upon its *content*. If the urge to power is an end in itself, if it is a matter of power and conquest for their own sake, then the man who has conquered and won power will never find his power and his conquests strong enough and complete enough; for he will not know what to do with them, his whole attention will be directed towards his 'rivals' (real and imaginary), and his power will become the power of fear, which breeds crime upon crime. Thus both Richard III and Macbeth pursued power for its own sake. But lust for power can have for its object some concrete plan or some goal to be attained. Thus Henry V knew the urge to power even while he was still Prince Hal. It was no accident that he tried on the crown even at his dying father's bedside. But his desire for power was not an end in itself; he wanted power in order to set his country's affairs in order at last, secure internal peace, conquer France, and the like. Even so, of course, he did not come out of it with 'clean hands'. For it was under his auspices that his brother Lancaster deceived the conspirators, offering them a chance to withdraw freely and then, when they had put down their arms, massacring them. This was indeed 'Machiavellianism', of the *authentic* sort – deceit in the interest of an objective. But the objective was a determinate one: to forestall further conspiracies so as to be able to govern in peace. Henry V attained that objective, and so his brother's Machiavellianism cannot be counted against him. In sum: Shakespeare again and again shows us that the violation of ethical norms is not always profitable, even in the sense of an ethic of consequences; indeed, it is often unprofitable. Ethics for him is a separate realm, but a concrete realm, no more easily captured through mere evaluation of the consequences than through abstract rosters of values. (Shakespeare, incidentally, never accepted the generalization that 'men are good' either, any more than he did the generalization that 'men are bad'.)

The separation of ethics from rosters of values is final with Machiavelli and Shakespeare only, of course, in historical perspective. Since that time (both during the Renaissance and later) there have been countless attempts to work out new fixed sets of values. In a way, Giordano Bruno trod new paths in his *Banishment of the Victorious Animal*. The purpose of this allegorical dialogue is

323

to work out a value-system in which not only the traditional 'virtues' will find a place, but indeed *all those properties, activities, and situations* which have played a positive role in historical development. Thus, of course, quite heterogeneous categories are thrown together, without any hierarchy or effort to create a hierarchy. Justice, Wisdom, Law, Providence, Fortune, Philosophy, Generosity, Force, Science, Art, Simplicity, Industry, Good Will, Gratitude, Loyalty, Sincerity, Mercy, Good Conscience, Joy, Repose, Health, the Supreme Delight, and the like are the new 'deities', or ideal values. This was a late attempt at a synthesis, *an effort to synthesize all the values of the Renaissance.* It is not here that the real significance of Bruno's ethics lies, however, but rather in its analysis of the content of certain virtues or values and in its examination of how far these values are realized.

For Bruno takes up the same question as Machiavelli: are all these virtues, or at least some part of them, realized intact in the world of the present? And he answers the question with a categorical 'no'. That 'no', however, is not at all inspired by despair. For Bruno does not regard it as a 'fault' that good is never realized in its full splendour:[181]

> When with the imitation of the divine action and the
> inclination of the spiritual capacities thereto, difficulties arose
> and *wants appeared, the mind of man was sharpened* as a result;
> men invented the branches of industry and discovered the arts,
> until now, *under the spur of necessity,* ever more wondrous
> new inventions pour forth day by day from the depths of the
> human mind. . . . *Do not wonder at the injustices and
> iniquities which have grown up side by side with man's
> aspirations for the good.* . . . In your golden age [Sloth is being
> addressed – A.H.] men were not yet virtuous, because they
> were not sinful; for there is a great difference between
> innocence and virtuousness. . . .

Bruno's ethical optimism springs from an almost enthusiastic affirmation of bourgeois progress: if bourgeois development generates evil, selfishness, and injustice, it also generates good.

Of course Bruno was not the only one to draw a distinction between goodness and virtue. Many writers, foremost among them Charron, analysed the difference between 'goodness' and 'merit'. The former was 'natural' and in harmony with innate traits of character, while the latter was 'artificial', mediated, consciously chosen; the former was easy, the latter difficult. For Bruno, however, it is not simply a matter of differences in character among men;

324

it is rather a *historical* question. Man gradually *breaks away from nature*; as his needs and his industry develop he changes more and more from an animal being into a conscious human being. Immediate goodness thus becomes historically antiquated. Historical development in all its complexity awakened such impulses in man and made social relations so complicated that *evil became inevitable*; but for the same reason *merit* also became necessary (though Bruno does not use precisely that expression), a human ethics which is mediated and based on consciousness, and which finds its way amid these complex relationships. Thus Bruno, who accepted the perspectives of capitalist development, accepted its ethical consequences, too, without denying the contradictoriness of bourgeois ethics. In that respect he is a forerunner of Diderot – of the Diderot who with good reason retorted to Rousseau: the question is not whether wrong has increased with civilization (for surely it has), but whether happiness has decreased, and enjoyment, and needs, and – merit.

The divorce of ethics from the roster of values made it particularly important to analyse the ethical functions of *custom* and *public opinion*. In a certain sense both were already problems in the ancient world, nor did they cease to be problems during the Christian era. But during antiquity and the Christian Middle Ages both custom and opinion were interpreted strictly with respect to the roster of values. 'Good' existed, and people could become habituated to good or to evil. 'Truth' existed, and opinion took its stand for the truth or against it. The famous anecdote about Plato, told by both Montaigne and Bacon, raises the question of 'custom' in the form of the alternatives of good and bad. Some children are playing in the street, throwing peppercorns about. When Plato, passing by, scolds them, they reply that they have done 'nothing', at least nothing wrong. To that Plato retorts: 'And custom, is that nothing?' Throwing things about, then, promotes bad qualities in people; those who start by throwing pepper about, which really is nothing, will soon go on to stones, which is already 'something', and so on. Similarly, public opinion, too, manifested itself only in terms of alternatives of good and bad, true and false. In the polis of classical antiquity public opinion was highly esteemed *generally*, however much it might err in individual cases; the institution of ostracism was based on public opinion, and the choruses of tragedy gave expression to the opinion of the community. In later antiquity – and during the Christian era – the notion of a 'bad' public opinion became more and more frequent. The New Testament thoroughly

325

condemns those who are unable to take an unequivocal stand towards public opinion in terms of 'truth' and 'falsehood', foremost among them Pontius Pilate, who is incapable of an unequivocal stand precisely by reason of his asking, 'What is truth?'

During the Renaissance, however, it became less and less common to view the matter as if there were one or another system of values which could be adopted, and one truth or another which could be advocated.

Above all, the question of virtue was *reversed*, at least in part.

Now it is not so simply a matter of people 'accustoming themselves' to virtue; now what men are generally accustomed to *is* virtue. 'Use maketh us many times to delite in, and to set little by the selfe same things', writes Castiglione;[182] 'the laws of conscience, which we say are born of nature, are born of custom', argues Montaigne.[183] Social demands and individual compliance, or lack of compliance, turn into a relationship of customary ethics – the relationship of *individual* usage to *social usage*, or to the usage of one class or stratum. Social custom, or the practice of a class or social stratum, is not necessarily 'good', any more than is the individual usage which may adopt them as a model. General social custom is extremely heterogeneous and contradictory in its value-content, and so may be a *source of both positive and negative motivation*. Often it is simply *conservative*; it carries the petrified demands and prejudices of outlived exigencies, so that its adoption would even hinder the unfolding of individual powers. It is a hindrance, moreover, not because in and of itself it is 'bad' or 'wrong', but because it has *become* bad, *become* wrong, for developing reality had pulled the carpet from under it. 'For in conjecturing what may be men set before them the example of what has been, and divine of the new with an imagination *preoccupied* and *coloured* by the old', writes Bacon.[184] Thus the *derivation* of ethical and behavioural norms from custom, and the examination of the constant possibility of their obsolescence, springs directly from the dynamic conception of man and from the first seeds of a future-oriented attitude.

This analysis of the dynamics of objective customary morality has far-reaching importance for the interpretation of *individual* usage as well. Since the adoption of 'customs' or quasi-virtues is not necessarily and unequivocally a positive thing any longer, it is necessary to make a many-sided analysis of the social and ethical components of individual usage. Usage remained a *shaper of character* – it was no accident that the anecdote about Plato was quoted with such readiness. As to whether knowledge or usage was more effective in shaping character – on that score there was as much controversy as during antiquity. As we move forward in time, however, from Petrarch to Bacon, we find that usage is more and more often awarded the palm. But usage is not simply a complement to knowledge, and hence a form of ascesis or practice, nor is it simply a kind of bad conditioning with which reason must contend. The very fact of conditioning or habit becomes a problem in itself: 'How much habit stupefies our senses!' exclaims Montaigne.[185] Or we might cite one argument of Bacon's (from among many): 'A man would wonder to hear men profess, protest, engage, give great words, and then do just as they have done before; as if they were dead images, and *engines* moved only by the *wheels of custom*.'[186] The fact of usage thus becomes contradictory in itself, for it turns a person's activity into something *mechanical*, stereotyping it so much that he no longer notices what he is doing and is even less capable of reflecting relatively objectively on his actions.

No doubt the stereotyping of action and judgment was not something new. Most forms of human activity, in *every* age, are stereotyped, thus freeing human energies for the accomplishment of tasks which are essential, as yet unsolved, individual, and concrete (compare A. Gehlen). With the advent of bourgeois society, however, stereotyping appeared in *forms* so new as to really make necessary a reinterpretation of the category of 'custom'. On one hand, an ever greater tension arose between an ethics which was not based on a system of virtues and which demanded far-reaching individual decisions, and the stereotypes which regulated conduct in all its details, between the possibility of freedom and the kind of freedom that really existed. On the other hand, as a result of the growing social and technical division of labour the stereotypes multiplied more and more, while encompassing the whole man as a creative being less and less, and increasingly carving up the personality in terms of a variety of often contradictory stereotypes. Finally, then, people ceased not only to think about the content of the demands which these stereotypes made, but also about the way they applied them. Thus Bacon's metaphor of machinery, of the 'wheels of custom', was very perceptive indeed. So was his observation (already discussed) that custom, precisely because of its mechanical character, always 'gives up' and becomes helpless in the face of new phenomena – which is the reason that in dealing with new phenomena an individual's real, not yet mechanized essence 'breaks out'.

In their judgment of the *significance* of public opinion, the thinkers of the Renaissance were in agreement. Opinion was the power which sooner or later enforced the demands of social custom against the individual. As to how seriously its content ought to be taken, there opinions differed considerably. It will hardly come as a surprise that the moralists were the ones who generally rejected public opinion most flatly – not because it was unjust, but because it was conformist, uncritical and prejudiced. I have already mentioned Pico in this connection, and I must also speak of Charron as a representative of this attitude. It is no wonder that the philosopher of *honnêteté*, writing amid the religious fanaticism of the Wars of Religion in France, should have spoken so scathingly of public opinion:

[It is] the hardest servitude to be led by opinion.[187]

[Opinion is] the guide of fools and of the herd.[188]

By contrast, the majority of Italian thinkers, especially the theorists of the polis, saw in public opinion a form of *wisdom*, a system of norms and experience free from the 'idol' of particularity, for in the mass particular interests 'cancelled out' one another, permitting *general* tendencies to make themselves felt. Thus Machiavelli always urges the prince to pay attention to the tone of public opinion, to 'win' opinion. Castiglione, too, emphasizes that people rarely form an entirely 'separate' opinion for themselves: 'You your selfe and all wee here have many times, and doe at this present credite the opinion of others, more than our owne.'[189] But he does not see that as in the least tragic, since 'for the most part the multytude, though they have no perfect knowledge, yet do they feele by the instinct of nature a certain savour of good and ill, and can give none other reason for it'.[190] The thinkers of the Renaissance were not yet able to perceive what a close, *organic* connection existed between particularity, the preconceptions inherent in public opinion, and the stereotyped acceptance of custom and opinion.

CHAPTER 10

Social philosophy, politics, Utopia

In appearance, the social philosophy of the Renaissance was as undifferentiated as that of antiquity. Machiavelli, More, and Bodin produced, like Plato and Aristotle, works which dealt at one and the same time with ethics, political theory, economics, and legal theory. The resemblance, however, is only superficial. In the time of Plato and Aristotle science itself had not yet set out on the path of differentiation. But the beginnings of bourgeois society – which were at the same time the beginnings of the bourgeois division of labour – made possible, and even necessary, a process of differentiation among the 'social sciences'. The immediate unity of economy, state, law, and ethics gave way increasingly to a mediated unity, and the discovery of their *special*, particular laws became a pressing scientific task. It was Machiavelli and Bodin above all who took up that task.

With them the problem became one of analysing specific social correlations, and of grasping the *characteristic* structure of particular social formations and movements which often complemented or crossed one another. Machiavelli also grasped the split in human conduct expressed in the fact that the integral man had entered a crossfire of different, often mutually contradictory expectations, precisely as a result of the new, peculiarly divided and conflict-ridden social structure. The apparent resemblance to antiquity is caused merely by the fact that this differentiation of content still found expression within the framework of a single science (philosophy), that the great representatives of Renaissance politics, economics, and jurisprudence were in no way specialists, that they always related their theories – in keeping with the nature of

329

philosophy – to practice and to conduct, and that they were public men in every sense of the word. Here is another area in which Marx and Engels rightly felt Renaissance thought to be a forerunner of their own aspirations and way of thinking.

Renaissance social philosophy was least modern in its way of apprehending the *general* movement of history. Even those who went the furthest in this area still explained social dynamics *on the analogy of the organism*. As Bacon formulated it: 'In the youth of a state, arms do flourish; in the middle of a state, learning; . . . in the declining age of a state, mechanical arts and merchandise.'[191] The examples, or precedents, were of course taken from the political history of antiquity. Thus even Bacon, a passionate exponent of technology, did not suspect that social conditions could exist in which industry and commerce were not destructive and were in no way peculiarities of 'old age'. Here too Machiavelli was the most radical, yet without stepping over the fundamental dividing line. Organic analogies are characteristic of his writing too. But Machiavelli does not regard 'old age' as being necessarily final; rather, he deems possible the constant 'renewal' of any given social formation, through a *cyclical* movement. Those forms survive longest which from time to time 'return' to their own origins. Thus the Church, for example, would long ago have perished if St Francis had not revived primitive Christianity, thereby carrying out the task of 'returning' it to its original purity.

> It may be observed that provinces amid the vicissitudes to which they are subject, pass from order into confusion, and afterward recur to a state of order again; for the nature of mundane affairs not allowing them to continue in an even course, when they have arrived at their greatest perfection, they soon begin to decline. In the same manner, having been reduced by disorder, and sunk to their utmost state of depression, unable to descend lower, they, *of necessity*, reascend; and thus from good they gradually decline to evil, and from evil again return to good.[192]

I have italicized the words 'of necessity'. For Machiavelli does not regard all this as simply a description of empirical facts, but rather as an absolute law. In *The Discourses* cyclical movement is represented as being universal and absolutely valid at all times. The brilliance of Machiavelli's social ontology manifests itself also in the fact that he does not make this law independent of the practical activity of the human beings who realize it. For him, there is no such thing as a social 'law' which can manifest itself 'independently' of the people involved, nor are the people involved independent of the 'law'. However absolute may be the law of 'cyclical movement', no renewal will take place if there are no men to carry through the work of 'returning' to the origins. *Thus the overall necessity of 'cyclical movement' is not in contradiction with the possibility that in concrete cases that movement may not take place*; at such times we witness not the start of a new cycle but the final destruction of the whole social formation. Machiavelli's other insight, related to the first, was that forms of society incapable of renewing themselves, and so doomed to destruction, give way to other, newer forms of society. If at one point on the earth's surface the cycle has finally ended, at another point the same process may still begin again. It is almost as if, in this cyclical movement, each country passed on the torch to another.

> Reflecting now upon the course of human affairs, I think that, as a whole, the world remains very much in the same condition, and the good in it always balances the evil; but the good and the evil change from one country to another. . . .[193]

But however brilliant an innovator Machiavelli may have been, the foregoing quotation shows clearly the limits beyond which he could not go. The concept of social development is unknown to him too. Successive social formations always take up the *same thing* and in the *same way*. If individual cities and countries perish, humanity – he assures us – still goes on; the destruction of 'our' world is not the destruction of 'the' world. In this he went far beyond antiquity, and operated with a modern concept of humanity. Through the destruction of particular social formations, however, humanity reproduces itself on the same level; the site is different but the constantly renewed process is the same. To that degree his notion of society is still based on the traditional category of the polis. The axiom 'nothing new under the sun' finds perfect expression in Machiavelli's view of the world, too.

I have said that Machiavelli's concept of society was based on the traditional category of the polis. That is true even if Rome does supply a good part of his empirical material, for even the history of the great Roman Empire was actually the history of a city. It is still true even though we know that Machiavelli's goal was the creation of a unified Italian monarchy. The experience on which he built, nevertheless, and from which his work drew its emotional power, was the experience of the polis. Not for nothing did he write the history of Florence, compose a commentary on ten books of Livy, and follow closely the Swiss struggle for liberty (the cantons, too, were based on direct democracy). He studies the vital processes of structures *relatively isolated from one another*, where the destruction of a given, concrete social formation meant the destruction of the whole culture, or, conversely, where the emergence of a concrete social formation brought about a flowering of the whole culture. He did not subject to study those national units (countries) which through different social formations, albeit at different tempos, were 'taking over the torch', in which the process of cumulative growth had taken the form of a spiral; and indeed it would have been difficult for him to study it, for that was something which first appeared during the transition from feudalism to capitalism (and even then only as a possibility), when isolated social structures ceased to exist. And it happened first in England and France, and only in Machiavelli's own lifetime; the further unfolding of the process falls into the period after his death. Thus we should not reproach Machiavelli for his theory of cultural cycles. He merely generalized those potentialities of previous history which had in fact been realized. Parenthetically, let it be said that the sort of lawfulness or regularity identified by Machiavelli does indeed apply to some relatively closed social structures. We can surely say even today of certain cities, institutions, journals, schools, or classes that they have had their rise and their flowering, which then necessarily gave way to decline – which in turn led either to renewal or resulted in their final oblivion. But the closer a social formation is to the 'backbone' of society, to overall social production *per se* (capitalist or socialist) and to fundamental social relations, the less will it follow its own autonomous laws of development; it will observe the organic rules of its purely internal structure all the less, and its fate will be determined all the more by the universal process of development and regression, which is, however, never simply cyclical. In a sense, then, Machiavelli repeats the Heraclitan *panta rhei* ('All human things are kept in a perpetual movement and can never remain stable', he writes),[194] nor has he any doubt that therein the prime conscious motive force is class struggle. *The affirmation of class struggle* – which I have already spoken of in my Introduction – was quite general during the Renaissance, from Petrarch to Bacon. (The fact that counter-tendencies also existed, as with Erasmus, does not in any way alter the case.) Here, too, however, Machiavelli's standpoint was unique. For in speaking of the struggle between 'the people' and 'the illustrious', and in urging the prince to rely on the people against the latter, he was replacing the traditional early Renaissance notion of the people with a novel and *modern* concept of it. The traditional Florentine *popolo* took in, in principle,

332

all the inhabitants of the city; but in practice it meant the more illustrious and more capable, those who participated in the direction of public affairs. With Machiavelli this notion of the people was reversed. The actual leading stratum (what had until now been called 'the people') was now included in the category of 'the illustrious' rather than in that of the people, and even there nobles and burghers formed two separate groups; the people are now the lower social strata, the poor and dispossessed. It is the struggle of *these* people which Machiavelli regards as desirable in the life of the state, and not just the struggle of the 'people' in the old sense, that is, the internal broils of patricians and plebeians. In speaking of struggle, then, he was indeed striving to broaden the concept of a struggle of social strata into a concept of class struggle. Thus – if I may make use of a modern term – *the basis of Machiavelli's social stratification is the economic system of bourgeois society and not the political structure of the polis.*

This new conception of the people has nothing to do, however, with the concept of the 'masses'. Indeed, the author of *The Discourses* sharply rejects the charge that the people are an undifferentiated 'mass', easily erring and infinitely susceptible to influence. He writes:[195]

> I say, then, about that fault of which writers accuse the
> multitude, that all men individually can be accused of it, and
> chiefly princes; for he who is not regulated by the laws will
> commit the same errors as the ungoverned multitude.

Thus Machiavelli makes no distinction in principle between the psychology of the individual and that of the mass – which means, as we shall see, that in political manipulation he did not recognize any separate 'mass manipulation'. On the contrary, his techniques of manipulation are aimed primarily at individuals, and indeed at rivals of the ruler ('the illustrious'), while we meet only scattered attempts to manipulate the masses, and then only in a preventive way. *For the people are a subject in politics rather than an object.* I might add in passing that in structure the psychology of the masses and the psychology of the individual are similar in Shakespeare's plays, too. It may be objected that *Julius Caesar* and *Coriolanus* show something different: the necessity of influencing and manipulating the masses. But that is only the appearance. For in Shakespeare's plays the popular masses can never be influenced *against their own interests*. Mark Antony's demagogy strikes its mark because Caesarism was in the interests of the masses to begin with (they

333

would like to see in Brutus, too, another Caesar); in *Coriolanus*, again, the tribunes work up the passions of the people precisely in the direction of the latter's particular interests. Coriolanus' successes are transitory because even though he represents a general national cause, he is *objectively* the *enemy* of the particular aspirations of the people, not because he refuses to flatter them (as in the oral tradition). There are no such precisely set limits, however, to how far the individual can be influenced. Henry VI proves possible to influence even against his own interests because he is weak. Othello falls victim to Iago's machinations in defiance of his every interest. If there is a difference in the ease with which the individual and the masses can be influenced, then surely the difference is always in favour of the masses. What creates the impression that here Shakespeare might be Machiavelli's opposite is only the gradual alteration of outlook and of the times. The judgments of the later, Jacobean Shakespeare were more pessimistic in these matters than those of Machiavelli almost a century earlier, with respect to *both* the masses and the individual.

The *limits* of the people's impressionability are very important from the point of view of Machiavelli's overall social conception. As we noted in the case of his theory of 'cyclical movement', Machiavelli conceived the dynamic of society as regular and lawful. This regularity – or, properly speaking, its realization – depends upon human beings, in so far as they are the ones who accomplish 'fate'. But at the same time it is independent of them in so far as they cannot change that regularity itself. The reason the people are not completely open to influence is that in the mass individual interests cancel one another out, so that in the end they work in the direction of the 'rule'. That rule or law is the *objective end* of society, which subjective purposes cannot alter. It is the inner movement itself which provides the end and the direction. This conception is what enables Machiavelli to apprehend social phenomena and actions from the standpoint of overall development, in a hierarchical order. In that hierarchy the distinction between *cause* and *occasion* has a particularly important place. Machiavelli often enters into polemics with those who ascribe certain turns of fate to accident, the conduct of one man, or the like. These he places in the category of 'occasions'. Thus he writes, for example, that the cause of Tarquinius Superbus' fall was that he changed the constitution into a tyrannical one (according to the theory of 'cyclical movement' every tyranny must necessarily fall). The violation of Lucretia served only as the occasion of his fall, for 'if the incident of Lucretia had not occurred, some other would have produced the same effect . . .'.[196]

334

Machiavelli brings out at one and the same time the immanent objectivity of the historic process, and the equally immanent possibilities of individual, subjective action, the freedom of the individual.[197]

It is not unknown to me how many have been and are of opinion that worldly events are so governed by fortune and by God, that men cannot by their prudence change them . . . and for this [reason] they may judge it to be useless to toil much about them, but let things be ruled by chance. This opinion has been more held in our day, *from the great changes that have been seen, and are daily seen, beyond every human conjecture. . . .* Nevertheless . . . I think it may be true that *fortune is the ruler of half our actions, but that she allows the other half or thereabouts to be governed by us.*[198]

This passage offers a variety of insights into the richness of Machiavelli's *Weltanschauung*. Of prime importance are the lines in which he speaks of events which are inexplicable to the human mind. Parenthetically I might remark that Shakespeare, in Hamlet's speech to Horatio, repeats Machiavelli's train of thought almost word for word. The author of *The Prince* pointed here to the confused and disintegrating world of his own time, just as Hamlet did, and to the inability of human thought to comprehend every reason, connection, and prospect inherent in that confusion. At the same time he pointed out that men's practical participation in the shaping of history does not cease even though that sort of theoretical comprehension becomes impossible. Though he did not put it in the form of a philosophical generalization, still Machiavelli *in concreto* anticipates the Marxian thesis that men 'do not know' what task history has thrust upon them, and yet 'they do it'. Even if they cannot explain the course of the world, events still 'half depend' on them.

But Machiavelli does not conceive the relationship between human action and destiny in any simplistic way. For he distinguishes between the 'fate' of any social formation, the 'fate' of some of its concrete phases, and the 'fate' of the individual. As we have seen, every social formation as a whole has in its course of development an objective end, and that is all which it is possible to attain. Machiavelli thought that in his own day the time had come for the state to 'return' to its origins. He entertained two different hopes. One was for the rejuvenation of the peoples of Italy by arms and ultimately their unification into one great monarchy; the other was for the birth of a new lawgiver for Florence. (Sometimes the two conceptions are even mingled.) Fate – in its broadest sense – could not be turned in any other direction. The influence of particular social formations, and especially of particular individuals, on their own destiny was, however, much greater – though not always in equal degree. The closer one stands to the summits of social activity and the more one is an active political being, the more essential it is that one's own (subjective) goals coincide with the objective ends. There are two prerequisites for that: the right character (and the knowledge of it), and the right moment (and the knowledge of it). 'Therefore, those of our princes who had held their possessions for many years *must not accuse fortune* for having lost them, *but rather their own remissness* . . . having never in quiet times considered that things might change. . . .'[199] I have already discussed the idea that a certain ossification of character can set a limit to the consistent ability to seize the time, and the notion that changing times may cast down a type of character which once advanced from success to success. Here I should only like to add that Machiavelli does not assert those two propositions of *every* human being in *equal* degree. The further someone stands from public life the more he can exercise control over his own life, and the greater likelihood there is that his awareness of his own character will be *solely* decisive for his conduct; he might as well live like a stoic, in the *procul negotiis*, and guide his fate in that way. True, Machiavelli does not very highly esteem this private manner of living. In an age when he saw his country 'without head, without order, beaten, despoiled, lacerated and overrun', he had little praise for those who strove only to create their own private freedom. I might say that so far as the mutual interaction of fate and freedom are concerned Machiavelli rests up *two different hierarchies of value*. The first extends from the person who governs his own fate to the one who does not, the second from private existence to public life; in those who are truly great the tops of the two hierarchies meet. Thus it is that he admires perhaps most of all Cincinnatus, who undertook to enter public life when he was needed and when it suited his character, but who also knew when it was time to retire. '. . . . it seems almost impossible that the same mind should be able to bear such great changes', he writes with enthusiasm.[200] Machiavelli's ideal is the man who exposes himself to the blows of fate if he must, who has no fear – as we shall see – of wrongdoing itself if it is necessary, but who serves without vanity.

In grasping the dialectic of political character and the 'moment' Machiavelli arrived at a paradoxical position. Though he had actually not yet discovered 'history' – for, as we have seen, he speaks of cyclic movement, renewal on the same level, social structures 'passing the torch' to one another rather than building upon one another – still Machiavelli discovered the *historicity of character*, and the *historic character*. His working-out of the dynamic of events and of the idea of the 'moment' brought him to constantly reiterate the fact that a certain character-type can be 'historic' (though he does not use that expression) only at a given moment in time, ceasing to be historic at the next juncture and giving way to other kinds of historic character.

That great discovery, whose theoretical point was, as we have seen, necessarily blunted by the fact that the dynamic conception of society had not yet yielded to historicity, burst out in its whole uncontradictory richness in the world of artistic representation. I have in mind the history plays of Shakespeare, which are indeed, in the strict sense of the word, *historical dramas*. What makes them historical is not that they depict events of a bygone age – for *Julius Caesar* and *Coriolanus* are *not* history plays – but rather the fact that they operate with historic characters. In Shakespeare's history plays every single character has its own concrete here and now. Still unsullied and heroic in *Richard II*, Hotspur in *Henry IV* becomes more and more anachronistic, almost grotesque; in the later tragic developments this kind of old-fashioned hero, with his code of knightly honour, no longer appears at all. The sort of opportunism displayed by York in the first play of the series no longer has any place, either, in the subsequent ones; there the Yorks have become Buckinghams, murderous upstarts. In *Richard II* Bolingbroke by a little Machiavellianism acquires a kingdom, but in *Henry VI* a much more subtle craft, and greater villainy, are needed to accomplish the same thing. Or, to put it the other way around: a type of man like Henry VII could never have become king in the age of Richard II or Henry V: a whole series of humiliations, families extirpated, horror and despair were necessary before a ruler of that sort could come to the throne. In their depiction of the mutual interaction of political character and historical situation, Shakespeare's history plays radiate the same atmosphere as Walter Scott's novels centuries later. The difference, of course – and this is what makes Scott the definitive creator of the historical genres – is that Scott grasps this dialectic of individual and history not only as between great personalities and the world, but also as between every man (the common man) and the world.

It became possible to apprehend the past as history because in Shakespeare's England *the present was first experienced as history*. Never before had so sudden a transformation of the *whole* social structure been seen as in the era of primitive accumulation in

England. I have stressed the word 'whole' deliberately. For we should recall that if Athens and Florence had dramatic histories, the dramatic events – the alternation of 'rise' and 'fall' – still took place on *one and the same* economic base (primitive accumulation at Florence was not nearly so sudden a process as in England and, as we have seen, it eventually petered out). In England, however, economic structure, state organization, and ideology (religion) were changed almost at one stroke. The awareness that 'from head to toe we are different from what we were a hundred years ago' was very strong. We need only look at another play, *The Famous History of the Life of King Henry VIII* (irrespective of whether Shakespeare wrote it or not); the noblemen and noblewomen pictured there, their attitudes and their behaviour simply have nothing to do with the 'historical nobility's' forms of behaviour. *To pass through history*, of course, does not necessarily mean *to become conscious of history*. The sense of life of the English bourgeoisie after the destruction of the Armada differed considerably from that of the citizens of Athens following the defeat of the Persians (we need only think of the plays of Aeschylus). The Greeks' reflections were oriented towards the past; those of the English were oriented towards the future. And that is still true even if this orientation towards the future did not find expression in historiosophical generalizations. For if history is to appear not only in everyday experience but also in philosophical consciousness, it is not enough that it should become explicit in one country: *the history of all humanity* must become the possible object of concrete personal experience *in order for the concept of historicity to emerge*. That, however, still had to wait a long time, until the French Revolution.

Of all the social sciences, politics was the one which first became individually differentiated. (The systematic study of the laws of economics would be characteristic of the following century, the seventeenth.) We can trace, in the works of Machiavelli and Bodin, the process by which politics became a science. True, the two men proceeded in quite different ways in making politics an object of scientific inquiry. *Machiavelli examines politics as technique*, studying the laws of political action. Central to the political questions which he raises, then, is the study of the *political personality*. Bodin analyses the *objective sphere of politics* in society, above all law and the state – in other words, *political institutions*. Machiavelli analysed politics at a time and place where the bourgeois state had not yet developed, Bodin at a time and place where certain of its outlines and its first (abstract) forms had already appeared, in the absolute monarchy.

338

In my view, Machiavelli's analysis was the more fundamental. In saying this I do not wish to minimize Bodin's importance, but I should like to point out that the problems and questions which he raised were fully developed in succeeding centuries; thus his contract theory was taken up in turn by Grotius, Hobbes, Spinoza, and Rousseau, in ever richer and more comprehensive treatments. But Machiavelli – however much he has been invoked, justifiably or (for the most part) unjustifiably – is a unique phenomenon; even today political science still owes us a satisfactory resolution of the issues he raised.

My assertion that politics became a science only during the Renaissance calls for some explanation. Plato and, in particular, Aristotle could be pointed to as examples to the contrary. So far as the question of politics as *techné* is concerned, it would not be particularly difficult to prove my contention. In 'natural communities', whether oligarchic, aristocratic, or democratic, politics can never be a 'craft'. There was, to be sure, a social division of labour there, but the social stratum which held the leading position in the social division of labour *was not subjected to any division of labour with respect to its leadership functions.* That is to say that within that stratum (be it broad or narrow) *anyone* could be adept at politics and expert in the direction of the state. Only thus was it possible for offices to be filled not through voting, but *by lot*. The only office in which the division of labour, and special abilities, made themselves felt was military leadership. The special role of military leaders was, however, rigorously restricted to the duration of hostilities, and the ancient polis-republics watched closely to make sure that these military leaders would not organize themselves into a separate leading stratum; hence the frequent charge that they were aiming for a tyranny, the practice of ostracism, and the like. Of course there were men even then who, objectively, acted according to the norms of political activity, but the separate categories of 'politician' and of a 'political activity' deviating from the general norms of social life did not emerge in life and thinking. I must add that there was a great deal more scope and opportunity for political action *par excellence* in Rome, especially during the time of the early Empire. Why that age, which saw the elaboration of the classic legal code, did not have its own political theorist is a question which I cannot attempt to answer within my present limits. It goes without saying, however, that in the loose political organization of the Middle Ages, where political activity was again closely determined by the 'natural community' and where a division of labour with respect to leadership did not yet exist even in germ, the problem lost all basis in reality. Even in the *De monarchia* of Dante there is not the slightest trace of political analysis. The bourgeois division of labour had to develop before politics could emerge as a 'craft', as the concern of the politician, a man with special abilities and duties and a special way of thinking; and, I might add, circumstances had to arise in which that sort of professional political activity became a life-and-death matter. And that brings me back again to Machiavelli.

It may be more difficult to see why I dispute Plato's or Aristotle's title to have formulated the problem raised by Bodin. The reason, first of all, is that neither Plato nor Aristotle made any distinction between state and society. As a result, objective political problems, analyses of institutions, and the like are, for them, interwoven with ethical problems. For Plato, especially, the Republic is identical with the polis. In the last analysis Aristotle did not go beyond that either. True, in his analysis he started out from the problem of slavery, i.e. from that social relation which was *common* to the various city-states he examined, and to that degree he strove for a more general comprehension of contemporary society than was Plato's. But statehood still remained identical with the *forms of state*, and the latter with *constitutions*. With Bodin, however, it is quite a different matter. Having witnessed the first appearance of the modern bourgeois state, he was able to grasp the general concept of 'the state' within the category of a *national state* rather than one of polis type. He was able to show the 'other side' of the problem raised by Machiavelli. His ideal monarch, which guaranteed bourgeois private property, personal liberty, civil legality, tolerance, religious freedom, and the like, first proclaims the new status quo of bourgeois existence (an existence divorced from that of the *citoyen*), a status quo which makes necessary the 'professional politician'.

If the division of labour made possible the general development of political technique and made special political abilities a necessity, that still does not mean, of course, that the division of labour was the *sole* cause of this new phenomenon. The division of labour was only *one aspect* of the evolution of bourgeois society as an *overall process*. I have already spoken of some other aspects, related to the foregoing but at least as important in their own right – above all the quicker tempo of history, which demanded ever more rapid decisions, adapted to new situations, and the decline in past-orientedness and growth in future-directedness, which left tradition and precedent uncertain and demanded individual resourcefulness. At least equally important, however, was the geometrical increase in international contacts and national conflicts, in which decision-making neces- sitated countless special kinds of knowledge – and the different

kinds of knowledge grew ever more numerous as the economic and
political fabric of society became more complex: a national politics
which here and there was expanding already into a world politics.
And the broader the unity which political activity sought for and
achieved, the weightier the consequences became; and the smaller
the part played in decision-making by precedent, the more the results
depended on the personal responsibility of politicians.

The Renaissance was an era which produced great political
personalities indeed. The politicians of the emerging bourgeois
world were statesmen, not mere functionaries (which they tended to
become in 'completed', less agitated periods of bourgeois development), and to that degree they were all representatives of what
Machiavelli regarded as political *techné*. For we must not imagine the
type of the 'politician' *par excellence* as some sort of ideal bureaucrat.
The autonomous movement of politics presupposes real movers,
autonomous individuals who are capable of setting the stamp of
their personalities on history. Be he legislator or consolidator,
ruler or councillor, warrior or peacemaker, an aggrandizer of his
country or the author of its economic flowering, the politician is
subordinated to the division of labour in so far as his ideas, and
especially their realization, demand a different kind of thinking and
conduct, and a different ethic and *modus operandi* from that of,
for example, the philosopher, artist, or ordinary burgher.
Machiavelli's politician was not the type of the Tory politician of
Victorian England.

The brilliance of Machiavelli's concept of the politician is to be
wondered at all the more in view of the fact that precious few
political talents were to be found in his own country. Even Cesare
Borgia was not one such; Machiavelli cites him rather for the sake of
example and paradox. But at the same time the poverty of politicians
in Italy explains Machiavelli's way of thinking. For Italy had no
politicians – that was the reason one was so sorely *needed*. In the
last analysis *The Prince* is an agonized cry for help, a cry for
personalities whose prototypes may have existed but were lacking
in greatness.

In Machiavelli, politics as *techné* appears in the form of several
of its different though ultimately unified components: as *political
knowledge*, as *political manipulation*, as *political practice*, and as
political ethics.

Political knowledge and political practice are always directed
towards *the end as a whole*. They are one another's indispensable
corollaries. The correctness of political knowledge and practice are
determined by the factors I have already discussed at length: a

341

recognition of the right moment, a sense for the tendencies of movement at work in society, the ability to 'take the current when it serves', a conception of reform in harmony with 'the times', and so forth. If a man is deficient in this general political knowledge and praxis he may be the subtlest, most cunning dissembler and employ all the right devices of politics, but he will still never be a serious politician. Nothing is further from Machiavelli's mind than to recommend a morality for politics, or forms of manipulation, independent of one's overall perception of the situation and overall practice. It was only later 'Machiavellians' who thought and acted in that way. If a man does not achieve the desired, and beneficent, results with the means permitted in politics – if, in other words, his political knowledge and practice 'misfire' – then neither his manipulative nor his ethical decisions will be praiseworthy or pardonable. To repeat once again: for Machiavelli consequences are the main criterion, and the chief moral criterion of overall political action. The basic requisite for achieving a successful result, however, is correct political knowledge and practice; political manipulation and political morality are only *subordinate*, though necessary, aspects of that.

Within the context of political knowledge and practice, however, Machiavelli places a great deal of emphasis on the matter of manipulation and ethics – though, it must be added, the emphasis varies from work to work. In *The Discourses* questions of knowledge and praxis occupy the foreground, while in *The Prince* it is more the aspect of manipulation and ethics that comes to the fore.

What is the essence of manipulation in Machiavelli? It is *the use of the totality of means* towards the practical implementation of political knowledge. None of the means is to be rejected if it is *necessary* to achieve the desired result: that, in brief summary, is the content of Machiavelli's theory of ends and means. In this connection there are two matters which must be stressed. The first is that Machiavelli always speaks of the means which are necessary to attain the end. Such means as divert us from the given end (and praxis) are to be rejected – whether they are good or evil means. *In a political sense, bad means are nothing but inadequate means.* And Machiavelli never denies that what is evil and reprehensible may often be, from a political standpoint, inadequate. Thus he stresses, for example, that a prince should not make himself hated by the people by laying hands on their money or their women. But he does plainly say that *there are cases*, and not infrequently, where the adequate means are morally bad or problematical. The prince, he writes, must 'not deviate from what is good, if possible but [must]

342

be able to do evil if constrained'.[201] The other thing which must be remarked in advance is that Machiavelli's thesis has nothing in common with the Jesuitical axiom that 'the end justifies the means'. For 'the end justifies the means' implies that in the light of the end even wicked means become good and 'just'. Machiavelli, however, insists stubbornly that even though we employ it for a good end, *the ethical character of the means remains unchanged.* A bad means is still a bad means even though we regard it as necessary. The point is a most important one, both theoretically and practically. I will analyse its theoretical implications later on; for the present let us examine it solely from the practical side. Machiavelli reveals the objective contradictions of political manipulation. If we are clear in our minds about these objective contradictions, then we will be able to analyse again and again the problem of what is 'adequate' and what is 'not adequate' – and to the degree an evil means loses its necessity (and so becomes no longer adequate), we can promptly reject it. If, on the other hand, we consider our means 'just' from the standpoint of the end in view, then our value-contents become transformed and we justify the use of such means *in itself.* In that case the contradiction ceases to be a conscious one and we lose not only our ethical but also our political powers of discernment; the need to make judgments constantly on the adequacy or inadequacy of our means disappears. 'Therefore it is necessary for a prince, who wishes to maintain himself, to learn how not to be good', writes Machiavelli, 'and to use this knowledge and not use it, according to the necessity of the case.'[202] Only the man who knows when he is being wicked, and who knows that he is being wicked, and who knows that he is being wicked only to the degree that it is necessary, can dispense with evil means just as easily as make use of them.

The need for *political manipulation* is rooted – as I have said – socio-anthropologically in the 'corruption' of men. 'If men were all good, this precept would not be a good one; but as they are bad, and would not observe their faith with you, so you are not bound to keep faith with them.'[203] Men's corruption is the reason they can be enlisted for certain ends (even right ends) only by appealing to their two basic emotions: interest and fear. If, however, the end is entirely opposed to their interests, then it becomes necessary to eliminate them. With respect to the latter, however, I must make one qualification: Machiavelli believed it was justified to employ violence (to whose ethical problems I shall return) only against the few, the 'illustrious', and against patently dangerous political enemies, but never against the people. In their case, 'intimidating the people' is the furthest permissible extreme. Machiavelli (the plebeian Machiavelli)

343

recognizes no end towards which genocide would be an 'adequate' means.

So there is no avoiding operating, in politics, with interest and fear, both in acquiring power and in maintaining it. Only in each concrete situation can it be determined when it is fear that is more important and when interest, or what concrete institutions are necessary to mobilize interests or maintain fear, or both; and that determination must be made over and over again.

> For it must be noted, that men must either be caressed or else
> annihilated; they will revenge themselves for small injuries,
> but cannot do so for great ones; the injury therefore that we
> do to a man must be such that we need not fear his vengeance.[204]

Of course the problem of violence extends far beyond the sphere of political manipulation. Thus eliminating political enemies, stripping them of the means of revenge, and the like belong essentially to the category of praxis. Manipulative features appear rather in the *indirect* effects of violence and in the striving for indirect results; *at such times violence is not the consummation of a historical mission* (as when the first Brutus had his children put to death, or a later Brutus assassinated Caesar), *but a means for 'keeping people in check'.* An example is the case of Cesare Borgia and the governor of Romagna. Cesare Borgia had his governor rule the province with a firm hand, but when he saw that he was beginning to be hated because of it,[205]

> having found the opportunity he had him [the governor] cut
> in half and placed one morning in the public square at Cesena
> with a piece of wood and blood-stained knife by his side. The
> ferocity of this spectacle caused the people both satisfaction
> and amazement.

At the same time, the category of political manipulation is much broader than that of violence 'to keep people in check'. *Simulation* and *dissimulation* play no less a part in it than violence (to stay only with means which are morally contradictory and ambiguous). The first apostle of the category of 'necessary evil' held simulation of prevailing moral judgments and prejudices to be one of the chief forms of political manipulation. We may recall our discussion, in connection with the problem of knowledge of men, of how and why hypocrisy developed at this time into a quite universal social and ethical problem. The fear of being 'seen through', which characterized the overall conduct of men motivated by the competitive struggle everywhere from economic life to science and ideology, necessarily appeared even more distinctly in relation to political activity. Using general, received moral principles as a cover also meant concealing one's deepest plans and intentions, hence it was an advantage in the competitive struggle. But of course it meant something else as well. *Men nearly always seek the moral principles and requirements (ideals) of everyday life in prominent people*, and so in politicians. The greater their confidence in the latter, the more they think to find in them these ideals. Arousing this sort of confidence is one of the methods of political manipulation. I cannot go on here to describe this fact more fully, much less analyse it. I should only like to remark that this expectation on the part of public opinion is a two-sided phenomenon. On one hand, trying to 'measure' the 'great man' by the average level of ideals of the age leads, in part, to an inability to understand real greatness; on the other hand – and for the most part this is what happens – it leads to a reinterpretation of greatness in terms of popular sensibility. At such times there appears the ideal of the 'great man in slippers', the military leader who is 'the best husband and father in the world', the political leader who is a 'pious, religious, benevolent man'. The possibilities of manipulating this kind of ideal image then become infinite. But the other side of the matter is no less important. The need to pay lip service to certain ideals – the homage vice pays to virtue, as La Rochefoucauld was to sum it up succinctly later on – is a confession of the fact that evil cannot be made universally attractive. It takes very mature politicians and a very mature people for the concept of 'necessary evil', and the acts which follow from it, to be accepted openly, without disguise.

Machiavelli neither recognized, nor did he describe, the type of statesman who would openly disclose necessary evil to his people. His ideal was the politician *who would lie least to himself*. 'Thus', he writes, 'it is well to seem merciful, faithful, humane, sincere, religious, and also to be so; but you must have a mind so disposed that when it is needful to be otherwise you may be able to change to the opposite qualities.'[206] At the same time, I must add that Machiavelli not only believed possible (as an extreme case) a type of politician who would not deceive himself – a man who would sham, but would know what he was doing and why, how far to go in deceit, and so on; *he also failed even to raise the question* of what happens when a prince himself starts to believe, more or less, in the values and ideals he has been simulating. At that point the world of praxis and the world of manipulation diverge too sharply from each other. While in praxis the general is always present (in the apprehension and pursuit of the general tendencies present in the world), manipulation is reduced to the creation of a sphere of action for the individual and to the preservation of his power; political *techné* dwindles from the exercise of power to a technique for the preservation of individual authority.

From this it follows that Machiavelli does not distinguish types of manipulation according to social and political forms, objectives, or social tendencies, but according to *how* a politician (the prince) has come to power – whether through inheritance or by his own devices, in wartime or peace, in his own country or in a conquered province, and so on. Not that this way of posing the question is meaningless; it is only one-sided. (In *The Prince* this tendency is stronger than in *The Discourses*.) I do not wish to detract thereby from the genius of Machiavelli, but I would like to remark that here too Shakespeare, in the depiction of his political characters, outshone the most brilliant theory. In Shakespeare the inheritance of a throne, or the winning of one, can act as a motivation (Henry IV versus Richard II), but this aspect is still a subordinate one. The content of every concrete tactical measure taken by a given politician (or his inability to take such steps, as in Henry VI's case) is determined in the first instance by his overall conception of society and its value-content, depth, and meaningfulness. That is why there are so many more resemblances between a Henry V (who becomes king by inheritance) and a Henry VII (who does not) than between any two kings who both succeed by inheritance, or who both come to the throne by other means. Mark Antony's funeral oration, a marvel of manipulation, is intimately bound up with his overall activity and overall ideology, with the state of social development as a whole, with the 'moment', and so on – and Mark Antony himself is not that sort of Machiavellian hero who deceives himself least, but rather the much more common type who, with few exceptions half believes and half disbelieves what he himself says.

If Machiavelli's method of distinguishing the various types of manipulation is one-sided, it still affords a way of depicting a wide range of instances. Since I have already discussed the subject of violence, and will be returning to it again (according to Machiavelli, it is the new prince who has just won power for himself who has most need of violence), I will merely quote one other passage in order to illustrate how the Florentine thinker saw the possibilities of governing an established absolute monarchy:[207]

A prince must also show himself a lover of merit, give preferment to the able, and honour those who excel in every art. Moreover, he must encourage his citizens to follow their callings quietly, whether in commerce, or agriculture, or any

other trade that men follow. . . . Besides this, he ought, at
convenient seasons of the year, to keep the people occupied
with festivals and shows; and as every city is divided either
into guilds or into classes, he ought to pay attention to all
these groups, mingle with them from time to time, and give
them an example of his humanity and munificence. . . .

Furthermore, let him gather around himself a number of astute men
who will always speak the truth to his face. In this political form,
then, morally contradictory and equivocal means recede, to a great
extent, into the background. And this in turn points to another
important aspect of Machiavelli's thinking, namely to the fact that
he never regarded necessary evil as something to be employed con-
stantly and regularly, but rather as a temporary means of securing
power more firmly. That is the reason it was so important to be aware
that certain means were necessary, but *evil*[208]

[Cruelties] well committed may be called those (if it is
permissible to use the word well of evil) which are perpetuated
once for the need of securing one's self, and which afterwards
are not persisted in, but are exchanged for measures as useful
to the subjects as possible. Cruelties ill committed are those
which, although at first few, increase rather than diminish with
time. . . .

Whence it is to be noted, that in taking a state *the conqueror*
must arrange to commit all his cruelties at once, so as not to
have to recur to them every day. . . .

Before turning to the last, but still important, aspect of political
techné, the question of political morality, I should like to stress once
more that Machiavelli's ethical statements – however much they
may be restricted to the realm of political morality – go far beyond
it in their significance, touching upon *universal questions of ethics.* I
must refer back to what has been said about how fixed rosters of
values lost their validity. Machiavelli declares, as a matter of general
validity, that it is impossible to act in keeping with abstract virtues
at all times and places, that such a thing is contrary to 'human
nature' and to the requirements of the time. In itself, of course,
that was hardly a new discovery. What was new was the establish-
ment of the fact that the infringement of the virtues (which in an
abstract ethical sense was bad) could, in certain concrete connections and from certain points of view, be adequate, necessary,
and, what is more, good. There exists, moreover, a criterion by

347

which its 'goodness' can be measured, a standard by which that goodness can be read. That is none other than the *consequence* of an action. An overall action may be proper even though it contains many partial actions which contradict accepted rosters of values, and an overall action may be wrong even though there is no single part of it which contradicts them. Machiavelli thus uncovered the internal contradiction between abstract morality and real social ethics (an ethics based not on any Ought, but on the unity of Ought and possibilities). And he pointed out as well that 'bearing' this contradiction, and eventually resolving it, is not a general, abstract, theoretical task but an eminently *practical* one, and a practical task of a sort which every single human being must solve again and again in each concrete situation, and for which he must bear personal responsibility. Machiavelli's ethics was the first great step which mankind had made since Aristotle's theory of the mean towards a theoretical solution of the contradictory character and thrust of ethics. Just as, with the emergence of a non-communal society, moral responsibility came to weigh more and more heavily on the individual's shoulders, so too Machiavelli proclaimed the need for the individual's acceptance of responsibility for good and evil, humanity's arrival at moral adulthood, and *the ethics of willingness to take a risk*. In a paradoxical way, Machiavelli's pointed propositions served to awaken men to the risky character of their actions and, among other things, to the fact that often they can only choose between the greater and the lesser evil and that in these cases neither God nor the law will decide for them what to choose.

And now I should like to conclude my own remarks with a paradox. *Machiavelli, seemingly the cynic, is in actuality a moralist.* For the cynical man does not acknowledge values. Machiavelli, however, thoroughly recognizes them, but he adds that *the value-world of reality is not homogeneous.* He does not at all deny the value-character of abstract norms, moral principles, and virtues. On the contrary, he points it up, since *he denies every action devoid of absolute value the name of moral good.* Is dissimulation good? No. Is violence good? No. What is that if not precisely a defence of the absolute purity of moral content and, moreover, eminently a moralist's defence? Only it is not just the abstract moral world of values which alone exists. Success is a value too, achievement of the goal is a value, the expression of personality in creation is a value (and we have already seen what an important one it was for the Renaissance), serving the welfare of mankind is a value. And if at times these can be attained only by breaking moral norms, it is not then a case of a non-value conflicting with a value, but of one kind

348

of value in conflict with another. 'For where the very safety of the country depends upon the resolution to be taken, no considerations of justice or injustice, humanity or cruelty, nor of glory or of shame, should be allowed to prevail', writes Machiavelli in *The Discourses*.[209] In this case, of the values in conflict, it is not the abstract moral ones which carry the most weight. Of course, there may be situations in which abstract moral values have more weight. But that is precisely what can only be decided, and must be decided, concretely, in concrete situations.

In fact Machiavelli was a moralist, and that was true even in the realm of political ethics itself, narrowly defined. Nor is it simply a matter of Machiavelli's having 'deprived' political action of its moral content – nor even the fact that he simply described the existing status quo (as indeed he did), but approved dreadful things and accepted them as the norm. There is another side to the question as well: Machiavelli's 'separation' was a dual one. For he separated the value-system from political practice just as effectively as he divorced political practice from the value-system. He takes note of what really exists, but at the same time he demands of men that they make themselves conscious of the inner laws and possibilities of actual social and political practice. *It is not simply a matter of his recommending dissimulation and the use of violence* (though that is a *part* of it too), *but also of his urging people to know they are dissembling, know they are using violence, know that dissimulation and violence are evil in themselves, and therefore know that they are to be used only so far as necessary, that you do not have 'clean hands' for having used them, and that you ought to accept that.* That is anything but cynicism.

Machiavelli then is not 'amoral'; but he explores the real possibilities of concrete social and political ethics from the point of view of a moralist who regards the demands of social practice and not those of an abstract morality as the highest value. And he did so in an age when every measure of social progress was, of necessity, morally contradictory. That was an acceptance of the contradictory character of progress, of a sort which was later to characterize many of the giants of bourgeois thought. Yet it would not be correct to confuse his attitude – especially his ethical attitude – with that of thinkers like Mandeville or Ricardo. For Mandeville and Ricardo really were cynics. (And by using that term I do not mean to lend a pejorative note to my evaluation – for a certain kind of cynicism may at times play a very positive role in the disclosure of truth, and the cynicism of Mandeville did in fact play such a positive role.) They saw economic development, or enrichment, as the sole criterion

349

of the success of social activity. And they declared – cynically, but in keeping with the truth – that the material abundance of capitalist society unfolds at the cost of the misery of the single individuals, and that the ethical motivations behind that development are private egoism and the vices which spring from it ('private vices', as Mandeville calls them). They approve enrichment, and so they consciously approve along with it 'private vices' of every kind. For them, there is no question of these vices being means towards the achievement of an ethical end, a necessary evil to be dispensed with when the necessity for such means has passed; for them vice is not a *temporary* evil, consciously chosen, but the *state* of social development. That is why an awareness that evil *is* evil, an awareness of deviating from the ethical value-system, and an acceptance of moral responsibility for it have no place in their writings. Where vice stems from private egoism, where it permeates *every* social stratum and *every* sphere of social activity, there virtue can only be hypocrisy or stupidity – there no functioning system of values exists at all, nor any risk, nor any individual moral responsibility. Nothing depends on the individual – either on his virtues or on his vices – because the world of private egoism is a smoothly working *mechanism*. Machiavelli's pathos, now revolutionary, now reformistic, but at all events oriented towards the transformation of the world, becomes for Mandeville and Ricardo only the twilight wisdom of Minerva's owl.

In saying that Machiavelli was the first to make a radical distinction between customary morality and ethics (including political ethics), we are undoubtedly on firm ground so far as his overall *conception* is concerned. In his *terminology*, however, Machiavelli is often uncertain; he struggles to accomplish his great theoretical task. Thus at one time he speaks (in connection with evil means) of vices, at another of *apparent* vices; at one point he speaks of 'good' in respect of the consequences, while at another he adds the qualification, 'if indeed evil can be called good'. Elsewhere, again, he calls a successful result a 'semblance' which also lends a 'semblance of dignity' to the means. The host of concrete examples and the frequently repeated theoretical formulas nevertheless still combine to give an unequivocal clarity to what is being said, despite any vacillation about terminology.

In analysing Machiavelli's political ethics I must return to the problem of *violence*. It was not theoretical speculation which made this question the order of the day, but the concrete situation of Italy. Machiavelli came to the problem of violence primarily by way of his inquiry into the reasons for the fall of Savonarola:[210]

350

Thus it comes about that all armed prophets have conquered and unarmed ones failed; for ... the character of peoples varies, and it is easy to persuade them of a thing, but difficult to keep them in that persuasion. And so it is necessary to order things so that when they no longer believe, they can be made to believe by force. ... In our own time ... Fra Girolamo Savonarola, who failed entirely in his new rules when the multitude began to disbelieve in him ... had no means of holding fast those who had believed nor of compelling the unbelievers to believe.

Thus the reason for Savonarola's fall was that he did not have recourse to violence as a means of manipulation. But a comparison with developments elsewhere, or a look at the prospects for Italy, could lead to the question of violence just as easily as could an examination of the past. Absolute monarchy had stabilized the social order of France and England. But before great 'legislators' could be born there it was first necessary for their rivals to be exterminated with fire and sword – violence once more. At home, Machiavelli looked forward to a unified national Italy in the form of a modern absolute monarchy. To create it – especially in the light of the very divergent interests of the smaller states and the Papacy – a strong hand was required, a man who would not respect anyone or anything in accomplishing his goals. Only after a united Italy had been achieved by force could the great work of 'legislation' begin, and the 'return' of the people to their own origins.

Here, however, we come up against the lone major difficulty with Machiavelli's political ethics, the fact that, leaving aside a few concrete examples, he in essence *makes political technique entirely independent of the economic sphere, and the governance of men quite independent of the management of things.* For that reason, the political struggle is for him a pure *power* struggle. The power struggle is conducted, so to speak, 'in a vacuum'. However often he may write that men fail because they are unable to understand 'the time', he always means by it the time of power and political activity alone. Consider the theory of *corsi e ricorsi*. The cycle it describes is one of forms of power and authority: republic, tyranny, aristocracy, oligarchy, and empire succeed one another in regular sequence, but on what sort of economic base – of that there is not the slightest indication. Nor could there be any indication, for according to Machiavelli these changes always take place uniformly and *in the same way*. The analysis of political activity in a vacuum, and its separation from the management of things, leads to a situation

351

where Machiavelli is not, and cannot be, capable of distinguishing *the various types of violence*. The successful seizure of a purely personal authority, and the violent deeds performed in doing so, are ranged without distinction alongside measure of violence taken in winning the liberation of one's country. And here we can blame Machiavelli not only for failing to recognize an ethical distinction, but for failing to recognize a *political distinction* as well. That is the source, and the sole source, of those feelings of repugnance which grip the reader on meeting certain passages in *The Prince*, and which aroused in Rousseau, undoubtedly an admirer of Machiavelli, the impression that *The Prince* was a satire. For when Machiavelli analyses Cesare Borgia's actions, describing how he tricked the Orsini, first bringing them gifts and then 'contriving to have them killed one and all', or when he writes that 'following the extermination of his enemies his power rested on a secure foundation', the only thing we do not find out is, why? Simply in order to make his own authority more secure? Or did that authority serve more far-reaching ends? And here we can turn to Shakespeare once again, because in his works the 'order' of violence was in fact restored. For he saw – and brilliantly – that murder committed for the sake of purely individual power does not even meet the Machiavellian criterion itself, because after making one's power secure it is not possible to stop, since it is *never* possible to make one's power finally secure and one crime brings another in its wake. Only the man for whom power is merely a means – a means for changing things, transforming social relations – can really make his authority secure and really knows where to stop in evil. Neither the unifying action of the absolute monarchy, nor its conquests, nor the aggrandizement of the country appeared to him in an abstract light, but rather as part of an overall conception. We need only think again of Henry V.

There is no denying that in this – truly problematical – connection there really is a difference of emphasis between *The Discourses* and *The Prince*. In *The Discourses* Machiavelli always strives to regard not only violence, but also power acquired (or confirmed) through violence as a means to an end. Consider two examples: 'He is to be reprehended who commits violence for the purpose of destroying, and not he who employs it for beneficient purposes', he writes in *The Discourses*.[211] And again: 'Whoever makes himself tyrant of a state and does not kill Brutus, or whoever restores liberty to a state and does not immolate his sons, will not maintain himself in his position long.'[212] If we compare this with the passage in *The Prince* where Cesare Borgia's actions in preparation for the papal election

352

are analysed, the difference in emphasis is clearly visible. Here, however, it is not so much a matter of a change of mind as of the fact that the two books have different subjects. *The Discourses* is properly speaking a historiosophical work, in which questions of political knowledge and practice are uppermost, while the real subject of *The Prince* is political technique, above all political morality and manipulation. And it was chiefly in his analysis of the latter that neglect of the economic structure limited Machiavelli, rather than in his exposition of broad historical conceptions, where the substantive relationships were more obvious.

But once political activity had been analysed in isolation from overall social activity, some uncertainty was bound to result, for Machiavelli sought to be *scientific*. Of course the fact that in given *concrete* cases violence was indispensable for winning freedom or preserving it was by no means a novelty, much less any discovery of Machiavelli's. Petrarch, for example, in his letter to Cola di Rienzo, insists almost hysterically on the necessity of violence, and after his hero falls he explains the event thus:[213]

> The man who cannot pursue what he wants as steadfastly as
> he should and as the times demand, deserves his punishment
> in the highest degree; for after he [Cola] had made himself
> the champion of liberty, he ought to have killed all his enemies
> at one stroke (an opportunity which the grace of Fortune never
> gave to any other ruler), but instead he let them all go, and
> let them go armed! Oh cruel and lamentable darkness, which
> amid the splendour of the most magnificent enterprises so often
> clouds the eyes of mortals. . . .

Here Petrarch formulates, *in concreto*, the ethic of consequences in politics. The fact that in certain circumstances violence was morally right was practically a commonplace. Thus, for example, Michelangelo's friend Gianotti, in one of his dialogues, puts these words in Michelangelo's mouth: 'Whoever dispatches a tyrant has not killed a human being, . . . but a wild beast that has crept into a human skin. . . . Thus Brutus and Cassius did not act wrongly when they killed Caesar.'[214] But – as we have seen – it is not individual cases that Machiavelli analyses, nor individual examples; he does not deal in possibilities, nor does he offer concrete advice for concrete situations. Rather he seeks the *general and necessary* modes of political activity (manipulation included). That is precisely what is so radically new in him. He could have avoided his difficulties completely only if he had discovered other aspects, other substantive sides of this same general validity itself.

If Machiavelli revealed the contradictions inherent in the politics and ethics of the new age, still he singled out for attention only *one* aspect of those contradictions. There were others who turned their minds to dealing with other aspects. The sixteenth century had brutally demonstrated already that the evolution of the human essence went hand in hand with the alienation of the human essence. No one, of course, saw or formulated it in general terms. Yet the fact that the development of the means of production was simultaneously both beneficial and harmful, the fact that the accumulation of wealth did not decrease but rather increased human misery, the fact that civilization did not put an end to demoralization, but rather reproduced it in sharpened form (and in growing measure) – all these things were becoming recognizable, and they were in fact recognized. Some only mentioned them, while for others they played a central role; some merely described them, recording the facts, while others attacked or defended them with passion.

It must be emphasized, however, that here we are in an age of transition. Neither the contradictions of wealth nor those of technology appeared as 'purely' a part of the problematics of capitalism. More, Bruno, and Campanella were perhaps the only ones to get past the traditional ways of posing the question, in order to distill the 'pure' problematics of bourgeois society. Let us first examine this in relation to the contradictory character of the development of the means of production.

For those who in later centuries reckoned with this phenomenon, the prime force at work to lame human beings was the technical division of labour (or the division of social labour). During the Renaissance, however, this problem was taken up only by the utopian writers, and even then indirectly, not so much in their critical analyses as in their positive (utopian) disquisitions. With others – as we have already seen in the case of Pomponazzi – the division of labour was something unequivocally affirmed; for the most part, however, they omitted to analyse it. For them, too, the moral contradictions of technology have both an individual side and a general social side. On the individual plane, they speak of its power to cripple human individuality and of its moral devastation. But this mutilation and moral devastation do not manifest themselves in the *use* of technology, in *labour*, but rather in the quest and *discovery* of new technical procedures. The man who devised new procedures was a kenner of *secrets* and the possessor of *power*. His devices were contradictory precisely because they were 'mysterious' and because they conferred power. That was how they enabled some to rise above the community of 'ordinary' men, made possible for them actions which were not within the power of others and into whose mechanics they could not see; with which, therefore, any evil could be committed, and at whose mercy all the others were placed. Here is the 'diabolism' of technology, the *Faustian problem*. Parenthetically be it added that when Bacon said that 'knowledge is power', he was talking about *this kind* of power too; there are no grounds for interpreting the phrase solely in terms of the modern notion of 'power over nature' (which is close to the Marxian notion).

The social side of the contradiction presents itself in the opposite possibility, that of the reduction of privilege, for the advances of technology even out inequalities; moreover, every technical innovation, and the spread of every technique, carries with it the danger that *they may be turned against mankind* or may, of themselves, without our having any power over it, turn against humanity. In connection with the idea of 'equalization' or 'levelling' I may refer back to the passage in which Ariosto laments the discovery of gunpowder. Gunpowder does away with military valour and puts an end to the distinction between courage and cowardice. Here, however, Machiavelli's response must also be appended. The Florentine writer replied that gunpowder did not obviate the martial virtues; it simply demanded new ones in place of the old. With that concrete reply he did not mean to imply, however, that the problem was a meaningless one. In discussions of how technology may turn against man two aspects have customarily been singled out: the growth of destructive forces and the increase in opportunities for luxury. 'Certainly human life is much indebted to [the mechanical arts]', wrote Bacon, 'and yet out of the same fountain come instruments of lust, and also instruments of death.'[215]

The ambiguous character of the wealth created by technology was a particularly favoured theme during the Renaissance. We should note in advance that among the thinkers of the age *not one* regarded the problem of poverty and wealth as an *individual* problem. The Catholic tradition was helpful here; it merely had to be secularized. For Catholicism (before the Counter-Reformation), poverty had been programme and ideal (and therefore could not be an individual fault); at the same time it was a 'station' determined by one's place in the feudal system, and so once again was ordained by God. The idea, if it can be called that at all, that the poor are poor because they do not work, while the rich have got that way as a result of their industry, became the ideology of a triumphant capitalism and found its most immediate expression in Protestantism. During the Renaissance, then, it was unknown. Wealth and poverty were seen as objective social phenomena, and their cause was sought in society itself, not in individuals.

As for the *process by which wealth was produced*, however – that was something which the men of the Renaissance scarcely began to examine. It was rather the problem of the *use of wealth* which was uppermost in their minds. Wealth could be employed 'well' or 'ill'. It was well used if it benefited trade, 'industry', and culture, ill used if it gave rise to idleness, luxury, and neglect of public affairs. We ought not to forget that this way of looking at the matter played an important part in later centuries too. Even the English classical economists distinguished between industries producing useful articles and those producing luxuries (although they still regarded the latter as productive), while Saint-Simon separated the class of 'idlers' from that of 'workers' (to which latter category, of course, capitalists also belonged). And yet – as Saint-Simon's own distinction indicates – in the heyday of classical political economy the capitalist class which was developing the means of production was ever more sharply set off (even where it *produced* luxuries) from the class which was purely a *consumer of luxuries*, the nobility. But during the Renaissance, especially during the sixteenth century, that was not at all the case. In Italy the pioneering bourgeois class *par excellence* set foot on the road of refeudalization; capital meant for production went more and more for luxury and 'idleness'. In England, Spain, and France, on the other hand, the noble class was bourgeoisified (though in varying degree) – the same nobility whose demand for luxuries had appeared not long before and now grew and grew. So 'useful' and 'useless' wealth could not be identified with specific classes, and for that reason no analysis of its social character was possible. Thus the thinkers of the Renaissance, from Petrarch all the way to Bruno, contented themselves with a mere *description* of wealth as a Janus-faced thing, without undertaking a deeper analysis of the phenomenon.

Renaissance thinkers were no less interested by the question of whether wealth was useful politically, from the standpoint of consolidating the state. Here opinions differed widely, and I have no wish to enumerate them all here. But I should like to point out how the undifferentiated state of the problem is indicated by the constantly recurring references to *Rome*. 'Rome, the conqueror of the world, was herself conquered by richness', wrote Petrarch,[216] without its occurring to him that the wealth of his own age and that of Rome were simply not commensurable. Machiavelli, too, loudly proclaimed how sorely riches corrupt morals, drawing again on Roman examples. But he was also the one to declare, citing both

SOCIAL PHILOSOPHY, POLITICS, UTOPIA

Rome *and* Florence, that the struggle of rich and poor is one of the basic prerequisites for correct and successful political manipulation. For only where it exists can the prince manoeuvre between the two groups, with their opposed interests, and so more easily attain his own objectives. Machiavelli saw that poverty was good for a new republic, while wealth (and poverty) was good for a monarchy.

It is no wonder that at a time when the contradictions bred of technological development, wealth and (as their result) private property were becoming the constant theme of everyday discussion (though not yet their organic unity), the image of the Ovidian 'golden age' should recur again and again. We can see this in the criticism of Bruno, in Erasmus' praise of 'folly', and in the arguments of Gratiano in Shakespeare's *Tempest*. It was the idea of a world in which there was no property, no state, no law, no compulsion to labour, no egoism and no evil – only tranquil enjoyment, constancy, repose, and pure morals. Many of the finer spirits 'hark back' to humanity's peaceful, paradisiacal past with nostalgia. The word 'paradisiacal' must be emphasized, for the revival of the myth of the 'golden age' is a sign of the fading of the Judaeo-Christian myth. Adam and Eve's God-given private paradise is replaced by humanity's great common social paradise.

But despite the nostalgia of finer spirits, the state of nature still did not engage thinkers of the first rank in a *scientific* way. The time for a *historical* interpretation of it was still a long way off. For that, more general principles of historicity were necessary, of the sort which were not available until the appearance of Rousseau's *Discourse on the Origin of Inequality*. As a *programme*, it was illusory – that is why Shakespeare's Gratiano is so grotesque. All the more numerous were the scholarly opponents of the ideal of a 'golden age'. For Bruno, the golden age has a *negative* value-content. A happy paradise, without wants and constant activity, and without progress, were repugnant to Giordano Bruno, one of the most passionate defenders of bourgeois society. He preferred to accept a world in which the stake existed and in which heroes like himself were burned to death, rather than idealize a social order in which even evil did not exist, because human self-consciousness did not exist:[217]

During the golden age, then, men were, thanks to Sloth, no more virtuous than are the beasts today. . . . But when with the imitation of the divine action and the inclination of the spiritual capacities thereto, difficulties arose and wants appeared, the mind of man was sharpened as a result; men

invented the branches of industry and discovered the arts, until
now, *under the spur of necessity, ever more wondrous new
inventions pour forth day by day from the depths of the
human mind. . . . Do not wonder at the injustices and iniquities
which have grown up side by side with man's aspirations for the
good. . . .* In your golden age men were not yet virtuous,
because they were not sinful; for there is a great difference
between innocence and virtuousness. . . .

The argument bears an almost uncanny resemblance to Diderot's
criticism of Rousseau's *Discourse*.

Some have mistakenly seen the great utopists of the Renaissance,
More and Campanella, as reviving the idea of a golden age, just as
others have erroneously seen in them a direct prefiguring of post-
French Revolution utopianism. I have already said that in More and
Campanella there is no trace of future-orientedness, but at the same
time there is no trace of past-directedness either. They do not differ
from Bruno by reason of any longing for a 'golden age', but in
which aspects of the present they accept, and in what they consider
necessary and what accidental. Bruno regards it as inevitable that
'under the spur of necessity' the world should advance, in a double
sense: in the sense that needs should go on growing, and in the sense
that property, the contradiction between wealth and poverty,
should continue to play a controlling part. More and Campanella,
however, assert that social conditions are *conceivable* under which
needs can be satisfied at the given level, and which are not governed
by 'necessity' in that double sense. It was the *model* of such a social
construction which they created.

But is private property and its subjective expression, individual
material interest, the sole adequate – even the best – regulator of
society? On this point turns the whole debate in More's *Utopia*. At
first the author himself is uncertain: 'For how can there be
abundaunce of goodes, or of any thing, where every man with-
draweth his hand from labour? Whome the regard of his own
gaines driveth not to worke . . .?' he asks.[218] Thereupon Raphael
replies with his description of the island of Utopia. And the final
conclusion is:[219]

In other places they speake stile of the commen wealth, but
every man procureth his owne private gaine. Here where
nothing is private, the commen affaires bee earnestlye looked
upon. . . . For in other countreys who knoweth not that he
shall sterve for honger, onles he make some severall provision,
though the commen wealthe floryshe never so muche in ryches?

And therefore he is *compelled even of verye necessitie* to have
regard to him selfe, rather then to the people, that is to saye,
to other.

Here, then, the category of 'necessity', normative for bourgeois
economics, appears again, but this time not as the motor of economic
progress, rather as a moral stumbling-block which from an economic
standpoint is indifferent at best. Thus the utopias of More and
Campanella should not be treated simply as ideal demands for
ethical norms, springing purely from moral indignation. They wished
– to use the expression of András Hegedüs – to satisfy at one and
the same time the demands of both optimalization and humanization. This optimalization differed from the expectations not only
of Marxism, but also of post-French Revolutionary utopianism,
in only one respect – though that was an essential respect: it explored
the possibilities of making maximum use of the means of production
in their *given* state of development, and did not take up at all the
problem of further developing the means of production, or of
raising productivity. And so of course the conception which they
were able to form of the satisfaction of human needs could only be a
static one. Still, there was no asceticism in it, no 'sharing the
poverty'. They desired and premised a way of life in keeping with
the needs of their time, but truly humanistic, and one that could
be enjoyed at the existing standard of the age.

In both works, the union of ethical and economic perspectives
gives rise to a special style. Passionate indignation and deep moral
pathos are combined with an expert, objective, scientific, and
detailed description of the model proposed. The unity of these two
styles is best achieved in More; in terms of composition his is the
better work, for Campanella too often gets lost in the details of his
model. Objectively, the paradoxical thing about both works is
that – partly as a result of the things I have been discussing – their
critical sections have universal validity, while their objective,
'scientific' sections turn out to be naïve. Since Campanella lays
more stress on the latter, the naïvety is more conspicuous in his
case. But the brilliance of both works shines through the naïvety.
It is particularly apparent in the fact that when the economic
structure is described, in both *Utopia* and *The City of the Sun*, the
emphasis falls at least as much on *production* as on distribution and
consumption. More and Campanella instinctively knew that 'in-
equities' in distribution are a function of how production is
organized. Here, moreover, the seemingly more naïve Campanella
was actually the more perceptive. For while More thought that the

elimination of private property would be sufficient to set a new productive mechanism in motion, that was still not enough for Campanella. In More, production is carried on in the family. Sons follow their father's trade, the family makes its own clothing, and so forth; only distribution, and in part consumption, are in common. Campanella, however, envisages production too as social, in large-scale workshops and work brigades. The fact that he could conceive of such a thing only at the cost of abolishing the family (among other things) bears witness not only to the Platonic tradition, but also to the influence of certain contemporary, especially Anabaptist, examples.

Thus both More and Campanella were in search of a model in which what was most useful for the community would also be most pleasant for the individual – though not necessarily for every individual, of course. Both on the island of Utopia and in the City of the Sun punitive sanctions are very important. Punishment awaits those who find individual enjoyment in anything which is *opposed* to the interests of the community. But More and Campanella assumed that they are few in number, for they were convinced that wrongdoing was 'unnatural' – it did not spring from 'human' nature, but was a necessary consequence of those factors which lead to wrongdoing. If we get rid of the causes which compel to wrong-doing, then wrong itself will cease to be typical. It is compelling need that makes man egotistical, grasping and crooked, makes him a thief and a pillager. For – as More wrote – there is no punishment which will restrain from pillage those who have no *other* way of acquiring their daily bread. Or – as Campanella asked – why should crime be typical if there is no reason to compete for position, no poverty and no wealth, no abuse of love, no ignorance?

More and Campanella sought, then, to create a model of a *free* society. *The stoic-epicurean concept of freedom becomes here a collective, socially formative principle;* the ontological conception of freedom becomes intertwined with the sociological conception of freedom. Freedom, they say, is achieved by 'living according to nature', through autonomy, through self-actualization. Only now the question is: how can the *conditions* and the *desire* to 'live according to nature' be created for every single human being? It is property, money, gold that distort human nature; they are what makes wrongdoing pleasing. If there were no longer any property, money, or gold, then work itself, helping others, and goodness would be pleasing, and the object of people's free choice. 'Everyone will work', writes Campanella, 'according to his own proper nature, and so will perform his work well and with pleasure for its being natural to him. . . .'[220] And again: 'The community makes them all rich and poor: rich, because they have and possess all things; poor, because they are not attached to the service of things, rather all things serve them.'[221] Their freedom manifests itself, then, in their pleasure in carrying out their work, in the reduction of the working day (to six hours in More, to four in Campanella), in the alternation of work and rest, and (in Campanella) in the study of the sciences and their application to every purpose.

Earlier I said that people today (and even the people of two centuries ago) would have felt they were in prison in More's or Campanella's ideal society. Why, then, do I assert that they sought to design a realm of freedom? Because the modern bourgeois individual, with his characteristic subjectivity and inner life, had not yet evolved; given the existence and consciousness of the men *of that age*, the utopias of More and Campanella really did depict a world of freedom. That is especially true in the case of More; in Campanella's case it is true only with qualifications – true only within the limits of the world he *knew*, the one immediately surrounding him.

But even supposing – though not conceding – that these utopias may not have described the structure of a (relatively) free society: their *philosophical tendency* was still in the direction of seeking after, and framing the outlines of, such a society. This philosophical attempt to unite the sociological and ontological concepts of freedom did not spring *ex nihilo*. It was an expression and reflection – even though a critical, polemical one – of an emerging society which would give birth to the 'free individual'. That society was bourgeois society, and that freedom was *bourgeois* freedom, as Marxian philosophy conceives of it. It gave birth to men who were 'liberated' from their means of production yet still had to toil, upon whose labour, moreover, all society rested. Without that, it would have been impossible even to imagine a human society in which *no one* owned the means of production but where, nevertheless, *everyone* still worked industriously. There was born the formal equality of 'all men' (rich and poor), occasionally in a real way, as for a time in Florence, but for the most part in ideal form. Without it no human society would have been imaginable in which everyone was equal – not in the sight of God, or through the mediation of divine law or will, but equal as a result of the immanent structure of society.

There are still slaves in the utopias of More and Campanella. Liberty and equality do not pertain to them at all. Their importance, however, is marginal. So long as the slave is not human and the serf is situated, by divine decree, at the foot of the social hierarchy, no 'social science' can arise – that is, no scientific study or programme aiming to transform the *entire* social structure in the interests of *every* human being. It was, then, bourgeois freedom and formal equality which made possible the contrasting of a realm of freedom with the realm of necessity, and the announcement of a society of equal opportunities. Capitalism, even at the moment of its birth, necessarily gave rise to its own critics, who attacked the reality of their own day on the grounds of its own inherent principles and possibilities.

CHAPTER 11

Fate, destiny, fortune

Fate, destiny, fortune – all these are categories of everyday life.
Their ontological content, none the less, varies greatly; even during
one and the same age it is labile and uncertain. Their lability,
however, is not just the result of a cloudy vision; it is a consequence
and at the same time a premise of the anthropomorphic teleology
of everyday life.

The notion of destiny implies irrevocability, immutability, man's
inability to change things – not, then, his absolute powerlessness.
It reflects a real fact: the irrevocable, the immutable, the unredeem-
able really do exist. But the concept always contains the idea of the
reason and substance of that irrevocability – the ontological function
of 'irrevocability', we might say. When the ancient Greeks referred
to destiny (*moira*), they meant by it the inevitable unfolding of the
fate of individuals and peoples, an evolution inherited from their
ancestors and ordained by the gods. For all that, man was still not
petty or helpless. Whoever acted in accordance with destiny
triumphed, whoever struggled against it failed; but the former was
not necessarily the greater of the two. (*Victrix causa diis placuit,
sed victa Catoni*, as was said later in Rome.) For victory was not the
'merit' of the victor (it was actually the gods who had triumphed),
any more than defeat was a fiasco for the vanquished (for it was
really his gods who had been beaten). There is no difference between
Hector and Odysseus so far as their order of greatness is concerned.
The hero can, of course, acquire great personal merit in carrying
destiny to victory (like Achilles), but that follows from his *personal*
qualities and human greatness, not in the first instance from his
function as an agent of destiny. The God of the Old Testament was

363

more circumspect in this regard. He 'elected' in advance those who displayed greatness to be the executors of His destiny. Esau ought to have succeeded to Isaac's position, but God, having seen Jacob's 'aptness', simply 'bestowed' on Jacob the mission of representing destiny. In the case of Moses, again, this individual election is even more significant, with its conditionality and its linkage to merit. For the rest, destiny may also originate with man – with the mediation of God or the gods. A curse, for instance, can 'take effect'; that is, through the mediation of the gods it can become destiny. The ontological structure of destiny remains essentially similar throughout the Middle Ages: general and special Providence guide men's fates.

The concept of destiny, then, is not at all synonymous with the concept of 'necessity'. Necessity, as the immanent and causal link joining objective processes in a series of 'if . . . then' connections, *may* form the ontological content of destiny, but it does not necessarily do so. In theological and teleological world-views, destiny most often is precisely that which does not spring from necessity. The whim or fancy of a god may become destiny. The accidental may become destiny, and so may an act that springs from 'free will'.

A number of non-teleological, immanent world-views have attempted to explain the category of destiny as some kind of 'inevitable necessity'. The 'destiny' of the epicureans is synonymous with the 'natural essence' of man. It is man's destiny that he must endure every consequence which flows from the natural essence of the human species; that is the only thing that is unavoidable. The prime 'inevitability' which we must embrace along with our existence is death. Our only normal conduct in the face of destiny – precisely because by its nature it is inevitable – is to have no concern about it. It is no business of ours, for we should be concerned only with the things which in some sense lie within our power, within the range of our freedom. *Thus Epicurus did not recognize any personal, individual destiny, just as he did not recognize any social destiny either.* The individual, as an individual and as a social being, is dependent only upon himself; he has a fate, but no destiny. In ancient stoicism – by contrast with the foregoing – the identification of destiny with 'inevitable necessity' was made rather in the spheres of social life and individual existence. That is why, in its case, autonomy became for the most part purely subjective. Since I have already discussed this subject, I will simply refer again to the fact that the stoicism of the Renaissance was far from a mere copy of ancient stoicism; in this respect, as in others, it was mixed to a great extent with fundamental principles drawn from epicureanism.

The terminology of Renaissance thought did not always make a distinction between destiny and fate. For the most part the word *fatum* served to designate both (the category of 'predestination' was used only in theological contexts, and 'fate' was often simply synonymous with *fatum*). But great emphasis was placed on making a *substantive* distinction between the two. The polemic between *fatum* as destiny and *fatum* as fate was one of the central topics of debate of the age.

With the progress of secularization the Christian concept of destiny faded away (to be revived, presently, in the form of Protestant predestination). It gave way to a new, *astrological* concept of destiny. Pomponazzi regarded both the historical world and the natural world as being the necessary outcome of the influence of the heavenly bodies. The movements of the stars determine the life of the larger structures and the fate of individual human beings as well. Such was the unshakeable conviction of the Renaissance 'man in the street', too. To repeat: here again, as with the notion of destiny generally, it is not a matter of a 'pure', consistently thought-out conviction, permeating every action and conception; rather it is a question of an axiom which has become a commonplace, and alongside which contrary theories and practices could simultaneously come into existence too.

The mutual influence of Renaissance science, and of the evidence of everyday life, was particularly strong in the case of the concept of astrological destiny. However paradoxical it may sound, science demythologized even in busying itself with astrology. What had seemed marvel, accident, or divine decree was now given, in the movement of the stars, a *natural* explanation. Society's complex, incomprehensible twists and turns received a 'scientific' grounding; nor did the fate of individual men any longer depend on God, either. The teleological structure of the world remained: as before, the fate of both society and individual had been played out in advance. But what directed the play was not God (and so not consciousness) any longer, but nature itself, 'objective purposefulness without a purpose', as Kant was later to express it. If we can take the measure of this tendency we will no longer wonder that even such a scientist as Kepler occupied himself with the preparation of horoscopes – and not just because his patron demanded it, but from personal conviction.

In many ways this attitude suited the man in the street. The demands of individualism were satisfied by a special destiny, one's 'own star'. Inexhaustible curiosity about one's fate was assuaged, in a fascinating way, by horoscopes and prophecies from the stars.

Those who had managed to climb aboard the last 'wave' in society 'thanked their lucky stars'; those who had inexorably gone under consoled themselves with the thought that the stars had been responsible. The lust for action did not diminish because of this; self-reproach merely became less common, for the men of that age respected lust for action, and did not think very highly of self-reproach.

But even in everyday life astrological destiny did not reign supreme. There, too, it was combined not only with ideas of religious predestination and freedom of will, but also with *fatum* in its interpretation as 'fate'.

The category of 'destiny' abstracts one real aspect of human life – inevitability and irrevocability – from the complex fabric of actual life, and places it 'above' men; it manifests itself in a person or in natural phenomena (God, the stars). To that degree even the stars are transcendent, since they stand outside the totality of human life. An immanent concept of destiny existed, indeed, only in epicureanism. Even today there is still validity in its precept that what is destined is only that which is biological, not social. But epicureanism provided the man in the street no explanation for the fact that there were still, in his life, events very much of social origin, inevitable and irrevocable, independent of human will, desire, and character, and quite transcendent by comparison with the latter; and that he was at the mercy of those events. The workers whom we meet in More's account, who were forced to steal in order not to starve, were in no position to hold discourse with epicurean philosophy; nor were those new burghers of More's who, driven by necessity, become grasping and evil. For them *fatum*, in the sense of destiny, existed. Until such time as a notion of social law developed – and that did not happen during the Renaissance – epicurean categories could not be generally accepted in this area. But there was something acceptable, something which competed with the concept of destiny. That – to repeat – was the interpretation of *fatum* as 'fate'.

For in what respect does 'fate' differ from 'destiny'? Precisely in the fact that the inevitable is only *one aspect* of it. Like 'destiny', it is applicable to peoples, groups, and individuals. *But it does not denote a predetermined path, but rather a range of possible courses.* It is no more synonymous with necessity than destiny is; like destiny it can also mean 'chance' or 'accident', or a series of accidents. *But it is social and objective in its point of departure as well as in its effect.* No deity ever impels or guides fate. It does not depend upon divine caprice, nor can it be changed through any form of 'persuasion' – prayer, oaths, or magic. For that reason it is more elastic than destiny, though at the same time harder too. It is more elastic because, leaving as it does some room for human action, it can be played with, shaped, compelled. Fate can be 'taken in hand', destiny never. But fate is also harder, because no powers are imagined behind it whose attitude can be changed. Fate is always immanent, and it remains so even if the individual feels it (and interprets it) as a force which tosses him this way and that; it remains so even when he personifies it and thinks of it in an allegorical way. *Fate* manifests itself in *other* men, in particular combinations of other men, in the movement of society, the cycle of the times, and the like. That is why fate is not 'written out in advance' and is not teleological. It is not present at the moment of birth – it evolves. It is possible for an individual's fate to take shape independently of him, or a people's fate independently of that people. But it is created through deeds, put together out of actions and decisions. This is the Greek *tuché*, which during the golden age of the Athenian polis was beginning to take the place of *moira* in everyday consciousness, and which has been present ever since alongside the concept of destiny, often overshadowed by it but still exercising its own influence.

During the Renaissance the opinions of ordinary men varied greatly as to how far the individual was responsible for his own fate, and how far it was independent of him; ideas on this subject were different at different times, and the opinions held in 'high places' differed from those held in low. Boccaccio, for example, wrote that 'all matters, which we foolishly call our own, are in her [Fortune's] hands, and therefore subject, at her inscrutable will, to every variety of chance and change without any order therein by us discernible'.[222] But however much fatalism there may be in Boccaccio's words, it is a fatalism which applies only to our goods, to the objects that belong to us, and not to our persons. At the same time Boccaccio assumes a certain lawful regularity (not purposefulness!) in the unfolding of fate, even though we may not recognize it. In doing so, he does not infringe upon the immanence of the concept of fate.

To make clear the attitude of the 'great individuals' of the age, I can do no better than to cite the words of Tamburlaine in Marlowe's drama:[223]

> I hold the Fates bound fast in iron chains,
> And with my hand turn Fortune's wheel about;
> And sooner shall the sun fall from his sphere
> Than Tamburlaine be slain or overcome.

Fate thus offers broad possibilities for autonomous action – in making use of one's range of movement, in seizing the 'moment', in recognizing the new, in searching out 'laws', in getting to know men and situations, and the like. As Machiavelli wrote:[224]

> It is not unknown to me how many have been and are of opinion that wordly events are so governed by fortune and by God, that men cannot by their prudence change them . . . and for this they may judge it to be useless to toil much about them, but let things be ruled by chance. . . . Nevertheless . . . I think it may be true that fortune is the ruler of half our actions, but that she allows the other half or thereabouts to be governed by us.

To that I need only add that Machiavelli conceives 'fate' as the common parent of both fortune and divine governance; thus empirically he distinguishes fate from destiny. Fate and fortune remain, however, undifferentiated even here. Nor is that a 'fault', for – as I have said – fuzziness and ambiguity are proper to these categories of everyday life. One thing more remains to be said: in the relationship of fate and autonomy the men of the Renaissance did not see any problem of 'acknowledging necessity'. Or rather, their thoughts did turn to it spontaneously, but only as one aspect of the whole. As we have seen, they had not even worked out a concept of social necessity; when they were thinking of something like it they spoke rather of the 'moment'. As for the stoic-epicurean thinkers, what characterized them was a view of knowledge and wisdom as freedom, as a liberation from the *morally* compelling force of external determination; for them, however, fate was taken, as I have said, rather in the sense of 'destiny'.

However much the notions of fortune and fate might be confounded with each other, a substantive distinction between the two began to be made even during antiquity. Aristotle speaks of 'goods of fortune'; for him, then, 'fortune' means the ensemble of those goods which are external to man's essence, to the moral character which shapes his fate, and to his personality, and which for the most part he receives 'ready-made' at the moment of his birth – such things as wealth, beauty, intelligence, social position, and the like. Of course these goods affect the unfolding of one's fate: only a man of a certain social position can be a great military leader, only a handsome youth can become a favoured and promising pupil of sages, and so on. Fortune is a raw material; it is up to the individual to make use of it. Of course this raw material does not necessarily remain stable. One man may lose his property, another be enslaved in war, a third be carried away by disease; good fortune may turn to bad. But whether it is the gods (i.e. destiny) who decide thus, or whether pure chance brings it about, man can do no better than bear it bravely, or lament it loudly – his fortune can never be his own doing.

During the Middle Ages fortune retained its character as a condition of life and a condition of action – and rightly so, for in communal society that, in fact, was what fortune was. The third son of the folk-tale, who 'makes' his own fortune, carving out for himself through his own abilities a place not indicated by his birth, is already the child of commodity production; 'each man is the master of his fate' is the watchword of youthful bourgeois society.

Fortune is not fate, only one aspect of it: success. Aristotle's 'goods of fortune' are the conditions of a successful fate – if a man loses them, he can no longer achieve success. The question of how far men shape their own fortunes, and how far those are determined by external goods, translates into the question of *which* properties, or objective conditions, are the ones we call 'fortunate', and hence are the surest pledges of success.

Both Ernst Cassirer and Max Dvořák devote considerable attention to the pictorial representation of fortune, and to the fact that with the passage of time its graphic portrayal changed. During the Middle Ages Fortune was depicted as a woman with a wheel, a wheel carrying away with it a helpless human figure. By contrast, Fortune during the early Renaissance was a woman controlling, with her hand, the sail of a ship; but the ship's tiller was in man's hand. In the case of the medieval Fortuna, the possession or lack of goods of fortune completely determines one's fate: Fortune is at once both fate and destiny. The Fortuna of the early Renaissance – the woman with the sail – offers only possibilities; the man at the helm then puts these possibilities (opportunities) to use. When Alberti writes that Fortune is silly and weak in the face of those who challenge it, that is only a poetic way of saying that a man need not accept as his destiny the possibilities defined for him by his birth alone. Not only could these opportunities be seized, they could also be created – and in that event man becomes master of his own fortune.

As is evident from the allegory of Fortune with the sail, Alberti took issue with the conception of fortune characteristic of communal societies. But he was no less eager to give a new meaning to the concept of fortune itself, and so, as I have said, not simply dethrone the prevailing medieval notion of fortune but also put a new kind of fortune in its place. If success really depends upon us, then can Fortune really be identified with birth, or other accident, or the play of chance?

369

Let us recall Bacon's saying that fortune is like a market where the price will often fall if one only waits a little. Elsewhere, he writes that 'if a man look sharply and attentively, he shall see Fortune'.[225] Here, then, it is not simply that a great deal depends on us and not just on fortune, nor even that a clever man can overcome weak Fortune, but rather that fortune itself is nothing but *the successful assertion of our personal capacities*. External circumstances dwindle to a mere *occasion* – and occasion is not the same thing as fortune. Only the occasion seized and realized is fortune; thus fortune is the individual personality itself. *There is no Fortune independent of men themselves*; there are only fortunate natures and unfortunate ones. That is the concept of fortune which reflects the entry upon the scene of the new bourgeois individual.

Such 'external properties' as birth and money are completely absent here – they have no part in 'fortune'. But virtue and courage do belong there – the ethical substance of man. And that is radically new, in comparison not only with the ancient and medieval concepts of fortune, but also with that of the early Renaissance, and it is related to the fortune of the popular fable. Now the only fortunate man is the one who succeeds through his own powers alone. That is the future luck of the Tom Joneses and Wilhelm Meisters, of those who set out, like the Biblical Saul, in search of their fathers' stock and found a kingdom instead – but not by divine decision, nor through destiny's decree, but by the strength of their own powers alone.

PART FOUR

Philosophical anthropology

PART FOUR

Philosophical anthropology

The Renaissance created philosophical anthropology, the science whose subject is man as a species being. Philosophers and poets had theorized ever since antiquity, of course, as to what was special about the humanity of human beings; Plato and Aristotle had formulated their concepts on the subject, while Sophocles celebrated man as the most wondrous of all creatures. But they were still not able to examine his most general species characteristics in terms of universal principles, because they were ignorant of the fact of anthropological equality. In Aristotle a free man is someone essentially different from a slave; the latter is in no sense a *zōon politikon*, and thus does not even come within the category of 'human being'. The male is the goal of nature's evolution; woman is only an imperfect male, and her human 'form' is thus by no means complete. The human essence was thus a pure end-concept, not the sum total of the potentialities of all men. In the Christian *Weltanschauung*, again, where everyone was equal in the sight of God, anthropological equality was inseparable from the idea of man's depravity and of his dependence upon the transcendent. It was during the Renaissance that a society first appeared – above all in Italy, and there chiefly at Florence – in which man's essential activity, work, appertained in principle and potentially to *every* citizen, where socially conscious activity could become the activity of *every* citizen. That is why labour and societality, and also freedom and consciousness (including knowledge), were necessarily perceived there as traits belonging, by the very essence of the human species, to every human being and to all mankind. Thus it was that mankind could awaken to a consciousness of its unitary species essence;

373

thus it was that philosophical anthropology was born, first and foremost, at Florence.

Philosophical anthropology was not, of course, a separate 'branch of science'. Its result, as we shall see, was nothing less than a dynamic concept of man – a concept formulated, however, always within the context of an overall *Weltanschauung*. The secularization of natural philosophy, a new examination of labour and technique, and an analysis of the process of knowledge were just as much a part of it, as was the examination of the problem-complexes surrounding human freedom and human substance. But the opposite is also true. The world-view of the Renaissance was sufficiently unitary and anthropomorphic so that no single philosophical problem can be understood without some examination of the anthropological questions which were posed at that time. Renaissance discussions of epistemology or philosophy of nature went, to be sure, beyond the consideration of those aspects of each subject having anthropological relevance; still, those aspects were always present. In setting out to discuss these problems, then, I must apologize in advance for doing so only from an anthropological standpoint.

CHAPTER 12

Nature and man

Until the seventeenth century, world-view, philosophy, and science were inseparable; and, as we have seen, a fourth element, religion, was often associated with the others. A scientific or philosophical credo – and I use the word 'credo' advisedly – invariably characterized the whole man. Even Gilbert uses ethical arguments in defence of the Copernican system. Only mean-spirited and fretful souls are 'afraid' of the Copernican explanation of the universe, he writes, for they feel they will lose their security in a universe where the earth moves. Bruno, too, calls Copernicus the liberator of mankind, for expanding man's self and his faculty for knowledge into the infinite. To be for or against Copernicus, then, was to be *pro* or *contra* on the question of human freedom, greatness, and dignity. Here, of course, we are already at the end of an epoch. The possibility that world-view, science, and philosophy might be divorced from one another, and indeed their actual separation, were already irreversible facts towards the end of Galileo's life. But it was not only *Weltanschauung*, philosophy, and science that were inseparable during the Renaissance; *philosophy of nature and natural science were not distinguished from the experience of nature either.* What is more, they were even *more* closely intermingled with that experience than during earlier epochs. Every new insight, every discovery set the whole man in motion, not only his faculty for knowledge but his world of feelings as well. Men's emotional relationship to nature was as *immediate* when they were speaking of the structure of substance as it was when they surveyed the wide landscape from a mountainside. There is a direct line leading from the allegorical character of Petrarch's ascent of Mont Ventoux to the

375

scientific spirit permeating the writings of Bruno. In Petrarch the beauty of the climb and the experience of conquest are allegories of *all* human life; the macrocosm of the philosophers of nature is reproduced in the microcosm. The joy and wonder which pertain to being-in-itself pertain to man as well. Dilthey was unjustified in interpreting this Renaissance unity of philosophy of nature and experience of nature in the spirit of *Lebensphilosophie*. For one of the greatest achievements of the scientific spirit of the Renaissance was precisely *the drawing of a sharp distinction between subject and object*. Immediate experience was increasingly evoked by the beauty and harmony of a nature interpreted as an object in itself. Humanity discovered the magnificence, the 'wonders' of its own world. The parallels between the wonders of human nature and those of the nature surrounding man did not indicate that men had subjectivized the world, but rather that man and humanity also had come to be regarded objectively; here, too, philosophical anthropology is inseparable from the universal exaltation of nature.

Georg Lukács, in analysing the history of the concept of being-in-itself,[1] reaches the conclusion that during antiquity an emotional relationship to being-in-itself was the exception, not the rule. All of Ionian natural philosophy, and even Aristotle himself, described and analysed the nature of things with cool objectivity. As that fact also demonstrates, a teleological conception of nature does not necessarily entail the immediacy of experience (it did not entail such a thing for Aristotle, nor for Hegel either). An 'emphatic relationship to being-in-itself' (Lukács's expression) characterizes Plato alone, for whom the ideas-in-themselves are the pure forms of the highest values (the Good, the True, the Beautiful) and for whom knowledge of being-in-itself is inseparable from experience of it. This emphatic relationship springs from the ideological character of Plato's work, and only finds enhancement in ancient Neoplatonism, most notably in Plotinus. In Christianity, both in antiquity and during the Middle Ages, enthusiasm for being-in-itself was transformed into experience of God: the world could be the object of adoration only as a creation of God. Here, then, experience was not *identical* with knowledge, as in Plato, but rather its *condition* and, what is more, very often its *surrogate*. Unquestionably, the end result of this process, historically, is modern science, which had emerged by the seventeenth century thanks to a relatively consistent application of the principle of de-anthropomorphization.

In between there intervened, however – in the perspective of world history only as an episode, to be sure – the age of the Renaissance.

First of all, being-in-itself was 'split', in the theory of double truth. Theology preserved the emphatic attitude, but at the same time that attitude became entirely foreign to those endeavouring to conduct a scientific exploration of reality. The world they analysed was no object either for our experience or for our love. The dry scientism of Duns Scotus is not just a stylistic peculiarity, just as the difference of style between Valla and Pomponazzi covers important substantive differences. Step by step, the Paduan school 'went over' from a Thomism interpreted in Aristotelian fashion, and from Averroism, to the preparation and reception of a modern, de-anthropomorphized science.

The mainstream of Renaissance philosophy of nature, nevertheless (notably Telesio, Bruno, and the young Bacon), was characterized by the opposite tendency. Within this mainstream it was, once again, emphasis which prevailed. This emphasis was, however, opposed in its basic tendencies to the sort of exaltation which had stretched from Plato to Aquinas. The object of emphasis was no longer transcendence, but rather the immanent world. *This philosophy of nature, permeated by immediate emotive experience, 'brings God back' into the world: hence it is pantheist.* And because it brings God back into the world, it reverses the relationship of emotive experience and knowledge, not only by comparison with the Christian tradition but also in contrast to the Platonic legacy. Emotive experience does not precede knowledge; it is not simultaneous with it, and in value it stands neither above it nor on a par with it. On the contrary, knowledge precedes emotive experience; what is more, knowledge is what *generates* this experience. The emphatic attitude is elicited by the experience that the world – this beautiful, complex, rich and inscrutable world – is something *in itself* and *for itself*, yet at the same time is *ours*.

In his poem, *De immenso*, the young Giordano Bruno describes how nature is everywhere beautiful. After becoming acquainted with Telesio's philosophy and setting out to explore nature's laws, he still retains the basic attitude of his youthful verses. Later, in his mature dialogues, the experience of nature's beauty often carries him away until, breaking the bounds of the dialogue form, he casts his experiential ideas in poetic form. Infinitude, motion, purposefulness, development, harmony fill him with enthusiasm. The world's infinitude expresses at the same time the boundlessness of man's capacity for knowledge and man's potential, nature's dynamism expresses man's dynamism, nature's purposefulness the purposefulness of human activity. This is how the Copernican discovery reverberates in his verse:[2]

Passing alone to those realms
The object erst of thine exalted thought,
I would rise to infinity: then I would compass the skill
Of industries and arts equal to the objects.

And again later:[3]

Henceforth I spread confident wings to space;
I fear no barrier of crystal or of glass;
I cleave the heavens and soar to the infinite.
And while I rise from my own globe to the others
And penetrate ever further through the eternal field,
That which others saw from afar, I leave far behind me.

He casts the movement of the universe into poetic form thus:[4]

Naught standeth still, but all things swirl and whirl
As far as in heaven and beneath is seen.
All things move, now up, now down,
Whether on a long or a short course,
Whether heavy or light;
Perchance thou too goest the same path
And to a like goal.
For all things move till overtaken,
As the wave swirleth through the water,
So that the same part
Moveth now from above downward
And now from below upward,
And the same hurly-burly
Imparteth to all the same successive fate.

It is not difficult to detect the anthropomorphism here. 'All things move, now up, now down' was the prime experience of the social life of the age, too. Infinity has a value-content, for it is 'exalted'. The theory of the crystalline heaven is not just false; it is a justification of human bondage. The emphatic attitude, however – and I repeat – still relates to being-in-itself. It anthropomorphizes it and so exalts it. But that does not alter the fact that it exalts it *as* being-in-itself.

Poetic formulation of a philosophy of nature is not a new phenomenon; nor is there anything new in the attempt to seek analogies in nature for the resolution of the conflicts of human existence. Both can be observed in Lucretius' *De rerum natura.* Yet Lucretius' attitude towards nature, like Epicurus' is not at all an emphatic one. Thus it is that his philosophical poetry is not really lyrical. It describes the facts of nature and the worthiest responses man can make, in his conduct, to those facts. But Bruno, and many of his contemporaries, must be separated from later posterity, i.e. from romanticism. In romanticism the attitude linking us to nature is lyrical once more, permeated by emotive experience. But in that passion fired by experience it is subjectivity that dominates. Thus the romantic experience of infinity, for example, reduces itself to the experience of the subject; its objective basis, the boundlessness of immanent nature, and wonder at the autonomous regularity of the cosmos, are subordinated to subjectivity, and later disappear altogether.

De-anthropomorphization, both in natural science and in the philosophy of nature, led necessarily to a situation where, among those striving for an objective picture of the world, spontaneous experience of nature and systematic investigation of nature went two different ways. De-anthropomorphization was, of course, a process that went forward only gradually, and which, indeed, is still in progress. As I have observed several times before (following Georg Lukács), Goethe was the great rearguard defender of the anthropomorphic view of nature, and so it is no accident that in him emotive experience, science, and philosophy are fused into an inseparable whole. The evocation of the experience of nature was increasingly displaced from science and philosophy and transferred to art; only now, moreover, did this become one of the special tasks of art. During the Renaissance we would seek in vain for a 'pure' art of landscape painting or a poetry 'purely' descriptive of landscape. The experience of landscape acquires an autonomy in artistic representation only after philosophy and science cease to have a part in it.

There is one more remark I should like to make here: it is superfluous, I think, to stress how much de-anthropomorphization and, in its wake, the dissolution of the unity of experience and science (philosophy of nature) meant in the history of modern science, and how much, all in all, this may be regarded as a necessary and positive process. But I must add that in the evolution of science from the seventeenth to the twentieth centuries the element of emotive experience, though in a suppressed form, was still preserved. Out of the immediate, spontaneous experience there developed a species of indirect experience. Now the scientist no longer considers the infinite sublime, or the crystalline sphere a prison; but whenever he conquers for mankind a small piece of being-in-itself, whenever in his researches he meets with something hitherto unknown, he still retains some sense of wonder, some experience of joy at the endless wealth of nature. Kant gave voice to this age-old attitude when he ranked his wonder at the starry heavens alongside his awe before the moral law. Whenever even this kind of enthusiasm and experience of nature vanish from natural science, and pure pragmatism comes to dominate the scientist's conduct, then we have to do with alienation. In his everyday life and everyday contacts a great natural scientist experiences and enjoys nature just as spontaneously as anyone else who leads a more or less conscious existence. Some connection must exist between his everyday experiences and his scientific attitude, for it is *one and the same* nature which appears, though from different aspects, in the Alps and in the laboratory – whether as being-in-itself, as untouched nature, or as humanized nature.

But to return to the Renaissance experience of nature: it must be stressed that the Copernican-Keplerian view of the universe, *in and of itself*, did not represent any great turning-point. The first disciples of a heliocentric universe saw the world as the embodiment of beauty and harmony, and imagined it by analogies with the human, just as much as did the proponents of a geocentric universe. Let me first take as an example a description of a geocentric experience of nature. Castiglione writes:[5]

Behold the state of this great Ingin of the worlde . . . the
heaven rounde besette with so many heavenly lights: and in
the middle, the earth environed with the Elements, and upheld
with the waight of it selfe. . . .

Again, the exaltation of the sun, the recognition and emphatic assertion of its central place, were widespread even before the appearance of the heliocentric world-view. Leonardo, for example, writes:[6]

I could wish that I had such power of language as should
avail me to censure those who would fain extol the worship of
men above that of the sun, for I do not perceive in the whole
universe a body greater and more powerful than this. . . .

The fusion of aesthetic, ethical, and strictly scientific statement is clearly visible in both quotations. But if we read Copernicus' own professions about his discovery, we will not come upon any essential difference in philosophical attitude:[7]

By no other arrangement have I been able to find so admirable
a symmetry of the universe, and so *harmonious* a connection of
orbits, as by placing the lamp of the world [lucernam mundi],

the sun, in the midst of the beautiful temple of nature as on a kingly throne, ruling the whole family of circling stars that revolve around him [circumagentem gubernans astrorum familiam].

Here the sun appears as an absolute monarch ruling peacefully over his subjects, and the demands of aesthetics – harmony, symmetry – are satisfied as well. Kepler again, in giving one of his works the title *Harmony of the World*, remained, in this regard, entirely within the tradition of Renaissance philosophy of nature. (The *Astronomia Nova*, however, is already the harbinger of a new era.)

In the last analysis, de-anthropocentrization and de-anthropomorphization are two sides of the same process, but they do not always appear simultaneously or in the same guise, or with the same value-content. We need only think of Montaigne, one of the most radical partisans of de-anthropocentrization, whose view of nature was, however, marked – partly for that very reason – by a far-reaching anthropomorphism.

Who has persuaded him [man] that that admirable motion of the celestial vault . . . [was] established and [has] lasted so many centuries for his convenience and his service? Is it possible to imagine anything so ridiculuous as that this miserable and puny creature . . . should call himself master and emperor of the universe, the least part of which it is not in his power to know, much less to command?

he writes of man.[8]

But precisely because he wished to combat the false semblance of man's central position in the universe, Montaigne assumed the existence of human characteristics in nature, above all in organic nature. His main argument against man's being the centre of the universe is that the specific characteristics which distinguish man are not exclusively human ones.

Do the swallows that we see on the return of spring ferreting in all the corners of our houses search without judgment, and choose without discrimination, out of a thousand places, the one which is most suitable for them to dwell in? And in that beautiful and admirable texture of their buildings, can birds use a square rather than a round figure, an obtuse rather than a right angle, without knowing their properties and their effects . . . ? Why does the spider thicken her web in one place and slacken it in another, use now this sort of knot, now that one, unless she has the power of reflection, and thought, and inference?[9]

In so far as it was pantheist, in so far as it denied creation, the act of a telos-setting God, even the most anthropocentric and anthropomorphic natural philosophy of the Renaissance was de-anthropomorphized and de-anthropologized by comparison with traditional Christian dogma and the traditional Christian world-view. Nature no longer 'serves' man. However teleological it may be, however much man and human society may be its 'end', that end is not a subjective but an objective one. A teleology of nature meant that nature necessarily *leads to man*, but not necessarily that it exists *for the sake of* man. Hence it was possible for the idea to arise again and again – though often in primitive form – that being-in-itself could be transformed into being-for-us. Mankind itself is no more 'completed' than nature is. By gaining knowledge of nature, and making use of her, man can make everything which hitherto contained him, as a goal, only objectively, into 'being-for-himself'. At bottom, even this idea was based on a new conception of the labour process, a matter I will return to later. I will also simply point out here that this idea of self-creation arose only with reference to nature, not social development. For the present it is enough to take note of the fact that, in every concrete respect, anthropomorphic traits and formulas were always based upon the conception of a nature external to man, immanent and self-creating, a nature to be conquered by man through an infinite process – a conception of nature, then, that was in essence de-anthropocentrized. When Paracelsus, for example, compared the relationship of nature and man to that of the fruit and the core of an apple, with man as the centre or core, he did not at all mean this distinctly anthropocentric comparison to imply that the whole fruit existed only for the sake of the core, only that since 'the fruit surrounds and supports it, it draws its nourishment from the fruit'.[10] As a physician, Paracelsus was speaking only of immediate consumption, but Leonardo, for example, knew that the 'fruit' also meant the instruments and objects of labour.

How difficult and complicated was the process of de-anthropomorphization and de-anthropocentrization is shown also by, among other things, the fact that one and the same thinker will often take radical steps in their direction, while in other places he will uncritically anthropomorphize or bear witness to an anthropocentric picture of the world. That is true even of Bacon, the crowning glory of Renaissance philosophy of nature. Here are two arguments from the same work, showing clearly how these two tendencies persist side by side. In the *Wisdom of the Ancients* Bacon writes that[11]

382

The sum total of matter remains always the same and the absolute quantum of nature suffers neither increase nor diminution. . . .

Now the agitations and motions of matter produced at first imperfect and ill-compacted structures of things, that would not hold together, – mere attempts at worlds. Afterwards in process of time a fabric was turned out which could keep its form.

Here Aristotle's great adversary simply repeats Aristotle's position.

In speaking of Bacon, however, I must mention a third precondition of the modern scientific spirit, one closely connected again with those already described. That is the *de-anthropologizing* of the process of scientific (or philosophical) knowledge. I have already described how the elimination of the 'idols of the tribe' was designed to divorce scientific knowledge from everyday thinking, since the latter is never separable from sensory experience and reflection and from comparative immediacy, and relates all knowledge to its potential use. Bacon discusses the various modes and relations of de-anthropologization. Knowledge is introduced as a relatively autonomous element between needs and praxis. Praxis itself is not simply *techné* or everyday practice either, but also experiment, serving to validate this autonomous element 'truth'. Man's sensory organs do not directly 'receive' reality; rather, 'instruments' are introduced between the sense organs and reality, which correct the 'distortions' of the sense organs or 'extend' their range, making them capable of more extensive and intensive knowledge than they naturally would be. It is already a commonplace that Bacon was incapable of realizing his own methodological claims – his theory and practice of induction are far from being de-anthropomorphized. But that does not detract in the slightest from the importance of his philosophical formulation of the postulate of de-anthropologization.

De-anthropologization was the epistemological and methodological side of that process whose ontological basis was provided by de-anthropocentrization and de-anthropomorphization. During the Renaissance these processes appeared in such close combination that de-anthropologizing often had a concrete basis in, and consequences for, ontology and *Weltanschauung*, just as de-anthropomorphization and de-anthropocentrization had epistemological and methodological consequences. Thus, for example, the heliocentric picture of the universe demanded a de-anthropologized conception of knowledge, for it was possible to accept that view of the world only if one could abstract from the apparent rotation of the sun around the earth and could elevate oneself above the level of immediate perception. Even those who, like Bruno, did not draw the epistemological and methodological consequences still thought, spontaneously, in this spirit. In such cases a situation arose temporarily where a picture or explanation of the world made necessary a de-anthropologizing of epistemology even without doing away with anthropomorphic ontology (as in Copernicus' analogy of the sun). At the same time, de-anthropologization could not be complete either so long as an 'emphatic relationship to being-in-itself' survived, so long as emotive experience and knowledge were not divorced from each other.

Despite contrary tendencies, Renaissance natural philosophy was – to repeat – essentially anthropomorphic, if we compare it with modern natural science or the thought of the seventeenth century, rather than with the theological view of the world. *The process of de-anthropomorphization was carried through using ideas created by the Renaissance itself, but at the same time it marked the end and abandonment of the prime aspirations of Renaissance philosophy*. At first there still remained the demand for harmony and an aesthetic image of the world, and the tendency to allegorize, as we have seen in the case of Copernicus and Kepler. According to Kepler, for example, the laws of the stars are analogues of the laws of music. But reality and nature *no longer have an organic structure*, as in classical Renaissance philosophy; rather, *they are mechanically structured*. In Kepler's view the universe was to be regarded not as a divine, living being, but as a divine watch-works. Its harmony, thus, was not organic but mechanical. The principle that moved the universe which for most Renaissance thinkers was none other than spirit, the world-soul, and for the later Telesio was 'force', the dynamic union of the energies of soul and body – that principle became mechanical in Kepler. It is true that he retained the term 'force', but precisely because he interpreted it within the framework of an inorganic, mechanical structure, the concept of 'force' was itself de-anthropomorphized, and changed its meaning.

A nature deprived of its 'soul', its 'God', and its 'force' could not contain objective values, or a hierarchy of values. Through this step the aesthetic (and often ethically coloured) interpretation of nature also lost its basis. Copernicus had still insisted that circular motion was the 'most perfect'. But Kepler already denied that, and Galileo expressly formulated the principle that neither in nature nor i ι geometrical figures is it possible to distinguish senior and junior, perfect and imperfect, noble and ignoble. Gilbert's theory of the magnet, as Dilthey has shown, put an end to the distinction between 'above' and 'below', or at least relativized it. That too was an

384

important step in the process by which the scientific, and philosophical, view of the world again parted, once and for all, from aesthetic contemplation.

With de-anthropomorphization and de-anthropologization was born natural science proper, and the mechanical picture of the universe which reflected its first period of development. It was the science, and world-view, which were at once the condition and result of the technical exigencies and developments that came into being in the course of production carried on for production's sake, and which served the bourgeois society that was born with it. This was the path taken by 'natural science' and 'science' generally, a path which in the end re-creates, or at least may re-create, the concept of a unified science: a union of all sciences founded on the unity of reality. But it was a concept which in its concrete content was remote from the Renaissance conceptions, at least so far as the mainstream is concerned.

The Renaissance concept of the unity of nature may be summarized briefly as follows: the same essential forces exercise their influence, in various forms and in varying degrees, throughout all of reality, from inorganic to living beings, from organic nature to man and human society. To the extent that one sphere ever evolves from another, such an evolution can take place only because entities similar or identical in their ultimate structures are involved.

The precondition of this unified world-view was the treatment of reality as immanent. This was almost never a declared, openly emphasized principle. Those who maintained the idea of a God independent of nature treated nature itself 'separately', as something unitary, complete and explainable in and of itself, something apart from divine being. According to Agrippa von Nettesheim, man is an indirectly created being: God created him but through the intermediary of the world, and thus any direct connection between God and man is excluded from the picture of the world. Pomponazzi, again, writes that 'no effect is produced upon us by God immediately but only through the means of his ministers'.[12] Those 'ministers', of course, are none other than natural forces and events. But of course it is only pantheism that is fully capable of consistently maintaining a theory of immanence. Here Bruno was the most consistent of all, more consistent even than Bacon. The principle of *natura est deus in rebus* – the thesis of Nicholas of Cusa despiritualized – expressed the most advanced synthesis of these efforts. (All this is not, of course, to say that in his handling of particular philosophical problems Bruno was equal to Bacon or Nicholas of Cusa.)

It was the *organic* outlook which was called upon to bring about the unity of a nature complete in itself and evolving from itself – a nature at once creating and created. Thus the great idea of the unity of nature was born in problematic form, in the concept of the identity of general laws. If 'spirit' and purpose exist in the world of man, that is possible only because the very universe is purposeful and has a 'spiritual' character. Otherwise the 'unity' would be lost. Thus was born the *theory of the parallelism of microcosm and macrocosm*, according to which man, the microcosm, contains 'in miniature' everything that the macrocosm contains, obeys the same laws and displays the same structure as the macrocosm, infinite nature.

From Nicholas of Cusa onward, the parallelism of microcosm and macrocosm became a commonplace of Renaissance philosophy. Let us consider one example, formulated at the highest level of the age. Paracelsus writes:[13]

> Thus man is like the image of the four elements in a mirror;
> if the four elements crumble, man too will perish. If what is in
> front of the mirror is at rest, then the image in the mirror
> will also be at rest. And so philosophy is nothing but
> knowledge and understanding of what is reflected in the
> mirror. And just as the image in the mirror will not enlighten
> anyone about his own essence, nor will anyone learn to know
> himself from it, since it is a dead image, so too is it with man
> by himself: From himself alone he can learn nothing. For
> knowledge can only spring from that external essence of
> which he himself is but the mirror-image.

Here we can grasp immediately one of the most inspired features of contemporary philosophical anthropology, the fact that it never tries to understand man in isolation, purely in and of himself, but as a being set in nature and part of it. But the quotation is illuminating also from the standpoint of the exaggerated parallelism of microcosm and macrocosm; man can *only* be regarded as a mirror, the mirror of nature, and he is understandable only in terms of *external* nature. We can gain adequate knowledge of man only through knowledge of external nature (in this case, by discovering the nature of the four elements). True, Paracelsus here is speaking expressly of the human organism, hence of man's biological state, leaving open the question of man as a social being. But I need hardly demonstrate at length how far this parallel disregards the *differentia specifica* of man and human nature. All the same, this conception must not be interpreted in the light of such later notions as, for example, the *homme machine* of La Mettrie. For in Paracelsus – as generally during the Renaissance – the human organism did not become mechanized; on the contrary, nature was regarded as organic and spiritual. Unity was created, then, through anthropomorphization.

Even more characteristic – and more brilliant – is the ontology of Carolus Bovillus, for whose discovery and interpretation we are indebted to Ernst Cassirer (in his *Individual and Cosmos in Renaissance Philosophy*). Bovillus, too, devised a unitary ontology, but applied the theory of the parallelism of macrocosm and microcosm in such a way as to preserve at the same time the *differentia specifica* of the human essence. For him, man emerges from nature – 'mother nature', as Bovillus calls it; or rather, man is himself 'mother nature' but at the same time rises above it, becoming its antithesis. *If for Paracelsus man was a 'microcosm' in the totality of his existence, for Bovillus he becomes a microcosm through knowledge.*

According to Bovillus, there are four grades of reality. They are characterized as *esse*, *vivere*, *sentire* and *intelligere*. A teleological sequence leads from inorganic existence through living and sentient beings to intelligence, which is incarnated in man. Man is the 'concept' of nature, the form of the substance, the goal of the universe. But man's existence is merely goal and concept in the universe. For man, when he comes into existence, must again traverse the four stages of nature. Thus the development of substance from mere existence through life and sensation to intelligence is repeated 'in miniature' – here is the microcosm – in the world of man. Here, however, man's free will 'intervenes'. Not every man necessarily passes through these four stages. One may stop on the first, second, or third, or slip back to an earlier 'stage'. A man arrives at 'intelligence' if he attains consciousness of his own human existence, and if he awakens to self-consciousness as a result of his own labours applied to himself. Then he is no longer man, but 'human man' (*homohomo*). *Homo potentia* becomes *homo in actu*, *homo ex principio* becomes *home ex fine*, and *homo ab natura*, *homo ab intellectu*.

Awakening to self-consciousness, becoming human a second time, is the precondition of knowledge of the world (i.e. of substance). To the degree that a man wakens to an awareness of his humanity and his human dignity (a category drawn from Pico's spiritual legacy), he becomes capable of reproducing the universe in thought. Thus man may become a microcosm, but this microcosm is not a replica of the macrocosm on a reduced scale, not a unity of matter and spirit *in the same way* as the macrocosm, as the traditional parallelism theory had interpreted it. *For according to Bovillus the microcosm is the reproduction in thought of the macrocosm*. The structure of the two systems is the same, but while the macrocosm is substantial, the microcosm is the intellectual mirror of that substantiality. 'The world has a maximum of substance, and a minimum of knowledge. Man has the minimum of substance, but a maximum of knowledge.'[14]

The expression of 'mirror' should not be taken, however, in the sense of a mere reflection. The mirror is not only subjective but objective as well, in the same sense that for Paracelsus man was the mirror of the world. Man's awakening to self-consciousness is a condition of the reproduction of the macrocosm because in *gaining self-knowledge man (the microcosm) finds in himself the same forms as in the macrocosm; more precisely, the same forms in a spiritual and intellectual projection.* That in turn makes possible a kind of epistemological reflection, for in the laws of the macrocosm man discovers and reveals the world outside himself, which 'agrees' with his own world because the latter is a derivative, a spiritual reproduction of the former.

The priority of the macrocosm is a notion common to Paracelsus' and Bovillus' microcosm-macrocosm theories, then, as is the structural parallelism of macrocosm and microcosm. Their difference lies in the fact that while Paracelsus postulates a parallelism not only of structure but also of substance, Bovillus' theory rests on a parallelism of structure but asserts a dissimilarity of substances – even though the higher order of essence does contain within itself the lower. That is why Paracelsus needs an anthropomorphic view of nature, while Bovillus does not. Bovillus de-anthropomorphizes. But – and here we can see again the contradictory evolution of Renaissance science – epistemologically the situation is the reverse. Paracelsus – precisely as a consequence of his principle of an anthropomorphic unity of nature – asserts that in gaining knowledge of the world man learns to know himself, and that otherwise he cannot learn to know himself; that is to say, he de-anthropocentrizes. Bovillus, since in his thought the unity of reality is based upon a marked emphasis on man's *differentia specifica*, holds by contrast that in order to unveil the universe or macrocosm it is enough for man to waken to self-consciousness, to learn to know himself, to discover his human structure: his view of the world, then, is anthropocentric.

Thus even Bovillus did not get over that stumbling-block in the way of Renaissance philosophy's efforts to unify reality, the notion of the parallelism of microcosm and macrocosm – something which does not at all detract from his extraordinary merit in conceiving it as a structural parallelism and in demonstrating theoretically, within a consistently thought-out system, both the natural origin of man and also his transcending of nature. We in no way enhance Bovillus' greatness, however, by treating him in isolation from Renaissance thought, and so modernizing him. Yet that is what Cassirer does when he sees in Bovillus' world-view a direct forerunner of the Hegelian system, and even describes Bovillus' views using Hegelian terms. He writes, for example, that in Bovillus – as in Hegel – substance becomes a subject. Yet Bovillus' concept of substance does not resemble Hegel's any more than do other teleological and pantheist Renaissance conceptions of nature in general, does not resemble Hegel's even in the fact that for Bovillus the most abstract and most general category is existence (*esse*), a category which for him exhausts the essence of *every* non-living entity. More interesting is his notion of how the subject reproduces the substance – only for Bovillus the subject is always the *individual* man. True, individual man is for him identical with man in general, since he always realizes the potentials of all humanity (that was self-evident during the Renaissance). Yet in Bovillus' system the problem of how this humanity as a whole arrived at the various forms of knowledge is a non-existent one, just as it is for his contemporaries generally. Every individual's knowledge has its history, but there is no history of mankind's knowledge. We need only think of the passage where Bovillus speaks of 'free will' in connection with the fact that a man may remain on the level of mere existence or may proceed to the plane of living, sensation, and intellect. The human individual here is really presented with alternatives – and so Bovillus is right – but since the whole problem is never raised in regard of all mankind, the question of mankind's alternatives is not even an issue in Bovillus' eyes. If we wanted to modernize considerably we could say that Bovillus arrived at the Hegelian category of 'subjective spirit' but could never formulate the categories of objective and absolute spirit, and so could not form a concept of actual history nor of a process of knowledge that is realized in historical objectifications. For Bovillus the man who knows himself (the microcosm), and who therefore is capable of reproducing the macrocosm, is the wise man, the sage. There are wise men and men who are not wise, there always have been and there always will be. How is it possible to identify that with a line of reasoning in which *philosophy* (not the sage as a subject) – and indeed a philosophy created by a concrete era – is the form in which 'spirit truly awakens to self-consciousness'?

I have disputed Cassirer's thesis in such detail because, if he were right, then Bovillus would be the first representative of a historical

anthropology. But this is surely not true and could not be true of
Bovillus. Yet Cassirer's association was not at all accidental. For
Hegel, in his striving after a unitary vision of reality, really was a
modern, historicizing successor of the Renaissance, even if he did
not know the thinkers we have been discussing, or knew them only
through an intermediary, Jacob Böhme.

It is also quite unwarranted to single out Bovillus in this way from
the ranks of Renaissance thinkers because many others tried (though
not within the context of a unitary ontological system) to interpret
the microcosm-macrocosm parallel in a non-schematic way, and
within that unity to place emphasis on the special complexity of man
(and of all organic nature). Bacon, for example, wrote:[15]

> For though the Alchemists, when they maintain that there is
> to be found in man every mineral, every vegetable, etc., or
> something corresponding to them, take the word *microcosm*
> in a sense too gross and literal, and have so spoiled the
> elegance and distorted the meaning of it, yet that the body of
> man is of all existing things both the most mixed and the
> most organic, remains not the less a sober and solid truth.
> And this is indeed the reason it is capable of such wonderful
> powers and faculties, for the powers of simple bodies, though
> they be certain and rapid, yet being less refracted, broken up,
> and counteracted by mixture, they are few; but abundance
> and excellence of power resides in mixture and composition.

It would be petty to balk at the fact that Bacon was wrong in
denying the possible existence of minerals and organisms in the
human system. For the tendency which he polemicized against was
indeed a primitive one: it interpreted the parallelism of microcosm
and macrocosm as if *everything* that existed in nature generally
could be found in man the microcosm and, moreover, in *just the
same form*. Bacon sought to combat the idea of extensive totality
with his own notion of *intensive totality*. He did not see man's pre-
eminence in the fact that man contains within himself all simpler
forms 'in miniature', hence not in any quantitative index, but rather
in the fact that man's structure is distinguished from more primitive
ones by reason of its *complexity*. The criterion of complexity, again,
is none other than the many-sidedness of functions, of forms of
activity. Bacon did not at all deny the notion – already familiar from
Aristotle – that the higher products of nature contain within themselves the lower ones, at least to some degree: 'Man has something
of the brute; the brute has something of the vegetable; the vegetable
something of the inanimate body. . . .'[16] Without this no unitary

conception of nature could have come into being. But in Bacon this unity is hierarchical and differentiated – though still, again, within the framework of an anthropomorphic outlook.

No less brilliant – though from a different standpoint – was Leonardo's position. We do not find in him a unitary ontological system either, but illuminating axioms are all the more numerous. He did not seek man's unity with nature as a thinking being or as a biological entity, as Bovillus and Paracelsus did; rather, he deemed man, as a *living being performing work*, to be a part of nature, even in his separation from it. On the one hand Leonardo saw that work was a specifically human trait, not characteristic of any other living being; on the other hand, he always emphasized that in work *nature acts upon nature*, self-creating 'second nature' transforms the 'first nature' from which it was born.

> She [nature] does not change the ordinary kinds of things which she creates in the same way that from time to time the things which have been created by man are changed; indeed, man is nature's chiefest instrument, [for] man from these elementary things produces an infinite number of compounds. . . .[17]

And again:

> Gravity and force together with material movement and percussion are the four accidental powers by which the human race in its marvellous and varied works seems to reveal itself as a second nature in this world. . . .[18]

Man, then, acts upon nature through these forces which are the most elemental and universal properties of physical nature, putting them to use through his work. Through his physical activities and their effects he makes himself a 'second' nature, distinct in principle from every other natural being. We should not overlook, however, that even Leonardo, who thoroughly grasped the fundamentally human character of work, still operated with anthropomorphizing comparisons – in calling man an 'instrument' of nature, for example. We might say that this was only an analogy. But in Renaissance philosophy analogies are far from accidental; they are the methodological and stylistic form in which anthropomorphic thinking appears.

Inherency and *analogy* in fact permeate all of Renaissance philosophical thought, playing a much greater part in it than the categories of causality or natural law. When Telesio asserts that all knowledge can be traced back to analogical inferences, he is expressing an idea which has much more than just logical or epistemological roots.

If reality is anthropomorphic and unitary, and its different spheres and entities are parallel, then analogy is the expression of an objective, ontological fact. We need only recall Copernicus' metaphor, cited above, in which he likens the sun to a prince enthroned. Behind this comparison there also lies the fact that Copernicus took harmony, beauty, and perfection (which, of all forms or motion, was represented best by cyclical motion) to be the common essence of all reality. Telesio in one place explains acceleration on a human analogy: just as one wishes to get through an unpleasant necessity quickly, so, too, falling bodies strive to hurry their descent towards the earth, which they feel as an unpleasant compulsion. This again is no mere 'metaphor'; it involves the ideas of the world spirit and of the 'soul of things', of the aestheticization and ethical colouring of nature. The parallelism of microcosm and macrocosm, again, was clearly based on the category of inherency; the notion of causality appeared only peripherally. Natural law was often synonymous with the categories of 'propriety' and 'regularity' and thus appeared in a thoroughly anthropomorphized and aestheticized form. All this does not mean, of course, that the concept of natural law is never present in its 'pure' form. Leonardo, for example, plainly expresses the notion of natural law when he writes:[19]

Experience the interpreter between resourceful nature and the human species teaches that that which this nature works out among mortals constrained by necessity cannot operate in any other way than that in which reason which is its rudder teaches it to work.

Yet an anthropomorphic comparison is not absent here either.

The prevalence of inherency and analogy only underscores what I have been saying about the unity of natural philosophy (science) and experience of nature. With the separation of emotive experience and science, the divorce of natural science from immediate everyday thinking, these categories were bound to lose their leading role and to be replaced, necessarily, by those of causality and natural law. At the same time, there can be no doubt that the seventeenth-century cult of exact science led to a certain impoverishment of categories. It was this process of impoverishment that Marx was referring to when he wrote that in mechanical materialism the concept of matter had lost the sensuous glow of the Renaissance category of substance.

The dynamic concept of man and the dynamic conception of nature were thus inseparable during the Renaissance: the experience that 'everything moves' in nature (only recall Bruno's poem) also

392

expressed the primary social experience of the heady pace of change. Abstract law and abstract substance had not yet emerged from the sensuous multifariousness of nature, just as the sensuous diversity of concrete forms of labour still veiled the notion of abstract labour, and just as the unevenness of development had not yet revealed the common tendencies at work in the various processes of social evolution. Speculation – sometimes incredibly abstruse speculation – blossomed out of a comprehension of the concrete, moving, sensuous world. It was a speculation of the imagination rather than of the concept; particularity prevailed even in the most general formulations. Synthesis, too, rested upon these concrete sensuous images – not on analysis. Truth was one; it could be compelled and could be grasped, in all its mystery and complexity; it bore a human face.

393

CHAPTER 13

Work, science, *techné*, art

In the course of history the essence of work has been approached, and described, from many sides; at different times different aspects of it have predominated in philosophy and everyday thinking. Naturally these approaches were related to one another, for they were all approaches to one and the same phenomenon; yet people were not always aware of the interrelationships, or of their significance. Taken in historical – not substantive – order, these approaches were as follows:

(1) description and analysis of the *structure* of work, of the *process* of some work-cycle;
(2) the *ethical* interpretation of work;
(3) discovery of the *social function* of work;
(4) analysis of work as a basic category of human *anthropology*;
(5) labour's contradictory effect on man, both *developing* and *stunting* him, and the disclosure of this conflict;
(6) the introduction of the *economic* concept of labour;
(7) the discovery of work as the motive force in the process by which *man becomes human*; and finally,
(8) *the synthetic, historical concept of work*, which embraces all these aspects at once.

When I assert that antiquity went furthest in the analysis of the structure of the work process, I must apply certain qualifications. This statement refers exclusively to *handicraft* labour. The analysis of slave labour was excluded from the very outset: 'free' and slave labour were interpreted not as two different modes of one and the same quality, but as two quite different qualities. In ancient Greek, two different words were even used to describe them, *banausis* and *techné*. Similarly, the possibility of raising the question of co-operation was also excluded. The work process appeared as an operation planned and executed by one man. Thus the analysis was directed towards the propensity of work to further the development of the human individual; work was regarded as the realization of some set goal, as the *shaping of matter*, an activity that conferred form. It is enough here to refer to Aristotle's master builder.[20]

It is surprising, perhaps, that on this point neither the Middle Ages nor the Renaissance went beyond the conclusions of antiquity. For my part I have not seen a single passage which goes beyond Aristotle on this subject. The new problems that the age raised concerning work pertained not to the structure of the individual artisan's abstract labour process, but to the *technical* aspects of that structure. Form-giving activity and purposefulness as such appeared 'natural' by now – more natural than during antiquity, for they were more *universal*, at least in the classic birthplaces of the Renaissance. The structures typical of the 'natural community', i.e. of the recent past (labour within the guild framework, for instance) no longer interested the men of the Renaissance; what was of interest to them were the things which had disrupted the 'natural community'. The labour of the cultivator also ceased to hold any interest. What engaged their minds was work *amid changing technical conditions* – work as a *dynamic* process which never repeats itself, never does anything twice *in exactly the same way*. Most writings on art (for some time yet art was not separated completely from handicrafts) dealt likewise with technical problems. Of course technique here – as we shall see – was in the service of efforts to mirror reality more perfectly. The time was past when it had been possible to abstract from the technique of labour, for that was possible only in past-oriented societies; and the day had not yet arrived when the technique of labour was only a practical concern for the individual worker, not a theoretical one: that came about only when modern factory industry took the place of early, small-scale manufacture. The fact of the technical modification of labour was, then, a universally valid fact, one that affected every human being and affected not only his existence but his thinking as well. That is why it obscured the more universal aspects of the work process and made relatively unimportant the analysis of what contemporary labour had in common with 'old' labour. *It was not the giving of form, but the changing 'how' of doing so that constituted the central problem of the age.*

Thus what became typical was not description of the work-process in general, but descriptive accounts of *concrete tasks* and *concrete techniques*, with arguments in their favour. But these accounts rested on the same theoretical foundations just described: they demanded of those who immersed themselves in the study of these concrete procedures not mere repetition, but rather that they should surpass those who had gone before them. As Dürer wrote: 'I know however that he who accepts it [viz., Dürer's techniques] will not only get a good start but will reach better understanding by daily practice; *he will seek farther and find much more than I now indicate.*'[21] No small part was played in all this by the socially significant polemic against 'stagnant' labour, the kind of labour performed within the guilds. Peter Apian, the mathematician and technician of Ingolstadt, wrote in 1532 that those 'who reject the best things because they are new, err, for without new inventions life would return to the state of the ancients who lived lawless and uncivilized like beasts'.[22] How could one have asked them to pay attention to the analyses of work by thinkers who lived in an 'uncivilized age', and to follow in their footsteps?

The thinkers and ordinary men of the Renaissance did not for a moment doubt that the wealth of society is the product of labour, not capital, that all goods were 'the gift of mind and hands' (Bruno), not of money. That age was the era of the *birth* of wealth. Thus wealth was regarded not as a starting-point but as a result. There were, of course, only a comparative few who interpreted the correlation of wealth and poverty in such a way as to suggest that the source of the fortunes of the rich was the labour of the poor, rather than just 'human discoveries generally'. (Among those few were the utopians, above all Campanella.) For the most part, however, men attributed it to *wit*, to *cunning*, to *human cleverness*, and it never entered their minds that wealth or money might become a value in itself, and the creator of values independent of man. This not yet fetishized thinking found expression also in the fact that when they spoke of the products, greatness, and dignity of human work (1) they never distinguished mental labour from physical, the 'mind' from the 'hands'; (2) they did not separate living and dead labour, the work-process and the tools and objects produced in the course of earlier work-processes; (3) they did not distinguish reified and non-reified forms of objectification. Vives, for example, writes in his allegorical *Fable about Man* that human inventions include 'towns and houses, the use of herbs, stones, and metals',[23] music, writing, foresight. Giannozzo Manetti, in his *De manectis*, writes that 'the things we have are, nevertheless (*macchinamenta*), human, for man created them . . . as houses and cities, pictures and statues, arts, sciences, inventions, languages. . . . The more we consider, the more wondrous must we find all these things'.[24]

Of course, the creations of the 'political' and the 'technical' man were often expressed in an undifferentiated conjunction in ancient thought, too. We need only recall the legend of Prometheus, or the chorus from *Antigone* mentioned several times before. It was not the fact that this concomitance was *undifferentiated* that was new in the Renaissance – for that is just the element that appears as 'old' by comparison with later capitalist thinking – but the fact that it was *necessary*. For during antiquity this concomitance had been random and transitory. In the Prometheus myth itself men acquire the use of fire (the mechanical arts) *separately*, and only later (and again separately) the capacity for state building, for social life. For the thinkers of the Renaissance, however, one was not imaginable without the other. We need only recall those passages in which Pomponazzi analyses man's faculties. All three faculties or 'intellects' – the speculative, ethical, and technical – are found in greater or lesser degree in *every* human being. Indeed, Pomponazzi emphasizes that in this synthesis it is the 'operative' or technical intellect which predominates in most men. Of course Aristotle, too, places *techné* among the faculties of the soul, regarding it as a universal human capacity; but for him it was so only *in posse*, not *in esse*. For Pomponazzi, however, every human being actually realizes this capacity; it belongs, to a degree, to his human completeness, just as abstract thought and ethical conduct do. And here Pomponazzi was only formulating the general conviction of Renaissance anthropology. For work activity was, in the eyes of Renaissance anthropology, an essential attribute of man, a species characteristic. And since it belonged to the species, it must belong to every human being, even though in varying degree.

After this, it hardly seems necessary to lay special stress on the fact that this kind of anthropological interpretation of work activity presupposes a recognition, both socio-philosophical and practical, of equality. And indeed both of these were among the basic principles from which the Renaissance utopias set out. Societies in which everyone – among other activities – worked, in which work activity was therefore a necessary aspect of human versatility for every individual, could not have been advanced as an ideal if work had not been regarded as the anthropological essence of man.

This kind of anthropological generalization was a new element in Renaissance thought, by comparison with the conceptions of antiquity. But within it, the underlying attitude of antiquity

397

persisted: work was interpreted only as an exchange of matter between nature and man, an activity that developed his capacities, a function giving rise to a 'second nature'. Any kind of labour that did not measure up to this ideal met with criticism and rejection. Theory and practice were inseparable in that ideal. In Campanella's City of the Sun labour is to be organized according to the book of sciences – knowledge of the canon of science is the prerequisite for correct practice.

However much the anthropological interpretation of work and the affirmation of work activity were common features of Renaissance thought, there were of course differing opinions heard of man's relationship to labour, of the meaning of technology, and the like, from those who occupied different positions in the social structure. But the problem of alienation does not arise, even in symbolic or incipient form, no matter where we look. We may note in passing that the great utopias of the day do not deal with the alienation of work or with industrial activity at all. The lot of the *peasantry*, the impoverishment and ruin of the peasant cultivator, the one-sidedness of peasant labour in contrast to the growth of luxury and wealth – these were the things that provided a social and moral basis for the utopian writers.

From a technical standpoint, as we have seen, the analysis of work during the Renaissance was remarkably *concrete*. At the same time it was, *in its social aspects*, highly *abstract*. The recognition in an anthropological sense of the general function of work in shaping and maintaining society still did not at all involve a concrete analysis of the labour, work structures, motives for working, and ethic of work of the various categories of labouring strata. Now and then, to be sure, it is possible to find an occasional observation along those lines. Machiavelli, for example, writes that 'men work either from necessity or from choice, and ... it has been observed that virtue has more sway where labour is the result of necessity rather than of choice'.[25] There was at least the glimmering of an awareness here of the connection existing between the society of his time and labour performed from necessity, and an intimation of the fact that labour springing from a need for activity, from inner compulsion and from a sense of satisfaction and self-realization was not necessarily the most efficient economically, nor by any means the basis of the real economy of society as given. Such observations are the exception, nevertheless, and even as such they do not represent a well thought out theory.

But let me return to my starting-point, the approach, from a number of different aspects, to the concept of work. I have already discussed descriptions of the structure of work and analyses of its social function – primitive ones to be sure, but still serving as points of departure for further analyses. So far as the ethical evaluation of labour is concerned, that was something which made itself felt during the Renaissance only *indirectly*, within the context of the anthropological interpretation of work. Immediate ethical evaluation of labour is subject most of all to the changing exigencies of class. During antiquity such evaluations appeared only occasionally, as in Hesiod's *Works and Days* or in some of Aristophanes' comedies – i.e. exclusively among those who glorified peasant labour. Only there was it declared (and only there could it be declared) that working was 'moral' and 'honourable', and conferred upon the one who worked a human superiority over those who did not work. In the Christian world-view of the Middle Ages the ethical interpretation of labour was adapted to the hierarchical order of society. Thus labour continued to be 'evaluated' as the performance of a duty, but only for a given social stratum, the peasantry. *Ora et labora* was not a universal obligation. That sort of hierarchical ethic was alien to the thought of the Renaissance, which operated to dissolve hierarchies. Ethics, as we have seen, rested upon a universal anthropological foundation, or else became stratified in accordance with concrete social activities and functions (political life, private life, and so on), not according to a social hierarchy. At the same time, an immediate ethical evaluation of labour would not have expressed the social status quo. Among the artisanate and in small-scale manufacture employing skilled workmen, what was pertinent for ethics was not the fact *that* one worked, but rather *how* one worked. The joy of enterprise – commercial, industrial, and financial – so filled the new bourgeoisie that the ethical element was *spontaneously* absorbed in the new anthropology, just as it was in scholarly or artistic activity. For those peasants evicted from their holdings, however, the labour performed in the great workshops – mainly in England, but to some extent in the Italian cities too – so obviously sprang from the compulsion of necessity that the thought of evaluating it ethically occurred neither to them nor to the 'ideologues' of the day. Even the notion, 'You must work', which was a natural one for the peasantry, was not so natural for the early industrial proletariat. From Marx's investigations we know that even a century later the English workers still did not complete a full work-week: they were minded to work only enough to make a bare living. Yet even at that time, with the rise of Protestantism, the bourgeoisie's own special – ethical – interpretation of labour had appeared, in which work as such became an ethical value.

399

Thus the immediate work-ethic was subordinated to an anthropological approach in which *work was not of value as the performance of a duty but rather for its unique role in developing human capacities*, and so the man who worked was superior to the one who did not work not because the latter was 'idle', but rather because the former's praxis enriched him more than others were enriched by mere pleasure – and so it was a good deal closer to the Marxian conception worked out centuries later than to the bourgeois ethic of work. That does not mean, of course, that labour as a fulfilment of duty played no part during the Renaissance – for in that event the idea would not have found expression in both More and Campanella – only that this interpretation was not of central importance.

The chief merit of the Renaissance was, then – to repeat – the interpretation of work as belonging to the anthropological essence of man. To this I ought to add that the recognition of work as an essential property of mankind was not necessarily coupled with the discovery of work as the motive force in the process of the hominization of man. Not infrequently it was seen – as the quotation from Leonardo cited in the preceding chapter indicates – as creating and developing a 'second nature', by which was understood both human 'nature's' system of social custom and the human world surrounding man, the world of dead, objectified labour incarnate. Yet this qualitative change was never analysed as a process in which work meant a transition from a non-human world to a human one. Here the writers of the Renaissance either anthropomorphized completely (recall Montaigne's analysis of the 'human labour of the animals'), or else they regarded human nature in the abstract, as a purely natural product, upon which labour begins to 'work', creating a second nature, only after man as a natural being has already emerged ready-made (compare Bovillus' analysis of how man is transformed from a mere 'existence' into an 'intellect'). *Here, then, the idea of a creation was preserved, even though in secularized form.* Nature created man (either as a link in a chain descending from God, or of its own accord), and it was as a being created by nature that man embarked on his own uniquely human life. Here those two opposite poles which I designated with the names of Montaigne and Bovillus actually meet. The endless allegory which is characteristic of the discussions of Renaissance anthropology is revealing. Here, too, it springs from the failure to think a problem through to its conclusion.

The economic problems of labour were left essentially untouched by the thinkers of the period. It had not yet become possible even in that age to formulate the philosophical and economic problem of

400

the quantitative equivalence of different qualities. Marx, analysing Aristotle's *Politics*, notes that the great Stagirite could not come upon the cause of the equivalence of exchanged goods if only for the reason that his whole way of thinking was based upon the inequality of men. By the time of the Renaissance this difficulty had already been overcome. Emerging bourgeois production already proclaimed that equivalence in principle. But prior to the beginnings of capitalist reproduction, or 'production for production's sake', the concrete quality of the various kinds of labour so obscured the quantitative side of the products of labour, and their use-value their character of exchange-values, that it proved impossible to get much closer to apprehending abstract labour than antiquity had done. There was one area where attempts at an economics were made and where the phenomenon of alienation was observed and analysed, much more radically than happened in connection with work: that was in the investigation of money. But I must add that even that did not happen until the late Renaissance, in the sixteenth century.

The result of all this was that a synthesis of the various aspects of work was not even attempted. Similarly, no attempt was made to discover the various forms in which work had appeared historically, or the relationship of those forms to the mode of labour, its object and instruments, its relationship to class, its structure or economic function. A systematic – historically synthesizing – analysis of work appears only with the investigations of Marx. Even the materials for such a synthesis – abstract structural analysis and abstract anthropological analysis excepted – were assembled only later. The Renaissance's real merit was simply to have *proclaimed* the fact of its anthropological universality. That was enough to make possible the elaboration of a dynamic concept of man. In all other respects we can speak, at most, only of first beginnings.

Most of the thinkers of the Renaissance fought stubbornly to see science and technique made 'open subjects'. That was as true of the science and technique of art (Alberti) as of the science and technique of nature (Leonardo, Bacon, Bruno), of politics (Machiavelli), and of ethical conduct (Charron). To make them open subjects meant to remove from them the veil of mystery, declaring them something usable by everyone and imitable by everyone. This democratic attitude in epistemology and anthropology was also in the interests of bourgeois production, then in its infancy. I speak of 'epistemological democratism' because the programmatic abolition of mystery was based on the premise that men *in general* could make use of the facts and procedures which science and technology had discovered, and thus assumed that men's capacities for knowing reality were – at least in principle – identical. And I say 'anthropological democratism' because the equality, in principle, of capacities for acquiring knowledge and making use of it was based on a theory of the essential, substantial identity of the human species – sometimes expressed openly, sometimes in tacit form. No great thinker of the Renaissance ever entertained any doubt that man was a 'rational' being, in other words that *every* man was a rational being. And that was true even of the more aristocratically tinged thinkers of aristocratic periods (the first generation of Florentine Neoplatonists, for example).

All this may seem to be contradicted by the fact that the Renaissance was the first age which seriously occupied itself with the idea of genius – the unique, unduplicatable set of abilities in an individual human being which distinguish him from others. But the contradiction is only an apparent one. The problem of genius – paradoxical though it may sound – came into being as the child of a democratic epistemology and anthropology. Kierkegaard put it very well when he contrasted the *genius* with the *apostle*. The genius is immanent, the apostle transcendent. The powers of the genius are, albeit to an especially intensified and enhanced degree, human powers, while the apostle is sent from God. The genius is a representative of the human species, the apostle a representative of supernatural powers.

Before the Renaissance there was no theory of genius, nor were 'geniuses' acknowledged in daily life. Where the application of human abilities and their opportunity for further development were narrowly circumscribed by the framework of the feudal order, even exceptional talents could assert themselves only within that framework. Exceptionalness grows out of the soil of common human activities. It represented them to an enhanced degree, to be sure, but *they* were what it represented. So long as past-orientedness prevailed, seizing upon or moulding something radically new was hardly possible, much less praiseworthy.

When, in myth and legend, men appear with abilities so outstanding that they cannot be explained as merely a high-order synthesis of the experience of the community or the social order, then they are regarded not as men but as 'heroes' or demigods, as in Greek or German mythology, or in the legends of the early Middle Ages. Exceptional greatness was of divine origin, either indirectly or directly through the medium of divine intervention. God or the gods could also be selective, as I have said. The God of Israel, for example, often postponed the decision to elect someone until He had become convinced of the right man's character and abilities, until He had put him to the test. His range of choice, however, was not large. In the case of Isaac's sons, for example, he had to choose either one or the other.

Respect for 'great men' is not, of course, a new phenomenon. In ancient Greece a special regard already surrounded those whose greatness was thought to be of this world; that was true above all of the seven sages, whose wisdom was not in any way held to be of divine derivation. But people, as I have said, did not find in their wisdom anything wondrous either. They saw in the sages the summation of their communal experiences, and a representation of their own ethics; hence the name 'sage', which implies a cumulative wisdom and ethical conduct. Respect surrounded great military leaders, too, since at any given moment they were the ones best fitted for their task, inasmuch as they knew *best* how to execute it; but the thought never arose that they were the *only* ones who knew how to do it. Even the capture of Troy did not depend solely on the 'hero' Achilles, as his great admirer, Alexander the Great, knew perfectly well; and it was not his contemporaries but posterity who styled Alexander a 'genius'.

In Christian ideology, regard for specifically human exceptionalness faded into the background; abilities without exception (not just those of heroes and saints) were viewed as being of divine origin, and were coupled, in their exercise, with humility. Here, too, the emergence of Renaissance individualism, and the Renaissance individual shattered the old ideology. The age was marked by a cult of the particular abilities of the individual.

The cult of individual greatness, however, was still not necessarily accompanied by the development and articulation of the concept of genius.

And here we return to our paradox. It was indeed a democratic anthropology that gave rise to those forms in which the conception of genius first appeared. In unbelievably rapid succession new inventions were made and new continents discovered; men rose swiftly in the social hierarchy; the quest of the new took the place of the perfecting of the old. And so it became necessary to comprehend this ability, this striving for and discovery of the new. But it could no longer be comprehended simply as a summation of the efforts of a given community, but rather as something that formulated anew the problems of *the entire human species* and revealed whole new worlds. Aeschylus and Phidias were honoured more by their communities than were Dante and Leonardo. Yet whoever would have written a biography of them? Whoever would have searched for what was unique in their abilities? Whoever would have regarded

403

them as spiritual champions of all mankind, discoverers of new worlds? Yet that is what they were; only people did not yet know that they were. During the Renaissance they began to know.

They knew that there are abilities which can open to men worlds yet unknown, can lead on to one or another 'promised land' – but without the help of God. For those abilities were regarded as *human* abilities and studied as such. At the same time, results had to be *intelligible to all and universally diffusable* – once more because they were results attained through human abilities. If someone discovered a new world, anyone could follow him there and indeed ought to do so. In their time Ionia and Attica had seven sages. Everyone respected their wisdom and understood it, too, yet others could not become 'that' wise. The saints and heroes of the Christian Middle Ages also merited respect. Men listened to the legends of their deeds, but – apart from the newly elect – they were too weak to follow them. The Renaissance, however, reasoned in the following way: the scientist, philosopher, discoverer, or artist of genius creates something that has never existed before. But he transmits his results and, even more important, the technique of inquiry and creation. And after that access is free: anyone can appropriate them. And if a new genius arises, he can build further on those results.

I have mentioned several times before that the notion of transcendental aid at the genius's command did not disappear. But divine assistance was no longer available; what remained was diabolical aid. The genius who broke completely with the community, whose results were non-transferable and incomprehensible, deserved only a very ambiguous kind of recognition. He found unequivocal rejection only in the Faust legend of the Protestant opposition – even though it too sprang from Renaissance soil.

Here, however, I should like to stress once more the extraordinary extension of superstition, magic, and witchcraft during the Renaissance. And yet even the science of secrets was losing its mystery. Astrology, magic, and the like had their own recipes, their own technical descriptions and textbooks, just like any genuine science. Here, too, the urge to disseminate one's results reared its head. Magical notions, and the truth or falsity of certain superstitions, were discussed with the help of the same scholarly apparatus employed on other ideas. Pico della Mirandola's polemic against magic is a classic example, and so is Pomponazzi's *De naturalium effectum admirandorum causis.*

The Renaissance had no integral theory of genius; what is more, it had no actual theory of genius at all, only a variety of notions about it. I must take issue with a very widespread preconception in emphasizing that there was not a single element in the Renaissance's conception of genius which pointed in any way towards romanticism. Despite its legacy of superstition and magic Renaissance science was, in this regard, the forerunner rather of the Enlightenment and of German classicism than of romanticism.

And that was so because of the decidedly democratic attitude which I have analysed already, but also because during the Renaissance the criterion of genius was not the grandeur of subjectivity in and of itself, but rather *objectivity*. We need only refer back to Machiavelli's conception of the political genius, which sees him as a function of the ability to 'seize the time', to find adequate means: the genius of a politician, and also his personality, can be measured by results, by consequences. We may recall, parenthetically, that according to Machiavelli there is no such thing as 'all-round' political genius. A politician can display genius only in some definite situation, only in response to some kind of challenge; and the emergence of political genius is always the result of the momentary coincidence of *two possibilities*, an objective and a subjective one. A great subjectivity is, then, bound to its age, and it is great only in its objectivization.

The same thing is true as well in the two spheres to which I now turn, those of science and art.

Inventors, writes Leonardo, are 'interpreters between Nature and Man'.[26] The interpreter understands more than men in general; he can apprehend things which are not apprehended by everyone. But the criterion of his status as an inventor is an objective one – the extent to which he really does know the *language of nature*; and at the same time it is a democratic one – the extent to which he is able to translate it into the language of men. Every morally and physically sound human being has a desire for knowledge: 'The natural desire of good men is knowledge.'[27]

Thus the 'translation' efforts of the interpreter have a fertile soil on which to work. Science can be transmitted in two ways – either directly as knowledge, or else indirectly as the practical application of knowledge or its fruits. 'Science is the captain, practice the soldiers', writes Leonardo.[28] But I must pause for a moment, for I touch here upon a new problem.

The extraordinary importance attached to the practice and transmittability of technique, and the ultimate democratism of scientific (theoretical and philosophical) thinking were both, in general, characteristic of Renaissance philosophy. But the two problems often appear separately; there are times, moreover, when ethical-political practice alone takes over the role of praxis (as in

Bruni and Bovillus, to mention two different types of thinkers). Yet there does exist a mainstream (and it still exists even where direct connections cannot be demonstrated) in which the relationships mentioned by Leonardo between direct and indirect transmission, between theory and practice, are all present at once. The line begins with Alberti and ends with Bacon; it really embraces the entire Renaissance. Thus it is justified to treat Leonardo's ideas as at least typical, even if not characteristic of every thinker of the Renaissance – and typical not only of those who emerged from the craft guilds, but of some of the academicians as well (the school of Padua).

It is an altogether traditional feature in Leonardo's theory of scientific *techné* that he subordinates technique to science (and we should note once again how he formulates the matter allegorically!). *What is new in him is the necessary correlation of the two*, apparent in the allegory as well. Just as a captain without soldiers is no captain, so, too, a science without a praxis is no science. Still, it would not be correct to equate Leonardo, in this respect, with Bacon. Leonardo nowhere writes that the process of scientific knowledge itself involves praxis,[29] that praxis is a part of the process of cognition itself and so pertains to the 'captain' proper. For Bacon, on the other hand, the 'sequence' of observation, reflection, and experiment is not a sequence leading from scientific cognition to the 'soldiers', or praxis; rather, *all three of those elements are themselves aspects of scientific cognition.* Leonardo's conception of sensory experience does not differ, in the abstract, from that of Duns Scotus, while Bacon's really does.

All in all, then, Bacon, in his judgment on the place of science and scientists and in his analysis of science (though not, of course, in the way he himself applied his own theory), was at least as much the beginning of a new era as the conclusion of an old one. Already he was raising the problems of bourgeois science, sometimes in a negative way through his critical posture, sometimes in a positive way.

The social situation of the artist and the scholar or scientist during the Renaissance can scarcely be called problematical as yet. Each was, on one hand, subject to the conventions of his craft and community, and, on the other hand, each had his patron, in some Italian cities an already rather bourgeoisifed university, elsewhere the cultivated bourgeoisie itself; in some places the Church for a while competed with the bourgeoisie in offering support and, for a time, patronage as well; while in such advanced bourgeois communities as Florence scholars could even aspire to high political office. Bacon was able to witness a new phenomenon, the emergence of a scientific (and artistic) *intelligentsia*, illustrative of the status of science and art in the bourgeois order: production has become a matter of separate professions, products have become commodities. More and more scholars and scientists are needed, and yet these – if they are outstanding – find it ever more difficult to 'succeed', because the 'professional' differences between them and their patrons, who mediate the expectations of society, grow wider day by day.

> For it does not *rest with* the same persons to cultivate sciences and to reward them. The growth of them comes from great wits; the prizes and rewards of them are in the hands of the people, or of great persons, who are but in very few cases even moderately learned.[30]

What I have just been saying is not a mere repetition of what was said before in analysing everyday life. Bacon's theory of the idols now appears in a new light; it was an attempt to separate science from everyday life. Bacon wanted to make science a specialized trade or profession, a high-level trade to be sure, but still a trade. One of the greatest geniuses of the Renaissance saw that a natural science founded on genius was not feasible, partly for scientific, partly for social reasons. Science must be based on method, a method for whose acquisition and practice geniuses are no longer necessary. For, writes Bacon, 'the course I propose for the discovery of sciences is such as leaves but little to the acuteness and strength of wits, but *places all wits and understandings nearly on a level*'.[31] We have arrived at the pioneering scientific methodicalness of the seventeenth century, the precondition of genuine, universal scientific progress, but also at its mechanistic conception of man and know-ledge. There is no longer a captain, only a host of soldiers, however excellently equipped.

Thus the Renaissance measured genius by the standards of objectivity and of the transmittability of objective results; yet it *was genius* which it measured by these standards. As we saw in analysing the concept of fate, opinions diverged as to what role the subject had in the meeting of objective and subjective possibilities and as to what extent that role depended on depth of insight and particular attributes of character. But little effort was made to grasp the *psychic* aspect of genius or how, in the process of creation, the genius was raised to the level of the human species, how starting out from a basis of particularity he eventually broke away from that same particularity. Most interesting, perhaps, in this connection is

407

the remark of Leonardo, who went beyond the customary allegories of the 'divine spark' and of the creator's 'elevation' to the ideal when he said:[52]

> The divinity which is the science of painting transmutes the painter's mind into a resemblance of the divine mind. With free power it reasons concerning the generation of diverse natures.

What is especially interesting in the quotation is that here the great adept of artistic technique sees the psychological basis of artistic genius not in technical skill, but in the artist's vision. That was connected with *techné*, of course, for it was 'science' which gave rise to a new way of seeing; yet without that new way of seeing science alone would not have been sufficient to produce creations of genius. And the opposite is also true: without the *sine qua non* of science the 'divine spirit', the free flight of imagination and creation could never have come to fruition of their own accord, on the strength of subjectivity alone.

But that condition *sine qua non*, 'science', was not just a science of technique, but above all a science of mimesis.

If, as I have said, Renaissance science and philosophy are filled with allegory, I ought to add that art theory *de-allegorizes*. We need only compare the illustrations which adorn the scientific and philosophical literature with works of art proper, full of life and independent: while the illustrations reveal an ever more complicated allegorical mode of representation, art proper is almost untouched by it. I would not say that in Renaissance art there was never, at the very beginning, any allegory anywhere – for then it would rightly be possible to cite such contrary instances as the 'virtues' and 'vices' of the Arena Chapel. Or one could write if off to the subjective taste of the author who deemed it no accident that Giotto's artistic genius is least evident in his allegories. The charge of subjective bias does not, however, alter the objective fact that in art and art theory alike allegory recedes into the background right up until the moment of crisis when, with the advent of mannerism, it flowers anew.

By contrast with the Christian requirement, Renaissance art theory rejected the principle that the purpose of art was to be morally edifying. In that believers and unbelievers alike were agreed. Boccaccio, as we have seen, wrote in defence of his tales that 'these stories, such as they are, may, like all things else, be baneful or profitable according to the quality of the hearer'.[33] Boccaccio thus makes the moral effectiveness (or counter-effectiveness) of art dependent upon the audience. Everything in the world is worthy of representation, and the latter should not be limited to what is 'edifying': it is not the artist's task to draw a moral from what exists, but the task of the reader, spectator, or listener. When, as a result of a crisis of conscience and the collapse of his world-outlook, Boccaccio took fright at the position he himself had taken, Petrarch still defended, by contrast, that same position. And with that he took over the 'torch' of the Renaissance.

The aesthetic 'relay' of the Renaissance passed along three axioms. The first held that art is imitation or *mimesis*. According to the second, art is a *science* (*techné*). According to the third, art is *hierarchical*: there are higher-order arts and lower-order arts. Science was only able to win, after a long struggle, a recognition of its demand to be 'democratic', commonly intelligible and accessible to all. For art, that was not necessary. Accessibility, transmittability, 'utility' (in the sense of universal enjoyability) never became axiomatic because they were natural.

According to Frederick Antal's studies the theory of mimesis was first revived by Cennini, a pupil of Gaddi, in 1390 in Padua, in his book on painting. Painting, in his view, was 'the imitation of nature'. In any event, the fact that the fine arts formed the dominant genre of the Italian Renaissance from the end of the fourteenth century, and the fact that in the hierarchy of the age they occupied the most distinguished place, made it easier to revive the theory of mimesis. It is in the fine arts that 'imitation' can most easily be verified.

The fact that the Renaissance theory got its start in connection with the fine arts entailed in itself the possibility that the ancient concept of imitation would be interpreted one-sidedly or at least imperfectly. Dénes Zoltai analysed it neatly when he wrote, with respect to the music theory of antiquity, that in the ancient world, in Plato or even in Aristotle, imitation never meant imitation of *nature*; it always meant, rather, the imitation of an *ethos*. But since during the Renaissance every kind of fixed ethos was in process of dissolution (as we saw in analysing ethics), the ancient interpretation was no longer timely. What was more natural, then, than combining the old theory with a demand for the depiction of nature (above all, for its visual depiction), and thus creating a new interpretation of mimesis. The ancient theory of mimesis gave precise expression to the fundamental attitude of the ancients towards art; the Renaissance theory of mimesis formulated, with its principle of the imitation of nature, not just the ideology of an actual mode of creation but a general principle. I cannot elaborate here on the difficulties to which

409

this general principle later gave rise. Nonetheless, the Renaissance did formulate for posterity, for the first time, certain immortal precepts, above all the theory of artistic *originality*.

It became a commonplace during the Renaissance to contrast the 'imitation of nature' with the imitation of the imitators. No greater recognition could be accorded the great innovators than to say of them that they had gone directly back to nature, to reality. According to Vasari – who summed up all these conceptions, which had already become commonplaces – Giotto threw open the 'gateway of reality', and with that became the founder of 'modern' art. Masaccio [8]imitated the phenomena of nature', and so on. Leonardo expressed the same idea in his own graphic and original way:[34]

> Those who took as their standard anything other than nature,
> the supreme guide of all the masters, were wearying
> themselves in vain. . . . Those who study only the authorities
> and not the works of nature are in art the grandsons and not
> the sons of nature, which is the supreme guide of the good
> authorities.

Nor does this contradict what Leonardo wrote about the psychology of the artistic genius or about his capacity for free creation. For the artist who has studied the forms of nature so thoroughly that they have got into his very blood is still able to create – freely – on the model of nature, via his own 'human' nature.

The revelation of the mimetic character of art was not only a description, but also a *programme*. The extension of the subject matter was another part of the programme, as discussed earlier, as was the divorcing of art from morality and didacticism. But the programme had its scientific and technical side as well. Thus the second 'axiom' was not independent of the first.

Alberti directly stated the paradox that art is a science. The interpretation of the paradox was, however, not so paradoxical. It proclaimed, first of all, a break with an artistic vision and technique based on the old guild organization and oriented towards the past. To be scientific was tantamount to becoming conscious of what one was doing. It was not enough for the artist to learn his art as a craft. He had to know what he was doing. He must be aware of the laws of his art and, what is more, of the laws of nature and reality which he is obliged to reproduce in his art. Finally, he must be conscious of the methods which make it possible to render as well as possible the observed relationships of nature. These methods are scientific and technical. Moreover, they can be developed further, just like the methods of science.

In order to be able to mirror nature and reality, then, the artist must be a philosopher of nature and a natural scientist, and – a technical innovator as well. One of the central categories of art was that of *convenientia*. This was the final goal of artistic effort. It would arise if the artist's intelligence was capable of recognizing the *ratio naturae* and bringing it into harmony with his sensuous experience, if, that is, he could bring about the unity of *nature perceived and nature comprehended*.

I do not propose to discuss the artistic theory of the age in detail. It is enough to mention that such central problems as those of perspective and anatomy sprang from the same endeavour. The theory of perspective was a science. Anatomy was a science. Yet without a thorough knowledge of these sciences *convenientia* could not come into being, for behind the sensuous experience the *ratio naturae* would be absent, and so mimesis would suffer injury.

The Renaissance expected of art, too, a constant process of technical innovation – not in order to de-anthropomorphize art as well, but in order to render its human truth complete. That technique was the means, and mimesis the goal was taken for granted – so much so that it did not even require discussion.

That was the mainstream tendency. If individual artistic theories of the age then went further in emphatic enthusiasm for science and technique, that does not alter the basic tendencies in any way. More than one anatomical analysis – even those of Leonardo and Dürer – sought to render every moment of movement with natural fidelity, reducing artistic truth here, too, to the truth of nature. It is unnecessary to go all the way to Lessing's magnificent analysis of the Laocoon to find a refutation of this conception. Lessing was not the first to discover that the validity, mimetic conviction, and truth of a work of art does not depend on whether the human or animal figure depicted can be found, with *exactly* the same movements, in nature – especially if the work represents motion. Michelangelo already saw that clearly; it was for that reason that he – among others – did not sympathize with many representatives of the mimesis theory of his age, not even with Leonardo and Dürer. Condivi wrote:[35]

> I know that when Michelangelo read Albrecht Dürer he found him very weak . . . for Albrecht actually dealt only with the proportions and variations of the body. . . . But of the most important things, of human activity and movement, he said nothing.

Michelangelo radically rejected theories which identified art and science, and, as Charles de Tolnay has shown, he deliberately refused to employ the laws of perspective. Of course his Platonic outlook played a part in that too, alongside his scepticism towards the artistic use of science and technique. For him mimesis meant the mirroring of the Ideal.

During the Renaissance, then, work, science, technique, and art represented, in the strict sense of the word, an *inseparable* manifestation and objectification of human abilities, and served the conquest of macrocosm and microcosm, of nature and human nature. In all this, *emotion and reason, experience and method acted in unison.* Man and his world appeared unified, and man himself – at least in his diverse objectivations – seemed unified too.

CHAPTER 14

Knowledge; body and soul

The Renaissance *still* had no theory of knowledge. Problems of cognition were subsumed partly under ontology, partly under anthropology. Nor did it yet have a psychology either. Cognition and other psychic phenomena were regarded as functions of the 'soul'. Opinions differed as to the characteristics and properties of the soul. But at the same time every Renaissance thinker – regardless of whether he held the soul to be form or substance, of natural or divine origin – agreed that the soul was *objective* and was in some way to be found in reality as a *whole*, if perhaps on different levels of existence.

The divorce of epistemology from the analysis of the 'soul' began only in the seventeenth century, and then it took two forms. (In this regard Descartes, Spinoza, and Leibniz were even more closely bound up with the Renaissance tradition, though on an incomparably higher level of scientific methodicalness.) One tendency sprang from Hobbes. Hobbes was indeed the first who detached the categories of cognition and mind from the concept of a 'soul'-substance. The second part of his philosophical trilogy bears – almost as if with polemical intent – the title of *De homine* rather than *De anima*. Here was a great beginning towards the creation of a unitary anthropology, especially as it still subordinated anthropology (and *within* it the fundamental questions of mind and knowledge) to philosophy of nature, whose problems had been treated in the first part of the trilogy. Most of the French materialists of the Enlightenment followed the same path, particularly Helvétius and (if unsystematically) Diderot. Hume, who divorced anthropology from the ontology of the philosophy of nature, in part broadened the

413

path opened by Hobbes, while at the same time blazing a new trail himself. And from there it was only a step to Kant who, departing from Hume's ambiguity, created an unambiguous theory. With Kant anthropology became synonymous with the analysis of individual faculties functioning in isolation from one another. The necessity of a *separate* psychology (not the real necessity, but the necessity inherent in this method) is a product of Kant's reasoning. Hegel's great attempt to transcend the Kantian 'soul-impasse' – once again on an incomparably higher theoretical and scientific level – led back to the thought of the Renaissance. Anthropology (phenomenology) was unified once more, and man – in all of his manifestations – was again a particular part of a unitary nature. But the 'soul' was smuggled back in again, now in the form of the world-spirit. Instead of a many-sided, sensuous universe and a human being appropriate to it, there was now a thinking universe, with man attaining his acme in philosophical knowledge. Eventually it was only the ontology and anthropology worked out by the Marxian method, a unitary social ontology and anthropology in which there were no separate 'epistemology' and 'psychology', as in Hobbes, but where *de cive* is not founded on *de homine*, that was able to surpass the Renaissance conception as a whole, not just in its details.

All of Renaissance thought preserved the premise, already widespread in antiquity and confirmed by Christianity, that man was 'body and soul'. Nature, too, was 'body and soul'. That in itself does not yet tell us anything about the content of various tendencies of thought or of their scientific character. The level of scientific value has to be measured by the analysis of the body-soul relationship and by the interpretation of the concept of soul, not by the mere assertion of the body-soul dichotomy.

With respect to the 'essence' of the soul, there was still a great deal of theological, magical, and other sorts of abstruse speculation. Out of the reaction against these there sprang one current of thought – even though not a central one – which programmatically turned away from analysis of the essence of the soul. Thus Valla argued that it was not the essence of the soul that ought to be known, but mental phenomena. Vives again, in his *De anima*, acted in accordance with that programme. He did not concern himself at all with theories of substance, but with anthropology, and within it (as we have seen) with the affects. When Telesio – partly following Vives, partly criticizing him – averred that this whole trend of thinking had to be subordinated to the philosophy of nature, he was, of course, in an abstract, theoretical way, undoubtedly correct. But for him, at the given level of development of the day, that necessarily meant returning to the concept of soul as substance, indeed to the conception of an 'immortal soul'.

It would be quite unwarranted to see in this current of thought, particularly in Valla's rejection of any search for the 'essence' of the soul, a species of positivism, as some of Cassirer's pupils (outstanding Renaissance scholars, in other ways) have done. Valla did not deny that there was such a thing as the essence of the soul, as he did not deny the essence, the substantiality of nature either. It was simply that he saw in the observation and description of mental phenomena a *better means* of gaining knowledge about 'the soul' than through speculation divorced from empirical reality. Such was the case with Vives as well.

Thus the debate did not turn on the existence or non-existence of the soul as a substance, but rather on whether the soul was immanent or not, hence whether it was an eternal, infinite, and necessary part of living nature, as, for example, Giordano Bruno asserted, or not; whether the human soul emanated from the soul of nature (as Bovillus said), or not; whether God conferred immortality on the soul indirectly, through the mediation of the soul of nature (as Ficino claimed), or not; whether its immortality was a collective immortality (as the Averroists said), or whether it was individual (as the Platonists and some of the Aristotelians claimed). Was it substance (as in the opinion of the Platonists), or form (as in the view of some Aristotelians)? Were its functions immanent or transcendent? Did its immortality – if it was immortal – have any influence on moral conduct, and if so what was that influence and was it a desirable one? What was its connection with the body? Did it exist in a parallel or a causal relationship with the latter? These were the questions, and more could be enumerated.

It must be noted that the socially progressive character and the intellectually progressive character of the various currents of thought did not always coincide. The social function of a given theory could be quite different in different circumstances, and it is always difficult to abstract from its intellectual context. I have already mentioned Ficino's view that the body, too, is immortal. This notion, ridiculous from a scientific point of view, was called upon to represent the unity of body and soul, the wholeness of the individual, and the equality of cognitive, ethical, and sensuous praxis. We have also described how the polemic of the Averroists against individual immortality was also, at the same time, an attack on individualism. There was little obligation to think problems through to a conclusion in connection with these questions; here, perhaps, philosophy remained closest to the plane of everyday life. In order to solve any theoretical problem, whether ethical or epistemological, the appropriate conception of the soul was fitted into place – was selected, that is, from the abundance of ready-made solutions. Or else it might not be selected and fitted into place, as in those brilliant passages where Montaigne analyses fancy and imagination. He concludes: 'But all this may be attributed to the narrow seam between the soul and body, through which the experience of the one is communicated to the other.'[36] But Montaigne does not elaborate on what this 'narrow seam' and this 'communication' consist of; he takes the attitude here that these categories are 'self-evident'.

The most scientific analysis of the soul appeared among the Aristotelians, whose attitude towards nature was a less experiential one, and among whom the object under study, the soul, was not simultaneously the object of passionate emphasis. Among them we may single out the most characteristic, Pomponazzi and Zabarella.

Pomponazzi wished above all else to demonstrate the *unity of the soul*. The duality of a sensitive and intellectual soul was, he argued, contradicted by experience:[37]

> First, this seems to contradict experience. For I who am writing
> these words am beset with many bodily pains, which are the
> function of the sensitive soul; and the same I who am tortured
> run over their medical causes in order to remove these pains,
> which cannot be done save by the intellect. But if the essence
> by which I feel were different from that by which I think, how
> could it possibly be that I who feel am the same as I who
> think? For then we could say that two men joined together
> have common cognitions, which is ridiculous.

The argument for the inseparability of sensing and thinking, and the final conclusion that it is impossible to have 'two men' in one man, are strongly reminiscent of Hobbes and of the arguments of the *philosophers*.

Indeed, this brief passage suggests, in its content and in its conclusions, several 'heretical' solutions. Affirming the unity of the 'sensitive' soul and the 'intellectual' soul does away with the ontological basis for a *hierarchy* of the two. In Christian ideology this hierarchy, originating actually with Aristotle, took on aspects which Aristotle would never have suspected. The inferiority of the passions, of those affects which had their seat in the 'sensitive soul', was a proof of the superiority of the 'intellect', the 'thinking soul'. Base corporeality contaminated the 'sensitive soul', while the

416

'intellect' soared high to God. Various schools of Renaissance thought restored Aristotle's original meaning, according to which the inferiority of mere perception meant only that this human faculty existed in organic nature as a whole. We may recall Bovillus' four stages: *esse, vivere, sentire, intelligere*. Pomponazzi, however, took a different tack – and in my opinion, a more productive one. He treated perception as a special *human* kind of perception, and as such he held it to be not only equivalent to, but co-substantial with, conceptual knowledge.

The restoration of the unity of the soul implied, however, the abolition of the body-soul duality. If the most corporeal sensation is just as much a phenomenon of the 'soul' as the purest reflection, then body or matter is not what Christianity called 'corporeality'. Body and soul, Pomponazzi reasoned, are not two separate substances. The soul – the unitary soul – is none other than the form of the body. The relationship of body and soul is the relationship of content and form. So far this is still Aristotelianism. But – adds Pomponazzi here – if something displays a form-content relationship, that still does not mean that the relationship is one of mover and moved. The relationship of mover and moved is not like that of ox and plough. The latter is not organic, while the former is organic. Pomponazzi, then, did not take over from Aristotle the notion that form animates matter. In his 'organic unity' there was no longer an active element and a passive one.

This whole line of reasoning must necessarily lead Pomponazzi to the notion of the mortality of the soul. And indeed he frequently comes close to it. I have said before that, from an ethical standpoint, he rejects the immortality of the soul. But in the ontological and epistemological contexts he is not entirely able to do so. The soul, he reasons, is in its essence mortal, because it is a form of matter and must perish with it; the soul is generated by its parents, not through some special creation. But, he adds, at the same time it 'participates' in immortality because – and here is the catch – otherwise it would not be able to grasp universal and immortal things.

Here, then, Pomponazzi recapitulates the common theme of the Renaissance, the theory of the parallelism of microcosm and macrocosm. If the whole of reality – the universe – is infinite and universal, then man (the microcosm) must also be infinite and universal, and so – inseparably – he must be capable of knowing the infinite and universal. And since experience shows that the body is neither infinite nor universal, there must be in man 'something' of the infinite and universal. The reflection cannot differ from that which the mirror reflects. In that faculty of knowledge in which the notion

of infinity and universality appears at all 'there must be something'
of infinity and universality. That something can be represented only
by the soul. If the single individual is not identical, even in his soul,
with immortal substance, and if his soul is thus partly mortal, still
he participates in that essence through his universal faculty of
knowing, and so his soul has an immortal aspect. To repeat: here is a
case where a thinker suffers shipwreck in seeking to solve a great
problem, and not at all through the ideologization of some social
or ethical need.

But Pomponazzi's pupil, Giacomo Zabarella, cut the Gordian
knot simply by *distinguishing between substance and function*,
between the organism and its functions. By so doing he exploded –
far more radically than did Bovillus – the principle of the parallelism
of microcosm and macrocosm. 'The body is not the act of the soul,
but the soul is the act of the body; it is not body, but something
belonging to body....'[38] The soul as the 'act' of the body is not
at all identical with the soul as a 'form'. A form is the form of some
material, but it also partakes of substantiality itself. But the 'act'
which pertains to some material no longer partakes of substantiality
itself, it is merely its *function*.

The two more primitive forms of the soul (those common to men
and animals alike) may indissolubly comprehend the organism and
its functions; that is, their *existence* determines their *function*
(*esse – operari*). But the connection between *esse* and *operari*, which
in Thomism was of universal validity, is not applicable to man.
Man's unique faculty for knowing, his intellect, is indeed concrete
in its substance, determinate, circumscribed, and constant, but its
function may transcend its mere existence. In its operation, in its
functioning the intellect is capable of grasping, processing and
knowing essences (like universality and infinity) which are *not* at all
present in its material or substance.

> For in its being it is a form of the body and truly informs
> matter, but in its operation it is more elevated above matter
> than the other parts of the soul, and in the reception of species
> does not use any part of the body as recipient,

writes Zabarella;[39] and again: 'It can receive intelligible species,
without the body's receiving them. By its operation man is said to
operate and know, for it is the form by which man is man....'[40]
Man may consequently be a microcosm, but of such a kind that
*he does not reproduce the macrocosm either in matter or structure, he
only acquires some knowledge of it*. The reflection of the universe in a
schematic way based on complete identity had to give way to the

outlines of a more modern theory of knowledge before science could take leave of the substantiality of the 'soul'.

It is clear that, with reference to the Renaissance, the usual typologies of epistemology are meaningless. Its controversies cannot be described by using the concept of 'rationalism' versus that of 'empiricism'. To cite just one example: Ficino's anthropology, and his whole basic conception, can be called rationalist, while that of Leonardo can be termed empiricist; but both are based on a very similar conception of anthropology, that of the interpretation of the concept of man. The distinction between 'idealism' and 'materialism' is even less useful. No materialist theory of knowledge in the strict sense of the word existed during the Renaissance, only such – and this is the essence of the matter – as pointed in certain respects towards certain kinds of questions and solutions and which could thus be recognized as forerunners, and utilized, by later materialist epistemologies. Telesio, who worked out a materialistic and naturalistic theory of sensation, still found a place in his argument for the concept of God, the creator of the soul; Zabarella, who came closest to a realistic conception of the 'link' between body and soul, still operated with scholastic forms; the thinking of Leonardo, the experimentalist, is shot through and through with the notion of an emphatic relationship to being-in-itself. Cardano speaks of three kinds of knowledge:[41]

> First, there is knowledge gained by my senses through the observing of innumerable things. . . . This aspect of knowledge assumes two questions: *What is it? Why is it . . . ?*
> Secondly, there is an understanding of higher things obtained through the examination of their beginnings and pursued by conforming to certain principles. This aspect of knowledge is called *proof* because it is derived from the effect based upon the cause. . . .
> The third form of my knowledge is that of things intangible and immaterial, and by this I have come wholly as a result of the ministrations of my attendant spirit. . . .

Thus even this outstanding empiricist and scientist, a man with few peers among those who first made the notion of methodical inferences drawn from empirical material a matter of common awareness, still attributed great importance to knowledge of immaterial essences mediated by an 'attendant spirit'.

Nevertheless, the arguments of Renaissance thinkers about knowledge were frequently polemical. These polemics almost invariably opposed to 'book' knowledge both experience *and* speculation directed towards the real world. When Valla writes that most human things are unknown to us and so we have no need of 'books', and when he then appeals to experience, he displays a general and *common* tendency of Renaissance scholarship. *'Experience', however, must not be taken to mean sensory experience alone.* If Valla had been thinking of that alone his own dialogues would be the best refutation of his thesis. 'Experience' means speculation too if it is oriented towards *reality*, if it analyses newly recognized phenomena from a *new* point of view rather than hashing over the traditional scholastic subject matter of philosophy. Experience is the starting-point of all those who use their *own* heads to think about their world. The line of demarcation must be drawn, then, between independent thought and lack of self-reliance in thinking, between 'free' and 'unfree' thinking, between scholasticism and the 'golden tree of life'. Any other way of categorizing Renaissance epistemology obscures the essential distinction and the essential similarity.

It may be objected that many Renaissance thinkers polemicized sharply against *sensatio*, while others wrote in defence of it. Yet we ought not to forget that the words *sensatio* and *sensus* were used in two quite different senses. Those expressions referred not only to sensory, empirical *knowledge* but also to sensual *pleasure* as well. When some writers (Ficino, for example) take up the cudgels against sensation, they mean by it not sensory, empirical knowledge but sensual pleasure, while they mean 'intellect', which is contrasted with the latter, to stand for *knowledge in general*. In that case the distinction between *sensus* and *intellectus*, and advocacy of the latter, means simply advocating the pleasures of knowledge versus sensual pleasures, taking a stand for the infinite (or the possibility of achieving it) against the limited and finite, for the anthropological essence against something they deemed to be, anthropologically, secondary.

The basic unity of Renaissance epistemology is summed up in the idea of knowing the *infinite*. 'We know nothing as yet' leads on again and again to action; to say that we know nothing is as much as to say that we *must* find out about it and that we must learn to know *everything*. To acquire knowledge of everything, however, is an *infinite process*. It was interpreted as such both by those who held reality to be infinite and constantly in motion, and by those whose world-view implied a finite universe. For the former, its inexhaustibility rested on an ontological concept of infinitude; for the latter it was a purely epistemological (and anthropological) problem –

they cited the finitude of individual men's knowledge. The continuous character of that infinite process, the aspect of *process*, must also be emphasized. Man progresses from ignorance towards knowledge. In that process illumination has no great role. The *result* (which according to this thinking can only be approximated to) may be illuminating, as for Nicholas of Cusa or Ficino, but it is not necessarily so. Progress is, nevertheless, an intellectual process; the greatness of the *human mind*, and the limitlessness of human capacities, are its source and its guarantee. Thus the doctrine of the infinite and process-like character of knowledge is a direct affirmation of human greatness.

I have said that nearly all of Renaissance thinking was characterized by an emphatic view of nature. Within it, however, we must still make certain distinctions so far as the goal and result of the infinite process of acquiring knowledge is concerned. Two tendencies must be distinguished – tendencies which, as I have said, cannot simply be identified with empiricism and rationalism. The first was characterized by the fact that the culmination of the process of gaining knowledge (regardless of whether that culmination can be attained or only approximated) *is the fusion of the individual with the whole*, the bliss of identification with the universe or with God; the second, by the fact that in the process of acquiring knowledge the subject's distance *vis-à-vis* the objective world is enhanced, in that the autonomy of the laws of that world becomes ever 'harder'.

The high point of the first tendency, and at the same time its exemplar, is Nicholas of Cusa. Cassirer writes perceptively that it was Nicholas who transformed the infinitude of the object (substance) into the infinitude of the process of cognition. And it was likewise Nicholas who saw in the infinite, continuous process of gaining knowledge proof of the 'divine' character of man. But however endless the process, and however much it was the process itself that was divine, the *goal* was still the absorption of the individual in the whole, through the absorption of the whole ('the All') in the individual. To be a child of God meant, according to Nicholas of Cusa, 'the dissolution of all otherness and difference and the resolution of All into One, which is the One, and at the same time the merging [*transfusio*] of the One in the All'.[42]

Ficino came to a similar conclusion. For him, there was a contradiction between the striving of the human reason after infinitude and the unattainability of the infinite; it was a paradox that the most characteristically human of all human aspirations could not find satisfaction. On earth it was only men who sought the infinite; the animals did not. The animals could find satisfaction (the satisfaction of the senses), but man could not (for the intellect is infinite and insatiable). In a brilliant analysis he describes that 'hardness' of the objective world which was to become the central point for the analyses of his less enthusiastic contemporaries and successors:[43]

> The intellect, led on by its own nature, restlessly seeks the causes and grounds of things. In that search *it often comes upon things which it did not at all intend.* . . . In reality it is always doubtful, wavering, distressed. Since it never rests while it is so much taken up with them, it never comes into possession of the desired goal.

Ficino, however, was not satisfied with the human mind's endless struggle to conquer hard reality. He sought resolution, harmony, union; and nothing could provide that but transcendence – that is, Beauty, for (as I have said) those were for Ficino synonymous concepts. The rapture of knowledge elevates us into the world of Beauty: here the individual really can merge with the whole, and the infinite can find itself again because it has found an infinity which does not induce dread, but rather rest and happiness. God 'emanates' into the world. When man[44]

> perceives [these emanations] through his senses, gathers them in through his imagination, purifies them through his reason and finally links them together through the general ideas of the spirit . . . his soul sets in order again the shaken world, since through his efforts the once-spiritual world, now grown corporeal, is gradually re-infused with spirit again.

Here, 'translated' into epistemological terms, the short-lived illusion of the Florentine golden age (the early period of Medici rule) appears again – the illusion that freedom and happiness can be attained *together*. The concept of happiness of ancient (Platonic) ethics and the modern (Florentine) concept of freedom are here united with Beauty. Human knowledge, in its struggle with 'hard objectivity', serves to discover what in the latter is 'divine' – that is, beauty. The boundlessness of the intellect (a modern notion) comes to rest and finds its harmony (a Platonic notion); the individual becomes identified with the general. The Aesthetic is what makes possible and embodies this union.

It would distort history to say that the alternation of enthusiastic and 'distanced' attitudes can be ascribed simply to changing times. True, Ficino's sort of emphasis, with its aesthetic content, disappears with the passing of the golden age of the Medici, when the ideal of beauty becomes problematical. But it is just as true that in the case of, for example, Giordano Bruno the epistemological crown of a *Weltanschauung* which is not at all aesthetic in content is still union with the universe and immersion in it. The advocates of a 'distanced' attitude towards objectivity stem likewise from the most diverse periods and currents of thought. Their ranks extend from Valla to Pomponazzi and from Leonardo to Telesio. Cassirer, who sensed their kinship in many things, called them 'naturalists'. But that expression is imprecise at best. Their basic common feature, in my opinion, is that in examining the relationship of subject and object they focus not on union (or the possibility of union) but on *differences* and *effects* (interactions). (I must stress once again that there is no Chinese wall between these two attitudes; I spoke earlier, for example, of the enthusiastic features of Leonardo's vision of the world.)

That tendency can best be documented in the case of Telesio. He agreed with Leonardo that sensory experience was the source of all knowledge. But what in Leonardo was aphoristic became, with Telesio, a carefully worked-out theory of sensation. The soul is a moving substance which is set in motion by external reality (cold and heat). Every concrete sensation arises as the result of some distinct movement. The highest-order sensation is that in which the object impinges directly on the subject: touch. All sensation can be traced back to touch. Moreover, every idea can be traced back to perception: in thought the soul, moved by the outer world, continues to 'move' further, and so thought too can be derived from touch. 'The intellect itself', writes Cassirer, 'is only a mediate and derivative sense. Precisely because of this mediateness it remains necessarily imperfect and preserves only a kind of outline, an analogue, a simile of the true composition of the impression.'[45]

Little argumentation is required to make it clear that such a theory of perception (and of thought) *a priori* excludes an emphatic identification of subject and object. For the *most immediate* connection between subject and object is at one and the same time the most inferior, the most primitive, and it is in no way a culmination. Nor is much required to demonstrate my thesis that the proponents of a 'distanced' (rather than an emphatic) attitude do not form any unitary school. Telesio links up directly with pre-Socratic thought (which was beginning to come back into fashion again at this time, as we see in Bacon); he interpreted his new observations with the help of Democritus. In his theory of sensation work plays no part, even though he explains sensation by the *movement* of the soul-substance. On the other hand, in Pomponazzi, for example, the productive intellect, technical work-praxis, has a fundamental role in creating the relationship between subject and object.

But why distinguish 'emphatic' and 'distanced' theories of knowledge when I have myself stressed first the relativity of the difference, and then the fact that the two do not constitute unitary currents of thought? The reason is that the *destiny* and *future* of the two tendencies were different. In the sixteenth century – the age when the development of the Italian and French Renaissance became problematical, the age of the Reformation and the Wars of Religion – the emphatic tendency lived on only in exceptional cases, like that of Bruno; by contrast, the theory of 'distance' and the questions it raised (which were at least as old, if not even – as with Valla – older) proved, by the nature of the case, to be the hardier. The great hopes for society went up in smoke, the illusion of freedom and happiness combined dissolved, and so there was no soil for the notion of a unity of subject and object based upon the boundlessness of knowledge, on the greatness and power of thought and of the human mind.[46] The emphatic attitude became more and more a mark of retrograde tendencies – as in the Counter-Reformation – and its source was no longer the cognitive intellect (for Ficino and Leonardo even love was the child of the intellect) but rather the ecstatic temper. The Reformation 'turned over' the intellect to the exact sciences, so that it might preserve its claim to shape views of the world. Luther, describing this state of affairs, said wittily that man could be a realist through the grace of God, but with the help of reason he could only be a nominalist.

And so, for the time being, the philosophical theory which had postulated the emphatic and ultimate identification of subject and object had collapsed. From its ruins grew a newly revived scepticism on one hand, and the Reformation on the other. 'It is a curious fact', writes Charron, 'that although man naturally wants to know the truth and tries every possible means to attain it, he cannot attain it.'[47] Do we not recognize here, almost word for word, Ficino's thesis? And yet for Ficino union with Beauty – with God – is achieved *in spite* of that. Now it is absent. For Charron only the erring human mind exists. His first precept is 'I do not know'. It is characteristic of the correlation between scepticism and the Reformation that Luther even makes use of scepticism in defence of his own tenets. 'For we are not well able', he writes,[48]

> to comprehend or know why those things happen which the
> eye sees; I do not understand how we can hear and speak
> distinct and clear words, when the tongue moves in the mouth

and we speak – yet these are all natural things. . . . How then can we grasp or understand through reason secret counsels, or the splendor of God?

It is not the examples here which are decisive, but rather the fact that scepticism becomes an argument for faith.

Let there be no misunderstanding: scepticism as a current of thought was not in the service of faith, not even (as we have seen) in Charron. I merely wish to point out that the Reformation very early on took note of the collapse of those 'realist' world-views erected upon the greatness of man; and in doing so it made use of sceptic arguments, even before a genuine philosophical scepticism could emerge.

'Distance' world-views – and Luther took these *too* to be nominalist – did not collapse, however. What is more, the natural science which was then emerging might justly refer to them – so far as their overall tendency was concerned – and could associate itself with them. It would be an easy matter to argue that the 'distanced' world-views were not scientific, either, in any modern sense; that Bacon failed to understand Harvey; that the later representatives of the school of Padua disputed Galileo's findings, and so on. Cardano's methodology was, *in concreto*, not a modern methodology; Telesio's theory of sensation was naïve and primitive, Bacon's induction was scientifically useless. But from the standpoint of philosophical and epistemological principles it is undeniable that a real connection existed between the early natural sciences and the theory of the 'hardness' of objects. Bacon was expressing this 'hardness' when he said that it is possible to dominate nature only by obeying her (abstracting for the moment from the ethical content of this thesis). And he gave expression to it not as a negative thing, as the representatives of enthusiastic tendencies had done, but rather as a positive thing. And when Bacon denigrated the passive admiration and exaltation of the human mind, but in the sense that 'while we falsely admire and extol the powers of the human mind we neglect to seek for its true helps',[49] he was recognizing the facts so often stressed by the sceptics to arrive at opposite conclusions – conclusions which were to encourage the development of science and technique.

The idea that it was possible to 'seek for helps' for the weaknesses of the human mind was not a strange one for Nicholas of Cusa either – for even he held that the mind was the only mirror of the world which was capable of clarifying and correcting itself. For him, however the fidelity of the mirror is designed only to receive an infinite world in a better (more infinite) way, to create a more perfect union. The 'perfection' of the mind means something different for Bacon, however; his was the first theoretical formulation of the idea that knowledge can *force* itself upon the world, for humanity as a whole is more than the individual man, more even than thinking humanity itself.

CHAPTER 15

What is man capable of?

Hitherto I have examined the forms in which the dynamic concept of man manifested themselves. These manifestations – in theory, reflection, and the facts of life – were summarized and systematized by Renaissance anthropology in the narrow sense of the term – that Renaissance anthropology which gave a direct answer to the questions, 'What is man?' and 'What is he capable of?' It is not by accident that I speak of systematization and direct answers; in analysing Renaissance anthropology we will no longer come upon new ways of posing questions or new solutions. I will be tracing only that process by which the dynamic concept of man coalesces to form a *unified whole*.

All the things that Renaissance thinkers profess and write about man become the modes and attributes of the 'eternally human' and 'generally human'. For them, dynamic man *is* 'man' – and if that has not yet been demonstrated, this in itself clearly shows that the dynamic concept of man was not a historical concept of man. They discovered and described the dynamic categories which, in their opinion, were characteristic of man; and they termed these dynamic categories eternal and general categories. Men change, are confronted with alternatives, choose, rise, and fall; they are autonomous, they have infinite possibilities – but they are such in every situation, at all times, in the past and also in the future. 'For', writes Vives, 'however much everything that springs from our wilful actions and postulates may change, *the natural conditions of events, the causes and manifestations of human affects and passions* will remain unshaken.'[50]

Today it is easy to smile at the concept of the 'eternally human', for we know that the human essence is the product of historical development, and is itself a historical category. For that very reason I cannot emphasize enough how great an achievement the elaboration of the concept of an 'eternally' and 'generally' human was *before* the notion of historicity developed, and how at that time it *pointed towards* a historical concept of man.

In the case of the 'generally human' this can easily be seen, for it was a polemical formulation of the idea that 'human' features pertained to every man hence to humanity as a whole. Everyone partook of the 'human' not only irrespective of caste, feudal order, or class; so also did, in equal measure, Christian and non-Christian, civilized and uncivilized peoples, whites and non-whites. The last was not at all a mere theoretical question at that time; in the age of the discovery of America and, presently, of the first wars of extermination against the Indians of the Americas, the concept of the 'generally human' implied a very real defence of the 'human' rights of the Indians. The discovery and proclamation of the *common* anthropological essence of mankind pointed directly towards the slogans of the French Revolution. Then it was that 'liberty, equality, and fraternity' first made their appearance as *at one and the same time, a political demand and an anthropological, ontological fact.*

If, however, liberty, equality, and fraternity are anthropological facts, 'eternal' manifestations of the human essence – and here I pass on from the 'generally' human to the concept of the 'eternally human' – then *depravity is not a primary anthropological fact.* Man may, of course, become perverted, but however perverted, however petty, wicked, or unfortunate he may become, the 'core' of his essence remains unchanged. Even those, like Machiavelli, who deemed the men of their own time evil, still believed that. Jan Kott is quite right to say that Shakespeare depicted the conflict between men's possibilities and their destiny. That, indeed, was a phenomenon common to the Renaissance, especially the late Renaissance. Man's possibilities were equivalent to his anthropological essence – hence depravity *could* be a man's destiny.

Depravity and 'fate' are not, of course, independent of man's essence. Still, they are only secondary manifestations of that essence. The essential force that mediates in 'depravity' is, however, none other than freedom (often synonymous with 'free will'): that is one of the greatest of essential human forces. Freedom (free will) is inherent in *every* human being. From the standpoint of freedom as *possibility*, then, one man cannot be compared against another – for the same potential exists in the one as in the other – he can only be compared with creatures in whom this potential is *lacking*. 'Man' comes to be contrasted with 'the animals' – and sometimes, on the other side, with God, the gods, the angels, and the like.

The inquiry into freedom becomes, then, a way of posing questions that are *primarily anthropological, rather than primarily ethical*, as they had been for Christianity. Christianity placed great stress on man's ability to choose between good and evil. During the Renaissance, however, that pair of alternatives, 'good' and 'evil', paled away, to be transformed into a conviction that men (by contrast with animals) had every ability to choose between *various* courses of action. That choice *could*, of course, be a choice between good and evil, but it was not necessarily limited to that.

Freedom as an anthropological category and freedom as a social and political category at first ran parallel to each other without being interrelated. When, for example, Petrarch wrote that 'it would be better to lose life itself than to lose liberty, without which life itself is a vain mockery',[51] he meant by liberty the freedom of the republic (liberation from the power of the Roman aristocracy), and it never occurred to him to make a connection between his ideas of political freedom and the concept of free will which he had taken over from Augustine. When Nicholas of Cusa writes that freedom is the essence of man, he means by freedom a primary ontological and epistemological mark (man has free will, hence he is a mirror which either clouds or clarifies itself, hence it depends on him whether or not he comes to know the infinite and finds union with it), and he does not in the least mean to apply this concept of freedom to man's other – non-cognitive and non-ethical – activities, much less to the economic and political situation of peoples or classes. Even with Valla it is still a matter of two quite distinct categories.

As soon as the dynamism of history becomes explicit, however, as soon as it becomes clear that social and political liberation, too, is a consequence of successfully deciding among concrete alternatives which are constantly reborn and that this – successful choice among constantly arising alternatives – is the essence of man's anthropological freedom, then the two distinct concepts of freedom begin to merge. Now it is no longer the abstract possibility of choice which is interpreted as anthropological freedom, but rather the *concrete process* by which a man chooses that conduct and mode of action which is most advantageous for him (for him as a total person, *for the assertion and realization of his individuality*). Reality, as Bacon said, is a sphinx whose riddle must be solved in practice; nor is that without risk, for 'the riddles of the Sphinx have always a twofold condition attached to them; distraction and laceration of mind, if you fail to solve them; if you succeed, a kingdom'.[52]

Political freedom, then, is a state of affairs which offers the optimum conditions for the realization of anthropological freedom.

But in order for the connection to be made between the political and the anthropological-ontological concept of freedom, it was first necessary for the anthropological-ontological concept of freedom itself to emerge. It is this process that we can witness in the line of development that runs from Nicholas of Cusa through Valla, Ficino, Pico, Bovillus, and Bruno to Bacon.

For the Renaissance's anthropological concept of freedom was itself the result of a synthesis. Its two sources were *the stoic-epicurean concept of freedom* and *the Christian conception of free will*.

Having already discussed the stoic-epicurean concept of freedom earlier, I will restrict myself here to recalling that it inherited from antiquity the injunction to 'live according to nature'. The heritage was complex; it meant living according to nature on one hand, maintaining control over unnatural, unruly passions on the other, freeing oneself from the fact and the thought of death; that was what made a man free. Originally, then, the stoic-epicurean anthropological concept of freedom was not a dynamic one, for it placed its emphasis on the state of freedom rather than on the process of becoming free. In order for this concept of freedom to develop into a dynamic one it had to undergo synthesis with the free-will principle of the Christian tradition.

In the Christian conception of 'free will' the emphasis was, *a priori*, not on passivity but on activity; for free will meant that man could choose between good and evil, and thus his life and fate depended on his own choices. The choice between good and evil did not take place, however, *procul negotiis*, but amid concrete conflicts, conflicts of moral content. I might add that through the mediation of Christianity the Aristotelian category of choice, or the alternative, found its way into the consciousness of the age, where it was erroneously interpreted as free will. But however erroneous the interpretation may have been on a verbal level, it still served to make one of the important notions of Aristotelian social ethics an integral part of the philosophical tradition.

The Christian concept of free will, however, severely restricted the implications of activity latent in the notion itself. They were limited by the dogma of providence, and also by the far from negligible qualification that man of his own free will can only choose evil – and so he is responsible only for his sins – while he does good only through the grace of God, and so he has no responsibility for positive actions. Hence the common observation that the dogma of free will only relieved God of the charge of being the author of

430

the world's evils, without giving man credit for being the *primus movens* of good.

Renaissance anthropology – in its beginnings – was directly bound up with the dogma of free will. But from the very outset there were two important differences. I have already mentioned one – the fact that what was under discussion was not just choice between good and evil, but choice in general. This was an extremely important circumstance. It implied no less than the appearance of work and production in the realm of human freedom and human alternatives. Work-activity and production are also carried out by choices between alternatives; the choice and attainment of the right alternative constitutes a realization of human freedom, of 'free will'. Yet it is not at all an ethical choice. Going even further, choice between alternatives broadens out to include political choice and choice with respect to social activity generally, and among these are choices of alternatives which, ethically, cannot be characterized unambiguously.

At this point 'free will' becomes a genuine anthropological-ontological category. True, for Christianity, too, it belonged to humanity in general, since every one of Adam's descendants had free will. But they had it in only one area, in the sphere of ethics. This category now became a universal anthropological category not just because it pertained to every human being, but also because *it now pertained to every human activity.*

The second difference was a consequence of the extension which I have just described. If the will is free to choose not only between good and evil but can decide 'freely' in every kind of human activity, then there is no sense in the Christian restriction that man can only be responsible for evil, while good is a gift of God; then man is responsible for *everything*, whether he decides one way or the other, whether he brings about his own success or failure, or the success or failure of some other enterprise.

The thinkers of the Renaissance knew very well, of course, that 'free will' was not limitlessly free, but only free within certain bounds and amid the possibilities presented by certain concrete alternatives; no one of them spoke of absolute freedom. The limitations to be found in the earliest attempts to deal with this question were due to the traditional body of ideas on which they drew, for at that time the concept of freedom still had to be reconciled with divine providence or at least divine foreknowledge. Later on, the stoic-epicurean concept of necessity became 'merged' with the concept of free will. It was necessity itself which provided the alternatives among which men could choose and, furthermore, often man had to choose the

431

necessary in order to be free. This extreme solution was that of Giordano Bruno who in a paradoxical way reminiscent of Hegel declared in his dialogue between the hero and the enthusiast that freedom and necessity are actually the same thing. But if Bruno's position was an extreme one, it is still true that more or less all of the thinkers of the Renaissance took the position that man's freedom, his alternatives, and his range of choice were to be found in the 'interstices' of necessity, that he could use his wits to ferret them out, and that by so doing he could forge his *own* life and fate, the life and fate that best suited his own personality.

The combination of the idea of free will with the idea of necessity realized the synthesis of the Christian and the stoic-epicurean concepts of freedom, of which I spoke before. That synthesis determined in two important respects the kinds of questions that would be raised in later centuries and, in part, the solutions to them. I have already discussed one of these, the synthesis of the anthropological and the sociopolitical concepts of freedom. To see what sort of 'school' the Renaissance created here it is enough to point to such diverse thinkers as Spinoza, Hobbes, Leibniz, Diderot, and Rousseau. In *this* particular respect, moreover, the line extends all the way to Marx. The other respect in which the Renaissance also created a school had the effect, however – in contrast with the former – of pointing in the wrong direction most later attempts at posing certain questions. It consisted in the fact that even those conceptions which polemicized against Christianity, which were atheistic in their practical orientation, still accepted critically the category of 'free will', or at least made use of it too (as synonymous with freedom, freedom of choice, and the like). The problem of freedom, pro and con, or of relative freedom, pro and con, thus became involved with the thoroughly meaningless set of problems surrounding free will, pro and con, and relatively free will, pro and con.

It must be said, however, that although Renaissance thought opened up a sterile line of reasoning by taking up the polemic over free will, Renaissance thinking itself did not suffer so much from the erroneous way of posing this question as did later philosophies. To a certain extent Renaissance thinkers used the concept of will in 'raw', unclarified form, often merely as a synonym allegory of consciousness and choice as a whole; most of them at least were far from defining it as a psychological category, circumscribing it with precision, or 'deriving' it. In Pico, for example, free will does not refer to individual actions but to the nature of man (man has free will so that he may become a nature of either a higher or a lower order), and in this context it is obvious that 'free will' does not simply denote the *will*, but is rather more a figurative expression for the possibility of becoming free. In analysing various anthropologies we will meet more identifications of this sort.

I do not wish to analyse various concepts of freedom in isolation from these anthropologies as a whole; it would be all the more impossible to do so since they form a basic, essential component of the latter. I will simply take a look at Valla's concept of freedom by way of introduction. Indeed, the transformation of freedom into an anthropological-ontological category was his chief accomplishment. With his *De libero arbitrio* he gave rise to a school with which the mainstream of anthropological thinking on free will was identified for centuries to come.

In the dialogue between Antonio and Lorenzo, Valla sought to forge the categories of free will, divine foreknowledge, and providence into a unity free of contradictions. Leibniz was right, however, in remarking that while the attempt to reconcile free will and foreknowledge proved successful, the attempt to do the same with free will and providence was a failure. The first (successful) reconciliation was a theological question only for an extremely superficial observer. In an earlier chapter I mentioned that Valla's use of pagan examples cannot be regarded as accidental, particularly the fact that he replaces the concept of a Christian God with Apollo and Jupiter. But those observers who, at the other extreme, speak of Valla's modern, positivist way of posing the question are equally superficial. Examining the possibility of divine foreknowledge, Valla asks how there can be any kind of foreknowledge *if* there really is free will, *if* man is really confronted with alternatives and can really choose; and yet without some kind of foresight or foreknowledge – and here is the paradox – no truly free action is possible (for in order for us to choose freely we must be able to foresee events in a rough way). This is anything but a positivist way of putting the matter (and at the same time it is not a theological way either). It is simply the first formulation on a philosophical plane of a problem that was to engage the Renaissance to the very end: how can we act as freely as possible in a changing world?

As regards the problem of providence, however (rather than foreknowledge), we can witness here a genuinely teleological, theological attempt at a solution. That is why Luther sympathized with Valla and why Leibniz took an interest in him in his *Theodicy*, with the difference that Luther failed to notice what Leibniz saw clearly – namely, that Valla had failed in his demonstration of providence and so in his teleological proof. And he failed not

433

because of its scientific absurdity but because as a Renaissance thinker he was unwilling to give up the possibility of a 'free will' which asserted itself within the framework of necessity.

Valla – to summarize his argument very sketchily – starts out from the proposition that there is no contradiction between (divine) foreknowledge and free will. We, too, foresee that night will follow after day, without our being the cause of the change. Yet it may be countered that we can only foresee what is certain. To that Valla rejoins that we *can* foresee actions that flow from free will, because 'something that can happen and something that *will* happen are very different'.[55] A man may often exercise choice and yet it may still be possible to foresee what he will choose, by reason of his character. When, for example, Sextus turned to Apollo to learn his future, the deity foretold that he would do wrong. Sextus asked that his fate be changed, whereupon Apollo replied that he could only prophesy, but could not alter fate:[54]

Jupiter as he created the wolf fierce, the hare timid, the lion brave, the ass stupid, the dog savage, the sheep mild, so he fashioned some men hard of heart, others soft, he generated one given to evil, the other to virtue, and, further, he gave a capacity for reform to one and made another incorrigible. To you, indeed, he assigned an evil soul with no resource for reform. And so both you, for your inborn character, will do evil, and Jupiter, on account of your actions and their evil effects, will punish sternly, and thus he has sworn by the Stygian swamp it will be.

Valla does not give us an answer to the question of what happens to foreknowledge in the case of a 'reformable' character, or how we can foresee in which 'moments' it will reform and in which it will not. In the dialectic of fate and character he puts the emphasis on the side of character more heavily than his successors did, and thus he ascribes to knowledge of men a greater role in foreknowledge than he does to knowledge of the situation. I have no desire to linger over the weaknesses in Valla's argument, and I will forego any analysis of how this position – strongly fatalistic as regards character even while preserving free will – was connected with the fact that Valla belonged to the old Roman patricianate, which was accommodating itself only with great difficulty to the new age. And yet his conception was important and productive, for it succeeded in grasping how freedom and foreknowledge presuppose each other. Now it became possible to apprehend and analyse scientifically the structure of reality notwithstanding the presupposition of freedom and even its necessity. Moreover, there appeared – if only in broad outline – the idea that although freedom is the anthropological essence of man, that still does not mean that men are *de facto* free, for (as Valla here analyses it) their own *earlier* actions and decisions go a long way to determine just how far the *ontologically given* alternatives open to men are *real* alternatives, and how far the possibility of choice represents a real choice. The contradiction which I have discussed before, between man's anthropological potential and his actual fate, is here taken note of for the first time with a claim to scientific objectivity.

The idea that man's possibilities and his fate might often be in conflict was, of course, not a strange one in ancient (and Christian) thought either. But there – as I have said in another context – this conflict was described in terms of the then-existing categories of happiness and unhappiness, which at that time were still ethical categories. Whoever possessed the right human forces, the virtues, had no need of anything else, except good fortune, in order to be happy. During the Renaissance the formula *sors bona, nihil aliud* was applied not to happiness, but to freedom. The man who possessed the right faculties – and these were not necessarily ethical ones, but could also have to do with overall solidity of human substance, with his astuteness and resourcefulness as a human being as well – still required circumstances in which his forces could unfold in order to set his stamp upon the world and to become free. The fact that 'freedom' was now becoming the central category of both ethics *and* anthropology was a sign that the old 'natural' communities were breaking up, and that mankind was entering a new era of its socialization, in which process (the process of becoming free) an unbounded activity would dominate.

Freedom as the mere possibility of becoming free did not, however, mediate only in the direction of a process of becoming free. As I have said freedom mediated in the direction of depravity as well. If *other* forces of human essence came to ruin and if thereby freedom – as process and result – was lost as well, then the root of the trouble lay in freedom itself. The link between freedom and depravity was not an 'event' in some prehistoric, mythical world. It did not begin with Adam's creation and end with Adam's sin; rather, it went on day after day. The thinkers of the Renaissance – as I have said – did not believe in 'original' sin. According to Valla, for example, man's punishment was not his 'sinfulness', but his *mortality*. For the philosophers of the Renaissance the concept of depravity had meaning, and was connected with free will, only in so far as any age, nation, social group, or person could 'become depraved'. Every man could, by reason of his freedom, throw away his essential humanity. We did not inherit Adam's sin; but we could follow his example. Thus man's wickedness was not a part of the essence of man, but a part of his essence as a free agent; it was a necessary attribute of his freedom that he *could* be evil, that for a time – perhaps even a whole lifetime – he could irreparably pervert himself. And that was true not only of individual men, but of whole generations as well. Man's smallness lay in the fact that he himself could squander his own greatness. In that, the concept of freedom represented the focal point of Renaissance anthropology.

Renaissance anthropology took over from antiquity two basic axioms. One was that man was a *natural being* (stoicism and epicureanism), the other that man was a *social being* (Aristotle). Whether the myth of creation was retained or reinterpreted (now, of course, consciously as a myth rather than as reality), or whether the question of the genesis of mankind and of the 'first' man was simply left aside, no one doubted the existence of a kind of 'primordial natural stage' of the development of man. The stoic-epicurean tradition was scientifically and critically extended. For stoicism and epicureanism – at least during antiquity – 'human nature' was a fact of the ontology of nature only to a very limited degree. The ensemble of concrete human affects was termed 'human nature', and the complex of socialized needs, wants, and passions was included in it as well. There were two points of contact with nature 'as a whole', with nature in itself: the satisfaction of needs, and death. The emphasis fell, then, on the passive endurance of nature and the natural. We know that for Aristotle, who first examined the process of work and the teleology of work in a scholarly way, labour was not an anthropological category; the Renaissance could not draw upon this source, either, for an active interpretation of the concept of 'human nature'. A *substantive* reinterpretation of the category of 'human nature' was the 'order of the day'. For an active relationship to nature – work – had, as I have already said, itself become an anthropological category. The fact that man was a 'natural being' *still* implied the necessity of coming to terms with the 'natural' passions and with death; but *now* it *also* implied an active relationship to nature as a whole (nature in itself), a relationship in which *like* would act upon *like*, the micro-cosm upon the macrocosm, and would thereby acquire 'power'. The best thinkers of the Renaissance were clearly aware that the reason why man could acquire command over nature and make an impact upon her was that he was a part of nature, and her laws operated in him as well as elsewhere. Thus he could, as Bovillus wrote, create actuality out of potentiality. 'Man is the brilliance, light, knowledge and soul of the world; while the whole world is as the body of man.'[55]

I have already mentioned how the traditional myths (above all the Biblical myths) were reinterpreted in order to demonstrate man's character as a 'natural being'. As an example, I might cite the views of Paracelsus:[56]

If man were not of the world, but rather of the heavens, then he would eat celestial bread from the skies, together with the angels. *But he is of the earth and made of elements, and that is why he must sustain himself upon them. And so he cannot survive without the world; without it he is dead. And so, like the world, he is dust and ashes.*

Here nature appears only as the indispensable basis for man's nourishment. But as we know from other sources, the notion that nature was the source of man's means of production had also become a commonplace.

The concept of *man's societality* was also modified. For antiquity, the social man was a man who belonged to a given community. During the Renaissance, however, *the concepts of societality and of membership in a given community or group became divorced from each other*. That became possible because of the discovery of 'the human species', or 'humanity'. More and more, then, man's societality came only to mean that every man was necessarily a part of humanity, and that his characteristics were the species characteristics of man. Every concrete social structure, whether family, polis, or nation, now appeared to be merely a 'part' of 'humanity'. 'For', as Pomponazzi wrote, 'the whole human race is like a single body composed of different members, also with different functions, yet ordered to the common advantage of the human race.'[57] This discovery, growing necessarily out of the evolution of the first forms of bourgeois production, went far beyond the 'cosmopolitanism' of the late Roman era. The attitude of the stoic cosmopolite was a *negative* one: it represented a simple turning-away from the bloody internal struggles of the Roman Empire, and strove to preserve every human achievement. The basic attitude underlying the Renaissance concept of humanity was a positive one: a turning towards this newly discovered universal humanity, and a constant, conscious effort to work for the betterment of this 'great whole'. At the same time, it cannot be stressed enough that the old 'cosmopolitan' attitude did not rest upon an anthropological foundation, for even

WHAT IS MAN CAPABLE OF?

late antiquity did not recognize the potential equality of all men and
thus had no concept of a unitary human species.

It was the general tendency of the Renaissance to award first
place in the hierarchy of larger and smaller communities to humanity
as a whole, as the community which comprehended within itself all
others. The measure of scientific and artistic achievements was the
degree to which they became the property of *all* mankind, even if
only potentially. Bacon consciously formulated this hierarchy
which appears spontaneously almost everywhere:[58]

> It will not be amiss to distinguish the three kinds and as it
> were grades of ambition in mankind. The first is of those who
> desire to extend their own power in their native country;
> which kind is vulgar and degenerate. The second is of those who
> labour to extend the power of their country and its dominion
> among men. This certainly has more dignity, though not less
> covetousness. But if a man endeavour *to establish and extend
> the power and dominion of the human race itself over the universe*,
> his ambition (if ambition it can be called) is without doubt
> both a more wholesome thing and a more noble than the other
> two.

Here, however, two questions arise. The first is whether the
Renaissance did not give recognition to the division of the human
species into races, and the second, whether the cohesiveness of the
nations which were emerging at that time did not overshadow the
appeal of humanity and of the concept of humanity.

The first question is easily answered. Racial theories were quite
unknown to the Renaissance. Georg Lukács has shown in his
Dethronement of Reason what a *late* philosophical development
such theories were. True, Campanella spoke of the 'breeding' of
the human species; that is why fascist historians have – unjustly –
referred back to him. But Campanella did not recognize *within* the
human species any distinctions between superior and inferior races,
nor did he recommend any kind of elite breeding; he simply tossed
off the idea that it might be possible to develop the *whole human
species* biologically, through eugenic methods. By 'race', then, he
meant the human species itself, all of humanity, setting out from
the scientifically false premise that it was possible, even necessary, to
improve mankind biologically. That, however, was merely a mistaken
anthropological notion, and not in the least an attempt at a theory of
race.

The answer to the second question is much more complicated. It is
common knowledge that the formation of national states took place

during the same age which saw the emergence of a consciousness of human universality, and that the problems created by the evolution of nations played a role of the first importance for more than one thinker (of whom I need only cite Machiavelli). During the Renaissance, however, the problem of the nation was never a problem of philosophical anthropology, but rather one of political philosophy. First of all, while 'human' qualities were regarded as being eternally and generally characteristic, national traits were never thought of in the same way. The genesis of the national state took place before the very eyes of the thinkers of the Renaissance; they were still too close to the process of the emergence of nations to entertain those kinds of illusions. National characteristics, whether in ancient peoples or modern nations were derived from political institutions, economic institutions, centuries-old systems of custom, and the like. It was a commonplace in the literature of the time that national characteristics *change* along with political institutions; what was constant in them was precisely what was 'human' and displayed kinship with all mankind.

It cannot be denied that later on many national features appeared in the *manner* of formulating anthropological questions; the history of national class struggles and other national experiences set its stamp on the way anthropological questions were posed, even where a supranational continuity is apparent, as in the line running from Hume to Rousseau to Kant. This difference in 'manner' was present during the Renaissance, too, though in lesser degree, as we have seen in connection with the problem of uneven development. That appears very clearly if we compare such contemporaries as Nicholas of Cusa and Ficino, or Telesio and Montaigne. (In addition to national differences, moreover, we must also reckon with local differences in the development of the various city-states.) But what is true of the 'manner' is not true of the subject matter of philosophy. The *prime subject of social philosophy* – the one that occupied the pinnacle of the hierarchy of concerns – *was always 'man', that is, the most highly and generally integrated society of the age.* During antiquity, to inquire about 'man' meant asking about 'the citizen of the polis', for the polis itself represented the highest kind of integration. Thus ancient social philosophy, when it asked about 'man', necessarily asked about the city-state at the same time. During the Renaissance – as we have seen – it became possible to recognize the highest-order integration of all: humanity. And yet here a striking conflict appears, for humanity becomes a 'being-for-us' before it becomes a 'being-for-itself'; in men's consciousness humanity appears at the summit of the hierarchy of integration, even while a being-for-itself it is not yet present but, on the contrary, is falling apart into nations in sharp conflict with one another. That same process of bourgeois development which made possible the recognition and the abstract idealization of humanity also made necessary an economic and political struggle between national states lasting for centuries and not yet concluded even in our own day. Philosophy, however – as I have said – is always oriented towards the widest possible integration; thus even in the age of great national upsurge the problematics of the nation did not become the subject of philosophy. Plato's ideal state sought to solve the conflicts of the Athenian polis; it was, as Marx said, 'an Athenian idealization of the Egyptian caste system'. More's *Utopia*, though it drew directly upon the experience of English primitive accumulation for its critique, set up a norm for *all* mankind. Art depicted the concrete development of nations, its events and conflicts (literature above all, though even then in such a way, of course, as always to point, in the last analysis, towards the problematics of mankind as a whole); history, too, reflected it (Aristotle correctly recognized the kinship between these two modes of representation) – but philosophy never did. Even when it dealt with politics, which during the Renaissance was pre-eminently national politics, even in Machiavelli, whose theories had the avowed goal of creating national unity, *what* was being discussed (in Machiavelli's case the relation between political morality and morality in general) was never a national matter, but a matter of mankind in general. When a Renaissance philosopher speaks of the nation, he always speaks of it as a part of mankind; if he speaks of national character, he means by it one kind of manifestation of 'man'; when he deals with politics he is not dealing with society in its entirety, but only with one, partial aspect of it.

Unquestionably, Christianity played an important part in the development of the concept of mankind as a 'being-for-us'. Here again I may refer to Engels's perceptive observation that 'equality in the sight of God' (brotherhood in Christ, and a common Christian consciousness) laid the groundwork for the concept of equality in general – and, I might add, for Renaissance anthropology only necessary to secularize the Christian concept of equality and thereby equate Christians and non-Christians. The thinkers of the Renaissance, who had grown up on the pre-sixteenth-century ideal of a universal Christendom and who in the sixteenth century protested almost to a man against the schism brought about in Christendom by the Reformation, found it much more natural to deal with the notion of a universal humanity and treated it as a

WHAT IS MAN CAPABLE OF?

self-evident fact much more than did their successors later on, raised as they were in a tradition of national struggles.

It may seem paradoxical that *the appearance in philosophy of humanity, the highest form of integration, was contemporary with a methodology which set out from the individual.* In the chapter dealing with the emergence of the individual I spoke at length of this methodological peculiarity. I described how it gradually gained ground and how, by the fifteenth and sixteenth centuries, it had become dominant. I noted that the analyses of Vives and Telesio, for example, both began strictly with the individual, with the society of individuals being bound together through the category of *commiseratio*. I pointed to the seeds of contract theory in Bodin. In other chapters I arrived from other directions at similar conclusions. Thus, for example, in examining the microcosm-macrocosm parallel we saw that in Carolus Bovillus it was the individual in whose consciousness the structure of the whole macrocosm is reproduced, and that the proponents of this thesis in general regarded the individual (as a microcosm) as a replica of the macrocosm. As striking examples to the contrary I can cite only the brilliant aphorism of Pico or the views of Pomponazzi, a man who lived within the bounds of the polis and was even more strongly influenced by Aristotle than was Pico.

I must repeat that this kind of methodology gained ground only *gradually*. It was most pronounced in those thinkers whose views were not conditioned by the polis, and even there it was a relatively late development. Dante, for example, was strongly influenced in his thinking by the city-state community, however much monarchy may have been his ideal. The same is true of Petrarch, even though he lived in voluntary or involuntary exile. Only those were not polis-determined who in their lives, in the social basis of the motives which guided their ethics and behaviour, did not belong to any group or stratum of communal character; these were neither aristocratic nor democratic, neither Guelph nor Ghibelline, but citizens in the modern sense of the word, Italians or Frenchmen in the modern sense.

I must reiterate that these higher-order and more general forms of integration (class, nation, humanity), appearing amid the circumstances of the extension of bourgeois production relations – hence of commodity production – and springing from a kind of thinking that was already bourgeois or becoming so, necessarily entailed the methodology of the individual (other kinds of integration, deeply rooted in some hierarchical structure, did not result in the formulation of any independent philosophical world-view; rather, each in its own way reproduced the religious outlook). So long as the

441

individual was *himself* only while he was a member of some community (Athenian or Florentine, that of the feudal order or that of
the craft guild), and could be deprived of his identity if he was
expelled from that community (so much so that not even an *ideal*
connection could be maintained), it was natural for everyone (and
for every philosopher) to see man as a *zoon politikon*, and so not
just a *social* being but also a *political* being, a member of a *given*
political (or other) community. With the dissolution of these natural
communities, however, and the appearance of higher-order forms of
integration, this 'naturalness' was at an end. Man remained, indeed,
a part of a whole – whether that whole was a class, a nation,
humanity, or all three – but he was a part of it only from the standpoint of the *division of labour*. He was not necessarily a 'political
being' with his *whole* essence. For these higher-order forms of
integration created the appearance that they themselves were not
primary entities (compared to the individual), but secondary ones.
It was individual men who produced commodities, entered into
contact with one another, and 'constituted' societies (sometimes by
means of a contract). The individual was the starting-point, and
society the result – a collection of individuals. Of course, this
appearance did not arise *simply* from commodity production. For
among the higher-order forms of integration there were two (class,
nation) where man had a certain amount of free choice, and so
these forms of integration did not relate to the essence of his
existence; what was essential was the individual, while his belonging
to one of these forms of integration was derivative. Without Athens
the Athenian was not a 'genuine' human being; every thought, deed
and desire of his was oriented towards the community. The same was
true of the Florentine citizen of the fourteenth century. A nobleman
could not lose his nobility so long as he lived – his nobility was the
essence of his individual existence. Now, however, a citizen of an
Italian city-state could easily put down roots – as a bourgeois – in
England, for example, and might even feel more at home there
than in his own country. A bourgeois could become ennobled (nor
was this a random occurrence, but rather a socially typical one),
while no one any longer 'saw' in an impoverished nobleman his
noble ancestors; he was 'himself', no more, no less, which was as
much as to say that he was *not* synonymous with his 'roots'; his
roots were no longer identical with his community.

It was only with respect to the most general of these integrations–
that with humanity – that this 'freedom of choice' did not apply. Of
course, each human being always had to choose over and over again
his character as a human being – he could become more elevated, or

more depraved – but he could not *entirely* lose his human essence, his freedom, his alternatives. But this kind of integration – the one available to everyone – was the most abstract and the most mediated.

Mediation is a far from negligible aspect of this whole complex of questions. The ties and relationships of the community preserved a great deal of the 'face-to-face' relations of groups. The citizens of a town all knew one another. Where formal democracy existed, all citizens met personally in the exercise of their social rights and obligations. The members of the guilds and of the various feudal orders also enjoyed the possibility of forming face-to-face acquaintanceships and other kinds of direct ties. Community integration was manifested through immediate human ties. This was true of hierarchical relations as well: employers and workers in the guilds, lord and peasant on the estate stood likewise in a personal relationship to each other – exploitation itself had not yet taken on an impersonal face. But in the higher-order integrations which were becoming fundamental during the Renaissance these immediate links were dissolved. One man was no longer connected personally with another man, in whose character as a member of a community he could recognize himself and his own nature as a community being; rather, he was 'connected' with him through institutions, and first and foremost through commodity relations. In this wider integration immediate communities did not, of course, cease to exist entirely. But since they had lost the fundamental role which they had enjoyed in human life, they themselves came to appear derivative. There arose the appearance that society was made up of individuals, and that this had 'generated' the primary communities. Only the family, perhaps, with its direct ties of blood, remained exempt from this appearance – and yet even the family did not always remain so. In the case of class, one's relation to the means of production and one's share in the distribution of income were, as was evident to everyone, mediated. Indeed, people were much more aware of this in a dynamic age, when in a matter of days men could 'change places' in the social hierarchy, than they were in the later centuries of bourgeois society, when class membership created the false impression that this was a natural, 'inborn' matter. Thus the link with humanity – the fact that every individual was a 'human being' – became the only link that was recognized as *natural*. At the same time it was the most abstract and most mediated one. It was not only that a man had no way of 'personally knowing' humanity, but also that there were, in that age, no institutions, no ways and means through which one could 'act for humanity' – at least not on the plane of social and political activity.

There were, nevertheless, some 'planes' on which 'acting for humanity' appeared feasible already in this age. Among them were firm moral conduct as a *way of setting an example*, successful 'navigation' in a value-system devoid of any fixed roster of values, and, moreover, the sort of objectification which could be enjoyed, *in principle*, by every human being: scientific and artistic activity and technical discovery. In the Renaissance's hierarchy of activities these came more and more to occupy the premier place. Of course, this was – to repeat – not the case everywhere, and it was not true of everyone. It was truer in those countries where national unity and a national monarchy had indeed developed (such as England, France, and Spain), and less true in those places – like Italy – where national unity, the indispensable condition of bourgeois progress, was never achieved (late fifteenth and early sixteenth centuries).

This complex process is reflected in the anthropologies of the time. It was the individual which they studied, and yet in his characteristics they sought for and analysed the *general*, the traits that were typical of *every* human being, hence of humanity as a species. Yet it was still as an individual that they examined him, and it was from a species essence perceived and analysed in the individual that they 'derived' or 'based' his social relations and the necessity of those social relations (and even this was not done everywhere). *The subject of Renaissance anthropology, then, was a primarily social being whose society was made up of its individuals.*

After this, it is unnecessary to spend much time demonstrating that it was not only from lack of scientific raw materials that the Renaissance had no conception of the evolution of man and society. Its writers did not even take up the question; their fancy did not even turn in this direction. Man was eternal and universal, and so there *had* to be a unitary human 'beginning'. Here the myth of genesis came to their assistance, a story which – to repeat – they treated *as myth*, interpreting it not at all in its literal religious content. But the fact that they *did* retain it as a myth – and practically *all* of them retained it, even Giordano Bruno and at times Bacon – betrays the absence of a real genesis.

To repeat: for every Renaissance thinker the theoretical point of departure in dealing with the essence of man was *free will*, or the existence of *alternatives*. The *culmination* of man's humanity, again, was *freedom* – but now it was a freedom interpreted in many different ways. There were those – in the stoic tradition – for whom the culmination of freedom was complete *self-rule*, while for others – in the epicurean tradition – it was the *humanization of every instinct and passion.* For others, again, it meant an absolute *awakening to self-consciousness*; in one of its interpretations this implied the *complete reproduction of the macrocosm in the microcosm*, while in another interpretation it meant *man's awakening to an awareness of his own essential powers*, those specific to him. Still another, later tendency understood by freedom a *dominion over the external world of objective nature*. The various solutions were interrelated, sometimes organically, sometimes not, sometimes consciously and sometimes unconsciously. One of the products of this interrelationship was the notion of *deification.*

All of these things, taken in their entirety, formed the subject of anthropology, broadly defined – the concept of man. That is why I have analysed them, with one exception, in the foregoing pages. The one exception was the interpretation of freedom according to which the goal for man was 'to awaken to a consciousness of his own essential forces'. That must be preceded by an analysis of those 'essential forces'. This is the subject of anthropology in the narrow sense. I will have more to say about it later on.

If freedom is the starting-point and the goal of the human essence, the means of achieving that goal are *intellect and work*. This again was a conception characteristic of all Renaissance thought generally. Giordano Bruno summed it up aptly when he wrote:[59]

> The gods endowed man with intellect and hands and made
> him like unto themselves, giving him power over the other
> animals; the which consists not only in being able to work
> according to the normal order of nature, but even going beyond
> her laws; so that, shaping or being able to shape other
> natures, other courses, other systems with his mind, with that
> freedom without which the said similarity would not exist, he
> comes to be like a god on earth.

What are those essential forces of men which develop on the foundation of freedom, with the aid of hand and intellect, and which in the end make man into an earthly god? They are (1) the capacity and the exercise of *creativity* (work, art, science, technique); (2) *self-creation* – including the development of his ethical substance and self-awareness; (3) *versatility*; (4) *dissatisfaction* (insatiability), and (5), as a manifestation of the latter, *limitlessness* with respect to knowledge, creation, and the satisfaction of needs.

If I wish to discuss Renaissance anthropology in the 'narrow sense', I must speak first and foremost of *Ficino* and *Pico della Mirandola*. Their arguments are the ones which analyse most cogently and most coherently those 'essential forces' which I mentioned before. Their philosophical hymns to human greatness were composed in the Florence of the fifteenth century. And they were written at that fortunate historical moment when the values worked out over the centuries in the Florentine polis – civil liberty, equality (even if only formal), many-sidedness in both senses of the word (relatively marked degree of versatility in individuals, and the beginnings of a many-sided bourgeois division of labour), creativity as an attribute of human life, and the like – were *still* a living tradition and in part an everyday praxis, and yet when the slackening of the bonds of the polis and the onset of its slow dissolution had *already* made possible an outlook on the problems of humanity which went beyond the perspectives of the polis.

I cannot stress enough, however, that the problems analysed by Ficino and Pico were not of their own invention; they inherited them, each in his own way, and their less fortunate successors inherited them from them in the same way. We have seen before, in many connections, how this happened. Here I should only like to cite a few examples, in order to bring home the *similarity of the reasoning*. Buckhardt cites the opinion of Petrarch that men are capable of doing anything on their own once they will it. Nicholas of Cusa, who defined man as the *nexus universitatis entitum*, had this to say in speaking of his essence:[60]

> Within the potentiality of man all exists, after its own
> fashion. In humanity all is human – as in the universe all unfolds
> universally. The world exists here as a human one. . . . Nothing
> sets bounds to the creative activity of humanity but humanity itself.

(Here we can trace clearly how the ideas of many-sidedness, limitless possibility, and the microcosm are connected.)

Giannozzo Manetti, his *De dignitate et excellentia hominis*, weighs, among other things, the difference between animals and men, noting that animals stick to *one* way of life because that is their instinct, while man has no such instinct and therefore is able to become the master of *every* art. Machiavelli talks a great deal about the boundlessness of human needs and the impossibility of satisfying them, and about the sources of 'eternal discontent'. What is more, even the opponents of Renaissance anthropology were unable to escape from the influence of its general truths. Colet recognized that the intellect strives after the infinite and cannot be satisfied, and that was why he wanted it to be restrained. Luther applied the idea of self-creation to that fancied figure of Christian mythology, the devil, who, he wrote, 'has grown very clever and shrewd from long practice'.[61]

446

In Ficino's anthropology, the comparison with the animals as living beings of a lower order serves very effectively to bring out the essence of man – that special natural being – as something transcending nature.

'We observe that they [the animals] never act except in so far as they are driven by a natural impulse toward a necessity of nature.'[62] As for men, by comparison, 'we see that by a natural instinct every soul strives in a continuous effort both to know all truth by the intellect and to enjoy all good things by the will'.[63] Here, then, the proposition is advanced that the natural instincts of animals and men are different. The animal's instinct prompts him to a limited existence, while man's instinct urges him towards the infinite. Human nature, then, is limitless and unsatisfiable. Here already, at the moment of its birth, we can observe one of the peculiarities of bourgeois anthropology, by which it generalizes the nature of the men of a given age into 'human nature' *per se*; the 'nature' of dynamic man, the man of emerging bourgeois society, an unsatisfiable being striving for the infinite, an individual constantly changing in his needs and desires, is hypostasized here into the 'eternally human'. Yet here this generalization (leaving the theoretical errors aside) still did not prove to be such a stumbling-block as it did for the anthropology of the seventeenth century. For it hypostasized as eternal properties which really always had been human properties – if in smaller measure and with a different content – ever since man rose from the animal world, and which really were coming to the surface forcefully in bourgeois production.

What is problematic in Ficino's arguments about the boundless aspirations of 'human nature' is the ambiguous position which he took towards them. On the one hand he greatly esteemed this dissatisfaction and discontent, but on the other hand he shared the notion of the teleology of antiquity that *what was perfect was that which attained its end*. Only those human strivings could be called fulfilled which attained their goal. That goal could not be reached on earth (that was contradictory to human nature) – and so the achievement of the goal could only be union with God in knowledge and love. We cannot hold this ambiguity against Ficino if we consider that even in Spinoza's *amor dei intellectualis* we still come upon traces of it.

The insatiability of human needs stands in a reciprocal relationship with the *limitless potential for the development of human work* (*creativity*). Not only does production (work) grow quantitatively, and needs along with it – needs are also transformed, and they expand; new branches of production are accompanied by new needs, and vice versa.

447

Every other creature gets along without any special skills, or else disposes of only one [cf. Manetti's notion – A. H.]; that skill, however, is not one which he has forged for himself, but which the law of fate has imposed upon him [*fatali lege trahuntur*]. That is shown by the fact that with the passage of time they do not make any progress in their skill, in manufacturing their products. Men, by contrast, are the discoverers of countless arts, and they practise them with a free will. That springs from the fact that any single man can practise several arts, and can alternate among them, and so with time he becomes much more adept.[64]

It is interesting to observe how Ficino, ambiguous in his judgment of the infinite insatiability of wants and desires, unambiguously comes down in favour of the *performance of labour* itself. That is an indication of how little labour was alienated in Florence in this period. The more alienated labour becomes, the more anthropology's judgment on it is reversed. Then it affirms more unequivocally the development of needs and their growing satisfaction, but affirms less strongly the process of work as the developer of human capacities.

Thus the universality of abilities and their development is what, according to Ficino, characterizes the process of work. Having analysed before the role of work in creating man, he now turns to the problem of creation in the objective world, in 'works', and to the problem of transforming nature. 'And what is wondrous: human arts bring forth everything that nature brings forth.'[65] The glass and metal with which man improves and perfects the works of inferior nature are a proof 'that we are not the slaves of nature, but rather her rivals'.[66] External and internal harmony in struggle, in many-sidedness, in growth and development: humanity rises to contest nature, and finds in that contest its happiness.

It is the limitless development of work (technique) which creates tools and materials (objects) for the satisfaction of wants, for enjoyment. 'Thus there arises that inexhaustible multitude of pleasures which delights the five senses of our body, and which we have produced for ourselves with the help of our own ingenuity.'[67] But the mind of man strives not only to gratify the desires of the five senses, but also to satisfy the demands of the world of imagination and fancy: thus art is born. (It was very much a Florentine notion to derive the origin of art and artistic creation directly from work and technique.) Again: 'The thinking spirit operates in a more serious way, and rushes forward to bring its children into being, and clearly shows the power of its ingenuity in the many fabrics of silk and cotton, in paintings, in statues, and in buildings.'[68] What then is the result of the development of technique and work? The growth of enjoyments, of their variety, and of the multitude of satisfactions: objects of use, objects of fancy, beauty, and so on.

Man is not content with one element. He uses *every* element as the object and instrument of his labour; yet he not only uses but beautifies them as well, as cultivation beautifies the earth. Only the 'heavenly material' is lacking for him to become a god. Here again are the lines I cited before in connection with the problem of deification:[69]

> Who could deny that man possesses as it were almost the same genius as the Author of the heavens? And who could deny that man could somehow also make the heavens, could he only obtain the instruments and the heavenly material, since even now he makes them, though of a different material, but still with a very similar order?

I have mentioned several times how Ficino, who looked upon the limitlessness of the development of work and technique with pleasure, regarded with ambiguity man's insatiability, that 'Faustian nature' which he called *inquietudo animi*. Here it is not a matter of a contradiction between the spirit and the body (the senses). According to Ficino – as is clear from the quotations – striving after the infinite, even with respect to pleasures, is a property of the mind. His genius saw that it was not physiological, biological needs themselves which remained 'unsatisfied'; it was, rather, the 'mind' which made it impossible to satisfy them. Nothing is either good or bad, as Hamlet said, speaking of ethics, but thinking makes it so. For Ficino, too, the insatiability of the senses is a question of the 'mind', that is of the whole man. He was not thinking of a *category* of 'socialized needs', yet it was that *fact* which he was trying to describe.

But to return to the ambiguity in his thought: the existence, on one hand, of non-alienated labour, satisfying to man, made enjoyment on the other very problematical indeed at that time, *in the given historical circumstances*. I have referred frequently to the fact that the process of bourgeois reproduction had not yet begun. Thus while the alienation of labour was still minor in extent, enjoyments were unevenly distributed (from luxury to the inadequate satisfaction of needs); moreover, the enjoyments of the rich could be increased, in principle, infinitely, for there was not the same necessity to 're-invest' as existed after the beginning of bourgeois reproduction. *Inquietudo animi* meant an unbelievably violent struggle for power and wealth, for boundless possibilities of sensual pleasure, or for

449

the acquisition of the nobler pleasures (works of art, for example). Physical gratification *no longer* defined the limits of pleasure, nor did accumulation set limits to it *as yet*. I have already discussed, in characterizing the individualism of the age, the psychological and moral consequences of this state of affairs. But now consider Ficino's description of it:[70]

> Thus man does not wish to have anyone above him, or on a par with him, and will not tolerate it if something remains outside his power. But that condition can only be God's. That is why man desires the status of a god.

This 'divine status' and the need for it do not, however, pertain only to mankind as a whole. The *individual* man wants this divine position *for himself*, and he asserts this insatiable desire *against* his fellow men: 'Many philosophers and princes have demanded for themselves a divine respect. They were not content to be seen as good men, but demanded at the same time that they be regarded as gods.'[71] It was the boundless and unrestrained individualism of this 'Faustian nature' which made ambiguous, in Ficino's eyes, that *inquietudo animi* which he analysed with such enthusiasm in relation to the boundlessness of knowledge and the limitless development of work, technique, and art. That is why Ficino requires – *ethically*, then – the postulate of rest in contemplation of God, the attainment of the goal, *perfection* as *contentment*.

If the creation, many-sidedness, restlessness and limitlessness which sprang from freedom occupy the centre of Ficino's anthropology, for Pico della Mirandola it is the idea of *self-creation* which becomes central. This modification reflects the difference in their overall ethics. We should recall that ethics for Ficino was customary ethics (*Sittlichkeit*), while for Pico it was morality (*Moralität*); Ficino was still rooted in the prevailing mores of the Florentine polis, while Pico opposed to their rapid dissolution a postulate of moral fortitude so rigorous, in many ways, as to point towards Savonarola. His stress on *individual responsibility* is reflected in his anthropology. He made use of everything that Ficino and Manetti had said before him, but he tied it all in with the main thread of self-creation. It is his brilliant *Oration on the Dignity of Man* to which I refer.

The work begins with a panegyric on man – nothing is more admirable than man. But having committed these – by now traditional – ideas to paper, Pico was aware that he had to go further: 'The many grounds for the excellence of human nature reported by many men failed to satisfy me. . . .'[72] He uses a reinterpretation of the Biblical myth to express his own concept of man.

The great work of creation was brought to completion when 'the best of artisans ordained that that creature to whom He had been able to give nothing proper to himself should have joint possession of whatever had been peculiar to each of the different kinds of being'.[73] Before proceeding I must pause over this brilliant notion, tossed off though it may be in the form of an aphorism. For here Pico did no less than sketch in outline the difference between the relationship of species and individual in the animal world, and the same relationship among mankind. In animals the characteristics of the species are identical with those of the individual; the individual is a direct representative of his species. In man the two do not coincide. What is 'human' is what the species as a *whole* represents, and the capacities of the individual do not coincide with the capacities of the species. In Ficino's anthropology 'man' was still identical with 'every human being'; here man is identified – if only aphoristically – with humanity. Pomponazzi – in whom we have observed similar tendencies – is in this respect directly linked with Pico. But to continue with the *Oration*:[74]

He therefore took man as a creature of indeterminate nature and, assigning him a place in the middle of the world, addressed him thus: 'Neither a fixed abode nor a form that is thine alone nor any function peculiar to thyself have We given thee, Adam, to the end that according to thy longing and according to thy judgment thou mayest have and possess what abode, what form, and what functions thou thyself shalt desire. The nature of all other beings is limited and constrained within the bounds of laws prescribed by Us. Thou, constrained by no limits, in accordance with thine own free will, in whose hand We have placed thee, shalt ordain for thyself the limits of thy nature.

For Ficino there still was a 'human nature'; dynamic man still possessed his *concrete characteristics*. But now his 'beginning' holds only two characteristics: free will, and universality solely as a *possibility*. The uniqueness of man is that he creates himself, *forms and shapes his own nature. The concept of 'human nature' has itself become dynamic.*

And yet the transformation of human nature into something dynamic is a brilliant aphorism and nothing more. For when Pico speaks of man's realizing his potential – of how and in what direction he can mould his nature, what sort of nature he can choose for himself through free will – then the material question *becomes narrowed to a moral and ethical one*. Pico sees in the development of human nature only two directions, up or down: bestialization and

451

depravity on one hand, deification on the other. He describes a human being in whom the Divine Father placed, at the moment of his birth, 'the seeds of all possibilities', a being who is a 'chameleon'. But in describing the concrete realization of those possibilities he says only that 'thou shalt have the power to degenerate into the lower forms of life, which are brutish. Thou shalt have the power, out of thy soul's judgment, to be reborn into the higher forms, which are divine'.[75] Here there is – by contrast with Ficino – scarcely anything about creativity, work, or the use of tools, and nothing at all about technical universality. Pico with his notion of the 'self-creation of nature' means only to say that man (or humanity) is always responsible for his own fate and, moreover, for his own nature as well; he cannot call upon 'eternal nature' as an excuse. It was, then – to repeat – a moralist who discovered the idea of self-creation.

After this we should not wonder that the ideas of individual perfection, rest, and attainment of the goal retained their validity for Pico just as much as they had for Ficino. At the end of the *Oration* he lists the three Delphic utterances through which 'we can attain to the true divine Apollo' – the precepts, then, of the finest human conduct:[76]

'Nothing too much,' [which] prescribes a standard and rule for all the virtues through the doctrine of the Mean, with which moral philosophy deals.

'Know thyself,' [which] urges and encourages us to the investigation of all nature, of which the nature of man is the connecting link. . . .

The theological greeting . . . 'Thou art,' [with which] we shall likewise in bliss be addressing the true Apollo on intimate terms.

The first precept is antiquity's, the second that of the modern world, the third that of a Christianity permeated with mysticism and the ideal of beauty. It is thus that past, present, and future are fused together.

The revolution of the Renaissance was a revolution in the conception of man. Liberty, equality, and fraternity *together* became an anthropological category, and with that humanity awakened for the first time, *as humanity*, to self-consciousness. Similarly, freedom, work, many-sidedness, boundlessness *together* represented the essence of man, his 'nature', and thereby it was declared that man was capable of *all things*. But the first explorations of the earth and, presently, of the universe, gave notice that in the process of realizing man's potentialities the present was not the end, but only the beginning. Amid the cataclysms of the sixteenth century, however, it became more and more doubtful whether man could live with his own potentialities. The devastating Wars of Religion and the inhumanities of primitive accumulation seemed all the more horrible because they were carried out by a mankind whom men knew to be 'great', 'sublime', 'capable of all things', 'able to guide its own fate'. For a time panegyric was replaced by scepticism and despair. But this mood did not persist long in anthropology. The philosophy of emerging bourgeois society did not reject the notion of self-creation, nor that of (technical) many-sidedness, nor that of infinite capacities. But it searched in a new direction; it sought the *motive* which impelled man to create. And it found that motive – which was no longer sublime, nor moral – in the real motivation of the bourgeois individual: egoism.

NOTES

Introduction: is there a 'Renaissance ideal of man'?

1 Karl Marx, *Grundrisse: Foundations of the Critique of Political Economy*, tr. Martin Nicolaus, New York: Random House, 1973, pp. 541–2 (emphasis in the original).
2 ibid., p. 488 (emphasis in the original).
3 ibid., p. 325.
4 Max Dvořak, *Geschichte der italienischen Kunst*, Munich: Pieper, 1927, I, p. 191.
5 Edgar Zilsel, 'The genesis of the concept of scientific progress', in Philip Wiener and Aaron Noland (eds), *Roots of Scientific Thought*, New York: Basic Books, 1957.
6 This is still true even if Goethe's theory of colour later turned out to be the starting-point for future endeavours.
7 Under the Empire the contrast between stoicism and epicureanism sometimes found expression in a plurality of virtues – but I cannot here enter into an analysis of this subject.
8 Frederick Antal, *Florentine Painting and Its Social Background*, London: Kegan Paul, 1947.
9 György Márkus, *Marxizmus és 'antropológia'* (*Marxism and 'Anthropology'*), Budapest: Akadémiai Kiadó, 1966.

PART 1 UNEVEN DEVELOPMENT

1 *Lettere di Francesco Petrarca delle cose familiari*, ed. Giuseppe Fracassetti, Florence, Le Monnier, 1863–7, V, p. 358.
2 For a detailed analysis of this question see my *Az aristotelési etika és az antik ethos* (*Aristotelian Ethics and the Ethos of Antiquity*), Budapest: Akadémiai Kiadó, 1966.
3 Max Weber, *Wirtschaftsgeschichte* (*Abriss*), Berlin: Duncker-Humboldt, 1958.

4 Jaroslav Kudrna, *Stát a spolécnost na usvite italské renesance*, Prague: Akadémie, 1964.
5 Karl Marx, *Capital*, New York: International Publishers, 1967, I, p. 716 note.
6 Niccolò Machiavelli, *History of Florence*, New York: Harper, 1960, p. 114.
7 Max Dvořak, *Geschichte der italienischen Kunst*, Munich: Pieper, 1927, I, p. 16.
8 ibid., p. 57.
9 Machiavelli, *History of Florence*, pp. 129–30.
10 Giovanni Pico della Mirandola, *Die Würde des Menschen*, Freiburg, Frankfurt am Main, and Vienna: Pantheon, n.d., p. 117.

PART 2 ANTIQUITY AND THE JUDAEO-CHRISTIAN TRADITION

1 For a discussion of symbol and allegory see Georg Lukács, *Die Eigenart des Aesthetischen*, Neuwied am Rhein: Luchterhand, 1963, II, pp. 727ff.
2 Charles de Tolnay, *Werk und Weltbild des Michelangelo*, Zürich: Rhein Verlag, 1949.

1 Secularization

3 C. Wright Mills, *Power, Politics and People*, ed. Irving L. Horowitz, New York: Ballantine Books, 1965, pp. 612–13.
4 Giovanni Boccaccio, *The Decameron*, First Day, Second Story, London: J. M. Dent; New York: E. P. Dutton, 1930 (Everyman's Library), I, p. 33.
5 Cited in Paul Piur, *Petrarchas 'Buch ohne Namen' und die päpstliche Kurie*, Halle: Niemeyer, 1925, pp. 1353–5.
6 Giorgio Vasari, *Lives of the Great Painters*, London: Bohn's Standard Library, 1888, V, p. 229.
7 This, of course, is only one of the existing interdependences, though a typical one. Among the deists there were many who were both moralists and practical atheists, while – conversely – subjective piety was often found together with superstitious attitudes.
8 Jerome Cardan, *The Book of My Life*, tr. Jean Stoner, New York: E. P. Dutton, 1930, pp. 181, 200.
9 *The Autobiography of Benvenuto Cellini*, tr. J. A. Symonds, New York: Modern Library, 1927, p. 333 (Book II, chapter 27).
10 *The Confessions of St. Augustine*, tr. Rex Warner, New York: New American Library, 1963, p. 63 (Book III, chapter 8).
11 Cardan, *The Book of My Life*, p. 36 (my italics – A.H.).
12 Jacob Burckhardt, *The Civilization of the Renaissance in Italy*, London: Phaidon, 1965, pp. 303–4.
13 Baldassare Castiglione, *The Book of the Courtier*, in Burton A. Milligan (ed.), *Three Renaissance Classics*, New York: Scribner's, 1953, p. 550 (my italics – A.H.).
14 Thomas More, *Utopia*, ed. Surtz, New Haven, Conn., and London: Yale University Press, 1964, p. 133.
15 ibid., p. 93.
16 Cited in Eugene Rice, *The Renaissance Idea of Wisdom*, Cambridge, Mass.: Harvard University Press, 1958, p. 115.

NOTES TO PAGES 80–102

17 Nicholaus Cusanus, *De conjecturis*, II.14, cited in Landmann, *De homine*, Freiburg and Munich: Karl Alber, 1962.

18 Giannozzo Manetti, *De dignitate et excellentia hominis*, cited in Landmann, *De homine*, p. 146.

19 *The Portable Renaissance Reader*, New York: Viking Press, 1965, p. 389 (from 'Ficino's *Platonic Theology*', *Journal of the History of Ideas*, April 1944).

20 Lane Cooper (ed.), *Fifteen Greek Plays*, New York: Oxford University Press, 1969, p. 222.

21 Cited in de Tolnay, *Werk und Weltbild des Michelangelo*, p. 38.

22 Dvořak, *Geschichte der italienischen Kunst*, II, p. 18.

23 ibid., II, pp. 18–19.

24 Text of the Protocols of the Council of Trent, cited in Robert Hoopes, *Right Reason in the English Renaissance*, Cambridge, Mass.: Harvard University Press, 1962, p. 98.

25 *Dr. Martin Luthers Tischreden oder Colloquia*, Leipzig: Reclam, n.d., p. 122.

26 Hoopes, *Right Reason in the English Renaissance*, p. 111.

27 Rice, *The Renaissance Idea of Wisdom*, p. 123.

28 *A Treatise on Christian Liberty*, in *Works of Martin Luther*, Philadelphia, Pa.: Muhlenberg Press, 1943, II, p. 331.

29 ibid., p. 318.

30 For a detailed analysis of Cardinal Bellarmine's thesis see the introduction to Georg Lukács, *Zur Ontologie des gesellschaftlichen seins*, Neuwied am Rhein: Luchterhand, 1900.

31 Charron, *De la sagesse*, cited in Rice, *The Renaissance Idea of Wisdom*, p. 183.

32 ibid., p. 213.

2 A glance at the past

33 Burckhardt, *The Civilization of the Renaissance in Italy*.

34 Castiglione, *The Book of the Courtier*, in Milligan (ed.), *Three Renaissance Classics*, p. 343 (my italics – A.H.).

35 Aristotle, *Nichomachean Ethics*, tr. J. E. Welldon, London: Macmillan, 1923, p. 46.

36 *Of the Wisdom of the Ancients*, in Francis Bacon, *Works*, ed. James Spedding, Robert L. Ellis, and Douglas D. Heath, London: Longmans, 14 vols, 1875–9; VI, p. 754.

37 ibid., VI, p. 730.

38 Cardan, *The Book of My Life*, p. 189.

39 Cited in A. C. Keller, 'Zilsel, the artisans, and the idea of progress in the Renaissance', in Philip Wiener and Aaron Noland (eds), *Roots of Scientific Thought*, p. 285 (my italics – A.H.).

3 Stoicism and epicureanism

40 The same may be said of scepticism; but I will not discuss it separately, since in such cases it is normally found together with either an epicurean or a stoic attitude, usually the latter.

41 Charron, *De la sagesse*, cited in Wilhelm Dilthey, *Autonomie des Denkens im 17. Jahrhundert*, in *Gesammelte Schriften*, Leipzig and Berlin: Teubner, 1914, II, p. 267.

42 As we shall see, ancient stoicism was aristocratic even in theory, but this was far from true of *every* variety of modern stoicism.

43 Boccaccio, *The Decameron*, Ninth Day, Introduction; Everyman's edition, II, p. 226.
44 *Lettere di Francesco Petrarca delle cose familiari* (Book II. 2), ed. Giuseppe Fracassetti, Florence: Le Monnier, 1863–7, I, p. 327.
45 Burckhardt, *The Civilization of the Renaissance in Italy*, p. 336.
46 ibid.
47 Pietro Pomponazzi, 'On the immortality of the soul', in Cassirer, Kristeller and Randall (eds), *The Renaissance Philosophy of Man*, University of Chicago Press, 1948, p. 377.
48 ibid., p. 358.
49 ibid. (my italics – A.H.).
50 ibid., p. 364 (my italics – A.H.).
51 ibid., p. 362.
52 Michel de Montaigne, *Complete Essays*, tr. Donald Frame, Stanford University Press, 1948, p. 65 (Book I, chapter 20).
53 ibid., p. 57 (Book I, chapter 20).
54 Bacon, *Essays*, in *Works*, VI, p. 604.
55 Montaigne, *Complete Essays*, tr. Frame, p. 64 (Book I, chapter 20) (my italics – A.H.).
56 Cf. the description of, and the quotations taken from, Alberti's three works *De Iciarchia*, *De obedientia*, and *De magnitudine*, in Bogdan Suchodolski, *Narodziny nowozytnej filozofii czlowieka* (*The Renaissance Man*), Warsaw: P.W.N., 1963, p. 619 (in Polish).
57 *As You Like It*, IV, 1.
58 ibid., II, 7 (my italics – A.H.).
59 Letter to Luise Kautsky, in Rosa Luxemburg, *Briefe an' Karl und Luise Kautsky 1896–1915*, Berlin: E. Taubsche, 1923, I, p. 26; translated in part in Paul Fröhlich, *Rosa Luxemburg*, New York: Howard Fertig, 1969, pp. 259–60 (my italics – A.H.).
60 Niccolò Machiavelli, *The Discourses*, ed. Bernard Crick, Baltimore: Penguin 1970, Book III, Discourse 22.
61 François Rabelais, *Gargantua and Pantagruel*, London: Everyman's Library, 1929, Book I, chapter 57.
62 ibid.
63 Cardan, *The Book of My Life*, tr. Stoner, p. 50.
64 Montaigne, *Complete Essays*, tr. Frame, p. 857 (Book III, chapter 13).
65 ibid., p. 617 (Book III, chapter 2).
66 Rice, *The Renaissance Idea of Wisdom*, p. 194.
67 Bacon, *Essays*, in *Works*, VI, p. 604.
68 ibid.
69 For a detailed analysis of how this attitude is related to catharsis and education see Georg Lukács, *Der Weg ins Leben: Der russische Realismus in der Weltliteratur*, in *Werke*, vol. 5, Neuwied: Luchterhand, 1965.
70 Pomponazzi, 'On the immortality of the soul', in Cassirer *et al.*, *The Renaissance Philosophy of Man*, p. 362.
71 Burckhardt, *The Civilization of the Renaissance in Italy*, p. 259.
72 Machiavelli, *The Discourses*, Book II, chapter 29 (my italics – A.H.).
73 Castiglione, *The Book of the Courtier*, in Milligan (ed.), *Three Renaissance Classics*, pp. 550–1.
74 ibid., p. 305 (my italics – A.H.).
75 ibid., p. 555 (my italics – A.H.).
76 ibid., p. 554 (my italics – A.H.).

77 I have analysed here only one type of educator; space is lacking to go more deeply into the various types of individual pedagogy which appeared above all in France (Rabelais, Montaigne).
78 *Julius Caesar*, I. 2.
79 ibid., II. 2.
80 ibid., III. 1.
81 ibid.
82 ibid.
83 ibid., V. 1.
84 ibid.
85 ibid., V. 3 (my italics – A.H.).
86 ibid.
87 ibid., V. 5.
88 ibid., I. 2.
89 ibid., I. 3.
90 ibid., II. 1 (my italics – A.H.).
91 ibid., IV. 3.
92 Rice, *The Renaissance Idea of Wisdom*, p. 197 (my italics – A.H.).
93 Wilhelm Dilthey, *Autonomie des Denkens im 17. Jahrhundert*, in *Gesammelte Schriften*, II, p. 265.
94 *Hamlet*, III. 2.

4 Ecce homo: *Socrates and Jesus*
95 Cited in Wilhelm Dilthey, *Auffassung und Analyse des Menschen im 15. und 16. Jahrhundert*, in *Gesammelte Schriften*, II, p. 54.
96 More, *Utopia*, in Milligan (ed.), *Three Renaissance Classics*, p. 149.
97 Pico della Mirandola, *Die Wrüde des Menschen*, Freiburg, Frankfurt am Main and Vienna: Pantheon, n.d., p. 122.
98 ibid., p. 123.
99 Castiglione, *The Book of the Courtier*, in Milligan (ed.), *Three Renaissance Classics*, pp. 311–12.
100 Montaigne, *Complete Essays*, tr. Frame, p. 86 (Book I, chapter 23).
101 ibid., pp. 793–4 (Book III, chapter 12).

PART 3 ETHICS AND LIFE: MAN'S PRACTICAL POSSIBILITIES

5 *Everyday life*
1 At that time, of course, there were no specialized branches of science in the modern sense.
2 Boccaccio, *The Decameron*, Fourth Day, Ninth Story; London: J. M. Dent; New York: E. P. Dutton, 1930 (Everyman's Library), I, p. 282.
3 ibid., Third Day, Sixth Story; I, p. 189.
4 *Autobiography of Benvenuto Cellini*, tr. J. A. Symonds, New York: Modern Library, 1927, pp. 155–6 (Book I, chapter 74).
5 Pomponazzi, 'On the immortality of the soul', in Cassirer, Kristellen, and Randall (eds), *The Renaissance Philosophy of Man*, University of Chicago Press, 1948, p. 346 (my italics – A.H.).
6 ibid.
7 ibid., pp. 353–4 (my italics – A.H.).

8 ibid., p. 354.
9 ibid. (my italics – A.H.).
10 ibid.
11 ibid., p. 355.
12 ibid.
13 ibid., p. 256 (my italics – A.H.).
14 ibid., p. 356.
15 Michel de Montaigne, *Complete Essays*, tr. Donald Frame, Stanford University Press, 1948, pp. 114–15 (Book I, chapter 26) (my italics – A.H.).
16 ibid., p. 116 (Book I, chapter 26).
17 Francis Bacon, *Essays*, London: Macmillan, 1900, pp. 123–4.
18 Francis Bacon, *Novum Organum*, in *Works*, ed. James Spedding, Robert L. Ellis, and Douglas D. Heath, London: Longmans, 1875–9, IV, p. 54.
19 ibid., p. 55.
20 ibid., p. 56.
21 I have dealt with this problem in 'Az előítélet problémája' ('The problem of prejudice'), in *Társadalmi szerep és előítélet* (*Social Role and Prejudice*), Budapest: Akadémiai Kiadó, 1966.
22 Bacon, *Novum Organum*, in *Works*, IV, p. 56.
23 ibid., p. 57.
24 ibid.

6 Time and space: past-orientedness and future-orientedness

25 For a detailed analysis of this distinction see the chapter on Hegel in Georg Lukács's new *Ontology*.
26 Bacon, *Novum Organum*, in *Works*, IV, p. 82 (my italics – A.H.).
27 *Richard II*, V. 5 (my italics – A.H.).
28 Dialogue between Inghirami and Sadoleto, cited in Eugene Rice, *The Renaissance Idea of Wisdom*, Cambridge, Mass.: Harvard University Press, 1958, p. 74.
29 Thomas Kyd, *The Spanish Tragedy*, ed. J. R. Mulryne, London: Ernest Benn, 1970, III, p. 13.
30 Niccolò Machiavelli, *The Prince*, New York: Random House, 1950, pp. 92–3.
31 Bacon, *Essays*, Macmillan edition, p. 53.
32 ibid.
33 In late Roman Christianity there did indeed develop a notion of continuity (as in Augustine), but the process it described was again composed of static, closed elements.
34 Giordano Bruno, *La cena de le ceneri*. First Dialogue, in G. Aquilecchia (ed.), *Dialoghi italiani*, Florence, Sansoni, 1958, pp. 39–41 (English translation by Richard E. Allen).
35 Bacon, *Novum Organum*, in *Works*, IV, p. 77.
36 *Henry VI*, Part III, II. 5.
37 *As You Like It*, III. 2.
38 Jerome Cardan, *The Book of My Life*, tr. Jean Stoner, New York: E. P. Dutton, 1930, p. 190.
39 Bacon, *Novum Organum*, in *Works*, IV, p. 87.
40 Cited in A. C. Keller, 'Zilsel, The artisans, and the idea of progress in the Renaissance', in Philip Wiener and Aaron Noland (eds), *Roots of Scientific Thought*, New York: Basic Books, 1957, p. 284.
41 Bacon, *New Atlantis*, in *Works*, III, p. 144.
42 Bacon, *Novum Organum*, in *Works*, IV, p. 113.

43 *Henry IV*, Part II, III. 1 (my italics – A.H.).
44 Jan Kott, *Shakespeare Our Contemporary*, New York: Anchor Books, 1966, pp. 176–7.

7 *Individuality, knowledge of man, self-knowledge, autobiography*
45 Giorgio Vasari, *Lives of the Great Painters*, London: Bohn's Standard Library, 1850, I, p. 115.
46 ibid., I, p. 348.
47 Cited in Rice, *The Renaissance Idea of Wisdom*, p. 74.
48 *The Taming of the Shrew*, I. 2.
49 ibid., II. 1.
50 *The Two Gentlemen of Verona*, II. 6.
51 Leonardo da Vinci, *Notebooks*, ed. Edward MacCurdy, New York: George Braziller, 1958, p. 278.
52 Dénes Zoltai, *A zeneesztétika története* (*History of the Aesthetics of Music*), Budapest: Zenemükiadó, 1966, I: Ethos and Affect.
53 Wilhelm Dilthey, *Auffassung und Analyse des Menschen im 15. und 16. Jahrhundert*, in *Gesammelte Schriften*, Leipzig and Berlin: Teubner, 1914, II, p. 55.
54 John Herman Randall, *The School of Padua*, Padua: Editrice Antenore, 1961, p. 80.
55 For a more thorough analysis of this problem see my study, 'A szerepfogalom marxista értelmezhetóségéról' ('On the marxist interpretability of the concept of "role"'), in *Társadalmi szerep és elóitélet* (*Social Role and Prejudice*).
56 Montaigne, *Complete Essays*, tr. Frame, p. 86 (Book I, chapter 23).
57 Charron, *De la sagesse*, cited in Dilthey, *Autonomie des Denkens im 17. Jahrhundert*, in *Gesammelte Schriften*, p. 265 (my italics – A.H.).
58 Lodovico Ariosto, *Orlando Furioso*, tr. John Harington, London: Centaur Press, 1962, p. 83 (Book VIII, Stanza 1).
59 Bacon, *Essays*, Macmillan edition, p. 97.
60 ibid., p. 13.
61 ibid.
62 ibid.
63 ibid., p. 14.
64 ibid., p. 12.
65 ibid. (my italics – A.H.).
66 ibid.
67 ibid.
68 *Henry VI*, Part III, III. 2.
69 *Richard III*, III. 5.
70 ibid., I. 3.
71 ibid., III. 4.
72 *Othello*, I. 1 (my italics – A.H.).
73 ibid., I. 3.
74 *King Lear*, I. 2.
75 *Othello*, I. 3.
76 *Pericles*, II. 2.
77 *Hamlet*, I. 2.
78 *The Tempest*, I. 2 (my italics – A.H.).
79 *Much Ado About Nothing*, IV. 1 (my italics – A.H.).

80 *Timon of Athens*, III. 6.
81 ibid., IV, 1.
82 *Othello*, I. 3.
83 *Henry IV*, Part II, IV. 4.
84 *Hamlet*, I. 2 (my italics – A.H.).
85 ibid., II. 2 (my italics – A.H.).
86 ibid., III, 2 (my italics – A.H.).
87 ibid.
88 ibid., III. 4.
89 ibid., IV. 7.
90 ibid., V. 2.
91 *The Tempest*, V. 1.
92 ibid.
93 *Julius Caesar*, II. 1.
94 ibid., III. 1.
95 ibid., I. 2 (my italics – A.H.).
96 ibid., V. 5 (my italics – A.H.).
97 *Hamlet*, III. 1.
98 Roy Pascal, *Design and Truth in Autobiography*, London: Routledge & Kegan Paul, 1960, p. 21.
99 Roy Pascal analysed in detail the aesthetic properties of autobiography; the passages relating to that subject are among the most interesting in his book. For our purposes, however, we must neglect that subject, for here we are considering autobiography only as expressive of certain features of the life of the day.
100 The word 'calling' is used here not in the narrow interpretation given it by Max Weber, but in its broader everyday sense.
101 Cardan, *The Book of My Life*, p. 270.
102 ibid., p. 124.
103 ibid., p. 36 (my italics – A.H.).
104 See his 'Afterword' to the *Collected Works* of Dante (in Hungarian), Budapest: Helikon, 1962, p. 974.
105 Cited in Pascal, *Design and Truth in Autobiography*, p. 10.

8 *Measure and beauty – emotional ties*

106 Marsilio Ficino, *Ueber die Liebe*, Leipzig: Meiner, 1914, p. 57.
107 Karl Marx and Frederick Engels, *Manifesto of the Communist Party*, in *Selected Works*, New York: International Publishers, 1968, pp. 37–8.
108 ibid., p. 38.
109 In my *Csernisevszkijetikai nézetei. Az értelmes önzés problémája* (*Chernyshevsky's Ethical Views: the Problem of Rational Egoism*), Budapest: Szikra, 1955.
110 Marsilio Ficino, *Theologia Platonica* in Landmann, *De homine*, Freiburg and Munich: Verlag Karl Alber, 1962, p. 152.
111 Randall, *The School of Padua,*, p. 130.
112 *The Tragical History of Dr. Faustus*, in *The Plays of Christopher Marlowe*, New York: E. P. Dutton, and London: J. M. Dent, 1950 (Everyman's Library), p. 162.
113 Max Dvořák, *Geschichte der italienischen Kunst*, Munich: Pieper, 1927, I, p. 137.

114 Sonnet LIV, in *Sonnets of Michel Angelo Buonarotti*, tr. J. A. Symonds, London: J. Murray [1926], p. 59.
115 'Madrigal', in *Complete Poems and Selected Letters of Michelangelo*, tr. Gilbert, New York: Random House, 1963, p. 101.
116 It should be added that in the sculpture of the late Michelangelo (e.g. the Milan *Pietà*) even this kind of beauty disappears too.
117 Ariosto, *Orlando Furioso*, tr. Allan Gilbert, New York: Vanni, 1954, I, p. 156 (Canto 11, Stanza 26).
118 *Hamlet*, III. 1 (my italics – A.H.).
119 Francis Beaumont and John Fletcher, *The Maid's Tragedy*, III. 2.
120 *Hamlet*, V. 1.
121 Montaigne, *Complete Essays*, Frame, p. 139 (Book I, Essay 28).
122 *Romeo and Juliet*, II. 3.
123 It is true that madrigals are enjoyed even today, but they never became part of the common store of human culture to anything like the same degree as Dante or Petrarch. The music of Monteverdi, on the other hand, is already distinctly mannerist.
124 Boccaccio, *The Decameron*, Fourth Day, Introduction, Everyman's edition, I, p. 240.
125 ibid., Eighth Day, First Story, Everyman's edition, II, p. 240.
126 ibid., Eighth Day, First Story, Everyman's edition, II, p. 150.
127 Marsilio Ficino, *Ueber die Liebe*, p. 53.
128 *The Book of the Courtier*, in Burton A. Milligan (ed.), *Three Renaissance Classics*, New York: Scribner's, 1953, p. 592.
129 *Amours de Cassandre*, CLXXII, in Ronsard, *Oeuvres Complètes*, ed. Gustave Cohen, Paris: Gallimard, 1950, I, p. 75 (my italics – A.H.). Prose translation by Richard E. Allen.
130 Tommaso Campanella, *La Città del Sole*, in A. Guzzo and R. Amerio (eds), *Opere di Giordano Bruno e di Tommaso Campanella*, Milan and Naples: Riccardo Ricciardi Editore, n.d. [1885–6] (La Letteratura Italiana, Vol. 33).
131 I will discuss the anthropological implications of this problem below.
132 Ariosto, *Orlando Furioso*, London: Centaur, 1962, p. 43 (Canto 4, Stanzas 50 and 53) (my italics – A.H.).
133 Shakespeare, Sonnet LXVI.
134 *Othello*, III. 3.
135 *Much Ado About Nothing*, I. 1.
136 ibid., IV. 1.

9 Values and ethics

137 Ficino, *Ueber die Liebe*, p. 60.
138 Pomponazzi, 'On the immortality of the soul', in Cassirer *et al.* (eds), *The Renaissance Philosophy of Man*, pp. 246, 351 (my italics – A.H.).
139 Castiglione, *The Book of the Courtier*, in Milligan (ed.), *Three Renaissance Classics*, p. 554.
140 Pomponazzi, 'On the immortality of the soul', in Cassirer *et al.* (eds), *The Renaissance Philosophy of Man*, p. 357.
141 ibid., p. 358.
142 Rice, *The Renaissance Idea of Wisdom*.
143 Cited in ibid., p. 117.
144 Boccaccio, *The Decameron*, Seventh Day, Ninth Story, Everyman's edition, II, pp. 135–6.

145 *As You Like It*, II. 3.
146 ibid.
147 *Twelfth Night*, III. 4.
148 Boccaccio, *The Decameron*, Author's Epilogue, Everyman's edition, II, p. 347.
149 Bacon, *Essays*, Macmillan edition, p. 11.
150 *Henry VI*, Part II, III. 1.
151 *Richard III*, I. 2.
152 ibid., III. 6.
153 *Richard II*, V. 1.
154 Montaigne, *Complete Essays*, tr. Frame, p. 528 (Book II, chapter 27).
155 More, *Utopia*, in Milligan (ed.), *Three Renaissance Classics*, p. 238.
156 Bacon, *Essays*, Macmillan edition, p. 19.
157 Montaigne, *Complete Essays*, tr. Frame, p. 491 (Book II, chapter 17).
158 Cardan, *The Book of My Life*, p. 36 (my italics – A.H.).
159 Ben Jonson, *Volpone or, The Fox*, I. 1.
160 Christopher Marlowe, *The Tragical History of Dr. Faustus*, I. 1; Everyman's edition, p. 121.
161 *Richard III*, IV. 4 (my italics – A.H.).
162 Ficino, *Ueber die Liebe*, p. 53.
163 Pico della Mirandola, *Die Würde des Menschen*, Freibourg, Frankfurt am Main and Vienna: Pantheon, n.d., p. 123.
164 ibid., pp. 123–4.
165 ibid., p. 117.
166 *The Discourses* (Book I, chapter 17), in Niccolò Machiavelli, *The Prince and The Discourses*, New York: Modern Library (copyright 1950), p. 166.
167 *The Discourses* (Book I, chapter 2), p. 114.
168 *The Discourses* (Book I, chapter 3), ibid., p. 117.
169 *The Discourses* (Book I, chapter 3), ibid., p. 118.
170 *The Discourses* (Book II, Introduction), ibid., p. 274.
171 *The Discourses* (Book I, chapter 16), ibid., p. 161.
172 *The Prince* (chapter 18), New York: Random House, 1950, p. 64.
173 *The Prince* (chapter 17), ibid., p. 61.
174 *The Prince* (chapter 6), ibid., p. 22 (my italics – A.H.).
175 *The Prince* (chapter 17), ibid., p. 61.
176 *The Prince* (chapter 17), ibid., p. 62.
177 *The Prince* (chapter 17), ibid., p. 60.
178 *The Prince* (chapter 18), ibid., p. 64.
179 *The Prince* (chapter 26), ibid., p. 98.
180 *The Prince* (chapter 3), ibid., p. 13.
181 Giordano Bruno, *Spaccio de la bestia trionfante*, in Guzzo and Amerio (eds), *Opere di Giordano Bruno e di Tommaso Campanella*, pp. 537–8 (my italics – A.H.).
182 *The Book of the Courtier*, in Milligan (ed.), *Three Renaissance Classics*, p. 251.
183 Montaigne, *Complete Essays*, tr. Frame, p. 83 (Book I, chapter 23).
184 Bacon, *Novum Organum*, in *Works*, IV (my italics – A.H.).
185 Montaigne, *Complete Essays*, tr. Frame, p. 78 (Book I, chapter 23).
186 Bacon, *Essays*, Macmillan edition, p. 98 (my italics – A.H.).
187 Cited in Rice, *The Renaissance Idea of Wisdom*, p. 188.
188 ibid.

189 *The Book of the Courtier*, in Milligan (ed.), *Three Renaissance Classics*, p. 380.
190 ibid., p. 249.

10 Social philosophy, politics, Utopia
191 Bacon, *Essays*, Macmillan edition, p. 143.
192 Niccolò Machiavelli, *History of Florence*, New York: Harper, 1960, p. 204 (Book V, chapter I) (my italics – A.H.).
193 *The Discourses* (Book II, Introduction), p. 272.
194 *The Discourses* (Book I, chapter 6), ibid., p. 129.
195 Machiavelli, *The Discourses*, (Book II, chapter 58), in Allan Gilbert (tr.), *Machiavelli: The Chief Works and Others*, Durham, NC: Duke University Press, 1965, I, p. 314.
196 *The Discourses* (Book III, chapter 5), 1950 edition, p. 408.
197 He does so on the basis of a dualism of 'circumstances' and 'human activity'; but it would of course be unwarranted for us to demand of him a Marxian concept of praxis.
198 *The Prince* (chapter 25), 1950 edition, p. 91.
199 *The Prince* (chapter 24), ibid., p. 90.
200 *The Discourses* (Book III, chapter 25), 1950 edition, p. 488.
201 *The Prince* (chapter 18), 1950 edition, p. 65.
202 *The Prince* (chapter 15), ibid., p. 56.
203 *The Prince* (chapter 18), ibid., p. 64.
204 *The Prince* (chapter 3), ibid., p. 9.
205 *The Prince* (chapter 7), ibid., p. 27.
206 *The Prince* (chapter 18), ibid., p. 65.
207 *The Prince* (chapter 22), ibid., p. 85.
208 *The Prince* (chapter 8), ibid., p. 34 (my italics – A.H.).
209 *The Discourses* (Book III, chapter 41), 1950 edition, p. 528.
210 *The Prince* (chapter 6), 1950 edition, p. 22.
211 *The Discourses* (Book I, chapter 9), 1950 edition, p. 139.
212 *The Discourses* (Book III, chapter 3), ibid., p. 405.
213 *Lettere di Francesco Petrarca delle cose familiari* (Libro XIII, 1), ed. Giuseppe Fracassetti, Florence: Le Monnier, 1863–7, III, pp. 229–30.
214 Cited in Charles de Tolnay, *Werk und Weltbild des Michelangelo*, Zürich: Rhein Verlag, 1949, p. 30.
215 Bacon, *Of the Wisdom of the Ancients*, in *Works*, VI, p. 735.
216 *Lettere di Francesco Petrarea delle cose familiari* (Book XI, Letter 16), ed. Fracassetti, III, p. 92.
217 Giordano Bruno, *Spaccio de la bestia trionfante*, in Guzzo and Amerio (eds), *Opere di Giordano Bruno e di Tommaso Campanella*, pp. 537–58 (my italics – A.H.).
218 More, *Utopia*, in Milligan (ed.), *Three Renaissance Classics*, p. 152.
219 ibid., p. 234 (my italics – A.H.).
220 Campanella, *La Città del Sole*, in Guzzo and Amerio (eds), *Opere di Giordano Bruno e di Tommaso Campanella*, p. 1094.
221 ibid., p. 1090.

11 Fate, destiny, fortune
222 *The Decameron*, Second Day, Third Story; Everyman's edition, I, p. 68.
223 Marlowe, *Tamburlaine the Great*, I, 3.
224 Machiavelli, *The Prince* (chapter 25), 1950 edition, p. 91.
225 Bacon, *Essays*, Macmillan edition, p. 100.

PART 4 PHILOSOPHICAL ANTHROPOLOGY

12 Nature and man

1 Georg Lukács, *Die Eigenart des Aesthetischen*, Neuwied am Rhein: Luchterhand, 1963, 2 vols.

2 Giordano Bruno, *On the Infinite Universe and Worlds*, tr. Dorothea Waley Singer, 'Introductory Epistle'; in D. W. Singer, *Giordano Bruno: His Life and Thought*, New York: Henry Schuman, 1950, p. 248 (my italics – A.H.).

3 ibid. (my italics – A.H.).

4 ibid., 'Third Dialogue', p. 303 (my italics – A.H.).

5 Castiglione, *The Courtier*, in B. A. Milligan (ed.), *Three Renaissance Classics*, p. 600.

6 Leonardo da Vinci, *Notebooks*, ed. Edward MacCurdy, New York: George Braziller, 1958, p. 278.

7 Cited in Alexander von Humboldt, *Cosmos*, tr. E. C. Otté, London: Bohn, 1849, II, p. 688.

8 Michel de Montaigne, *Complete Essays*, tr. Donald Frame, Stanford University Press, 1948, pp. 328–9 (Book II, chapter 12).

9 ibid., p. 333 (Book II, chapter 12).

10 Theophrastus Paracelsus, *Lebendiges Erbe*, Zürich and Leipzig: Rascher Verlag, 1942, p. 48.

11 Francis Bacon, *Works*, ed. James Spedding, Robert L. Ellis, and Douglas D. Heath, London: Longmans, 1875–9, VI, pp. 723–4.

12 Cited in Randall, *The School of Padua*, Padua: Editrice Antenore, p. 103.

13 Paracelsus, *Lebendiges Erbe*, p. 34.

14 Cited in Eugene Rice, *The Renaissance Idea of Wisdom*, Cambridge, Mass.: Harvard University Press, 1958, p. 113.

15 Bacon, *Of the Wisdom of the Ancients*, in *Works*, VI, p. 747.

16 ibid., VI, p. 710.

17 Leonardo da Vinci, *Notebooks*, ed. MacCurdy, p. 142.

18 ibid., p. 588.

19 ibid., p. 57.

13 Work, science, techné, art

20 For the Aristotelian analysis of *techné* see my *Az aristotelesi etika és az antik ethos* (*Aristotelian Ethics and the Ethos of Antiquity*), Budapest: Akadémiai Kiadó, 1966.

21 Cited in Edgar Zilsel, 'The genesis of the concept of scientific progress', in Philip Wiener and Aaron Noland (eds), *Roots of Scientific Thought*, New York: Basic Books, 1957, p. 260 (my italics – A.H.).

22 Cited ibid., pp. 269–70.

23 Juan Luis Vives, *A Fable about Man*, in Cassirer, Kristeller and Randall (eds), *The Renaissance Philosophy of Man*, University of Chicago Press, 1957, p. 392.

24 Giannozzo Manetti, *De manectis*, in Landmann, *De homine*, Freiburg and Munich: Verlag Karl Alber, 1962, p. 146.

25 Machiavelli, *The Discourses* (Book I, chapter 1), New York: Modern Library (copyright 1950), p. 107.

26 Leonardo da Vinci, *Notebooks*, ed. MacCurdy, p. 57.

27 ibid., p. 88.

28 ibid., p. 72.

465

29 Here, of course, I am using the concept of praxis in the sense of praxis with regard to nature, not in the Marxian meaning of the word.
30 Bacon, *Novum Organum*, in *Works*, IV, p. 90.
31 ibid., IV, pp. 62–3 (my italics – A.H.).
32 Leonardo da Vinci, *Treatise on Painting*, tr. A. Philip McMahon, Princeton University Press, 1956, I, p. 113.
33 Giovanni Boccaccio, *The Decameron*, Author's Epilogue, London: J. M. Dent, 1930 (Everyman's Library), II, p. 347.
34 Leonardo da Vinci, *Notebooks*, ed. McCurdy, p. 903.
35 Cited in Charles de Tolnay, *Werk und Weltbild des Michelangelo*, Zürich: Rhein Verlag, 1949, p. 87.

14 Knowledge; body and soul

36 Montaigne, *Complete Essays*, tr. Frame, p. 74 (Book I, chapter 21).
37 Pomponazzi, *De immortalitate animae*, in Cassirer et al. (eds), *The Renaissance Philosophy of Man*, p. 298.
38 Cited in Randall, *The School of Padua*, p. 108.
39 ibid., p. 109.
40 ibid., p. 110.
41 Jerome Cardan, *The Book of My Life*, tr. Jean Stones, New York: E. P. Dutton, 1930, pp. 245–6.
42 Nicolaus Cusanus, *Drei Schriften vom verborgenen Gott*, Hamburg: Felix Meiner Verlag, 1958, p. 36.
43 Marsilio Ficino, *Theologia Platonica*, in Landmann, *De homine*, p. 152.
44 ibid., p. 54.
45 Ernst Cassirer, *The Individual and the Cosmos in Renaissance Philosophy*, New York: Harper, 1963, p. 147.
46 This idea was to become important again later in those two spiritual heirs of the Renaissance, Spinoza and Goethe (in later life).
47 Cited in Rice, *The Renaissance Idea of Wisdom*, p. 184.
48 *Dr. Martin Luthers Tischreden oder Colloquia*, Leipzig: Reclam, n.d., p. 30.
49 Bacon, *Novum Organum*, in *Works*, IV, p. 48.

15 What is man capable of?

50 Vives, *De tradentis disciplinis*, cited in Ernst Cassirer, *Das Erkenntnisproblem*, Berlin: Verlag Bruno Cassirer, 1906, II, p. 157 (my italics – A.H.).
51 Florence: Le Monnier, 1863–7, *Lettere di Francesco Petrarca delle cose familiari*, ed. Giuseppe Fracassetti, V, p. 398.
52 Bacon, *Of the Wisdom of the Ancients*, in *Works*, VI, p. 757.
53 Lorenzo Valla, *De libero arbitrio*, in Cassirer et al., *The Renaissance Philosophy of Man*, p. 168 (my emphasis – A.H.).
54 ibid., p. 173.
55 Cited in Rice, *The Renaissance Idea of Wisdom*, p. 117.
56 Cited in August Riekel, *Die Philosophie der Renaissance*, Munich: Ernst Reinhard, 1925, p. 77.
57 Pomponazzi, *De immortalitate animae*, in Cassirer et al. (eds), *The Renaissance Philosophy of Man*, p. 353.
58 Bacon, *Novum Organum*, in *Works*, IV, p. 114 (my italics – A.H.).
59 Giordano Bruno, *Spaccio dela bestia trionfante*, in Guzzo and Amerio (eds), *Opere di Giordano Bruno e di Tommaso Campanella*, pp. 536–7.
60 Nicolaus Cusanus, *De coniecturis*, II, 14, in Landmann, *De homine*, p. 136.

61 *Dr. Martin Luthers Tischreden oder Colloquia*, p. 195.
62 Marsilio Ficino, *Five Questions Concerning the Mind*, in Cassirer *et al.* (eds), *The Renaissance Philosophy of Man*, p. 206.
63 ibid., p. 201.
64 Marsilio Ficino, *Theologia Platonica*, in Landmann, *De homine*, p. 147.
65 ibid., p. 148.
66 ibid.
67 ibid., pp. 148–9.
68 ibid., p. 149.
69 Ficino, *Platonic Theology*, extract in *The Portable Renaissance Reader*, New York: Viking Press, 1965, p. 389.
70 Ficino, *Theologia Platonica*, in Landmann, *De homine*, p. 152.
71 ibid.
72 Giovanni Pico della Mirandola, *Oration on the Dignity of Man*, in Cassirer *et al.* (eds), *The Renaissance Philosophy of Man*, p. 223.
73 ibid., p. 224.
74 ibid., pp. 224–5.
75 ibid., p. 225.
76 ibid., p. 235.

INDEX

Abélard, Peter 231
acceptance 140
actions 125–6, 175
activity 120
affection 121–3, 128–9, 168
afterworld 108–12; *see also* hell
Alberti, Leone: economics 158;
   Florence 38; fortune 369; gods
   123; life 143; man 129; the
   mean 246; pleasure 121–2;
   science of art 401, 410; social
   life 114–17, 195; versatility 51
Alexander VI, pope 66–7
alienation 10, 22
allegory 60, 406–8
analogy 391–2
anarchy 45
Angelico, Fra 253
animals 421, 428–9, 446–7
animi see soul
Antal, Frederick 19, 47–8, 409
anthropocentrism 167, 378–93
anthropology 21, 34, 373–4, 397–9,
   413–14, 428–53; *see also* man
anthropomorphism 378–93, 400
anti-values 299, 302–5; *see also* sin
antiquity 59–65, 98, 394–9, 409;
   see also Greek; Roman
Apian, Peter 191, 396
Apollo 61–2
Aquinas, Thomas 12, 49, 87
architecture 46–7, 50, 67, 94; *see*
   also art

Aretino 24, 31
Ariosto, Lodovico: chivalry 256–9;
   deceit 208; gunpowder 355;
   love 268, 275–6; poetry 203;
   Tasso 36
aristocracy 7, 36, 38, 45–6; *see also*
   class
Aristophanes 250, 399
Aristotelianism 39–40, 77, 305–6,
   415–17
Aristotle: affections 129; courage
   300; cult 63; fate 368; friendship
   263; good 129, 232, 283;
   happiness 285; laughter 298; man
   14, 373, 436; the mean 305, 348;
   metaphysics 103; morality 19;
   motives 320; nature 129, 390;
   philosophy 95–9; politics 25,
   339–40; 'real' 59; soul 415–17;
   stoic 107; *techné* 397; thought
   158–9; time 172–5, 183; work
   395
army 51–2
art: beauty 250, 252–3; capitalism
   251; class 48, 50; daily life 150–
   2; derivative 93–4; ethics 152;
   Florence 40, 43, 47–51, 151, 253;
   fortune 369; goal 151; imitation
   158; industry 43; Italian 94; love
   267–8; mannerism 33–4; myths
   59–64, 152; nationalism 440;
   official 203; patronage 36, 53;
   perspective 172; philosophy 40;

reality 250–1, 387, 417–18
reason 13–14, 77, 84, 87
recantation 32–3
reciprocity, in love 266, 270–1
redemption 125
refeudalization 13, 30–1, 86, 276
Reformation 30, 67–8, 77, 83–6,
    276, 424–5, 440; *see also*
    Counter-Reformation; religion
Regius 99, 186, 191
religion: art 18, 61–2, 68, 141, 143,
    145; attitudes 67; changes
    12–13; city-states 41; conven-
    tional 67–8; daily life 104;
    decline 68–9, 75; freedom 75;
    philosophy 76–7; revival 53,
    83–6, 330; science 83, 87; state
    75; uniformity 77; *see also*
    Calvanism; Christianity;
    Protestantism; Reformation
Renaissance: defined 2–3; High
    31, 95
reversibility 126
revival, religious 53, 83–6, 330
revolt, workers 49, 51–2
revolution: and capital 42; French
    91–2, 117, 181, 428;
    Renaissance as 2
rhythm of time 173, 185–96
Ricardo, David 349–50
Rice, Eugene 290
Richard II 175, 186–7, 303, 309,
    337, 346
Richard III: contempt 302–3;
    evil 309; family 260; man 220;
    role 213–14, 227, 229, 305; time
    118; values 23, 313, 323
role-behaviour 206–7
Romans 16, 81, 91–4
romanticism, 250, 379
Rome 30, 35–6, 59–61, 83, 150,
    316, 331, 356
Ronsard, Pierre de 268, 272
Rousseau, J.-J. 8, 21, 120, 234,
    249–50, 316, 339, 357

Sadoleto, Giacomo 30, 83
saints 79
Saint-Simon 356
Salutati, Coluccio 38, 50, 142
Sartre, J.-P. 90
Satan 310–12

Savonarola 8, 41, 65–6, 86, 253,
    318, 350–1
scepticism 166, 424–5
scholarship 148, 239
Scott, Walter 181, 251, 337
sculpture 40, 43, 82, 94, 151;
    see also art
science: and art 401, 410–11;
    Bacon 11, 184–5, 244, 355, 401,
    406–7; city-states 150; daily
    life 148–50, 158, 163–9;
    development 13, 100, 355, 379,
    385; identified 19; individuality
    244–5; knowledge 98–9; magic
    148–9; natural 40, 78, 87, 379,
    385; 'new' 99; philosophy 83,
    88; religion 68, 78, 83, 87; social
    87, 183–4; time 182, 192–3;
    wisdom 291–2; work 401, 405–
    12; *see also* nature
secularization 47, 81–9, 107, 203, 236
self: conception *see* vocation;
    creation 81; criticism 235;
    deception 217–18; development
    120; enjoyment 200; interest
    238–40, 249; knowledge 230–1;
    love 304; portraits 241; preserva-
    tion 123, 204; realization 120,
    200–3; sacrifice 122
senses 420, 423
sensuality 269–71, 279
sexuality 275, 310–11
Shakespeare, William: appeal
    152; autobiography 242–3;
    baroque 34; beauty 259–60;
    comedy 299; conflict 309;
    courage 301–2; cowardice 302–3;
    cynicism 305; death 113; destiny
    428; ethics *see* values; fidelity
    296–7; history 188, 337–8;
    incognito 212; interest 261; law
    155; life 116; love 265–8, 272,
    276–9; morality 154; myth 61;
    naïve characters 217–21, 227;
    the people 333–4; poetry 244;
    politics 346; power 323; property
    201–2; rational characters 221–9;
    reversibility 126; riches 85; Rome
    93–4; society 3; stoic-epicureans
    102, 107, 129–35; time 174–7,
    186–8, 195–6; tragedies 308;
    values 19, 144, 322; villains

479